The Brothers Karamazov

A Powerful Story of Faith, Family, and Morality

A Modern Translation

Adapted for the Contemporary Reader

Fyodor Dostoevsky

Table of Contents

Preface - Message to the Reader

Rebuilding the Greatest Library in Human History

Thousands of years ago, the Library of Alexandria was the heart of global knowledge — a sanctuary where the wisdom of every known civilization was gathered and shared freely.

And then, it was lost.

Now, we're rebuilding it — and you are invited to join us.

At the Library of Alexandria, we've set out to make every book available to *every person on Earth* — not just in print, but in every language, every format, and for every reader.

Here's how we do it:

- **Deluxe Print Editions at True Printing Cost** - Order any book as a high-quality paperback, elegant hardcover, or stunning boxset — and only pay what it costs to print. No markups. No middlemen.

- **Unlimited Access to the Greatest Works** - Enjoy thousands of timeless classics — from Plato to Shakespeare to Tolstoy — in beautiful, modern eBook and audiobook editions. Read and listen without limits — for every reader, everywhere.

- **Modern Translations for Every Language & Dialect** - We're reimagining the classics in clear, accessible language — and translating them into every dialect imaginable. Everyone deserves to understand humanity's greatest ideas.

When you visit **LibraryofAlexandria.com**, you're not just accessing books — you're joining a global movement to restore, preserve, and share the wisdom of civilization.

Join us today at LibraryofAlexandria.com

Together, we'll ensure the light of human wisdom never fades again.

With gratitude,
The Modern Library of Alexandria Team

Visit:

www.libraryofalexandria.com

Or scan the code below:

Introduction

"Man is a creature that can get accustomed to anything, and I think that is the best definition of him."
~ Fyodor Dostoevsky

While other authors may have been content to tell stories, Dostoevsky compelled his readers to confront life's raw complexities. His characters, flawed and deeply human, are mirrors of the struggles we all face: our battles with guilt, faith, freedom, and identity. Through his unflinching gaze into the darkest recesses of the human mind, Dostoevsky has left an indelible mark on world literature and thought. Dostoevsky understood that the most harrowing conflicts are not those waged between nations but within the hearts and minds of individuals. His works portray human beings as creatures torn between sin and redemption, darkness and light, despair and hope. He explored existential questions—not in an abstract, philosophical sense but in the lived reality of ordinary people. This skill has made his writing resonate across cultures and generations, as readers recognize themselves in the struggles and moral dilemmas of his characters.

Dostoevsky's significance stems from his unparalleled exploration of universal themes. Chief among them is suffering—a theme that permeates his writing as both a curse and a catalyst. For Dostoevsky, suffering is the crucible through which redemption, growth, and understanding are achieved. He portrays suffering as an unavoidable part of existence, yet one that can lead to spiritual transformation if confronted with courage and faith. Alongside suffering, his works grapple with freedom, the moral consequences of choice, and the eternal conflict between good and evil—all set against a backdrop of a society in flux. His exploration of faith and doubt speaks directly to modern readers who struggle to find meaning in a secular, fragmented world.

Through his vision, Dostoevsky reaches out to anyone who has ever questioned their place in the world, anyone who has ever felt trapped by their circumstances, and anyone who has struggled to reconcile their actions with their conscience.

Fyodor Dostoevsky: A Life of Suffering, Redemption, and Genius

Fyodor Mikhailovich Dostoevsky was born in 1821 in Moscow, the second of seven children. From an early age, Dostoevsky was immersed in an environment of faith, hardship, and empathy for the downtrodden. His father, a strict and devout man, worked as a physician at a charity hospital for the poor. This setting exposed young Dostoevsky to the stark realities of suffering, illness, and poverty—experiences that would deeply influence his later works. He developed a profound understanding of human frailty and a deep compassion for those enduring life's harshest trials.

Dostoevsky's mother died when he was just 16, followed by the sudden and violent death of his father, who was rumored to have been murdered by serfs on his estate. These losses marked Dostoevsky's early years with an acute awareness of mortality and suffering. It was during this time that he turned to literature as both a refuge and a means of making sense of his world. The emotional intensity of his childhood laid the foundation for his exploration of themes like loss, guilt, and redemption in his later works.

In his early twenties, Dostoevsky's life took a dramatic turn. After achieving modest success as a writer with his first novel, Poor Folk, he became involved with a group of intellectuals known as the Petrashevsky Circle. This group engaged in discussions about socialism, reform, and the oppressive nature of Tsarist rule. Though their activities were relatively harmless by modern standards, they were seen as treasonous by the authorities.

In 1849, Dostoevsky was arrested, imprisoned, and sentenced to death. At the last moment, as he stood before a firing squad, his execution was commuted to hard labor in Siberia—a harrowing experience that left an indelible mark on his soul. The mock execution was a psychological trauma from which he would never fully recover, but it also served as a turning point for his beliefs. It was during his years in a Siberian prison camp that Dostoevsky confronted the depths of human suffering, the harshness of existence, and the redemptive power of faith. He witnessed firsthand the struggles of criminals, peasants, and outcasts, and this encounter with humanity's rawest condition would inform his portrayal of characters torn between despair and salvation.

Following his release from Siberia, Dostoevsky emerged a changed man. The experience had stripped away any remnants of youthful idealism and left him with a deep, unshakable belief in the importance of faith and personal redemption. For Dostoevsky, human suffering was no longer something to be eradicated but something to be endured and transcended through love, forgiveness, and spiritual awakening.

This renewed outlook fueled his return to literature. He began producing works of immense philosophical and moral depth, exploring the spiritual struggles of humanity with an intensity that had rarely been seen before. In his writing, Dostoevsky sought to reconcile his experiences in Siberia with his understanding of faith, freedom, and redemption. His characters wrestle with the same questions that haunted him: the existence of God, the meaning of suffering, and the nature of good and evil. His return to literature marked the beginning of a creative period that would solidify his place as one of the greatest writers of all time.

Despite his growing reputation, Dostoevsky's life remained fraught with hardship. He struggled with crippling poverty, largely due to his compulsive gambling addiction. On more than one occasion, he lost everything at the gambling tables, leaving himself and his family destitute. These personal struggles found their way into his works, where gambling often serves as a metaphor for humanity's desperate search for meaning and transcendence in a chaotic world.

His first wife, Maria, died young, and he lost several children in infancy—griefs that compounded his already fragile emotional state. Yet, it was in the face of these hardships that Dostoevsky produced some of his greatest works. His ability to persevere through suffering, and to channel that suffering into art, became a testament to his strength as both a writer and a human being. He wrote not from a place of privilege or detachment but from the depths of lived experience—a quality that lends his works their raw power and emotional authenticity.

In the final decade of his life, Dostoevsky solidified his legacy with works that remain unparalleled in their psychological and philosophical depth. He completed The Brothers Karamazov, a towering exploration of faith, doubt, morality, and the human condition. In it, he wove together the themes that had defined his career: the eternal struggle between good and evil, the redemptive power of suffering, and the search for meaning in a broken world. Dostoevsky's final years were marked by a growing recognition of his genius. He became a revered figure in Russian literature and beyond, celebrated for his ability to capture the complexities of the human experience.

In 1881, at the age of 59, Dostoevsky died of a pulmonary hemorrhage. Thousands attended his funeral, mourning the loss of a writer whose words had touched their hearts and souls. His legacy endures not only in the pages of his novels but in the countless readers who have found solace, challenge, and inspiration in his works. Through his life of suffering and redemption, Dostoevsky created literature that transcends time—a body of work that continues to illuminate the deepest truths of what it means to be human.

Part 1

Book 1: The History of a Family

Chapter 1: Fyodor Pavlovitch
Karamazov

Alexey Fyodorovich Karamazov was the third son of Fyodor Pavlovich Karamazov, a landowner well known in our district during his time and still remembered among us because of his tragic and dark death, which took place thirteen years ago, and which I will describe in its proper place. For now, I'll just say that this "landowner"—as we used to call him, even though he hardly spent a single day of his life on his own estate— was a peculiar character, though one you could frequently meet, someone who was both disgraceful and wicked, and at the same time foolish. But he was one of those foolish men who are very capable of managing their worldly matters, and apparently nothing else. Fyodor Pavlovich, for example, started with next to nothing; his estate was tiny; he was known to dine at other people's tables, attaching himself to them as a parasite, but by the time he died, it turned out he had a hundred thousand rubles in hard cash. Despite this, he was one of the most absurd, wild men in the whole district all his life. I repeat, it wasn't stupidity—the majority of these wild men are clever and smart enough—but pure senselessness, and a particular kind of national senselessness.

He was married twice and had three sons: the eldest, Dmitri, from his first wife, and two others, Ivan and Alexey, from his second wife. Fyodor Pavlovich's first wife, Adelaida Ivanovna, came from a fairly wealthy and noble family, also landowners in our district, the Miüsovs. How it happened that an heiress, who was also a beauty, and one of those strong, intelligent girls—so common in this generation, but sometimes found in the last— could marry such a worthless, weak, and frail man, as we all called him, I won't attempt to explain. I knew a young woman from the previous "romantic" generation, who, after years of some mysterious passion for a man whom she could have easily married at any time, created insurmountable obstacles to their union, and in the end, threw herself, on a stormy night, into a deep and fast-moving river from a high bank, almost a cliff, and so perished, all to satisfy her own whim and to imitate Shakespeare's Ophelia. Indeed, if this cliff, her favorite spot, had been less picturesque, if instead there had been a dull, flat bank, most likely the suicide would never have occurred. This is a fact, and probably there have been quite a few similar cases in the last two or three generations. Adelaida Ivanovna Miüsov's actions were undoubtedly, in some way, an echo of other people's thoughts, and a result of the frustration she felt due to a lack of mental freedom. She may have wanted to show her feminine independence, to rise above social class distinctions and the oppression of her family. And a creative imagination may have briefly convinced her, we can suppose, that Fyodor Pavlovich, despite his parasitic behavior, was one of the bold, ironic figures of that progressive time, though in reality, he was simply a mean buffoon and nothing more. The marriage was made more exciting by the fact that it was preceded by an elopement, which greatly appealed to Adelaida Ivanovna's imagination. Fyodor Pavlovich's situation at that time made him especially eager for such a venture, as he was passionately determined to make a career in one way or another. The idea of connecting himself to a good family and securing a dowry was an attractive option. As for mutual love, it clearly did not exist, neither in the bride nor in him, despite Adelaida Ivanovna's beauty. This was perhaps the only time in Fyodor Pavlovich's life where his usual lustful nature was not aroused, though he was always the type to chase after any woman who showed even the slightest interest. She seems to have been the only woman who didn't stir him in that way.

Immediately after the elopement, Adelaida Ivanovna realized that she felt nothing but contempt for her husband. The truth about their marriage revealed itself very quickly. Even though her family quickly accepted what had happened and gave her the dowry, the couple began to lead a very chaotic life, filled with constant arguments. It was said that the young wife showed much more generosity and dignity than Fyodor Pavlovich, who, as we now know, took hold of all her money—up to twenty-five thousand rubles—as soon as she received it, so that she lost it forever. The small village and the rather nice town house that were part of her dowry, he tried for a long time to get transferred into his name, through some kind of legal arrangement. He probably would have succeeded, merely due to her exhaustion and desire to get rid of him, and from the contempt and hatred his constant and shameless demands created. But luckily, Adelaida Ivanovna's family stepped in and prevented him from taking what was left. It is known for certain that the husband and wife often fought, but the rumor was that Fyodor Pavlovich didn't hit his wife; instead, she beat him, for she was a hot-tempered, bold, dark-browed, and impatient woman, with remarkable physical strength. Eventually, she left him and ran away with a poor theology student, leaving their three-year-old son, Dmitri, in Fyodor Pavlovich's care. Immediately after, Fyodor Pavlovich filled his house with a sort of harem and gave himself over to wild drinking sprees. In between his bouts of drunkenness, he traveled around the province, crying to everyone about how Adelaida Ivanovna had left him, going into details about their marriage that were far too disgraceful for a husband to share. What seemed to please him most was playing the ridiculous role of the wronged husband and telling his story with added embellishments.

"Anyone would think you'd gotten a promotion, Fyodor Pavlovich, you seem so happy despite your suffering," people would say to him mockingly. Some even added that he was enjoying the new comic role he had found, and that he exaggerated his misery to make it even funnier. But who knows, maybe it was just simplicity. In the end, he managed to find out where his runaway wife was. The poor woman had gone to Petersburg with her theology student and had thrown herself into a life of complete freedom. Fyodor Pavlovich immediately began preparing to go to Petersburg, though even he didn't know what he planned to do once he got there. He probably would have gone, but having made up his mind, he felt he deserved to prepare for the trip with another bout of heavy drinking. Just then, her family received word of Adelaida Ivanovna's death in Petersburg. She had died suddenly in an attic, either from typhus, or according to another version, from starvation. Fyodor Pavlovich was drunk when he received the news, and the story goes that he ran out into the street, shouting with joy and raising his hands to the sky, saying, "Lord, now lettest Thou Thy servant depart in peace." Others say he wept uncontrollably, like a small child, so much so that people actually felt sorry for him, despite the disgust he inspired. It's quite possible that both versions are true: that he felt joy at his newfound freedom and sorrow for the woman who had given it to him. As a general rule, people, even the wicked, are much more naïve and simple than we think. And so are we.

Chapter 2: He Gets Rid of His Eldest Son

You can easily imagine what kind of father such a man would be and how he might raise his children. His behavior as a father was exactly what you'd expect. He completely neglected the child from his marriage to Adelaida Ivanovna, not out of malice or because of his marital issues, but simply because he forgot about him. While he was exhausting everyone with his tears and complaints and turning his house into a den of debauchery, a loyal family servant, Grigory, took the three-year-old Mitya into his care. If he hadn't done this, there would have been no one to even change the boy's little shirt.

It also happened that the child's relatives on his mother's side forgot about him at first. His grandfather had already passed away, and his grandmother, Mitya's maternal grandmother, had moved to Moscow and was seriously ill. Meanwhile, her daughters were all married, so Mitya remained in old Grigory's care for almost a year, living with him in the servant's cottage. But even if his father had remembered him (though he couldn't have been completely unaware of his existence), he would have sent him back to the cottage since the child would only have gotten in the way of his wild lifestyle. However, a cousin of Mitya's mother, Pyotr Alexandrovitch Miüsov, happened to return from Paris. He spent many years abroad after this but was then a young man known among the Miüsovs for his progressive ideas and European sophistication. He had traveled to the capitals and abroad, and later in life, he became a Liberal, like many in the 1840s and 1850s. During his life, he met many of the most Liberal minds of the time, both in Russia and abroad. He even knew Proudhon and Bakunin personally, and in his old age, he liked to tell stories about the three days of the Paris Revolution of February 1848, hinting that he almost fought on the barricades. It was one of his fondest memories from his youth. He owned independent property of about a thousand souls, to use the old way of counting. His grand estate was near our little town, bordering the land of our famous monastery. Pyotr Alexandrovitch almost immediately got into a long legal dispute with the monastery over the rights to fish in the river or cut wood in the forest, though I'm not sure exactly which. He saw it as his duty as a citizen and a cultured man to challenge the "clericals."

Upon hearing about Adelaida Ivanovna, whom he remembered and had once been interested in, and learning about the existence of Mitya, he stepped in, despite his youthful anger and contempt for Fyodor Pavlovich. He met Fyodor Pavlovich for the first time and directly told him that he wanted to take charge of the boy's education. Pyotr Alexandrovitch later told the story, saying that when he first mentioned Mitya, Fyodor Pavlovich looked as if he didn't understand what child he was talking about and was even surprised to hear that he had a son in the house. The story might have been exaggerated, but it was probably close to the truth.

Fyodor Pavlovich liked to act unpredictably throughout his life, sometimes playing strange roles without any real reason, even when it hurt him, as it did in this case. This trait, however, is common in many people, some of them very clever—unlike Fyodor Pavlovich. Pyotr Alexandrovitch took charge of the situation energetically and was appointed, along with Fyodor Pavlovich, as co-guardian of the boy, who had a small property, including a house and land, left to him by his mother. Mitya was placed under his cousin's care, but since Pyotr Alexandrovitch had no family of his own and, after securing the income from his estate, was eager to return to Paris, he left the boy in the care of one of his cousins, a woman living in Moscow. After settling in Paris permanently, he also forgot about the child, especially when the February Revolution broke out, making a lasting impression on him. The Moscow lady passed away, and Mitya ended up in the care of one of her married daughters. I believe he changed homes a fourth time later. I won't go into detail about that now since I'll have much more to say about Fyodor Pavlovich's firstborn later on, so for now, I'll stick to the essential facts about him, which are important before I begin my story.

To start with, this Mitya, or rather Dmitri Fyodorovich, was the only one of Fyodor Pavlovich's three sons who grew up believing that he had some property and that he would be financially independent when he came of age. His childhood and youth were irregular and troubled. He didn't finish his studies at the gymnasium, ended up at a military school, went to the Caucasus, was promoted, fought a duel, was demoted, earned promotion again, lived wildly, and spent a lot of money. He didn't receive any income from Fyodor Pavlovich until he came of age and was in debt by then. He saw and met his father, Fyodor Pavlovich, for the first time when he reached adulthood and visited our area to settle matters regarding his inheritance. It seems he didn't like his father. He didn't stay with him for long and quickly left after securing some money and arranging future payments from the estate, though he didn't manage (and this is important to note) to get a clear statement of the estate's revenues or value from his father during this visit.

Fyodor Pavlovich noted for the first time (this is also important to note) that Mitya had a vague and inflated idea of his inheritance. Fyodor Pavlovich was pleased with this since it fit his own plans. He understood that the young man was reckless, impulsive, passionate, impatient, and prone to excess, and that he would be satisfied with some quick money, though only for a short time. Fyodor Pavlovich began taking advantage of this, sending him small payments at various times. Eventually, four years later, when Mitya lost patience and returned to our little town to settle things once and for all, he was shocked to discover that he had nothing left, that it was difficult to get any accounting, and that he had already received the full value of his inheritance from Fyodor Pavlovich in small payments. He might even have owed his father money. Through various agreements, which he had willingly entered into over the years, Mitya had no right to expect anything more.

The young man was stunned, suspected he had been cheated, and became almost frantic. This situation led to the catastrophe, which is the subject of my first introductory story, or rather, its external cause. But before I get into that story, I need to say a little about Fyodor Pavlovich's other two sons and how they came into the picture.

Chapter 3: The Second Marriage and The Second Family

Very soon after getting rid of his four-year-old son Mitya, Fyodor Pavlovitch married again. His second marriage lasted eight years. He married his second wife, Sofya Ivanovna, who was also a very young girl, from another province, where he had gone on some small business trip with a Jew. Although Fyodor Pavlovitch was a drunk and a wicked man, he never neglected his finances and handled his business very successfully, though certainly not honestly. Sofya Ivanovna was the daughter of a poor deacon and had been an orphan since childhood, with no relatives. She was raised in the house of a general's widow, a rich old woman of high standing, who was both her benefactor and tormentor. I don't know all the details, but I've heard that this orphaned girl, who was quiet and gentle, was once found hanging by a noose from a nail in the attic because she was so miserable from the constant nagging and cruelty of the old woman. The widow wasn't necessarily a bad person, but she had turned into a tyrant out of boredom.

Fyodor Pavlovitch proposed to her, but when people inquired about him, the offer was refused. However, just like in his first marriage, he suggested that they elope. It's almost certain that Sofya would never have married him if she had known more about him in time. But she lived in a different province, and what could a sixteen-year-old girl know except that anything would be better than staying with her cruel benefactor? So, the poor girl traded one tyrant for another. This time, Fyodor Pavlovitch didn't get any money from the marriage because the general's widow was furious. She gave them nothing and cursed them both. But Fyodor hadn't expected a dowry; what attracted him was the girl's extraordinary beauty, especially her innocent appearance, which was particularly appealing to such a depraved man, who had previously only admired women of a rougher kind of beauty.

"Those innocent eyes cut through me like a razor," he used to say later, with a disgusting grin. In a man so corrupt, this was most likely nothing more than physical attraction. Since he didn't receive a dowry with his wife and, in a way, had "saved her from the noose," he didn't treat her with any respect. Making her feel like she owed him something, he took advantage of her extreme meekness and submission, trampling over the basic decency of marriage. He filled the house with loose women and held wild parties in front of his wife. To give an idea of how bad things were, I'll mention that even Grigory, the gloomy, stubborn, and argumentative servant who had always hated Fyodor's first wife, Adelaida Ivanovna, stood up for the new mistress. He defended her, scolding Fyodor Pavlovitch in a way that was very unbefitting of a servant. On one occasion, Grigory even broke up one of Fyodor's drunken parties and kicked all the disorderly women out of the house.

In the end, this poor young woman, who had been living in fear since childhood, developed a nervous condition similar to what people often call being "possessed by demons," which is most common among peasant women. At times, after severe fits of hysteria, she even lost her mind. Still, she gave birth to two sons, Ivan and Alexey—the first born in the first year of their marriage and the second three years later. When she died, little Alexey was just four years old, and although it may seem strange, I know that he remembered his mother for the rest of his life, though it was like a distant dream.

After her death, the same thing happened to Ivan and Alexey that had happened to their older brother Mitya. They were completely forgotten and abandoned by their father. Once again, Grigory took care of them, and they lived in his cottage, where they were found by the same tyrannical old lady who had raised their mother. She was still alive and had never forgotten the insult she had suffered eight years before. All that time, she had been keeping track of how Sofya was living, and when she heard about her illness and terrible living conditions, she said out loud to her servants several times, "She deserved it. God punished her for her ingratitude."

Exactly three months after Sofya Ivanovna's death, the general's widow suddenly arrived in our town and went straight to Fyodor Pavlovitch's house. She stayed in town for only half an hour, but she accomplished a lot. It was evening when Fyodor Pavlovitch, who hadn't seen her in eight years, came in, drunk. The story goes that as soon as she saw him, without saying a word, she slapped him twice across the face, grabbed a handful of his hair, and shook him up and down three times. Then, without another word, she went straight to the cottage where the two boys were.

Seeing at first glance that they were dirty and unwashed, she immediately gave Grigory a slap on the ear, and announced that she was taking the children away. She wrapped them in a rug, just as they were, put them in her carriage, and drove off to her town. Grigory took the slap like a devoted servant, without saying a word, and as he escorted the old lady to her carriage, he gave her a deep bow and said solemnly, "God will repay you for caring for the orphans." "You're an idiot anyway," the old lady shouted back as she drove off.

Fyodor Pavlovitch thought about it and decided that it was for the best. He didn't refuse the general's widow when she asked for formal consent to raise his children. As for the slaps, he drove around town telling everyone about the incident.

It so happened that the old lady died soon after, but in her will, she left the boys a thousand rubles each for their education, with the condition that the money be spread out until they turned twenty-one, as it was more than enough for "such children." The will was written in a strange, whimsical way, or so I've heard—I haven't read it myself. The main heir, Yefim Petrovitch Polenov, the Marshal of Nobility for the province, turned out to be an honest man. He wrote to Fyodor Pavlovitch, and realizing that he wouldn't get any real cooperation from him for the children's education—although Fyodor never directly refused, he just kept stalling and sometimes got overly emotional—Yefim Petrovitch took a personal interest in the orphans. He grew especially fond of the younger boy, Alexey, who lived with his family for a long time. Please note this from the beginning. It was thanks to Yefim Petrovitch, a man of rare generosity and kindness, that the boys received their education and upbringing. He kept the two thousand rubles left to them by the general's widow untouched, so that by the time they came of age, the money had doubled due to the accumulated interest. He paid for their education himself and spent far more than a thousand rubles on each of them. I won't go into the details of their childhood and youth, but I will mention a few important events.

As for the older brother, Ivan, I will only say that he grew into a somewhat gloomy and reserved boy, though far from shy. By the time he was ten, he understood that they were living not in their own home, but on someone else's charity, and that their father was a man too shameful to even talk about. People say that from a very young age, Ivan showed a remarkable talent for learning. I don't know the exact reason, but when he was barely thirteen, he left Yefim Petrovitch's household and went to a gymnasium in Moscow, living with a well-known and respected teacher, an old friend of Yefim Petrovitch. Ivan later said that this was all because of Yefim Petrovitch's enthusiasm for "good deeds" and his belief that a boy as gifted as Ivan should be trained by a gifted teacher. But by the time Ivan finished the gymnasium and entered the university, both Yefim Petrovitch and the teacher had passed away. Since no arrangements had been made for the money left by the general's widow, which had grown from one thousand to two, it was delayed due to the inevitable bureaucracy of Russia. This left Ivan in financial trouble during his first two years at university, as he had to support himself while studying. It should be noted that he never tried to contact his father, perhaps out of pride, contempt, or simply because his common sense told him that nothing good would come from such a man. No matter how things had turned out, the young man didn't feel discouraged and managed to find work. At first, he gave sixpenny lessons and later started writing short articles about street incidents for the newspapers under the name "Eye-Witness." These articles were said to be so engaging and sharp that they were quickly accepted. This alone proved the young man's practical and intellectual superiority over the many poor and unfortunate students of both genders who lingered around the offices of the newspapers, unable to think of anything better than constantly begging for copying or translating work from French. Once Ivan Fyodorovitch had made contact with the editors, he maintained his relationships with them, and in his later years at university, he published brilliant reviews of books on various specialized subjects, earning him recognition in literary circles. However, it was only in his final year that he unexpectedly caught the attention of a much broader audience, making many people take note of and remember him. It was a rather curious incident.

After he had just graduated from the university and was preparing to travel abroad with his two thousand roubles, Ivan Fyodorovitch published a strange article in one of the more prominent journals. It attracted significant attention and was on a topic he seemed to know nothing about, given that he was a student of natural sciences. The article was about the topic that was being widely debated at the time—the role of ecclesiastical courts. After discussing several opinions on the matter, he went on to explain his own view. What stood out most about the article was its tone and its unexpected conclusion. Many members of the Church believed without question that he was on their side. And yet, not only secularists but even atheists joined in praising it. Finally, some astute individuals suggested that the article was nothing more than a cheeky satirical burlesque. I mention this incident specifically because the article reached the famous monastery in our area, where the residents, who were particularly interested in the issue of ecclesiastical courts, were utterly baffled by it. When they learned the author's name, they became intrigued by the fact that he was a native of the town and the son of "that Fyodor Pavlovitch." And just at that time, the author himself appeared among us.

I remember asking myself with some unease why Ivan Fyodorovitch had come to visit us. This fateful visit, which marked the beginning of many subsequent events, was something I never fully explained to myself. On the surface, it seemed strange that a young man who was so well-educated, proud, and seemingly cautious would suddenly visit such a notorious house and a father who had ignored him all his life, barely knew him, never thought of him, and wouldn't have given him money under any circumstances—though he was always worried that his sons, Ivan and Alexey, would come to ask him for it. And yet, here was the young man staying in his father's house, living with him for two months, and they were getting along perfectly well. This fact puzzled many people besides myself.

Pyotr Alexandrovitch Miüsov, whom we've already mentioned, was the cousin of Fyodor Pavlovitch's first wife and happened to be visiting his estate in the neighborhood again. He had come from Paris, which was his permanent home. I remember that he was more surprised than anyone else when he met the young man, who fascinated him greatly, and with whom he sometimes argued, not without a feeling of inner unease when comparing his own knowledge to the young man's. "He's proud," he used to say, "he'll never be in need of money; he has enough to go abroad now. What could he want here? Everyone can see that he didn't come for money, as his father would never give him any. He's not interested in drinking and wild living, yet his father seems to depend on him. They get along so well together!"

This was true; the young man had a clear influence over his father, who seemed to be behaving more decently and even appeared ready to listen to his son's advice at times, though he could still be extremely difficult and even spiteful. It wasn't until later that we learned Ivan had come partly at the request of his elder brother, Dmitri, whom he met for the first time during this visit, although they had corresponded by letter before about an important matter that concerned Dmitri more than Ivan. What this matter was will be explained in due course. Yet even after learning of this particular circumstance, I still found Ivan Fyodorovitch to be a mysterious figure, and I thought his visit rather puzzling.

I should add that Ivan seemed to be acting as a mediator between his father and his elder brother, Dmitri, who was openly at odds with his father and was even planning to take legal action against him. The family, I repeat, was united for the first time, and some of its members were meeting each other for the first time in their lives. The youngest brother, Alexey, had already been with us for a year, having been the first of the three to arrive. It is about this brother, Alexey, that I find it hardest to speak in this introduction. Yet I must give a brief description of him, if only to explain one strange fact: I must introduce my hero to the reader while he's wearing the robes of a novice. Yes, for the past year, he had been living in our monastery, and he seemed ready to remain there for the rest of his life.

Chapter 4: The Third Son, Alyosha

He was only twenty years old, while his brother Ivan was twenty-four, and their older brother Dmitri was twenty- seven. First, I must explain that this young man, Alyosha, was not a fanatic, and in my opinion, not even a mystic. I might as well give my full opinion right from the start. He was simply someone who loved humanity from an early age, and the reason he chose the monastic life was that, at that time, it seemed to him like the perfect way to help his soul escape from the darkness of worldly wickedness into the light of love. And the reason this life appealed to him was that he found, or thought he had found, an extraordinary person in it: our famous elder, Zossima, to whom he became attached with all the warmth of his passionate heart's first love. But I do not deny that Alyosha was very unusual even back then and had been so from the time he was born. I have already mentioned that although he lost his mother when he was four, he remembered her for the rest of his life—her face, her tenderness, "as if she were still alive in front of me." Such memories can stay with a person, as everyone knows, even from an earlier age, perhaps even from two years old, but it's rare for them to stand out for a lifetime like a bright spot in the middle of darkness, like a piece torn from a large picture, with the rest of it faded and gone except for that fragment. That's how it was with him. He remembered one still summer evening, an open window, the slanting rays of the setting sun (that's what he recalled most clearly); in the corner of the room, there was a holy icon, a lit lamp in front of it, and his mother kneeling before it, sobbing hysterically with cries and moans. She snatched him up in her arms, squeezed him so tightly it hurt, and prayed over him to the Mother of God, holding him out in front of the icon as if offering him up to the Virgin's protection... and suddenly, a nurse ran in and, terrified, snatched him away from her. That was the image! And Alyosha remembered his mother's face in that moment. He used to say that it looked wild, but beautiful, as he remembered it. But he rarely liked to talk about this memory with anyone.

In his childhood and youth, Alyosha wasn't very outgoing, and he didn't talk much at all, but not because he was shy or unsociable; quite the opposite, in fact. It came from something else, a kind of personal, inner focus that had nothing to do with other people but was so important to him that it seemed to make him forget others. Yet he cared for people; all his life, he seemed to have complete trust in them, though no one ever thought of him as a fool or naive. There was something about him that made people feel right away (and this stayed with him throughout his life) that he wasn't the type to judge others—that he would never criticize anyone or condemn them for anything. It was like he accepted everything without the slightest hint of judgment, though he often felt deep sadness. This was true to such an extent that nothing could shock or scare him, even when he was very young. When he came to his father's house at twenty, a house filled with horrible depravity, he, as chaste and pure as he was, would simply leave the room in silence whenever what he saw was too unbearable, but he did so without the slightest sign of disgust or condemnation. His father, who had once been in a lowly position himself and was quick to take offense, at first met him with suspicion and gruffness. "He doesn't say much," his father would say, "but he thinks all the more." Yet, within two weeks, Fyodor Pavlovitch took to embracing him and kissing him far too often, with drunken tears and sentimental speeches, though he clearly felt a real and deep affection for Alyosha, something he had never been capable of feeling for anyone else before.

Everyone, indeed, loved this young man wherever he went, and it had been that way since he was a child. When he went to live with his benefactor and patron, Yefim Petrovitch Polenov, he won the hearts of the whole family, who treated him as their own child. He entered their home at such a young age that it couldn't have been from any plan or cleverness that he gained their affection. So, it seemed that the ability to make people love him instantly and without trying was part of his nature. It was the same at school, although he seemed to be one of those children who were often distrusted, sometimes teased, and even disliked by their classmates. He was dreamy and preferred to be alone. From an early age, he liked to sit in a corner and read, yet he was still a general favorite while at school. He was rarely playful or cheerful, but anyone could see right away that this wasn't because he was moody. On the contrary, he was bright and kind. He never tried to show off to his classmates. Maybe because of this, he was never afraid of anyone, and the boys immediately understood that he wasn't proud of his courage and didn't even seem aware that he was bold. He never held a grudge. If someone offended him, it wasn't uncommon for him to speak to the person an hour later, answering a question with the same open and trusting expression, as if nothing had happened between them. It wasn't that he seemed to have forgotten or deliberately forgiven the offense, but more that he didn't see it as an insult in the first place, and this won over his classmates.

There was one thing about him that made all the other boys, from the youngest to the oldest, want to tease him—not out of cruelty, but because it amused them. This was his extreme, almost fanatical modesty and chastity. He couldn't stand to hear certain words or conversations about women. Unfortunately, there are certain words and conversations that are impossible to avoid in schools. Even boys with pure minds and hearts, practically still children, talk at school about things, images, and ideas that even soldiers might hesitate to bring up. In fact, much of what soldiers don't even know about is familiar to very young children from our upper classes. There's no real corruption in it, no deep moral depravity, but it has the appearance of it, and it's often seen among them as something clever, daring, and worth imitating. When the boys saw that Alyosha Karamazov would cover his ears when they talked about "those things," they would sometimes crowd around him, pull his hands away, and shout vulgar things into both his ears. Alyosha would struggle, slip to the floor, and try to hide without ever saying a single word of abuse, enduring the insults silently. But eventually, they left him alone and stopped teasing him about being a "regular girl." What's more, they even began to look on it as a weakness and felt sorry for him. He was always one of the top students in his class, though he was never the best.

At the time of Yefim Petrovitch's death, Alyosha had two more years left to finish at the provincial gymnasium. The grieving widow left almost immediately after his death for a long trip to Italy, taking her entire family with her, which consisted only of women and girls. Alyosha went to live with two distant relatives of Yefim Petrovitch, women he had never met before. He didn't know what kind of relationship he had with them. It was very typical of Alyosha that he never cared about whose expense he was living on. In this way, he was a sharp contrast to his older brother Ivan, who struggled with poverty during his first two years at university, supported himself through his own efforts, and had been painfully aware since childhood of living on his benefactor's generosity. But this strange quality in Alyosha shouldn't be judged too harshly, for anyone who spent even a little time with him would soon realize that Alyosha was the kind of person who, if he suddenly came into a large fortune, would not hesitate to give it all away to anyone who asked, whether for good causes or even to a cunning swindler. Overall, he seemed hardly to understand the value of money—not in a literal sense, of course. When he was given pocket money, which he never asked for, he was either incredibly careless with it, spending it all at once, or he kept it for weeks, not knowing what to do with it.

In later years, Pyotr Alexandrovitch Miüsov, a man very particular about money and bourgeois honesty, made the following statement after getting to know Alyosha: "Here is perhaps the only man in the world whom you could leave without a penny, in the middle of an unknown city with a million inhabitants, and he wouldn't come to any harm. He wouldn't die of hunger or cold, because he would be fed and sheltered immediately. And if he wasn't, he would find a place to stay on his own, and it would cost him no effort or humiliation. In fact, giving him shelter wouldn't be a burden at all; it would probably feel like a pleasure."

He didn't finish his studies at the gymnasium. A year before the course was over, he suddenly told the ladies he was staying with that he was going to visit his father about a plan he had come up with. They were sad to see him go and didn't want him to leave. The trip wasn't expensive, and the ladies wouldn't let him pawn his watch, which had been a parting gift from his benefactor's family. They gave him plenty of money and even bought him new clothes and linens. However, he returned half the money, saying he planned to travel third class. When he arrived in town, he didn't answer his father's first question about why he had come before finishing his studies, and they say he seemed unusually thoughtful. It soon became clear that he was searching for his mother's grave. He practically admitted at the time that this was the main reason for his visit, though it probably wasn't the only one. It's likely that he himself didn't fully understand what had suddenly stirred in his soul and drawn him into a new, unknown, but inevitable path. Fyodor Pavlovitch couldn't tell him where his second wife, Alyosha's mother, was buried, as he had never visited the grave since throwing dirt on her coffin and had completely forgotten where she was buried over the years.

By the way, Fyodor Pavlovitch hadn't been living in our town for some time. Three or four years after his wife's death, he went to southern Russia and eventually ended up in Odessa, where he stayed for several years. He first became acquainted, as he put it, "with a lot of low Jews, Jewesses, and Jewkins," and eventually was accepted by "Jews high and low alike." It seems that during this time he developed a knack for making and saving money. He returned to our town only three years before Alyosha's arrival. His old acquaintances found him looking much older, though he wasn't an old man. He didn't behave with more dignity, but with more arrogance. The old fool had turned into someone who liked to make fools of others. His behavior with women had become not just wicked, but even more disgusting. Soon, he opened several new taverns in the area. It was clear that he had at least a hundred thousand rubles, if not more. Many people in town and the surrounding district were soon in debt to him, of course having provided good security. Recently, he had started to look more bloated and seemed more unpredictable and inconsistent. He had become scattered, starting one thing and then moving on to something else, as if he was losing control of himself. He was also drunk more and more often. If it hadn't been for his old servant, Grigory, who had also aged a lot by that time and now looked after him almost like a caretaker, Fyodor Pavlovitch might have ended up in serious trouble. Alyosha's arrival even seemed to stir something in him morally, as if something that had long been dead in his soul had awakened.

"Do you know," he often said, looking at Alyosha, "you look just like her, 'the crazy woman'"—that's what he used to call his dead wife, Alyosha's mother. It was Grigory who pointed out "the crazy woman's" grave to Alyosha. He took him to the town cemetery and showed him a modest iron tombstone in a remote corner. It was simple, but well-kept, with her name, age, and the date of her death, along with a four-line verse typical of old-fashioned middle-class graves. To Alyosha's surprise, Grigory had arranged for this tombstone. He had paid for it himself after Fyodor Pavlovitch, who Grigory had pestered many times about the grave, left for Odessa, abandoning the grave and all memories of it. Alyosha didn't show any strong emotions at the sight of his mother's grave. He simply listened to Grigory's detailed and serious explanation of how the tombstone had been put up, stood with his head bowed, and left without saying a word. It was probably a year before he visited the cemetery again. But this little event had an odd effect on Fyodor Pavlovitch. He suddenly took a thousand rubles to the monastery to pay for prayers for the soul of his first wife, Adelaida Ivanovna, who used to beat him, but not for his second wife, Alyosha's mother, the "crazy woman." That same evening, he got drunk and insulted the monks in front of Alyosha. He was far from religious himself and probably had never even lit a candle in front of a saint's icon. Strange outbursts of emotion and sudden thoughts are common in people like him.

I already mentioned that he looked bloated. His face at that time showed clear signs of the life he had lived. Besides the long, fleshy bags under his small, always insolent, suspicious, and mocking eyes, and the deep wrinkles on his chubby face, his Adam's apple hung below his sharp chin like a large, fleshy lump, which gave him a particularly ugly, sensual appearance. Add to that his long, greedy mouth with thick lips, through which you could see small, rotting black teeth. He would drool whenever he started talking. He loved making fun of his own appearance, though I think he was secretly proud of it. He especially liked to point to his nose, which wasn't large, but was very thin and noticeably hooked. "A real Roman nose," he would say. "With my goiter, I look like an ancient Roman patrician from the decadent period." He seemed proud of it.

Not long after visiting his mother's grave, Alyosha suddenly announced that he wanted to join the monastery, and that the monks were willing to accept him as a novice. He explained that this was his strong desire, and that he was formally asking for his father's permission. The old man knew that the elder Zossima, who lived in the hermitage of the monastery, had made a special impression on his "gentle boy."

"That's the most honest monk among them, of course," he said after listening quietly to Alyosha, not really surprised by his request. "Hmmm... So that's where you want to go, my gentle boy?" He was half-drunk and suddenly grinned his slow, tipsy grin, which had a touch of slyness. "Hmmm... I had a feeling you'd end up like this. Can you believe it? You were heading straight for it. Well, at least you've got your own two thousand roubles. That's a dowry for you. And don't worry, I won't abandon you, my angel. I'll pay whatever's needed for you there if they ask for it. But of course, if they don't ask, why should we bother them? What do you think? You know, you spend money like a bird—just a little bit each week. Hmmm... You know, there's a place near one monastery, outside of town, where everyone knows that 'the monks' wives' live, as they call them. Thirty women, I think. I've been there myself. It's interesting in its own way, I guess, for variety's sake. The worst part is, it's so very Russian. No French women there. Of course, they could get them easily if they wanted; they've got plenty of money. If they find out about it, they'll show up. But there's none of that here—no 'monks' wives,' just two hundred monks. They're honest. They follow the fasts. I'll admit that... Hmmm... So you want to be a monk? And you know, I'm sorry to lose you, Alyosha; would you believe it, I've really grown fond of you? Well, it's a good opportunity. You'll pray for us sinners—we've sinned way too much here. I've always wondered who would pray for me, and if there was anyone in the world who would do it. My dear boy, I'm so dumb about that. You wouldn't believe it. Really dumb. You see, even though I'm so stupid about it, I still keep thinking, from time to time, of course—not all the time. It's impossible for me to believe that the devils would forget to drag me down to hell with their hooks when I die. Then I start thinking—hooks? Where would they get them? What would they be made of? Iron hooks? Do they have some kind of foundry down there? The monks in the monastery probably believe that there's a ceiling in hell, for example. Now, I'm willing to believe in hell, but without a ceiling. It makes it more refined, more enlightened, more Lutheran, you know? And really, does it even matter if it has a ceiling or not? But, you know, there's a tricky question in all of this. If there's no ceiling, then there can't be hooks, and if there aren't any hooks, then the whole thing falls apart, which is unlikely, because then there'd be no hooks to drag me down to hell. And if they don't drag me down, where's the justice in the world? They'd have to invent those hooks just for me, on purpose, because if you only knew, Alyosha, what a scoundrel I am."

"But there are no hooks," said Alyosha, looking at his father gently and seriously.

"Yes, yes, only the shadows of hooks, I know, I know. That's how a Frenchman once described hell: 'I saw the shadow of a coachman brushing the shadow of a carriage with the shadow of a brush.' How do you know there are no hooks, my boy? When you've lived with the monks, you'll change your mind. But go find out the truth there and then come back and tell me. Anyway, it's easier to face the next world if you know what's waiting there. Besides, it's probably better for you to be with the monks than here with me, with a drunken old man and young women... though you're like an angel, nothing seems to touch you. And I bet nothing will touch you there either. That's why I'm letting you go, because I have hope for that. You've got your head on straight. You'll burn, and you'll burn out; you'll be healed and then come back. And I'll wait for you. I feel like you're the only person in the world who hasn't condemned me. My dear boy, I feel it, you know. I just can't help feeling it."

And he even started crying. He was emotional. He was both wicked and emotional.

Chapter 5: Elders

Some of my readers might think that this young man was weak, overly emotional, or underdeveloped, a pale, sickly dreamer. But on the contrary, Alyosha was, at this time, a well-developed, red-cheeked, clear-eyed young man of nineteen, glowing with health. He was also very handsome, with a graceful figure, moderately tall, dark brown hair, a regular, rather long, oval face, and wide-set, bright, dark gray eyes. He was very thoughtful and seemed very calm. Perhaps someone will tell me that red cheeks are not incompatible with fanaticism and mysticism; but I believe Alyosha was more of a realist than anyone. Oh, no doubt, in the monastery, he fully believed in miracles, but I think that miracles are never a stumbling block for a realist. Miracles are not what make realists believe. A true realist, if he doesn't believe, will always find the strength and ability to not believe in the miraculous. And if he is confronted with a miracle as an undeniable fact, he would rather doubt his own senses than admit the fact. Even if he does admit it, he accepts it as a fact of nature that he had not previously understood. Faith doesn't come from miracles for a realist, but miracles come from faith. If a realist begins to believe, then his realism itself forces him to also accept the miraculous. The Apostle Thomas said that he wouldn't believe until he saw it for himself, but when he did see it, he said, "My Lord and my God!" Did the miracle force him to believe? Most likely, it didn't; he believed because he wanted to believe, and perhaps he already fully believed in his heart, even when he said, "I won't believe until I see it."

Perhaps someone will say that Alyosha was stupid, undeveloped, that he hadn't finished his studies, and so on. It's true that he didn't finish his studies but saying that he was stupid or dull would be a great injustice. I'll simply repeat what I've already said. He chose this path because, at that time, it alone captured his imagination and presented itself to him as the ideal way to free his soul from darkness and bring it into the light. Add to that the fact that he was, in some sense, a young man of his time—honest in his nature, searching for the truth, seeking it, and believing in it, wanting to serve it immediately with all the strength of his soul, seeking immediate action, and ready to sacrifice everything, even his life, for it. However, these young men often fail to realize that sacrificing one's life is, in many cases, the easiest sacrifice of all. To sacrifice five or six years of their passionate youth to hard and tedious studies, just to multiply their power to serve the truth and the cause they have chosen, is a sacrifice that is beyond the strength of many. The path Alyosha chose was one that went in the opposite direction, but he chose it with the same thirst for swift achievement. As soon as he seriously reflected on it, he became convinced of the existence of God and immortality, and immediately said to himself, "I want to live for immortality, and I won't accept any compromise." In the same way, if he had decided that God and immortality didn't exist, he would have immediately become an atheist and a socialist. Because socialism is not just about the labor question; it is, above all, the atheistic question—the form atheism takes today, the question of building the Tower of Babel without God, not to reach heaven from the earth, but to create heaven on earth. Alyosha would have found it strange and impossible to keep living the way he had before. It is written: "Give all that you have to the poor and follow Me, if you wish to be perfect."

Alyosha said to himself, "I can't just give two roubles instead of everything and go to mass instead of truly following Him." Perhaps the memories of his childhood brought back thoughts of the monastery, where his mother might have taken him to mass. Perhaps the slanting sunlight and the image of the holy icon, to which his poor "crazy" mother had held him up, still stirred his imagination. Reflecting on all this, he may have come to us to see whether here he could sacrifice everything or only "two roubles," and in the monastery, he met this elder. I must digress for a moment to explain what an "elder" is in Russian monasteries, and I regret that I don't feel very competent to do so. I'll try, however, to give a brief account of it. Experts on the subject say that the institution of "elders" is a relatively recent development, no more than a hundred years old in our monasteries, although it has existed in the Orthodox East, especially in Sinai and Athos, for over a thousand years. It's claimed that it existed in ancient Russia as well, but because of the disasters that befell Russia—the Tatar invasions, civil wars, and the interruption of ties with the East after the fall of Constantinople—this institution fell into oblivion. It was revived in Russia towards the end of the last century by one of the great ascetics, Païssy Velitchkovsky, and his followers. But even now, it exists only in a few monasteries and has sometimes been almost persecuted as an innovation in Russia. It flourished especially in the famous Optina Monastery in Kozelsk. When and how it came to our monastery, I cannot say. By the time of this story, there had already been three such elders, and Zossima was the last. But he was very ill and weak, and they had no one to replace him. This was an important issue for our monastery, as it had not been particularly famous for anything else: it had no relics of saints, no miracle-working icons, no glorious traditions, no notable historical events. It had become well-known throughout Russia because of its elders, whom pilgrims traveled thousands of miles to see and hear.

So, what was an elder? An elder was someone who took your soul and your will into his own soul and his own will. When you chose an elder, you gave up your own will and surrendered it completely to him in full submission, complete self-denial. This novitiate, this difficult school of self-denial, was taken up voluntarily in the hope of mastering oneself. After a life of obedience, the goal was to achieve perfect freedom—freedom from oneself—in order to escape the fate of those who live their whole lives without ever finding their true selves. This institution of elders was not founded on theory but grew out of a thousand years of practice in the East. The obligations to an elder were not the same as the ordinary obedience that had always existed in Russian monasteries. It involved confessing everything to the elder, and there was an unbreakable bond between the elder and the person who submitted to him.

There's a story, for instance, from the early days of Christianity. A novice, who had failed to fulfill a command given to him by his elder, left his monastery in Syria and went to Egypt. There, after great efforts, he was eventually deemed worthy to suffer torture and die a martyr for the faith. But when the Church was preparing to bury him as a saint, something strange happened. At the deacon's call, "Depart all ye unbaptized," the coffin containing the martyr's body was thrown out of the church, not once, but three times. It was only then that they learned this holy man had broken his vow of obedience by leaving his elder, and because of this, he could not be forgiven without the elder's absolution, despite his great deeds. Only after this could the funeral take place. Of course, this is just an old legend. But here is a more recent example...

A monk was suddenly ordered by his elder to leave Athos, which he cherished as a holy place and a safe refuge, and to first go to Jerusalem to pay homage to the Holy Places, then to head north to Siberia: "That is where you belong, not here." The monk, filled with sorrow, went to the Ecumenical Patriarch in Constantinople and begged him to release him from his vow of obedience. But the Patriarch answered that he had no power to release him and that no one on earth had such power except the elder who had given him the order. This shows that elders, in certain cases, possess unexplainable and limitless authority. This is why, in many of our monasteries, the institution of elders was initially met with resistance, almost to the point of persecution. Meanwhile, the elders quickly gained great respect among the people. Large numbers of ordinary people, as well as people of distinction, came to the elders in our monastery to confess their doubts, sins, and troubles, seeking advice and comfort. Seeing this, the opponents of the elders argued that the sacrament of confession was being degraded, treated lightly, though the act of opening one's heart to the elder, whether by a monk or a layperson, was not the same as the sacrament of confession. However, the institution of elders has persisted and is now firmly established in Russian monasteries. Perhaps it is true that this practice, which has endured for a thousand years as a tool for transforming a person from spiritual slavery to freedom and moral perfection, can be a double-edged sword. In some cases, instead of leading to humility and self-control, it might lead to pride, which is the opposite of freedom—it becomes a kind of slavery.

Elder Zossima was sixty-five years old. He came from a family of landowners and had served as a young officer in the army, stationed in the Caucasus. There was no doubt that he had deeply impressed Alyosha with some special quality of his soul. Alyosha lived in the elder's cell, as the elder was very fond of him and allowed him to serve him. It should be noted that Alyosha was not under any strict obligations and could go where he wished, sometimes being absent for days at a time. Although he wore the monastic robes, it was by choice, so as not to be different from the others. No doubt he enjoyed wearing them. Perhaps his youthful imagination was deeply stirred by the elder's power and fame. It was said that for many years, people came to confess their sins to Father Zossima and ask for his advice and prayers, and that he had developed such keen intuition that he could tell, just by looking at an unfamiliar face, what a person needed and what troubled their conscience. He sometimes astonished and even frightened visitors by knowing their secrets before they had spoken.

Alyosha noticed that almost everyone who came to see the elder for the first time was filled with nervousness and unease, but they left with bright and joyful faces. Alyosha was particularly struck by the fact that Father Zossima was not at all harsh or stern. On the contrary, he was always cheerful. The monks said that the elder seemed to be especially drawn to those who had committed the greatest sins, and the worse the sinner, the more he loved them. Of course, even up to the end of his life, there were a few monks who disliked and envied him, but they were few in number and kept quiet, though some of them held important positions in the monastery. One, for example, was an older monk known for his strict fasting and vows of silence. But the majority of the monks were on Father Zossima's side, and many of them loved him with all their hearts, deeply and sincerely. Some were almost fanatically devoted to him and quietly proclaimed that he was a saint, that there could be no doubt. And as his death neared, they expected miracles and great fame for the monastery because of his relics. Alyosha had complete faith in the elder's miraculous powers, just as he fully believed in the story of the coffin that flew out of the church. He saw many people who brought their sick children or relatives to the elder, begging him to lay hands on them and pray. These people would soon return—some as early as the next day—falling at the elder's feet in tears, thanking him for healing their loved ones.

Whether these people had truly been healed or if their conditions had simply improved naturally wasn't something Alyosha ever questioned, because he wholeheartedly believed in the spiritual power of his teacher and took joy in the elder's fame and glory, as if it were his own triumph. His heart would pound with excitement, and his face would light up whenever the elder came out to greet the crowds of pilgrims, mostly humble people, who had traveled from all over Russia just to see him and receive his blessing. They would fall down before him, weeping, kissing his feet, kissing the ground where he stood, while women held up their children to him and brought their sick, those said to be "possessed by demons." The elder would speak to them, say a short prayer, bless them, and send them away. Recently, he had become so weak from illness that he sometimes couldn't leave his cell, and the pilgrims would wait for several days for him to come out. Alyosha didn't wonder why people loved him so much, why they would fall before him and weep just at the sight of his face. He understood that for the humble souls of Russian peasants, worn out by hardship and endless injustice—both their own and the world's—it was a deep need and comfort to find someone or something holy to bow before and worship.

"Among us, there is sin, injustice, and temptation, but somewhere on earth, there is someone who is holy and pure. He holds the truth; he knows the truth. So, it is not dead on the earth. And one day, the truth will come to us, too, and rule over the entire earth as it was promised." Alyosha knew that this is exactly how the people felt and even thought. He understood it, and that Elder Zossima was this saint and keeper of God's truth—he had no more doubt about this than the weeping peasants and the sick women who held out their children to the elder. The belief that, after his death, the elder would bring great glory to the monastery was even stronger in Alyosha than in anyone else. And lately, a deep fire of inner excitement burned more and more brightly in his heart. He wasn't troubled at all by the fact that the elder was the only example of holiness before him. "No matter. He is holy. He carries within his heart the secret to renewing the world: the power that will finally bring truth to the earth, so that all men will be holy and love one another. There will be no rich or poor, no one high or low, but all will be like the children of God, and the true Kingdom of Christ will come." That was the dream burning in Alyosha's heart. The arrival of his two brothers, whom he had not known before, seemed to make a strong impression on Alyosha.

He became friends with his half-brother Dmitri (who arrived later) more quickly than with his own brother Ivan. He was extremely interested in Ivan, but even after two months in the town, though they had seen each other often, they still weren't close. Alyosha was naturally quiet, and he seemed to be waiting for something, feeling embarrassed about something, while Ivan, although Alyosha noticed at first that he looked at him long and curiously, seemed to stop thinking about him after a while. Alyosha noticed this with some discomfort. He first thought his brother's lack of interest might be because of their difference in age and education. But he also wondered whether there might be some other reason for Ivan's distance that he didn't understand. He kept imagining that Ivan was focused on something—something important and difficult to achieve—and that this was why he had no thoughts for him. Alyosha also wondered if Ivan, as a learned atheist, might look down on him as a foolish novice. He knew for sure that his brother was an atheist, and if Ivan felt any contempt, Alyosha couldn't take offense. Still, with a quiet discomfort that he didn't fully understand, he waited for his brother to draw closer to him. Dmitri often spoke of Ivan with deep respect and seriousness. From him, Alyosha learned all the details about the important matter that had recently created a strong bond between the two older brothers. Dmitri's enthusiastic praise of Ivan stood out even more to Alyosha, since Dmitri was almost uneducated compared to Ivan, and the two brothers were so different in personality and character that it would be hard to find two people more unlike.

It was around this time that the meeting, or rather the gathering, of these family members, who were so at odds with one another, took place in the cell of the elder who had such a powerful influence on Alyosha. The reason for the meeting wasn't genuine. At the time, the conflict between Dmitri and his father was at its most intense, and their relationship had become unbearably strained. It seems that Fyodor Pavlovitch was the first to suggest, apparently as a joke, that they should all meet in Father Zossima's cell. He suggested that, even without directly asking the elder to intervene, they might be able to reach some understanding under the influence of his calming presence. Dmitri, who had never met the elder before, naturally assumed that his father was trying to frighten him, but feeling guilty about his recent outbursts toward his father, he accepted the challenge. It should be noted that Dmitri wasn't staying with his father like Ivan was, but was living at the other end of town. It so happened that Pyotr Alexandrovitch Miüsov, who was staying in the district at the time, eagerly seized upon the idea. A liberal thinker from the 1840s and 1850s, and an atheist, Miüsov might have been motivated by boredom or by the hope of some lighthearted entertainment. He was suddenly struck by the desire to visit the monastery and see the holy man. Since he was still involved in a lawsuit with the monastery, he used this as an excuse to meet with the Superior in hopes of resolving the matter peacefully. A visitor coming with such a respectable purpose might be received with more attention and respect than one who came just out of curiosity. The elder, who had hardly left his cell recently due to illness and had turned away even his usual visitors, was finally persuaded by those within the monastery to agree to the meeting. In the end, he consented, and the day was set. "Who made me their judge?" was all he said to Alyosha with a smile.

Alyosha was deeply troubled when he heard about the planned visit. Out of all the quarreling, argumentative family members, Dmitri was the only one who might take the meeting seriously. Alyosha knew well that the others were coming with more trivial or disrespectful intentions toward the elder. Ivan and Miüsov would likely come out of mere curiosity, perhaps of the worst kind, and his father might be planning some kind of joke. Although he didn't say anything, Alyosha fully understood his father. The boy, I should note, was far from being as simple as people thought. He awaited the day with a heavy heart. It's clear that he was always thinking about how the family's conflict might be resolved, but his main concern was for the elder. He trembled with worry for him, for his honor, and he feared any insult to him, especially the polite but mocking attitude of Miüsov and the condescending remarks from the highly educated Ivan. He even thought about warning the elder, telling him something about what to expect, but after thinking it over, he decided to say nothing. The day before the meeting, he sent a message through a friend to Dmitri, telling him that he loved him and hoped he would keep his promise. Dmitri was puzzled because he couldn't remember making any promise, but he wrote back, saying that he would do his best not to let himself be provoked "by anything vile." He added that although he had deep respect for the elder and for Ivan, he was certain that the meeting was either a trap for him or just a pointless joke. "Even so," he concluded, "I'd rather bite my tongue off than show any disrespect to the holy man whom you hold in such high regard." Alyosha was not greatly reassured by the letter.

Book 2: An Unfortunate Gathering

Chapter 1: They Arrive at The Monastery

It was a warm, bright day at the end of August. The meeting with the elder had been set for 11:30, right after the late mass. Our visitors did not attend the service but arrived just as it was ending. First, an elegant open carriage drawn by two valuable horses arrived, carrying Miüsov and a distant relative of his, a young man of twenty named Pyotr Fomitch Kalganov. This young man was preparing to go to university. Miüsov, with whom he was staying, was trying to persuade him to study abroad at the University of Zurich or Jena. The young man had not yet made up his mind. He was thoughtful and often lost in his own world. He was good-looking, strongly built, and rather tall. At times, there was a strange fixedness in his gaze. Like many absent-minded people, he would sometimes stare at someone without actually seeing them. He was quiet and somewhat awkward, but at times, when alone with someone, he could become talkative and animated, laughing at things that were either small or nothing at all. Yet, his liveliness would fade as quickly as it appeared. He was always dressed well, and even a bit too elaborately. He already had some independent fortune and expected much more in the future. He was a friend of Alyosha's.

In an old, rattling but roomy rented carriage, with a pair of old pinkish-gray horses, far behind Miüsov's carriage, came Fyodor Pavlovitch and his son Ivan. Dmitri was late, even though he had been informed of the time the evening before. The visitors left their carriages at the hotel outside the monastery grounds and walked to the gates of the monastery on foot. None of the group, except Fyodor Pavlovitch, had ever been to the monastery before, and Miüsov had likely not even been to church in thirty years. He looked around with curiosity, trying to appear at ease. But aside from the church and the simple domestic buildings, which were quite ordinary, he found nothing of interest inside the monastery. The last of the worshippers were leaving the church, bareheaded and making the sign of the cross. Among the humble folk were a few people of higher rank—two or three women and a very old general. They were all staying at the hotel. Our visitors were immediately surrounded by beggars, but none of them gave anything, except for young Kalganov, who nervously took a ten- copeck piece from his purse and, for some reason embarrassed, quickly handed it to an old woman, saying, "Share it equally." None of his companions commented on it, so he had no reason to feel awkward, but realizing this only made him feel even more self-conscious.

It was strange that their arrival did not seem to be expected and that they were not greeted with any special honors, even though one of them had recently donated a thousand roubles, and another was a wealthy and well-educated landowner, on whom the monastery somewhat depended. A ruling on a lawsuit could soon put the monastery's fishing rights into his hands. Yet, no official came out to meet them.

Miüsov absent-mindedly glanced at the tombstones around the church and was about to comment that the dead buried there must have paid a considerable sum for the privilege of being buried in this "holy place," but he held his tongue. His liberal sarcasm was quickly turning into frustration.

"Who are we supposed to ask for directions in this ridiculous place? We need to find out; time is slipping by," he said, almost to himself.

Just then, an elderly, bald man with small, eager eyes approached them. He was wearing a full summer coat. Lifting his hat, he introduced himself in a sweet, lisping voice as Maximov, a landowner from Tula. He immediately understood their dilemma.

"Father Zossima lives in the hermitage, separate from the monastery, about four hundred paces away, on the other side of the woods."

"I know it's on the other side of the woods," Fyodor Pavlovitch replied, "but we don't remember the way. It's been a long time since we've been here."

"This way, through this gate, straight across the woods... the woods. Come with me, won't you? I'm going that way myself. This way, this way."

They exited the gate and turned toward the woods. Maximov, a man of sixty, moved more like he was running than walking, turning sideways to stare at them all with an almost wild curiosity. His eyes seemed to bulge from his head.

"You see, we've come to the elder on personal business," Miüsov said sharply. "He's agreed to meet with us, so while we appreciate your guidance, we can't ask you to join us."

"I've been there! I've already been! A true knight!" Maximov snapped his fingers in the air.

"A knight? Who's a knight?" Miüsov asked.

"The elder! The great elder! The pride and joy of the monastery, Zossima. What a great elder!"

But his rambling was interrupted by a pale, tired-looking monk of medium height, wearing a monk's cap, who had caught up to them. Fyodor Pavlovitch and Miüsov stopped.

The monk, with a deep, polite bow, announced, "The Father Superior invites all of you gentlemen to join him for dinner after your visit to the hermitage. At one o'clock, no later. And you too," he added, addressing Maximov.

"I'll definitely be there," Fyodor Pavlovitch said, clearly delighted by the invitation. "And I promise we've all agreed to behave ourselves here. What about you, Pyotr Alexandrovitch? Will you come?"

"Yes, of course. Why else would I be here, if not to observe everything? The only problem is having to put up with you…"

"And Dmitri Fyodorovitch is still nowhere to be found."

"It'd be great if he didn't show up at all. Do you think I'm enjoying all this nonsense, especially with you? Fine, we'll go to dinner. Thank the Father Superior," he said to the monk.

"It's my duty to escort you to the elder now," the monk replied.

"Well then, I'll head straight to the Father Superior... straight to the Father Superior," Maximov babbled.

"The Father Superior is busy at the moment, but as you wish," the monk hesitated.

"What a rude old man!" Miüsov said out loud as Maximov hurried back toward the monastery.

"He reminds me of von Sohn," Fyodor Pavlovitch said suddenly.

"That's all you can think of? How does he remind you of von Sohn? Have you even met von Sohn?"

"I've seen his portrait. It's not the facial features, it's something else. I can't explain it. He's a second von Sohn. I can always tell by looking at someone's face."

"Oh, I'm sure you're an expert at that. But listen, Fyodor Pavlovitch, you mentioned earlier that we promised to behave ourselves. Don't forget that. I suggest you control yourself. But if you start acting up, I'm not staying with you. Look at him," he said, turning to the monk, "I'm afraid to be seen with him in decent company."

The monk's pale lips curled into a slight, amused smile, but he remained silent, clearly out of respect for the situation. Miüsov frowned even more.

"Ugh, to hell with all this!" Miüsov thought angrily. "Centuries of elaborate tradition, and underneath it all, just lies and nonsense."

"Look, here's the hermitage! We've arrived," Fyodor Pavlovitch exclaimed. "The gates are shut."

And he repeatedly made the sign of the cross toward the saints painted above and on the sides of the gates.

"When in Rome, do as the Romans do. Here in this hermitage, there are twenty-five saints being saved. They watch each other and eat cabbages. Not a single woman enters through this gate. That's what's remarkable. And it's true. But I've heard the elder does see ladies," Fyodor Pavlovitch suddenly said to the monk.

"Women of the people are here now, lying in the portico, waiting. But for ladies of higher rank, two rooms have been built next to the portico, outside the main grounds. You can see the windows from here. The elder goes to see them through a private passage when he feels well enough. They always stay outside the grounds. Right now, a lady from Harkov, Madame Hohlakov, is waiting there with her sick daughter. He has probably promised to see her, though he's been so weak lately that he's hardly come out, even for the people."

"So, there are ways to sneak out of the hermitage to visit the ladies. Don't get me wrong, holy father, I don't mean anything bad by that. But did you know that at Athos, not only are women not allowed, but no female creature at all—no hens, turkeys, or cows?"

"Fyodor Pavlovitch, I'm warning you. I'll leave and let them throw you out once I'm gone."

"But I'm not bothering you, Pyotr Alexandrovitch. Look!" he suddenly shouted, stepping inside the grounds, "What a beautiful place they live in!"

Though there were no roses at this time of year, there were many rare and beautiful autumn flowers growing wherever they could, clearly cared for by a skillful hand. Flower beds were placed around the church and between the graves, and the small, one- story wooden house where the elder lived was also surrounded by flowers.

"And was it like this when the last elder, Varsonofy, was here? He didn't care about all this elegance. They say he used to jump up and beat ladies with a stick," Fyodor Pavlovitch remarked as he walked up the steps.

"Elder Varsonofy could seem a bit strange at times, but a lot of what people say is just nonsense. He never beat anyone," the monk replied. "Now, gentlemen, if you'll wait a moment, I'll go announce you."

"Fyodor Pavlovitch, for the last time—remember our agreement, do you hear? Behave yourself, or I'll make sure you regret it!" Miüsov muttered again.

"I don't know why you're so upset," Fyodor Pavlovitch said sarcastically. "Are you worried about your sins? They say the elder can tell why you've come just by looking into your eyes. And you care so much about what he thinks! You, a man from Paris, so sophisticated. I'm really surprised."

But Miüsov didn't have time to reply to this remark. They were invited to come inside. He entered, already feeling annoyed.

"I know myself too well. I'm going to get angry, start arguing, and embarrass myself and my beliefs," he thought.

Chapter 2: The Old Buffoon

They entered the room almost at the same moment the elder came in from his bedroom. Two monks from the hermitage were already in the cell, waiting for the elder—one was the Father Librarian, and the other was Father Païssy, who, according to reports, was a very learned man, though he was in poor health, despite not being old. There was also a tall young man, who looked about twenty-two, standing quietly in the corner throughout the meeting. He had a broad, fresh face, sharp, observant brown eyes, and he was dressed in ordinary clothing. He was a divinity student, living under the protection of the monastery. His expression showed unquestioning but self-respecting reverence. Being in a lower, dependent position, and therefore not on equal footing with the guests, he didn't greet them with a bow.

Father Zossima entered the room accompanied by a novice and Alyosha. The two monks stood up and greeted him with deep bows, touching the floor with their fingers, and then kissed his hand. After blessing them, the elder bowed just as deeply in return and asked for their blessing. The entire ceremony was done with great seriousness and genuine emotion, unlike a daily ritual. But Miüsov thought it was all done deliberately to leave an impression. He stood in front of the other visitors. He had considered the night before that, out of simple politeness and because it was the custom here, he ought to have gone up to receive the elder's blessing, even if he did not kiss his hand. But when he saw all the bowing and kissing from the monks, he changed his mind instantly. Instead, he made a dignified, conventional bow and stepped back to take a seat. Fyodor Pavlovitch did the same, imitating Miüsov like a monkey. Ivan bowed with great dignity and courtesy, but he kept his hands at his sides, while Kalganov was so confused that he did not bow at all. The elder lowered his hand, which he had raised to bless them, bowed again, and asked everyone to sit down. Alyosha's face flushed red. He felt embarrassed. His worst fears were coming true.

Father Zossima sat on a very old-fashioned mahogany sofa covered with leather and had his visitors sit down in a row along the opposite wall on four mahogany chairs with worn-out black leather. The monks took seats, one by the door and the other by the window. The divinity student, the novice, and Alyosha remained standing. The cell wasn't very large and looked faded. It had only the most basic furniture, all of it coarse and poor in quality. There were two pots of flowers on the windowsill and a number of holy icons in the corner. In front of one large, ancient icon of the Virgin, a lamp was burning. Nearby were two other holy pictures in bright frames, and next to them were carved cherubim, china eggs, a Catholic cross made of ivory with a Mater Dolorosa embracing it, and several foreign engravings from famous Italian artists of centuries past. Next to these expensive and artistic engravings were some of the crudest Russian prints of saints and martyrs, the kind sold cheaply at fairs. On the other walls were portraits of Russian bishops, both from the past and the present.

Miüsov gave a quick glance at all these "traditional" surroundings and then focused his attention on the elder. He had a high opinion of his own judgment, a trait understandable for a man of fifty, a time when a clever, worldly man of established position can't help but take himself rather seriously. At first glance, he didn't like Zossima. There was something in the elder's face that others besides Miüsov might also dislike. The elder was short, bent, with very weak legs, and though he was only sixty-five, he looked at least ten years older. His face was thin, lined with a fine web of wrinkles, especially around his eyes, which were small, light-colored, quick, and bright like two shining points. He had a sprinkling of gray hair around his temples. His pointed beard was small and sparse, and his lips, which smiled often, were as thin as two threads. His nose wasn't long, but sharp, like a bird's beak.

"To all appearances, a malicious soul, full of petty pride," thought Miüsov, feeling unhappy with the situation.

A cheap little clock on the wall quickly struck twelve, signaling the start of the conversation.

"Right on time!" Fyodor Pavlovitch exclaimed, "but no sign of my son Dmitri. I must apologize for him, dear elder!" (Alyosha shuddered at the words "dear elder.") "I'm always punctual, down to the minute, because I remember that punctuality is the courtesy of kings."

"But you're not a king," Miüsov muttered, immediately losing control of his temper.

"Yes, that's true. I'm not a king, and, would you believe it, Pyotr Alexandrovitch, I'm aware of that myself. But, there! I always say the wrong thing. Your reverence," he suddenly cried with dramatic intensity, "you see before you a fool, a fool in all seriousness! I introduce myself as such. It's an old habit, alas! And if I sometimes talk nonsense at the wrong time, it's with the aim of amusing people, making myself likable. You have to be likable, don't you? Seven years ago, I was in a small town for business, and I made friends with some merchants. We went to see the chief of police for some reason and invited him to dine with us. He was a tall, fat, fair-haired, grumpy man—the most dangerous kind in these situations. It's all because of their liver, you see. I went

23

up to him confidently, like a man of the world, and said, 'Mr. Ispravnik, be our Napravnik.' 'What do you mean by Napravnik?' he asked. I knew right away my joke had failed; he stood there looking so serious. 'I meant it as a joke,' I explained, 'for the sake of good humor. Mr. Napravnik is our well-known Russian conductor, and for harmony, we need someone like him.' I thought I explained it quite well, didn't I? 'Excuse me,' he said, 'I'm an Ispravnik, and I do not tolerate puns on my position.' He turned and walked away. I followed him, shouting, 'Yes, yes, you're an Ispravnik, not a Napravnik.' 'No,' he replied, 'since you called me Napravnik, I'm Napravnik now.' And would you believe it? That ruined our business! I always do this. I always ruin things with my politeness. Once, many years ago, I said to an important person, 'Your wife is a sensitive woman,' meaning it as a compliment to her character. But he asked me, 'Why, have you tickled her?' And I, trying to be polite, said, 'Yes,' and he gave me quite a beating on the spot. That was a long time ago, so I'm not ashamed to tell the story now. I always end up hurting myself like this."

"You're doing it again," Miüsov muttered in disgust.

Father Zossima observed them both in silence.

"Am I? Would you believe it, Pyotr Alexandrovitch, I was aware of it even before you pointed it out. And let me tell you, I also foresaw that you would be the first to notice. As soon as my joke fails, your reverence, both my cheeks feel as if they're being pulled down to my jaw, and there's almost a spasm in them. It's been like this since my youth, when I had to make jokes to earn a living in noblemen's houses. I've been a clown my whole life, your reverence, as if it's some sort of mania. I think there's a little devil inside me, but only a small one. A bigger one would have chosen a better person to possess. But not you, Pyotr Alexandrovitch; you're not worth possessing either. But I do believe—I believe in God, though I've had my doubts lately. But now I sit here, waiting for words of wisdom. I'm like the philosopher Diderot, your reverence. Did you ever hear, most Holy Father, how Diderot went to see Metropolitan Platon during Empress Catherine's reign? He walked in and said right away, 'There is no God.' To that, the great bishop raised a finger and said, 'The fool hath said in his heart there is no God.' Diderot immediately fell at his feet, shouting, 'I believe! I will be baptized!' And so he was. Princess Dashkov was his godmother, and Potyomkin was his godfather."

"Fyodor Pavlovitch, this is unbearable! You know you're lying, and that silly story isn't true. Why are you acting like a fool?" Miüsov shouted, his voice trembling.

"I've suspected all my life that it wasn't true," Fyodor Pavlovitch said, sounding convinced. "But I'll tell you the whole truth, gentlemen. Dear elder! Forgive me, I just made up the part about

Diderot's christening right now. I never thought of it before. I made it up to make things more interesting. I act like a fool, Pyotr Alexandrovitch, to make people like me. Though, to be honest, I'm not even sure why I do it sometimes. And as for Diderot, I've heard the phrase 'the fool has said in his heart' a dozen times from the upper class around here when I was young. I even heard your aunt, Pyotr Alexandrovitch, tell the story. They all still believe that the atheist Diderot came to argue about God with Metropolitan Platon."

Miüsov stood up, unable to control his frustration. He was furious and embarrassed, aware of how ridiculous the situation had become.

What was happening in the room was truly unbelievable. For the past forty or fifty years, ever since the times of previous elders, no visitors had entered this room without the deepest sense of respect. Almost everyone admitted into the elder's cell felt that they were receiving a great honor. Many remained kneeling for the entire visit. Many of these visitors had been people of high status and learning, some even freethinkers, drawn by curiosity, but all of them had shown the deepest reverence and respect. Money wasn't involved here; on one side, there was love and kindness, and on the other side, there was repentance and the desire to resolve a spiritual crisis. So this clownish behavior shocked and confused those present, or at least some of them. The monks, their faces unchanged, waited, watching the elder closely, eager to hear what he would say. But they looked like they were about to stand up, just like Miüsov. Alyosha stood with his head down, almost in tears. What struck him as most strange was that his brother Ivan, the one he had placed all his hopes in, who was the only one who could influence their father and stop him, sat quietly, not moving, with his eyes down, as if he were waiting to see how it would all end, like he wasn't involved at all. Alyosha didn't dare to look at Rakitin, the theology student, whom he knew well. He was the only one in the monastery who knew what Rakitin was thinking.

"Forgive me," Miüsov began, turning to Father Zossima, "I seem to have gotten caught up in this shameful nonsense. I made a mistake in thinking that even someone like Fyodor Pavlovitch would know how to behave in front of such a respected figure as yourself. I never thought I would have to apologize just for coming here with him."

Pyotr Alexandrovitch could say no more, overwhelmed with embarrassment, and was about to leave the room.

"Please don't trouble yourself, I beg you," the elder said as he got up on his weak legs. He gently took Pyotr Alexandrovitch by both hands and made him sit down again. "Please don't be upset. I especially ask you to stay as my guest." And with a polite bow, he returned to his little sofa.

"Dear elder, tell me! Am I annoying you with my liveliness?" Fyodor Pavlovitch suddenly asked, gripping the arms of his chair like he was ready to jump up if the answer wasn't what he wanted.

"I also beg you not to worry, and not to be anxious," the elder said calmly and with authority. "Don't trouble yourself. Make yourself completely at home. And most of all, don't be so ashamed of yourself—that's the root of the problem."

"Make myself at home? Be my true self? Oh, that's asking too much, but I gladly accept with joy! Do you know, blessed Father, it might not be the best idea to invite me to be my true self. Don't take the risk… I won't even go that far myself. I'm warning you for your own sake. Well, the rest is still unclear, but there are people who would be happy to describe me to you. I mean you, Pyotr Alexandrovitch. But as for you, holy elder, let me tell you, I am filled with ecstasy."

He got up and raised his hands, exclaiming, "Blessed is the womb that bore you, and the breasts that fed you—especially the breasts. When you just said, 'Don't be so ashamed of yourself, for that is the root of it all,' you cut right through me with that remark and saw right into my soul. Truly, I always feel when I meet people that I am lower than everyone, and that they all see me as a fool. So I say, 'Let me really act like a fool. I don't care what you think, because all of you are worse than I am.' That's why I act like a fool. It's from shame, dear elder, from shame; it's just being overly sensitive that makes me behave so badly. If I had only known that everyone would accept me as the kindest and wisest person, oh, Lord, what a good man I could have been! Teacher!" he suddenly dropped to his knees. "What must I do to gain eternal life?"

Even now, it was hard to tell whether he was joking or if he was really moved.

Father Zossima looked up at him and smiled as he spoke. "You have known for a long time what you must do. You're smart enough to know: don't give in to drunkenness or speaking without thinking; don't give in to lust; and most importantly, don't be greedy for money. And close your taverns. If you can't close them all, at least close two or three. And most of all—don't lie."

"You mean about Diderot?"

"No, not about Diderot. Above all, don't lie to yourself. The person who lies to themselves and listens to their own lies ends up unable to recognize the truth in themselves or in the world around them. They lose all respect for themselves and others. And without respect, they stop loving. To distract themselves without love, they give in to passions and crude pleasures, sinking into animal-like vices—all because they've been lying to others and to themselves. The person who lies to themselves gets offended more easily than anyone. You know, it's sometimes quite enjoyable to be offended, isn't it? A person might know that no one has really insulted them, but they've made it up in their head, exaggerating the situation to make it seem worse. They take a simple comment and turn it into something big—they know this themselves, but they'll still be the first to get offended and will wallow in their resentment, finding a kind of pleasure in it, until it turns into real bitterness. But get up now, sit down, I beg you. This, too, is just false posturing..."

"Blessed man! Let me kiss your hand."

Fyodor Pavlovitch hurried over and quickly kissed the elder's thin hand. "You're right, it is pleasant to take offense. You said it better than I've ever heard it before. Yes, my whole life, I've been taking offense for my own pleasure, taking offense even on aesthetic grounds. Sometimes it's not just pleasant, it's distinguished to be insulted—that's the part you left out, great elder—it's distinguished! I'll make a note of that. But the truth is,

I've been lying—lying constantly my entire life, every day, every hour. I am a lie, the father of lies. Well, maybe not the father of lies; I'm mixing up my Bible verses. Call me the son of lies— that's enough. But, my angel, can I sometimes talk about Diderot? Diderot won't hurt anyone, although sometimes words can do harm. By the way, great elder, I almost forgot. For two years now, I've been meaning to come here to ask you something. Just tell Pyotr Alexandrovitch not to interrupt me. Here's my question: Is it true, great Father, that there's a story in the Lives of the Saints about a holy saint who was martyred for his faith, and when they finally cut off his head, he stood up, picked up his own head, and, 'politely kissed it,' then walked a long way holding it in his hands? Is that true or not, honored Father?"

"No, it's not true," the elder replied.

"There's nothing like that in any of the Lives of the Saints. Which saint did you say the story was about?" the Father Librarian asked.

"I don't know the saint's name. I don't know, and I can't say. I was misled. Someone told me the story. Do you know who told me? It was Pyotr Alexandrovitch Miüsov right here, the same man who got so mad about Diderot just now. He's the one who told me the story."

"I've never told you that. I never talk to you at all."

"You're right, you didn't tell it to me, but you told it when I was there. It was three years ago. I bring it up because that ridiculous story shook my faith, Pyotr Alexandrovitch. You didn't know it, but I went home with my faith in pieces, and it's been getting more and more broken ever since. Yes, Pyotr Alexandrovitch, you were the cause of my great fall. And that wasn't even about Diderot!"

Fyodor Pavlovitch grew more dramatic and emotional, though by now, it was obvious to everyone that he was acting. Still, Miüsov was irritated by his words.

"What nonsense, this is all nonsense," Miüsov muttered. "I may have told it, at some point... but not to you. I heard it from someone else. A Frenchman told me in Paris. He said it was read at our mass from the Lives of the Saints. He was a very learned man, who had studied Russian history for years and lived in Russia a long time. I've never read the Lives of the Saints myself, and I'm not going to read them. People say all sorts of things at dinner— we were dining then."

"Yes, you were dining, and that's when I lost my faith!" Fyodor Pavlovitch mimicked him.

"What do I care about your faith?" Miüsov was about to shout but caught himself and said with disdain, "You ruin everything you touch."

Suddenly, the elder stood up from his seat. "Excuse me, gentlemen, for leaving you for a few minutes," he said, addressing all the guests. "I have visitors waiting for me who arrived before you. But don't lie, all the same," he added, turning to Fyodor Pavlovitch with a good-natured expression. He walked out of the room. Alyosha and the novice rushed to accompany him down the steps. Alyosha was relieved to get away, but he was also glad the elder was in a good mood and hadn't been offended. Father Zossima was heading toward the portico to bless the people waiting for him there, but Fyodor Pavlovitch still stopped him at the door.

"Blessed man!" he cried with emotion. "Let me kiss your hand one more time. Yes, with you, I feel like I can still talk, I can still connect. Do you think I'm always like this, always lying and playing the fool? Believe me, I've been acting this way on purpose to test you. I've been testing you the whole time, seeing if I could get along with you. Is there room for my humility alongside your pride? I'm ready to give you a glowing recommendation—one can get along with you! But now I'll be quiet; I'll stay silent the rest of the time. I'll sit in a chair and hold my tongue. Now it's your turn to speak, Pyotr Alexandrovitch. You're the main person left now—for the next ten minutes."

Chapter 3: Peasant Women Who Have Faith

Near the wooden porch below, which was attached to the outer wall of the monastery grounds, there was a crowd of about twenty peasant women. They had been told that the elder was finally coming out, and they had gathered there in anticipation. Two ladies, Madame Hohlakov and her daughter, had also come out to the porch to wait for the elder, but they were in a separate section of the porch reserved for women of higher rank.

Madame Hohlakov was a wealthy lady, still young and attractive, and always dressed tastefully. She had a rather pale complexion and lively black eyes. She was no older than thirty-three and had been a widow for five years. Her daughter, a fourteen-year-old girl, was partially paralyzed. The poor child hadn't been able to walk for the last six months and had to be wheeled around in a long reclining chair. She had a charming little face, though somewhat thin from illness, but still full of cheerfulness. Her large dark eyes, framed with long lashes, had a mischievous sparkle in them. Her mother had been planning to take her abroad since the spring, but they had been delayed all summer due to business related to their estate. They had been staying in town for a week, mostly for business, though they had visited Father Zossima once already, three days before. Although they knew that the elder rarely saw visitors, they had shown up again and were urgently requesting "the blessing of seeing the great healer one more time."

The mother sat on a chair beside her daughter's wheelchair, and standing two steps away from her was an old monk, not from our monastery, but a visitor from a remote religious house in the far north. He too was seeking the elder's blessing.

But when Father Zossima entered the porch, he went first to the peasants, who were crowded around the bottom of the three steps leading up to the porch. Father Zossima stood on the top step, put on his stole, and began blessing the women gathered around him. A woman, clearly troubled, was brought up to him. As soon as she saw the elder, she began screaming and thrashing about as if in labor. He placed the stole on her forehead, said a short prayer over her, and she immediately calmed down and became quiet.

I'm not sure if things are the same now, but when I was a child, I often saw and heard these "possessed" women in the villages and monasteries. They would be brought to mass, barking and squealing like dogs, so loudly that the whole church could hear them. But when the sacrament was brought out and they were led to it, their "possession" would stop instantly, and the sick women would always calm down for a time. I was greatly amazed by this as a child, but later I heard from local villagers and teachers that the whole thing was just an act, to avoid work, and that these women could be cured with strict discipline. Many stories were told to back up this claim. But later, I was surprised to learn from medical experts that there was no faking involved. It was a real and terrible illness, one that afflicted women especially in Russia, caused by the harsh lives peasant women led. It was a disease, they said, that came from exhaustion after hard, abnormal, and unassisted labor during childbirth, and from the hopeless suffering, beatings, and other hardships that some women couldn't endure as well as others. The strange and sudden healing of these tormented women when they were brought to the sacrament, which I had once thought was due to trickery, probably happened in the most natural way. Both the women supporting the sick woman and the woman herself fully believed, without question, that the evil spirit tormenting her couldn't stand up to the power of the sacrament and would be forced to leave her. And so, in a nervous and mentally disturbed woman, this belief triggered a kind of convulsive reaction in her body, which always happened when she bowed before the sacrament, driven by her expectation of a miracle and her absolute faith that it would occur. And it did occur, even if only briefly. It was exactly the same now, as soon as the elder touched the sick woman with the stole.

Many of the women in the crowd were moved to tears of joy by what they saw. Some tried to kiss the hem of his robe, while others called out in high-pitched, sing-song voices. He blessed them all and spoke with a few of them. He already knew the troubled woman. She came from a village only six miles from the monastery, and she had been brought to him before.

"But here is one from far away," he said, pointing to a woman who was not very old, but very thin and worn, with a face not just tanned but almost blackened from exposure. She was kneeling, staring at the elder with a wild, desperate look in her eyes.

"From far away, Father, from far away! I've come two hundred miles to see you. From far away, Father, from far away!" the woman began chanting in a mournful tone, swaying her head from side to side, resting her cheek in her hand.

Among the peasants, there is a silent, long-enduring kind of grief that withdraws into itself and remains quiet. But there is also a kind of grief that breaks out, and when it does, it pours out in tears and wailing. This kind of grief is especially common among women. But it is no less painful than the silent kind. Tears don't bring comfort; instead, they only make the heart ache more. Such grief doesn't seek consolation. It feeds on its own hopelessness, and crying only comes from the constant desire to reopen the wound.

"You are a tradeswoman?" asked Father Zossima, looking at her closely.

"We are townsfolk, Father, we live in the town. But we are peasants, even though we live in town. I've come to see you, Father! We heard about you, Father, we heard. I buried my little son, and I've come on a pilgrimage. I've been to three monasteries, but they told me, 'Go, Nastasya, go to them,' meaning you. So I've come. I was at the service yesterday, and today I've come to you."

"What are you crying for?"

"I'm grieving for my little boy, Father. He was three years old— three years, almost three months. I'm mourning for my little boy, Father. He was our last one. My husband Nikita and I had four children, but now we have none. All our dear children are gone. I buried the first three without much grieving, but now that I've buried the last one, I can't stop mourning. I see him everywhere, standing before me. He's never gone from my thoughts. He's broken my heart. I look at his little clothes, his tiny shirt, and his little boots, and I wail. I lay out everything that's left of him, all his little things, and I cry. I say to my husband, 'Let me go on a pilgrimage, my dear.' My husband is a driver. We're not poor, Father, not poor at all. He drives our own horse, and the horse and carriage are ours. But what good is it to us now? Since I left home, Nikita has started drinking again. He always does when I'm away. It's been three months since I left. I've forgotten about him, forgotten about everything. I don't want to remember anything anymore. And what would life be like for us now, living together? I'm done with him, I'm done with everything. I don't want to look at our house or our belongings. I don't want to see anything anymore!"

"Listen, my dear," said the elder. "Long ago, a holy saint saw a mother like you, weeping in the Temple for her only child, whom God had taken. The saint said to her, 'Don't you know how bold these little ones are before the throne of God? Truly, there is no one bolder than they are in the Kingdom of Heaven. They say to God, "You gave us life, O Lord, and just as we were beginning to see it, You took it back." And so they ask and ask again, and God grants them the rank of angels right away. So,' the saint said, 'you too, mother, should rejoice and not cry, because your little son is with the Lord, among the angels.' That's what the saint said to the grieving mother long ago. He was a great saint, and he wouldn't have spoken falsely. So you too, mother, should know that your little one is surely before the throne of God, happy and rejoicing, and praying for you. So don't cry, but rejoice."

The woman listened to him, her cheek resting in her hand as she looked down. She sighed deeply.

"My Nikita tried to comfort me with the same words you're saying. 'Foolish one,' he said, 'why are you crying? Our son is surely singing with the angels before God.' He tells me that, but I see that he cries too, just like me. 'I know, Nikita,' I told him. 'Where else could our son be if not with the Lord God? But here, with us, he isn't like he used to be, sitting beside us.' And if I could only see him just one more time, even if I didn't go up to him or say anything, if I could just hide in a corner and see him for one little minute, hear him playing in the yard, calling out with his little voice, 'Mommy, where are you?' If I could just hear his little feet running through the house, just once—just once; I remember so often how he used to run to me, laughing and shouting. If I could only hear his little feet, I would know him! But he's gone, Father, he's gone, and I'll never hear him again. Here's his little sash, but I'll never see him or hear him now."

She pulled her boy's small, embroidered sash out of her dress, and as soon as she looked at it, she started shaking with sobs. She covered her eyes with her fingers, and tears poured out in a sudden rush.

"It is like Rachel of old," said the elder, "weeping for her children and refusing to be comforted because they are no more. This is the fate given to you mothers on earth. Don't look for comfort. Comfort is not what you need. Weep, and don't be consoled, just weep. But each time you cry, remember that your little son is one of God's angels. He is watching you from up there, and he rejoices at your tears and shows them to the Lord God. You will carry that great mother's grief for a long time yet, but eventually, it will turn into quiet joy. Your bitter tears will become gentle ones of tender sorrow, the kind that purify the heart and free it from sin. And I will pray for your child's soul to be at peace. What was his name?"

"Alexey, Father."

"A beautiful name. After Alexey, the man of God?"

"Yes, Father."

"What a saint he was! I will remember him, mother, and your grief in my prayers. And I will also pray for your husband's health. It is a sin for you to leave him. Your little one will see from heaven that you've left his father and will cry for you. Why are you disturbing his happiness? He's still alive, because the soul lives forever, and even though he's not in the house, he's close to you, unseen. How can he come into the house if you say the house is hateful to you? Who will he come to if you and his father are not together? He comes to you in your dreams now, and you feel sorrow. But soon, he will send you peaceful dreams. Go back to your husband, mother. Go today."

"I will go, Father, because you have told me to. I will go. You've touched my heart. My Nikita, my Nikita, you are waiting for me," the woman began to say in a sing-song voice. But the elder had already turned to an old woman in the crowd. She was dressed more like a townsperson than a pilgrim. Her eyes showed she had something important to say. She explained that she was the widow of a non-commissioned officer and lived nearby in the town. Her son, Vasenka, was in the commissariat service and had gone to Irkutsk in Siberia. He had written two letters from there, but it had been a year since she last heard from him. She had asked around about him but didn't know where to go to get real information.

"Just the other day, Stepanida Ilyinishna—a rich merchant's wife—said to me, 'You should go, Prohorovna, and put your son's name down for prayers in church and pray for the peace of his soul as if he were dead. His soul will be troubled,' she said, 'and he will write you a letter.' Stepanida Ilyinishna said this was certain, that it had worked many times before. But I have doubts. Oh, dear Father, tell me, is it true or false? And is it right?"

"Don't even think about it. It's wrong to ask such a thing. How can you pray for the peace of a living soul? And from his own mother too! It's a great sin, like sorcery. But because you don't know any better, you're forgiven. Instead, pray to the Queen of Heaven, who helps us all, for your son's good health, and ask her to forgive your mistake. And let me tell you something else, Prohorovna. Either your son will soon return to you, or you will surely get a letter from him. Go now and be at peace. Your son is alive, I promise you."

"Dear Father, may God bless you, our protector, who prays for all of us and for our sins!"

But the elder had already noticed another pair of eyes watching him from the crowd. A thin, frail peasant woman who looked very sick was gazing at him without speaking. Her eyes pleaded with him, but she seemed too scared to approach.

"What is it, my child?"

"Forgive my soul, Father," she whispered, and slowly sank to her knees, bowing down at his feet. "I have sinned, Father. I am afraid of my sin."

The elder sat down on the lower step. The woman crawled closer to him, still on her knees.

"I've been a widow for three years," she began in a quiet, trembling voice. "I had a hard life with my husband. He was an old man, and he used to beat me terribly. When he was sick, I thought to myself, if he gets better, if he recovers, what will happen then? And then a thought came to me—"

"Stop," said the elder, leaning in to hear her better.

She continued in a hushed voice, so low that it was almost impossible to catch what she was saying. She finished quickly.

"Three years ago?" the elder asked.

"Yes, three years. At first, I didn't think much about it, but now I've gotten sick, and the thought won't leave me." "Did you come from far away?"

"Over three hundred miles." "Have you confessed this before?" "Yes, twice."

"Have you taken Communion?"

"Yes. But I'm afraid. I'm afraid to die."

"Don't be afraid, and don't worry. As long as you don't lose your repentance, God will forgive everything. There is no sin so great on this earth that the Lord won't forgive if you truly repent. Man cannot commit a sin so terrible that it exhausts God's infinite love. Could there ever be a sin greater than God's love? Think only of repentance—constant repentance—and let go of your fear. Believe that God loves you more than you could ever understand. He loves you, even in your sin, with your sin. It's been said that there is more joy in heaven over one repentant sinner than over ten righteous people. Go now, and don't be afraid. Don't be bitter toward people. Don't hold on to anger if you're wronged. Forgive the dead man in your heart for the wrongs he did to you. Make peace with him in your soul. If you are truly repentant, you love. And if you love, you are with God. Everything can be forgiven, and everything can be saved by love. If I, a sinner like you, can feel kindness and compassion for you, how much more will God? Love is such a priceless treasure that it can redeem the whole world. It can make up for not just your sins, but the sins of others too."

He made the sign of the cross over her three times, took a small icon from around his neck, and gave it to her. She bowed down to the ground, speechless.

He stood up and smiled warmly at a healthy-looking peasant woman holding a small baby.

"From Vyshegorye, dear Father."

"You've come five miles with that baby in your arms. What can I do for you?"

"I came to see you. I've been here before—don't you remember? You must have a poor memory if you've forgotten me. They told us you were sick, and I thought, I'll go see him myself. But now I see you, and you're not sick! You'll live another twenty years. God bless you! So many people are praying for you. How could you be ill?"

"Thank you for everything, daughter."

"By the way, I have something small to ask. Here are sixty copecks. Please give them to someone poorer than me. I thought as I walked here, better to give it through you. You'll know who to give it to."

"Thank you, dear, thank you! You are a good woman, and I love you. I'll make sure it goes to someone in need. Is this your little girl?"

"Yes, Father, my little girl, Lizaveta."

"May the Lord bless both you and your baby, Lizaveta! You've brightened my heart, mother. Farewell, dear children, farewell, my dears."

He blessed them all and bowed low to them.

Chapter 4: A Lady of Little Faith

A visitor watching the scene of the elder speaking with the peasants and blessing them shed silent tears and wiped them away with her handkerchief. She was a sentimental lady from high society with a truly kind nature in many ways. When the elder finally approached her, she greeted him enthusiastically.

"Oh, what I have been feeling, watching this touching scene!" She couldn't continue because she was overwhelmed with emotion. "Now I understand why the people love you. I love the people too. I want to love them. And who could help loving our wonderful Russian people, so simple and yet so great in their way!"

"How is your daughter's health? You wanted to speak with me again?" asked the elder.

"Oh, I have been praying for this moment, begging for it! I was ready to kneel at your windows for three days until you let me in. We have come, great healer, to express our deepest gratitude. You have healed my Lise, completely healed her, just by praying over her last Thursday and laying your hands on her. We hurried here to kiss your hands and pour out our heartfelt thanks and respect."

"What do you mean by healed? But she is still lying in her chair," said the elder.

"But her night fevers have completely stopped since Thursday," said the woman quickly. "And that's not all. Her legs are stronger. This morning, she got up without any trouble; she slept all night. Just look at her rosy cheeks, her bright eyes! She used to cry all the time, but now she laughs and is cheerful. This morning, she insisted on standing up, and she stood for a whole minute without any help. She even says that in two weeks, she'll be dancing! I called Doctor Herzenstube, and he just shrugged his shoulders and said, 'I am amazed; I don't understand it.' And do you think we could just stay away and not thank you? Lise, thank him— thank him!"

Lise's pretty, laughing face suddenly became serious. She tried to rise in her chair as far as she could, clasping her hands before the elder, but then couldn't hold back and burst into laughter.

"It's because of him," she said, pointing at Alyosha, annoyed with herself for laughing.

If anyone had looked at Alyosha, standing just behind the elder, they would have seen his face turn bright red instantly. His eyes sparkled, and he looked down.

"She has a message for you, Alexey Fyodorovitch. How are you?" Lise's mother said, holding out her exquisitely gloved hand to Alyosha.

The elder turned around and suddenly looked carefully at Alyosha. He stepped closer to Lise and, smiling awkwardly, held out his hand to her. Lise took on a more serious air.

"Katerina Ivanovna sent this through me for you." She handed him a small note. "She urgently asks you to visit her as soon as possible and says you must not fail her but must come."

"She asks me to go and see her? Me? What for?" Alyosha muttered in astonishment. His face suddenly became anxious.

"Oh, it's all to do with Dmitri Fyodorovitch and... what has happened recently," the mother explained hurriedly. "Katerina Ivanovna has made up her mind about something, but she needs to see you about it. I don't know why, but she wants to see you right away. And of course, you will go. It's your Christian duty."

"I have only met her once," Alyosha said, still confused.

"Oh, she's such a noble, incomparable woman! Just think of all she has been through, what she is enduring now! And what still awaits her—it's all terrible, terrible!"

"All right, I will go," Alyosha decided after quickly scanning the brief, mysterious note, which only contained an urgent request for him to come without any explanation.

"Oh, how sweet and generous that is of you!" Lise suddenly cried out with excitement. "I told mamma you wouldn't go. I said you were busy saving your soul. You're wonderful! I've always thought you were wonderful. I'm so happy to tell you that!"

"Lise!" her mother said, trying to sound stern, though she smiled as she said it.

"You've completely forgotten us, Alexey Fyodorovitch," she added. "You never come to visit us. And yet Lise has told me twice that she is never happy except when she's with you."

Alyosha lifted his eyes and blushed again, smiling without really knowing why. But the elder was no longer looking at him. He had started speaking with a monk who, as mentioned earlier, had been waiting near Lise's chair for the elder. The monk seemed to be of a humble background, a peasant by origin, with a narrow outlook but a true believer, and firm in his own way. He said he had come from the far north, from Obdorsk, from Saint Sylvester's monastery, which consisted of only ten monks. The elder gave him his blessing and invited him to visit his cell whenever he wished.

"How can you dare to do such things?" the monk suddenly asked, pointing meaningfully at Lise. He was referring to her "healing."

"It's too soon to talk about that. Relief isn't the same as a complete cure, and it can come from many causes. But if there has been any healing, it is not by my power but by God's will. Everything comes from God. Visit me, Father," he added to the monk. "I don't see visitors often. I am sick, and I know my days are numbered."

"Oh no, no! God will not take you from us yet. You will live many more years!" the lady cried. "And how are you sick? You look so well, so cheerful."

"I feel extraordinarily well today. But I know it's only for a moment. I fully understand my illness now. If I seem happy to you, you couldn't have said anything better. People are made for happiness, and anyone who is truly happy can say, 'I am doing God's will on earth.' All the righteous, all the saints, all the holy martyrs were happy."

"Oh, the way you speak! Such bold and beautiful words!" the lady exclaimed. "You seem to pierce right through me with your words. But still—happiness, happiness—where is it? Who can truly say they are happy? Oh, since you've been so kind to let us see you again today, let me tell you what I couldn't say last time, what I didn't dare to say. I've been suffering for so long! Forgive me! I'm suffering!"

With a rush of emotion, she clasped her hands together in front of him.

"What are you suffering from?" "I suffer... from a lack of faith." "A lack of faith in God?"

"Oh, no, no! I wouldn't dare think that. But the idea of life after death—it's such a mystery! And no one, no one can explain it. Listen! You're a healer, you understand the human soul deeply, and I don't expect you to believe me completely, but I swear to you, I'm being serious. The thought of life after death fills me with agony, with terror. And I don't know who to turn to, I've been afraid to ask anyone all my life. But now, I'm bold enough to ask you. Oh, God! What must you think of me now?"

She clasped her hands again.

"Don't worry about what I think of you," said the elder. "I completely believe in the sincerity of your suffering."

"Oh, how grateful I am to you! You see, I close my eyes and ask myself, if everyone has faith, where did it come from? And then they say it all came from fear of nature, and that none of it is real. And I ask myself, 'What if I've believed my whole life, and when I die, there's nothing but weeds growing on my grave?' I read that somewhere. It's terrifying! How—how can I get my faith back? I only believed when I was a little child, without thinking about it. How, how can anyone prove it?"

I've come now to lay my soul before you and ask you about it. If I let this chance slip, no one will answer me for the rest of my life. How can I prove it? How can I convince myself? Oh, how unhappy I am! I look around me and see that hardly anyone else cares; no one thinks about it, and I'm the only one who can't stand it. It's unbearable—unbearable!"

"Of course. But there's no way to prove it, though you can be convinced of it."

"How?"

"By the experience of active love. Try to love your neighbor actively and tirelessly. The more you grow in love, the more certain you will become of the reality of God and the immortality of your soul. If you reach the point of forgetting yourself completely in the love of others, then you will believe without any doubt, and no doubt will ever enter your soul. This has been tested. It's certain."

"In active love? There's another question—and such a big one! You see, I love humanity so much that—would you believe it?—I often dream of giving up everything, leaving Lise, and becoming a nurse. I close my eyes, and I imagine it, and in those moments, I feel like I could overcome anything. No wounds, no horrible sores could frighten me. I would wash them with my own hands, bandage them, and care for those who are suffering. I would even kiss those wounds."

"It's good that you have such dreams, and not others. Someday, without realizing it, you might do a good deed for real."

"Yes, but could I endure that kind of life for long?" the woman went on, almost frantically. "That's the main question—that's what torments me the most. I shut my eyes and ask myself, 'Could you stay on that path?

And what if the person whose wounds you're cleaning doesn't thank you, but instead complains, doesn't appreciate your kindness, yells at you, and even complains about you to the authorities (which happens when people are suffering)—what then? Would you still be able to love them, or not?' And you know, I realized with horror that if anything could kill my love for humanity, it would be ingratitude. In short, I'm like a hired worker, expecting to be paid right away—that is, I want praise, and I expect love in return. If I don't get it, I can't love anyone."

She was overwhelmed with self-criticism, and after finishing, she looked defiantly at the elder.

"That reminds me of something a doctor once told me," said the elder. "He was an older man, and quite clever. He spoke as honestly as you have, but with a touch of bitter humor. 'I love humanity,' he said, 'but I'm amazed at myself. The more I love people in general, the less I love them individually. In my dreams, I've often come up with great plans for serving humanity, and I might even face crucifixion if necessary; but I can't live with someone in the same room for two days. As soon as anyone is near me, their presence disturbs me, bothers me, and limits my freedom. In twenty-four hours, I start hating even the best of people: one because he takes too long to eat, another because he has a cold and keeps blowing his nose. I start disliking people the moment they come near me. But the more I dislike people individually, the more passionate my love for humanity becomes.'"

"But what can one do? What can someone do in that case? Should they give up hope?"

"No. It's enough that you're upset about it. Do what you can, and that will count for something. Much has already been achieved in you if you can see yourself so clearly and honestly. But if you're only being this sincere with me just to gain my approval, as you did just now, then you won't reach true love; your dreams won't go anywhere, and your life will pass by like a shadow. In that case, you'll stop thinking about the life to come, and eventually, you'll calm down in your own way."

"You've crushed me! Only now, hearing you speak, do I realize that I was really just seeking your approval when I told you I couldn't stand ingratitude. You've shown me who I really am. You've seen through me and explained me to myself!"

"Are you telling the truth? Well then, after such a confession, I believe you are sincere and good at heart. If you don't find happiness, always remember that you're on the right path, and try not to leave it. Above all, avoid falsehood—every kind of falsehood—especially lying to yourself. Watch closely for your own deceitfulness, and examine it constantly. Avoid being scornful, both toward others and yourself. What seems bad to you inside will improve just because you're paying attention to it. And avoid fear, too, because fear comes from falsehood. Don't be afraid of your own weakness when it comes to love. Don't worry too much, even about your wrong actions. I'm sorry I can't offer you more comfort, because love in action is a harsh and frightening thing compared to love in dreams. Love in dreams craves quick action, something big and done in front of everyone. People will even give their lives if it's over quickly, with everyone watching and cheering. But active love requires hard work and endurance, and for some people, it's a whole way of life. But I predict that just when you see, with horror, that despite all your efforts, you seem to be getting farther from your goal instead of closer, that will be the moment when you'll reach it, and you'll see clearly the miraculous power of the Lord, who has been loving and guiding you all along. Forgive me for not being able to stay longer with you. They are waiting for me. Goodbye."

The woman began to cry.

"Lise, Lise! Bless her—bless her!" she cried, suddenly jumping up.

"She doesn't deserve to be loved. I've seen her naughtiness all along," the elder said playfully. "Why have you been teasing Alexey?"

Lise had, in fact, been quietly mocking Alyosha the whole time. She had noticed earlier that he was shy and tried to avoid looking at her, and she found this very amusing. She waited intently, trying to catch his eye. Alyosha, unable to resist her constant stare, would glance at her, and she would immediately smile triumphantly. This made him even more embarrassed. Eventually, he turned away completely and hid behind the elder. But after a few minutes, driven by the same irresistible urge, he looked again to see if she was still watching, and found her almost hanging out of her chair, leaning sideways to catch his eye. As soon as he looked, she burst into laughter so hard that the elder couldn't help but say, "Why are you teasing him like that, you naughty girl?"

Lise suddenly blushed. Her eyes flashed, and her face became serious. She started speaking quickly and nervously, her voice warm and slightly upset.

"Why has he forgotten everything? He used to carry me around when I was little. We used to play together. He even taught me to read, did you know that? Two years ago, when he left, he promised he'd never forget me, that we'd be friends forever—forever! And now, he's suddenly afraid of me. Does he think I'm going to eat him? Why won't he come near me? Why doesn't he talk to me? Why won't he visit us? It's not that you won't let him. We know he goes everywhere. I can't invite him—it wouldn't be proper— but he should have thought of it first, if he hasn't forgotten me.

But now he's busy saving his soul! And why did you put that long robe on him? If he runs, he'll trip and fall."

Suddenly, she covered her face with her hand and started laughing again, this time uncontrollably, with nervous, silent laughter. The elder watched her with a smile and gently blessed her. As she kissed his hand, she suddenly pressed it to her eyes and began crying.

"Don't be angry with me. I'm silly and useless… and maybe Alyosha is right, completely right, not to want to visit such a foolish girl."

"I will certainly send him," said the elder.

Chapter 5: So Be It! So Be It!

The elder had been away from his cell for around twenty-five minutes. It was already past half-past twelve, but Dmitri, the reason they had all gathered there, still had not arrived. However, it seemed as though they had almost forgotten about him, and when the elder reentered the cell, he found his guests deeply engaged in conversation. Ivan and the two monks were the ones most involved in the discussion. Miüsov, too, was making an effort to participate, and with great eagerness. Yet, he wasn't succeeding. He was evidently being overshadowed, and his comments were largely ignored, which only made his irritation grow. He had engaged in intellectual debates with Ivan before, and he couldn't bear the carelessness that Ivan seemed to show toward him.

"I have always stood in the front ranks of all that is progressive in Europe, and now this younger generation is blatantly disregarding us," he thought.

Fyodor Pavlovitch, who had promised to sit quietly, had indeed been silent for some time. However, he watched his neighbor Miüsov with a sly, ironic smile, clearly enjoying his frustration. He had been waiting for an opportunity to settle old scores, and now he wasn't about to miss the chance. Leaning over, he began to tease him again in a whisper.

"Why didn't you leave earlier, right after the 'courteous kiss'? Why did you agree to stay in such unpleasant company? You felt offended and hurt, and you stayed to defend yourself by showing off your intelligence. Now, you won't leave until you've demonstrated your brilliance."

"You again?… On the contrary, I'm just about to go."

"You'll be the last, the very last to leave!" Fyodor Pavlovitch gave him another jab, right before Father Zossima returned.

The conversation paused briefly, but the elder, seating himself back in his usual place, looked at them all as though warmly encouraging them to continue. Alyosha, who could read every expression on his face, saw that he was utterly exhausted and was pushing himself to keep going. Recently, he had been prone to fainting spells due to overexertion. His face was pale, as it always was before such episodes, and his lips were white. However, he clearly did not want to dismiss everyone just yet. It seemed as though he had some special reason for wanting them to stay. What could it be? Alyosha watched him closely.

"We were just discussing this gentleman's very interesting article," said Father Iosif, the librarian, addressing the elder and motioning toward Ivan. "He presents a number of fresh ideas, but I believe the argument cuts both ways. His article is a response to a book by a church authority on the issue of church courts and their jurisdiction."

"I'm sorry I haven't had the chance to read your article, but I have heard of it," said the elder, looking at Ivan with a sharp and focused gaze.

"He takes a very intriguing position," Father Iosif continued. "As far as church jurisdiction is concerned, he seems to be firmly against the separation of church and state."

"That's quite interesting. In what way, exactly?" Father Zossima asked Ivan.

Finally, Ivan responded, but not in the condescending manner that Alyosha had feared. Instead, he spoke with modesty and caution, showing a genuine sense of goodwill, and without the slightest trace of hidden intent.

"My argument begins with the premise that this blending of elements—meaning the core principles of the church and state— will, of course, continue indefinitely. Even though they are inherently unable to fully integrate, this blending cannot result in any consistent or normal outcomes because there is a fundamental flaw at its base. In my opinion, a true compromise between the church and state on issues such as jurisdiction is impossible. My opponent claims that the church has a fixed and well-defined role within the state. I, on the other hand, argue that the church should encompass the entirety of the state, not merely occupy a small portion of it. And if, for some reason, this is not achievable at the present time, it should nonetheless be the ultimate goal for the future development of Christian society!"

"Absolutely correct," Father Païssy, the reserved and scholarly monk, agreed passionately and firmly.

"Purest Ultramontanism!" Miüsov burst out impatiently, crossing and recrossing his legs.

"Oh, well, we have no mountains," Father Iosif joked, and then turning back to the elder, he continued: "Notice how he responds to his opponent's key 'fundamental and essential' points, an opponent who is, by the way, an ecclesiastic. First, the claim that 'no social organization should have the power to determine the civic and political rights of its members.' Second, that 'criminal and civil jurisdiction should not belong to the church and is contrary to its nature, both as a divine institution and as an organization of people with religious aims.' And finally, the third point, that 'the church is a kingdom not of this world.'"

"What a disgraceful play on words for a churchman!" Father Païssy interrupted again. "I have read the book to which your article responds," he said, addressing Ivan, "and I was appalled by the statement 'the church is a kingdom not of this world.' If it is not of this world, then it cannot exist on earth at all. In the Gospels, the phrase 'not of this world' is not meant in that sense. To twist the words like this is unforgivable. Our Lord Jesus Christ came to establish the church on earth. The Kingdom of Heaven is indeed not of this world, but it is only accessible through the church, which was founded and established here on earth. To manipulate words in such a serious context is both inappropriate and inexcusable. The church is truly a kingdom, destined to rule, and in the end, it will surely become the ruling kingdom over all the earth. We have been given this divine promise."

He stopped speaking suddenly, as though restraining himself. After listening attentively and with respect, Ivan continued, once again addressing the elder calmly and with the same open, friendly manner.

"The central point of my article lies in the fact that for the first three centuries, Christianity only existed on earth within the church and was nothing more than the church. When the pagan Roman Empire chose to become Christian, the church was naturally incorporated into the state. However, the state remained largely pagan in many of its practices. This was inevitable. The Roman state held onto much of its pagan civilization and culture, even in its basic aims and guiding principles. When the Christian church entered the state, it could not compromise any of its fundamental principles—the rock upon which it is built. Nor could the church pursue any other goals than those ordained and revealed by God Himself, including the goal of drawing the entire world—and thus, the ancient pagan state itself—into the church. Therefore, the church should not seek a distinct and fixed position within the state, like 'any social organization' or as 'an organization of people with religious purposes,' as my opponent describes the church. On the contrary, every earthly state should, in the end, be completely transformed into the church and become nothing but the church, rejecting all purposes that are incompatible with the church's mission. This transformation would not diminish the state's honor or its glory as a great power, nor would it lessen the prestige of its rulers. Instead, it would guide the state away from a false and still pagan path toward the true and rightful path, the only path that leads to the eternal goal. That is why the author of the book On the Foundations of Church Jurisdiction would have been correct if, in seeking and establishing those foundations, he had regarded them as a temporary compromise, necessary in our sinful and imperfect times. But as soon as the author claims that the foundations he now outlines—some of which Father Iosif just mentioned—are the permanent, essential, and eternal foundations, he directly contradicts the church and its sacred and eternal purpose. That is the core of my article."

"That means," Father Païssy began again, emphasizing each word, "according to certain theories, which were made very clear in the nineteenth century, the Church should be changed into the State. This change is viewed as progress, as if it would be a step up from a lower to a higher form. The Church would then disappear into the State, making room for science, the spirit of the age, and modern civilization. And if the Church resisted, not wanting to go along with this, it would be allowed a small corner in the State, but even then, it would be under control. This would happen everywhere in all modern European countries. But Russian hopes and ideas are not that the Church should change into the State, as if it were a move from a lower to a higher form. No, it is the opposite. The State should end up being worthy of becoming only the Church, and nothing else. So be it! So be it!"

"Well, I must admit you've reassured me somewhat," Miüsov said, smiling and crossing his legs again. "From what I understand, achieving such an ideal is infinitely far off, something for the second coming of Christ. That's fine with me. It's a beautiful, utopian dream—getting rid of war, diplomacy, banks, and so on. It sounds a lot like socialism, really. But I thought you meant this seriously, and that the Church might now start judging criminals and sentencing them to beatings, prison, or even death."

"But even if only the Church had power, it would not now sentence criminals to prison or death," Ivan replied calmly, without showing any reaction. "Crime, and how people view it, would inevitably change—not all at once, of course, but pretty soon."

"Are you serious?" Miüsov asked, looking at him sharply.

"If everything became the Church, the Church would exclude all the criminals and disobedient people, but it wouldn't cut off their heads," Ivan went on. "I ask you, what would happen to those who were excluded? They would be cut off not only from people, as they are now, but from Christ. By committing their crime, they wouldn't just be breaking the law of man but also going against the Church of Christ. This is already true now, of course, strictly speaking, but it's not made very clear. Today's criminal often tries to make peace with his conscience. He says, 'I steal, but I don't oppose the Church. I'm not an enemy of Christ.' This is what criminals today often tell themselves. But when the Church takes the place of the State, it will be much harder for them to say, 'All people are wrong, everyone is mistaken, all of humanity is the false Church. I, a thief and murderer, am the only true Christian.' It will be very hard for them to say that to themselves. It would require an unusual set of circumstances to believe such a thing. Now, consider the Church's own view of crime. Wouldn't it have to change its current, almost pagan attitude? It would no longer simply cut off its tainted members in order to preserve society. Instead, it would have to fully and honestly adopt the goal of reforming and saving the person."

"What do you mean? I don't understand again," Miüsov interrupted. "Is this another dream? Something vague and even incomprehensible. What is excommunication? What sort of exclusion are you talking about? I suspect you're just amusing yourself, Ivan Fyodorovitch."

"But you know, in reality, this is how it is now," said the elder suddenly, and everyone immediately turned toward him. "If it weren't for the Church of Christ, there would be nothing stopping the criminal from committing evil, and there would be no real punishment afterward—only the mechanical punishment we talked about earlier, which, in most cases, just makes the heart bitter. What's missing is real punishment, the only kind that works, the only kind that softens the heart, which comes from a person's own conscience recognizing their sin."

"And how exactly does that work?" Miüsov asked, now showing real curiosity.

"Well," began the elder, "all these sentences to exile and hard labor, and in the past, even flogging, don't reform anyone. What's more, they hardly ever stop a criminal, and the number of crimes isn't going down, it's actually increasing. You have to admit that. So, society isn't really protected. While we send away one criminal, another one soon takes his place—sometimes two. If anything is keeping society safe today, and if anything is changing and transforming the criminal, it's only the law of Christ speaking to their conscience. It's only by recognizing their wrongdoing as a member of Christian society—that is, the Church—that a criminal realizes their sin against society, which is really a sin against the Church. So, today, it's only through the Church, and not the State, that a criminal can truly see that they have sinned. If society, as the Church, had legal authority, it would know when to bring those who had been excluded back in, and it would know when to reunite them with society. But now, since the Church has no real authority—only the power of moral judgment—it withdraws from actively punishing criminals. The Church doesn't excommunicate them, but instead, keeps guiding them with motherly care. In fact, the Church tries to maintain a Christian connection with the criminal. It lets them come to services, receive the holy sacrament, gives them charity, and treats them more like someone who has been captured than like a convict. And what would happen to a criminal, Lord, if even the Christian society—that is, the Church—rejected him, just like the civil law does and cut him off? What would happen if the Church punished him with excommunication, following the law of the State? It would be unbearable despair, at least for Russian criminals, who still have faith. And who knows, maybe something terrible would happen then. Maybe the criminal's despairing heart would lose its faith, and then what would become of him? But the Church, like a loving and tender mother, holds back from punishing them actively because they are already being punished too severely by the civil law, and someone needs to show them some pity. The Church holds back, above all, because its judgment is the only one that is true, and so it cannot be mixed with any other judgment—not even as a temporary compromise. The Church can't make any deal on that.

Foreign criminals, they say, rarely repent. The ideas they follow today tell them that their crime isn't really a crime, just a reaction against an unjust force. Society cuts them off by force, beating them mechanically, and (at least that's what they say in Europe) follows this exclusion with hatred, forgetfulness, and total indifference to the criminal's fate. And all this happens without the Church's compassionate involvement, because in many cases, there are no churches there anymore. While there are still priests and grand church buildings, the churches themselves long ago tried to turn from being the Church into being the State and to disappear into it completely. That's how it seems, at least, in many Protestant countries. As for Rome, it was turned into a State instead of a Church a thousand years ago. And so, the criminal no longer feels like he belongs to the Church and falls into despair. If he returns to society, it is often with such hatred that society instinctively cuts him off again. You can imagine what that leads to. It seems that the same thing could happen here too, but we have something more. Besides the regular law courts, we still have the Church, which always keeps a connection with the criminal, treating him as a beloved and valuable son. And, besides that, we still have the Church's judgment, at least in thought, which no longer exists in practice but still lives on as a dream for the future. And the criminal instinctively knows this in his heart. What was said earlier is true: if the Church's legal authority were put into practice, if society were completely changed into the Church, then not only would the Church's judgment influence the criminal's reformation more strongly than it does now, but crime itself would likely decrease. There's no doubt that the Church would look at crime and criminals differently, and it would be able to bring back those who had been excluded, stop those planning to commit evil, and save those who had fallen. It's true," Father Zossima added with a smile, "that Christian society isn't ready yet, and it's only being held up by a handful of righteous people, but as long as those people are there, society will keep going, waiting for the time when it will be transformed from a society that is almost pagan into one, single, universal, and all-powerful Church. So be it, so be it! Even if it only happens at the end of time, for it is destined to come to pass! And there's no need to worry about when it will happen, for the secret of the times is in God's wisdom, foresight, and love. What seems far away to us may, by God's will, be closer than we think, already on the verge of happening. So be it, so be it!"

"So be it, so be it!" Father Païssy repeated firmly and with reverence.

"Strange, extremely strange!" Miüsov said, not so much with anger as with hidden frustration.

"What do you find so strange?" Father Iosif asked cautiously.

"It's unbelievable!" Miüsov suddenly burst out. "The State is being erased, and the Church is taking its place! This isn't just Ultramontanism, it's extreme Ultramontanism! It goes beyond anything Pope Gregory the Seventh could have dreamed of!"

"You are completely misunderstanding this," Father Païssy said sternly. "Understand, the Church is not becoming the State. That's the dream of Rome. That's the third temptation of the devil. No, the State will become the Church, it will rise and transform into the Church over the whole world. This is the exact opposite of Ultramontanism and Rome, and of your interpretation. This is the glorious destiny that awaits the Orthodox Church. This star will rise in the East!"

Miüsov remained silent, his body language showing great personal pride. A condescending smile appeared on his lips. Alyosha watched everything with a pounding heart, deeply affected by the conversation. He glanced at Rakitin, who stood still by the door, listening closely but with his eyes cast down. From the color in Rakitin's cheeks, Alyosha guessed that he was probably just as stirred by the conversation, and Alyosha knew what was causing his excitement.

"Let me tell you a little story, gentlemen," Miüsov said dramatically, with a particularly dignified tone. "A few years ago, not long after the coup d'état of December, I happened to be visiting a very important figure in the government in Paris. While there, I met a fascinating man. He wasn't exactly a detective, but he was in charge of a whole group of political detectives—a very powerful position in its own way. Out of curiosity, I struck up a conversation with him. Since he wasn't there as a guest but on official business to deliver a special report, and because he saw how his boss treated me, he allowed himself to speak with me somewhat openly, though only to a certain extent. He was polite rather than truly open, as the French know how to be, especially with foreigners. But I understood him perfectly. The topic of our conversation was the socialist revolutionaries who were being persecuted at the time. I will share just one particularly interesting remark this man made. 'We're not too worried,' he said, 'about all these socialists, anarchists, atheists, and revolutionaries. We keep an eye on them and know what they're up to. But there are a few strange men among them who believe in God and are Christians, but they are also socialists. These are the ones we fear the most. They are dangerous! A socialist who is a Christian is far more dangerous than a socialist who is an atheist.' These words struck me at the time, and now they've come back to me in this conversation, gentlemen."

"You think we are socialists and compare us to them?" Father Païssy asked directly, not beating around the bush.

But before Pyotr Alexandrovitch could think of a reply, the door opened, and Dmitri Fyodorovitch, the guest they had been waiting for, finally came in. They had actually stopped expecting him, so his sudden arrival caused a moment of surprise.

Chapter 6: Why Is Such a Man Alive?

Dmitri Fyodorovitch, a young man of twenty-eight, of average height and a pleasant face, looked older than he really was. He was strong and muscular, clearly showing his physical power. Yet, there was something unhealthy in his appearance. His face was rather thin, his cheeks sunken, and his skin had an unhealthy yellowish tint. His large, dark eyes showed determination, but there was also a vague, uncertain look in them. Even when he got excited and spoke angrily, his eyes didn't always match his mood and often seemed to reveal something different, something that didn't fit with what he was saying. "It's hard to tell what he's thinking," people who talked to him would sometimes say. People who saw something sad or thoughtful in his eyes were often surprised by his sudden laughter, which revealed cheerful and lighthearted thoughts, even when his eyes looked so gloomy. The tension in his face at this moment was easy to understand. Everyone knew, or had heard, about the wild and reckless life he had been living lately, as well as the intense anger he had felt during his arguments with his father. There were many stories in the town about these fights. It was true that he had a quick temper and an "unstable and unbalanced mind," as our local justice of the peace, Katchalnikov, once described him.

He was dressed in an elegant, perfectly tailored frock coat that was carefully buttoned. He wore black gloves and carried a top hat. Having only recently left the army, he still wore a mustache but no beard. His dark brown hair was cut short and combed forward over his temples. He had the long, confident stride of a military man. He paused for a moment in the doorway, looked at everyone in the room, and then walked straight toward the elder, guessing that he must be the host. He bowed deeply and asked for his blessing. Father Zossima, rising from his chair, gave him his blessing. Dmitri respectfully kissed his hand and, with strong emotion, almost anger, said:

"Please be kind enough to forgive me for being so late, but Smerdyakov, the servant my father sent, told me twice that the appointment was for one o'clock. Now I suddenly find out—"

"Don't worry about it," the elder interrupted. "You're just a little late. It's no big deal..."

"Thank you so much, I expected no less from your kindness."

With this, Dmitri bowed again. Then, turning suddenly toward his father, he made a similar deep, respectful bow. It was clear that he had thought about this beforehand and made the bow seriously, feeling it was his duty to show respect and good intentions.

Although Fyodor Pavlovitch was caught off guard, he quickly reacted. He jumped up from his chair and bowed just as deeply in return. His face suddenly became serious and impressive, but it gave him a malicious look. Dmitri then bowed to everyone else in the room and, without saying a word, walked to the window with his long, determined stride. He sat down in the only empty chair, which was near Father Païssy, and leaned forward, ready to listen to the conversation he had interrupted.

Dmitri's entrance took no more than two minutes, and the conversation resumed. But this time, Miüsov decided it wasn't necessary to answer Father Païssy's persistent and slightly irritated question.

"Allow me to step back from this discussion," he said with a calm, polite air. "It's a delicate issue anyway. Ivan Fyodorovitch is smiling at us. I'm sure he has something interesting to add. Ask him."

"Nothing special, just a small observation," Ivan replied immediately. "European Liberals in general, and even our own liberal thinkers, often confuse the ultimate results of socialism with those of Christianity. This confusion is, of course, a strange feature. But it's not only Liberals and thinkers who mix up socialism and Christianity. It seems that, in some cases, even the police—the foreign police, of course—do the same. Your story about Paris fits perfectly with that, Pyotr Alexandrovitch."

"I ask once again that we drop this subject entirely," Miüsov repeated. "Instead, gentlemen, let me tell you another interesting and rather fitting story about Ivan Fyodorovitch himself. Just five days ago, at a gathering, mostly with ladies, he argued that there is nothing in the world that makes people love their neighbors. He said there's no natural law that requires people to love each other and that if love has existed on Earth, it's only because people have believed in immortality. Ivan Fyodorovitch added, as a side note, that this belief is the foundation of all natural laws, and if humanity ever lost its belief in immortality, not only love but all life's forces that keep the world going would immediately dry up. He even went further, saying that without belief in immortality, nothing would be immoral anymore, and everything would be allowed— even cannibalism. That's not all. He concluded by saying that for anyone who doesn't believe in God or immortality, the moral law of nature would immediately reverse itself. Selfishness, even to the point of crime, would not only become allowed but would be seen as the most logical, rational, and even honorable way to live. From this paradox, gentlemen, you can get a sense of the rest of our eccentric and paradoxical friend Ivan Fyodorovitch's ideas."

"Excuse me," Dmitri suddenly interrupted, "did I hear correctly that crime must not only be allowed but should be considered the most logical outcome for anyone who doesn't believe in God or immortality? Is that what he's saying?"

"That's correct," said Father Païssy. "I'll remember that."

After saying this, Dmitri fell silent as quickly as he had started. Everyone looked at him with curiosity.

"Is that really what you believe would happen if people stopped believing in immortality?" the elder asked Ivan suddenly.

"Yes, that's my belief. Without immortality, there's no virtue."

"You are blessed if you truly believe that—or else, you are very unhappy."

"Why would I be unhappy?" Ivan asked, smiling.

"Because, most likely, you don't truly believe in the immortality of your soul, nor in what you've written in your article about Church authority."

"Maybe you're right... But I wasn't completely joking," Ivan admitted suddenly, blushing.

"You weren't completely joking. That's true. This question is still troubling your heart, and you haven't found an answer yet. But sometimes, in your despair, you try to distract yourself, almost playing with your hopelessness. Meanwhile, even in your despair, you keep yourself busy with writing articles and debating with people, though deep down you don't believe in your own arguments. You secretly mock them with a heavy heart... But this question remains unanswered, and it's your greatest sorrow because it demands an answer."

"But can I give that answer? Can I say yes?" Ivan asked strangely, still looking at the elder with the same puzzling smile.

"If it can't be answered with yes, it will never be answered with no. You know this. That's the trouble with your heart, and all its suffering comes from it. But thank the Creator, for He has given you a great heart, capable of such deep suffering, of thinking and searching for higher truths, for our home is in heaven. God grant that you will find the answer on Earth, and may He bless your path."

The elder raised his hand, intending to make the sign of the cross over Ivan from where he stood. However, before he could do so, Ivan rose from his seat, walked over to him, and humbly received his blessing. After kissing the elder's hand, Ivan quietly returned to his place. His face showed a firm and serious expression. This gesture, along with everything Ivan had said previously, struck everyone in the room with its oddity and a sense of gravity, creating a strange and solemn atmosphere. The unexpected nature of Ivan's actions had left everyone in stunned silence for a moment. Even Alyosha, who knew his brother well, had a look of unease, as if sensing that something deeper was stirring. But just then, Miüsov shrugged his shoulders with a gesture that seemed to dismiss everything. At that very same moment, Fyodor Pavlovitch suddenly jumped up from his seat, as if unable to restrain himself any longer.

"Most pious and holy elder," Fyodor Pavlovitch cried, dramatically pointing at Ivan, "that young man over there is my son—my own flesh and blood, the very dearest part of me! He is my most obedient Karl Moor, so to speak, while this son who has just walked in, Dmitri, the very one I am seeking justice against before you, is the disobedient Franz Moor. They're both straight out of Schiller's Robbers, and as for me, I must be the reigning Count von Moor! So judge us, save us, wise elder! We need not just your prayers but your prophecies as well, for we are lost!"

"Speak with seriousness and respect," the elder replied, his voice faint and growing weaker, "and do not start by insulting your own family." It was clear to everyone in the room that the elder was becoming more and more exhausted, as his frail body showed signs of his strength ebbing away.

"This ridiculous scene is exactly what I expected when I came here!" Dmitri cried out, his voice filled with frustration. He, too, jumped up from his seat, his face flushed with indignation. "Forgive him, Father," he added quickly, turning respectfully to the elder. "I'm not an educated man, and I don't even know how to speak to you properly, but let me tell you this: you've been tricked, and you've been far too kind to let this meeting happen. The only thing my father wants is a scandal. Why he wants it, only he knows. He always has some hidden motive. But I think I have an idea of what it is—"

"They all blame me, every single one of them!" Fyodor Pavlovitch interrupted, raising his voice and turning the focus back to himself. "Even Pyotr Alexandrovitch here blames me! You've been blaming me, haven't you, Pyotr Alexandrovitch, haven't you?" He suddenly turned toward Miüsov, though Miüsov hadn't said a word and wasn't even thinking of interrupting. "They all accuse me of hiding my children's money in my boots and cheating them out of it! But tell me, isn't there a court of law? The court can figure out for you, Dmitri Fyodorovitch, from your notes, your letters, and your agreements, exactly how much money you had, how much you've spent, and how much is left! Why doesn't Pyotr Alexandrovitch want to pass judgment on this? Dmitri isn't a stranger to him, after all! But no, they're all against me! Meanwhile, Dmitri Fyodorovitch owes me money—not just a little, but thousands of rubles, and I've got all the documents to prove it. The whole town is buzzing about his reckless behavior. And back when he was stationed somewhere else, he spent a fortune, thousands of rubles, trying to seduce respectable young women—we know all the sordid details, Dmitri Fyodorovitch, every last one! And I'll prove it, too... Holy Father, can you even believe it? He's managed to win the heart of a young lady from a good family—the daughter of a gallant colonel, a man who once held a high rank, who received many honors, and who wore the Anna Order on his chest. He promised to marry her, and now this poor orphaned girl is here, engaged to him, while at the same time, right in front of her, he's chasing after another woman. And this other woman, let me tell you, has practically lived in what you might call a civil marriage with a respectable man! She's an independent woman, untouchable, just like a real wife—because, yes, holy Fathers, she is virtuous! And yet, Dmitri Fyodorovitch wants to win her over with money! That's why he's acting so rude to me now, trying to squeeze more money out of me. He's already wasted thousands on this woman, and now he keeps borrowing more. Do you want to know who he's borrowing it from? Should I tell them, Mitya?"

"Shut up!" Dmitri shouted furiously, his face turning red. "Wait until I'm gone! Don't you dare say anything about her in front of me! It's a disgrace for you to even speak of such an honorable girl, and I won't allow it!"

He was breathing heavily, barely able to control his rage. "Mitya! Mitya!" Fyodor Pavlovitch cried out in a hysterical voice, forcing out a tear for added effect. "Does my fatherly blessing mean nothing to you? What will you do if I curse you instead?"

"You shameless hypocrite!" Dmitri shouted back, his anger exploding.

"He says that to his own father! His own father! Imagine how he'd treat others! Gentlemen, just picture this: there's a poor but honorable man living here in town, a captain who has fallen on hard times, with a large family to support. He was discharged from the army under a cloud, but not publicly, not by court-martial, and with no stain on his honor. Just three weeks ago, Dmitri grabbed him by the beard in a tavern, dragged him outside, and beat him in full view of everyone, all because this poor man works as an agent for me in a small business deal."

"It's all lies! Outwardly, it may seem true, but inside it's a complete lie!" Dmitri shouted, trembling with fury. "Father, I don't deny what I did. Yes, I admit it openly, I acted like a beast toward that captain, and I'm disgusted with myself for it now. I regret it deeply. But your agent, this captain you're talking about, went to the woman you call an enchantress and suggested, on your behalf, that she should take the IOUs you've been holding over me and sue me for the money, so you could get me thrown into prison if I kept asking you to give me an account of my inheritance. And now you accuse me of being infatuated with that woman, even though it was you who pushed her into trying to seduce me! She told me herself—she laughed at you! She told me everything and laughed at your foolishness! You wanted to lock me up because you're jealous of me! And I know all about how you've been trying to force your attentions on her—she laughed at you for that too! Do you hear me? She laughed at you as she told me about it! So here's this man, this father, accusing his wicked son! Gentlemen, forgive me for my anger, but I knew from the very beginning that this sly old man would bring us all together just to stir up trouble. I came here ready to forgive him if he would offer me his hand, to forgive him and ask for his forgiveness!

But now, after he has insulted not only me but also an honorable young woman, someone I respect so much that I won't even say her name, I've decided to expose his dirty schemes, even though he's my father..."

Dmitri couldn't continue. His eyes were blazing with fury, and his chest heaved as he struggled to catch his breath. The tension in the room had reached its peak, and everyone was visibly affected. All of them, except for Father Zossima, stood up from their seats, clearly uneasy. The monks maintained their stern expressions, but they looked to the elder for direction, waiting for his guidance. The elder, however, remained seated, pale, not from the excitement in the room but from his own weakening condition. A soft, pleading smile appeared on his face, and from time to time, he raised his hand as if to calm the storm brewing in the room. It was obvious that one simple gesture from him would have been enough to put an end to the entire scene, but he seemed to be waiting for something, watching them closely as if trying to understand something that wasn't fully clear to him yet. Finally, Miüsov, feeling completely humiliated and ashamed, broke the silence.

"We're all responsible for this disgraceful scene," he said heatedly. "But I didn't expect this when I came here, even though I knew full well who I was dealing with. This must stop immediately! Believe me, your reverence, I had no idea about the details that have just been revealed. I didn't want to believe them, and I'm hearing them for the first time now. A father, jealous of his son's relationship with a woman of questionable morals, conspires with her to throw his own son in prison! And this is the company I've been forced to keep! I want it to be known that I was deceived, just like everyone else here."

"Dmitri Fyodorovitch," Fyodor Pavlovitch suddenly yelled in a voice that sounded completely unnatural, "if you weren't my son, I would challenge you to a duel right now... with pistols, at three paces... across a handkerchief!" He finished with a dramatic stomp of both feet.

With old liars who have been acting all their There are moments in life when people play their role so well that they actually tremble or cry real tears, even though at the same time—or just a second later—they can whisper to themselves, "You know you're lying, you shameless old sinner! You're acting right now, even though you pretend to be full of 'righteous anger.'"

Dmitri frowned deeply and looked at his father with intense disgust.

"I thought... I thought," he said in a soft, controlled voice, "that I was coming back to my hometown with the angel of my heart, my fiancée, to care for you in your old age. But instead, I find nothing but a vile, corrupt man, a pitiful clown!"

"A duel!" the old man yelled again, breathless and sputtering. "And you, Pyotr Alexandrovitch Miüsov, let me tell you, there has never been in your whole family a more noble, honest woman—you hear me, more honest—than this 'creature' you've dared to insult! And you, Dmitri Fyodorovitch, you've left your fiancée for that 'creature,' so you must think she's better than your fiancée. That's the woman you call a 'creature'!"

"Shameful!" Father Iosif muttered.

"Shameful and disgraceful!" Kalganov, his face red, shouted in a trembling, boyish voice. He had been silent until then.

"How can a man like that be allowed to live?" Dmitri growled, consumed with rage. His voice was low, and his shoulders hunched up until he looked almost deformed. "Tell me, can we really let him go on defiling the earth?" He looked around at everyone and pointed at his father. He spoke slowly and clearly.

"Listen, listen, monks, to the parricide!" Fyodor Pavlovitch shouted, rushing up to Father Iosif. "That's his answer to your 'shameful!' What's shameful? That 'creature,' that 'woman of loose morals,' might be holier than you monks who are seeking salvation! Maybe she fell in her youth, destroyed by her surroundings. But she loved much, and Christ himself forgave the woman 'who loved much.'"

"That's not the kind of love Christ forgave her for," Father Iosif said impatiently.

"Yes, it was, monks, it was! You save your souls here by eating cabbage and think you're righteous. You eat a little fish every day and think you can bribe God with fish."

"This is unbearable!" came angry murmurs from all sides of the room.

But the unseemly scene came to an unexpected end. Father Zossima suddenly stood up. Alyosha, almost frantic with worry for the elder and everyone else, managed to support him by the arm. Father Zossima walked toward Dmitri, and when he reached him, he sank to his knees in front of him. Alyosha thought the elder had fallen from weakness, but that wasn't the case. Zossima intentionally and calmly bowed down at Dmitri's feet until his forehead touched the floor. Alyosha was so shocked that he didn't move to help him when the elder got up again. There was a faint smile on Zossima's lips.

"Goodbye! Forgive me, all of you!" he said, bowing to everyone in the room.

Dmitri stood there, stunned. Bowing down to him—what could it mean? Suddenly, he cried out, "Oh, God!" He covered his face with his hands and ran out of the room. All the guests hurried out after him in confusion, without saying goodbye or acknowledging their host. Only the monks came up to Zossima again to receive his blessing.

"What did that mean, bowing at his feet like that? Was it symbolic or what?" Fyodor Pavlovitch asked. He had suddenly calmed down and was trying to restart the conversation, but didn't direct his question at anyone in particular. They were all walking out of the hermitage at that moment.

"I can't speak for madmen and asylums," Miüsov snapped angrily, "but I'll make sure I never have to be in your company again, Fyodor Pavlovitch, trust me on that. Now, where's that monk?"

The monk, the one who had invited them to dine with the Superior, didn't keep them waiting. He met them as soon as they came down the steps from the elder's room, as though he had been waiting for them the whole time.

"Reverend Father, please do me a favor. Convey my deepest respect to the Father Superior, and apologize to him on my behalf," Miüsov said irritably to the monk. "Tell him I regret that, due to unforeseen circumstances, I'm unable to attend his dinner, even though I greatly desired to."

"And of course, the 'unforeseen circumstance' is me," Fyodor Pavlovitch cut in immediately. "Do you hear that, Father? This gentleman doesn't want to stay in my company, or he'd come right away. So go ahead, Pyotr Alexandrovitch, go to the Father Superior and enjoy your dinner. I'll decline, not you. I'll eat at home. I don't feel up to eating here, Pyotr Alexandrovitch, my dear relative."

"I'm not your relative, and I never was, you despicable man!"

"I said it on purpose to make you mad because you always deny it, even though you really are related to me, no matter how much you try to wriggle out of it. I can prove it using the church records. Ivan, you can stay if you want. I'll send the horses for you later. But, Pyotr Alexandrovitch, you should go to the Father Superior and apologize for the commotion we caused."

"Are you really going home? Or are you lying?"

"Pyotr Alexandrovitch! How could I lie after what's happened? Forgive me, gentlemen, I got carried away! I'm upset! And honestly, I'm ashamed. Some men have the heart of Alexander the Great, and others have the heart of a little dog. I'm like the little dog. I'm ashamed! After all this, how could I go to dinner and gobble up the monastery's sauces? I'm ashamed. I can't. You'll have to excuse me!"

"The devil only knows if he's telling the truth," Miüsov thought, still hesitating, watching the retreating buffoon with suspicious eyes. Fyodor Pavlovitch turned around and, noticing that Miüsov was watching him, blew him a kiss.

"Well, are you going to the Superior?" Miüsov asked Ivan abruptly.

"Why not? I was invited yesterday."

"Unfortunately, I feel like I have to go to this ridiculous dinner," Miüsov grumbled, still irritated, despite the monk standing nearby. "At the very least, we should apologize for the disturbance and explain that it wasn't our fault. What do you think?"

"Yes, we need to make it clear it wasn't our fault. Besides, Father won't be there," Ivan replied.

"Well, I hope not! Curse this dinner!"

They all continued walking, the monk listening in silence. As they walked through the woods, the monk finally said something: the Father Superior had been waiting a long time, and they were more than half an hour late. No one responded. Miüsov glared at Ivan.

"Look at him, going to dinner like nothing happened," he thought. "That brazen face! He has the conscience of a true Karamazov!"

Chapter 7: A Young Man Bent on A Career

Alyosha helped Father Zossima to his bedroom and sat him down on his bed. It was a small room with only the essentials. There was a narrow iron bed with just a piece of felt for a mattress. In the corner, under the icons, was a reading desk with a cross and a Gospel on it. The elder sank down onto the bed, exhausted. His eyes sparkled, and he was breathing heavily. He looked closely at Alyosha, as if thinking about something.

"Go, my dear boy, go. Porfiry will take care of me. Hurry, you are

needed elsewhere. Go wait at the Father Superior's table." "Let me stay here," Alyosha begged.

"You are more needed there. There is no peace over there. You will wait and be useful. If evil spirits rise up, say a prayer. And remember, my son," the elder liked to call him that, "this is not your place in the future. When God calls me, you must leave the monastery. Leave for good."

Alyosha was shocked.

"What is it? This is not your place for now. I bless you for great work in the world. You will go on a long journey. And you will have to marry as well. You will face much before you return. There is a lot to do. But I have no doubt in you, and so I send you out. Christ is with you. Do not leave Him, and He will not leave you. You will see great sorrow, but in that sorrow, you will find happiness. This is my final message to you: in sorrow, seek happiness. Work, work without stopping. Remember my words, because even though I will speak to you again, my days—and even my hours—are numbered."

Alyosha's face showed deep emotion. The corners of his mouth quivered.

"What is it now?" Father Zossima asked with a gentle smile. "Worldly people cry for the dead, but here we rejoice for the father who is leaving. We rejoice and pray for him. Leave me now, I must pray. Go, and hurry. Stay close to your brothers. And not just to one, but to both of them."

Father Zossima raised his hand to bless him. Alyosha couldn't object, though he wanted badly to stay. He also wanted to ask about the elder bowing to Dmitri. The question was on the tip of his tongue, but he didn't dare ask. He knew the elder would have explained if he thought it necessary. But it seemed that it was not his will. That action had made a powerful impression on Alyosha; he believed without question that it had deep, perhaps even frightening, meaning.

As he hurried out of the hermitage to make it to the Father Superior's dinner in time, Alyosha suddenly felt a sharp pain in his heart and stopped. He seemed to hear Father Zossima's words again, predicting his own death. Everything the elder had said would definitely happen, Alyosha believed that completely. But how could he live without him? How could he go on without seeing him or hearing his voice? Where would he go? The elder had told him not to cry and to leave the monastery. Good God! It had been a long time since Alyosha felt such deep sorrow. He rushed through the forest that separated the monastery from the hermitage. Unable to bear his thoughts, he stared at the ancient pines along the path. He didn't have far to go—only about five hundred steps. He wasn't expecting to meet anyone at that hour, but at the first turn in the path, he saw Rakitin waiting for someone.

"Are you waiting for me?" asked Alyosha, catching up to him.

"Yes," Rakitin grinned. "You're rushing to the Father Superior, aren't you? He's having a banquet. There hasn't been a feast like this since the Superior entertained the Bishop and General Pahatov. Remember that? I won't be there, but you can go and serve the sauces. Tell me something, Alexey—what did that vision mean? That's what I want to ask you."

"What vision?"

"That bowing to your brother Dmitri. Didn't the elder even touch his forehead to the ground?"

"Are you talking about Father Zossima?" "Yes, Father Zossima."

"He touched the ground?"

"Ah, what a disrespectful way to say it! But still, what do you think it meant?"

"I don't know what it means, Misha."

"I knew he wouldn't explain it to you! There's nothing strange about it, really, just the usual holy nonsense. But there was a reason behind it. The pious folks in town will talk about it, spread the story throughout the province, and wonder what it meant. I think the old man has a good nose. He smelled a crime. Your house reeks of it."

"What crime?"

It was clear that Rakitin had something he was eager to talk about.

"The crime will happen in your family. Between your brothers and your rich old father. That's why Father Zossima bowed down, to prepare for whatever's coming. If something happens later, people will say, 'Ah, the holy man saw it coming, he predicted it!' even though it's a cheap prophecy, bowing like that. They'll say, 'It was symbolic, an allegory,' and who knows what else! It'll be remembered in his honor: 'He predicted the crime and marked the criminal!' That's always how it is with these fanatics; they cross themselves in a tavern and throw stones at the temple. Like your elder—he hits a righteous man with a stick and bows at the feet of a murderer."

"What crime? What murderer? What are you talking about?" Alyosha stopped in his tracks. Rakitin stopped too.

"What murderer? As if you don't know! I'll bet you've thought about it already. That's interesting, by the way. Tell me the truth, Alyosha. You always do. Have you thought about it or not? Answer me."

"I have," Alyosha replied quietly. Even Rakitin was surprised. "What? You really have?"

"I... I didn't exactly think about it," Alyosha muttered, "but as soon as you started talking so strangely, I felt like maybe I had thought it myself."

"You see? And you said it so well! Just by looking at your father and brother today, you thought of a crime. So I wasn't wrong?"

"But wait a minute," Alyosha said, feeling uneasy. "What made you think of all this? Why does it matter to you? That's my first question."

"Two questions, actually, but they're connected. I'll answer them one by one. What made me think of it? I wouldn't have thought of it if I hadn't suddenly understood your brother Dmitri, if I hadn't seen straight into his heart in a single moment. I figured him out from one small trait. These very honest but passionate people—they have a line you mustn't cross. If someone does, he'll go after them with a knife. And your father is a drunken, immoral old man who doesn't know how to draw the line. If they both lose control, it'll end in disaster."

"No, Misha, no. If that's all, you've made me feel better. It won't go that far."

"Then why are you trembling? Let me tell you, Mitya may be honest (he's stupid, but honest), but he's a sensualist. That's the very heart of who he is. He gets it from your father. I'm honestly surprised at how you, Alyosha, have stayed pure. You're a Karamazov, too, you know! In your family, sensuality is almost a disease. And now, these three sensualists are circling each other, with knives ready. They're butting heads, and you might end up being the fourth."

"You're mistaken about that woman. Dmitri—he despises her," said Alyosha, with a slight shudder.

"Grushenka? No, brother, he doesn't despise her. Since he has openly abandoned his fiancée for her, he doesn't despise her. There's something here, my dear boy, that you don't understand yet. A man will fall in love with some beauty, with a woman's body, or even with a part of a woman's body (a sensualist would understand that), and he'll abandon his own children for her, sell his father and mother, and his country, Russia, too. If he's honest, he'll steal; if he's humane, he'll murder; if he's faithful, he'll deceive. Pushkin, the poet of women's feet, sang of their feet in his verse. Others don't sing their praises, but they can't look at their feet without a thrill— and it's not only their feet. Contempt's no help here, brother, even if he did despise Grushenka. He does, but he can't tear himself away."

"I understand that," Alyosha jerked out suddenly.

"Really? Well, I dare say you do understand, since you blurt it out at the first word," said Rakitin, malignantly. "That escaped you unawares, and the confession's the more precious. So it's a familiar subject; you've thought about it already, about sensuality, I mean! Oh, you virgin soul! You're a quiet one, Alyosha, you're a saint, I know, but the devil only knows what you've thought about, and what you know already! You are pure, but you've been down into the depths... I've been watching you a long time. You're a Karamazov yourself; you're a thorough Karamazov—no doubt birth and selection have something to answer for. You're a sensualist from your father, a crazy saint from your mother. Why do you tremble? Is it true, then? Do you know, Grushenka has been begging me to bring you along. 'I'll pull off his cassock,' she says. You can't think how she keeps begging me to bring you. I wondered why she took such an interest in you. Do you know, she's an extraordinary woman, too!"

"Thank her and say I'm not coming," said Alyosha, with a strained smile. "Finish what you were saying, Misha. I'll tell you my idea after."

"There's nothing to finish. It's all clear. It's the same old tune, brother. If even you are a sensualist at heart, what of your brother, Ivan? He's a Karamazov, too. What is at the root of all you Karamazovs is that you're all sensual, grasping, and crazy! Your brother Ivan writes theological articles in joke, for some idiotic, unknown motive of his own, though he's an atheist, and he admits it's a fraud himself—that's your brother Ivan. He's trying to get Mitya's betrothed for himself, and I fancy he'll succeed, too. And what's more, it's with Mitya's consent. For Mitya will surrender his betrothed to him to be rid of her, and escape to Grushenka. And he's ready to do that in spite of all his nobility and disinterestedness. Observe that. Those are the most fatal people! Who the devil can make you out? He recognizes his vileness and goes on with it! Let me tell you, too, the old man, your father, is standing in Mitya's way now. He has suddenly gone crazy over Grushenka. His mouth waters at the sight of her. It's simply on her account he made that scene in the cell just now, simply because Miüsov called her an 'abandoned creature.' He's worse than a tomcat in love. At first, she was only employed by him in connection with his taverns and in some other shady business, but now he has suddenly realized all she is and has gone wild about her. He keeps pestering her with his offers, not honorable ones, of course. And they'll come into collision, the precious father and son, on that path! But Grushenka favors neither of them, she's still playing with them, and teasing them both, considering which she can get most out of. For though she could filch a lot of money from the papa, he wouldn't marry her, and maybe he'll turn stingy in the end and keep his purse shut. That's where Mitya's value comes in; he has no money, but he's ready to marry her. Yes, ready to marry her! To abandon his betrothed, a rare beauty, Katerina Ivanovna, who's rich and the daughter of a colonel, and to marry Grushenka, who has been the mistress of a dissolute old merchant, Samsonov, a coarse, uneducated provincial mayor. Some murderous conflict may well come to pass from all this, and that's what your brother Ivan is waiting for. It would suit him down to the ground. He'll carry off Katerina Ivanovna, for whom he is languishing, and pocket her dowry of sixty thousand. That's very alluring to start with, for a man of no consequence and a beggar. And, take note, he won't be wronging Mitya, but doing him the greatest service. For I know as a fact that Mitya only last week, when he was with some gypsy girls drunk in a tavern, cried out aloud that he was unworthy of his betrothed, Katya, but that his brother Ivan, he was the man who deserved her. And Katerina Ivanovna will not in the end refuse such a fascinating man as Ivan. She's hesitating between the two of them already. And how has that Ivan won you all, so that you all worship him? He is laughing at you, and enjoying himself at your expense."

"How do you know? How can you speak so confidently?" Alyosha asked sharply, frowning.

"Why do you ask, and are frightened at my answer? It shows that you know I'm speaking the truth."

"You don't like Ivan. Ivan wouldn't be tempted by money."

"Really? And the beauty of Katerina Ivanovna? It's not only the money, though a fortune of sixty thousand is an attraction."

"Ivan is above that. He wouldn't make up to anyone for thousands. It is not money, it's not comfort Ivan is seeking. Perhaps it's suffering he is seeking."

"What wild dream now? Oh, you aristocrats!"

"Ah, Misha, he has a stormy spirit. His mind is in bondage. He is haunted by a great, unsolved doubt. He is one of those who don't want millions but an answer to their questions."

"That's plagiarism, Alyosha. You're quoting your elder's phrases. Ah, Ivan has set you a problem!" cried Rakitin, with undisguised malice. His face changed, and his lips twitched. "And the problem's a stupid one. It is no good guessing it. Rack your brains—you'll understand it. His article is absurd and ridiculous. And did you hear his stupid theory just now: if there's no immortality of the soul, then there's no virtue, and everything is lawful. (And by the way, do you remember how your brother Mitya cried out: 'I will remember!') An attractive theory for scoundrels!—(I'm being abusive, that's stupid.) Not for scoundrels, but for pedantic poseurs, 'haunted by profound, unsolved doubts.' He's showing off, and what it all comes to is, 'on the one hand we cannot but admit' and 'on the other it must be confessed!' His whole theory is a fraud! Humanity will find in itself the power to live for virtue even without believing in immortality. It will find it in love for freedom, for equality, for fraternity."

Rakitin could hardly restrain himself in his heat, but suddenly, as though remembering something, he stopped short.

"Well, that's enough," he said, with a still more crooked smile. "Why are you laughing? Do you think I'm a vulgar fool?"

"No, I never dreamed of thinking you a vulgar fool. You are clever but... never mind, I was silly to smile. I understand your getting hot about it, Misha. I guess from your warmth that you are not indifferent to Katerina Ivanovna yourself; I've suspected that for a long time, brother, that's why you don't like my brother Ivan. Are you jealous of him?"

"And jealous of her money, too? Won't you add that?"

"I'll say nothing about money. I am not going to insult you."

"I believe it, since you say so, but confound you, and your brother Ivan with you. Don't you understand that one might very well dislike him, apart from Katerina Ivanovna? And why the devil should I like him? He condescends to abuse me, you know. Why haven't I a right to abuse him?"

"I never heard of his saying anything about you, good or bad. He doesn't speak of you at all."

"But I heard that the day before yesterday at Katerina Ivanovna's he was abusing me for all he was worth—you see what an interest he takes in your humble servant. And which is the jealous one after that, brother, I can't say. He was so good as to express the opinion that, if I don't go in for the career of an archimandrite in the immediate future and don't become a monk, I shall be sure to go to Petersburg and get on to some solid magazine as a reviewer, that I shall write for the next ten years, and in the end become the owner of the magazine, and bring it out on the liberal and atheistic side, with a socialistic tinge, with a tiny gloss of socialism, but keeping a sharp look out all the time, that is, keeping in with both sides and hoodwinking the fools. According to your brother's account, the tinge of socialism won't hinder me from laying by the proceeds and investing them under the guidance of some Jew, till at the end of my career I build a great house in Petersburg and move my publishing offices to it, and let out the upper stories to lodgers. He has even chosen the place for it, near the new stone bridge across the Neva, which they say is to be built in Petersburg."

"Ah, Misha, that's exactly what will happen, every word of it," Alyosha said, unable to stop himself from smiling kindly.

"You think you're being funny, Alexey Fyodorovitch."

"No, no, I'm just joking. Forgive me. I have something else on my mind. But tell me, how did you hear all this? You couldn't have been at Katerina Ivanovna's yourself when he was talking about you, right?"

"I wasn't there, but Dmitri Fyodorovitch was. I heard it from him myself. Actually, I didn't hear it directly from him, but I overheard it by accident, of course. I was sitting in Grushenka's bedroom, and I couldn't leave because Dmitri Fyodorovitch was in the next room."

"Oh, right, I forgot she was a relation of yours."

"A relation? That Grushenka, a relation of mine?" Rakitin shouted, his face turning red. "Are you crazy? Have you lost your mind?"

"Wait, isn't she a relation of yours? That's what I heard."

"Where did you hear that? You Karamazovs love to brag about being some ancient, noble family, even though your father was nothing but a fool at other people's tables and only got into the kitchen out of pity. I may only be a priest's son and mean nothing to noblemen like you, but don't insult me so casually. I've got a sense of honor too, Alexey Fyodorovitch. I could never be related to Grushenka, a common woman. Understand that!"

Rakitin was clearly upset.

"Forgive me, I had no idea... besides, how can you call her that? Is she really... that kind of woman?" Alyosha blushed suddenly. "I tell you again, I heard she was related to you. You visit her often, and you told me yourself that you aren't her lover. I never thought you, of all people, would think so lowly of her! Does she really deserve that?"

"I might have my own reasons for visiting her. That's none of your business. But as for being related, your brother—or even your father—is more likely to make her related to you than I am. Anyway, here we are. You'd better head to the kitchen. Wait, what's going on? Are we late? They can't have finished dinner already! Have the Karamazovs caused trouble again? I bet they have. Look, there's your father and your brother Ivan behind him, coming out of the Father Superior's place. And see, Father Isidor is shouting something at them from the steps. And your father's yelling and waving his arms around. He's probably cursing. And look, Miüsov's carriage is driving away. He's leaving! And there's old Maximov running!—there must've been a big fight. I doubt they even had dinner. Do you think they beat up the Father Superior? Or maybe they got beaten? It would serve them right!"

Rakitin's outburst wasn't without reason. There had been a scandal—an outrageous and unexpected scene. It all happened in a moment of impulse.

Chapter 8: The Scandalous Scene

Miüsov, being a man who prided himself on his good manners and refinement, couldn't help but feel a twinge of guilt as he and Ivan approached the Father Superior's residence. The memory of his outburst earlier weighed heavily on him, and he was genuinely ashamed of the way he had allowed himself to lose his temper. As a gentleman, he felt he should have been above such things, too detached and dignified to be rattled by a man as base and ridiculous as Fyodor Pavlovitch. He realized, as he climbed the steps, that he had failed to keep his composure in the presence of the monks, especially in Father Zossima's cell, where dignity and decorum should have been his guiding principles. "The monks had done nothing wrong," he reflected. "They weren't at fault in any way." He knew, in fact, that if anyone had been wronged by the situation, it was the monks themselves.

"They deserve respect, not animosity," Miüsov thought. "If the Father Superior is the nobleman I've heard he is, and if the monks are as honorable as they seem, it would only be proper for me to behave politely and with the utmost courtesy. Why not be friendly and agreeable with them? I'll go along with everything. I won't argue, I'll be compliant, and by showing them respect, I'll win them over." He paused for a moment, thinking about how he had been caught up in the commotion. "And besides, I need to make it clear that I have absolutely nothing in common with that vile buffoon, Fyodor Pavlovitch," he mused. "I was dragged into this just as much as the monks were. I'll let them know I was fooled just like they were."

With this thought, Miüsov made an important decision: he would drop his lawsuit against the monastery. He resolved to relinquish his claims to the rights to the wood-cutting and fishing privileges immediately, without delay. After all, those rights had diminished in value over the years, and in truth, Miüsov hardly knew where the woods and rivers involved were located. His determination to make peace strengthened as he neared the dining room, filled with a growing sense of purpose and resolution.

When Miüsov finally entered the Father Superior's dining room, his resolve to be gracious only deepened. Technically speaking, the room wasn't exactly a dining room, given that the Father Superior had only two rooms in his modest quarters. However, these two rooms were significantly larger and more comfortable than the bare, ascetic accommodations of Father Zossima. Yet, despite their size, there was no sense of luxury or extravagance about them. The furniture was old-fashioned, crafted from sturdy mahogany and covered in leather, reminiscent of a style popular in the 1820s. The floors were simple and unstained, yet everything gleamed with cleanliness, as though the space had been lovingly cared for over many years. The windows were lined with carefully tended flowers, adding a touch of warmth and life to the room. Still, the most striking feature of the room, at that moment, was undoubtedly the dining table itself. It was beautifully set, with a clean white tablecloth and dishes that sparkled in the light.

The table boasted three types of bread, baked to perfection, along with two bottles of wine, two bottles of exquisite mead, and a large glass jug of kvas, a fermented drink made in the monastery and highly regarded in the surrounding region. However, there was no vodka present on the table, a fact that might have been notable to some guests. According to Rakitin, who later recounted the details, the meal consisted of five distinct dishes: a fish soup made with sterlets, accompanied by small fish patties; then a dish of boiled fish prepared in a unique style; followed by salmon cutlets, ice pudding, a compote of fruits, and finally, blancmange. Rakitin had been unable to resist sneaking into the kitchen, where he already had established connections, to find out exactly what would be served. He had always been a restless, curious individual, driven by an intense need to know everything. His talent for gathering information was well known, as was his ability to cultivate relationships wherever he went.

Rakitin was a man who had long been troubled by a sense of unease and envy. He was well aware of his own intelligence and abilities, yet he often exaggerated them in his mind, becoming more and more self-important with each passing day. He believed himself destined for a prominent role in society, though his aspirations often seemed more rooted in vanity than in any real plan for success. His good friend Alyosha, who admired him in some ways, was saddened by Rakitin's lack of true integrity. Despite his intellect, Rakitin didn't seem to recognize his own dishonorable behavior. Instead, he saw himself as a man of principle, considering himself morally upright simply because he wouldn't stoop to stealing money left on a table. No one, not even Alyosha, could sway him from this belief, and Rakitin remained unaware of the many ways in which he fell short.

Of course, Rakitin was not important enough to be invited to this particular dinner. The gathering was small, with only a few select guests. Father Iosif, Father Païssy, and one other monk from the monastery had been invited to join the Father Superior for the meal. When Miüsov, Kalganov, and Ivan arrived, these guests were already waiting. Another man, Maximov, stood off to the side, waiting quietly for the meal to begin. The Father Superior stepped into the center of the room to greet his guests. He was a tall, thin man, yet there was a certain vitality about him, a strength that belied his age. His black hair was streaked with gray, and his face was long, solemn, and ascetic, bearing the marks of a man who had lived a life of devotion and discipline. He bowed in silence to his guests as they entered.

This time, the guests made a point of approaching him to receive his blessing, a gesture of respect. Miüsov, in particular, made an effort to be humble, even attempting to kiss the Father Superior's hand, though the Father Superior pulled his hand back just in time to avoid the kiss. Ivan and Kalganov, on the other hand, approached the ritual with sincerity, bowing and kissing the Father Superior's hand in the simple, heartfelt way that peasants might do.

"We must humbly apologize, Your Reverence," Miüsov began, adopting a polite and gracious tone as he addressed the Father Superior. His words were carefully chosen, his manner respectful. "Please forgive us for arriving without Fyodor Pavlovitch, the gentleman you so kindly invited. He felt it necessary to decline the honor of your hospitality. It seems that the unfortunate quarrel he had with his son in Father Zossima's cell left him feeling upset, and he spoke words that were, frankly, quite inappropriate and out of place." Miüsov glanced toward the monks, acknowledging their presence. "I'm sure Your Reverence is aware of the situation. Fyodor Pavlovitch deeply regrets his actions. He recognizes his fault and feels genuine remorse. He has asked me, along with his son Ivan Fyodorovitch, to convey his apologies and express his hope to make amends in the future. He asks for your blessing and humbly begs you to forget the incident."

As Miüsov finished speaking, a sense of calm settled over him. He felt that he had handled the situation well, and his earlier frustration had completely dissipated. With his irritation gone, he found himself once again in a state of good humor, feeling a renewed sense of compassion for his fellow man.

The Father Superior listened to Miüsov's speech with a dignified air. He bowed his head slightly and responded, "I am truly sorry to hear of his absence. Perhaps, if he had joined us at the table, we might have come to appreciate each other more, and he might have found us agreeable as well. But please, gentlemen, take your seats."

The Father Superior then turned toward the holy icon and began to say grace aloud. Everyone bowed their heads in reverence. Maximov, standing near the back, clasped his hands in prayer with a fervor that seemed out of place given his usual demeanor.

It was at this exact moment that Fyodor Pavlovitch decided to pull one final stunt. It's important to note that he had originally intended to go home. After the disgraceful scene he had caused in Father Zossima's cell, he felt that it would be improper to attend the Father Superior's dinner. Not that Fyodor Pavlovitch was particularly ashamed of his behavior—on the contrary, he was proud of his ability to stir up trouble—but he still recognized that it would be inappropriate to act as though nothing had happened. However, just as he had settled into his carriage at the hotel, he suddenly paused, struck by a thought. He remembered his own words in Father Zossima's cell: "I always feel that I am lower than everyone I meet, and that they all see me as a fool. So I say, let me be the fool, for you are all even more foolish and lowly than I am."

This thought filled him with a desire for revenge. He recalled how, once, someone had asked him, "Why do you hate that person so much?" and, with shameless audacity, he had replied, "I'll tell you why: he never did anything to me. But I played a dirty trick on him once, and ever since then, I've hated him."

With a malicious smile, Fyodor Pavlovitch decided that if he had already made a spectacle of himself, he might as well continue. He hesitated for only a moment, his eyes gleaming with mischief, before telling his coachman to wait while he returned to the monastery. His primary thought was to shame everyone for the way they had treated him. He would show them that he didn't care what they thought of him—that he had no need for their approval.

With quick steps, Fyodor Pavlovitch made his way back to the Father Superior's dining room. He had no real plan, but he knew that his temper could easily push him to the edge of obscene behavior—though nothing criminal, of course. He always took pride in his ability to stop himself from crossing that line. As he entered the dining room, the prayer had just ended, and the guests were preparing to sit down to eat. Standing in the doorway, Fyodor Pavlovitch looked around the room, then burst into a loud, mocking laugh. He looked each guest in the eye, his laughter ringing through the room. "They thought I had left, but here I am again," he announced, grinning at the shocked faces before him.

For a brief moment, the entire room was silent. Then, it became immediately clear that something terrible was about to happen— something grotesque, scandalous, and deeply inappropriate. Miüsov, who had just been feeling calm and collected, suddenly flew into a rage. All the feelings of anger and irritation that he had suppressed came rushing back, overwhelming him.

"No! This is intolerable!" he shouted, barely able to contain his fury. "I simply cannot—absolutely cannot— stand for this!"

His face turned red with anger, and he grabbed his hat, ready to leave the room in a huff.

"What is it that you cannot stand, my dear sir?" Fyodor Pavlovitch called out, his voice dripping with mockery. "What is it that you cannot tolerate, cannot endure? Your Reverence," he said, turning to the Father Superior with a sarcastic smile, "am I welcome here or not? Will you receive me as your guest?"

"You are welcome with all my heart," the Father Superior replied calmly. "Gentlemen," he added, addressing the room, "I humbly ask that you all set aside your differences and come together in the spirit of love and family harmony. Let us join in prayer at our humble table."

"No, no, this is impossible!" Miüsov shouted, his anger boiling over.

"Well, if it's impossible for Pyotr Alexandrovitch, then it's impossible for me too," Fyodor Pavlovitch declared. "That's why I came back. I'll stick with Pyotr Alexandrovitch from now on. Wherever he goes, I'll go. If he leaves, I'll leave too. If he stays, I'll stay. Father Superior, you've offended him with all that talk of family harmony. He won't admit that he's related to me. Isn't that right, von Sohn? Oh look, here's von Sohn himself. How are you, von Sohn?"

"Do you mean me?" muttered Maximov, looking confused.

"Of course, I mean you," cried Fyodor Pavlovitch. "Who else? The Father Superior can't be von Sohn."

"But I'm not von Sohn either. I'm Maximov."

"No, you're von Sohn. Father Superior, do you know who von Sohn was? It was a famous murder case. He was killed in a house of ill-repute—that's what you call those places, right? He was killed and robbed, and despite his old age, they nailed him up in a box and shipped him from Petersburg to Moscow in the luggage van. And while they were nailing him up, the harlots sang and played the piano. So, this is that very von Sohn. He's risen from the dead, hasn't he, von Sohn?"

"What's going on? What is this?" voices murmured from the monks.

"Let's go," said Miüsov, speaking to Kalganov.

"No, wait," Fyodor Pavlovitch broke in loudly, taking another step into the room. "Let me finish. Earlier in the cell, you accused me of being disrespectful just because I talked about eating gudgeon, Pyotr Alexandrovitch. Miüsov, my relative, prefers to have 'more nobility than sincerity' in his words, but I prefer to have 'more sincerity than nobility,' and—forget nobility! Isn't that right, von Sohn? Father Superior, let me tell you, though I'm a fool and act like one, I'm a man of honor, and I have something to say. Yes, I am the soul of honor, while Pyotr Alexandrovitch is full of wounded pride and nothing else. Maybe I came here to check things out and speak my mind. My son, Alexey, is here, saving his soul. I'm his father; I care about him, and I have a duty to care. While I've been playing the fool, I've been paying attention, and now I'm ready to give you the final act of the show. You know how things are? As a thing falls, so it lies. But no! I want to get up again. Father Superior, I'm upset with you. Confession is a holy sacrament, and I bow down to it. But in the cell earlier, people were confessing out loud. How is that right? It was ordained that confession should be in secret. Then it stays a mystery. But how can I confess in front of everyone that I did this or that... well, you know what I mean—some things aren't meant to be said out loud. It's a scandal! No, Fathers, you could drag me into being a Flagellant. I'll write to the Synod, and I'm taking my son, Alexey, home with me."

It's important to note here that Fyodor Pavlovitch had hit on a sensitive subject. There had once been nasty rumors, even reaching the Archbishop, that in monasteries with elders, like this one, the elders were given too much authority, even overshadowing the Superior. Some even accused them of misusing the sacrament of confession. These ridiculous accusations had faded away over time. But Fyodor Pavlovitch, caught up in his own foolishness, was blindly repeating these old slanders, not even realizing what he was saying. No one had knelt or confessed out loud in the elder's cell, so he couldn't have seen it. He was just recalling confused rumors from the past. As soon as he finished his rant, he realized he'd been talking nonsense. But instead of stopping, he pushed forward, trying to prove to everyone—and to himself— that he hadn't been talking nonsense at all.

"How disgraceful!" cried Pyotr Alexandrovitch.

"Pardon me," said the Father Superior calmly. "It was said long ago, 'Many have spoken against me, saying evil things. And hearing this, I said to myself: It is the Lord's correction, sent to heal my proud soul.' So, we humbly thank you, dear guest," and he bowed deeply to Fyodor Pavlovitch.

"Tut-tut-tut—sanctimonious words and gestures! Old phrases and bows. All lies and fake humility. We know all about that. A kiss on the lips and a knife in the heart, like in Schiller's Robbers. I don't like lies, Fathers. I want the truth. And the truth isn't found in eating gudgeon! I'll tell you that much! Why do you fast,

Fathers? For what? To earn a reward in heaven? Well, if that's what you're after, I'll come and fast too! No, saintly Fathers, try being virtuous in the world, doing good for society without hiding in a monastery, and without expecting some heavenly reward. That's much harder! I can talk sense, too, Father Superior. What have we got here?" He approached the table. "Old port wine, mead brewed by the Eliseyev Brothers. Look at that, Fathers! This is more than just gudgeon! Look at the bottles they've set out! Ha, ha! And who paid for it all? The poor Russian peasant, the laborer, brings his last farthing, earned by the sweat of his brow, wringing it from his starving family! You bleed the people dry, holy Fathers!"

"This is disgraceful," said Father Iosif.

Father Païssy remained silent. Miüsov stormed out of the room, and Kalganov followed him.

"Well, Father, I'll go with Pyotr Alexandrovitch! I won't be coming back here. Even if you beg me, I won't return. I sent you a thousand roubles, and now you're keeping an eye on me! Ha! But no, I'll say no more. I'm taking revenge for my youth, for all the humiliation I suffered." He slammed his fist on the table in a fake show of emotion. "This monastery has played a big part in my life! It's cost me many tears. You even turned my wife against me! You cursed me, spread stories about me everywhere. Enough, Fathers! This is the age of Liberalism, the age of steam engines and railways! You'll get no more money from me!"

Again, it should be noted that the monastery had never played any real part in his life, and he had never shed a tear because of it.

But he was so caught up in his act that, for a moment, he almost believed his own story. He was even close to tears. But then he realized it was time to pull back.

The Father Superior bowed his head and said calmly, "It is written again, 'Bear the dishonor that comes to you through no fault of your own with patience and humility, and do not hate the one who dishonors you.' And so we shall."

"Tut-tut-tut! More old sayings and advice. Well, Fathers, I'm leaving. But I'm taking my son, Alexey, away from here for good, as his father. Ivan Fyodorovitch, my loyal son, I order you to come with me. Von Sohn, what are you waiting for? Come to town with me. It's fun there. It's not far, just one short verst. I'll give you something better than Lenten oil. How about some roasted pig and porridge, with brandy and liqueur? I've got some cloudberry wine. Hey, von Sohn, don't miss out!" He left, shouting and waving his arms.

Just then, Rakitin pointed him out to Alyosha.

"Alexey!" Fyodor Pavlovitch shouted from a distance when he saw him. "Come home with me today, for good. Bring your pillow and mattress and don't leave a trace behind."

Alyosha stood still, silently watching. Meanwhile, Fyodor Pavlovitch got into the carriage, and Ivan, without a word or even looking at Alyosha, was about to follow him. But then, another strange and ridiculous scene unfolded. Maximov suddenly ran up to the carriage, panting, afraid he was too late. Rakitin and Alyosha watched him. He was in such a rush that he stepped on the carriage as Ivan was still getting in, grabbing onto the door, and laughing wildly.

"I'm coming with you!" he shouted, his face full of reckless joy. "Take me with you!"

"There!" Fyodor Pavlovitch cried, delighted. "Didn't I tell you he was von Sohn? He's risen from the dead! How did you escape? What did you vonsohn in there? And how did you get away from the dinner? You must be a shameless fellow! I'm like that too, but even I'm surprised at you! Jump in, jump in! Let him in, Ivan. It'll be fun. He can lie at our feet. Will you lie at our feet, von Sohn? Or ride up front with the driver? Jump up there, von Sohn!"

But Ivan, who was already in the carriage, suddenly shoved Maximov hard in the chest, sending him stumbling back. He nearly fell.

"Drive!" Ivan shouted angrily at the driver.

"What are you doing? Why did you do that?" Fyodor Pavlovitch protested.

But the carriage was already moving. Ivan didn't reply.

"Well, you're something else," Fyodor Pavlovitch said, after a pause.

After a couple of minutes, he added, "A drop of brandy would be nice right now."

Ivan said nothing.

"You'll have some when we get home," Fyodor Pavlovitch went on.

Ivan still said nothing.

After another pause, Fyodor Pavlovitch spoke again. "But I'm taking Alyosha out of that monastery, even though you won't like it, my dear Karl von Moor."

Ivan shrugged dismissively and turned to look out at the road. They didn't speak again for the rest of the ride home.

Book 3: The Sensualists

Chapter 1: In The Servants' Quarters

The Karamazov house wasn't exactly in the middle of town, but it wasn't too far out either. It was a cozy, old two-story house painted gray with a red iron roof. The place was spacious and comfortable, and it seemed like it could last for many more years. There were all kinds of unexpected little cupboards, closets, and staircases. The house had rats, but Fyodor Pavlovitch didn't really mind them. "You don't feel so alone when they're around in the evenings," he used to say. He often sent the servants away to the lodge for the night and locked himself inside alone. The lodge, which was in the yard, was a sturdy, spacious building. Fyodor had the meals cooked there, even though the house had a kitchen, because he didn't like the smell of cooking. So, whether it was winter or summer, the food was always carried across the yard to the house. The house was big enough to fit a large family—five times as many people as there were, along with their servants. But at the time of this story, only Fyodor Pavlovitch and his son Ivan lived there. In the lodge, there were only three servants: old Grigory, his wife Marfa, and a young man named Smerdyakov. We need to talk about these three. We've already said a little about Grigory. He was a man who, once he believed something was right (and the reasons were often very illogical), would stubbornly stick to it. He was honest and couldn't be bribed. His wife, Marfa Ignatyevna, had always followed his will throughout their marriage, but after the serfs were freed, she bothered him endlessly about leaving Fyodor Pavlovitch and starting a small shop in Moscow with their savings. But Grigory decided, once and for all, that "the woman's talking nonsense, because all women are dishonest," and that they shouldn't leave their old master, no matter who he was, because "it was their duty now."

"Do you even know what duty is?" he asked Marfa Ignatyevna.

"I know what duty means, Grigory Vassilyevitch, but I'll never understand why it's our duty to stay here," Marfa replied confidently.

"Well, you don't have to understand. But that's how it's going to be. And keep quiet about it."

So, they stayed, and Fyodor Pavlovitch agreed to pay them a small wage, which he gave them regularly. Grigory also knew that he had some influence over his master. And it was true—he was well aware of it. Fyodor Pavlovitch was stubborn and tricky, but while he had a strong will "in some parts of life," as he put it, he was surprised to find himself very weak when it came to certain situations. He knew his own weaknesses, and they scared him. There were moments when you had to be very careful, and that wasn't easy without a reliable person by your side. And Grigory was definitely reliable. Many times in his life, Fyodor Pavlovitch had barely escaped a good beating because of Grigory's help, and each time, the old servant would give him a good talking-to. But it wasn't just physical beatings that scared Fyodor Pavlovitch. There were more serious moments, complicated and subtle, when he couldn't explain his sudden, strong need for someone loyal and devoted, which sometimes hit him out of nowhere. It was almost like an illness. Corrupt and often cruel in his desires, like some nasty insect, Fyodor Pavlovitch would sometimes, during his drunken fits, be overcome by superstitious fear and a moral shock that felt almost physical. "My soul feels like it's stuck in my throat at those times," he used to say. In those moments, he liked knowing there was a strong, faithful man nearby, either in the lodge or in the house itself. Someone who was good and unlike him, who had seen all his worst behavior and knew all his secrets but was still loyal enough to overlook it all. Someone who wouldn't go against him, especially not scold him or threaten him with anything, either in this world or the next, and who, if needed, would protect him—from what? From someone unknown, but terrifying and dangerous. What Fyodor Pavlovitch needed was to feel like there was another person, an old and trusted friend, whom he could call in his moments of sickness just to look at or exchange a few random words with. And if the old servant wasn't angry, he would feel better. If the servant was angry, he would feel worse. Sometimes (but this was rare), Fyodor Pavlovitch would go to the lodge at night to wake Grigory and have him come over for a moment. When Grigory arrived, Fyodor Pavlovitch would start talking about meaningless things and then send him back to bed, sometimes even making a joke. Afterward, Fyodor Pavlovitch would get into bed, cursing, and sleep soundly.

This sort of thing happened when Alyosha came to visit, too. Alyosha "touched his heart" by "living with him, seeing everything, and saying nothing." More than that, Alyosha brought something with him that Fyodor Pavlovitch had never experienced before: a complete lack of contempt and a constant kindness. Alyosha showed him a pure, natural, and unaffected loyalty that the old man didn't deserve. All this was a total shock to the old sinner, who had long cut himself off from family. It was a new and surprising experience for a man who had only ever loved "evil." When Alyosha left, Fyodor Pavlovitch admitted to himself that he had learned something he'd never wanted to know before.

I already mentioned that Grigory had hated Adelaida Ivanovna, Fyodor Pavlovitch's first wife and Dmitri's mother. On the other hand, he had always stood up for Sofya Ivanovna, the poor "crazy woman," against anyone who insulted her, including his master. His sympathy for the unhappy wife became sacred to him. Even twenty years later, he couldn't stand to hear anyone speak ill of her and would immediately shut them down. Outwardly, Grigory was cold, dignified, and quiet. He spoke carefully, without being frivolous. You couldn't tell right away whether he loved his gentle, obedient wife, but he really did, and she knew it.

Marfa Ignatyevna was no fool. In fact, she was probably smarter than her husband or at least more practical about worldly things. And yet, from the day they were married, she never questioned him and followed his lead in everything. She respected him for his spiritual strength. What was strange was how little they talked to each other during their life together. They only spoke about the most necessary daily matters. The serious and dignified Grigory dealt with all his concerns and responsibilities on his own, so Marfa had long accepted that he didn't need her advice. She knew he respected her silence and saw it as a sign of her good sense. He had only hit her once, and even then, it wasn't hard. It happened the year after Fyodor Pavlovitch married Adelaida Ivanovna. The village women and girls, who were still serfs back then, were called to sing and dance in front of the house. They started with "In the Green Meadows," and Marfa, who was still a young woman, stepped forward and danced the Russian Dance. But she didn't dance it the way they did in the village; she danced the way she had learned when she was a servant for the wealthy Miüsov family, where a Moscow dance instructor had taught the servants to perform in their private theater. Grigory saw how his wife danced, and an hour later, at home in their cottage, he pulled her hair a little to "teach her a lesson." But that was the end of it. He never hit her again, and Marfa Ignatyevna gave up dancing.

God had not blessed them with children. They had one child, but it died. Grigory loved children and wasn't ashamed of showing it. When Adelaida Ivanovna ran away, Grigory took care of Dmitri, who was just three years old. He combed his hair, washed him in a tub with his own hands, and looked after him for almost a year. Later, he also took care of Ivan and Alyosha, though for that, the general's widow rewarded him with a slap in the face— but I've already told that story. The only joy his own child had brought him was in the time he waited for its birth. When the baby was born, Grigory was struck with grief and horror. The baby had six fingers. Grigory was so devastated by this that he didn't speak until the day of the christening and kept to himself in the garden. It was spring, and he spent three days digging in the kitchen garden. The third day was set for the christening, and by then, Grigory had made up his mind.

He walked into the cottage, where the priest and guests, including Fyodor Pavlovitch, who was to be the godfather, had gathered. He suddenly announced that the baby "shouldn't be christened at all." He said this quietly and briefly, forcing out the words while staring at the priest with a dull, serious look.

"Why not?" asked the priest, smiling. "Because it's a dragon," Grigory mumbled. "A dragon? What do you mean?"

Grigory stayed silent for a while, then muttered vaguely but firmly, "It's a mistake of nature." He clearly didn't want to say more.

They all laughed, and of course, they christened the poor baby anyway. Grigory prayed earnestly during the ceremony, but his feelings about the baby didn't change. Still, he didn't interfere. While the sick baby lived, Grigory barely looked at it, trying not to notice it, and mostly stayed out of the house. But when the baby died of thrush two weeks later, Grigory himself laid the child in its tiny coffin. He looked at it with deep sadness, and when they were filling the shallow grave, he fell to his knees and bowed to the ground. For years afterward, he never mentioned the child, and Marfa never spoke of the baby in front of him. Even when Grigory wasn't around, she only mentioned it in whispers. Marfa noticed that, from the day of the burial, Grigory devoted himself to "religion." He took to reading the Lives of the Saints, mostly sitting alone in silence, always wearing his big, round silver-rimmed glasses. He rarely read aloud, maybe only during

Lent. He loved the Book of Job, and had somehow gotten a copy of the sayings and sermons of "the God-fearing Father Isaac the Syrian," which he read for years, even though he understood little of it. Maybe that was why he loved it so much. Recently, he had started listening to the teachings of the Flagellants, a religious sect that had settled nearby. He seemed moved by their beliefs but thought it wasn't right to convert. His habit of reading religious texts gave him an even more serious expression.

He might have always been drawn to mysticism. The birth and death of his deformed child, as if by some strange plan, were followed by another mysterious and amazing event, which, as Grigory later said, left a "mark" on his soul. On the very night after his child was buried, Marfa was woken up by the sound of a newborn baby crying. She was terrified and woke her husband. He listened and said it sounded more like someone groaning, "maybe a woman." He got up and got dressed. It was a warm night in May. As he went down the steps, he clearly heard groans coming from the garden. But the gate from the yard to the garden was locked at night, and there was no other way to get in, as the garden was surrounded by a tall, strong fence. Grigory went back inside, lit a lantern, grabbed the garden key, and, ignoring his wife's frightened pleas (she still thought she was hearing her own baby crying for her), he silently went into the garden. Once inside, he immediately heard that the groaning was coming from the bathhouse near the garden gate. It was definitely a woman.

When he opened the door of the bathhouse, he was shocked. Inside was Lizaveta Smerdyastchaya (Stinking Lizaveta), a simple-minded girl who wandered the streets and was known to everyone in town. She had somehow gotten into the bathhouse and had just given birth to a child. She lay there, dying, with the baby beside her. She didn't speak, as she had never been able to talk. But her story needs its own telling.

Chapter 2: Lizaveta

There was something that caught Grigory's attention and confirmed a suspicion that disturbed him. Lizaveta was a small woman, "not even five feet tall," as many of the old, pious women would say sadly after her death. Her wide, healthy, red face had a blank, stupid look, and the fixed stare in her eyes was unsettling, despite their gentle expression. She wandered around, summer and winter, barefoot, wearing only a rough, hempen dress. Her thick, almost black hair curled like lamb's wool and formed a big, messy cap on her head. It was always caked with mud and had leaves, twigs, and bits of dirt stuck in it, since she slept on the ground in the dirt.

Her father, a homeless, sickly drunkard named Ilya, had lost everything and worked for years for some wealthy tradesmen. Her mother had been dead for a long time. Bitter and diseased, Ilya would beat Lizaveta cruelly whenever she returned to him, though she rarely did, because everyone in town took care of her. She was considered an idiot and, therefore, especially dear to God. Ilya's employers and many other people in town, particularly the tradesmen, tried to dress her better, giving her high boots and a sheepskin coat for the winter.

Though she let them dress her, she usually left and went to the cathedral porch, where she would take off everything they had given her—boots, scarf, coat—and walk away barefoot in her dress, just as before.

Once, a new governor came to inspect the town and was offended when he saw Lizaveta. Even though he was told she was an idiot, he said it was improper for a young woman of twenty to walk around in just a dress, and he declared that it shouldn't happen again. But the governor left, and Lizaveta stayed the same. When her father died, people in town thought even more kindly of her since she was now an orphan. Everyone seemed to like her; even the boys didn't tease her, though the schoolboys in our town were usually mischievous. Lizaveta would walk into strangers' houses, and no one would chase her away. Everyone was kind to her and gave her something.

If she was given a coin, she would take it straight to the church or prison and drop it in the donation box. If someone gave her a roll or bun in the market, she would hand it to the first child she saw. Sometimes, she would stop a wealthy woman in town and give her the bread instead, and the woman would accept it with a smile. Lizaveta herself only ate black bread and drank water. She would walk into expensive shops where valuable items and money were lying around, but no one watched her because they knew that even if she saw thousands of rubles, she wouldn't touch a single one. She almost never went to church, and she usually slept in the church porch or climbed over fences into kitchen gardens.

At least once a week, Lizaveta would show up at the home of her father's former employers, and during the winter, she went there every night to sleep in the hallway or the barn. People were amazed at how she could survive such a rough life, but she was used to it, and even though she was so small, she was tough. Some people in town said she acted this way out of pride, but that's hard to believe. She could barely speak, and only occasionally made a low, grunting sound. How could she have been proud?

One warm, clear, moonlit night in September, years ago, five or six drunken men were coming back from the club late at night by our town's standards. They were taking the back road, which led between the back gardens of the houses, with fences on either side. This path led to the bridge over the long, stinking pool we used to call a river. Among the nettles and weeds by the fence, the men saw Lizaveta sleeping. They stopped, laughing, and started making crude jokes. One of the young men asked, half-seriously, if anyone could actually see Lizaveta as a woman. They all laughed and said it was impossible. But Fyodor Pavlovitch, who was with them, suddenly jumped in and said it wasn't impossible at all. In fact, he said, there was something exciting about the idea.

At the time, Fyodor was acting like a fool on purpose. He enjoyed putting himself in the spotlight and trying to entertain others, pretending to be their equal, though in reality, he was beneath them. It was right around the time he had found out about his first wife's death in Petersburg, and even though he wore mourning clothes, he was drinking heavily and behaving so badly that even the most reckless people were shocked. The men laughed at his unexpected comment, and one of them even dared him to act on it. The others firmly rejected the idea, though still laughing, and eventually, they all moved on.

Later, Fyodor Pavlovitch swore he had left with them, and maybe he had. No one really knows for sure, and no one ever found out. But five or six months later, the whole town was outraged when they noticed Lizaveta was pregnant, and everyone was trying to figure out who had done it. Then, suddenly, a terrible rumor spread that Fyodor Pavlovitch was responsible. No one knows who started the rumor. Of the drunken men, five had already left town, and the only one still living there was an older, respected civil servant with grown daughters, who would never have spread such a rumor, even if there had been any truth to it. But everyone pointed to Fyodor Pavlovitch, and the rumor wouldn't go away. It didn't bother him much; he didn't care what the townspeople thought. Back then, he was proud and only talked to people in his own circle of officials and nobles, whom he entertained well.

At the time, Grigory defended his master strongly. He got into arguments and fights with people over it and even convinced some to believe his side. "It's the girl's own fault," he insisted, and he blamed Karp, a dangerous criminal who had escaped from prison and was hiding in our town. This explanation seemed believable because people remembered that Karp had been nearby that autumn and had robbed three people. But even with all the talk, no one stopped feeling sorry for Lizaveta. In fact, she was cared for more than ever. A wealthy merchant's widow named Kondratyev decided to take Lizaveta into her home at the end of April, planning to keep her there until the baby was born. They kept a close watch on her, but despite their efforts, Lizaveta escaped on the very last day and somehow ended up in Fyodor Pavlovitch's garden.

How she managed to climb the high, strong fence in her condition was a mystery. Some people thought someone had lifted her over the fence, while others whispered about something more supernatural. The most likely explanation is that Lizaveta, used to climbing fences to sleep in gardens, had somehow managed to climb this one, despite her condition, and had jumped down, injuring herself.

Grigory ran to Marfa and sent her to Lizaveta, while he went to fetch an old midwife who lived nearby. They were able to save the baby, but Lizaveta died at dawn. Grigory took the baby home, placed it in Marfa's arms, and said, "A child of God—an orphan belongs to all of us, but especially to us. Our lost little one has sent us this one, born from the devil's son and a holy innocent. Take care of him, and don't cry anymore."

So Marfa raised the child. He was named Pavel, and soon people started calling him Pavel Fyodorovitch (son of Fyodor). Fyodor Pavlovitch didn't mind this at all; in fact, he found it amusing, though he kept denying that he was responsible. The townspeople were pleased that he had taken in the orphan. Later on, Fyodor Pavlovitch made up a last name for the boy, calling him Smerdyakov, after his mother's nickname.

So, Smerdyakov became Fyodor Pavlovitch's second servant, and at the beginning of our story, he was living in the lodge with Grigory and Marfa. He worked as the cook. I should say more about Smerdyakov, but I feel bad about taking up so much of the reader's time on these ordinary servants, so I will return to the main story and talk more about Smerdyakov later on.

Chapter 3: The Confession of A Passionate Heart—In Verse

Alyosha stood there for a while, unsure of what to do after hearing his father shout from the carriage. But even though he felt uneasy, he didn't just stand still. That wasn't his way. He went straight to the kitchen to find out what his father had been doing upstairs. Then, he set off, trusting that as he walked, he would find an answer to the troubling thoughts that were bothering him. I should add that his father's orders for him to come back home "with his mattress and pillow" didn't scare him at all. Alyosha knew perfectly well that those loud commands were just a way for his father to make a scene. It was similar to how a shopkeeper in town once threw a party, and when he got mad because he wasn't given more vodka, he smashed his own plates and furniture, tore up his and his wife's clothes, and even broke the windows—just to get attention. Of course, the next day when he was sober, he regretted breaking all the dishes. Alyosha knew that his father would let him return to the monastery the next day, or maybe even that evening. He was sure that, while his father might hurt someone else, he would never hurt him. Alyosha believed that no one in the world would want to hurt him, and even more, he believed that no one could hurt him. This

was something he had accepted without question, and he moved forward without any hesitation, relying on that belief.

But right then, another kind of worry was troubling him, and it bothered him even more because he couldn't put it into words. It was a fear of a woman—of Katerina Ivanovna—who had urgently asked him in a note, through Madame Hohlakov, to come and see her. This request, and the need to visit her, had sparked a sense of unease in his heart, which had only grown stronger throughout the morning, despite everything that had happened at the hermitage and with the Father Superior. He wasn't nervous because he didn't know what she would talk about or how he should respond. And he wasn't afraid of her just because she was a woman. Even though he didn't know much about women, he had spent his entire life, from childhood until he entered the monastery, surrounded by women. What he was afraid of was this woman, Katerina Ivanovna. He had been afraid of her from the first time he saw her. He had only seen her two or three times, and had only spoken a few words to her. He thought of her as a beautiful, proud, and commanding girl. It wasn't her beauty that troubled him, but something else. And not being able to pinpoint exactly what worried him only made his fear worse. He knew that her intentions were noble—she was trying to help his brother Dmitri, even though Dmitri had treated her poorly. Alyosha recognized and respected her kindness, but still, a shiver ran down his spine as he got closer to her house.

He thought that he wouldn't find Ivan, who was a close friend of hers, there, because Ivan was most likely with their father. He was even more sure that Dmitri wouldn't be there, and he had a strong feeling he knew why. That meant he would have to speak to her alone. He really wanted to see his brother Dmitri before that serious meeting. Even without showing him the letter, he could talk to him about it. But Dmitri lived far away, and Alyosha was sure he wouldn't be home anyway. After standing still for a moment, he made up his mind. Crossing himself quickly, with a familiar gesture, and smiling, he turned and headed straight toward the house of the woman who scared him so much.

He knew where she lived. If he went through the High Street and crossed the market square, it would take longer. Even though our town is small, it's spread out, and the houses are far apart. Meanwhile, his father might still be waiting for him, and might still be thinking about the command he had given. His father might act unreasonably, so Alyosha needed to hurry there and back. He decided to take a shortcut through the back streets, since he knew the area so well. It meant he would have to go around fences, climb over barriers, and cross through people's backyards, where everyone knew him and greeted him. That way, he could reach the High Street in half the time.

He had to pass the garden next to his father's house, which belonged to a small, rundown home with four windows. The owner of this house, as Alyosha knew, was an old bedridden woman who lived with her daughter. The daughter had worked as a maid for wealthy families in Petersburg but had been back home for a year taking care of her sick mother. Even though they were now very poor, the daughter still dressed in fancy clothes, and they came every day to Fyodor Pavlovitch's kitchen for soup and bread, which Marfa always gave them. Though the young woman came for soup, she never sold any of her expensive dresses, and one even had a long train— a fact that Alyosha had learned from Rakitin, who always seemed to know everything going on in town. Alyosha had forgotten this until he reached the garden, but now he remembered the dress with the train. Lifting his head, which had been bent down in thought, he saw something completely unexpected.

Over the garden fence, Dmitri was standing on something, leaning forward and waving his arms wildly, motioning for Alyosha to come over, obviously afraid to speak out loud. Alyosha ran to the fence.

"It's good you looked up. I was about to shout for you," Dmitri said in a joyful, hurried whisper. "Climb in here, quick! It's great that you've come! I was just thinking about you!"

Alyosha was happy too, but he didn't know how to get over the fence. Dmitri put his strong hand under Alyosha's elbow to help him jump. Tucking up his cassock, Alyosha jumped over the fence with the quickness of a street kid.

"Well done! Now come on," said Dmitri, still whispering excitedly.

"Where?" Alyosha whispered back, looking around and realizing they were alone in the empty garden. The garden was small, and the house was at least fifty paces away.

"There's no one here. Why are you whispering?" asked Alyosha.

"Why am I whispering? Oh, forget it!" Dmitri shouted loudly. "You see what tricks your mind can play. I'm here secretly, hiding, and on the lookout. I'll explain later, but since I'm hiding,

I started whispering like a fool, even though there's no reason. Let's go. Over there. Until then, be quiet. I want to kiss you.

'Glory to God in the world, Glory to God in me...'

I was just repeating that to myself before you came."

The garden was about three acres in size, with trees planted along the fence on all four sides. There were apple trees, maples, limes, and birch trees. The center of the garden was an open grassy area, where they harvested a lot of hay in the summer. The garden was rented out for a few rubles during the summer. There were also rows of raspberries, currants, and gooseberries along the sides. Near the house, a vegetable garden had been recently planted.

Dmitri led his brother to the most hidden corner of the garden. There, in a thicket of lime trees and old bushes of black currants, elderberries, snowball bushes, and lilacs, stood an old, run-down green summerhouse, blackened with age. Its walls were made of latticework, but it still had a roof that could offer shelter. No one knew exactly when the summerhouse had been built, but there was a story that it had been put up around fifty years earlier by a retired colonel named von Schmidt, who had owned the house back then. The summerhouse was falling apart; the floor was rotting, the boards were loose, and the wood smelled damp. Inside, there was a green wooden table fixed to the ground, with green benches around it that were still strong enough to sit on.

Alyosha immediately noticed how excited his brother was, and when they entered the summerhouse, he saw a half-empty bottle of brandy and a wineglass on the table.

"That's brandy," Dmitri laughed. "I see the way you're looking at me—'He's drinking again!' Don't trust your eyes. Don't trust the lying crowd, and set aside your doubts. I'm not drinking, I'm just 'indulging,' as that pig, Rakitin, likes to say. He'll be a civil servant one day, but he'll always say 'indulging.' Sit down. I could hug you, Alyosha, and squeeze you until I crush you, because in the whole world—in real life—in real life (can you understand?) I love no one but you!"

He said these last words with a kind of passion.

"No one but you and one woman I've fallen in love with, to my ruin. But being in love doesn't mean loving. You can be in love with a woman and still hate her. Remember that! I can still laugh about it. Sit here at the table, and I'll sit beside you and talk. You can just listen, and I'll keep talking, because now's the time. But, on second thought, I should talk quietly, because here—here— you never know who might be listening. I'll explain everything, as they say, 'the story will continue.' Why have I been longing for you? Why have I been dying to see you these past few days? (I've been hiding out here for five days.) Because you're the only one I can tell everything to. I need to talk to you because tomorrow, everything ends and begins. Have you ever felt, or dreamt, that you were falling down a cliff into a deep pit? That's how I'm falling, but not in a dream. And I'm not scared, and you shouldn't be either. Well, I am scared, but I'm enjoying it. No, it's not enjoyment, it's something more like ecstasy. Whatever it is, let's praise nature. Look at the sunshine, how clear the sky is, the leaves are still green—it's still summer. It's four in the afternoon, and everything is so still. Now, where were you going?"

"I was going to father's, but I meant to go to Katerina Ivanovna's first."

"To her, and to father! Oh, what a coincidence! Why was I waiting for you? Craving you with every fiber of my soul and even in my bones? Why, to send you to father and to her, Katerina Ivanovna, so I could be done with her and with father. I wanted to send an angel. I could have sent anyone, but I wanted to send an angel. And here you are, already on your way to see father and her."

"Did you really plan to send me?" cried Alyosha with a distressed look.

"Wait! You knew it! I see that you understood everything right away. But stay quiet, stay quiet for a moment. Don't be upset, and don't cry."

Dmitri stood up, thought for a moment, and put his finger to his forehead.

"She asked you, didn't she? Wrote you a letter or something, that's why you're going to see her? You wouldn't be going if she hadn't?"

"Here's her note." Alyosha took it out of his pocket. Dmitri glanced through it quickly.

"And you were taking the back way! Oh, gods, I thank you for sending him by the back way, and he came to me like the golden fish to the foolish old fisherman in the fairy tale! Listen, Alyosha, listen, brother! Now I'm going to tell you everything, because I must tell someone. I've already told an angel in heaven, but I want to tell an angel on earth. You are an angel on earth. You'll hear me, judge me, and forgive me. And that's what I need—that someone above me should forgive. Listen! If two people break away from everything on earth and fly off into the unknown, or at least if one of them does, and before they fly off or fall to ruin, they come to someone and say, 'Do this for me'—some favor never asked before, one that could only be asked on their deathbed—would that friend or brother refuse them?"

"I'll do it, but tell me what it is, and please hurry," said Alyosha.

"Hurry? H'm!... Don't rush, Alyosha, don't rush yourself. There's no need to hurry now. The world has taken a new turn. Ah, Alyosha, it's a shame you don't understand ecstasy. But what am I saying? Of course you understand it. What an idiot I am! What am I saying? 'Be noble, O man!'—who says that?"

Alyosha decided to wait. He felt that perhaps, indeed, this was where his work lay. Dmitri sat in silence for a moment, resting his elbow on the table and holding his head in his hand. Both of them were quiet.

"Alyosha," said Dmitri, "you're the only one who won't laugh. I want to start—my confession—with Schiller's Hymn to Joy, An die Freude! I don't know German, I just know it's called that. Don't think I'm talking nonsense because I'm drunk. I'm not drunk at all. Brandy is fine, but I need two bottles to really get drunk:

'Silenus with his rosy face Riding his stumbling donkey.'

But I haven't even had a quarter of a bottle, and I'm not Silenus. I'm not Silenus, even though I'm strong," he chuckled, "because I've made up my mind, once and for all. Forgive me the pun; you'll have to forgive me a lot more than puns today. Don't worry. I'm not dragging this out. I'm talking sense, and I'll get to the point soon. I won't keep you in suspense. Now, how does it go?"

He lifted his head, thought for a minute, then began with excitement:

"Wild and fearful in his cave, Hid the naked caveman,
And the wandering nomad wandered, Ruining the fertile land.
With spear and arrow,
The hunter roamed the forest... Woe to all poor souls
Stranded on those cruel shores!

"From the peak of high Olympus,
Mother Ceres came down,
Searching in those savage places
For her lost daughter, Proserpine.
But the goddess found no refuge,
No warm welcome anywhere,

And no temple stood to witness
To the worship of the gods.

"From the fields and vineyards
Came no fruits for festive feasts,
Only the flesh of bloodstained victims
Smoldered on the altar fires.
And wherever the grieving goddess
Turned her sorrowful gaze,
In his lowest degradation,
Man revealed his loathsomeness."

Dmitri burst into tears and grabbed Alyosha's hand.

"My dear, my dear, even now there's so much suffering and degradation for men on earth, so much pain. Don't think I'm just a brute in an officer's uniform, rolling in filth and drink. I think about this all the time—the suffering of man—if I'm not lying to myself. I hope I'm not lying or just trying to show off. I think about that man because I am that man.

'If he wants to cleanse his soul of filth
And reach the light and truth,
He must turn and cling forever
To his ancient Mother Earth.'

But the problem is, how do I cling forever to Mother Earth? I don't kiss her. I don't hold her close. Am I supposed to become a peasant or a shepherd? I keep moving, and I don't know if I'm heading for shame or for light and joy. That's the trouble, because everything in the world is a riddle! And whenever I've sunk into the lowest filth—and it happens often—I always read that poem about Ceres and man. Has it reformed me? Never! Because I'm a Karamazov. When I fall into the pit, I dive in headfirst with my heels in the air, and I enjoy it. I even take pride in it. And down in the deepest depths, I start singing a hymn of praise. Let me be cursed. Let me be vile and dirty, but at least let me kiss the hem of the veil that covers my God. Even if I'm following the devil, I am Your son, O Lord, and I love You, and I feel the joy that keeps the world going.

'Everlasting joy feeds
The soul of all creation.
It's the secret fire
That fills the cup of life.
It's at her call that the grass
Turns each blade toward the light,
And solar systems form
Out of chaos and dark night,
Filling the endless space
Beyond what the wise can see.'

At nature's generous breast,
Everything that breathes drinks joy.
Birds and beasts and creeping things
All follow where She leads.

Her gifts to man are friends in need,
The wine, the wreath of flowers,
To angels—the vision of God's throne,
To insects—sensual lust."

"But enough poetry! I'm crying, so let me cry. It may seem foolish, something everyone would laugh at. But you won't laugh. I can see it in your eyes. Enough poetry. Now I want to talk about those insects to whom God gave 'sensual lust.'

'To insects—sensual lust.'

I'm that insect, brother, and that line is especially about me. All of us Karamazovs are like those insects, and, angel that you are, that insect is inside you too. One day, it will stir up a storm in your blood. A storm, because sensual lust is a storm—worse than a storm! Beauty is a terrible and terrifying thing! It's terrifying because we can't understand it, and we never will, because God only gives us riddles. This is where all boundaries meet, and all contradictions exist side by side. I'm not an educated man, brother, but I've thought a lot about this. It's terrifying how many mysteries there are! Too many riddles weigh people down on this earth. We have to solve them as best we can and try not to drown in the process. Beauty! I can't stand the thought that a man with a noble heart and mind starts with the ideal of the Madonna and ends with the ideal of Sodom. But what's even worse is that a man with the ideal of Sodom in his soul doesn't give up on the ideal of the Madonna. His heart can still burn with that ideal, truly burn, just like in the innocent days of his youth. Yes, man is too broad, far too broad. I wish he were narrower. Only the devil knows what to make of it all! What seems shameful to the mind can be beautiful to the heart. Is there beauty in Sodom? Believe me, for most people, beauty is found in Sodom. Did you know that secret? The awful thing is that beauty is both mysterious and terrible. God and the devil are fighting over it, and the battlefield is the heart of man. But a man always talks about his own pain. Now, let me get to the facts."

Chapter 4: The Confession of A Passionate Heart— In Anecdote

I was living recklessly back then. My father just said I spent a lot of money on seducing young girls. That's a total lie, nothing like that happened. And even if it had, I didn't need money for it. Money to me was just an extra, something that came from the overflow of my feelings. Today one girl would be special to me, and the next day I'd find someone else. I treated them both the same. I threw money around like it meant nothing, spending it on music, wild parties, and gypsies. Sometimes I gave money to the girls too, because they'd take it eagerly and be happy about it. Women liked me back then—not all of them, but some did, it happened. But I always preferred the side streets, the dark alleys off the main road. That's where you find adventures and surprises, and sometimes, valuable things in the dirt. I'm speaking metaphorically, brother. In the town I was in, there weren't any real alleys like that, but there were moral ones. If you were like me, you'd know what I mean. I loved vice, I loved the shame that came with it. I loved cruelty; am I not a disgusting bug, a harmful insect? I'm a true Karamazov! Once, a big group of us went on a sleigh ride, seven sledges in total. It was dark, it was winter, and I started holding a girl's hand, making her kiss me. She was an official's daughter, sweet, gentle, and obedient. She let me do it, let me do a lot more in the dark. She thought, poor girl, that I would come the next day and propose to her (people thought I was a good match). But I didn't speak to her for five months. I saw her sometimes at dances (we were always having dances), and I could see her watching me, her eyes full of fire—a fire of gentle anger. This just excited that low desire I had inside me. Five months later, she married an official and left town, still mad at me, maybe still in love. Now they live happily. And you know, I never told anyone. I didn't brag about it. Even though I'm full of low desires, and love what's shameful, I'm not dishonorable. You're blushing; your eyes flashed. Enough of this filth with you. And all this was nothing special—just some petty moments like those cheap novels by Paul de Kock—even though the cruel part of me had already grown strong inside. I have a whole album of memories, brother. God bless them, those girls. I tried to end things without fights. And I never betrayed them. I never boasted about any of them. But that's enough. You can't think I brought you here just to talk about this nonsense. No, I'm going to tell you something much more interesting; and don't be surprised that I'm glad to tell you, instead of being ashamed."

"You say that because I blushed," Alyosha said suddenly. "I wasn't blushing at what you were saying or at what you did. I blushed because I'm the same as you are."

"You? Come on, that's going a bit far!"

"No, it's not too far," Alyosha said warmly (it was clear he'd thought about this before). "The ladder's the same. I'm on the bottom step, and you're further up, somewhere around the thirteenth step. That's how I see it. But it's the same. Absolutely the same kind. Anyone on the bottom step will end up on the top one."

"Then one shouldn't step on at all." "Anyone who can avoid it should." "But can you?"

"I don't think so."

"Hush, Alyosha, hush, my dear! I could kiss your hand, you've touched me so. That Grushenka has an eye for men. She once told me she'd devour you one day. There, there, I won't! Let's move from this field of corruption, fouled by flies, to my tragedy, also fouled by flies, that is, by every kind of filth. Though the old man made up lies about me ruining innocent girls, there was some truth to it in my tragedy, though it only happened once, and nothing came of it. The old man, who blamed me for something that didn't happen, doesn't even know about this. I never told anyone. You're the first, except for Ivan, of course—Ivan knows everything. He knew about it long before you did. But Ivan's like a grave."

"Ivan's like a grave?"

"Yes."

Alyosha listened closely.

"I was a lieutenant in an infantry regiment, but I was still under watch, like a sort of convict. Even so, I was very well-liked in the town. I threw money around like crazy. People thought I was rich; I thought so too. But I guess I pleased them in other ways as well. Though they often shook their heads at me, they liked me. My colonel, an old man, suddenly took a dislike to me. He was always criticizing me, but I had powerful friends, and, besides, the whole town was on my side, so he couldn't do much to hurt me. I didn't help matters by refusing to treat him with respect. I was proud. This stubborn old man, who was actually a good person, kind and generous, had been married twice, but both wives were dead. His first wife, who came from a modest family, left behind a daughter who was as humble as her mother. She was about twenty-four when I was there, living with her father and her mother's sister. The aunt was simple and uneducated; the niece was simple but cheerful. I like saying nice things about people. I never met a more delightful woman than Agafya—can you believe her name was Agafya Ivanovna! She wasn't bad-looking either, in a typical Russian way: tall, full-figured, with beautiful eyes, though her face was a bit coarse. She hadn't married yet, even though she had two suitors. She turned them down but stayed just as cheerful. I was close with her, but not 'that' way—it was just friendship. I've often been friends with women without any romance. I used to talk to her very openly, and she would just laugh. A lot of women like that kind of honesty, and she was a girl too, so it was fun. Another thing, you could never think of her as a 'lady.' She and her aunt lived in her father's house with a kind of voluntary humility, not trying to be on the same level as other people. She was well-liked by everyone and very helpful because she was a talented dressmaker. She was good at it. She didn't ask for money but didn't refuse if someone offered it. The colonel, though, was a different story. He was one of the most important people in the district. He hosted everyone, threw big dinners and dances. Right when I arrived and joined the battalion, the whole town was buzzing about the colonel's other daughter, a real beauty, who was coming back from a fancy school in the capital. This second daughter was Katerina Ivanovna, the child of the colonel's second wife, who came from a high-ranking general's family; although, as I found out from a reliable source, she didn't bring any money either. She had connections, and that was it. Maybe there had been some expectations, but nothing came of them.

"When this young lady came back from school to visit, the whole town came alive again. Our most important ladies—two wives of high-ranking officials and a colonel's wife—and everyone else following their lead, immediately made a fuss over her, throwing parties in her honor. She was the star of the balls and picnics, and they even organized living pictures to raise money for struggling governesses. I didn't care; I kept on living wildly as before. One of my escapades at the time had the whole town talking. I noticed her watching me one evening at the battery commander's house, but I didn't go over to her, acting like I didn't care. Later, at another party, I finally spoke to her, and she barely looked at me, pressing her lips together in a scornful way. 'Wait, I'll get my revenge,' I thought. I acted like a complete idiot so many times back then, and I knew it. What made it worse was knowing that 'Katenka' wasn't some innocent schoolgirl, but a woman of real character, proud and with strong principles. She was educated and intelligent, and I had none of that. Did you think I planned to propose to her? No, I just wanted to get back at her, because I thought I was something special, and she didn't seem to think so."

Meanwhile, I spent my days drinking and partying, until the lieutenant-colonel arrested me for three days. Around that time, my father sent me six thousand roubles because I had sent him a paper that gave up all my claims on him—basically settling everything between us and saying I wouldn't expect anything else. I didn't understand a word of it at the time. Even now, Alyosha, maybe even until recently, I still don't really get my financial situation with my father. But don't worry about that, we can talk about it later.

Just when I received the money, I got a letter from a friend telling me something that caught my attention. I learned that the authorities weren't happy with our lieutenant-colonel. He was suspected of doing something wrong, and his enemies were planning to catch him off guard. Then the division commander arrived and caused a huge commotion. Shortly after, the lieutenant-colonel was ordered to retire. I won't explain how it all went down. He definitely had enemies. Suddenly, people in town became very cold towards him and his family. His friends all turned their backs on him. That's when I made my first move. I met Agafya Ivanovna, who I'd always been friends with, and said, "Do you know there's a missing 4,500 roubles of government money in your father's accounts?"

"What do you mean? Why are you saying that? The general was here not long ago, and everything was fine." "It was fine then, but now it's not."

She was terrified.

"Don't scare me!" she said. "Who told you that?"

"Don't worry," I said. "I won't tell anyone. You know I'm as quiet as the grave. I just wanted to say that if they ask your father for the 4,500 roubles, and he can't come up with it, he'll be put on trial and forced to serve as a common soldier in his old age— unless, of course, you secretly send me your young lady. I just got some money, and I'll give her four thousand if you agree, and I'll keep it all secret."

"You scoundrel!" she shouted. "You wicked scoundrel! How dare you!"

She stormed away, furious, but I shouted after her again that I'd keep the secret safe. Agafya and her aunt, I should say, acted like angels throughout all of this. They absolutely adored their 'Katya,' thought of her as better than them, and treated her with the greatest care. But Agafya told her about our conversation. I found that out later. She didn't keep it secret, and of course, that's what I wanted all along.

Then the new major came to take over the battalion. The old lieutenant-colonel suddenly got sick, couldn't leave his room for two days, and didn't hand over the government money. Dr. Kravchenko said he was really sick. But I knew for a fact—and had known for a while—that for the last four years, the money was never in his hands except when the Commander came for inspections. He used to lend it to a trusted man in town, a merchant named Trifonov, an old widower with a big beard and gold-rimmed glasses. Trifonov would take the money to the fair, do some profitable business, and then return it all to the colonel with a gift from the fair and some interest. But this time (I learned all this by chance from Trifonov's son, a foolish and very wicked young man)—this time, Trifonov didn't bring anything back from the fair. The lieutenant-colonel rushed to him. "I never got any money from you, and I couldn't have gotten any," was all Trifonov said. So now the lieutenant-colonel is stuck at home, with a towel wrapped around his head, and they're all putting ice on it. Then suddenly, an orderly arrived with the book and the order to hand over the battalion money immediately, within two hours. He signed the book (I saw the signature later), said he was going to put on his uniform, ran to his bedroom, loaded his gun, took the boot off his right foot, set the gun against his chest, and started feeling for the trigger with his foot. But Agafya, remembering what I had told her, suspected something. She snuck up and peeked into the room just in time. She rushed in, grabbed him from behind, threw her arms around him, and the gun went off, but hit the ceiling and didn't hurt anyone. The others ran in, took the gun away, and held him down. I heard about all this later. I was at home, it was getting dark, and I was just getting ready to go out. I had dressed, combed my hair, sprayed some cologne on my handkerchief, and picked up my hat when suddenly the door opened, and standing there in the room was Katerina Ivanovna.

It's strange how things happen sometimes. No one saw her in the street, so no one in town knew. I lived with two old ladies who took care of me. They were very kind and would do anything for me, and I asked them to keep quiet about it afterward. Of course, I understood the situation right away. She walked in and looked directly at me, her dark eyes firm, even defiant, but I could see uncertainty on her lips and around her mouth.

"My sister told me," she began, "that you would give me 4,500 roubles if I came to you myself. So, I've come... give me the money!"

She couldn't hold it together. She was out of breath, scared, her voice was shaky, and her mouth trembled. Alyosha, are you listening, or have you fallen asleep?"

"Mitya, I know you'll tell the whole truth," said Alyosha, clearly upset.

I'm telling it all. If I tell the whole truth as it really happened, I won't spare myself. My first thought was a typical Karamazov one. Once, a centipede bit me, brother, and I was sick with a fever for two weeks because of it. Well, I felt like a centipede was biting at my heart then—a poisonous bug, you get it? I looked her up and down. You've seen her, right? She's beautiful. But back then, she was beautiful in a different way. She was beautiful because she was noble, and I was a scoundrel. She was standing there, full of grace and sacrifice for her father, and me—I was like a bug! And, as much of a scoundrel as I was, she was completely at my mercy, both body and soul. She was trapped. I'll admit to you honestly, that thought, that horrible thought, completely took over my heart, and I almost passed out from how tense I felt. It seemed like there was no way to fight it, like I was going to act like a bug, like a venomous spider, with no pity at all. I could barely breathe. Understand, I would've gone to her the next day to propose to her, so that everything could end honorably, so to speak, and so no one would ever know. Because even though I have low desires, I'm still an honest man. And right then, a voice seemed to whisper in my ear, "But when you come tomorrow to propose, she won't even look at you. She'll tell her coachman to throw you out. She'd say, 'Go tell the whole town, I'm not afraid of you!'" I looked at the young woman, and I knew that my voice hadn't lied to me. That's exactly how it would be, without a doubt. I could see from her face right then that I'd be thrown out of the house. My anger flared up. I wanted to play the nastiest, dirtiest trick on her: to look at her with a smirk, and right where she was standing, stun her with a tone of voice that only a shopkeeper would use.

"Four thousand! What are you talking about? I was just joking. You've been counting your chickens too soon, miss. Two hundred, if you want, that's fine with me. But four thousand? That's not a sum to just throw away on something like this. You've made this trip for nothing."

I would've lost everything, of course. She would've run off. But it would've been such a mean, evil revenge. It would've been worth it all. I would've regretted it for the rest of my life, but I would've loved playing that trick. Can you believe it? That's never happened to me with any other woman, not one, to look at her in a moment like that with such hatred. But I swear, I looked at her for three seconds, or maybe five, with a deep hatred—the kind of hate that's just a tiny step away from love, from the craziest kind of love!

I went to the window, pressed my forehead against the cold glass, and I remember the ice burned my skin like fire. I didn't keep her waiting long, don't worry. I turned around, went over to the table, opened the drawer, and took out a five-thousand-rouble banknote (it was inside a French dictionary). Then, without saying a word, I showed it to her, folded it, handed it over, opened the door to the hallway, and stepped back. I gave her a deep bow, a really respectful and impressive bow, believe me! She shivered all over, stared at me for a second, turned as white as a sheet, and then, all of a sudden—not in a rush but softly, gently—she bowed down to my feet. Not a polite schoolgirl curtsy, but a full Russian bow, her forehead touching the floor. She jumped up and ran off. I had my sword with me. I pulled it out and almost stabbed myself with it right then—why, I don't know. It would've been incredibly stupid, of course. I guess it was from joy. Can you understand that someone might kill themselves out of pure joy? But I didn't stab myself. I just kissed my sword and put it back in its sheath— which I didn't even need to tell you, really. And I think that by telling you all this about my inner struggle, I've made it sound a bit more dramatic than it really was, just to make myself look good. But let's forget about that, and to hell with anyone who tries to look too deeply into a person's heart! Well, that's the end of that 'adventure' with Katerina Ivanovna. So now Ivan knows about it, and so do you—no one else."

Dmitri stood up, took a few steps in his excitement, pulled out his handkerchief, wiped his forehead, and then sat down again, not in the same place as before, but on the opposite side, so that Alyosha had to turn around to face him.

Chapter 5: The Confession of a Passionate Heart — "Heels Up"

"Now I understand the first part," said Alyosha.

"You understand the first part. That part is a drama, and it happened back there. The second part is a tragedy, and it's happening here."

"And I still don't understand the second part," Alyosha admitted. "And do you think I understand it?" Dmitri asked.

"Wait, Dmitri. There's something important I need to ask. Were you engaged to her? Are you still engaged?"

"We weren't engaged right away—not until three months after that incident. The day after it happened, I convinced myself that it was over, that nothing more would come of it. It felt wrong, even shameful, to propose to her after what had happened. And she didn't reach out to me at all during the six weeks she stayed in town— except for one thing. The day after her visit, a maid brought me an envelope. Inside was the leftover money from the banknote. She only needed four thousand five hundred roubles, but exchanging it cost about two hundred, so she sent me back what was left—about two hundred and sixty roubles, though I can't remember exactly. Not a note, not even a word. I looked through the envelope hoping for a little scribble—nothing. Well, I spent what was left of the money on a wild binge that ended with the new major giving me a stern warning.

"Somehow, the lieutenant-colonel managed to produce the battalion money, shocking everyone since nobody believed he still had it untouched. As soon as he handed it over, he fell seriously ill. He took to his bed, and three weeks later, he started losing his mind. Five days after that, he died. They gave him a proper military funeral because he hadn't officially been discharged yet. Ten days after his funeral, Katerina Ivanovna, her aunt, and her sister left for Moscow. And on the very day they left—without saying goodbye to me or letting me see them off—I got a small note. It was written on thin blue paper, just one line in pencil: 'I will write to you. Wait. K.' That was it.

"Now, I'll explain the rest quickly. In Moscow, their lives changed like a fairy tale. A general's widow, their closest relative, suddenly lost her two nieces—her heirs. Both of them died in the same week from smallpox. The old lady was devastated and clung to Katya like she was her own daughter. She changed her will to make Katya her sole heir. That was for the future, though. For the moment, she gave Katya eighty thousand roubles to use however she liked. The old lady was emotional and unpredictable. I met her later in Moscow.

"Then, out of nowhere, I received four thousand five hundred roubles in the mail. I was stunned. A few days later, the letter she promised arrived. I still have it with me—you should read it. In the letter, she offers herself to me. 'I love you madly,' she wrote, 'and even if you don't love me back, it doesn't matter. Be my husband. Don't worry, I won't burden you. I'll be like your servant. I'll be the ground beneath your feet. I just want to love you forever. I want to save you from yourself.' Alyosha, I feel ashamed to repeat those words in my clumsy, rough way. That letter still pierces my heart. Do you think it doesn't bother me? It does, even now. I replied right away, since I couldn't go to Moscow myself. I wrote to her with tears in my eyes. But there's one thing I'll regret forever. I made the mistake of mentioning her wealth, her dowry. I wrote about how she was rich and I was just a poor, arrogant fool. I shouldn't have said anything about the money. I should've stayed silent, but I couldn't stop myself from writing it down. Then, I wrote a long letter to Ivan—six pages— and told him everything. I sent him to her.

"Why are you looking at me like that? Yes, Ivan fell in love with her. He's still in love with her, I know it. People say I acted foolishly, but maybe that foolish decision will end up saving us all. Don't you see how much she respects Ivan? How highly she thinks of him? When she compares us, do you really think she could love someone like me after everything that's happened?"

"But I believe she does love someone like you, not someone like him," Alyosha said.

"She only loves her own virtue, not me," Dmitri said bitterly, almost spitting out the words. He forced a laugh, but his face flushed, and a moment later, he slammed his fist on the table in frustration.

"I swear to you, Alyosha," he shouted, angry at himself. "You may not believe me, but as God is holy, and as Christ is God, I swear that even though I just laughed at her high ideals, I know I'm far worse than she could ever be. And I know that her feelings are as pure as an angel's. That's what makes it tragic—I know it for certain. Who doesn't put on a bit of a show sometimes? I do it too, and I'm still sincere. And as for Ivan... I can only imagine how bitter he must feel, with all his intelligence, watching someone like me get chosen over him. A man like me, who can't even keep himself in check—who can't stop disgracing himself right in front of his fiancée's eyes! And yet, she chooses me while rejecting someone like Ivan. Why? Because she feels grateful. It's absurd. I've never talked to Ivan about any of this, and he's never said a word to me about it either. But things will play out as they must. The better man will move on, and I'll be left behind in the gutter—my filthy gutter, where I belong, where I'll sink deeper into the muck, happily drowning in it. I've been talking nonsense. I've run out of words, but it doesn't matter. What I said will happen. I'll drown in that gutter, and she'll marry Ivan."

"Stop, Dmitri," Alyosha said urgently. "You still haven't answered my question. You are engaged to her, aren't you? How can you end the engagement if she doesn't want to?"

"Yes, we're officially engaged. It was all arranged when I went to Moscow, with all the rituals—icons, blessings, everything. The general's widow even congratulated Katya and told her she had made a good choice. 'I can see right through him,' she said. Would you believe it? She didn't even like Ivan—barely acknowledged him. I had many serious talks with Katya while I was in Moscow.

I told her everything about myself—honestly and openly. She listened closely.

"There were sweet moments, tender words. But there were also proud words, too. She got me to make a serious promise to change my ways, and I gave her my word. And now—"

"What?"

"Now, today—remember this—I've called you out here to send you to her."

"To tell her what?"

"To tell her that I'll never see her again. Tell her, 'He sends his regards.'"

"Is that really possible?"

"That's why I'm sending you, because I can't do it myself. How could I tell her in person?"

"And where are you going?" Alyosha asked. "To the gutter."

"To Grushenka, then!" Alyosha exclaimed in despair, clasping his hands. "So Rakitin was telling the truth? I thought you'd only visited her once, and that was all."

"Can a man who is engaged go to a woman like that? Is it even possible, especially when everyone knows about the engagement? Damn it, I still have some honor! As soon as I started visiting

Grushenka, I stopped being engaged, and I stopped being an honest man. I know that. Why are you looking at me? Listen, I went there at first to hurt her. I had heard—and now I know it for sure—that the captain, my father's agent, gave Grushenka an I.O.U. from me so she could demand I pay her and ruin me. They wanted to scare me. I went there to hurt her. I had seen her before. She doesn't look impressive at first. I knew about her old merchant, who's sick now, paralyzed, but he's leaving her some money. I also knew she liked money, that she saved it and lent it at a high interest rate, that she was ruthless and a cheater. I went to hurt her, and I stayed. The storm hit—it knocked me down like a plague. I'm still sick from it, and I know it's all over for me, that nothing else will ever happen for me. The circle of life is complete. That's my situation. And even though I'm poor, I had three thousand roubles in my pocket at the time. I went with Grushenka to Mokroe, a place twenty-five versts from here. I hired some gypsies and got champagne, and I got all the peasants there drunk, along with the women and girls. I threw the money away. In three days, I had nothing left, but I felt like a hero. Do you think I got what I wanted? Not a chance. Grushenka is slippery, her whole body has this smooth curve. You can see it even in her little foot, in her little toe. I saw it, and I kissed it, but that's all, I swear! 'I'll marry you if you want,' she said, 'but remember, you're poor. Promise you won't beat me and that you'll let me do whatever I want, and maybe I'll marry you.' She laughed, and she's still laughing!"

Dmitri jumped up angrily, like he was drunk. His eyes suddenly turned red.

"And you really want to marry her?" Alyosha asked.

"Right now, if she'll have me. And if she won't, I'll stay anyway. I'll be the doorman at her house. Alyosha!" he shouted, stopping right in front of him. He grabbed Alyosha by the shoulders and started shaking him violently. "Do you understand, you innocent boy, that this is all madness, complete madness, and there's a tragedy here. Let me tell you, Alexey, I may be a low man with low, base desires, but Dmitri Karamazov will never be a thief or a pickpocket. Well, let me tell you, I am a thief and a pickpocket. That morning, just before I went to Grushenka's, Katerina Ivanovna called me in secret (for some reason I still don't know) and asked me to go to the main town and send three thousand roubles to Agafya Ivanovna in Moscow, without anyone here knowing about it. So I had that three thousand in my pocket when I went to see Grushenka, and that's the money we spent at Mokroe. Afterward, I pretended I had gone to town, but I didn't show her the receipt from the post office. I told her I had sent the money and would bring the receipt later, but I haven't brought it yet. I forgot about it. Now, what do you think you'll say to her today? 'He sends his regards,' and she'll ask, 'What about the money?' You could still say, 'He's a weak man with no control over his base desires. He didn't send your money then, because, like a low animal, he couldn't control himself.' But at least you could add, 'He's not a thief though. Here's your three thousand roubles back. You can send it yourself to Agafya Ivanovna. But he wanted me to say he sends his regards.' But, as it is, she will ask, 'Where is the money?'"

"Mitya, you're unhappy, yes, but not as unhappy as you think. Don't torture yourself with despair."

"What, do you think I'd shoot myself just because I don't have three thousand to pay back? That's the thing. I won't shoot myself. I don't have the strength right now. Maybe later. But right now, I'm going to Grushenka's. I don't care what happens."

"And then what?"

"I'll marry her if she'll have me, and when her lovers come, I'll go to the next room. I'll clean their boots, light their fire, and run their errands."

"Katerina Ivanovna will understand everything," Alyosha said seriously. "She'll understand how big this trouble is, and she'll forgive you. She has a good heart, and no one could be more miserable than you are right now. She'll see that herself."

"She won't forgive everything," Dmitri said with a grin. "There's something she can never forgive. Do you know what the best thing to do would be?"

"What?"

"Pay back the three thousand."

"Where are we going to get it? Listen, I have two thousand. Ivan can give you another thousand—that makes three. Take it and pay her back."

"And where would you get that three thousand? You're not even of age yet. Besides, you have to—you absolutely have to—take my message to her today, with or without the money, because

I can't keep dragging this out. Things have gotten too serious. Tomorrow will be too late. I'm sending you to my father."

"To father?"

"Yes, to father first. Ask him for three thousand."

"But, Mitya, he won't give it to you."

"As if he would! I know he won't. Do you know what despair is, Alexey?"

"Yes."

"Listen. Legally, he owes me nothing. I've already taken everything from him, I know that. But morally, doesn't he owe me something? You know he started with twenty-eight thousand of my mother's money and made a hundred thousand with it. Let him just give me three out of the twenty-eight thousand, and he'll save my soul from hell, and it will make up for some of his sins. For that three thousand—I swear to you—I'll put an end to everything, and he won't hear from me again. This is his last chance to be a father. Tell him God Himself is giving him this chance."

"Mitya, he won't give you the money."

"I know. I know perfectly well he won't—especially now. But that's not the whole story. There's more. Just a few days ago, maybe even yesterday, he finally realized—really realized—that Grushenka might actually be serious about marrying me. He knows what she's like. He knows how she operates. Do you think he's going to give me money to help me marry her when he's madly in love with her himself? Of course not. And there's even more to it.

"For the past five days, he's had three thousand roubles taken out of the bank, exchanged into hundred-rouble notes, and packed into a big envelope. He sealed it with five seals and tied it up with red tape. I know all about it. On the front, he wrote: 'To my angel, Grushenka, when she will come to me.' He wrote it himself, secretly, without telling anyone—except for his valet, Smerdyakov, who he trusts completely. Now, for the past few days, he's been sitting around, waiting for her to come and take the money. He's already sent her a message about it, and she replied that she might come. And if she does go to him, how could I marry her after that? Now you understand why I'm hiding out here and watching."

"For her?"

"Yes, for her. Foma has a room here in this house with these women. He's from our hometown—he used to serve in our regiment. Now he does odd jobs for them. He works as a night watchman and spends his days hunting grouse to get by. I've moved into his room, but neither he nor the women know what I'm really doing—they have no idea that I'm here to watch and wait."

"So, only Smerdyakov knows?"

"Yes, just him. He'll tell me if she goes to the old man."

"He's the one who told you about the money?"

"Yes. It's a complete secret. Even Ivan doesn't know about the money—or anything else, for that matter. The old man is sending Ivan on a two- or three-day trip to Tchermashnya to finalize the sale of some timber. A buyer offered eight thousand roubles for the lot, and the old man wants Ivan to handle the deal. That's his plan—get Ivan out of the way so Grushenka can come while he's gone."

"So, do you think she'll come today?"

"No, she won't. I can tell. Smerdyakov thinks so too. Father's drinking right now—he's sitting at the table with Ivan. Go to him, Alyosha, and ask him for the three thousand."

"Mitya, what's wrong with you?" Alyosha jumped up, alarmed by the wild look in his brother's eyes. For a moment, he thought Dmitri had gone mad.

"What's wrong? I'm not insane," Dmitri said, staring hard at him. "I know exactly what I'm saying. I want you to go to Father. I believe in miracles."

"Miracles?"

"Yes, a miracle from God. God knows what's in my heart. He sees my despair. He sees everything. I believe He won't let something terrible happen. Go now, Alyosha."

"I'm going. Will you wait here for me?"

"Yes. I know it'll take time. You can't just confront him right away—especially not when he's been drinking. I'll wait three, four, five hours if I have to. Just remember—you absolutely must go to Katerina Ivanovna today, even if it's at midnight, whether you have the money or not. And tell her, 'He sends his compliments.' That's what I want you to say: 'He sends his compliments.'"

"Mitya, what if Grushenka comes today—or tomorrow, or the day after?"

"If she comes, I'll stop her. I'll run out and stop her." "And if—?"

"If it happens, it'll be murder. I won't be able to bear it." "Murder? Who?"

"The old man. I won't kill her." "Mitya, what are you saying?"

"I don't know... I really don't know. Maybe I won't kill him. Or maybe I will. I'm terrified that when I see his face in that moment, I'll hate him so much I won't be able to stop myself. I can't stand the way he looks—

his throat, his nose, his sneering grin. It disgusts me. That's what I'm afraid of. I don't know if I'll be able to hold myself back."

"I'll go, Mitya. I believe that God will make sure everything turns out the way it should, and nothing terrible will happen."

"And I'll wait here for the miracle. And if it doesn't happen—"

Alyosha turned and headed toward his father's house, deep in thought.

Chapter 6: Smerdyakov

He did in fact find his father still at the table. Although there

was a dining room in the house, the table was set as usual in the drawing room, which was the largest room and furnished with old-fashioned, showy decor. The furniture was white and very old, covered with old, red, silky material. In the spaces between the windows, there were mirrors in elaborate white and gilt frames, with old-fashioned carvings. On the walls, which were covered in white wallpaper that was torn in many places, there were two large portraits—one of a prince who had been governor of the district thirty years before, and the other of a bishop, also long dead. In the corner opposite the door, there were several religious icons, in front of which a lamp was lit at nightfall— not so much for religious devotion as to light the room. Fyodor Pavlovitch usually went to bed very late, around three or four in the morning, and he would wander around the room at night or sit in an armchair, thinking. This had become a habit of his. He often slept alone in the house, sending his servants to the lodge, but Smerdyakov usually stayed, sleeping on a bench in the hall.

When Alyosha came in, dinner was over, but coffee and preserves had been served. Fyodor Pavlovitch liked sweet things with brandy after dinner. Ivan was also at the table, sipping coffee. The servants, Grigory and Smerdyakov, were standing nearby. Both the gentlemen and the servants seemed to be in unusually good spirits. Fyodor Pavlovitch was laughing loudly. Before Alyosha even entered the room, he could hear his father's shrill laugh, which he knew so well, and from the sound of it, Alyosha could tell that his father was in a good mood and far from being completely drunk.

"Here he is! Here he is!" Fyodor Pavlovitch shouted, clearly delighted to see Alyosha. "Join us! Sit down. Coffee is a fasting dish, but it's hot and good. I won't offer you brandy, since you're keeping the fast. But would you like some? No, wait—better yet, I'll give you some of our famous liqueur. Smerdyakov, go to the cupboard, the second shelf on the right. Here are the keys. Be quick!"

Alyosha began to refuse the liqueur.

"Never mind. If you won't have it, we will," said Fyodor Pavlovitch, grinning. "But wait—have you had dinner?"

"Yes," answered Alyosha, who had only eaten a piece of bread and drank a glass of kvas in the Father Superior's kitchen. "Though I'd be happy to have some hot coffee."

"Bravo, my dear! He'll have some coffee. Does it need to be warmed up? No, it's boiling. It's excellent coffee—Smerdyakov made it. My Smerdyakov is an artist when it comes to making coffee, fish patties, and fish soup, too. You should come by one day and have some fish soup. Just let me know ahead of time…

But wait, didn't I tell you this morning to bring your mattress and pillow and stay here? Did you bring your mattress? Ha ha ha!"

"No, I didn't," said Alyosha, smiling too.

"Ah, you were scared this morning, weren't you? My dear, I couldn't bring myself to upset you. Do you know, Ivan, I can't resist when he looks me straight in the face and laughs? It makes me laugh too. I'm so fond of him. Alyosha, let me give you my blessing—a father's blessing."

Alyosha stood up, but Fyodor Pavlovitch had already changed his mind.

"No, no," he said. "I'll just make the sign of the cross over you for now. Sit down. Now, we've got a treat for you, something you'll love. It'll make you laugh. Balaam's donkey has started talking to us—and he sure talks a lot!"

It turned out that Balaam's donkey was the valet, Smerdyakov. He was a young man, about twenty-four years old, and very unsociable and quiet. Not that he was shy or embarrassed. On the contrary, he was arrogant and seemed to look down on everyone.

But we need to pause here to say a few words about him. He was raised by Grigory and Marfa, but the boy grew up "without a shred of gratitude," as Grigory put it. He was an unfriendly child who seemed to view the world with suspicion. As a child, he liked to hang cats and bury them with great ceremony. He would dress up in a sheet, pretending it was a priest's robe, sing, and wave something over the dead cat as if it were incense. He did all of this in secret. Grigory caught him doing it once and gave him a harsh beating. After that, the boy sulked in a corner for a week. "He doesn't care about you or me," Grigory would say to Marfa, "and he doesn't care about anyone. Are you even human?" he asked the boy directly. "You're not human. You grew out of the mold in the bathhouse." It seemed Smerdyakov could never forgive him for those words. Grigory taught him to read and write, and when he was twelve, he began teaching him the Bible. But this teaching didn't get far. During the second or third lesson, the boy suddenly grinned.

"What's that for?" asked Grigory, glaring at him from under his glasses.

"Oh, nothing. God created light on the first day, but the sun, moon, and stars on the fourth day. Where did the light come from on the first day?"

Grigory was stunned. The boy looked at him sarcastically. There was something condescending in his expression. Grigory couldn't control himself. "I'll show you where!" he shouted and gave the boy a hard slap on the cheek. The boy didn't say a word, but retreated to his corner again for several days. A week later, he had his first attack of the disease that would stay with him for the rest of his life—epilepsy. When Fyodor Pavlovitch heard about it, his attitude toward the boy changed immediately. Until then, he hadn't paid him much attention, though he never scolded him and would always give him a coin when they crossed paths. Sometimes, when Fyodor Pavlovitch was in a good mood, he would send the boy sweets from his table. But as soon as he heard about his illness, he became very interested in him, sent for a doctor, and tried different treatments, but the disease turned out to be incurable. The seizures happened about once a month, but at different intervals. Some seizures were mild, while others were very severe. Fyodor Pavlovitch strictly forbade Grigory from ever hitting the boy again and started allowing him to come upstairs. He also forbade any more lessons for a while. One day, when the boy was about fifteen, Fyodor Pavlovitch noticed him lingering by the bookcase, reading the titles through the glass. Fyodor Pavlovitch owned quite a few books—over a hundred— but no one ever saw him reading them. He immediately gave Smerdyakov the key to the bookcase. "Go ahead, read. You can be my librarian. It's better for you to sit here reading than hanging around the courtyard. Here, try this one," and he handed him Evenings on a Farm Near Dikanka.

Smerdyakov read a little but didn't like it. He didn't smile once and ended up frowning.

"Why? Isn't it funny?" asked Fyodor Pavlovitch.

Smerdyakov didn't say a word.

"Answer me, idiot!"

"It's all made up," the boy muttered with a grin.

"Then go to hell! You've got the soul of a servant. Here, take Smaragdov's Universal History. That's all true. Read that."

But Smerdyakov didn't get through ten pages of Smaragdov. He found it boring. So the bookcase was locked up again.

Shortly afterward, Marfa and Grigory told Fyodor Pavlovitch that Smerdyakov had started to become extremely picky. He would sit in front of his soup, take a spoonful, look at it closely, lean over and inspect it, then hold it up to the light before finally taking a bite.

"What is it? A beetle?" Grigory would ask.

"Maybe a fly," Marfa would say.

The picky boy never answered, but he did the same with his bread, his meat, and everything he ate. He'd hold a piece of food on his fork up to the light, inspect it carefully, and only after a long pause would he finally put it in his mouth.

"Look at him, acting all fancy!" Grigory muttered, watching him.

When Fyodor Pavlovitch heard about this new development, he decided to make Smerdyakov his cook and sent him to Moscow for training. He spent a few years there and returned looking remarkably different. He looked much older than his age, with wrinkled, yellowed skin and a strange, almost feminine appearance. His personality, however, seemed nearly the same as before. He was just as unsociable and showed no interest in any kind of friendship. In Moscow, as we later learned, he had also been very quiet. The city itself didn't interest him much; he saw very little and paid little attention to anything. He went to the theater once but returned silent and unimpressed. However, he came back to us from Moscow well-dressed, in a clean coat and fresh clothes. He brushed his clothes carefully twice a day and was especially fond of polishing his fine leather boots with a special English shoe polish, making them shine like mirrors. He turned out to be an excellent cook. Fyodor Pavlovitch paid him a salary, almost all of which Smerdyakov spent on clothes, pomade, perfumes, and other personal items. But he seemed to look down on women just as much as he did men. He was reserved and almost untouchable with them. Fyodor Pavlovitch began to view him a little differently. His seizures became more frequent, and on the days he was sick, Marfa had to do the cooking, which didn't suit Fyodor Pavlovitch at all.

"Why are your seizures getting worse?" Fyodor Pavlovitch asked, giving his new cook a sideways look. "Do you want to get married? Should I find you a wife?"

But Smerdyakov turned pale with anger and didn't answer. Fyodor Pavlovitch waved him off impatiently. The important thing was that he had complete trust in Smerdyakov's honesty. Once, when Fyodor Pavlovitch was drunk, he dropped three hundred-rouble notes in the muddy courtyard, money he had just received. He only noticed they were missing the next day and was about to start searching his pockets when he saw the notes lying on the table. Where had they come from? Smerdyakov had picked them up the day before and brought them inside.

"Well, my boy, I've never met anyone like you," Fyodor Pavlovitch said briefly, and gave him ten roubles. We can add that he not only trusted Smerdyakov's honesty but also, for some reason, liked him, even though the young man looked at him gloomily, just like he did with everyone else, and was always quiet. He rarely spoke. If anyone had wondered at that time what Smerdyakov was interested in or what was going on in his mind, they wouldn't have been able to tell just by looking at him. Still, sometimes he would suddenly stop inside the house or even in the yard or the street and stand still for ten minutes, lost in thought. A person who studied faces would have said there wasn't much thinking going on, no deep reflection, just a kind of staring or "contemplation."

There's a famous painting by the artist Kramskoy called Contemplation. It shows a forest in winter, and on a road cutting through the forest, a peasant in a torn coat and bark shoes stands completely alone. He stands there as if lost in thought, but he's not really thinking; he's just "contemplating." If someone touched him, he would flinch and look at them as though waking up, confused. He would quickly return to normal, but if you asked him what he had been thinking about, he wouldn't remember anything. Still, he probably holds on to some impression that was on his mind during that moment of contemplation. Those impressions are precious to him, and he likely stores them up without even realizing it. How and why he does this, he doesn't know either. He might, after hoarding these impressions for many years, suddenly leave everything behind and go on a pilgrimage to Jerusalem to save his soul—or maybe he'll set fire to his village, or maybe even do both. There are quite a few "contemplative" types among the peasants.

Well, Smerdyakov was probably one of those types, and he was likely gathering up impressions greedily, without fully understanding why.

Chapter 7: The Controversy

But Balaam's ass had suddenly spoken. The topic of conversation was strange. That morning, Grigory had gone

out to buy supplies and heard from the shopkeeper, Lukyanov, a story printed in the newspaper. It was about a Russian soldier who had been captured in a remote part of Asia. The soldier was told that he would be tortured and killed unless he gave up his Christian faith and converted to Islam. Refusing to abandon his beliefs, he was brutally tortured, skinned alive, and died while praising Christ.

Grigory shared the story at the table. Fyodor Pavlovitch always enjoyed talking and joking after dinner, even if it was just with Grigory. That afternoon, he was in an especially good mood, sipping brandy while listening to the story. He remarked that a soldier like that should be made a saint, and they should take his skin to a monastery. "That would bring people in and rake in the donations," he added with a smirk.

Grigory frowned, realizing that Fyodor Pavlovitch wasn't moved by the story but was, as usual, making fun of it. At that moment, Smerdyakov, who was standing by the door, smiled. It wasn't unusual for him to wait at the table toward the end of dinner, and ever since Ivan had come to town, Smerdyakov had been doing it every day.

"What are you grinning at?" Fyodor Pavlovitch asked sharply, noticing the smile right away and knowing it was directed at Grigory.

"Well, in my opinion," Smerdyakov began suddenly, in a loud and deliberate voice, "if that soldier's actions were truly admirable, there wouldn't have been anything wrong if, in such a desperate situation, he had renounced Christ and his baptism just to save his life. He could have made up for it later by living a good life and making up for his cowardice over time."

"How could that not be a sin? That's nonsense! For that, you'd go straight to hell and roast like a lamb," Fyodor Pavlovitch interrupted.

Just then, Alyosha entered the room, and Fyodor Pavlovitch, as we saw, was delighted by his arrival.

"We're discussing something right up your alley," Fyodor Pavlovitch said cheerfully, motioning for Alyosha to sit.

"There's no roasting like lamb for that," Smerdyakov continued, unfazed. "There's no punishment for it at all—there shouldn't be, if we're talking about true justice."

"What do you mean by 'justice'?" Fyodor Pavlovitch asked, laughing and nudging Alyosha with his knee.

"He's a scoundrel, that's what he is!" Grigory snapped, glaring at Smerdyakov with fury.

"Scoundrel or not, let me explain, Grigory Vassilyevitch," Smerdyakov said calmly. "If I were captured by enemies of Christianity, and they demanded that I curse God and reject my baptism, I would have the right to act according to reason, because it wouldn't really be a sin."

"You've said that already. Stop talking in circles and prove it," Fyodor Pavlovitch interrupted, chuckling.

"Soup-maker!" Grigory muttered with contempt.

"Soup-maker or not, hear me out, Grigory Vassilyevitch, before you start cursing me," Smerdyakov responded. "The moment I say to those enemies, 'I am not a Christian, and I curse my God,' I immediately, in God's eyes, become excommunicated, cut off from the Church as if I were a heathen. In fact, even thinking of saying it—before I can even speak the words—would already separate me from the Church. Isn't that right, Grigory Vassilyevitch?"

Although Smerdyakov was addressing Grigory, he was clearly directing his words at Fyodor Pavlovitch, fully aware of what he was doing. He intentionally acted as if Grigory had asked the question, all the while knowing he was really answering Fyodor Pavlovitch's challenge.

"Ivan!" Fyodor Pavlovitch called suddenly. "Come here, I need to whisper something."

Ivan leaned down, his expression serious.

"He's putting on this whole show just for you," Fyodor Pavlovitch whispered excitedly. "He wants your approval. Go ahead—praise him."

Ivan listened quietly to his father's drunken whisper.

"Hold on, Smerdyakov. Be quiet for a minute," Fyodor Pavlovitch interrupted. "Ivan, come here again."

Ivan leaned down once more, his face still calm and composed.

"I love you, you know, just like I love Alyosha. Don't think I don't. Want some brandy?"

"Yes. But you've had a bit too much already," Ivan thought, keeping his gaze steady on his father. He turned his attention back to Smerdyakov, watching him with curiosity.

"You're excommunicated already!" Grigory suddenly burst out. "And how dare you talk like this, you scoundrel?"

"Don't scold him, Grigory. Don't scold him," Fyodor Pavlovitch said, cutting him off.

"Just listen a little longer, Grigory Vassilyevitch, and let me finish," Smerdyakov said, maintaining his calm. "At the exact moment I'm excommunicated, I become the same as a heathen. My baptism no longer counts for anything. Isn't that so?"

"Finish what you're saying, my boy," Fyodor Pavlovitch urged, taking another sip of his drink.

"And since I would no longer be a Christian, I wouldn't be lying to the enemy by denying my faith. God would already have removed my baptism from me the moment I even thought about denying Him. And if I'm no longer a Christian, I can't deny Christ because there's nothing left for me to deny. Just like no one would blame a heathen Tatar in heaven for not being born a Christian, right? You can't take two skins off the same ox. Even God Himself wouldn't hold the Tatar accountable for not being born Christian—He would only give him a light punishment. After all, it wouldn't be the Tatar's fault that he was born to heathen parents. And would God lie by calling the Tatar a Christian? No, because God cannot tell a lie, not even once."

Grigory stood stunned, staring at Smerdyakov as if he had run headfirst into a wall. His eyes were wide with shock. He didn't fully understand what Smerdyakov had said, but something about it had unsettled him deeply.

Fyodor Pavlovitch emptied his glass and burst into his high- pitched laugh.

"Alyosha! Alyosha! What do you think of that?" he cried. "What a slippery little devil! Ivan, this guy must have been hanging around Jesuits somewhere. You sly Jesuit! Who taught you all this? But it's all nonsense—complete nonsense! Isn't it, Ivan? Just nonsense, nonsense, nonsense. Don't cry, Grigory. We'll deal with him soon enough."

Then Fyodor Pavlovitch turned back to Smerdyakov with a mischievous grin.

"So tell me this, my clever little ass—maybe you can justify yourself before your enemies. But in your heart, you've still abandoned your faith. And by your own admission, the moment you did that, you became excommunicated. And if you're excommunicated, they won't exactly be patting you on the back in hell, will they? So what do you have to say to that, my fine Jesuit?"

"Yes, I admit I've given up my faith in my heart," Smerdyakov replied calmly. "But that's not a serious sin. And if it is, it's just an ordinary one."

"What do you mean, ordinary?" Fyodor Pavlovitch asked, intrigued.

"You lie, cursed one!" hissed Grigory.

"Think about it, Grigory Vassilyevitch," Smerdyakov continued, calm and unshaken, feeling confident in his victory, but still being generous to his defeated opponent. "Think about it, Grigory Vassilyevitch. It says in the Bible that if you have faith, even as small as a mustard seed, and you tell a mountain to move into the sea, it will move without hesitation. Well, Grigory Vassilyevitch, if I have no faith, and you have such great faith that you're always swearing at me, then try it yourself. Tell this mountain—no, not to move to the sea, since that's far away—but just to move into our little smelly river at the bottom of the garden. You'll see that it won't budge, no matter how much you shout at it. That proves, Grigory Vassilyevitch, that you don't have the kind of faith you claim, and you just scold others about it. And besides, considering the fact that no one today—not you, not anyone, from the highest person to the lowest peasant—can move mountains into the sea, except maybe one or two people in the whole world, and they're probably hiding somewhere in the Egyptian desert, so you wouldn't be able to find them. If that's true, and no one has real faith, will God curse all the rest of us? That means, would God curse the whole population of the earth, except for those two hermits in the desert? And in His great mercy, wouldn't He forgive the rest of us? So I believe that even though I may have doubted at one point, I will be forgiven if I shed tears of repentance."

"Wait!" cried Fyodor Pavlovitch, overjoyed. "So you think there really are two people who can move mountains? Ivan, make a note of that, write it down. There's the Russian attitude for you!"

"You're right, that does reflect the people's faith," Ivan agreed with a smile.

"You agree? Then it must be true, if you agree. Isn't that right, Alyosha? That's the Russian faith, isn't it?"

"No, Smerdyakov doesn't have the Russian faith at all," Alyosha said seriously.

"I'm not talking about his faith. I mean the idea of those two in the desert. That's Russian, right?"

"Yes, that idea is purely Russian," Alyosha said with a smile.

"Your words are worth gold, O donkey, and I'll give you a gold coin today. But everything else you said is nonsense, nonsense, nonsense. Let me tell you, you fool, the reason we all have little faith is only because we're careless and don't have time; life is too much for us. Plus, God has given us so little time—just twenty-four hours in a day—that we don't even have enough time to sleep properly, let alone repent for our sins. But you denied your faith to your enemies when you had nothing else to worry about except proving your faith! So I believe, brother, that it is definitely a sin."

"It may be a sin, but think about it, Grigory Vassilyevitch, it also lessens the guilt if it is. If I had truly believed the way I was supposed to at that time, then yes, it would have been a terrible sin if I hadn't been willing to face torture for my faith, and instead converted to the pagan Muslim religion. But, of course, it wouldn't have come to torture, because all I would have had to do was say to the mountain, 'Move and crush my torturer,' and it would have moved and crushed him right away like a bug, and I would have walked away unharmed, praising and thanking God. But imagine I had tried that and shouted at the mountain, 'Crush these torturers,' and the mountain didn't move. How could I have avoided doubting my faith at that moment, in such a terrifying situation? And besides, I would already know that I couldn't reach the fullness of the Kingdom of Heaven (since the mountain didn't move when I commanded it, they must not think very highly of my faith up in Heaven, so there wouldn't be a great reward waiting for me in the next life). So why should I let them skin me alive for no reason? Even if they flayed the skin off my back, the mountain still wouldn't move at my command. And in that kind of moment, not only could doubt take over, but fear might make someone lose their mind, making it impossible to think clearly. So how can you say I'm especially to blame if, seeing no benefit or reward in this life or the next, I at least saved my skin? And so, trusting fully in the Lord's grace, I would hope that I might be completely forgiven."

Chapter 8: Over The Brandy

The argument was over. But, strangely enough, Fyodor Pavlovitch, who had been in such a cheerful mood, suddenly started frowning. He frowned and gulped down some brandy, which was already one glass too many.

"Get out of here, Jesuits!" he yelled at the servants. "Go away, Smerdyakov. I'll send you the gold piece I promised today, but go now! Don't cry, Grigory. Go to Marfa, she'll comfort you and put you to bed. These rascals won't let us enjoy our dinner in peace," he added irritably, as the servants quickly left the room at his command.

"Smerdyakov always hangs around after dinner now. He's interested in you. What have you done to make him so fascinated with you?" he asked Ivan.

"Nothing at all," Ivan replied. "He just thinks highly of me for some reason; he's a lackey with a low spirit. But he's the type that could fuel a revolution when the time comes."

"A revolution?"

"There will be better ones, but people like him will come first.

His kind will start it, and then better people will follow."

"And when will this happen?"

"Maybe the rocket will take off and then just fizzle out. The peasants aren't very interested in these 'soup-makers' yet."

"Ah, brother, but a donkey like him keeps thinking and thinking, and who knows where his thoughts will take him."

"He's storing up ideas," said Ivan, smiling.

"You know, I can tell that he can't stand me, or anyone else for that matter, even you, though you think he respects you. Worse still, he despises Alyosha. But at least he doesn't steal, and he doesn't gossip. He keeps his mouth shut and doesn't air our dirty laundry in public. And he makes excellent fish pies. But, damn it, is he worth talking about this much?"

"Of course he isn't."

"And as for the ideas he's brewing, the Russian peasant needs a good beating, in general. I've always said that. Our peasants are cheats, and they don't deserve pity. It's a good thing they still get flogged sometimes. Russia is rich in birch trees. If they cut down the forests, it would ruin the country. I support the clever people. We've stopped beating the peasants because we've gotten too smart, but they still beat themselves. And that's a good thing. 'With what measure you use, it will be measured back to you,' or something like that? Anyway, it will be measured. But all of Russia is full of filth. If you only knew how much I hate Russia…

Well, not Russia itself, but all this vice! But maybe I do mean Russia. All of it is just filth… You know what I do like? I like wit."

"You've had another glass. That's enough."

"Wait a minute. I'll have one more, and then another, and then I'll stop. No, wait, you interrupted me. At Mokroe, I was talking to an old man, and he told me, 'There's nothing we enjoy more than sentencing girls to be whipped, and we always have the boys do the whipping. And the girl he whipped today, he'll ask to marry tomorrow. So the girls don't mind either,' he said. Now that's something clever, don't you think? Shall we go check it out? Alyosha, are you blushing? Don't be embarrassed, boy. I'm sorry I didn't stay for dinner with the Superior and tell the monks about the girls at Mokroe. Alyosha, don't be mad that I insulted your Superior this morning. I lost my temper. If there is a God, if He really exists, then I'm to blame, and I'll have to answer for it. But if there isn't a God, what do your monks deserve? Cutting off their heads wouldn't be enough for holding back progress. Can you believe it, Ivan, that this really troubles me? No, I can see by the look in your eyes that you don't believe it. You think I'm just a clown, don't you? Alyosha, do you think I'm just a clown?"

"No, I don't think so."

"And I believe you. You look honest and you speak honestly. But not Ivan. Ivan is arrogant… Still, I'd get rid of your monks all the same. I'd wipe out all that mystical nonsense in one go, all over Russia, just to bring everyone to their senses. And imagine the gold and silver that would pour into the treasury!"

"But why get rid of it?" Ivan asked. "So that Truth can win. That's why."

"Well, if Truth won, you'd be the first one to be robbed and shut down, you know."

"Ah! You're probably right. I'm a fool!" Fyodor Pavlovitch burst out, lightly hitting his forehead. "Well, your monastery can stay then, Alyosha, if that's the case. And we clever folks will sit comfortably and enjoy our brandy. You know, Ivan, maybe this is how God Himself planned it. Ivan, tell me, is there a God or not? Wait, tell the truth, seriously. Why are you laughing again?"

"I'm laughing because you just made a smart comment about Smerdyakov's belief in two saints who could move mountains."

"What, am I like him now?" "Very much."

"Well, that just proves I'm Russian, too, and that I've got a Russian trait. You might get caught up in it too, even though you're a philosopher. What do you bet I'll catch you tomorrow? Come on, tell me, is there a God or not? Seriously, I want a serious answer now."

"No, there's no God."

"Alyosha, is there a God?"

"There is."

"Ivan, is there any kind of immortality, even a little bit, just a tiny bit?"

"No, there's no immortality."

"None at all?"

"None at all."

"So, it's just absolute nothingness? Maybe there's something? Anything's better than nothing!"

"Absolute nothingness."

"Alyosha, is there immortality?"

"There is."

"God and immortality?"

"God and immortality. Immortality is in God."

"Hmmm! Maybe Ivan is right. Good Lord! To think of all the faith, all the energy man has poured into that dream, and for how many thousands of years. Who's laughing at man, Ivan? For the last time, tell me once and for all, is there a God or not? I'm asking for the last time!"

"And for the last time, there is not." "Who's laughing at mankind, Ivan?"

"It must be the devil," Ivan said with a smile.

"And the devil? Does he exist?" "No, there's no devil either."

"That's too bad. Damn it all, I'd love to punish the man who first invented God! Hanging him on a bitter aspen tree wouldn't be enough."

"There wouldn't have been any civilization if they hadn't invented God."

"Really? No civilization without God?"

"No. And there wouldn't be brandy either. But I think I should take your brandy away from you, anyway."

"Wait, wait, wait, dear boy, just one more little glass. I've hurt Alyosha's feelings. You're not mad at me, Alyosha? My dear little Alexey!"

"No, I'm not mad. I understand your thoughts. Your heart is better than your head."

"My heart better than my head, is it? Oh, Lord! And you're the one saying that. Ivan, do you love Alyosha?"

"Yes."

"You must love him." (By this point, Fyodor Pavlovitch was very drunk.) "Listen, Alyosha, I was rude to your elder this morning. But I was upset. Don't you think the elder has some wit, Ivan?"

"Probably."

"Yes, yes. There's some wit in him. He's a Jesuit, a Russian Jesuit, I mean. He's an honorable person, but inside, there's hidden frustration at having to pretend to be holy."

"But, of course, he believes in God."

"Not at all. Didn't you know? He tells that to everyone. Well, not to everyone, but to the clever people who come to him. He said straight out to Governor Schultz recently: 'Credo, but I don't know in what.'"

"Really?"

"Yes, he did. But I still respect him. There's something like Mephistopheles in him, or maybe more like that character from The Hero of Our Time… Arbenin, or whatever his name is. You see, he's a sensualist. He's such a sensualist that I'd be afraid for my daughter or wife if they went to confess to him. You know, when he starts telling stories… A couple of years ago, he invited us to tea—tea with liqueur (the ladies send him liqueur)—and he started telling us about old times, and we nearly died laughing. Especially when he talked about how he once cured a paralyzed woman. 'If my legs weren't bad, I know a dance I could show you,' he said. What do you make of that? 'I've done a lot of tricks in my time,' he said. He tricked the merchant Dernidov out of sixty thousand rubles."

"What, he stole it?"

"He brought the money to Dernidov, saying, 'Take care of this for me, friend. There's going to be a police search at my place tomorrow.' And then he kept it. 'You've given it to the Church,' he said. I told him, 'You're a scoundrel,' I said. 'No,' he said, 'I'm not a scoundrel, I'm just broad-minded.' But wait, that wasn't him. That was someone else. I got mixed up without realizing it. Come on, one more glass and that's enough. Take away the bottle, Ivan. I've been lying. Why didn't you stop me, Ivan, and tell me I was lying?"

"I knew you'd stop on your own."

"That's a lie. You did it out of spite, just to get back at me. You look down on me. You come into my house and treat me with contempt."

"Well, I'm leaving. You've had too much brandy."

"I've begged you, for Christ's sake, to go to Tchermashnya for a day or two, and you won't go."

"I'll go tomorrow if you really want me to."

"You won't go. You want to keep an eye on me, that's why. That's what you're up to, you spiteful man. That's why you won't leave."

The old man wouldn't let it go. He had reached that point in drunkenness when a person, who had been harmless up until then, starts picking fights and trying to assert themselves.

"Why are you looking at me like that? Why do you stare at me? Your eyes are saying, 'You ugly drunk!' Your eyes are suspicious. They're filled with contempt… You've come here with some scheme. Alyosha looks at me, and his eyes are shining. Alyosha doesn't look down on me. Alexey, you must not love Ivan."

"Don't be mean to my brother. Stop attacking him," Alyosha said firmly.

"Oh, all right. Ugh, my head is killing me. Take away the brandy, Ivan. This is the third time I've told you."

He paused, and then a slow, sneaky grin spread across his face.

"Don't be mad at a weak old man, Ivan. I know you don't love me, but don't be angry. There's no reason for you to love me. Go to Tchermashnya, and I'll come to visit you there myself. I'll bring you a gift. I'll show you a little girl I've had my eye on for a long time. She's still running around barefoot. Don't be afraid of barefoot girls—don't look down on them—they're like pearls!"

And he kissed his hand with a loud smack.

"In my opinion," he suddenly perked up, seeming to sober up the moment he started talking about his favorite subject. "In my opinion… Oh, you boys! You children, little piglets, in my opinion… I've never thought any woman was ugly in my life— that's always been my rule! Can you understand that? No, you couldn't possibly understand it. You've got milk in your veins, not blood. You're still too young. My rule is that you can always find something interesting, something unique, in every woman that you wouldn't find in any other. The key is knowing how to find it—that's the real talent! In my mind, there's no such thing as an ugly woman. The fact that she's a woman is half the battle. But how could you understand that? Even in old spinsters, you can find something that makes you wonder how men could have been so blind as to let them grow old without noticing them.

Barefoot girls or plain-looking ones—you have to catch them by surprise. Didn't you know that? You have to shock them so they're fascinated, ashamed that such a fine gentleman could fall for such a simple girl. It's a wonderful thing that there are always going to be masters and servants in the world. So there will always be a little maidservant and her master, and that's all you need for happiness. Wait… listen, Alyosha, I used to surprise your mother, but in a different way. I would ignore her completely, and then, when the time was right, I'd act like I was totally devoted to her, get down on my knees, kiss her feet, and every single time—I remember it as if it were yesterday—I'd get her to do that quiet, nervous little laugh. It was so peculiar. I knew that her nervous fits always started with that laugh. The next day, she would be screaming hysterically, but that little laugh wasn't a sign of joy, even though it sounded like one. That's the secret, knowing how to handle everyone. Once, Belyavsky—he was handsome and rich—used to hang around here and flirt with her. One time, he slapped me right in front of her. And she—such a gentle soul—I thought she was going to knock me out for letting that happen. How she scolded me! 'You've been humiliated now,' she said. 'You let him hit you. You've been trying to sell me to him,' she said. 'And how dare he hit you in my presence! Don't you dare come near me again, never, never! You'd better go challenge him to a duel!'… I took her to the monastery after that to bring her back to her senses. The holy Fathers prayed for her, and she got better. But I swear to you, Alyosha, I never insulted that poor, crazy girl! Well, maybe just once, in the first year. She loved praying back then. She always celebrated the feasts of Our Lady and would kick me out of the room during them. I thought, 'I'll get rid of this mysticism!' I said, 'Look, here's your holy icon. I'm taking it down. You think it's miraculous, but here, I'll spit on it, and nothing will happen to me!'… When she saw me do it, good Lord, I thought she'd kill me. But instead, she just jumped up, wrung her hands, then covered her face, started shaking all over, and collapsed to the floor… she just fell like a heap. Alyosha, Alyosha, what's the matter?"

The old man jumped up in alarm. As soon as he started talking about Alyosha's mother, something began to change in Alyosha's face. His cheeks flushed bright red, his eyes sparkled, and his lips trembled. The old drunk kept rambling on, unaware of what was happening, until something very strange overtook Alyosha. Exactly what he had been describing about the hysterical outbursts of the mad woman suddenly repeated itself in Alyosha. He leapt from his seat just as his mother was said to have done, wrung his hands, buried his face in them, and collapsed back into his chair, shaking uncontrollably as a wave of silent, intense sobbing overcame him. The resemblance to his mother was so striking that it startled the old man.

"Ivan, Ivan! Get water—quick!" the old man cried. "He's just like her! Exactly like his mother used to be. Spray some water on him—just like I used to do with her. It's because he's upset about his mother. His mother," he mumbled toward Ivan.

"But she was my mother too, wasn't she?" Ivan snapped, his voice full of barely restrained anger and disgust.

The old man shrank under Ivan's furious gaze. For a moment, something strange happened—it was as if the old man had completely forgotten that Alyosha's mother had been Ivan's mother too.

"Your mother?" he stammered, confused. "What are you talking about? What mother do you mean? Was she…? Oh, of course! Damn it, of course she was your mother too! Damn it all! My mind's never been this clouded before. Forgive me. I was thinking… Ivan…" He trailed off with a slurred laugh. A broad, drunken, and almost senseless grin spread across his face.

At that moment, a loud commotion erupted from the hall. There were shouts and angry voices, and suddenly the door was thrown wide open. Dmitri stormed into the room, wild and furious.

The old man, terrified, ran toward Ivan.

"He'll kill me! He'll kill me! Don't let him get to me!" he shrieked, clutching desperately at the edge of Ivan's coat.

Chapter 9: The Sensualists

Grigory and Smerdyakov ran into the room right after Dmitri. They had been trying to stop him in the hallway, following the orders Fyodor Pavlovitch had given them days earlier. Dmitri paused for a moment as he entered the room, looking around, and Grigory took the chance to run around the table. He quickly shut the double doors leading to the inner rooms and stood in front of them, spreading his arms wide, ready to defend the entrance with all his strength.

Seeing this, Dmitri let out a scream more than a shout and rushed at Grigory.

"She's in there! You're hiding her! Get out of my way, you scoundrel!"

He tried to shove Grigory aside, but the old servant pushed back. Enraged, Dmitri lashed out, striking Grigory with all his might. The old man fell to the floor like a log, and Dmitri leaped over him, bursting through the door. Smerdyakov stayed frozen on the far side of the room, pale and trembling, pressed against Fyodor Pavlovitch.

"She's here!" Dmitri shouted. "I just saw her heading toward the house, but I couldn't catch her! Where is she? Where is she?"

That cry—"She's here!"—had an overwhelming effect on Fyodor

Pavlovitch. His fear vanished in an instant.

"Grab him! Stop him!" he yelled and ran after Dmitri.

Grigory had gotten up from the floor but still seemed dazed. Ivan and Alyosha rushed after their father. In the third room, they heard a loud crash. Dmitri had knocked over a large glass vase on a marble stand as he ran through, shattering it.

"Stop him!" Fyodor Pavlovitch shouted. "Help!"

Ivan and Alyosha grabbed their father and pulled him back.

"Why are you chasing him? He'll kill you!" Ivan shouted angrily at his father.

"Ivan! Alyosha! She's got to be here. Grushenka must be here. Dmitri said he saw her running!"

He was out of breath, trembling all over. The idea that Grushenka might be in the house made him frantic.

"But you've seen yourself—she isn't here," Ivan said. "She could've come in through the other entrance!" "You know that door is locked, and you've got the key."

Just then, Dmitri reappeared in the drawing room. He had tried the other entrance, but it was locked, with the key still in Fyodor Pavlovitch's pocket. All the windows were closed, so Grushenka couldn't have entered or left through them.

"Grab him!" Fyodor Pavlovitch screamed as soon as he saw Dmitri. "He's been stealing money from my room!"

The old man tore himself from Ivan's grip and charged at Dmitri, but Dmitri raised both hands and grabbed the two tufts of hair left on the old man's temples. With a violent yank, he pulled the old man to the floor and kicked him in the face two or three times with his heel. Fyodor Pavlovitch let out a sharp moan. Ivan, though not as strong as Dmitri, managed to wrap his arms around him and pull him back with all his strength. Alyosha jumped in to help, holding Dmitri from the front.

"You're mad! You've killed him!" Ivan shouted.

"Serves him right!" Dmitri gasped. "If he's not dead, I'll come back and finish him. You can't protect him!"

"Dmitri, leave now!" Alyosha commanded.

"Alexey, tell me—was she here or not? You're the only one I can trust. I saw her sneaking along the fence. I shouted, and she ran off."

"I swear she hasn't been here, and no one expected her."

"But I saw her! I'll find out where she went. Goodbye, Alexey!

Don't say anything to that old man about the money. And make sure you go to Katerina Ivanovna—tell her, 'He sends his compliments.' Compliments, understand? Just that, and goodbye. Tell her exactly what happened."

Meanwhile, Ivan and Grigory had helped Fyodor Pavlovitch into a chair. Blood covered his face, but he was conscious, listening eagerly to every word Dmitri shouted. He still believed that Grushenka was somewhere in the house. Dmitri looked at him with hatred as he turned to leave.

"I don't regret spilling your blood!" Dmitri shouted. "Beware, old man—beware of your dreams, because I have my own dreams too. I curse you! You mean nothing to me anymore!"

He stormed out of the room.

"She's here. She must be," the old man whispered weakly. "Smerdyakov! Smerdyakov!" He beckoned to him with a trembling finger.

"No, she's not here, you crazy old fool!" Ivan snapped angrily. "He's passing out—get water! A towel! Quickly, Smerdyakov!"

Smerdyakov ran to fetch water. They undressed Fyodor Pavlovitch and put him to bed, wrapping a wet towel around his head. Exhausted by the brandy, the shock, and the beating, he closed his eyes and fell asleep as soon as his head touched the pillow.

Ivan and Alyosha returned to the drawing room. Smerdyakov began sweeping up the broken glass from the shattered vase, while Grigory stood by the table, staring gloomily at the floor.

"Shouldn't you put a cold cloth on your head and get some rest too?" Alyosha asked gently. "We'll watch over him. My brother hit you hard."

"He insulted me," Grigory muttered darkly, his words slow and deliberate.

"He insulted his father too, not just you," Ivan said with a bitter smile.

"I used to bathe that boy in his tub," Grigory repeated grimly. "And he insulted me."

"Damn it, if I hadn't pulled him off, he might have killed the old man," Ivan whispered to Alyosha. "It wouldn't take much to finish him off."

"God forbid!" Alyosha cried.

"Why should God forbid it?" Ivan whispered back with a twisted grin. "One snake devouring another—that's all it would be. It's what they both deserve."

Alyosha shuddered.

"Of course, I won't let him be murdered," Ivan added quietly. "That's why I stopped him just now. Stay here, Alyosha. I need some air—my head is starting to ache."

Alyosha went to sit by his father's bedside, staying behind the screen for about an hour. At one point, the old man opened his eyes. He stared at Alyosha for a long time, as if remembering everything that had happened. Suddenly, his face changed, full of nervous excitement.

"Alyosha," he whispered anxiously, "where's Ivan?" "In the yard. He has a headache. He's keeping watch."

"Give me that mirror. The one over there. Bring it to me."

Alyosha handed him a small round folding mirror from the chest of drawers. The old man stared at his reflection—his nose was swollen, and a large, red bruise had formed on the left side of his forehead.

"What does Ivan say? Alyosha, my dear boy, my only son, I'm afraid of Ivan. I fear him more than the other one. You're the only one I'm not afraid of."

"Don't be afraid of Ivan either. He's angry, but he'll protect you."

"Alyosha, what about Dmitri? He's run off to Grushenka. Tell me the truth—was she here just now or not?"

"No one saw her. It was a mistake. She hasn't been here."

"You know Dmitri wants to marry her. He's determined to marry her."

"She won't marry him."

"She won't? She won't! She won't!" The old man's face lit up, as though those words had given him the greatest comfort.

Overjoyed, he grabbed Alyosha's hand and pressed it against his heart. Tears sparkled in his eyes.

"That icon of the Mother of God I mentioned earlier," he said, "you take it. Keep it for yourself. I'll let you go back to the monastery. I was only joking this morning—don't be upset with me. My head is pounding, Alyosha. Please, comfort me. Be an angel and tell me the truth!"

"You're still asking if she was here?" Alyosha replied sadly.

"No, no. I believe you. But listen—go to Grushenka yourself. Try to see her somehow. Find out for yourself—does she want him, or does she want me? Can you do that?"

"If I see her, I'll ask," Alyosha muttered awkwardly.

"No, no, she won't tell you the truth," the old man interrupted. "She's tricky. She'll start kissing you and pretend it's you she wants. She's a sly, shameless woman. Don't go to her—promise me you won't!"

"No, father, I won't. It wouldn't be right."

"Where was Dmitri sending you just now? He shouted at you to go somewhere."

"To Katerina Ivanovna."

"For money? Did he ask you to get money from her?" "No, not for money."

"He doesn't have a penny to his name. I'll try to settle down for the night and think things through. You can go, but come see me tomorrow morning. I have something important to tell you. Will you come?"

"Yes."

"When you come, act like it was your idea. Don't tell anyone I asked you to. And don't mention it to Ivan."

"All right."

"Goodbye, my angel. You stood up for me just now. I'll never forget that. I have something to tell you tomorrow, but I need to think about it first."

"How are you feeling now?"

"Tomorrow I'll be fine. I'll get up and go out—completely fine!"

When Alyosha crossed the yard, he found Ivan sitting on a bench near the gate, writing something in a notebook with a pencil. Alyosha told him their father was awake, conscious, and had allowed him to return to the monastery.

"Alyosha, I'd be glad to meet you tomorrow morning," Ivan said warmly, standing up. His friendly tone surprised Alyosha.

"I'll be at the Hohlakovs' tomorrow," Alyosha replied. "I might visit Katerina Ivanovna too, if I don't see her tonight."

"You're going to see her now, right? For that 'compliments and farewell' message?" Ivan asked with a knowing smile. Alyosha looked uncomfortable.

"I think I understand what Dmitri was shouting about," Ivan continued. "He's sending you to say he's leaving her, isn't he?"

"Brother, how will all of this end—this madness between father and Dmitri?" Alyosha asked.

"It's impossible to say for sure. It might amount to nothing in the end. That woman is a menace. In any case, we need to keep the old man inside and make sure Dmitri doesn't get back into the house."

"Let me ask you something else," Alyosha said. "Does anyone have the right to decide who deserves to live?"

"Why talk about worth? People decide such things for other reasons—reasons that come naturally. And as for rights—who doesn't have the right to wish for something?"

"Even to wish for someone's death?"

"Why not? Why lie to ourselves? Everyone has those thoughts. Maybe people can't help it. Are you talking about what I said earlier—about one snake devouring another? Let me ask you this: do you think I'm capable of killing the old man, like Dmitri?"

"Ivan, what are you saying? That thought never even crossed my mind. And I don't think Dmitri could do it either."

"Thanks, at least for that," Ivan said with a faint smile. "I'd defend him if it ever came to that. But I reserve the right to think whatever I want about the situation."

"Goodbye for now. Don't judge me, Alyosha. Don't think I'm a villain," he added with a smile.

They shook hands warmly—more warmly than ever before. Alyosha felt that Ivan had taken a step toward him, and he knew his brother had done it for a reason.

Chapter 10: Both Together

Alyosha left his father's house feeling even more exhausted and downhearted than when he had first entered. His thoughts were scattered, and he was afraid to gather the broken pieces and try to make sense of all the troubling and conflicting experiences from the day. A sense of despair began to creep over him—something he had never felt until now. Towering over everything else was the grim, unsolvable question: how would things end between his father, Dmitri, and that dangerous woman? Now, having witnessed it all for himself—standing right there while they confronted each other—he could see how deeply entangled it had become. It seemed inevitable that Dmitri would suffer the most, possibly beyond repair. Alyosha felt that trouble was coming for his brother, and perhaps others were involved more than he had previously imagined. There was an unsettling air of mystery surrounding it all.

Ivan, in particular, had taken a step toward him, something Alyosha had wanted for a long time. But now that it had happened, it filled him with unease. And then there were the women. Strangely enough, that morning, Alyosha had felt embarrassed about going to see Katerina Ivanovna. Now, however, he found himself hurrying to meet her, almost as if he believed she might provide him with some kind of guidance. Yet delivering Dmitri's message was harder than ever. The matter of the three thousand rubles was final—no way to reverse it now. Dmitri, having lost his last hope and honor, seemed likely to fall into complete despair. On top of that, Dmitri had told him to describe the entire scene with their father to Katerina Ivanovna.

It was already seven in the evening, and darkness was falling as Alyosha reached Katerina Ivanovna's large, elegant house on the High Street. Alyosha knew she lived with two aunts. One was the aunt of her half-sister, Agafya Ivanovna, who had cared for her in their father's home when she first returned from boarding school. This aunt was not well-educated. The other aunt was a more refined woman from Moscow, though she now lived in reduced circumstances. It was said that both aunts gave in to Katerina Ivanovna's wishes in everything, serving as her chaperones. However, Katerina Ivanovna deferred only to the general's widow, her benefactor, who was bedridden in Moscow. Katerina wrote to her twice a week, updating her on all her affairs.

When Alyosha knocked and gave his name to the maid, it was clear that they had been expecting him— perhaps someone had seen him approaching from a window. Alyosha heard quick footsteps and the swishing of skirts, as if two or three women had just rushed out of the room. He found it strange that his arrival caused such excitement. Still, the maid led him directly to the drawing room.

The drawing room was spacious and beautifully decorated, with none of the usual provincial style. There were several sofas, lounges, and tables scattered throughout. The walls were adorned with paintings, and the tables held vases, lamps, and fresh flowers. An aquarium stood by the window. In the dim light, Alyosha noticed a silk shawl thrown over one of the sofas, as though someone had just left it there. On a nearby table were two half-empty cups of chocolate, along with cakes, a dish of blue raisins, and another plate filled with sweets. It was obvious that Alyosha had interrupted some visitors, and the realization made him frown.

Just then, the curtain over the doorway lifted, and Katerina Ivanovna entered the room quickly. She held out both hands toward him, her face glowing with a warm, joyful smile. At the same moment, a servant followed behind her, placing two lit candles on the table.

"Thank God! You're finally here! I've been praying all day that you would come!" she exclaimed. "Please, sit down."

Alyosha had been struck by Katerina Ivanovna's beauty the first time he met her, three weeks earlier. At her request, Dmitri had introduced them, though Alyosha had not spoken much during that first meeting. Katerina assumed he was shy, so she directed most of her conversation to Dmitri, trying to make things easier for him. Alyosha had observed everything silently but attentively.

What had stood out most to him was Katerina's commanding presence and the way she carried herself with complete confidence. Her large, dark eyes were striking, especially against her pale, almost sallow face. But there was also something about her beauty that felt unsettling to Alyosha—something Dmitri might fall deeply in love with, though perhaps not forever. After the visit, Dmitri had asked for Alyosha's honest impression, and Alyosha had reluctantly given his opinion.

"You'll be happy with her," Alyosha had said, "but it may not be a peaceful kind of happiness."

"Exactly," Dmitri had replied. "People like her never bend to fate. So you think I won't love her forever?"

"No, maybe you will love her forever. But you might not always be happy with her."

Alyosha had regretted saying those words as soon as they left his mouth. He felt embarrassed for offering such a bold opinion about a woman, and he had scolded himself for speaking so foolishly. But now, as Katerina

Ivanovna stood before him, her face radiant with kindness and sincerity, Alyosha wondered if he had been completely wrong about her. The pride he had noticed before now seemed like nothing more than strength—a kind of determined faith in herself.

Alyosha could see right away that Katerina Ivanovna knew the full weight of her situation with Dmitri. She likely understood everything, perhaps even more than Alyosha did. Yet despite knowing all this, her face remained bright and full of hope. Alyosha felt ashamed for having judged her so harshly in his thoughts. Her genuine warmth and kindness quickly won him over. But alongside her kindness, Alyosha could sense that she was unusually excited—so excited that it bordered on ecstasy.

"I've been so eager to see you," she said with urgency, "because I know you'll tell me the truth. Only you can tell me everything I need to know."

"I've come," Alyosha stammered awkwardly. "He sent me."

"Ah, I knew it! I knew he would send you!" she said, her eyes lighting up with sudden excitement. "Now I understand everything!"

She paused for a moment, catching her breath. "Listen, Alexey Fyodorovich, I'll tell you why I've been waiting for you so desperately. I probably know more than you do, so there's no need for explanations. What I want is simple. I need to know your last impression of him—what you thought of him today, after meeting with him. Tell me plainly, even bluntly. Don't hold anything back. It would be better than any conversation I could have with him since he won't come to see me himself. Do you understand what I'm asking? Now, tell me—what message did he send? I knew he would send you with one."

"He told me to give you his compliments—and to say that he won't come again—but to give you his compliments," Alyosha said, feeling awkward.

"His compliments?" she repeated sharply. "Was that his exact word?"

"Yes."

"Could he have used the wrong word by accident?"

"No, he insisted on it. He made me promise not to forget to say it exactly that way."

Katerina Ivanovna flushed, and her excitement grew.

"Help me, Alexey Fyodorovich," she said urgently. "I need your help now. I'll tell you what I think, and you tell me if I'm right. Listen! If he had sent his compliments casually, without stressing the words, that would mean everything is over between us. But if he emphasized those words—if he made sure you wouldn't forget them—then he was probably upset, maybe even scared of the decision he made. He wasn't leaving me calmly; he was running away in a panic. His insistence might have been nothing more than bravado."

"Yes, yes!" Alyosha exclaimed. "I believe you're right!"

"And if that's the case, he's not completely lost. I can still save him. Wait! Didn't he tell you something about money—about three thousand roubles?"

"He did mention it, and that's what's bothering him the most. He said he's lost his honor and that nothing matters anymore," Alyosha replied earnestly, feeling a surge of hope and thinking that maybe there was still a way to help his brother. "But do you know about the money?" he asked and suddenly stopped.

"I've known about it for a while; I sent a telegram to Moscow to check and found out a long time ago that the money hadn't been sent. He never sent it, but I didn't say anything. Last week, I learned that he still needed money. My only goal in all of this was for him to know who he could rely on, who his real friend was.

90

But no, he won't see me as his truest friend; he won't understand me and only sees me as a woman. I've been so worried all week, trying to figure out how to stop him from being embarrassed in front of me because of the money he spent. Let him feel ashamed in front of other people, but not me. He can confess everything to God without feeling ashamed. Why doesn't he understand how much I'm willing to endure for him? Why, why doesn't he know me? How dare he not know me after everything that's happened? I want to save him forever. Let him forget about me as his fiancée. And here he is, thinking he's dishonored in my eyes. Why, he wasn't afraid to open up to you, Alexey Fyodorovitch. Why can't I deserve the same?"

She said the last words in tears. Tears streamed from her eyes.

"I need to tell you," Alyosha began, his voice trembling, "about what happened earlier between him and my father."

He explained the entire scene, how Dmitri had sent him to get the money, how he had forced his way in, knocked their father down, and then insisted that Alyosha pass on his greetings and farewell. "He went to that woman," Alyosha added quietly.

"And do you think I can't deal with that woman? Does he think I can't? But he won't marry her," she suddenly laughed nervously. "How could such a passion last forever in a Karamazov? It's not love, it's passion. He won't marry her because she won't marry him." Katerina Ivanovna laughed strangely again.

"He might marry her," Alyosha said sadly, looking down.

"He won't marry her, I'm telling you. That girl is an angel. Do you know that? Do you know that?" Katerina Ivanovna suddenly exclaimed with great warmth. "She's one of the most amazing people I've ever met. I know how enchanting she is, but I also know she's kind, strong, and noble. Why are you looking at me like that, Alexey Fyodorovitch? Are you surprised by what I'm saying, do you not believe me? Agrafena Alexandrovna, my angel!" she suddenly called to someone in the next room, "come in and meet us. This is a friend. This is Alyosha. He knows everything about us. Show yourself to him."

"I was just waiting for you to call me," said a soft, almost sugary feminine voice.

The curtain lifted, and Grushenka came out, smiling brightly. A strong wave of disgust hit Alyosha. He couldn't take his eyes off her. Here she was, that terrible woman, the "beast," as Ivan had called her just half an hour ago. But now she seemed so ordinary, like a good-natured, kind woman—yes, she was beautiful, but in a very normal way. She was definitely beautiful, with that Russian charm many men found irresistible. She was tall, though a little shorter than Katerina Ivanovna, who was exceptionally tall. She had a full figure, and her movements were soft, almost too soft, like her voice. She moved differently than Katerina Ivanovna, who had a bold, confident step; Grushenka's movements were quiet and graceful. Her footsteps made no sound on the floor. She sank gently into a low chair, her rich black silk dress making a soft rustling sound as she did so, and she nestled her milk-white neck and broad shoulders into a luxurious cashmere shawl. She was twenty-two years old, and her face looked exactly that age. Her skin was pale, with a faint pink blush on her cheeks. Her face was broad, and her lower jaw stuck out slightly. Her upper lip was thin, but the lower lip was much fuller, giving her a bit of a pout. Her thick, dark brown hair, sable-colored eyebrows, and striking gray-blue eyes with long lashes would have made anyone passing by notice her. Alyosha was struck by the childlike innocence in her expression. There was something childlike in her eyes, a look of pure delight. She walked to the table, beaming with happiness, as though expecting something exciting with childlike eagerness and trust. The brightness in her eyes was infectious— Alyosha felt it. There was something else about her he couldn't quite understand, something that subtly influenced him, though he couldn't explain it. It was her softness, the almost sensual way she moved, that quiet, feline grace. Yet her body was strong and full. Under the shawl, her broad shoulders and still-girlish chest were visible. Her figure reminded one of the Venus of Milo, though her proportions were a bit more exaggerated. An expert in Russian beauty could have predicted that by the age of thirty, her youthful beauty would start to fade; her face would become puffier, and wrinkles would soon appear around her forehead and eyes. Her complexion might become coarser and redder—in short, she had the kind of fleeting beauty often seen in Russian women. Alyosha didn't think of this, of course, but even though he was captivated by her, he felt an uncomfortable sensation, almost a kind of regret, wondering why she spoke in such a slow, exaggerated way instead of talking normally. She clearly thought this overly sweet, drawn-out speech was charming. It was really just a bad habit, showing poor education and a misunderstanding of what good manners were. But despite all that, her voice and way of speaking seemed oddly out of place with the innocent and joyful expression on her face, the childlike happiness in her eyes. Katerina Ivanovna immediately had her sit in a chair across from

Alyosha, kissing her repeatedly on her smiling lips. She seemed completely infatuated with her.

"This is the first time we've met, Alexey Fyodorovitch," she said joyfully. "I wanted to meet her, to see her. I wanted to go to her, but as soon as I wished it, she came to me. I knew we'd work everything out together. My heart told me it was the solution, and I was right. Grushenka has explained everything to me, told me all she plans to do. She flew here like an angel and brought us peace and joy."

"You didn't look down on me, kind, sweet lady," Grushenka said in her slow, singsong voice, still smiling brightly.

"Don't talk to me like that, you enchantress, you witch! Look down on you? Here, I must kiss your bottom lip again. It looks swollen, and now it's going to be even more so. Look how she laughs, Alexey Fyodorovitch! It does the heart good to see this angel."

Alyosha blushed, feeling faint shivers run through him.

"You're so kind to me, dear lady, but maybe I'm not worthy of your kindness."

"Not worthy? Not worthy?" Katerina Ivanovna exclaimed warmly. "You know, Alexey Fyodorovitch, we're a bit stubborn, a bit proud, but deep in our hearts, we're noble and generous. We've only been unlucky. We were too willing to give everything for a man who might have been unworthy or fickle. There was a man—an officer, in fact—we loved him and gave up everything for him. That was five years ago, and he's forgotten about us now, married someone else. Now he's a widower and has written to us. He's coming back here, and do you know, we've loved him all this time, for our entire lives! He's coming, and Grushenka will be happy again. For five years she's been miserable. But who can blame her, who can brag about winning her favor? Only that bedridden old merchant, but he's more like a father to her, a friend, a protector. He found her in despair, abandoned by the man she loved. She was ready to drown herself then, but the old merchant saved her—saved her!"

"You are very kind to defend me, dear lady, but you seem to be in quite a rush," Grushenka said in her slow, drawling tone.

"Defend you? Me? Do you think I have the right to defend you? Grushenka, my angel, give me your hand. Look at her lovely, soft little hand, Alexey Fyodorovitch! Look at it! It's brought me happiness and lifted me up, and I will kiss it—on the outside, the inside, here, here, and here!"

She kissed Grushenka's charming, though somewhat plump, hand three times, as if overcome with joy. Grushenka held out her hand with a light, playful laugh, watching the excited young lady and clearly enjoying the attention.

"A little too much excitement," Alyosha thought to himself. He blushed, feeling strangely uncomfortable.

"You're not going to make me blush by kissing my hand in front of Alexey Fyodorovitch," Grushenka said with a grin.

"Do you think that's what I was trying to do?" Katerina Ivanovna replied, sounding a bit surprised. "Oh, my dear, you really don't understand me!"

"And maybe you don't really understand me either, dear lady. Maybe I'm not as good as you think I am. I have a selfish heart—I always want things my way. I flirted with poor Dmitri Fyodorovitch that day just for fun."

"But now you'll help him, right? You promised me. You'll explain everything to him and tell him you've loved someone else all along, someone who's ready to marry you now."

"Oh no, I didn't promise that. You were the one talking about it, not me. I never gave you my word."

"So... I misunderstood you?" Katerina Ivanovna said slowly, turning pale. "But you said—"

"No, my dear lady, I made no promises," Grushenka answered gently, with the same lighthearted smile. "You see, I'm stubborn and unpredictable compared to you. When I want something, I just do it. Maybe I did say something like that earlier, but now I'm thinking I might stick with Mitya after all. I liked him a lot that day—well, at least for an hour. Who knows? Maybe I'll tell him to stay with me from now on. I change my mind all the time."

"But just now... you said something entirely different," Katerina

Ivanovna whispered, her voice faint.

"Yes, I did. But I'm such a foolish, soft-hearted creature. Just think about what he's gone through because of me! What if, when I go home, I feel sorry for him? What then?"

"I never thought..." Katerina began, trailing off.

"Oh, dear lady, you're so much kinder and nobler than I am! Now that you know what I'm like, you might not want anything to do with someone as silly as me. Give me your lovely hand, angel," Grushenka said tenderly, taking Katerina Ivanovna's hand with an almost reverent touch.

"Here, my dear, I'll kiss your hand, just like you kissed mine. You kissed mine three times, but I ought to kiss yours three hundred times to even things out. But let's not count. Let's leave everything up to God. Maybe I'll become your devoted servant, doing whatever you ask, like a slave. Let it be however God wills. Such a sweet hand—what a sweet hand you have! You beautiful, wonderful young lady!"

She slowly lifted Katerina's hand to her lips, determined to return the same kindness.

Katerina Ivanovna didn't pull her hand away. She listened, a flicker of hope rising within her, though Grushenka's talk of being her "slave" sounded odd. Katerina looked into her eyes, still seeing the same innocence and cheerful spirit as before.

"She might be a little too simple," Katerina thought, a hopeful glimmer in her mind.

Grushenka seemed delighted by the "sweet little hand," raising it toward her lips. But she paused, holding it near her mouth as if thinking something over.

"You know what, angel?" Grushenka suddenly said in an even softer voice, stretching her words sweetly. "I've decided I won't kiss your hand after all." She let out a playful laugh.

"Do whatever you like! What's gotten into you?" Katerina Ivanovna exclaimed, startled.

"I just thought it would be nice for you to remember that you kissed my hand, but I didn't kiss yours."

A sly glimmer flashed in Grushenka's eyes as she looked at

Katerina Ivanovna with unsettling intensity.

"You insolent woman!" Katerina Ivanovna shouted, her face suddenly flushing red as she leapt from her seat.

Grushenka stood up too, though much more calmly.

"So, I'll tell Mitya how you kissed my hand, but I didn't kiss yours. Imagine how he'll laugh!"

"You vile creature! Get out of here!" Katerina Ivanovna screamed.

"Oh, come now, dear lady! That's not a word you should be using," Grushenka said lightly. "It doesn't suit someone like you."

"Get out! You're nothing but a shameless woman for sale!" Katerina Ivanovna shrieked, her face twisting in anger.

"For sale, am I? Didn't you once meet gentlemen in secret for money? You sold your beauty too. I know all about it."

Katerina Ivanovna screamed and lunged at her, but Alyosha grabbed her, holding her back with all his strength.

"Not another step, not another word! Don't respond to her. She'll leave—just let her go," Alyosha urged.

At that moment, Katerina Ivanovna's two aunts and a maid rushed into the room. They hurried to comfort her.

"I'm leaving," Grushenka said, picking up her mantle from the sofa. "Alyosha, dear, walk me home."

"Please, just go—quickly!" Alyosha begged, clasping his hands.

"Come with me, Alyosha! I've got a little story to tell you on the way. You'll be glad you came, trust me. I planned this whole scene just for you," Grushenka said with a teasing laugh as she headed out the door.

Alyosha turned away, wringing his hands in frustration. Grushenka left the house, her musical laughter trailing behind her.

Katerina Ivanovna collapsed into a fit of hysterics, her body shaking with sobs and convulsions. Everyone crowded around her, trying to help.

"I warned you," said the elder aunt. "I told you not to get involved. You're too impulsive. How could you do this? You don't understand these kinds of people. They say she's worse than any of them. You're too stubborn."

"She's a wild beast!" Katerina Ivanovna cried. "Why did you hold me back, Alexey Fyodorovitch? I would've beaten her—I would've beaten her!"

She didn't hold back her emotions in front of Alyosha, and perhaps she didn't even care to.

"She should be whipped in public!" she shouted angrily. Alyosha slowly backed away toward the door.

"But my God!" cried Katerina Ivanovna, clasping her hands together. "Him! Him! How could he be so dishonorable, so cruel! Why, he told that woman what happened on that awful, cursed day! 'You sold your beauty, dear young lady.' She knows it! Your brother is a scoundrel, Alexey Fyodorovitch."

Alyosha wanted to say something, but no words came. His heart was in pain.

"Go away, Alexey Fyodorovitch! This is too shameful, too horrible for me! Please, I beg you, come tomorrow. Don't judge me. Forgive me. I don't know what I'll do with myself now!"

Alyosha stumbled into the street, feeling dizzy. He could have cried just like she did. Suddenly, the maid caught up with him.

"The young lady forgot to give you this letter from Madame Hohlakov; it's been here since dinner."

Alyosha took the small pink envelope without thinking and slipped it, almost automatically, into his pocket.

Chapter 11: Another Reputation Ruined

It was only about three-quarters of a mile from the town to the monastery. Alyosha walked quickly down the road, which was deserted at that time. It was nearly night, and too dark to see anything clearly thirty paces ahead. There was a crossroad halfway. A figure appeared under a lone willow tree at the crossroad. As soon as Alyosha reached it, the figure moved out and rushed toward him, shouting fiercely:

"Your money or your life!"

"So, it's you, Mitya!" cried Alyosha in surprise, though he was still shocked.

"Haha! You didn't expect me? I wondered where to wait for you. By her house? There are three roads from there, and I might have missed you. Finally, I thought of waiting here because you had to pass this way—there's no other route to the monastery. Come, tell me the truth. Crush me like a bug. But what's wrong?"

"Nothing, brother—it's just that you startled me. Oh, Dmitri! Just now, father's blood..." (Alyosha began to cry. He had been holding back tears for a long time, and now something seemed to break inside him.) "You nearly killed him—cursed him—and now—here—you're making jokes—'Your money or your life!'"

"Well, what about it? It's not appropriate—is that it? Not fitting for me?"

"No, it's just—"

"Wait. Look at the night. You see how dark it is, how the clouds look, and how the wind has picked up. I was hiding under the willow, waiting for you. And, by God, I suddenly thought, why keep suffering any longer? What's left to wait for? There's the willow, I have a handkerchief, a shirt—I can make a rope in a minute. I even have my suspenders! Why keep burdening the earth, disgracing it with my vile existence? And then I heard you coming. It felt like something flew down to me all of a sudden. So there's someone I love after all. Here he is, that person, my dear brother, the one I love more than anyone in the world—the only one I love in this world. And I loved you so much at that moment, I thought, 'I'll just throw myself into his arms.' Then a silly idea hit me: I'll joke with you and scare you. I shouted like an idiot, 'Your money!' Forgive me for being foolish—it was just nonsense. There's nothing wrong in my soul. Forget it. Tell me what happened. What did she say? Hit me, crush me, don't hold back! Was she furious?"

"No, not that... It wasn't like that, Mitya. I found them both there." "Both? Who?"

"Grushenka and Katerina Ivanovna."

Dmitri was speechless.

"Impossible!" he shouted. "You're crazy! Grushenka, with her?"

Alyosha explained everything that happened from the moment he entered Katerina Ivanovna's house. It took him about ten minutes to tell the story. He didn't explain it very smoothly or in a straight line, but he made sure to clarify everything important, not leaving out any key moments, and often describing his own feelings in just a word. Dmitri listened silently, staring at him with an intense, terrifying gaze, but Alyosha could tell that he understood everything. He caught every detail. As Alyosha continued, Dmitri's face became not just dark but threatening. He scowled, gritted his teeth, and his hard stare grew even more intense, until suddenly, as if something snapped, his angry, wild expression changed, his tightly pressed lips parted, and Dmitri Fyodorovitch burst into loud, uncontrollable laughter. He shook with laughter, unable to stop for a long time.

"So she wouldn't kiss her hand! So she didn't kiss it, and then she ran away!" he kept exclaiming with hysterical joy. It was a kind of smug delight, though it seemed too natural to be just mean. "And the other one called her a tigress! And a tigress she is! She should be whipped on a scaffold! Yes, yes, that's exactly what I think. She should've been whipped a long time ago. But listen, brother, she deserves to be punished, but I need to get better first. I understand her boldness—that's who she is! You saw it in that hand-kissing moment—the she-devil! She's magnificent in her own way! So she ran home? I'll go—no—I'll run to her! Alyosha, don't be mad at me, I agree that even hanging is too good for her."

"But what about Katerina Ivanovna!" Alyosha cried, feeling sad.

"I see her too! I see her more clearly than I ever have! It's like discovering all five continents at once! What a thing to do! That's

so typical of Katya—she wasn't afraid to confront a rude officer and risk a serious insult just to save her father! But the pride, the recklessness, the daring against fate—such limitless daring! You said her aunt tried to stop her? That aunt, you know, is full of herself too. She's the sister of the widow of a general in Moscow, and she's even more arrogant. But her husband got caught stealing government money. He lost everything—his estate and all—and the proud wife had to bow her head, and she's never raised it since. So she tried to stop Katya, but Katya wouldn't listen! She thinks she can overcome everything, that the world will bend to her will. She believed she could charm Grushenka if she wanted, and she convinced herself of it. She's just playing out her own fantasy. And whose fault is that? Do you think she kissed Grushenka's hand on purpose, with some hidden motive? No, she was genuinely enchanted by Grushenka—not by Grushenka herself, but by the idea of her, her own fantasy! Alyosha, my dear, how did you escape from them, those women? Did you pick up your cassock and run? Ha ha ha!"

"Brother, don't you realize how much you hurt Katerina Ivanovna by telling Grushenka about that day? And Grushenka threw it back at her, saying she'd met gentlemen in secret to sell her beauty! Brother, what could be worse than that insult?"

What troubled Alyosha most was that, incredibly, his brother seemed to be pleased by Katerina Ivanovna's humiliation.

"Bah!" Dmitri scowled, hitting his forehead with his hand. He had only now realized it, even though Alyosha had just told him about the insult and Katerina Ivanovna's cry: "Your brother is a scoundrel!"

"Yes, maybe I did tell Grushenka about that 'fatal day,' as Katya calls it. Yes, I remember! It was that time at Mokroe. I was drunk, the gypsies were singing... But I was crying. I was crying back then, kneeling and praying to Katya's image, and Grushenka understood. She got it all back then. I remember, she cried too... Damn it all! But it has to be like this now... Back then, she cried, but now it's 'a dagger in the heart'! That's how women are."

He looked down and fell silent.

"Yes, I'm a scoundrel, a complete scoundrel!" he suddenly said in a low, gloomy voice. "It doesn't matter if I cried or not, I'm a scoundrel! Tell her I accept the name if that makes her feel better. Come on, that's enough. Goodbye. There's no point in talking about this—it's not fun. You go your way, and I'll go mine. And I don't want to see you again unless it's absolutely necessary. Goodbye, Alexey!"

He squeezed Alyosha's hand warmly and, still looking down, without lifting his head, as if pulling himself away, quickly turned and walked back toward the town.

Alyosha stood there, watching him, unable to believe he would just leave like that.

"Wait, Alexey, one more confession, just for you alone!" Dmitri suddenly called, turning back. "Look at me—really look at me.

Do you see? Right here—there's a terrible disgrace waiting for me." (As he said "here," Dmitri pounded his chest with his fist, as if the shame was located exactly there, in some particular spot—perhaps in a pocket or hanging around his neck.) "You know me now—yes, a scoundrel, a confessed scoundrel. But let me tell you, I've never done anything before, and I will never do anything again, as shameful as what I am carrying now, at this very moment, right here on my chest. And what's worse is that I am perfectly free to stop it. I could stop it if I wanted to, or I could go through with it. But let me be clear—I won't stop it. I will go through with it.

"I told you everything earlier, but I didn't tell you this part because even I didn't have the nerve to say it. I could still turn back. If I did, I'd get back half of the honor I've already lost. But I won't turn back. I'll follow through with my disgraceful plan, and you will be my witness that I warned you ahead of time. Darkness and ruin—there's no need for me to explain further. You'll understand soon enough. The filthy back alley and the she-devil await me. Goodbye. Don't waste your prayers on me—I'm not worth it. And I don't need them. Not in the slightest. Now go!"

He turned away sharply and walked off, this time for good.

Alyosha continued on his way toward the monastery.

"What? Will I never see him again?" Alyosha thought to himself, feeling lost. "What does he mean by that? I'll see him tomorrow for sure. I'll find him—I'll make sure of it. What could he be talking about?"

He walked around the monastery and through the pine forest toward the hermitage. Though visitors weren't allowed at this hour, the door was opened for him. As he entered Father Zossima's cell, his heart trembled.

"Why? Why did he send me into the world?" Alyosha wondered. "Here there is peace. Here there is holiness. But out there—it's nothing but confusion and darkness. Out there, you can lose your way and go astray so easily…"

Inside the cell, Alyosha found the novice Porfiry and Father Païssy, who had been checking on Father Zossima every hour. Alyosha was deeply worried to hear that the elder's condition had worsened. He hadn't been able to meet with the monks as usual. Every evening after prayer, the brothers would gather in his cell to confess their sins out loud—their bad thoughts, their temptations, and any arguments they'd had that day. Some of them knelt as they confessed. Father Zossima would forgive them, offer advice, assign penance when needed, bless them, and send them on their way.

Many in the monastery opposed these open confessions, saying they dishonored the sacrament of confession and bordered on sacrilege. Some even complained to the diocesan authorities, arguing that these public confessions led to more sin and temptation rather than preventing it. Some of the monks disliked the practice but felt pressured to participate so they wouldn't be seen as proud or rebellious. Alyosha knew that, sometimes, monks would even plan their confessions ahead of time—agreeing to admit small faults like losing their tempers, just so they'd have something to confess. He also knew that some monks were unhappy that personal letters from family members were given to the elder first to be opened and read by him before they reached the intended recipients.

Officially, this was all voluntary and meant to provide spiritual guidance, but in reality, there was often insincerity and discomfort involved. Still, the older monks insisted that obedience and sacrifice were necessary for those truly seeking salvation. They argued that anyone who found it burdensome or resented it wasn't suited for monastic life and should return to the world. Even in the temple, they said, no one was safe from sin or the devil.

"He's weaker now, drifting in and out of sleep," Father Païssy whispered to Alyosha, blessing him. "We mustn't wake him. He only woke briefly to give his blessing to the brothers and ask for their prayers tonight. He plans to take the sacrament again tomorrow morning. When he woke, he asked about you, Alexey. He wanted to know if you were still in town. 'I gave him my blessing for his work there,' he said. 'For now, his place is in the world, not here.' Those were his words about you. He remembered you with love and concern. Do you see how much honor he gives you? But for him to say you must spend time in the world—he must have seen something in your future. Remember, Alexey, if you return to the world, you must do the work he has given you. Don't let yourself get caught up in vanity or worldly pleasures."

Father Païssy left. Alyosha knew in his heart that Father Zossima was dying, though he might live for another day or two. Alyosha made a firm decision—despite the promises he had made to his father, to Madame Hohlakov, and to Katerina Ivanovna, he would not leave the monastery the next day. He would stay with Father Zossima until the very end. His heart burned with love, and he felt deeply ashamed for having allowed himself, even for a moment, to forget about the elder, who now lay on his deathbed—the man Alyosha honored more than anyone in the world.

Alyosha went into Father Zossima's bedroom, knelt down, and bowed to the ground before the elder, who lay sleeping quietly, his breathing soft and steady, his face peaceful.

Alyosha returned to the other room, where Father Zossima had received guests earlier that morning. He took off his boots and lay down on the narrow leather sofa he had been using as a bed. He brought only a pillow—not the mattress his father had fussed over that morning. That mattress had long since been forgotten. Alyosha removed his cassock and used it as a blanket. But before lying down, he knelt and prayed for a long time.

In his prayer, Alyosha did not ask God to take away his confusion. Instead, he simply longed for the joy that always came after his evening prayers—a joy that filled his heart with peace and brought him restful sleep. As he prayed, his hand brushed against the small pink note in his pocket—the one the servant had given him when he left Katerina Ivanovna's house. The memory disturbed him, but he finished his prayer. Then, after a moment of hesitation, he opened the envelope.

Inside was a letter from Lise, the young daughter of Madame Hohlakov—the same Lise who had teased him that morning in front of the elder.

"Alexey Fyodorovitch," she wrote, "I'm writing this without anyone knowing—not even Mama. I know it's wrong, but I can't keep it to myself anymore. I need to tell you what's in my heart, and for now, it has to stay between just the two of us. But how do I even say it? They say paper doesn't blush, but I swear it does—I feel like this paper is blushing as much as I am.

"Dear Alyosha, I love you. I've loved you since we were children, back in Moscow, when you were so different from how you are now. I will love you for the rest of my life. My heart has chosen you, and I want us to spend our lives together, growing old side by side. But for that to happen, you'll have to leave the monastery. We'll wait until the time the law allows. By then, I'll be healthy again—walking and dancing, I'm sure of it.

"You see, I've thought it all through. But the one thing I can't figure out is what you'll think of me when you read this. I know I'm always laughing and acting silly. I even made you angry this morning. But before I wrote this letter, I prayed in front of the Image of the Mother of God. I'm still praying now—and almost crying.

"My secret is in your hands. When you come tomorrow, I don't know how I'll face you. What if I can't stop myself from laughing again? You'll think I'm just teasing you and won't believe any of this. So, please, when you come tomorrow, don't look me in the eyes—look at Mama, or out the window, but not at me, at least not right away.

"Oh no, I've written you a love letter! Alyosha, please don't be angry. If I've done something wrong, forgive me. My reputation is in your hands now.

"I know I'll cry today. Goodbye until we meet again—though I'm terrified of it. —Lise

"P.S. Alyosha, you must come. You must!"

Alyosha read the letter in amazement, then read it again. He thought for a moment, then let out a soft, joyful laugh. But he quickly stopped, startled by his own laughter—it felt almost wrong. A moment later, though, he laughed again, just as softly. He slipped the letter back into the envelope, crossed himself, and lay down. The unrest in his heart faded away.

"God, have mercy on all of them. Guide these troubled souls onto the right path. All paths are Yours. Save them according to Your wisdom. You are love, and You will bring joy to them all," Alyosha murmured as he crossed himself again and drifted into peaceful sleep.

Part 2

Book 4: Lacerations

Chapter 1: Father Ferapont

Alyosha was awakened early, before daybreak. Father Zossima had woken up feeling very weak, though he wished to get out of bed and sit up in a chair. His mind was completely clear; his face looked tired, yet it was bright and almost joyful. There was an expression of cheerfulness, kindness, and warmth on his face. "Perhaps I shall not live through the coming day," he said to Alyosha. Then he expressed a desire to confess and take the sacrament immediately. He always confessed to Father Païssy. After receiving communion, the service of extreme unction followed. The monks assembled, and the cell gradually filled up with the residents of the hermitage. By that time, it was daylight. People began to arrive from the monastery. After the service, the elder wished to kiss and bid farewell to everyone. As the cell was so small, the earlier visitors withdrew to make space for others. Alyosha stood beside the elder, who had seated himself once more in his chair. He spoke as much as he was able. Though his voice was weak, it was fairly steady.

"I have been teaching you for so many years, and as a result, I have been talking aloud for many years, that I have become so accustomed to speaking, it is almost more difficult for me to hold my tongue than to speak, even now, despite my weakness, dear Fathers and brothers," he joked, looking with emotion at the group surrounding him. Alyosha remembered afterward some of the things he said to them. Though he spoke distinctly, and his voice was mostly steady, his speech was somewhat disjointed. He spoke about many things, as if before the moment of death, he felt anxious to say all that had not been said in his life. Not merely for the sake of instructing them, but as if he longed to share his joy and ecstasy with all people and all creation, and to open his heart one last time in his life.

"Love one another, Fathers," said Father Zossima, as far as Alyosha could recall later. "Love God's people. For though we have come here and shut ourselves within these walls, we are no holier than those outside; on the contrary, by coming here, each one of us has admitted that he is worse than others, worse than all men on earth. The longer a monk lives in seclusion, the more keenly he must recognize this. Otherwise, there would have been no reason for him to come here. When he realizes that not only is he worse than others, but that he is responsible for all people and everything, for all human sins, both national and individual, only then is the goal of our seclusion accomplished. For know, dear ones, that each of us is undoubtedly responsible for all people and everything on earth, not only through the general sinfulness of creation but personally, for all humanity and every individual person. This understanding is the crown of life for the monk and for every person. Monks are not a special type of men, but only what all men ought to be. Only through that understanding does our heart become soft with infinite, universal, inexhaustible love. Then every one of you will have the power to win over the world through love and to wash away the sins of the world with your tears... Each of you must keep watch over your heart and confess your sins to yourself constantly. Do not be afraid of your sins, even when you recognize them, so long as there is repentance, but make no conditions with God. Again, I say, do not be proud. Be proud neither to the little nor to the great. Do not hate those who reject you, who insult you, who abuse and slander you. Do not hate atheists, teachers of evil, materialists—and I do not mean only the good ones, for there are many good ones among them, especially in our day—do not even hate the wicked ones. Remember them in your prayers, saying: 'Save, O Lord, all those who have no one to pray for them, save also all those who do not pray.' And add: 'It is not in pride that I make this prayer, O Lord, for I am lower than all men...' Love God's people, do not allow strangers to lead the flock astray, for if you slumber in laziness and disdainful pride, or worse, in greed, they will come from all sides and steal your flock. Preach the Gospel to the people constantly… be not extortionate... do not love gold and silver, do not hoard them... Have faith. Cling to the banner and lift it high."

Yet, the elder spoke more disconnectedly than Alyosha reported his words afterward. Sometimes he paused completely, as though to catch his breath and regain his strength, but he was in a state of ecstasy. They listened to him with emotion, though many were puzzled by his words and found them difficult to understand. But later, everyone remembered those words. When Alyosha left the cell for a moment, he was struck by the general excitement and anticipation among the monks gathered outside. In some, this showed itself in anxiety, in others, devout solemnity. All were expecting some miracle to happen immediately after the elder's death. From one perspective, their anticipation was almost childish, but even the most severe monks were affected by it. Father Païssy's face looked the most serious of all.

Alyosha was discreetly called by a monk to see Rakitin, who had arrived from town with an unusual letter for him from Madame Hohlakov. In the letter, she informed Alyosha of a strange and timely event. It seemed that among the women who had come the previous day to receive Father Zossima's blessing, there had been an old woman from the town, a sergeant's widow, named Prohorovna. She had asked whether she might pray for the soul of her son Vassenka, who had gone to Irkutsk and had not sent her any news for over a year. Father Zossima had sternly forbidden her, telling her that praying for the living as though they were dead was a form of sorcery. He then forgave her, because of her ignorance, and added, "as though reading the book of the future" (this was Madame Hohlakov's expression), some words of comfort: that her son Vassya was alive and that he would either return soon himself or send a letter, and that she should go home and wait for him. "And would you believe it?" Madame Hohlakov wrote with excitement, "the prophecy has been fulfilled literally, and even more than that!" The old woman had scarcely returned home when a letter from Siberia, which had been waiting for her, was handed to her. But that was not all; in the letter, written on the road from Ekaterinburg, Vassya told his mother that he was returning to Russia with an official, and that three weeks after she received the letter, he hoped "to embrace his mother."

Madame Hohlakov earnestly urged Alyosha to share this new "miracle of prediction" with the Superior and all the brotherhood. "Everyone should know about it!" she concluded. The letter was written in haste, and the excitement of the writer was evident in every line. However, Alyosha had no need to tell the monks, for they all already knew. Rakitin had asked the monk who delivered the message "to most respectfully inform Father Païssy that he, Rakitin, had a matter of such importance to discuss with him that he dared not delay it for a moment, and humbly begged forgiveness for his boldness." Since the monk had delivered the message to Father Païssy before speaking to Alyosha, when Alyosha finished reading the letter, there was nothing left for him to do but hand it to Father Païssy to confirm the story.

Even that strict and cautious man, though he frowned while reading the news of the "miracle," could not completely restrain a feeling of inner emotion. His eyes shone, and a serious, solemn smile appeared on his lips. "We shall see greater things!" he exclaimed. "We shall see greater things, greater things yet!" the monks around him repeated. But Father Païssy frowned again and urged everyone, at least for a time, not to speak of the matter "until it is more fully confirmed, since there is so much credulity in the world, and indeed, this might have occurred naturally," he added cautiously, as if to satisfy his conscience, although he barely believed his own disavowal, a fact that his listeners clearly understood.

Within the hour, the "miracle" was, of course, known throughout the entire monastery and among many visitors who had come for the mass. No one appeared more affected by it than the monk who had arrived the day before from St. Sylvester's, a small monastery in Obdorsk in the far North. It was he who had been standing near Madame Hohlakov the day before and had asked Father Zossima, earnestly referring to the "healing" of the lady's daughter, "How can you presume to do such things?"

He was now a little confused and didn't know who to believe. The evening before, he had visited Father Ferapont in his secluded cell behind the beehives and had been deeply impressed and somewhat intimidated by the visit. Father Ferapont was the old monk who had been mentioned earlier, very strict with fasting and silence, and known for opposing Father Zossima and the idea of "elders," which he considered a harmful and silly new practice. He was a tough opponent, even though he rarely spoke to anyone because of his dedication to silence. What made him so intimidating was that several monks agreed with him, and many visitors saw him as a great saint and ascetic, although they were sure he was mad. But it was precisely this madness that attracted people.

Father Ferapont never went to see the elder. Even though he lived in the hermitage, they didn't pressure him to follow its rules, mainly because he acted as though he were insane. He was seventy-five or older and lived in a corner past the beehives in an old, crumbling wooden cell that had been built long ago for another great ascetic, Father Iona, who had lived to be one hundred and five. Many interesting stories about his saintly life were still told in the monastery and nearby villages. Father Ferapont had managed to get himself settled in this same lonely cell seven years before. It was just a simple peasant's hut, but it looked like a chapel because it was filled with so many icons, with lamps burning constantly in front of them. These icons were offerings from people to the monastery, and Father Ferapont had been tasked with taking care of them and keeping the lamps lit. It was said (and it was true) that he ate only two pounds of bread every three days. The beekeeper, who lived nearby, would bring him the bread every three days, but even to this man, Father Ferapont rarely spoke. The four pounds of bread, along with the sacramental bread sent to him every Sunday after the late mass by the Father Superior, made up his weekly food. His water jug was refilled daily. He rarely showed up for mass. Visitors who came to honor him would sometimes see him kneeling all day in prayer, without even looking around. If he did speak to them, it was brief, blunt, strange, and often rude. Very rarely, though, he would talk to visitors, but usually, he would say something odd that was a complete mystery, and no pleading could get him to explain. He wasn't a priest, just a simple monk. There was a strange belief, mostly among the less educated people, that Father Ferapont could talk to heavenly spirits and only communicated with them, which is why he stayed silent with people.

The monk from Obdorsk, having been directed to the beehives by the beekeeper—a silent and grumpy monk as well—went to the spot where Father Ferapont's cell stood. "Maybe he'll speak since you're a stranger, or maybe you'll get nothing from him," the beekeeper had warned him. The monk, as he later told the story, approached with great nervousness. It was rather late in the evening. Father Ferapont was sitting outside his cell on a low bench. A large, old elm tree was gently rustling above. There was a coolness in the evening air. The monk from Obdorsk bowed deeply before the saint and asked for his blessing.

"Do you want me to bow down to you, monk?" said Father Ferapont. "Get up!"

The monk stood up.

"Blessing, be blessed! Sit with me. Where are you from?"

What surprised the monk the most was that despite Father Ferapont's strict fasting and old age, he still looked like a strong man. He was tall, stood up straight, and his face, though thin, looked fresh and healthy. There was no doubt that he still had a lot of strength. He was broad-shouldered. Despite his age, he wasn't entirely gray yet and still had thick hair and a full beard, which had once been black. His eyes were large, gray, and bright, but they stuck out noticeably. He spoke with a heavy accent. He wore a long reddish peasant's coat made from rough convict cloth (as it used to be called) and had a thick rope around his waist. His chest and throat were bare. Beneath his coat, his shirt, made from the roughest linen, looked almost black with dirt from not being changed in months. People said he wore irons weighing thirty pounds under his coat. His bare feet were stuck in old slippers that were falling apart.

"From the small Obdorsk monastery, from St. Sylvester," the monk answered humbly, while his sharp and curious, but rather frightened, little eyes stayed fixed on the hermit.

"I've been to your Sylvester's. I used to stay there. Is Sylvester doing well?"

The monk hesitated.

"You're a foolish bunch! How do you keep your fasts?"

"Our diet follows the old monastic rules. During Lent, we don't have meals on Monday, Wednesday, or Friday. On Tuesday and Thursday, we have white bread, fruit stewed with honey, wild berries, or salted cabbage and whole-grain porridge. On Saturday, we have cabbage soup, noodles with peas, and porridge, all with hemp oil. On weekdays, we have dried fish and porridge with cabbage soup. From Monday to Saturday night, during the six days of Holy Week, nothing is cooked, and we eat only bread and water, and even that sparingly, not eating every day if we can help it. This is the same as in the first week of Lent. On Good Friday, we eat nothing at all. In the same way, on Saturday, we fast until three o'clock and then eat a little bread and water and drink one cup of wine. On Holy Thursday, we drink wine and have something cooked without oil or uncooked, as the Laodicean council says for Holy Thursday: 'It is improper to dishonor the fast of Lent by breaking it on Holy Thursday.' That's how we keep our fast. But what is that compared to you, holy Father," added the monk, feeling more confident, "for you eat nothing but bread and water all year long, even at Easter. What we would eat in two days lasts you a full seven. Your great self-discipline is truly amazing."

"And mushrooms?" asked Father Ferapont suddenly. "Mushrooms?" repeated the surprised monk.

"Yes. I could give up their bread, not need it at all, and go live in the forest, eating mushrooms and berries, but they can't give up their bread here, and because of that, they are enslaved to the devil. Nowadays, the unclean deny the need for fasting. Arrogant and unclean is their thinking."

"Oh, very true," sighed the monk.

"And have you seen devils among them?" asked Ferapont. "Among them? Among whom?" the monk asked nervously.

"I went to the Father Superior on Trinity Sunday last year, but I haven't been back since. I saw a devil sitting on one man's chest, hiding under his cassock with only its horns sticking out. Another devil was peeking out from a monk's pocket, its sharp eyes full of fear when it saw me. One devil nestled in a man's belly, and another clung to a man's neck, riding along without him even noticing."

"You... can see spirits?" the monk asked cautiously.

"I tell you, I can see them as clear as day. When I left the Superior's cell, I spotted one hiding behind the door. It was huge—over a yard and a half tall—with a thick, long gray tail. The tip of its tail was stuck in the door's crack. I was quick and slammed the door on it. It squealed and squirmed, but I made the sign of the cross over it three times. It died right there, just like a crushed spider. It's probably still rotting in the corner, stinking, but no one notices it or smells it. That was a year ago. I'm telling you this because you're a stranger."

"Your words are frightening! But, holy Father," the monk pressed, growing bolder, "is it true, as people say even in distant places, that you're always in contact with the Holy Spirit?"

"He flies down sometimes," Father Ferapont replied. "How does He come down? What form does He take?" "As a bird."

"The Holy Spirit in the form of a dove?" the monk asked.

"There's the Holy Spirit, and there's the Holy Ghost. The Holy Spirit might appear as different birds—sometimes a swallow, other times a goldfinch, or even a blue tit."

"How do you know it's not just a regular bird?" the monk asked curiously.

"He speaks."

"In what language?" "In human language."

"What does He say to you?"

"Today, He told me that a fool would visit and ask me foolish questions. And here you are, monk."

The monk shook his head, unsettled. "Your words are terrifying, holy Father."

Father Ferapont paused, then pointed at a tree nearby. "Do you see that tree?"

"Yes, Father, I see it."

"You think it's just an elm. But at night, it changes."

"What does it turn into?" the monk asked after waiting for an answer.

"At night, those two branches become Christ, with His arms stretched out, reaching for me. I see Him, and I tremble. It's terrifying."

"Why is that frightening if it's Christ Himself?" the monk asked, confused.

"He might grab me and carry me away." "Alive?"

"Yes, like Elijah, taken up in glory. Haven't you heard? He could lift me in His arms and take me with Him."

The monk returned to the shared cell later that evening, his mind swirling with thoughts. Though he was deeply puzzled, he felt a greater respect for Father Ferapont than for Father Zossima. His admiration for fasting made it easier for him to believe that someone like Father Ferapont, who fasted so strictly, could witness miracles. The old monk's words had been strange, but who could know what truths lay hidden in them? Hadn't many saints performed acts and spoken words that seemed strange to the ordinary mind, all for the glory of God? He was ready to believe Father Ferapont's story about the devil's tail—both literally and figuratively.

Before coming to the monastery, the monk had already been skeptical of the institution of "elders." He had only heard of it from rumors and thought it was a dangerous innovation. During his time at the monastery, he noticed that some of the brothers secretly complained about the elders, which only reinforced his doubts. He had a curious and meddlesome nature, always poking into things, and this added to his confusion when he heard about Father Zossima's latest miracle. Alyosha later recalled how the inquisitive monk had wandered back and forth among the groups of monks, eavesdropping and asking questions as they gathered inside and outside the elder's cell. At the time, Alyosha hadn't paid much attention to him, but he remembered it afterward.

In truth, Alyosha had little time to think about the monk from Obdorsk. After Father Zossima, feeling tired again, returned to bed, he sent for Alyosha just as he was closing his eyes. Alyosha came running at once. Only Father Païssy, Father Iosif, and the novice Porfiry were with the elder. When Alyosha entered, Father Zossima opened his weary eyes and looked at him intently.

"Are your people expecting you, my son?" the elder asked suddenly.

Alyosha hesitated.

"Don't they need you? Didn't you promise someone you'd see them today?"

"I did promise… my father, my brothers, and some others too." "Then you must go. Don't be troubled. I promise, I won't die

before you come back to hear my final words. I will say them

to you alone—they'll be my last gift to you. You, my dear son, because you love me. But for now, go and keep your promise."

Even though it was hard for him to leave, Alyosha obeyed immediately. The thought that he would hear the elder's final words, that they would be a personal gift to him, filled Alyosha with joy. He hurried to finish his tasks in town so he could return as soon as possible. As they left the elder's cell together, Father Païssy spoke to Alyosha in a way that moved and surprised him deeply.

"Remember this always, young man," Father Païssy began without any introduction. "The science of this world has become powerful, especially over the past century. It has tried to analyze everything divine that was passed down to us in the holy scriptures. But after all their analysis, the scholars have stripped away what was sacred and left nothing behind. They study the parts, but they miss the whole picture. Their blindness is astonishing. The truth stands right before them, but they don't see it. Yet the truth still lives, and the gates of hell will not overcome it. Hasn't it lasted for nineteen centuries? Isn't it still alive and working in the hearts of individuals and entire communities? Even in the souls of those who reject it, Christianity remains strong. Many atheists who attack the faith still follow the ideals of Christ deep within themselves, even if they don't realize it. For all their cleverness, they haven't found a higher ideal of goodness and virtue than the one Christ gave us. Whenever they try, they end up with something ridiculous.

"Keep this in mind, young man, as you go out into the world. Your elder is sending you, and you'll need this knowledge to protect yourself. Remember my words—they come from the heart and are meant to guide you. The world's temptations are powerful, and you'll need strength to resist them. Now, go, my orphan."

With these words, Father Païssy blessed Alyosha. As Alyosha left the monastery, he thought over everything the monk had said. Suddenly, he realized that Father Païssy had become an unexpected friend and a kind mentor. Though the old monk had always seemed stern before, it now felt as if Father Zossima had entrusted him to Païssy's care. Perhaps that was exactly what had happened, Alyosha thought. The monk's unexpected advice reflected the warmth of his heart. It was clear that he wanted to prepare Alyosha for the struggles ahead and protect the young soul left in his care with the best wisdom he could offer.

Chapter 2: At His Father's

First, Alyosha went to his father. On the way, he remembered that his father had insisted the day before that he should come without his brother Ivan seeing him. "Why?" Alyosha wondered suddenly. "Even if my father has something to tell me in private, why should I sneak in? Most likely, in his excitement yesterday, he meant to say something different," he thought. Still, he was relieved when Marfa Ignatyevna, who opened the garden gate for him (Grigory was apparently sick in bed at the lodge), told him

that Ivan Fyodorovitch had gone out two hours earlier. "And my father?"

"He's up, having his coffee," Marfa answered a bit dryly.

Alyosha went inside. The old man was sitting alone at the table, wearing slippers and a worn-out overcoat. He was amusing himself by looking at some papers, but not paying much attention to them. He was all alone in the house since Smerdyakov had also gone out to the market. Though he had gotten up early and was trying to act tough, he looked tired and weak. His forehead, where large purple bruises had formed overnight, was wrapped in a red handkerchief. His nose had swollen terribly during the night, and smaller bruises dotted his face, giving him a particularly angry and irritable look. The old man knew this and shot a hostile glance at Alyosha as he entered.

"The coffee's cold," he barked. "I won't offer you any. I've only ordered Lenten fish soup today, and I'm not inviting anyone to share it. Why are you here?"

"I came to see how you are," Alyosha replied.

"Yeah, and besides, I told you to come yesterday. Doesn't matter though, you didn't need to bother. But I knew you'd come nosing around anyway."

He said this with nearly hostile energy. At the same time, he stood up and anxiously checked the mirror (maybe for the fortieth time that morning), inspecting his nose. He also started adjusting the red handkerchief on his forehead to make it look better.

"Red's better. A white one would make me look like I'm in the hospital," he muttered thoughtfully. "So, how are things over there? How's your elder?"

"He's very bad; he could die today," Alyosha answered. But his father hadn't been listening and had already forgotten his own question.

"Ivan's gone out," he said suddenly. "He's doing everything he can to steal Mitya's fiancée. That's why he's still hanging around," he added maliciously, twisting his mouth as he looked at Alyosha.

"Did he really tell you that?" Alyosha asked.

"Yes, he did, a long time ago. Can you believe it? He told me three weeks ago! Do you think he's come to kill me, too? He must have had a reason for coming."

"What do you mean? Why are you saying that?" Alyosha asked, troubled.

"It's true he hasn't asked me for money, but he won't get a cent from me. I plan on living as long as possible, you know that, my dear Alexey Fyodorovitch, so I need every penny, and the longer I live, the more I'll need it," he continued, pacing from one side of the room to the other, his hands stuffed into the pockets of his loose, greasy, yellow cotton overcoat. "I can still pass as a man at fifty-five, but I want to keep up the act for another twenty years. As I get older, you know, I won't be a pleasant sight. The girls won't come to me on their own, so I'll need my money. I'm saving it all for myself, my dear son Alexey Fyodorovitch, just so you know. I plan to continue in my sins until the end, let me tell you. Sin is sweet; everyone talks badly about it, but everyone lives in it. Others do it in secret, but I do it openly. That's why all the other sinners attack me for being honest. And your paradise, Alexey Fyodorovitch, it's not for me. I'll tell you that right now; it's not a place for a gentleman, your paradise, even if it exists. I believe I'll just fall asleep and never wake up again, and that's it. You can pray for my soul if you want, and if you don't, then don't, damn you! That's my philosophy. Ivan talked well yesterday, even though we were all drunk. Ivan is full of himself, but he's not particularly smart... or educated either. He just sits there, quiet, smiling at people without saying a word— that's how he gets by."

Alyosha listened silently.

"Why won't he talk to me? And when he does, he acts all high and mighty. Your Ivan is a scoundrel! And I'll marry Grushenka tomorrow if I want to. If you've got money, Alexey Fyodorovitch, all you need to do is want something, and it's yours. That's what Ivan is scared of; he's watching me to make sure I don't marry her. That's why he's pushing Mitya to marry Grushenka himself. He thinks he'll stop me from marrying her that way (as if I'd leave him any money if I don't marry her!). And if Mitya marries Grushenka, Ivan plans to run off with Mitya's rich fiancée. That's what he's counting on! He's a scoundrel, your Ivan!"

"How angry you are! It's because of yesterday; you should lie down," Alyosha said.

"There, you say that," the old man said suddenly, as though it had just occurred to him, "and I'm not mad at you. But if Ivan said it, I'd be furious. I only have good moments with you; otherwise, you know I'm a mean old man."

"You're not mean, just twisted," Alyosha said with a smile.

"Listen, I was planning this morning to get that thug Mitya locked up, but now I don't know what to do. Of course, these days, parents are seen as a nuisance, but even now, the law doesn't allow a son to drag his old father by the hair, kick him in the face in his own home, and brag about killing him right in front of witnesses. If I wanted to, I could crush him and get him locked up right now for what he did yesterday."

"Then you're not going to press charges?"

"Ivan talked me out of it. I wouldn't care about Ivan's opinion, but there's something else."

Leaning in closer to Alyosha, he continued in a confidential half-whisper.

"If I send that thug to prison, she'll hear about it and rush to see him. But if she hears that he nearly beat me to death, an old, weak man, maybe she'll leave him and come to me... because that's how she is, always doing the opposite of what you'd expect. I know her inside and out! Won't you have a little brandy? Take some cold coffee, and I'll pour a bit of brandy in it—it's delicious, my boy."

"No, thank you. I'll take that roll with me, if I may," Alyosha said, taking a small French roll and putting it in the pocket of his cassock. "And you probably shouldn't have any brandy either," he suggested carefully, watching the old man's face.

"You're right. It irritates my nerves instead of calming them. Just one little glass. I'll get it from the cupboard."

He unlocked the cupboard, poured himself a glass, drank it, then locked the cupboard again and put the key in his pocket.

"That's enough. One glass won't kill me."

"You see? You're already in a better mood," Alyosha said, smiling.

"Hmm. I love you, even without the brandy. But with scoundrels, I act like a scoundrel. Ivan isn't going to Tchermashnya—why is that? He wants to spy on how much I give Grushenka if she comes.

They're all scoundrels! But I don't know Ivan at all. Where did he even come from? He's not one of us. As if I'd leave him anything! I won't leave a will at all, just so you know. And I'll crush Mitya like a bug. I squash bugs with my slipper at night—they crunch when you step on them. And your Mitya will crunch too. Your Mitya, because you love him. Yes, you love him, and I'm not afraid of you loving him. But if Ivan loved him, I'd be scared for myself. But Ivan loves nobody. Ivan isn't one of us. People like Ivan are like dust. When the wind blows, the dust is gone... I had a silly thought when I told you to come today; I wanted to ask you about Mitya. If I gave him a thousand or maybe two thousand now, would that loser agree to disappear for five years or, even better, thirty-five, and give up Grushenka for good?"

"I—I'll ask him," Alyosha muttered. "If you gave him three thousand, maybe he—"

"That's nonsense! You don't need to ask him now; forget it! I've changed my mind. It was a stupid idea. I won't give him a single penny. I need my money," the old man cried, waving his hand. "I'll crush him like a bug without it. Don't say anything to him or he'll start hoping. There's nothing for you to do here, you can go. That fiancée of his, Katerina Ivanovna, the one he's been hiding from me, is she going to marry him or not? You went to see her yesterday, didn't you?"

"Nothing will make her leave him."

"You see how these proper young ladies adore a scoundrel and a rascal? They're pathetic, I tell you—those pale young women. They're nothing like—Ah, if I had his youth and the looks I once had (because I was better-looking than him at twenty-eight), I would've been a hero, winning hearts just like he is. But he's nothing but a low cad! And he won't have Grushenka, no, he won't! I'll crush him!"

His anger flared up again as he spoke those last words.

"There's nothing more for you to do here today," he barked. "You can go."

Alyosha walked over to say goodbye and kissed him lightly on the shoulder.

"What was that for?" his father asked, surprised. "Are you thinking we won't see each other again?"

"No, not at all. That wasn't what I meant."

"Nor did I mean anything by it," his father said, looking at him closely. "Listen—come back soon, all right? Next time, I'll make you a proper fish soup, a good one, not like today's. Be sure to come! Come tomorrow, do you hear? Tomorrow!"

As soon as Alyosha left, his father walked over to the cupboard and poured himself another half-glass of brandy.

"This is the last one," he muttered, clearing his throat. He locked the cupboard again and tucked the key into his pocket. Then he shuffled into his bedroom, lay down on the bed, and within a minute, he was sound asleep.

Chapter 3: A Meeting with The Schoolboys

"Thank goodness he didn't ask me about Grushenka,"

Alyosha thought as he left his father's house and headed toward Madame Hohlakov's. "Otherwise, I might've had to tell him about meeting her yesterday."

Alyosha felt troubled, realizing that both his father and Dmitri seemed more determined and angrier than the day before. "Father's angry and stubborn; he's come up with a plan, and he won't back down. And Dmitri— he's probably more fired up today too, angrier, with some scheme of his own. I need to find him today, no matter what."

But Alyosha didn't have much time to dwell on these thoughts. Something happened on the way that, though it seemed small, left a lasting impression on him. After crossing the square and turning the corner onto Mihailovsky Street, which was separated from the High Street by a small ditch (our town is full of ditches), he noticed a group of boys, about nine to twelve years old, gathered near a bridge. They were on their way home from school, carrying bags or leather satchels, some in short jackets and others in little coats. A few even wore fancy high boots with folds around the ankles—likely spoiled sons of wealthy parents. The boys were deep in conversation, huddled together as if holding a meeting.

Alyosha had always noticed children, even since his days in Moscow. Though he especially loved toddlers around three years old, he liked older schoolboys too. Despite the worries on his mind, he couldn't resist the urge to approach them. Their excited faces caught his attention, and he immediately saw that each boy was holding a stone.

On the other side of the ditch, about thirty paces away, stood another boy, also with a satchel slung at his side. He looked about ten years old, pale and thin, but his dark eyes sparkled with defiance. He kept a close watch on the group of boys, who were clearly his classmates. It was obvious that there was some kind of grudge between them.

Alyosha approached a rosy-cheeked boy with curly blond hair who was wearing a black jacket. "When I carried a satchel like yours," Alyosha said casually, "I always kept it on my left side, so I'd have my right hand free. But you've got yours on your right side. Won't that make it harder for you?"

There was no particular plan behind Alyosha's comment. He just knew instinctively that starting with a practical remark was the best way for an adult to connect with children, especially a group of them. It helped create an equal footing right away.

"But he's left-handed," another boy, a sturdy eleven-year-old, answered quickly. The other boys all turned to look at Alyosha.

"He even throws stones with his left hand," a third boy chimed in.

Just then, a stone flew from across the ditch. It barely missed the left-handed boy, but it had been thrown with force by the lone boy standing by the fence.

"Get him, Smurov! Hit him back!" the boys yelled. But Smurov, the left-handed boy, didn't need any encouragement. He quickly hurled a stone back, though it missed and hit the ground instead.

The boy on the other side of the ditch, whose coat pocket bulged with stones, threw another one. This time, it struck Alyosha hard on the shoulder.

"He aimed for you, Karamazov! That one was meant for you!" the boys shouted, laughing. "Let's all throw at him at once!"

Six stones flew toward the boy by the fence. One hit him on the head, knocking him down, but he jumped back up right away and started throwing stones fiercely in return. Both sides kept pelting each other with stones, and many of the boys had more stored in their pockets.

"What are you doing? Aren't you ashamed? Six against one! You'll hurt him!" Alyosha cried, running forward to shield the lone boy from the flying stones. A few of the boys stopped for a moment.

"He started it!" one boy in a red shirt shouted angrily. "He stabbed Krassotkin with a penknife in class the other day! There was blood, but Krassotkin didn't tattle on him. He needs to be punished!"

"Why? Do you pick on him?" Alyosha asked.

At that moment, another stone flew and hit Alyosha in the back. "See? He knows you!" the boys laughed. "He's throwing at you now, not us! Come on, hit him again, Smurov!"

The boys resumed their attack with even more fury. One stone hit the boy in the chest, making him cry out. He burst into tears and ran up the hill toward Mihailovsky Street.

"Aha! He's scared! He's running away! Wisp of tow!" the boys shouted, taunting him.

"You have no idea what a monster he is, Karamazov!" the oldest boy said, his eyes flashing. "Even killing him wouldn't be enough."

"What's so bad about him?" Alyosha asked. "Is he a tattletale or something?"

The boys exchanged amused glances, as if the question was silly.

"Are you going up Mihailovsky Street?" the older boy asked. "You'll catch up to him—he's stopped and is waiting for you."

"He's looking right at you!" the others chimed in.

"Ask him if he likes being called a 'wisp of tow.' Go on, ask him!"

The boys burst into laughter. Alyosha looked at them, then back at the boy standing in the distance.

"Don't go near him! He'll hurt you!" Smurov warned.

"I won't ask him about the 'wisp of tow.' I'm sure you use that to tease him somehow," Alyosha said. "But I'll find out why you hate him so much."

"Go ahead! Find out!" the boys laughed.

Alyosha crossed the bridge and climbed the hill, walking straight toward the boy by the fence.

"Watch out!" one of the boys called after him. "He won't be scared of you! He'll stab you, just like he did Krassotkin!"

The boy didn't move as Alyosha approached. He was small and thin, about nine years old, with a pale face and large, angry dark eyes. His old, worn-out coat was far too small for him, and his bare arms stuck out past the sleeves. There was a big patch on the right knee of his pants, and his right boot had a hole in the toe, carefully blackened with ink to make it less noticeable. Both of his coat pockets bulged with stones.

Alyosha stopped a few steps away, studying him quietly. The boy, seeing that Alyosha wasn't going to hurt him, lowered his guard a little and spoke first.

"I'm all alone, and there are six of them. But I'll fight them all by myself!" he said fiercely, his dark eyes flashing.

"One of those stones must've hurt you pretty badly," Alyosha said gently.

"But I hit Smurov on the head!" the boy said with pride.

"The other boys told me you knew who I was and threw a stone at me on purpose," Alyosha said.

The boy's expression darkened. "I don't know you," he muttered. "Do you know me?" Alyosha asked again.

"Leave me alone!" the boy snapped irritably. But he didn't move, as if waiting for something, and the anger in his eyes flickered again.

"All right, I'm going," Alyosha said. "I just wanted you to know that I don't tease you. The others told me how they tease you, but I have no interest in doing that. Goodbye."

"Monk in silk trousers!" the boy shouted after Alyosha, his face still full of spite and defiance. He dropped into a defensive stance, convinced Alyosha would come at him now. But Alyosha only glanced back at him and kept walking. He had taken no more than three steps when the largest stone from the boy's pocket struck him hard in the back.

"So you hit people from behind! They weren't lying when they said you fight dirty," Alyosha said, turning around. The boy responded by hurling another stone, this time aiming right at Alyosha's face. Alyosha managed to block it, but the stone slammed into his elbow instead.

"Aren't you ashamed? What did I ever do to you?" Alyosha cried out.

The boy stood silently, still glaring at him, waiting for Alyosha to attack. When Alyosha didn't, the boy's anger exploded like that of a wild animal. He lunged at Alyosha and, before Alyosha could react, grabbed his left hand with both of his own and bit down hard on Alyosha's middle finger. The boy sank his teeth into the finger near the nail, clamping down for a full ten seconds before letting go. Alyosha cried out in pain, pulling his hand back with all his strength.

Finally, the boy released his grip and stepped back to where he had been standing before. Blood welled from the deep bite on Alyosha's finger. He pulled out a handkerchief and wrapped it tightly around the wound, taking a full minute to finish. The boy stood still the entire time, watching him in silence.

When Alyosha was done, he looked up at the boy with the same calm expression. "All right," he said gently. "You've bitten me pretty badly. Isn't that enough? Now, tell me—what did I do to you?"

The boy stared back at him in shock.

"Even though I don't know you, and this is the first time we've ever met," Alyosha continued, speaking just as calmly, "I must have done something to you. You wouldn't have hurt me like this for no reason. So what did I do? How have I wronged you? Tell me."

Instead of answering, the boy burst into loud, tearful sobs. Then, without another word, he turned and ran off. Alyosha slowly followed him, heading toward Mihailovsky Street. For a long time, he could see the boy running ahead in the distance, still crying and not looking back even once. Alyosha decided that as soon as he had time, he would find the boy and get to the bottom of this strange encounter. But for now, he had other things to take care of.

Chapter 4: At The Hohlakovs'

Alyosha soon arrived at Madame Hohlakov's house, a grand two-story stone building, one of the finest in our town. Although Madame Hohlakov usually spent most of her time in another province, where she had an estate, or in Moscow, where she owned a house, she also had a house in our town, inherited from her forefathers. The estate in our district was the largest of her three estates, yet she had spent very little time in our province before now. She ran out to meet Alyosha in the hall.

"Did you get my letter about the new miracle?" she asked quickly, sounding nervous.

"Yes," Alyosha replied.

"Did you show it to everyone? He brought the son back to his mother!"

"He's dying today," Alyosha said.

"I heard, I know. Oh, how I wish I could talk to you—or someone—about all of this. No, it has to be you! And I'm so sad I can't see him! The whole town is in suspense. But guess what— do you know Katerina Ivanovna is here now?"

"Ah, that's great," Alyosha exclaimed. "Then I'll see her here. She told me yesterday to make sure I came by today."

"I know, I know everything. I heard exactly what happened yesterday—and the awful behavior of that— creature. It's tragic, and if I were in her shoes, I don't know what I would have done. And your brother Dmitri Fyodorovitch—what do you think of him? My goodness! Oh, Alexey Fyodorovitch, I almost forgot— your brother Ivan Fyodorovitch is in there with her right now, not the dreadful one from yesterday. They're having a serious conversation. If you could only imagine what's happening between them—it's terrible! It's like a horror story. They're ruining their lives, and for no reason anyone can understand. They both know it, but they can't stop. I've been waiting for you! I've been dying to see you! It's all too much for me. But I have to tell you something else, something more important—I almost forgot the most important thing! Tell me, why has Lise been having hysterics? As soon as she heard you were here, she started having a fit!"

"Maman, you're the one being hysterical now, not me," Lise's voice came through a tiny crack in the door at the side. Her voice sounded like she was trying not to laugh. Alyosha immediately noticed the crack and realized Lise was peeking through it, though he couldn't see her.

"No wonder, Lise, no wonder... your capricious behavior will make me hysterical too! But she's been so sick, Alexey Fyodorovitch — so ill all night, with a fever and moaning! I could barely wait for morning and for Herzenstube to come. He says he can't figure it out and that we'll have to wait. Herzenstube always says he can't figure it out. As soon as you got near the house, she screamed, had a fit, and demanded to be wheeled into this room."

"Mamma, I didn't know he was coming. It wasn't because of him that I asked to be wheeled in here," Lise said.

"That's not true, Lise! Yulia ran to tell you that Alexey Fyodorovitch was coming. You were watching for him."

"My dear mamma, that's not clever at all. But if you want to make up for it and say something clever, you should tell our guest, Alexey Fyodorovitch, that he's made a big mistake coming here after everything that happened yesterday, especially since everyone's laughing at him."

"Lise, you've gone too far. I'll have to be strict with you. Who's laughing at him? I'm glad he came—I need him, I can't do without him. Oh, Alexey Fyodorovitch, I'm so miserable!"

"But why, mamma, what's wrong?" Lise asked.

"Your capriciousness, Lise, your restlessness, your illness, that awful night with the fever, and that never-ending Herzenstube— it's all too much! Even the miracle! It's shaken me so much, Alexey Fyodorovitch! And then the drama happening in the drawing room—it's more than I can handle. I can't bear it. Maybe it's more of a comedy than a tragedy. Tell me, will Father Zossima live until tomorrow? Oh, my God! What's happening to me?

Every minute I close my eyes, and I feel like it's all nonsense, all of it."

"I would really appreciate it," Alyosha interrupted suddenly, "if you could give me a clean rag to wrap my finger. I hurt it, and it's very painful."

Alyosha unwrapped his bitten finger, which was bleeding badly. The handkerchief was soaked with blood. Madame Hohlakov screamed and shut her eyes.

"Heavens, what a terrible wound!"

As soon as Lise saw Alyosha's finger through the crack, she threw the door wide open.

"Come here!" she demanded. "No more fooling around! Good grief, why didn't you say something about it earlier? You could have bled to death, mamma! How did this happen? Water! You need to wash it first—just hold it in cold water to stop the pain. Keep it there, don't take it out. Hurry, mamma, get some water in a basin! But hurry!" she finished nervously, clearly alarmed by Alyosha's wound.

"Should we send for Herzenstube?" Madame Hohlakov asked. "Mamma, you'll be the death of me. Herzenstube will just say he can't figure it out! Water! Mamma, go yourself and tell Yulia to hurry up! She's so slow, she never gets anything done quickly. Hurry, mamma, or I'll die."

"It's not that bad," Alyosha said, alarmed by the fuss.

Yulia ran in with water, and Alyosha dipped his finger into it.

"Get some lint, mamma, and that antiseptic solution. What's it called? We've got some! You know where it is, in your bedroom cupboard. There's a big bottle of it in the right-hand side with the lint."

"I'll bring it all in a minute, Lise, but stop yelling and fussing. Look at how bravely Alexey Fyodorovitch is handling it. How did you get such a terrible wound, Alexey Fyodorovitch?"

Madame Hohlakov hurried away. Lise had been waiting for this moment.

"First of all, tell me how you got hurt like this," she asked Alyosha quickly. "Then I'll talk to you about something else. Well?"

Knowing that her mother's absence was a rare moment of privacy, Alyosha quickly told her about his strange encounter with the schoolboys, summarizing it briefly. Lise clasped her hands in surprise.

"How can you—dressed like that—be hanging out with schoolboys?" she asked angrily, as if she had the right to control him. "You're just a boy yourself if you do things like that—a complete child! But you must find out more about that horrible boy and tell me everything. There's something mysterious about it. Now for the second thing, but first—does your pain stop you from talking about silly, unimportant things?"

"Not at all, and it doesn't hurt much now," Alyosha said.

"That's because your finger is in the water. We'll need to change it soon before it gets warm. Yulia, bring some ice from the cellar and another bowl of water. Now that she's gone, I can talk. Will you give me back the letter I sent you yesterday, dear Alexey Fyodorovitch? Hurry, before mamma comes back—I don't want her to see."

"I don't have the letter."

"That's not true—you do. I knew you'd say that. It's in your pocket. I've been regretting that joke all night. Give me the letter back right now. Hand it over."

"I left it at home."

"But you can't treat me like a child after that silly joke! I'm sorry for the joke, but you have to bring me the letter. If you don't have it now, bring it today—you must, you must."

"Today I can't possibly stay because I'm going back to the monastery, and I won't be able to visit for the next two or three days—maybe even four—because of Father Zossima," Alyosha explained.

"Four days? That's ridiculous! Tell me, did you laugh at me a lot?" Lise asked.

"I didn't laugh at all." "Why not?"

"Because I believed everything you said."

"Now you're insulting me!"

"Not at all. As soon as I read your letter, I thought it would all happen, because when Father Zossima dies, I'll have to leave the monastery. Then I'll go back to finish my studies, and once you're of age, we'll get married. I'll love you. I haven't had much time to think about it, but I'm sure I couldn't find a better wife than you. And Father Zossima says I should get married."

"But I'm a cripple, stuck in a wheelchair," Lise laughed, blushing deeply.

"I'll push you around myself, but I'm sure you'll be better by then."

"You're crazy," Lise said nervously. "You're turning all this nonsense into something serious! Oh, here comes mamma, just in time. Mamma, why are you always so slow? How can you take so long? And here's Yulia with the ice!"

"Oh, Lise, don't scream, please don't scream. That scream drives me mad. How can I help it when you keep moving the lint? I've been searching everywhere—I bet you did it on purpose."

"How could I have known he would come with a hurt finger? Maybe I would've done it on purpose then. My dear mamma, you're finally saying something clever!"

"Never mind my being clever, but I must say, you're not showing much concern for Alexey Fyodorovitch's pain! Oh, Alexey Fyodorovitch, what's wearing me down isn't just Herzenstube, but everything at once—that's what's too much for me."

"That's enough, mamma, enough about Herzenstube," Lise laughed cheerfully. "Hurry up with the lint and the lotion, mamma. That's Goulard's water, Alexey Fyodorovitch—I remember the name now, and it's a great lotion. Can you believe it, mamma? On his way here, he got into a fight with some boys in the street, and one of them bit his finger. Isn't he just a child himself? Is he really ready to get married after something like that? Just imagine, he wants to get married, mamma. Wouldn't it be funny? Or maybe terrible?"

Lise kept laughing her high-pitched, nervous giggle, sneaking glances at Alyosha.

"But why are you talking about marriage, Lise? Where did that come from? And what if the boy was rabid?"

"Mamma! As if there were such a thing as rabid boys!"

"Why not, Lise? It's not like I said something stupid. Your boy might have been bitten by a mad dog, and he'd go mad and bite anyone nearby. Look how well she bandaged it, Alexey Fyodorovitch! I couldn't have done it that nicely. Do you still feel the pain?"

"It's much better now."

"You're not afraid of water, are you?" Lise teased.

"That's enough, Lise. Maybe I was too quick to say the boy might've been rabid, and you jumped on it right away. Katerina Ivanovna just heard that you're here, Alexey Fyodorovitch. She came rushing to me, she's dying to see you!"

"Oh, mamma, go see her yourself. He can't go now; he's still in pain."

"Not at all, I can go," Alyosha said.

"What? You're leaving already?" Lise asked.

"Well, after I see them, I'll come back, and we can talk as much as you like. But I really want to see Katerina Ivanovna now, and I need to return to the monastery as soon as I can."

"Mamma, take him away quickly. Alexey Fyodorovitch, don't bother coming back to see me after; just go straight to your monastery. I want to sleep. I didn't sleep at all last night."

"Oh, Lise, you're just teasing, but how I wish you would sleep," Madame Hohlakov said.

"I don't know what I've done.   I'll stay another three minutes, or five if you want," Alyosha muttered.

"Even five! Mamma, take him away quickly; he's a monster."

"Lise, you're impossible. Let's go, Alexey Fyodorovitch. She's too moody today. I'm afraid of crossing her. Oh, the struggles we have with nervous girls! Maybe she really will sleep after seeing you. Look how quickly you've made her tired—how fortunate!"

"Oh, mamma, how sweet you are! I have to kiss you for that."

"And I'll kiss you too, Lise. Listen, Alexey Fyodorovitch," Madame Hohlakov began mysteriously, lowering her voice to a quick whisper. "I don't want to suggest anything, I'm not trying to lift the veil. You'll see for yourself what's going on. It's shocking. It's a complete farce. She loves your brother Ivan, but she's trying to convince herself that she loves your brother Dmitri. It's awful! I'll go in with you, and if they don't kick me out, I'll stay until the end."

Chapter 5: A Laceration in The Drawing Room

When Alyosha and Madame Hohlakov entered the drawing room, the conversation had already ended. Katerina Ivanovna was visibly agitated, but she appeared resolute. At the moment Alyosha and Madame Hohlakov came in, Ivan Fyodorovitch was standing up, ready to leave. His face was rather pale, and Alyosha looked at him with concern. This moment was critical for Alyosha, as it would answer a troubling question that had haunted him for some time. Throughout the past month, several people had suggested that his brother Ivan was in love with Katerina Ivanovna, and more than that, that he intended to "take her away" from Dmitri. Up until recently, this idea seemed monstrous to Alyosha, though it worried him deeply. He loved both his brothers and dreaded the thought of such rivalry between them.

Meanwhile, Dmitri had said openly the day before that he was glad Ivan was his rival, and that it actually helped him, Dmitri, in some way. But how could it help him? To marry Grushenka? To Alyosha, that seemed the worst possible outcome. Furthermore, until the previous evening, Alyosha had fully believed that Katerina Ivanovna had a steady and passionate love for Dmitri. He had also thought she could never love a man like Ivan, and that her love for Dmitri was genuine, despite how strange it might seem.

But during the scene with Grushenka the day before, Alyosha had been struck by another thought. The word "lacerating," which Madame Hohlakov had just spoken, nearly startled him, because while half-awake at dawn that morning, he had cried out the word "Laceration, laceration," likely in response to his dream. He had dreamt all night about the previous day's events at Katerina Ivanovna's. Now, Madame Hohlakov's blunt and persistent claim that Katerina Ivanovna was in love with Ivan, but deceiving herself with some sense of "self-laceration" and torturing herself with a fake love for Dmitri out of a misplaced duty of gratitude, made Alyosha think that perhaps the truth lay in those words. "Yes," he thought, "maybe that is the real truth." But then, what did that mean for Ivan? Alyosha instinctively felt that Katerina Ivanovna's strong-willed character could only dominate someone like Dmitri, but never someone like Ivan. Dmitri might eventually accept her domination and perhaps even find happiness in it (which was what Alyosha hoped), but Ivan would never submit to her, and such submission would never make him happy. Alyosha was certain of this when it came to Ivan.

And now, all these doubts and reflections raced through Alyosha's mind as he entered the drawing room. Another thought suddenly forced its way into his mind: "What if she doesn't love either of them—neither Ivan nor Dmitri?"

It should be noted that Alyosha felt ashamed of these thoughts and often blamed himself for repeatedly thinking them over the past month. "What do I know about love or women, and how can I possibly judge such things?" he reproached himself whenever such doubts surfaced. Yet, he couldn't stop thinking about it. He had a strong sense that this rivalry between his brothers was of immense importance in their lives, and that much depended on its outcome.

"One snake will devour the other," Ivan had said the day before, angrily referring to their father and Dmitri. So Ivan saw Dmitri as a "snake," and perhaps had seen him this way for some time. Could it have started when Ivan first met Katerina Ivanovna? That phrase, spoken unthinkingly by Ivan, carried greater significance because of its unintended honesty. If Ivan truly felt this way, how could there ever be peace between them? Instead, it seemed that their family had more reasons for hatred and conflict. Whose side should Alyosha take? What should he wish for each of them? He loved both his brothers deeply, but what could he desire for each of them amidst all these conflicting emotions and interests? Alyosha feared he could lose his way in this tangled maze of feelings. His heart couldn't endure such uncertainty because his love was always active. He was incapable of passive love. If Alyosha loved someone, he would immediately set out to help them. But in order to help them, he needed to know for sure what was best for each person, and once he knew, he would naturally try to help them both. But instead of a clear goal, all he found was confusion and uncertainty. "It's lacerating," as Madame Hohlakov had just said. But what did he even understand about this "laceration"? He didn't even understand the first thing about this perplexing situation.

When Katerina Ivanovna saw Alyosha, she immediately and joyfully said to Ivan, who was already standing to leave, "Wait! Stay just a minute longer! I want to hear the opinion of someone I trust completely." She glanced at Alyosha. "Don't leave yet," she added, turning to Madame Hohlakov. She made Alyosha sit beside her, and Madame Hohlakov took a seat opposite them, next to Ivan.

"You are all my dear friends here—the only friends I have in the world," Katerina Ivanovna began warmly, her voice trembling with genuine emotion, and Alyosha's heart was moved by her sincerity. "Alexey Fyodorovitch, you were there yesterday and saw that horrible scene, you saw everything I did. Ivan Fyodorovitch didn't see it, but you did. I don't know what Ivan Fyodorovitch thought of me yesterday, but I know one thing: if the same thing were to happen again today, right this minute, I would act the same way. I would say and do the exact same things. You remember what I did, Alexey Fyodorovitch? You stopped me at one point..." As she said this, her cheeks flushed and her eyes shone brightly. "I can't seem to get past it. Listen, Alexey Fyodorovitch. I don't even know if I still love him. I feel pity for him, and that's a bad sign for love. If I loved him—if I truly loved him—then maybe I wouldn't feel sorry for him right now. I might even hate him."

Her voice shook, and tears glistened on her eyelashes. Alyosha felt a tremor within himself. "She's honest, she's telling the truth," he thought, "and she no longer loves Dmitri."

"That's exactly right!" cried Madame Hohlakov.

"Wait, my dear, I haven't told you the most important thing yet—the final decision I made last night. I believe this decision may be terrible for me, but I feel certain that I won't change my mind—nothing will make me change it. This is how things will be for the rest of my life. My dear, kind, loyal, and wise friend, Ivan Fyodorovitch, who understands the human heart so well, approves of my decision. He knows everything."

"Yes, I do approve of it," Ivan said quietly but firmly.

"But I also want Alyosha to tell me—Ah! Alexey Fyodorovitch, please forgive me for calling you just 'Alyosha,'" she said, smiling warmly. "I want Alexey Fyodorovitch to tell me in front of my two friends whether I'm doing the right thing. I feel in my heart that you, Alyosha, my dear brother (because you are like a brother to me)," she said again with great emotion, taking his cold hand in her hot one, "I feel that your approval, your decision, will bring me peace, no matter how much I suffer. After hearing your words, I will be calm and accept my decision—I'm sure of it."

"I don't know what you're asking me," Alyosha replied, blushing. "I only know that I care about you and right now I want your happiness more than my own!... But I don't know anything about matters like this," he added quickly.

"In matters like this, Alexey Fyodorovitch, the most important things are honor, duty, and something even higher—though I don't know what it is, but it's higher than duty. I feel this overwhelming sense of duty in my heart, and I cannot resist it. But really, it all boils down to this: I've already decided that even if he marries that... creature"—she said with emphasis—"whom I will never, ever forgive, I still won't abandon him. From now on, I will never, ever abandon him!" she cried, her voice growing more emotional. "But that doesn't mean I'll constantly follow him around, bothering him. Oh no! I'll move away to another town— any town—but I will watch over him for the rest of my life. When he becomes unhappy with her, which is bound to happen soon, he can come to me. He will find a friend, a sister... only a sister, of course, but always a sister. And he will realize that I'm truly his sister, who loves him and has sacrificed her entire life for him. I will make sure of that. I'll make him understand me, make him trust me completely, without holding anything back," she cried, almost in a fevered state. "I will be like a god to him, someone he can pray to—and that's the least he owes me after his betrayal and the pain he put me through yesterday. He will see that I will be faithful to him my whole life, keeping my promise, even though he was unfaithful and betrayed me. I will... I will become nothing but an instrument for his happiness—or how should I put it?—a machine for his happiness, for my entire life, and he will see that for the rest of his life!" she declared passionately. "That's my decision, and Ivan Fyodorovitch completely agrees with me."

She was breathless after speaking. She had probably intended to express herself with more composure and grace, but her words had come out rushed and awkward, revealing the rawness of her emotions. It was clear that she was still deeply hurt by the events of the previous day, and her pride demanded some form of redemption. She became aware of this shift in herself. Her face suddenly darkened, and an unpleasant expression appeared in her eyes. Alyosha immediately noticed the change and felt a wave of sympathy for her. His brother Ivan only made things worse by adding...

"I've only expressed my own opinion," he said. "If someone else had said this, it might have sounded fake or exaggerated, but not from you. Any other woman would have been wrong, but you're right. I can't quite explain why, but I see that you are completely sincere, and that's why you are right."

"But that's just for now. And what does this moment even mean? It's nothing but yesterday's insult," Madame Hohlakov remarked. Although she hadn't planned to interrupt, she couldn't resist making this fair point.

"Exactly, exactly," Ivan exclaimed eagerly, though he was obviously irritated by the interruption. "For someone else, this moment would only be a passing reaction to yesterday's events. But with Katerina Ivanovna, it will stay with her forever. What would be a simple promise to someone else becomes, for her, a constant and heavy duty—a serious obligation. And she will draw strength from knowing that she is fulfilling it. From now on, Katerina Ivanovna, your life will be filled with endless thoughts about your own feelings, your own bravery, and your own suffering. But in time, that suffering will soften and turn into a quiet satisfaction as you reflect on the bold and proud plan you've carried out. Yes, proud—and maybe reckless, too. But it will be your triumph. And knowing that will eventually bring you peace and help you accept everything else."

Ivan's words were clearly laced with malice, and he made no effort to hide the sarcasm in his tone.

"Oh dear, how completely wrong that is!" Madame Hohlakov cried out again.

"Alexey Fyodorovich, I really want to know what you think!" Katerina Ivanovna exclaimed, bursting into tears. Alyosha stood up from the sofa.

"It's nothing, really," she said through her tears. "I'm just upset. I didn't sleep at all last night. But with two friends like you and your brother by my side, I feel strong—I know you two will never leave me."

"Unfortunately, I have to return to Moscow, maybe even tomorrow. And I'll have to stay away for a long time," Ivan said suddenly.

"To Moscow—tomorrow?" Katerina's face twisted with emotion. "But—wait! That's wonderful!" she suddenly exclaimed in a completely different voice. In an instant, there was no trace of her tears left. Alyosha watched, amazed, as she changed from a weeping, hurt young woman into someone calm and even cheerful, as though something good had just happened.

"Oh, not wonderful because I'm losing you, of course not," she quickly added, flashing a charming, polite smile. "A friend like you wouldn't think that. I'll be terribly unhappy to lose you." She rushed over to Ivan, grabbed both his hands, and squeezed them warmly. "But it is wonderful that you'll be in Moscow and can see Auntie and Agafya. You can tell them everything about how miserable things are for me right now. You can be completely open with Agafya, but please be gentle with Auntie. You'll know how to handle it. You can't imagine how anxious I've been, trying to figure out how to write them such an awful letter—some things just can't be put into words on paper. But now that you'll see them in person, it'll be much easier for me to write. Oh, I'm so relieved! But it's only because of that, believe me. Of course, no one could ever take your place." She ended her speech abruptly and started to walk toward the door, as though she were going to leave the room.

"And what about Alyosha? Didn't you say you were desperate to hear what he thought?" Madame Hohlakov called out, her voice sharp with sarcasm and frustration.

"I haven't forgotten!" Katerina Ivanovna exclaimed, stopping suddenly. "And why are you being so hostile right now?" she added, her voice full of hurt and frustration. "What I said still stands. I need his opinion. In fact, I need his decision! Whatever he says, that's what I'll do. You can see how much I care about your words, Alexey Fyodorovich... But what's wrong?"

"I just can't believe it. I don't understand!" Alyosha cried out, his voice filled with distress.

"What? What do you mean?" Katerina asked urgently.

"He's leaving for Moscow, and you said you were glad. You said that on purpose! Then you tried to explain that you weren't really happy, only sad to lose him as a friend. But even that was an act— it was like something out of a play!"

"A play? What are you saying?" Katerina asked, shocked. Her face flushed with embarrassment, and she frowned deeply.

"You say you'll miss him, but at the same time, you're telling him it's good that he's leaving. You're not being honest," Alyosha said, his voice trembling as he stood by the table, refusing to sit down.

"What do you mean? I don't understand."

"I don't fully understand it either," Alyosha admitted, his voice shaky. "It just hit me suddenly... I know I'm not explaining it well, but I have to say it anyway. I think... maybe you never really loved Dmitri. Maybe you never loved him from the start. And Dmitri... he never loved you either. He just respects you. I don't know how I dare to say this, but someone needs to tell the truth— because no one else will."

"What truth?" Katerina demanded, her voice shaky and filled with hysteria.

"I'll tell you," Alyosha said quickly, as though he were leaping off a cliff. "Call Dmitri here. I'll bring him. Let him take your hand and Ivan's hand and let the two of you hold hands. You're hurting Ivan because you love him. And you're hurting yourself by pretending to love Dmitri—it's not real. You've just convinced yourself that it is."

Alyosha stopped speaking, his words hanging heavily in the room.

"You... You... You're nothing but a little religious fool!" Katerina snapped angrily, her face pale, her lips trembling with rage.

Ivan suddenly burst out laughing and stood up, holding his hat in his hand.

"You are mistaken, my dear Alyosha," Ivan said, with an expression Alyosha had never seen on his face before—a look of youthful sincerity and overwhelming, genuine emotion. "Katerina Ivanovna has never loved me! She always knew that I loved her—though I never said a word about it—she knew all along, but she never cared. I was never really her friend, not even for a moment. She's too proud to need my friendship. She only kept me by her side to use me as part of her revenge. She took out all the insults and humiliations she has suffered from Dmitri on me, and she used me to get back at him. Ever since the day they first met, she's carried that moment like a wound in her heart, nursing it like an insult—that's just the kind of person she is! All she ever talked to me about was her love for him, over and over.

"I'm leaving now, but, believe me, Katerina Ivanovna, you really do love him. The more he insults you, the more you love him— that's the nature of your suffering. You love him exactly the way he is, with all his flaws. You even love him because he hurts you. If he ever changed—if he became a better man—you'd stop loving him. You need him to stay the same so you can always feel like you are the noble, faithful one, holding onto your sense of pride, while blaming him for being unfaithful. That's where it all comes from—your pride. Yes, there's humiliation and even some self-abasement in it, but at its core, it's still your pride.

"I'm too young, and I've loved you too deeply. I know I shouldn't be saying all this—it would have been more dignified for me to leave quietly, and it would have spared you some pain. But I'm going far away, and I won't be coming back. This is goodbye forever. I can't sit beside your misery anymore, watching you suffer. I don't even know how to say this properly. But I've said everything now... Goodbye, Katerina Ivanovna. You can't be angry with me. I've been punished far more than you—just knowing I'll never see you again is punishment enough. Goodbye. I won't take your hand. You've hurt me too deliberately for me to forgive you right now. I will forgive you later, but not now. Right now, I can't take your hand."

With a forced smile, he added, "Den Dank, Dame, begehr ich nicht," quoting Schiller by heart—something that Alyosha would never have imagined Ivan capable of doing. Without saying another word, Ivan turned and left the room, not even offering a farewell to Madame Hohlakov. Alyosha clasped his hands together.

"Ivan!" he cried out desperately. "Come back, Ivan! No, he won't come back now," Alyosha whispered sadly, realizing that it was hopeless. "It's all my fault. I started this! Ivan spoke out of anger—he was wrong, unfair, and angry, but it's my fault. He must come back! He has to come back!" Alyosha kept repeating, frantic with guilt.

Katerina Ivanovna suddenly stepped into the next room, disappearing behind the door.

"You did nothing wrong. You behaved beautifully, like an angel," Madame Hohlakov whispered eagerly to Alyosha. "I will do everything in my power to stop Ivan Fyodorovitch from leaving."

Her face shone with excitement, but Alyosha only felt more troubled. A moment later, Katerina Ivanovna returned, holding two 200-rouble notes in her hand.

"I have a favor to ask of you, Alexey Fyodorovitch," she began, speaking in a calm, even voice, as if nothing unusual had happened. "A week ago—yes, I think it was a week—Dmitri Fyodorovitch behaved terribly. He did something disgraceful. There is a low tavern in town, and while he was there, he ran into an officer—someone your father used to hire for business. Dmitri lost his temper, grabbed the officer by the beard, and dragged him out into the street, pulling him along in that humiliating way. The officer's young son—a little boy from the school here—saw everything. The boy ran beside them, crying and begging for someone to help his father, but everyone just laughed. I can't think about it without feeling disgusted—it was such a shameful act. Only Dmitri, with his wild anger, could do something like that.

"I found out that the officer's name is Snegiryov, and he's fallen into terrible poverty. He was dismissed from the army for some offense—though I don't know the full story—and now his family is in complete ruin. His children are sick, and I've heard that his wife has gone mad. He used to work as a copying clerk, but now he earns nothing. I wanted to ask if you could visit him for me. Find a reason to see him—oh, I'm explaining this so poorly! What I mean is, please bring him these 200 roubles. You'll know how to give it to him in a way that won't offend him." Alyosha blushed deeply.

"I think he'll accept the money if you approach him the right way. This isn't a bribe to stop him from taking legal action—he may still plan to—but rather a small gesture of kindness, from me, as Dmitri Fyodorovitch's fiancée. It's not from Dmitri—it's from me. I thought of going myself, but I know you'll do it much better. He lives on Lake Street, in a house owned by a woman named Kalmikov. Please, Alexey Fyodorovitch, do this for me. I'm feeling rather tired now. Goodbye."

Before Alyosha could reply, she slipped behind the curtain and disappeared. He wanted to say something—to apologize, to blame himself—but he couldn't. His heart was too heavy, and the words wouldn't come. He couldn't bear to leave without speaking, but Madame Hohlakov took his hand and led him from the room. In the hall, she stopped him again.

"She's so proud, fighting her feelings, but she's also kind, generous, and wonderful," Madame Hohlakov whispered. "Oh, how much I admire her! And I'm so happy with how everything is turning out. Did you know? All of us—her aunts, Lise, and I—we've been hoping for the past month that she would give up Dmitri. He doesn't love her, and she knows it. We've been praying she'd marry Ivan Fyodorovitch instead. He's such a good, cultured young man, and he loves her more than anything. I even stayed longer to help make it happen."

"But she was crying—she's hurt again," Alyosha said, full of sorrow.

"Never trust a woman's tears, Alexey Fyodorovitch. In situations like these, I always side with the men."

"Mama, you're spoiling him!" Lise's voice came from behind the door.

"No, it's all my fault. I behaved terribly," Alyosha said, covering his face with his hands, consumed with guilt.

"Not at all! You acted like an angel — an absolute angel! I'd say it a thousand times over."

"Mama, how exactly did he act like an angel?" Lise called out again.

"I suddenly felt that she loved Ivan, so I said something stupid. What's going to happen now?" Alyosha wondered aloud, his voice trembling.

"To whom? To whom?" Lise demanded impatiently. "Mama, you'll drive me mad if you don't tell me!"

Just then, the maid came rushing in.

"Katerina Ivanovna is having a fit—she's crying and thrashing!"

"What's wrong with her?" Lise asked, suddenly alarmed. "Mama, I'll end up having a fit too!"

"Lise, please stop shouting! You're too young to understand everything. I'll explain later. Oh, dear, I'm coming, I'm coming! Alexey Fyodorovitch, it's actually a good sign—these fits and tears are perfectly normal. I always distrust women's tears, but this is exactly what should happen. Go tell her I'll be there soon, Yulia. It's her own fault Ivan left, but he won't stay away. Lise, stop shouting—oh wait, it's me who's shouting! Forgive me, dear! I'm just so happy. Did you see how young Ivan Fyodorovitch looked just now, Alyosha? I always thought he was so serious, but he acted so warm and open, with such youthful energy. It was wonderful—just like you! And the way he recited that German verse—it was exactly like something you would do! But I must hurry, I must hurry! Alexey Fyodorovitch, please take care of her request, and come back quickly. Lise, do you need anything? Please, don't hold him up—he'll come back right away."

At last, Madame Hohlakov rushed off. Alyosha started to open the door to check on Lise.

"Don't you dare!" Lise called out. "Just talk to me through the door. How did you become such an angel? That's all I want to know."

"Because I did something really foolish, Lise! Goodbye!" "Don't leave like that!" Lise started to protest.

"Lise, I have real sorrow to deal with! I'll be back soon, but I have a great, great sorrow right now!"

And with that, he ran out of the room.

Chapter 6: A Laceration in The Cottage

He was truly upset in a way he rarely had been before. He had rushed in foolishly, interfering in what? A love affair. "But what do I know about this? What could I possibly understand about such things?" he kept repeating to himself for the hundredth time, blushing deeply. "Oh, being embarrassed is nothing; it's just the punishment I deserve. The problem is I must have caused more harm.... And Father Zossima sent me to make peace and bring them together. Is this how I was supposed to do that?" Then he suddenly recalled how he had tried to join their hands, and he felt even more embarrassed. "Even though I was sincere, I need to be more careful next time," he concluded suddenly, and didn't even smile at his realization.

Katerina Ivanovna's task took him to Lake Street, and his brother Dmitri lived nearby, down a side street from Lake Street. Alyosha decided he would visit him before seeing the captain, even though he had a feeling his brother wouldn't be there. He suspected Dmitri was purposely avoiding him now, but he had to find him regardless. Time was passing, and the thought of his dying elder hadn't left Alyosha for a moment since he left the monastery.

One part of Katerina Ivanovna's task particularly interested him; when she mentioned the captain's son, the schoolboy who had run alongside his father crying, it immediately struck Alyosha that this was likely the same boy who had bitten his finger when Alyosha asked what had hurt him. Alyosha now felt almost certain of this, though he couldn't explain why. Thinking about something else was a relief, and he decided to stop worrying about the "trouble" he had caused and not punish himself with guilt, but instead focus on what needed to be done, whatever the outcome. With that thought, he felt completely reassured. As he turned down the street where Dmitri was staying, he felt hungry, and took the roll he had brought from his father's place out of his pocket and ate it. It gave him more energy.

Dmitri wasn't home. The people in the house, an old cabinet-maker, his son, and his elderly wife, looked at Alyosha with clear suspicion. "He hasn't been here for the last three nights. Maybe he's left," the old man replied to Alyosha's repeated questions. Alyosha could tell he was answering according to some instructions.

When Alyosha asked if Dmitri was either with Grushenka or hiding at Foma's (he purposely spoke so openly), all three of them looked at him nervously. "They care about him, they're doing what they can for him," Alyosha thought. "That's good."

Eventually, he found the house on Lake Street. It was an old, crooked little building, leaning to one side, with three windows facing the street and a muddy yard, where a lone cow stood. He crossed the yard and found the door that led into the hallway. On the left side of the hall lived the old woman who owned the house, along with her elderly daughter. Both seemed hard of hearing.

After repeated questions about the captain, one of them finally understood that he was asking about their tenants and pointed to a door across the hall. The captain's apartment was a simple, rustic room. Alyosha put his hand on the iron latch to open the door, but the strange silence inside stopped him. From what Katerina Ivanovna had said, he knew the man had a family. "Either they're all asleep or maybe they've heard me and are waiting for me to come in. I should knock first," and so he knocked. Someone answered, but not immediately— there was a pause of about ten seconds.

"Who's there?" someone shouted in a loud, angry voice.

Alyosha opened the door and stepped inside. He found himself in a typical peasant's room. Though the space was large, it was cluttered with all sorts of household items, and there were several people inside. On the left was a big Russian stove. A string stretched across the room from the stove to the window, with rags hanging from it. There was a bed along each wall, right and left, both covered with knitted quilts. The one on the left had a tall pile of four pillows, each smaller than the one underneath. The bed on the right had only one small pillow. The opposite corner was hidden by a curtain or sheet strung across a line. Behind this curtain, there was a bed set up on a bench and a chair. The rough, square wooden table had been moved to the middle window. The three windows, each with four tiny greenish panes of glass, let in little light and were tightly shut, so the room was dim and a bit stuffy. On the table sat a frying pan with the remains of some fried eggs, a half-eaten piece of bread, and a small bottle with just a few drops of vodka left.

A woman with a refined appearance, wearing a simple cotton dress, sat in a chair by the bed on the left. Her face was thin and pale, and her sunken cheeks showed immediately that she was ill. But what struck Alyosha the most was the look in the poor woman's eyes—a mix of surprised curiosity and proud defiance. And while Alyosha spoke to her husband, her large brown eyes moved between the two of them with that same proud and questioning expression. A young girl stood by the window next to her, rather plain, with sparse reddish hair, dressed very modestly but neatly. She gave Alyosha a scornful look as he came in. Another female figure sat by the other bed. She was a pitiful sight—a young woman about twenty years old, but hunched over and crippled, "with shriveled legs," as Alyosha would later be told. Her crutches stood in the corner beside her. The beautiful and gentle eyes of this poor girl looked at Alyosha with a calm, peaceful gaze. A man, around forty-five years old, was sitting at the table, finishing the fried eggs. He was small, thin, and frail. He had reddish hair and a sparse light-colored beard that looked like a tuft of straw (for some reason, this comparison and the phrase "tuft of straw" instantly popped into Alyosha's mind, and he remembered it later). It was clearly this man who had shouted earlier, as there was no other man in the room. But when Alyosha entered, he jumped up from the bench he was sitting on, quickly wiped his mouth with a ragged napkin, and rushed over to Alyosha.

"It's a monk, come to beg for the monastery. A fine place to come for that!" said the girl standing in the corner on the left. The man spun around towards her and answered in a high, trembling voice:

"No, Varvara, you're mistaken. Allow me to ask," he turned back to Alyosha, "what brings you to—our humble abode?"

Alyosha looked closely at him. It was the first time he had seen him. There was something awkward, jittery, and irritated about him. Though he had obviously been drinking, he wasn't drunk. There was an odd boldness in his expression, but at the same time, an undercurrent of fear. He looked like a man who had been oppressed for a long time and had finally rebelled, now trying to assert himself. Or, perhaps even more accurately, he looked like someone who desperately wanted to hit you but was terrified you'd hit him first. His voice, high-pitched and shaky, carried a kind of nervous humor that alternated between being spiteful and groveling, shifting from one tone to the next. His question about "our humble abode" was delivered with a tremor, his eyes rolling, as he stepped so close to Alyosha that it made him instinctively take a step back. The man wore a very shabby, dark cotton coat, patched and stained. His pants were an extremely light-colored checkered pattern, long out of style and made of thin material. They were so wrinkled and short that he looked like he had outgrown them, like a boy.

"I'm Alexey Karamazov," Alyosha began in response.

"I understand that perfectly well, sir," the man snapped quickly, trying to show he already knew who Alyosha was. "I'm Captain Snegiryov, sir, though I'd still like to know exactly what brings you here—"

"Oh, I didn't come for anything specific. I just wanted to talk to you—if you don't mind," Alyosha said.

"In that case, here's a chair, sir. Please, sit down. That's what they used to say in those old comedies, 'please be seated,' " the man said, quickly grabbing an empty chair (a rough wooden chair, not upholstered) and setting it almost in the middle of the room for Alyosha. Then, grabbing a similar chair for himself, he sat down facing Alyosha, so close that their knees almost touched.

"Nikolay Ilyitch Snegiryov, sir. Formerly a captain in the Russian infantry. Shamed because of my vices, but still a captain. Though I may not sound like it anymore, since for the last half of my life I've learned to say 'sir.' It's what you say when life knocks you down."

"That's very true," Alyosha said with a smile. "But do people say it without meaning to, or do they say it on purpose?"

"As God is my witness, it's without meaning to! I never used the word 'sir' before in my life, but once I hit hard times, I started saying it all the time. It's like a higher power making me do it. I can see you're interested in what's going on in the world today, but how could I have caught your interest when I live in such poor conditions, hardly fit to offer any kind of hospitality?"

"I came to talk about that situation."

"What situation?" the captain interrupted impatiently.

"About when you met my brother Dmitri Fyodorovitch," Alyosha blurted out awkwardly.

"What meeting are you talking about? You don't mean that meeting? About my 'wisp of straw,' right?" He moved closer until his knees were practically bumping into Alyosha. His lips were tightly pressed together, like a thread.

"What wisp of straw?" Alyosha mumbled.

"He's come to complain about me, Father!" shouted a familiar voice from behind the curtain. It was the voice of the schoolboy Alyosha had met earlier. "I bit his finger just now." The curtain was pulled back, and Alyosha saw the boy who had attacked him lying on a small bed, made up on the bench and a chair in the corner beneath the icons. The boy was covered with his coat and an old quilt. He clearly wasn't feeling well, and judging by the feverish glow in his eyes, he was sick. He looked at Alyosha without fear, as if he felt safe in his own home and untouchable.

"What! He bit your finger?" The captain jumped up from his chair. "Was it your finger?"

"Yes. He was throwing stones with some other boys. There were six of them against him alone. I went up to him, and he threw a stone at me and then another at my head. I asked him why he was doing it, and then he rushed at me and bit my finger badly. I don't know why."

"I'll give him a good beating right now, sir, right this minute!" The captain jumped up from his seat.

"But I'm not complaining. I'm just telling you what happened. I don't want him to be beaten. Besides, he looks sick."

"And do you really think I'd beat him? That I'd take my Ilusha and thrash him right in front of you to make you feel better? Would you prefer that I do it now, sir?" the captain suddenly turned to Alyosha, acting like he might attack him instead. "I'm sorry about your finger, sir. But instead of beating Ilusha, how about I chop off four of my own fingers with this knife right here, in front of you, to settle your anger? Would four fingers be enough to satisfy your need for revenge? You won't ask for the fifth one too, will you?" He stopped abruptly, choking on his words. His whole face was twitching, and he looked very defiant, like he was in a frenzy.

"I think I understand everything now," said Alyosha gently, his voice sad, as he stayed seated. "Your boy is a good boy, and he loves you. He attacked me because I'm the brother of the man who hurt you.... Now I get it," he said again thoughtfully. "But my brother Dmitri Fyodorovitch regrets what happened. I know he does. And if he can, or better yet, if he meets you in the same place, he will apologize in front of everyone—if that's what you want."

"So, after he pulled out my beard, he's going to apologize? And he thinks that will be good enough?"

"Oh, no! He'll do whatever you ask him to do, in any way you want him to do it."

"So, if I asked him to kneel before me in that tavern—the 'Metropolis,' or whatever it's called—or out in the marketplace, he'd do it?"

"Yes, he'd even kneel before you."

"You've really touched me deeply, sir. Moved me to tears and touched my heart! I can't help but appreciate your brother's generosity. Let me introduce you to my family, my two daughters and my son—my 'litter,' as you might say. If I die, who will look after them? And while I'm alive, who but them will take care of a miserable man like me? That's something every man like me has—someone who still loves him, even a man like me."

"Ah, that's so true!" Alyosha exclaimed.

"Oh, stop acting like a fool! Some stranger walks in, and you're making a spectacle of us!" shouted the girl by the window, turning to her father with a look of disdain and contempt.

"Hold on, Varvara!" her father cried, speaking sternly but giving her a look of approval. "That's just her personality," he said, addressing Alyosha again.

"And in all of nature there was nothing That could please her eyes—

Or rather, in this case, nothing that could please her eyes. But let me introduce you to my wife, Arina Petrovna. She's disabled, she's forty-three; she can move around, but not very much. She's from a humble background. Arina Petrovna, get yourself ready. This is Alexey Fyodorovitch Karamazov. Stand up, Alexey Fyodorovitch." He grabbed Alyosha's hand and, with surprising strength, pulled him up. "You must stand up when you're introduced to a lady. And it's not the Karamazov you've heard of, Mama, who's... well, let's say, troubled, but his brother, who's shining with modest virtues. Come now, Arina Petrovna, give your hand to be kissed."

And he kissed his wife's hand, respectfully and even tenderly. The girl at the window turned her back on the scene in disgust, while an expression of extraordinary kindness appeared on the proud, questioning face of the woman.

"Good morning! Sit down, Mr. Tchernomazov," she said.

"Karamazov, Mama, Karamazov. We come from humble origins," the captain whispered again.

"Well, Karamazov, or whatever it is, but I always think of Tchernomazov.... Sit down. Why did he make you stand up? He calls me crippled, but I'm not. My legs are just swollen like barrels, and I'm all shriveled up now. I used to be so fat, but now it's like I swallowed a needle."

"We're from humble origins," the captain mumbled again.

"Oh, Father, Father!" said the hunchbacked girl, who had been sitting quietly in her chair, suddenly covering her face with her handkerchief.

"Clown!" the girl at the window burst out.

"Have you heard our news?" the mother asked, pointing to her daughters. "It's like dark clouds rolling in, but then they pass, and we have music again. When we were with the army, we had lots of visitors. I'm not comparing, mind you—everyone has their own tastes. The deacon's wife used to come over and say, 'Alexandr Alexandrovitch is such a noble man, but Nastasya Petrovna,' she'd say, 'she's a demon from hell.' 'Well,' I told her, 'that's just your opinion, but you're a little spitfire yourself.' And she said,

'You need to learn your place.' 'And who asked you to teach me?' I said. 'At least my breath is fresh, unlike yours,' she said. 'You ask any of the officers if my breath isn't fresh,' I told her. And that stayed on my mind ever since. Not long ago, I was sitting here, just like I am now, and I saw that same general come in, the one who came here for Easter. I asked him, 'Your Excellency, is it possible for a lady's breath to smell bad?' 'Yes,' he said, 'you should open a window or a door, the air in here is stale.' They all carry on like that! And why do they care about my breath? The dead smell worse! 'I won't spoil the air,' I told them, 'I'll get some slippers and go.' My dear ones, don't blame your mother! Nikolay Ilyitch, why can't I make you happy? Ilusha is the only one who comes home from school and loves me. Yesterday, he even brought me an apple. Please, forgive your poor lonely mother! Why has my breath become unpleasant to you?"

And the poor, delusional woman began to sob, with tears streaming down her face. The captain rushed over to her.

"Mama, Mama, my dear, stop! You're not alone. Everyone loves you, everyone adores you." He kissed both her hands and gently stroked her face, then grabbed a napkin to wipe away her tears. Alyosha thought he saw tears in the captain's own eyes as well. "You see, you hear?" the captain said fiercely to Alyosha, gesturing towards the sobbing woman.

"I see and hear," Alyosha muttered.

"Father, how can you act this way, with him here! Leave him alone!" cried the boy, sitting up in his bed, staring at his father with glowing eyes.

"Stop showing off with your foolish antics that never amount to anything!" Varvara shouted, stamping her foot in frustration.

"You're right this time, Varvara, and I'll make it up to you quickly. Come, Alexey Fyodorovitch, put on your hat, and I'll put on mine. We need to talk seriously, but not here. This girl sitting here is my daughter, Nina. I forgot to introduce her to you. She's an angel, sent down from heaven... if you can understand."

"He's trembling like he's having a seizure!" Varvara went on, outraged.

"And that one there, stamping her foot and calling me a fool, she's an angel too, and she has every right to call me that. Come on, Alexey Fyodorovitch, let's go and finish this."

And grabbing Alyosha's hand, the captain pulled him out of the room and into the street.

Chapter 7: And In the Open Air

"The air outside is fresh, but it's not the same in my apartment, in any way you can think of. Let's walk slowly, sir. I'd be glad to have your kind interest."

"I have something important to talk to you about too," said Alyosha, "but I'm not sure how to start."

"Of course, you must have some reason to talk to me. You wouldn't have come to see me for no reason. Unless you're here to complain about my son, but that doesn't seem likely. Speaking of the boy, I couldn't explain earlier, but I can tell you now what happened. My beard was thicker a week ago—that's what they call my 'tow,' especially the schoolboys. Well, your brother Dmitri Fyodorovitch was pulling me by the beard. I didn't do anything, he was just in a rage and happened to see me. He dragged me out of the tavern and into the marketplace. That's when the boys were leaving school, and Ilusha was with them. As soon as he saw me in that state, he rushed over to me. 'Father,' he cried, 'father!' He grabbed me, hugged me, and tried to pull me away, shouting to my attacker, 'Let go! Let go! It's my father, forgive him!' Yes, he actually begged, 'forgive him.' He held onto that hand—that hand—with his little hands and kissed it. I remember his little face at that moment. I've never forgotten it, and I never will!"

"I swear," cried Alyosha, "my brother will sincerely regret his actions. He'll even get on his knees in that same marketplace if he has to! I'll make sure of it, or he's no brother of mine!"

"Aha, so it's just a suggestion! And it didn't come from him, but from the generosity of your own heart. You should've said so. Still, let me tell you about your brother's 'chivalrous' behavior at the time. He stopped pulling me by my beard and let me go. He said, 'You're an officer, and I'm an officer. If you can find someone decent to be your second, send me your challenge. I'll give you satisfaction, even though you're a scoundrel.' That's what he said. Very noble, isn't it? I left with Ilusha, and that moment is forever imprinted on his heart. No, people like us don't get to claim the privileges of noblemen. Look around at what you've just seen in our home. What did you find? Three women—one is disabled and not right in the head, one is a hunchback, and the other is smart but far too clever for her own good. She's a student, eager to return to Petersburg to fight for women's rights on the banks of the Neva. I won't even mention Ilusha—he's only nine. I'm all alone in the world. What would happen to them if I died? I just want to know. If I challenge your brother and he kills me, what then? What would happen to them? Or worse, what if he doesn't kill me, but cripples me? I couldn't work, but I'd still need to be fed. Who would feed me? And who would feed them? Would I have to take Ilusha out of school and send him to beg on the streets? That's what it means if I challenge him to a duel. It's just silly talk, nothing more."

"He will beg for your forgiveness. He'll bow at your feet in the middle of the marketplace," cried Alyosha again, his eyes glowing with emotion.

"I did think about taking him to court," the captain continued, "but have you seen our legal code? How much could I really get for a personal injury? And then Agrafena Alexandrovna sent for me and screamed, 'Don't even think about it! If you take him to court, I'll tell the world that he beat you up because you were dishonest, and then you'll be the one facing charges.' I swear by God, whose dishonesty was it? Wasn't I just following orders, hers and Fyodor Pavlovitch's? 'And if you go through with it,' she added, 'I'll fire you for good, and you'll never earn another cent from me. I'll talk to my merchant too' (that's what she calls her husband), 'and he'll fire you too!' And if he fires me, what would I have left? Your Fyodor Pavlovitch has already stopped giving me work, for other reasons, and now he plans to use the papers I signed to take me to court. So, I stayed quiet, and you've seen the state we're living in. But tell me this: did Ilusha hurt your finger badly? I didn't want to bring it up in front of him back home."

"Yes, it hurt a lot. He was very angry, and now I understand he was taking revenge on me because I'm a Karamazov. But if you had seen him throwing stones at the other boys! It's really dangerous. They might hurt him badly. They're just kids, and they're foolish. A stone could hit someone and break their head."

"That's exactly what happened. He got hit by a stone today. Not in the head, but in the chest, right above his heart. He came home crying and groaning, and now he's sick."

"And you know he's the one who starts these fights. He's angry at them because of you. They say he even stabbed a boy named Krassotkin with a penknife recently."

"I've heard about that too. It's dangerous. Krassotkin is an official's son, so we might hear more about it."

"I'd suggest," Alyosha continued, "that you don't send him to school for a while, at least until he calms down... and his anger subsides."

"Anger," the captain repeated. "That's exactly what it is. He's a little boy, but his anger is powerful. You don't know the full story, sir. Let me tell you more. Since that incident, the boys have been teasing him about the 'wisp of tow.' Schoolboys are merciless. Individually, they're angels, but when they're together, especially at school, they can be cruel. Their teasing has sparked a fierce spirit in Ilusha. Any other boy, a weaker boy, would have been ashamed of his father. But Ilusha? He stood up for me, his father, against all of them. He stood up for what's right. Only God knows—and I know—what he went through when he kissed your brother's hand and begged him to forgive me. Our children— not your children, but ours, the children of poor men like me— learn about justice early, even when they're only nine years old. How could the rich ever understand? They never experience such deep things. But at that moment in the marketplace, when Ilusha kissed your brother's hand, he understood what justice really means. And that truth hit him hard. It crushed him," the captain said passionately, almost in a frenzy, as he slammed his right fist into his left palm, trying to show how "the truth" crushed Ilusha. "That very day, sir, he fell ill with a fever, and he was delirious all night. He barely spoke to me all day, but I could tell he was watching me from the corner of his eye, even though he acted like he was focusing on his schoolwork. I knew his mind wasn't on his lessons. The next day, I got drunk to forget my troubles. Yes, I'm a sinner, and I don't remember much. His mother started crying too—I love her very much—and I spent my last penny drowning my sorrows. Don't look down on me for that, sir. In Russia, the men who drink are often the best of men. Our best men are the ones who drink the most. I passed out, and I don't remember what happened with Ilusha. But that day, the boys were mocking him at school. 'Wisp of tow,' they shouted, 'your father was dragged out of the tavern by his wisp of tow, and you ran by, begging for forgiveness.'"

"The air is fresh, but in my apartment it is not in any way, in any sense of the word. Let us walk slowly, sir. I would appreciate your kind interest."

"I have something important to say to you as well," Alyosha replied, "but I don't quite know how to begin."

"Of course, you must have some business with me. You wouldn't have come to see me without a reason. Unless, of course, you've come simply to complain about the boy, but that seems unlikely. And speaking of the boy, I couldn't explain it to you inside, but now I'll tell you what happened. My beard was thicker a week ago— that's what they call my 'tow,' especially the schoolboys. Well, your brother Dmitri Fyodorovitch was pulling me by my beard. I hadn't done anything; he was just in a rage and came across me. He dragged me out of the tavern into the marketplace, and right then, the boys were leaving school, and Ilusha was with them. The moment he saw me in that condition, he ran up to me. 'Father,' he cried, 'father!' He grabbed me, hugged me, tried to pull me away, and begged my attacker, 'Let go, let go, it's my father, forgive him!' Yes, he actually said, 'forgive him.' He held that hand—that hand—with his little hands and kissed it. I can still remember his face at that moment. I've never forgotten it, and I never will!"

"I swear," cried Alyosha, "that my brother will express his most deep and sincere regret, even if he has to kneel down in that very marketplace... I'll make him do it, or he's no brother of mine!"

"Aha, so it's only a suggestion! It's not coming from him, but from your own generous heart. You should have said so from the beginning. Still, let me tell you about your brother's noble, soldierly generosity, because he did show it in that moment. He let go of my beard and said, 'You're an officer, and I'm an officer. If you can find someone respectable to act as your second, send me your challenge. I'll give you satisfaction, even though you're a scoundrel.' That's what he said. Quite the chivalrous spirit, wouldn't you agree? I left with Ilusha, and that scene is imprinted forever in his memory. No, we are not the kind of people who can claim the privileges of noblemen. Judge for yourself. You've been in our humble home—what did you see there? Three women—one crippled and not in her right mind, another crippled and hunchbacked, and the third not crippled, but far too clever. She's a student, eager to return to Petersburg to work for the emancipation of women on the banks of the Neva. And then there's Ilusha, who is only nine. I'm alone in this world, and if I die, what will happen to them? I simply ask you that. And if I challenge your brother, and he kills me, what then? What will become of them? Or worse, if he doesn't kill me, but only wounds me—cripples me—I won't be able to work anymore. But I'll still need to be fed. Who would feed me? And who would feed them? Should I take Ilusha out of school and send him to beg in the streets? That's what it would mean if I challenged him to a duel. It's nonsense, just foolish talk."

"He will beg for your forgiveness. He will bow down at your feet in the middle of the marketplace," cried Alyosha again, with glowing eyes.

"I did think about suing him," the captain went on, "but if you look at our legal code, how much could I really get for personal injury? Then Agrafena Alexandrovna sent for me and yelled at me, 'Don't even think about it! If you go through with it, I'll make sure everyone knows he beat you up because you were dishonest, and then you'll be the one facing charges.' I swear by God, whose dishonesty was it? Wasn't I just following orders from her and Fyodor Pavlovitch? 'And if you press charges,' she said, 'I'll fire you for good, and you'll never earn another penny from me. I'll talk to my husband' (that's what she calls her merchant) 'and he'll fire you too!' And if they fire me, what would I have left? Your Fyodor Pavlovitch has already stopped hiring me for other reasons, and now he's planning to use the papers I signed to take me to court. So, I kept quiet, and you've seen what kind of life we're living. But let me ask you, did Ilusha hurt your finger badly? I didn't want to bring it up in front of him back there."

"Yes, it hurt quite a lot, and he was very angry. Now I see that he was taking revenge on me as a Karamazov. But if only you had seen how he was throwing stones at the other schoolboys! It's really dangerous. They might kill him. They're children, and they don't know any better. A stone could hit someone and crack their skull."

"That's exactly what happened. He was hit by a stone today—not in the head, but in the chest, just above his heart. He came home crying and groaning, and now he's sick."

"And you know he attacks them first. He's bitter toward them because of you. They say he recently stabbed a boy named Krassotkin with a penknife."

"I've heard about that too. It's dangerous. Krassotkin is the son of

an official, so we might hear more about it."

"I'd advise you," Alyosha continued, "not to send him back to school for a while, at least until he calms down... and his anger fades."

"Anger," the captain repeated. "Yes, that's exactly what it is. He's just a little boy, but his anger is fierce. You don't know the whole story, sir. Let me tell you more. Since that incident, the boys have been teasing him about the 'wisp of tow.' Schoolboys are merciless creatures. Individually, they're angels, but when they're together, especially in school, they're cruel. Their teasing has stirred up a strong sense of pride in Ilusha. Any other boy, a weaker one, would have been ashamed of his father. But not Ilusha. He stood up for me—his father—against all of them. He stood up for what's right. Only God knows—and I know—what he went through when he kissed your brother's hand and begged him, 'Forgive father, forgive him.' Our children—not yours, but ours, the children of poor men like me—understand justice, even at nine years old. How could the rich ever grasp such things? They never experience these depths in their lives. But in that moment, when Ilusha kissed your brother's hand in the marketplace, he understood what justice is. And that truth hit him hard. It crushed him," the captain said, his voice filled with passion, as he struck his right fist against his left palm, as though showing how "the truth" had crushed Ilusha. "That very day, sir, he fell ill with a fever, and he was delirious all night. All day, he hardly said a word to me, but I noticed him watching me from the corner of his eye, even though he pretended to be focusing on his lessons. But I could see his mind wasn't on his studies. The next day, I got drunk to forget my troubles—yes, I'm a sinner—and I don't remember much. His mother cried too—I love her dearly—and I spent my last penny drowning my sorrows. Don't look down on me for that, sir. In Russia, the men who drink are often the best of men. Our finest men are often the biggest drinkers. I passed out, and I don't remember what happened with Ilusha that day. But all day long, the boys were teasing him at school. 'Wisp of tow,' they shouted, 'your father was dragged out of the tavern by his wisp of tow, and you ran after him, begging for forgiveness.'"

They were both standing by the large stone near the fence, with no one else around. The money seemed to have a huge impact on the captain. He was startled, but at first, it was just from surprise. He had never expected this outcome from their conversation. Help from anyone—especially such a large amount—was the last thing on his mind!

He took the money, and for a moment, he couldn't even speak. His expression completely changed.

"For me? This much money—two hundred roubles! Good heavens! I haven't seen that much money in four years! Dear Lord! And you say it's from a sister... Is that really true?"

"I swear, everything I told you is true," Alyosha exclaimed. The captain's face turned red.

"Listen, listen closely, my dear. If I take this, I won't be a scoundrel, will I? In your eyes, Alexey Fyodorovitch, I won't be a scoundrel, right? No, Alexey Fyodorovitch, listen, please," he said urgently, touching Alyosha's hands. "You're encouraging me to take it, saying it's from a sister, but deep down, in your heart, will you despise me for taking it?"

"No, no, I swear on my soul I won't! And no one will ever know but me—you, I, and her, and another lady, her close friend."

"Forget about the lady! Listen, Alexey Fyodorovitch, you have to understand how much these two hundred roubles mean to me right now." The poor man was getting more excited, his words rushing out faster and faster, almost as if he was afraid he wouldn't get to say everything. He seemed completely thrown off balance, speaking with a kind of wild enthusiasm.

"Besides the fact that it comes from a respected and honorable 'sister,' do you realize that now I can take care of my mother and Nina, my sweet hunchbacked daughter? Doctor Herzenstube came out of kindness and examined them both for an hour. He said, 'I don't know what to make of it,' but he prescribed some mineral water from the pharmacy. He said it would definitely help her, and he also recommended baths with medicine. The mineral water costs thirty copecks a bottle, and she might need to drink forty bottles! I took the prescription and put it on the shelf under the icons, and it's still lying there. And he prescribed hot baths for Nina with something dissolved in them, morning and evening. But how can we manage all that in our house, without any servants, without help, without even a bath or water? Nina's rheumatic all over—I don't think I told you. Her whole right side aches every night, she's in terrible pain, but the little angel endures it silently so she won't wake us. We eat whatever we can get, and she only takes the leftovers, what you wouldn't even give a dog. 'I'm not worth it. I'm taking food away from you. I'm just a burden on you,' that's what her angelic eyes are trying to tell us. We take care of her, but she doesn't like it. 'I'm a useless cripple, no good to anyone,' she says. But how can she think that, when her angelic presence is what keeps us all going? Without her sweet, gentle spirit, it would be hell for all of us! She even softens Varvara. And don't judge Varvara too harshly—she's an angel too. She's been wronged. She came to stay with us for the summer and brought sixteen roubles that she'd saved from giving lessons. She planned to return to Petersburg in September—that's now. But we took her money to live on, so now she has nothing to go back with. Not that she could go back anyway, because she's been working for us like a slave. She's like a worn-out horse, carrying us all on her back. She does everything—cooking, cleaning, taking care of mother, doing the laundry. And mother is demanding, tearful, and half-mad! But now, with this money, I can finally hire a servant! Do you understand, Alexey Fyodorovitch? I can get medicine for my dear ones, I can send my student daughter back to Petersburg, I can buy proper food, I can buy beef to feed them! Good Lord, it's like a dream!"

Alyosha was overjoyed that he had brought the captain such happiness, and that the man was willing to accept the help.

"Wait, Alexey Fyodorovitch, wait," the captain continued, his words pouring out rapidly in a new burst of excitement. "Do you realize that Ilusha and I might actually be able to live out our dream now? We can buy a horse and cart, a black horse—he insists it has to be black—and we'll set out just like we pretended we would the other day. I have an old friend, a lawyer in the K. province, and I've heard from a reliable source that if I go there, he'd give me a job as a clerk in his office. Who knows, maybe he will. I could put mother and Nina in the cart, and Ilusha could drive, and I'd walk. Yes, I'd walk. If I could only get one of my debts paid, I'd have enough for that too!"

"There would be enough!" cried Alyosha. "Katerina Ivanovna will send you even more if you need it, and you know I have money too. Take what you need from me, like you would from a brother, from a friend. You can pay it back later… (You'll get rich, you'll get rich!) And there's no better idea than moving to another province. It'll save you, especially your boy—you should leave before the winter comes, before it gets cold. Write to us when you're settled, and we'll always be like brothers… No, it's not a dream!"

Alyosha felt like hugging him, he was so happy. But then he stopped short when he noticed the captain's expression. The man was standing with his neck stretched forward, his lips pressed together, his face pale and full of wild emotion. His lips were moving like he was trying to say something, but no words came out. It was unsettling.

"What's wrong?" asked Alyosha, startled.

"Alexey Fyodorovitch… I… you," the captain muttered, stammering, staring at him with a strange, desperate look. There was also a twisted grin on his face. "I… you, sir… would you like me to show you a little trick I know?" he whispered suddenly, his voice now firm and quick.

"What trick?"

"A fun trick," the captain whispered. His mouth twisted on the left side, and his left eye squinted. He was still staring at Alyosha.

"What's the matter? What trick?" Alyosha asked, now completely alarmed.

"Why, look!" the captain suddenly shrieked, holding up the two notes he had been clutching between his thumb and forefinger. He angrily crumpled them up and squeezed them tightly in his hand. "Do you see? Do you see?" he screamed, pale and furious. Then, raising his hand, he threw the crumpled notes onto the sand. "Do you see?" he shouted again, pointing at them. "Look there!"

In a fit of rage, he started stomping on the notes, grinding them into the ground with his heel and shouting as he did so, "So much for your money! So much for your money! So much for your money!"

Suddenly, he stepped back and stood tall in front of Alyosha, his entire posture filled with pride.

"Tell the people who sent you that the 'wisp of tow' doesn't sell his honor!" he cried, raising his arm in the air. Then he quickly turned and started running. But after five steps, he stopped, turned back, and blew a kiss to Alyosha. He ran another five steps, stopped again, and turned around one last time. This time, his face was no longer twisted with laughter, but trembling with emotion, his whole expression filled with tears. In a faltering, tearful voice, he called out, "What could I tell my son if I took money for our shame?"

Then he ran off without turning back. Alyosha stood there, heartbroken. He realized that up until the very last moment, the captain hadn't known he was going to crumple up the notes and throw them away. He didn't turn back. Alyosha knew he wouldn't. He didn't try to follow him or call him back; he understood why. Once the captain was out of sight, Alyosha bent down to pick up the two crumpled notes. They were wrinkled and pressed into the sand, but otherwise undamaged. They still made that crisp sound like new banknotes when Alyosha unfolded them and smoothed them out. After smoothing them, he folded them again, put them in his pocket, and headed to Katerina Ivanovna to tell her how her task had turned out.

Book 5: Pro And Contra

Chapter 1: The Engagement

Madame Hohlakov was the first to meet Alyosha again. She was flustered; something important had happened. Katerina Ivanovna's hysteria had ended in a fainting spell, and then "a terrible, awful weakness followed. She lay with her eyes rolled back and was delirious. Now she had a fever. They had sent for Herzenstube; they had sent for the aunts. The aunts were already here, but Herzenstube hadn't come yet. Everyone was sitting in her room, waiting. She was unconscious now, and what if it turned into brain fever!"

Madame Hohlakov looked deeply worried. "This is serious, serious," she repeated after every sentence, as if nothing that had happened before was serious. Alyosha listened with concern and started to describe his day, but she interrupted him almost immediately. She didn't have time to listen. She asked him to sit with Lise and wait there.

"Lise," she whispered almost in his ear, "Lise surprised me a lot just now, dear Alexey Fyodorovitch. She really touched me, and so my heart forgives her for everything. Can you believe it? As soon as you left, she started feeling truly sorry for laughing at you today and yesterday, even though she wasn't really laughing at you—she was just joking. But she felt so bad about it, she was almost ready to cry, which really surprised me. She's never been sorry for laughing at me; she always just jokes about it. And you know she laughs at me every chance she gets. But this time, she was serious. She thinks a lot of your opinion, Alexey Fyodorovitch, so don't be mad or hurt if you can help it. I'm never hard on her because she's such a clever little thing. Would you believe she just said you were a friend from her childhood? 'The greatest friend of her childhood,' can you imagine that— 'the greatest friend'! And what about me? She has such strong feelings and memories, and she uses the most unexpected words sometimes. She said something about a pine tree earlier. There used to be a pine tree in our garden when she was little. It's probably still there, so there's no reason to talk about it in the past tense. Pine trees aren't like people, Alexey Fyodorovitch, they don't change quickly. She said, 'Mamma, I remember that pine tree like a dream,' but she added something so unique that I can't even repeat it. Besides, I've forgotten it. Well, goodbye! I'm so worried, I feel like I'll lose my mind. Oh, Alexey Fyodorovitch, I've lost my mind twice before in my life. Go to Lise, cheer her up as you always do so charmingly." Then she called out, "Lise, I've brought Alexey Fyodorovitch, the one you insulted. He's not angry at all, I promise you. In fact, he's surprised you even thought he would be."

"Merci, maman. Come in, Alexey Fyodorovitch."

Alyosha went in. Lise looked a little embarrassed and immediately blushed. She was clearly ashamed about something, and like people often do in those situations, she started talking about other things, as if they were the most interesting topics at that moment.

"Mamma just told me all about the two hundred roubles, Alexey Fyodorovitch, and how you took it to that poor officer... and she told me the whole awful story of how he was insulted... and you know, even though mamma mixes things up and jumps from one thing to another, I cried when I heard about it. So, did you give him the money? How is that poor man doing?"

"Well, I didn't give it to him, and it's a long story," Alyosha replied, as though he, too, could only think about his regret over not giving the money. But Lise could tell he was avoiding the real topic, just like she was.

Alyosha sat down at the table and started telling his story. As he spoke, his embarrassment disappeared, and he gained Lise's full attention. He spoke with deep emotion, still under the strong impression of what had just happened, and he told the story in great detail. Back when they were in Moscow, Alyosha had often come to Lise and told her about his day—what he had read or what he remembered from his childhood. Sometimes they had created daydreams and made up stories together, usually cheerful and fun. Now, both of them felt as though they were suddenly back in those days in Moscow, two years ago. Lise was deeply moved by his story. Alyosha spoke about Ilusha with great warmth. When he finished describing how the unfortunate man had trampled on the money, Lise couldn't help clasping her hands and crying out:

"So you didn't give him the money! You let him run away! Oh, no, you should've run after him!"

"No, Lise, it's better that I didn't," Alyosha said, getting up from his chair and pacing thoughtfully across the room.

"How is that better? Now they have no food, and their situation is hopeless!"

"It's not hopeless, because the two hundred roubles will still get to them. He'll take the money tomorrow. I'm sure he'll take it tomorrow," Alyosha said, pacing back and forth, thinking. "You see, Lise," he continued, suddenly stopping in front of her, "I made one mistake, but even that mistake was for the best."

"What mistake? And how could it be for the best?"

"I'll explain. He's a man with a weak and nervous character. He's suffered a lot, and he's a very kind person. I keep wondering why he got so upset so suddenly because, up until the last moment, I'm sure he didn't know he was going to trample the money. But now I realize that there were a lot of things that hurt his pride, and it couldn't have been any other way in his situation. First of all, he was embarrassed that he had been so happy about the money in front of me and hadn't tried to hide it. If he had been a little less excited, if he had acted like he didn't care so much, or if he had pretended to be hesitant about taking the money, like other people do, he might have been able to accept it. But he was too genuinely happy, and that embarrassed him. Lise, he's a good and honest man, and that's what made everything so painful for him. While he was talking, his voice was so weak, so shaky. He was talking so fast, and sometimes he laughed, but I think he was really crying— yes, I'm sure he was crying, he was so happy. He talked about his daughters and the job he could get in another town. But after he poured out his heart like that, he felt ashamed for showing me everything he was feeling. So, he started to hate me right away. He's one of those very sensitive poor people. What really hurt him the most was that he had accepted me as a friend too quickly. You see, at first, he was almost aggressive toward me, trying to scare me off. But as soon as he saw the money, he started hugging me and touching me. That's when he felt humiliated. And then I made my mistake—a big one. I told him that if he didn't have enough money to move to another town, we would give it to him, and I would give him whatever he needed from my own money. That really hit him hard. He wondered why I was stepping in to help him. You see, Lise, it's very hard for someone who's been hurt to accept help from someone who looks at them like they're a charity case. I've heard that before—Father Zossima told me. I don't know how to explain it, but I've seen it myself, and I feel it too

132

sometimes. And the worst part is that even though he didn't know until the last second that he was going to trample the money, I'm sure he had a feeling it was going to happen. That's what made him so excited. And even though it was terrible, it was all for the best. In fact, I think nothing better could've happened."

"Why? Why could nothing better have happened?" Lise cried, looking at Alyosha in great surprise.

"Because if he had taken the money, by the time he got home, he would've been crying with shame. That's exactly what would've happened. He probably would've come to me early tomorrow and maybe even thrown the money back at me, just like he did today. But now he's gone home feeling proud and triumphant, even though he knows he's 'ruined himself.' So now, it'll be much easier to get him to accept the two hundred roubles tomorrow. He's already defended his honor, tossed the money aside, and stomped on it. He didn't know that I would bring it to him again tomorrow, but he's in desperate need of it. Even though he feels proud of himself now, he'll be thinking about what he lost. Tonight, it'll weigh on his mind, and he'll dream about it. By tomorrow morning, he might even be ready to come to me and ask for forgiveness. That's when I'll show up. 'You're a proud man,' I'll tell him, 'you've shown it. Now take the money and forgive us!' And then he'll take it!"

Alyosha was filled with joy as he spoke those last words, "And then he'll take it!" Lise clapped her hands.

"Ah, that's true! Now I understand completely. Alyosha, how do you know all this? You're so young, yet you seem to know what's in people's hearts... I would never have figured it out."

"The important thing now is to convince him that he's on equal footing with us, even though he's taking money from us," Alyosha said, still excited. "In fact, not just equal, but even on a higher footing."

" 'On a higher footing'—I love that phrase, Alexey Fyodorovitch! But go on, go on!"

"You mean there's no such phrase as 'on a higher footing,' but that doesn't matter because—"

"Oh, no, it doesn't matter at all. Forgive me, Alyosha, dear... You know, I never really respected you until now—that is, I respected you but as an equal. But now, I'm going to start respecting you on a higher footing! Don't be mad at me for joking," she added quickly, with emotion. "I'm silly and small, but you—you! Listen, Alexey Fyodorovitch, aren't we showing contempt for him, that poor man, by analyzing his soul like this, as if we're above him? Aren't we looking down on him by assuming he'll take the money?"

"No, Lise, it's not contempt," Alyosha replied, as if he had already thought about this. "I was thinking about it on my way here. How could it be contempt when we're just like him, when we're no different than he is? You know, we're exactly the same. If we're better off, it's only because we haven't been in his shoes. I don't know about you, Lise, but I feel like I have a lot of bad qualities, and his soul isn't like that. On the contrary, it's full of noble feelings. No, Lise, I don't have any contempt for him. You know, Lise, my elder once told me that we should care for most people the way we care for children, and for some people, we should care for them like we would for the sick in hospitals."

"Ah, Alexey Fyodorovitch, dear, let's care for people as we would for the sick!"

"Yes, let's do that, Lise. I'm ready, even though I'm not completely ready inside. Sometimes I get impatient, and other times I don't notice things. You're different."

"Ah, I don't believe that! Alexey Fyodorovitch, I'm so happy!" "I'm glad you're happy, Lise."

"Alexey Fyodorovitch, you're wonderfully kind, but sometimes you're a bit formal... And yet you're not really formal at all. Go to the door, open it quietly, and see if mamma is listening," Lise said in a nervous, hurried whisper.

Alyosha got up, opened the door, and came back to say no one was listening.

"Come here, Alexey Fyodorovitch," Lise went on, blushing even more. "Give me your hand—that's right. I have something to confess. I didn't write to you yesterday as a joke—it was serious," and she covered her eyes with her hand. It was clear she was very embarrassed by the confession.

Suddenly, she grabbed his hand and kissed it impulsively three times.

"Ah, Lise, this is wonderful!" Alyosha cried happily. "You know, I was completely sure you were serious."

"Sure? Really?" She pushed his hand away a little but didn't let go, blushing even more and laughing a little. "I kiss your hand, and you say, 'What a good thing!' "

But her teasing wasn't fair. Alyosha, too, was deeply moved.

"I just want to make you happy, Lise, but I don't know how to do it," he murmured, blushing as well.

"Alyosha, you're cold and rude. Do you see? He's decided I'm going to be his wife, and he's completely certain about it. He's sure I was serious. What a thing to say! That's so bold, really."

"Why, was it wrong of me to be sure?" Alyosha asked, suddenly laughing.

"Ah, Alyosha, no, it was perfectly right," Lise said, smiling at him tenderly and happily.

Alyosha stood still, holding her hand in his. Suddenly, he bent down and kissed her on the lips.

"Oh, what are you doing?" Lise cried, startled. Alyosha was deeply embarrassed.

"Oh, forgive me if I shouldn't have... Maybe I'm being really stupid. You said I was cold, so I kissed you... But I realize now it was stupid."

Lise laughed and covered her face with her hands. "And in that dress!" she said through her laughter. But then she suddenly stopped laughing and became serious, almost stern.

"Alyosha, we need to stop kissing. We're not ready for that yet, and we'll have to wait a long time," she said seriously. "Tell me instead, why would someone like you—so clever, so observant— choose a little idiot like me, an invalid? Ah, Alyosha, I'm so happy, but I don't deserve you at all."

"You do deserve me, Lise. I'm leaving the monastery in a few days. If I'm going to live in the world, I have to marry. I know that. My elder even told me I should marry. Who could I marry better than you? And who else would even want me besides you? I've thought about it a lot. First of all, you've known me since we were children, and you have so many qualities that I don't have. You're more light-hearted than I am, and most of all, you're more innocent than I am. I've already been exposed to so many things... You don't know, but I, too, am a Karamazov. It doesn't matter if you laugh and joke, even if it's at my expense. Keep laughing. I'm glad you do. You laugh like a child, but you think like a martyr."

"Like a martyr? How so?"

"Yes, Lise, the question you asked earlier—whether we were looking down on that poor man by talking about him—that was a question that comes from someone who understands suffering. You see, I don't quite know how to explain it, but anyone who thinks about those kinds of questions is capable of feeling pain. Sitting in your chair, you've probably thought a lot about things already."

"Alyosha, give me your hand. Why are you pulling it away?" murmured Lise, her voice soft with happiness. "Listen, Alyosha, what will you wear when you leave the monastery? What kind of suit? Don't laugh, don't be angry, it's really, really important to me."

"I haven't thought about it, Lise, but I'll wear whatever you want me to."

"I'd like you to wear a dark blue velvet coat, a white piqué waistcoat, and a soft gray felt hat... Tell me, did you believe me when I said I didn't care about you in my letter?"

"No, I didn't believe it."

"Oh, you impossible person, you're incorrigible."

"You see, I knew you seemed to care about me, but I pretended to believe you didn't, to make it easier for you."

"That makes it worse! Worse, but also better! Alyosha, I care about you so much. Just before you came this morning, I decided to test you. I thought I'd ask you for my letter, and if you calmly handed it back to me (like I expected you would), it would mean you didn't care about me at all, that you felt nothing, and that I was ruined. But when you left the letter at home, I was relieved. You left it on purpose, didn't you? So, you wouldn't have to give it back to me, because you knew I would ask for it. Was that it?"

"Oh, Lise, that wasn't it at all. I have the letter with me right now, and I had it this morning, in this pocket. Here it is."

Alyosha pulled the letter out, laughing, and held it up at a distance for her to see.

"But I'm not going to give it to you. You can look at it from here." "So, you lied? You, a monk, lied!"

"I lied if you want to call it that," Alyosha laughed, too. "I lied because I didn't want to give the letter back. It's very precious to me," he added suddenly, with deep emotion, and he blushed. "It always will be, and I'm not giving it to anyone!"

Lise looked at him joyfully. "Alyosha," she murmured again, "look at the door. Isn't mamma listening?"

"All right, Lise, I'll check, but wouldn't it be better not to assume she's eavesdropping? Why suspect her of something like that?"

"Why call it something bad? A mother has every right to listen to her daughter. It's not a bad thing!" Lise fired up. "You can be sure, Alexey Fyodorovitch, if I ever have a daughter like me, I will definitely spy on her!"

"Really, Lise? That's not right."

"Oh, my goodness! What does 'right' have to do with it? If she were listening in on some ordinary conversation, maybe it would be wrong, but when her own daughter is alone with a young man... Listen, Alyosha, you know I'm going to spy on you when we're married, right? And let me tell you, I'm going to open all your letters and read them. So, you might as well be prepared."

"Yes, of course, if you must," mumbled Alyosha. "But it's still not right."

"Ah, how disdainful! Alyosha, my dear, let's not fight on the first day. I might as well tell you the truth. Yes, it's wrong to spy, and yes, you're right and I'm not. But I'm still going to spy on you."

"Go ahead then, you won't find anything," Alyosha laughed.

"And Alyosha, will you give in to me? We need to decide that, too."

"I'll be happy to, Lise, and I'm sure I will, except when it comes to the most important things. Even if you disagree with me, I'll still do what I know is right in those matters."

"That's good; but let me tell you, I'm ready to give in to you in everything, not just the most important things. And I'm willing to promise it right now—in everything, for the rest of my life!" Lise cried passionately. "I'll even swear that I'll never spy on you, not once, and I'll never open a single one of your letters. Because you're right, and I'm not. And even though I'll be tempted, I won't do it, because you think it's dishonorable. You're my conscience now... Listen, Alexey Fyodorovitch, why have you been so sad lately? Yesterday and today? I know you have a lot on your mind, but I feel like there's something else—something personal, a secret sadness."

"Yes, Lise, there's a secret sadness, too," Alyosha answered sadly. "I can tell you care about me, since you noticed that."

"What is it? Can you tell me?" Lise asked softly, almost pleading.

"I'll tell you later, Lise—another time," said Alyosha, looking a little lost. "You might not understand it now—and I might not be able to explain it."

"I know your brothers and your father are causing you worry." "Yes, my brothers too," Alyosha muttered, lost in thought.

"I don't like your brother Ivan, Alyosha," Lise said suddenly. He noticed her remark with some surprise, but didn't respond.

"My brothers are ruining themselves," he continued, "and my father too. And they're pulling others down with them. It's what Father Païssy called 'the primitive force of the Karamazovs,' a

wild, uncontrolled, earthly force. Does the spirit of God move within that force? I don't even know. All I know is that I'm a Karamazov too... Me, a monk! Am I really a monk, Lise? You just called me that."

"Yes, I did."

"And maybe I don't even believe in God."

"You don't believe? What's the matter?" Lise asked quietly and gently. But Alyosha didn't respond. There was something too mysterious, too personal in those last words, maybe even unclear to him, but still deeply troubling.

"And on top of everything, my dearest friend, the best man in the world, is dying, leaving this earth! If you knew, Lise, how closely I'm connected to him! And soon I'll be left all alone... But I'll come to you, Lise... For the future, we'll be together."

"Yes, together, always! From now on, we'll be together for the rest of our lives! Listen, kiss me—I'll let you."

Alyosha kissed her.

"Now, go. May Christ be with you!" she said, making the sign of the cross over him. "Go back to him while he's still alive. I've kept you too long. I'll pray for him and for you today. Alyosha, we're going to be happy! We will be happy, won't we?"

"I believe we will, Lise."

Alyosha decided it would be better not to see Madame Hohlakov, and he was about to leave the house without saying goodbye to her. But as soon as he opened the door, he found Madame Hohlakov standing in front of him. From her first words, Alyosha realized she had been waiting for him on purpose.

"Alexey Fyodorovitch, this is ridiculous, just childish nonsense! I trust you won't take any of this seriously—it's all just foolishness, nothing but foolishness!" she said, immediately confronting him.

"Just don't tell her that," Alyosha said, "or it will upset her, and that's not good for her right now."

"Good advice from a sensible young man. Should I take it that you only went along with her because of compassion for her condition, so you wouldn't upset her by arguing?"

"Oh, no, not at all. I meant everything I said," Alyosha replied firmly.

"To be serious about this is impossible, unthinkable! And I'll tell you this, I won't let you visit anymore, and I'll take her away— you can be sure of that."

"But why?" asked Alyosha. "It's all so far off, we might not need to worry about it for another year or more."

"Ah, Alexey Fyodorovitch, of course, that's true, and you'll have plenty of time to argue and break up a thousand times over in a year and a half. But I'm so miserable! Even though it's nonsense, it's still a huge blow to me. I feel like Famusov in the final scene of Sorrow from Wit. You're Tchatsky, and she's Sofya. Just imagine,

I ran down to meet you on the stairs, and in the play, the big dramatic scene happens on the staircase. I heard everything—I almost fainted. So, this is the reason behind her terrible nights and recent hysterics! It means love for the daughter but death for the mother. I might as well be in my grave already. And what's worse, what's this letter she wrote? Show it to me immediately!"

"No, there's no need. Please, tell me—how is Katerina Ivanovna now? I need to know."

"She's still delirious; she hasn't regained consciousness. Her aunts are here, but all they do is sigh and act all superior. Herzenstube came, and he was so worried that I didn't know what to do with him. I nearly called another doctor just to treat him! He was taken home in my carriage. And on top of all that, there's you and this letter! It's true, nothing can happen for a year and a half, but for the love of all that's holy, in the name of your dying elder, show me that letter, Alexey Fyodorovitch. I'm her mother! Hold it in your hand if you must but let me read it."

"No, I won't show it to you. Even if she allowed it, I wouldn't. I'll come tomorrow, and if you'd like, we can discuss many things, but for now, goodbye!"

And with that, Alyosha ran down the stairs and out into the street.

Chapter 2: Smerdyakov with A Guitar

He really didn't have any time to lose. Even as he was saying goodbye to Lise, the thought came to him that he needed to come up with a plan to find his brother Dmitri, who was clearly avoiding him. It was getting late—almost three o'clock. Alyosha's heart was pulling him toward the monastery, to his dying elder, but the urgency of seeing Dmitri took priority over everything else. The feeling that a major disaster was about to happen grew stronger in Alyosha's mind with every passing hour. He couldn't have said exactly what that disaster would be, or what he would say to his brother when the time came, but he knew one thing for sure: "Even if my benefactor dies without me being there, at least I won't spend the rest of my life regretting that I could have done something but didn't. If I do this, I'll be following his greatest teaching."

His plan was simple: to catch Dmitri off guard. He would climb over the fence, like he had the day before, sneak into the garden, and sit in the summerhouse. If Dmitri wasn't there, Alyosha decided he wouldn't let Foma or any of the women of the house know he was there. He'd stay hidden in the summerhouse, even if it meant waiting all day. If Dmitri was still waiting for Grushenka to come, he'd probably end up in the summerhouse at some point. Alyosha hadn't thought out all the details, but he was determined to go through with it, even if it meant not getting back to the monastery that day.

Everything went smoothly. He climbed over the fence at almost the same spot as the day before and slipped into the summerhouse without being seen. He didn't want anyone to notice him. The women in the house, or even Foma if he was around, might be loyal to Dmitri and refuse to let Alyosha into the garden or warn Dmitri that he was looking for him.

There was no one in the summerhouse. Alyosha sat down and began to wait. He glanced around; the place looked much older and more rundown than it had the day before. Even though the day was just as nice, the summerhouse now seemed like a shabby little spot. He noticed a ring on the table, probably left from the brandy glass spilled the day before. Silly and random thoughts drifted through his mind, as they often do when you're waiting for something. He wondered, for example, why he had sat in the exact same spot as yesterday and not in the other chair. Eventually, he started to feel really down—nervous and uncertain about what might happen. But he hadn't been sitting there for more than fifteen minutes when he suddenly heard the sound of a guitar nearby. Someone was sitting—or had just sat down—in the bushes, no more than twenty paces away. Alyosha remembered that, when he had left the summerhouse the day before, he'd caught a glimpse of an old green garden bench hidden among the bushes near the fence. Whoever it was must be sitting on it now. But who were they?

A man's voice suddenly began singing in a sugary falsetto, accompanying himself on the guitar:

"With invincible force
I am bound to my dear.
O Lord, have mercy
On her and on me!
On her and on me!
On her and on me!"

The voice stopped. It was a servant's tenor, and it sounded like a servant's song. Then, a woman's voice chimed in, shyly and a little flirtatiously:

"Why haven't you visited us for so long, Pavel Fyodorovitch? Why do you always ignore us?"

"Not at all," the man's voice answered politely but with an air of superiority. It was clear that the man held the upper hand, and the woman was trying to win his favor. "That must be Smerdyakov," Alyosha thought, recognizing the voice. "And the woman must be the daughter of the house who came from Moscow—the one with the fancy dress who goes to Marfa for soup."

"I love all kinds of poetry, as long as it rhymes," the woman's voice continued. "Why don't you sing some more?"

The man started singing again:

"What do I care for royal wealth
If but my dear one be in health?
Lord, have mercy
On her and on me!
On her and on me!
On her and on me!"

"It was better last time," the woman commented. "You sang 'If my darling be in health'—that sounded sweeter. I guess you forgot today."

"Poetry is nonsense," Smerdyakov said curtly. "Oh no, I love poetry."

"As long as it's poetry, it's just foolishness. Think about it—who talks in rhyme? And if we all started talking in rhyme, even if the government made it a rule, we wouldn't say much, would we? Poetry is worthless, Marya Kondratyevna."

"You're so smart! How did you get to be so knowledgeable about everything?" the woman's voice grew even more flirtatious.

"I could've done even more. I could've learned more if it weren't for my fate since childhood. I would've shot a man in a duel if he had insulted me because I come from nothing and have no father. They used to hold that against me in Moscow—it spread there from here, thanks to Grigory Vassilyevitch. Grigory blames me for rebelling against my lowly birth, but I would've rather they killed me before I was born than come into this world like this. They used to gossip about it in the market, and even your mother, without any delicacy, would tell me her hair was as rough as a mat and that she was just under five feet tall by 'a wee bit.' Why say 'a wee bit' when she could have just said 'a little'? She wanted to make it sound sentimental, like a peasant's way of talking. But can a Russian peasant really feel the same way as an educated person? No, they don't have any real feelings because they're so ignorant. From the time I was a child, whenever I hear 'a wee bit,' it makes me want to explode with anger. I hate all of Russia, Marya Kondratyevna."

"If you had been a soldier, or a young hussar, you wouldn't talk like that. You'd have drawn your saber to defend Russia."

"I don't want to be a hussar, Marya Kondratyevna. In fact, I'd like to get rid of all soldiers."

"And when an enemy comes, who will defend us?"

"There's no need for defense. In 1812, Napoleon, the first Emperor of the French and the father of the current one, invaded Russia. It would've been better if they had conquered us. A smart nation would have taken over a very foolish one, and we would have had better institutions."

"Are things so much better in their country than here? I wouldn't trade a certain young man I know for three young Englishmen," said Marya tenderly, likely giving him a flirtatious look.

"That's a matter of personal taste."

"But you're just like a foreigner—like a very refined, foreign gentleman. I feel shy telling you that."

"If you're curious, the people there and the people here are just the same when it comes to vice. They're cheats, but over there, the scoundrel wears polished boots, while here, he rolls around in the dirt and doesn't see anything wrong with it. The Russian people need a good beating, just like Fyodor Pavlovitch said yesterday, even though he's mad, as are all his children."

"You said yourself that you had such respect for Ivan Fyodorovitch."

"But he called me a stinking lackey. He thinks I could be difficult to deal with. He is wrong about that. If I had a certain sum of money in my pocket, I would have left this place a long time ago. Dmitri Fyodorovitch is lower than any lackey, in both his behavior and his mind, and in his poverty. He doesn't know how to do anything at all, and yet everyone respects him. I may only be a soup-maker, but if things had gone right for me, I could have opened a café or restaurant in Petrovka, in Moscow, because my cooking is something special. There's no one in Moscow, except the foreigners, whose cooking is anything special. Dmitri Fyodorovitch is a beggar, but if he challenged the son of the most important count in the country to a duel, he would fight him. But what makes him better than I am? He's far more foolish than I am. Just look at how much money he has thrown away for no reason!"

"A duel must be lovely," Marya Kondratyevna suddenly remarked. "Why do you say that?"

"It must be both dreadful and brave, especially when young officers, with pistols in their hands, fire at each other over some lady. What a perfect picture! Oh, if only girls were allowed to watch! I'd give anything to see a duel!"

"It's all fine when you are the one shooting, but when he is aiming straight at your face, you must feel pretty ridiculous. You'd be wishing you could run away, Marya Kondratyevna."

"You don't mean that you would run away?" But Smerdyakov didn't bother to respond. After a brief pause, the guitar played again, and he began singing once more in the same falsetto voice:

"Whatever you may say,
I shall go far away.
Life will be bright and gay

139

In the city far away.
I shall not grieve,
I shall not grieve at all,
I don't intend to grieve at all."

Then something unexpected happened. Alyosha suddenly sneezed. They both stopped talking. Alyosha stood up and walked toward them. He saw Smerdyakov, dressed up, wearing polished boots, his hair slicked back with pomade, and possibly curled. The guitar lay on the garden bench. His companion, Marya Kondratyevna, wore a light-blue dress with a train about two yards long. She was young and might not have been unattractive, if not for her round face, which was terribly freckled.

"Will my brother Dmitri be back soon?" Alyosha asked, trying to stay as composed as possible.

Smerdyakov stood up slowly; Marya Kondratyevna also stood.

"How am I supposed to know where Dmitri Fyodorovitch is? It's not as though I'm his keeper," answered Smerdyakov calmly, clearly, and with a hint of superiority.

"But I only asked if you happened to know," Alyosha clarified.

"I don't know anything about his whereabouts, and I don't care to."

"But my brother told me that you keep him informed of everything going on in the house and that you promised to let him know when Agrafena Alexandrovna arrives."

Smerdyakov gave him a slow, indifferent look.

"And how did you get in this time? The gate was locked over an hour ago," he asked, looking straight at Alyosha.

"I came through the back alley, climbed over the fence, and went straight to the summerhouse. I hope you'll forgive me," he added, addressing Marya Kondratyevna. "I was in a hurry to find my brother."

"Oh, as if we could hold that against you!" drawled Marya Kondratyevna, clearly pleased by Alyosha's apology. "Dmitri Fyodorovitch often comes to the summerhouse that way. We don't know he's here, and he's just sitting in the summerhouse."

"I am really anxious to find him or at least learn from you where he is. Believe me, it's something of great importance to him."

"He never tells us," lisped Marya Kondratyevna.

"Even though I used to come here as a friend," Smerdyakov resumed, "Dmitri Fyodorovitch still bothers me relentlessly with questions about the master. 'What's new?' he'll ask. 'What's happening inside now? Who's coming and going?' He always wants to know more. He has already threatened me with death twice."

"With death?" Alyosha exclaimed, surprised.

"Do you think he'd think twice about it, with the temper he has, which you saw yourself yesterday? He says that if I let Agrafena Alexandrovna into the house and she stays the night, I'll be the first to suffer for it. I am terribly afraid of him, and honestly, if I weren't even more afraid of what might happen, I should probably inform the police. God only knows what he might do!"

"The master said to him the other day, 'I'll crush you like a bug!'" added Marya Kondratyevna.

"Oh, if it's just that, it's probably only talk," said Alyosha. "But if I could meet him, I might speak to him about that, too."

"Well, the only thing I can tell you," said Smerdyakov, after a moment's thought, "is that Ivan Fyodorovitch sent me this morning to your brother's place on Lake Street, without a letter but with a message inviting Dmitri Fyodorovitch to join him for dinner at the restaurant here, in the marketplace. I went there, but Dmitri Fyodorovitch wasn't home. It was eight o'clock. His landlady told me, 'He's been here, but now he's gone.' It seems like they were in on it together. So perhaps right now, he is at the restaurant with Ivan Fyodorovitch. After all, Ivan hasn't been home for dinner, and Fyodor Pavlovitch ate alone an hour ago and has gone to lie down. But please, whatever you do, don't mention me or what I've told you—he'd kill me for no reason at all."

"So, my brother Ivan invited Dmitri to the restaurant today?" Alyosha repeated quickly.

"That's right."

"The Metropolis tavern in the marketplace?" "Yes, that's the one."

"That's very likely," Alyosha said, sounding excited. "Thank you, Smerdyakov; that's important. I'll go there right away."

"Don't let him know I said anything," Smerdyakov called after him.

"Oh, don't worry. I'll go to the tavern as though I just happened to stop by. You can relax."

"Wait a minute, I'll open the gate for you," called Marya Kondratyevna.

"No, it's a shortcut. I'll climb over the fence again."

What Alyosha had heard made him very agitated. He ran toward the tavern. It wasn't possible for him to walk into the tavern wearing his monk's robes, but he could ask for his brothers at the entrance and call them down. But just as he arrived at the tavern, a window opened, and his brother Ivan called down to him from it

"Alyosha, can't you come up here to me? I'd really appreciate it." "Of course I can, but I'm not sure it's appropriate in this robe—"

"But I'm in a private room. Come up the steps; I'll come down and meet you."

A minute later, Alyosha was sitting next to his brother. Ivan was eating alone.

Chapter 3: The Brothers Make Friends

Ivan was not, however, in a private room but in a space sectioned off by a screen, so that he was hidden from the other people in the room. It was the first room from the entrance, with a buffet along one wall. Waiters were constantly rushing back and forth. The only customer in the room was an old retired military man, drinking tea in a corner. But the usual bustle was happening in the other rooms of the tavern—shouts for the waiters, the popping of corks, the clatter of billiard balls, and the low hum of an organ. Alyosha knew that Ivan didn't usually visit this tavern and generally disliked taverns. So, he must have come here, Alyosha thought, just to meet Dmitri as they'd planned. But Dmitri wasn't there.

"Shall I order you some fish, soup, or something else? You don't live on tea alone, I assume," Ivan said cheerfully, clearly happy to have Alyosha with him. He had finished his meal and was drinking tea.

"Let me have some soup, and tea after that. I'm hungry," Alyosha replied with a smile.

"And cherry jam? They have it here. Do you remember how much you loved cherry jam when you were little?"

"You remember that? Let me have the jam too. I still like it." Ivan rang for the waiter and ordered soup, jam, and tea.

"I remember everything, Alyosha. I remember you until you were eleven, and I was nearly fifteen. There's a big difference between fifteen and eleven, so brothers aren't really companions at those ages. I don't even know if I was fond of you. When I first went to Moscow, for the first few years, I didn't think about you at all. Then when you came to Moscow, we only met once, I think. And now I've been here for over three months, and we've barely spoken. Tomorrow I'm leaving, and as I was sitting here, I was thinking about how I could see you to say goodbye. And just then, you walked by."

"Were you really eager to see me?" Alyosha asked.

"Very much so. I want to finally get to know you, and I want you to know me. Then we can say goodbye. I think it's best to get to know people right before you leave them. I've noticed how you've been looking at me these past three months. There's always been this look of expectation in your eyes, and I can't stand that. That's why I've kept my distance. But in the end, I've learned to respect you. I thought to myself, 'The little man stands firm.' And even though I'm laughing, I'm serious. You do stand firm, don't you? I like people who stand firm, no matter what they stand for, even if they're little guys like you. Your expectant eyes stopped annoying me after a while, and in the end, I started to like them. You seem to love me for some reason, Alyosha."

"I do love you, Ivan. Dmitri says about you, 'Ivan is a tomb!' But I say, 'Ivan is a mystery.' You're still a mystery to me, even now. But I've understood something about you today that I didn't understand before."

"What's that?" Ivan laughed.

"You won't get mad?" Alyosha laughed too. "Well?"

"That you're just as young as other men your age. You're a fresh, nice, young boy—green, even! Have I insulted you terribly?"

"On the contrary, that's quite a coincidence," Ivan cried out, warmly and cheerfully. "Would you believe it, ever since that scene with her, I've been thinking about nothing but my own youthful greenness. And here you are, bringing it up, as if you read my mind. You know, I've been sitting here thinking that even if I didn't believe in life, if I lost faith in the woman I love, or lost faith in the way things are, or if I became convinced that everything is just a chaotic, devil-ridden mess, and if I experienced all the horrors of human disillusionment— still, I would want to keep living. Once I've had a taste of life, I wouldn't turn away from it until I had drained the cup dry. But when I turn thirty, I think I'll leave the cup, even if I haven't finished it, and I'll walk away— where to, I don't know. But until I'm thirty, I know my youth will carry me through everything—through all disillusionment, through every disgust with life. I've asked myself many times if there's any despair in the world that could overcome this crazy thirst for life I have, and I've decided there isn't. At least not until I'm thirty. Then, I think, I'll lose it naturally. Some sentimental moralists—and especially poets—often call that thirst for life base. The Karamazovs have it, that's for sure. I'm sure you have it too. But why is it base? The force that pulls us to life is still incredibly strong, Alyosha. I crave life, and I keep living in spite of logic. Even if I don't believe in the universe's order, I still love the sticky little leaves that sprout in spring. I love the blue sky. I love certain people, people you sometimes love without knowing why. I love the great deeds done by men, even if I stopped believing in them long ago. Yet out of habit, my heart still values them. Oh, look—they've brought your soup. Eat it, it'll do you good. This soup is top-notch, they really know how to make it here. I want to travel through Europe, Alyosha. That's where I'll go from here. And yet, I know I'm only going to a graveyard. But it's a special graveyard, that's what it is. Precious are the dead who lie there. Every stone speaks of such burning life in the past, of such passionate belief in their work, their truth, their struggles, and their science. I know I'll fall to the ground, kiss those stones, and weep over them, even though I know deep down it's just a graveyard now. I won't weep from despair, but from happiness. I'll soak my soul in that emotion. I love the sticky leaves in spring, the blue sky—that's what it is. It's not about intellect or logic. It's about loving with your gut, with your very insides. You love the strength of your youth. Do you understand anything of what I'm saying, Alyosha?" Ivan suddenly laughed.

"I understand it too well, Ivan. You want to love with your insides, with your gut. You put that so well, and I'm so glad that you have this longing for life," Alyosha exclaimed. "I think everyone should love life more than anything else in the world."

"Love life more than its meaning?"

"Absolutely, love it regardless of logic, as you said. Only then can you truly understand its meaning. I've thought this way for a long time. You've already done half the work, Ivan. You love life. Now you just need to do the second half, and you'll be saved."

"You're trying to save me, but maybe I'm not lost. And what's the second half?"

"You need to bring the dead back to life, those who might not really be dead after all. Come, let me have some tea. I'm really happy about our talk, Ivan."

"I see you're feeling inspired. I love hearing these declarations of faith from people who are just starting out. You're a steady person, Alexey. Is it true you're leaving the monastery?"

"Yes, my elder is sending me out into the world."

"Then we'll see each other in the world. We'll meet again before I turn thirty, before I start turning away from life's cup. Father doesn't plan to turn away from his cup until he's seventy—he even dreams of hanging on until eighty. He's quite serious about it, even though he acts like a fool. He's standing firm, clinging to his sensuality. But once we pass thirty, there might be nothing left to stand on. Hanging on until seventy is nasty— better to stop at thirty, when you can still deceive yourself with 'a shadow of nobility.' Have you seen Dmitri today?"

"No, but I saw Smerdyakov," Alyosha replied, and he quickly, but thoroughly, described his meeting with Smerdyakov. Ivan listened closely, then asked some questions.

"But Smerdyakov begged me not to tell Dmitri that he told me about him," Alyosha added. Ivan frowned and thought deeply.

"Are you frowning because of Smerdyakov?" Alyosha asked.

"Yes, because of him. Damn him. I wanted to see Dmitri, but now it doesn't seem necessary," Ivan said, reluctantly.

"But are you really leaving so soon, brother?"

"Yes."

"What about Dmitri and father? How will it all end?" Alyosha asked, worried.

"You're always going on about this! What does it have to do with me? Am I my brother Dmitri's keeper?" Ivan snapped irritably, but then suddenly smiled bitterly. "That's Cain's answer about his murdered brother right? Is that what you're thinking? Well, damn it, I can't stick around to be their keeper, can I? I've done what I needed to do, and now I'm leaving. Do you really think I'm jealous of Dmitri, that I've been trying to steal his beautiful Katerina Ivanovna for the past three months? Nonsense. I had my own business. I finished it. I'm leaving. You were there, you saw me finish it."

"At Katerina Ivanovna's?"

"Yes, and I've freed myself once and for all. And what does Dmitri have to do with it? He's got nothing to do with this. I had my own issues to settle with Katerina Ivanovna. You know, it was actually Dmitri who acted like there was something going on between us. I never asked him to, but he solemnly handed her over to me and gave us his blessing. It's ridiculous! Oh, Alyosha, if you only knew how light my heart feels right now! Can you believe it, I sat here eating my dinner and almost ordered champagne to celebrate my first hour of freedom

Tfoo! This has been going on for nearly six months, and just like that, I threw it all off. I wouldn't have guessed, even yesterday, that it would be this easy to end it if I wanted."

"Are you talking about your love, Ivan?"

"My love, if you want to call it that. I fell in love with her, I worried about her, and she worried about me. I sat by her... and suddenly, it all collapsed! I spoke this morning like I was inspired, but I left and burst out laughing. Can you believe it? Yes, it's the honest truth."

"You seem very happy about it now," said Alyosha, watching his brother's face brighten suddenly.

"How could I have known I didn't care for her at all? Ha ha! Turns out I didn't. And yet, how she drew me in! Even just now, when I gave my little speech, she was still so attractive. And even now, she still attracts me, but it's so easy to walk away from her. Do you think I'm bragging?"

"No, maybe it wasn't really love."

"Alyosha," Ivan laughed, "don't try to reflect on love, it's not your thing. Remember how you jumped into the conversation this morning? I forgot to kiss you for that... But oh, how she tortured me! She knew how much I loved her! She loved me, not Dmitri," Ivan insisted, smiling. "Her feelings for Dmitri were just her punishing herself. Everything I told her just now was completely true, but the worst part is, it might take her 15 or 20 years to figure out that she doesn't care about Dmitri and that she really loves me, the one she tormented. Or maybe she'll never realize it, even after today's lesson. Well, it's better this way. I can just leave for good. By the way, how is she now? What happened after I left?"

Alyosha told him she had a fit and was now unconscious and delirious.

"Is Madame Hohlakov exaggerating?" "I don't think so."

"I'll have to find out. Nobody dies from hysterics, though. They don't matter. God gave women hysterics as a way to release their emotions. I won't go back to her. Why should I get involved again?"

"But you told her she never really cared for you."

"I did that on purpose. Alyosha, should I order some champagne? Let's toast to my freedom. If you only knew how happy I am!"

"No, brother, we'd better not drink," said Alyosha suddenly. "Besides, I'm feeling a bit down."

"Yes, you've been down for a while, I've noticed that." "Have you decided to leave tomorrow morning, then?"

"Morning? I didn't say I was leaving in the morning... But maybe I will. Can you believe I had dinner here just to avoid eating with the old man? I hate him so much. I would've left a long time ago if it weren't for him. But why are you so worried about me leaving? We've got plenty of time before I go—an eternity!"

"If you're leaving tomorrow, what do you mean by 'an eternity'?"

"But what does it matter to us?" Ivan laughed. "We've got enough time to talk, enough time for whatever brought us here. Why do you look so surprised? Answer me—why are we meeting here? To talk about my love for Katerina Ivanovna? About the old man and Dmitri? About foreign travel? About Russia's problems? About Emperor Napoleon? Is that why?"

"No."

"Then you know why. Other people don't care, but for us, in our youth, we have to tackle the eternal questions first. That's what matters to us. Young Russia is obsessed with eternal questions these days, just as the older generation is busy with practical issues. Why have you been looking at me with such expectation for the past three months? Was it to ask me, 'Do you believe in God, or do you believe in nothing at all?' Isn't that what you've been wanting to ask?"

"Maybe," smiled Alyosha. "You're not mocking me now, Ivan?"

"Mocking you? No, I don't want to hurt my little brother who's been watching me so expectantly for three months. Alyosha, look me straight in the eye! I'm just as much a kid as you are, though I'm not a novice anymore. And what have Russian boys like us been doing all this time? Some of them, I mean? They sit in places like this, in taverns. They've never met before, and after they leave, they won't see each other again for 40 years. And what do they talk about during that brief moment in the tavern? The eternal questions, the existence of God, and immortality. And those who don't believe in God talk about socialism or anarchism, about how to transform all of humanity into something new. It all boils down to the same thing—it's the same questions, just turned inside out. And so many Russian boys do nothing but talk about these eternal questions! Isn't that right?"

"Yes, for real Russians, the questions of God's existence and immortality, or as you said, the same questions flipped around, come first and foremost. And that's how it should be," said Alyosha, still watching his brother with the same gentle, curious smile.

"Well, Alyosha, it's sometimes a mistake to be Russian at all, but you can hardly imagine anything dumber than the way Russian boys waste their time. But there's one Russian boy named Alyosha whom I'm very fond of."

"That was well said!" Alyosha laughed suddenly.

"Well, tell me where to start. What do you want me to talk about? The existence of God?"

"Start wherever you like. Yesterday at father's, you declared there was no God." Alyosha looked at his brother intently.

"I said that yesterday at dinner just to tease you. I saw how your eyes lit up. But now I'm open to discussing it seriously. I want to be friends with you, Alyosha. I have no friends, and I want to give it a try. Who knows, maybe I do believe in God," Ivan laughed. "That would surprise you, wouldn't it?"

"Yes, of course—if you're not joking," Alyosha replied.

"Joking? Yesterday, at the elder's, I was told I was joking. You know, my dear boy, there was an old sinner in the 18th century who said that if there were no God, people would have to invent one. S'il n'existait pas Dieu, il faudrait l'inventer. And man has indeed invented God. What's amazing isn't that God might really exist; the real marvel is that such an idea—the idea that God is necessary—could even enter the mind of a savage and cruel creature like man. It's so holy, so touching, so wise, and such a great credit to man. As for me, I've long decided not to think about whether man created God or God created man. And I won't go over all the basic points Russian boys argue about, all taken from European theories; because what's a theory over there is considered a fact by Russian boys, and not just by boys but by their teachers too, because even our Russian professors can act like boys. So, I'll skip all the theories.

What am I trying to explain? I'm trying to show you quickly what kind of person I am, what I believe, and what I hope for, right? That's what you're asking. So, here it is—I accept God, just like that. But listen, if God exists, and if He really created the world, then He created it based on Euclid's geometry, with the human mind only able to understand three dimensions of space. But there have been and still are mathematicians and philosophers— some of the best—who doubt that the whole universe, or all of existence, was created according to Euclid's rules. Some even dare to imagine that two parallel lines, which Euclid says can never meet on Earth, might meet somewhere in infinity. So, I've concluded that since I can't even understand that, I definitely can't understand God. I admit humbly that I don't have the ability to answer such questions. I have an earthly, Euclidean mind. How could I ever solve problems that don't belong to this world? And I suggest that you don't think about it either, dear Alyosha—especially when it comes to God, whether He exists or not. Questions like that are completely inappropriate for a mind designed to think in only three dimensions.

So, I accept God and I'm happy to do so. And what's more, I accept His wisdom, His purpose, which are way beyond our understanding. I believe in the hidden order and meaning of life. I believe in the eternal harmony we'll be part of one day. I believe in the Word that the universe is striving toward, which was 'with God' and is God, and so on, and so on, to infinity. There are all kinds of ways to phrase it. I'm on the right path, right? Yet, believe it or not, in the end, I don't accept this world that God made. Even though I know it exists, I don't accept it at all.

It's not that I reject God, you understand. It's the world He created that I don't and can't accept. Let me explain. I believe, like a child, that all suffering will be healed and made right. I believe that all the ridiculous contradictions of human life will disappear, like a bad dream, like a pathetic trick of the small and powerless human mind. I believe that, in the end, when eternal harmony comes, something so precious will happen that it will be enough to heal all hearts, to comfort all resentments, to atone for all of humanity's crimes and all the bloodshed. It will make it possible, not just to forgive but to justify everything that has happened to people. But even if all that happens, I won't accept it. I refuse to accept it. Even if parallel lines do meet and I see it with my own eyes, I'll acknowledge that they met, but still, I won't accept it. That's who I am, Alyosha. That's my belief. I'm being sincere. I started our conversation stupidly on purpose, but I've led up to my confession, which is really what you wanted. You didn't want to hear about God, but to know what kind of man your brother, who you love, really is. And now I've told you."

Ivan ended his long speech with an unexpected intensity of feeling.

"But why did you start 'as stupidly as you could'?" Alyosha asked dreamily.

"First, because I'm Russian. Russian conversations on topics like this are always unbelievably stupid. Second, the more stupid you are, the closer you are to reality. The more stupid, the clearer things become. Stupidity is simple and honest, while intelligence hides and wriggles around. Intelligence is sly, but stupidity is straightforward and honest. I've dragged this conversation down into despair, and the more stupidly I did it, the better it is for me."

"You'll explain why you don't accept the world?" Alyosha asked.

"Of course I will. It's no secret. That's what I've been building up to. My dear little brother, I don't want to corrupt you or take you away from your beliefs—maybe I even want you to heal me." Ivan smiled suddenly, with the innocence of a gentle child. Alyosha had never seen him smile like that before.

Chapter 4: Rebellion

"I need to confess something, Alyosha," Ivan began. "I've never understood how anyone can truly love their neighbors.

It's our neighbors, specifically, that are impossible to love, even though it might be easier to love someone far away. I once read about a saint named John the Merciful. When a starving, freezing beggar came to him, he took the man into his bed, held him close, and even breathed into his mouth, even though the man's breath was foul and rotting from some terrible disease. I'm convinced the saint did it out of some kind of self-punishment, forcing himself to act out of duty rather than real love. To love someone, I think, they need to stay hidden—because once you see them up close, the love fades away."

"Father Zossima has spoken about this many times," Alyosha said. "He said that for many people, it's the face of another person that makes it hard to love them. But I believe there's real love in people, even love that's close to Christ's. I've seen it myself."

"Well, I haven't seen it, and I can't understand it. And I think most people would agree with me. The real question is whether people are just bad by nature, or if it's simply part of being human. To me, the kind of love Christ showed is impossible on earth. He was God, but we're not. Take me, for example—if I suffer deeply, no one else can ever truly understand my suffering because they aren't me. And people rarely even acknowledge someone else's pain, as if admitting it would somehow elevate the sufferer. And why don't they acknowledge it? Maybe because I smell bad, or because I look stupid, or because I accidentally stepped on their foot once.

"On top of that, there's a difference between types of suffering. Someone might tolerate my hunger and help me with food—that's a kind of suffering people understand. But suffering for a cause, for an idea? People don't recognize that as easily. They expect someone suffering for an idea to look a certain way, to fit their image of what a person like that should be. And when I don't meet those expectations, they stop caring—not because they're cruel, but because I just don't match what they imagined. Honestly, beggars—especially those who try to act polite—shouldn't even show their faces. They'd have better luck asking for help through a newspaper ad. It's easy to love someone in the abstract, or from a distance, but up close, it becomes almost impossible.

"If beggars were like those in ballets—wearing silk rags and dancing gracefully while they asked for alms—maybe people would enjoy watching them. But even then, they still wouldn't love them. Anyway, enough of that. I only brought it up to make my point. I meant to talk about the suffering of humanity as a whole, but I think we'd better focus just on children. That narrows things down, though it makes my argument weaker. Still, it's better to talk about children because people can love children, even when they're dirty or ugly—though, really, I think children are never ugly.

"As for adults, they're not just hard to love—they've earned their suffering. They ate the forbidden fruit, learned about good and evil, and became 'like gods,' as the Bible says. And they keep eating that fruit to this day. But children haven't eaten anything. They're still innocent. You love children, don't you, Alyosha? I know you do, and that's why you'll understand why I want to focus on them. If children suffer terribly in this world, it must be because they're being punished for the sins of their parents— the ones who ate the fruit. But that kind of reasoning belongs to another world. It doesn't make sense to the human heart here on earth. It's not right for innocent children to suffer because of others' sins.

"You might be surprised, Alyosha, but I really love children too. Even cruel people—violent ones, like the Karamazovs—can love children. I've noticed that. Children are so different from adults, almost like they belong to another species. I once knew a criminal in prison who had killed entire families, including children, during his time as a thief. But in prison, he developed a strange affection for children. He spent his days at the window, watching the kids play in the yard. He even made friends with a little boy who came to his window every day.

"Do you know why I'm telling you all this, Alyosha? My head hurts, and I feel really sad."

"You sound strange," Alyosha said uneasily, "like you're not quite yourself."

"Recently, I met a Bulgarian in Moscow," Ivan continued, as if he hadn't heard Alyosha. "He told me about the horrible things the Turks and Circassians were doing in Bulgaria. They were afraid the Slavs would rebel, so they burned villages, killed people, and attacked women and children. They'd nail prisoners by their ears to fences and leave them there until morning—then hang them the next day.

"People talk about 'bestial cruelty,' but that's unfair to animals. Animals could never be as cruel as humans. A tiger, for instance, only tears and eats. That's all it knows how to do. It would never think to nail someone's ears to a fence, even if it could. Humans, on the other hand, enjoy cruelty. These Turks tortured children too— cutting unborn babies from their mothers' wombs and throwing infants into the air to catch them on their bayonets, all while their mothers watched. That was the part they enjoyed the most—doing it right in front of the mothers.

"Here's another example: picture a mother holding her baby, surrounded by Turkish soldiers. They want to entertain themselves. They smile at the baby, tickling him until he laughs. Then one of them takes out a pistol, holds it just inches from the baby's face, and pulls the trigger. The baby's brains are blown out right in front of his mother. The soldiers enjoyed that, don't you think? By the way, Turks are known to have a sweet tooth."

"Brother, what are you trying to say?" Alyosha asked, deeply troubled.

"I think if the devil doesn't exist, then humans must have created him in their own image."

"Just like they created God?" Alyosha said quietly.

"You're clever with words, aren't you?" Ivan laughed. "That's exactly what Polonius says in Hamlet: 'It's amazing how you can twist words.' Well, I'm glad you caught me."

"Yours must be quite the God if man created Him in his own image and likeness," Ivan began. "You asked me earlier what I was getting at. You see, I like collecting certain facts, and, believe it or not, I even copy down specific stories from newspapers and books. I've already gathered a pretty good collection. Of course, the Turks are included, but they're foreigners. What's more interesting to me are the stories I've found right here at home— stories even worse than what the Turks have done. You know, we prefer beatings—rods and whips— that's our national tradition. Nailing ears to fences? That's unimaginable to us, since we are Europeans, after all. But beatings—we've always had those, and no one can take them away from us.

"In other countries, they barely beat people anymore. Either their manners have become more civilized, or laws have been passed that make it illegal. But they've found other ways to express their cruelty, methods that are just as national to them as beatings are to us. Their ways are so tied to their culture that we would have trouble imitating them here, though we might be learning from them—especially since the religious movement has taken hold among the aristocracy.

"I have a fascinating pamphlet, translated from French, that tells the story of a man named Richard who was executed about five years ago. He was only twenty-three, and right before his execution, he supposedly found God. Richard was born illegitimate, and when he was six years old, his parents gave him away to some shepherds in the Swiss mountains. They treated him like an animal, teaching him nothing and barely feeding or clothing him. When he was seven, they made him herd sheep out in the cold and rain, and they didn't feel the least bit guilty about it. They believed they had every right to treat him that way, since he was just a burden handed over to them.

"Richard later described how, like the Prodigal Son in the Bible, he was so hungry that he longed to eat the food given to the pigs they were fattening for sale. But they wouldn't even let him have that. And when he tried to steal from the pigs, they beat him. That's how he spent his childhood and youth—until he grew strong enough to leave and try to survive as a thief.

"In Geneva, he worked as a laborer, drank away whatever he earned, lived like a brute, and finally ended up killing and robbing an old man. He was arrested, put on trial, and sentenced to death. They don't have much patience for sentimentality there. But in prison, Richard found himself surrounded by pastors, Christian volunteers, and kind-hearted ladies. They taught him to read and write and preached the Gospel to him non-stop. They wore him down until he finally confessed to his crime. He became religious, writing to the court to declare himself a monster, but one who had found God's grace in the end.

"All of Geneva was stirred by his story—especially the religious and upper-class circles. Everyone flocked to the prison, showering Richard with kisses and calling him their brother. 'You have found grace,' they told him. And Richard couldn't stop weeping. 'Yes,

I've found grace,' he said. 'All my life, I wanted to eat pig slop, but now even I have found God.' And the pastors and judges told him, 'Yes, Richard, you've found grace, but you still have to die. You've shed blood, and now you must pay with your life.'

"On the day of his execution, Richard was overwhelmed with emotion. He kept saying, 'This is the happiest day of my life. I am going to the Lord.' The pastors, judges, and kind-hearted ladies agreed: 'Yes, Richard, this is your happiest day.' They followed the prison van to the scaffold, all of them calling him their brother and urging him to die joyfully. And so, they led him to the guillotine, kissed him one last time, and beheaded him—because, after all, he had found grace.

"That pamphlet was translated into Russian by some aristocrats with religious leanings, and they've been distributing it for free, hoping it will educate the people. It's interesting because it shows a national custom—though to us, it's ridiculous to kill someone right after welcoming him as a brother. But we have our own traditions, and they might be even worse. Our national pastime is inflicting pain purely for the pleasure of it.

"Nekrasov wrote about this in a poem where he describes a peasant whipping a horse in the eyes—those 'meek eyes.' It's the kind of thing every Russian has seen at least once. In the poem, a weak, overworked horse collapses under the weight of a heavy load. The peasant, instead of helping the horse, starts beating it furiously. He keeps whipping the horse, caught up in a frenzy, no longer aware of what he's doing. 'You must pull,' he shouts, 'even if it kills you!' The poor horse trembles and gasps, dragging the load with unnatural, jerking movements, barely able to breathe. It's an awful scene, but that's just a horse. And horses, after all, were given to us to be beaten. The Tatars left us the whip as part of their legacy.

"But it's not just animals we beat. We beat people too. I once read about a well-educated man and his wife who beat their seven-year- old daughter with a birch rod. The father even bragged about how the twigs made it sting more. 'It stings better this way,' he said as he whipped his child. Some people become almost intoxicated by the act of beating. Each blow gives them more pleasure, driving them into a frenzy. They beat harder and harder, until the child can't scream anymore. All she can do is gasp, 'Daddy, daddy!'

"By some strange twist of fate, this case ended up in court. The father hired a lawyer, and the lawyer defended him, arguing that it was just normal discipline. 'This is a private family matter,' the lawyer said. 'It's shameful that it even reached the courts.' The jury agreed and found the father not guilty. The public cheered, thrilled that the man had been acquitted. Oh, how I wish I'd been there! I would've suggested we start a collection in his honor, just to celebrate his victory.

"But I've saved the worst stories for last, Alyosha. I've gathered so many terrible accounts about children. For example, I read about a little girl, only five years old, who was hated by her parents. They were well-educated and respected people, but for some reason, they took pleasure in tormenting their own child. It's strange how some people are kind to everyone else but take pleasure in hurting children. Children's innocence and helplessness seem to provoke something dark in them.

"These people, who act civilized toward adults, are drawn to the powerlessness of children. It's the child's trust, their complete dependence, that stirs something vile within these people. Every person carries a demon inside—a demon of rage, of cruel desire. That demon wakes up when they see someone defenseless. It feeds off the child's screams, their helpless cries.

"And every person carries other demons too—demons born from indulgence and vice, from the diseases they bring upon themselves, like gout and kidney problems."

"This poor child, only five years old, was tortured in every way by her 'cultured' parents. They beat her, kicked her, and punished her without reason until her whole body was covered in bruises. Then they took it further—they locked her outside all night in the freezing cold. Because she didn't wake up and ask to be taken inside at night (as if a child that age could know to do that), they smeared her face and filled her mouth with filth. And it was her mother, her own mother, who did this to her. That mother could sleep peacefully while listening to her child's cries of pain! Can you understand why this little creature, who didn't even know why she was being hurt, would hit her aching chest with her tiny fists in the cold and dark, crying her gentle tears and praying to a 'dear, kind God' for help? Can you understand that, my friend and brother, you, a humble and pious novice? Can you understand why this horrible cruelty must be allowed to happen? People say that without it, man could never know good and evil. But why should we need to know this terrible good and evil if it costs so much? Why, the whole world's knowledge isn't worth that one child's prayer to 'dear, kind God'! I won't even talk about the suffering of adults—they've eaten the apple, and they can go to hell! But these children? I'm hurting you, Alyosha. You're not yourself. I'll stop if you want."

"Never mind. I want to suffer, too," mumbled Alyosha.

"Just one more story, one more picture, because it's so strange, so typical, and I just read it in some old Russian history. I've forgotten the name of the book—I'll have to look it up. It happened during the darkest days of serfdom, in the early 19th century. God bless the liberator of the people! There was a general back then, a man with aristocratic connections and huge estates. He was one of those men—rare even in those days—who, after retiring from the military, believed they had absolute power over their serfs. He had kennels full of hounds and almost a hundred dog boys, all in uniform. One day, a little serf boy, just eight years old, accidentally threw a stone that hurt the paw of the general's favorite dog. 'Why is my dog limping?' the general asked. He was told the boy had thrown a stone and hurt the dog. 'So you did it,' the general said, staring the boy up and down. 'Take him away.' They locked the boy up all night, away from his mother. The next morning, the general went out riding with his dogs and his servants, all in full hunting gear. He ordered the little boy to be brought out. It was a cold, foggy autumn morning—perfect for hunting. The general ordered the boy to be stripped naked. The poor child shivered, terrified, too scared to even cry. 'Make him run,' the general commanded. The boy ran. 'Sic him!' yelled the general, and he set the whole pack of dogs on the boy. They tore the child to pieces in front of his mother. I think the general was later declared unfit to manage his estate. So, what should have been done to him? Should he have been shot? For the sake of our moral feelings, should he have been executed? Tell me, Alyosha!"

"He should have been shot," whispered Alyosha, raising his pale, trembling face to Ivan.

"Bravo!" Ivan cried happily. "Even you say so! You're not such a good monk after all, Alyosha Karamazov! There's a little devil inside you too!"

"What I said was absurd, but—"

"That's exactly the point! That 'but' is the key!" Ivan shouted. "Let me tell you, little monk, that absurdity is necessary in this world. The world stands on absurdities, and maybe nothing would happen without them. We know what we know."

"What do you know?"

"I understand nothing," Ivan continued, almost as if he were in a daze. "And I don't want to understand anything. I just want to stick to the facts. I decided long ago that if I tried to understand anything, I'd be lying to myself. So I've made up my mind to just stick to the facts."

"Why are you testing me?" Alyosha cried, suddenly distressed.

"Will you finally say what you mean?"

"Of course, I will. That's what I've been leading up to. I care about you, I don't want to lose you, and I'm not giving you up to Zossima."

For a minute, Ivan fell silent, and his face became very sad.

"Listen, I only used the example of children to make my point clearer. I won't even talk about the other tears of mankind that soak the earth from top to bottom. I narrowed my focus on purpose. I'm just a bug—I can't understand why the world is the way it is. I guess it's man's fault. We were given paradise, but we wanted freedom and stole fire from heaven, even though we knew it would make us unhappy. So there's no need to feel sorry for us. With my small, earthly mind, all I know is that there's suffering and that no one is truly guilty. Cause follows effect, everything flows naturally—but that's just Euclidian logic. I know it's nonsense, and I refuse to live by it! What good is it to me that there's no guilt and that cause follows effect? I demand justice, or I'll destroy myself. And I don't want justice far off in some distant time and space—I want it here on earth, where I can see it. I've believed in it. I want to see it with my own eyes, and if I die before it happens, I want to rise from the dead to witness it. I refuse to believe that my suffering, my sins, will only be used to 'fertilize the soil' for some future harmony that I won't even get to experience. I want to be there when the lamb lies down with the lion, and when the victim embraces the murderer. I want to understand it all. All religions are built on this hope, and I believe in it too. But what about the children? What am I supposed to do about them? I can't accept their suffering. I've only talked about children because it makes my point clearer. If all humanity must suffer for the eternal harmony, what do children have to do with it? Why should they pay for it? I can understand grown men being punished for their sins, but children? What about them? If children must suffer for the crimes of their fathers, that truth is beyond my understanding. It's not fair. Imagine an eight-year-old boy torn to pieces by dogs—he didn't even get the chance to grow up and sin! What sense does that make? Alyosha, I'm not blaspheming! I understand what a huge thing it will be when the whole universe finally understands the reason behind everything and we all shout, 'Thou art just, O Lord!' But I can't accept that harmony."

"I can't accept it, and while I'm here on earth, I'll do what I can to protest. Maybe, when the time comes, I'll join in and shout with everyone else, 'Thou art just, O Lord!' But I don't want to shout it now. I'm giving back my ticket to that harmony. It's not worth the tears of that tortured child, not worth the tears of a child who prayed to God with no answer. I don't want that kind of justice. I refuse to accept it, even if it's the truth. I'm giving back my entrance ticket."

"That's rebellion," Alyosha murmured.

"Rebellion? It's sad that you call it that," Ivan said seriously. "I'm not rebelling. I want to live. But answer me this—if you had to build a perfect world where everyone would be happy forever, but the price was torturing just one innocent child, would you do it?"

"No, I wouldn't," whispered Alyosha.

"And do you think the people who live in that perfect world would be able to live happily knowing their peace was built on the blood of one child?"

"No, I can't believe that," said Alyosha, his eyes glowing. "But there is someone who can forgive everything. Someone who gave His innocent blood for all and can forgive everything."

"I haven't forgotten Him," Ivan said softly. "In fact, I've been wondering when you'd bring Him up. Usually, people on your side mention Him right away. Let me tell you something, Alyosha. I wrote a poem last year. If you have a little time, I'll tell it to you."

"You wrote a poem?"

"Well, not exactly. I didn't write it down, but I made it up. You'll be the first to hear it. It's called 'The Grand Inquisitor.' Would you like to hear it?"

"I'm all ears," said Alyosha.

Chapter 5: The Grand Inquisitor

"Even this needs a bit of an introduction—a kind of literary preface," Ivan said with a laugh. "And I'm not the best at writing one. You see, the events in my story take place in the sixteenth century, and back then, as you probably learned in school, it was common in poetry to bring heavenly beings down to earth. Not just Dante—monks and clerics in France used to stage performances where the Madonna, saints, angels, and even God Himself appeared on stage. In those times, it was done with complete simplicity. For example, in Victor Hugo's Notre Dame de Paris, there's a scene in which a public play is performed in the Hôtel de Ville during the reign of Louis XI to celebrate the birth of the dauphin. The play was called Le bon jugement de la très sainte et gracieuse Vierge Marie, and the Virgin Mary herself appears on stage to pronounce her judgment. Similar religious plays, mostly based on Old Testament stories, were performed in Moscow too, right up until the time of Peter the Great. Along with these plays, there were also countless legends and poems that circulated, featuring saints and angels stepping into the world whenever they were needed.

"In our monasteries, the monks spent their time translating, copying, and even writing these kinds of poems—yes, even under the rule of the Tatars. One such poem, which of course came from Greek origins, is called The Wanderings of Our Lady through Hell. It's just as bold as Dante's work. In the poem, the Virgin Mary visits Hell, guided by the Archangel Michael, and she witnesses the suffering of the damned. Among the sinners in Hell, some are trapped at the bottom of a burning lake, unable to swim to the surface, and these are described as 'those whom God forgets'—a phrase with extraordinary depth and power. Overwhelmed by what she sees, Our Lady falls before the throne of God, pleading for mercy on behalf of all the souls in Hell. She refuses to give up, even when God points to the wounds of His Son, who was nailed to the Cross, and asks, 'How can I forgive His tormentors?' In response, she calls on all the saints, martyrs, angels, and archangels to join her in praying for mercy for everyone, without exception.

"In the end, she wins a brief reprieve for the souls in Hell—a break from their torment each year, from Good Friday until Trinity Day. As soon as this mercy is granted, the souls raise a chorus of thanks from the depths of Hell, chanting, 'Thou art just, O Lord, in this judgment.' My poem would have been something like that if it had been written back then. He appears in my poem too, but He says nothing. He just passes through silently. It has now been fifteen centuries since He promised to return in His glory, fifteen centuries since His prophet wrote, 'Behold, I come quickly.' He Himself said, 'Of that day and hour knoweth no man, neither the Son, but the Father.' Yet people have waited for Him with unshaken faith and love all this time. In fact, their faith has only grown stronger.

"For fifteen centuries, people have gone without signs from heaven, clinging only to the faith in their hearts.

No signs from heaven come today
To strengthen what the heart must say.

"There were miracles in those days—saints performing healing miracles and some holy people being visited by the Virgin Mary herself. But even then, doubt was creeping into people's hearts. A new heresy was spreading in northern Germany, where some claimed that miracles no longer occurred. These heretics mocked the idea of divine intervention. Still, the faithful clung to their beliefs with even greater fervor. People continued to cry out to Him, yearning for His return, loving Him, hoping for Him, and longing to suffer and even die for Him. For so many generations, humanity had prayed with all its heart, 'O Lord, come quickly,' and at last, in His infinite mercy, He answered their call.

"In the past, He had appeared to saints, martyrs, and hermits, as recorded in their stories. The poet Tyutchev even wrote with complete conviction that Christ had come to Russia:

Bearing the Cross in humble guise,
Weary and worn, the Heavenly King

Blessed our land and wandered on,
Touching the souls of suffering men.

"And I believe that is exactly what happened. He came down once more to walk among His children—those who were suffering and sinful, yet still loved Him like children.

"My story is set in Spain, in the city of Seville, during the darkest days of the Inquisition, when heretics were burned at the stake in the name of God. Fires were lit every day, and in grand autos- da-fé, crowds gathered to watch the condemned burn. Kings, cardinals, noble knights, and elegant ladies all attended these events, believing it was for the glory of God. One day, amidst the chaos and cruelty, He came—not in His promised final return, with all His heavenly glory shining like lightning from the east to the west—but quietly, just for a moment, to visit His people.

"He came in the same human form He had worn during His time on earth fifteen centuries ago. He walked the streets of Seville, where the day before, nearly a hundred heretics had been burned at the stake by the Grand Inquisitor in a grand spectacle attended by the king and all of Seville's elite.

"He arrived silently, unnoticed at first, but somehow, everyone recognized Him. That might be one of the most powerful moments in my poem—the way they recognized Him. The people couldn't help but gather around Him. They flocked to Him, following Him wherever He went. He moved among them with a gentle smile full of infinite compassion. There was a radiance in His eyes, a light that filled the hearts of those around Him with love.

"He stretched out His hands to bless the people, and healing flowed from Him, even through His clothes. An old man who had been blind since birth cried out, 'O Lord, heal me so I can see You!' And at that very moment, the man's eyes were opened, and he saw.

"The crowd wept with joy and kissed the ground beneath His feet. Children threw flowers in His path, singing and crying out, 'Hosanna!' Again and again, the people whispered, 'It's Him—it must be Him!'

"At that moment, He stopped on the steps of the Seville cathedral. A group of mourners was bringing in a small white coffin. Inside lay the body of a seven-year-old girl, the only daughter of a well- known citizen. Her lifeless body was covered in flowers.

"'He will raise her!' the crowd shouted to the grieving mother.

"The priest leading the procession hesitated, unsure what to do, but the mother threw herself at His feet, crying out, 'If it's really You, raise my child!' She held out her hands, begging for a miracle.

"The procession came to a halt, and the little coffin was laid at His feet. With deep compassion in His eyes, He looked down at the child. Then, softly, He spoke the words, 'Maiden, arise.'

"And the little girl sat up in the coffin. She looked around, wide- eyed with wonder, holding the bouquet of white roses that had been placed in her hands."

There were cries, sobs, and confusion spreading through the crowd, and just at that moment, the cardinal—the Grand Inquisitor himself—passed by the cathedral. He was an old man, almost ninety years old, tall and upright despite his age, with a face deeply lined by wrinkles and sunken eyes that still retained a flicker of sharp awareness. But he was not dressed in the majestic robes of a cardinal, as he had been the day before while presiding over the executions of those deemed enemies of the Church. Now, he wore a simple, coarse monk's cassock, worn and faded, a far cry from the splendid garments that marked him as the highest authority in the Church. Following him at a distance were his stern assistants, his attendants, and the so-called "holy guard," the enforcers of the Inquisition's will.

The Grand Inquisitor stopped abruptly, standing still when he noticed the commotion near the cathedral. His gaze swept over the scene from a distance, his sharp eyes observing everything with the precision of someone used to maintaining control over every situation. He saw how the people laid the coffin at the Prisoner's feet. He witnessed the miracle—the little girl who had been dead, rising from the grave at His words. In that instant, the cardinal's expression darkened, his face tightening as if an invisible shadow had fallen over him. His thick gray brows furrowed, and a fire flickered in his old, tired eyes—a fire not of wonder but of deep resentment, perhaps even fear. Slowly, the old man raised a hand, pointing with a single, bony finger at the Prisoner. He gave the guards a silent command: "Seize Him."

And so overwhelming was the cardinal's authority, so thoroughly had the people been trained into submission, that the crowd parted without hesitation, making way for the guards to approach. The guards advanced quietly, their movements precise, as though they were enacting a routine they knew all too well. In absolute silence, without protest, they laid their hands on Him and led Him away. Not a murmur rose from the crowd. No one dared to speak, let alone intervene. As if guided by a single will, the entire crowd fell to the ground in unison, bowing deeply before the Grand Inquisitor. The old man responded by raising his hand in a silent gesture of blessing. Then, without another glance, he resumed his walk, disappearing into the distance, his worn cassock swaying slightly as he moved away.

The guards, meanwhile, escorted the Prisoner through the winding streets of the ancient city, leading Him to the grim, vaulted chambers within the palace of the Holy Inquisition. These were dark, cold rooms, built for the sole purpose of breaking the will and spirit of those held within. They placed Him inside one such cell, an oppressive space made even more stifling by the thick stone walls. The heavy iron door slammed shut with a dull, resonating thud, locking Him in.

The day gave way to night—an oppressive night, heavy with the humid air of Seville. The streets outside lay silent under the cover of darkness, while the scent of laurel and lemon leaves drifted faintly on the still breeze. In the pitch-blackness of the cell, the iron door creaked open unexpectedly. A sliver of light cut through the darkness, and the Grand Inquisitor himself entered, holding a small lantern in his hand. He was alone, having dismissed his attendants. The door groaned shut behind him, leaving the two figures alone in the suffocating silence.

The old man stood still for a moment, gazing intently at the Prisoner's face, as if searching for some hidden meaning. His expression was stern, his weathered face a mask of both awe and bitterness. Slowly, with deliberate steps, he approached the Prisoner and placed the lantern on a small table in the corner of the cell. For a long moment, he stood there silently, as though waiting for something. At last, he began to speak, his voice low and deliberate.

"Is it really You? Is it truly You?" he asked, his words sharp and penetrating, as if he already knew the answer. He paused briefly, as if expecting a response, but when the Prisoner remained silent, the old man continued. "No, don't speak. Be silent. What could You say that I do not already know? I know everything You would say, and You have no right to say anything more than what You said long ago. So why have You come now? Why have You returned to disrupt everything we've built? Because that's what You're doing—you've come to interfere, and You know it well."

He leaned in closer, narrowing his eyes as though trying to read the Prisoner's thoughts. "Do You understand what will happen tomorrow? I don't know if You are truly Him, or just a shadow of Him. It doesn't matter. Tomorrow, I will condemn You. You will be burned at the stake as the worst of heretics. And the same people who kissed Your feet today—those same people, at the smallest gesture from me, will rush to throw more wood on Your fire. Do You know that? Yes, I believe You do," he added with a grim smile, his gaze never wavering from the Prisoner's face.

Alyosha, who had been listening quietly all this time, finally spoke, his voice hesitant and unsure. "I don't understand, Ivan. Is this just a strange fantasy? Or is it a misunderstanding—a mistake made by the old man?"

Ivan laughed softly. "Think of it however you like. If you prefer to believe it's just a case of mistaken identity, go ahead. After all, the old man is nearly ninety years old. Perhaps his mind is slipping, and he was simply overcome by the excitement of burning a hundred heretics the day before. Maybe he saw the Prisoner and, in his madness, believed it was truly Him. But does it really matter whether it's a mistake or not? What matters is that the old man finally says aloud what he has kept inside for ninety long years."

"And the Prisoner doesn't say anything? He just stands there silently?" Alyosha asked.

Ivan nodded, a small smile playing at the corners of his lips. "Exactly. The old man told Him He isn't allowed to say anything new. That's the essence of the Church's claim: everything that needed to be said was entrusted to the Pope, and there is no place for new revelations. That's what they write in their theological texts. 'Do You have the right to reveal anything new?' the old man asks Him. Then he answers his own question: 'No, You don't. Anything You reveal now would take away the freedom You gave to mankind. Any miracle would force belief, and You valued their freedom more than anything else when You walked the earth. Didn't You say, "I will make you free"? But now look at these free people,' the old man adds bitterly. 'Yes, we've paid a high price for that freedom, but at last, we have won. For fifteen centuries, we fought against it, and now we have finally conquered it.'"

Alyosha frowned slightly. "Is he being sarcastic? Or does he truly believe that?"

"He's entirely serious," Ivan said firmly. "He believes it's the Church's greatest achievement that they took away people's freedom—because only by doing that could they make them happy. 'The Inquisition's work,' the old man says, 'was to bring people happiness by freeing them from the burden of free will.

People were born rebels, and rebels can never be at peace. You were warned, but You didn't listen. You rejected the only way to bring them lasting happiness. But fortunately, You left the task to us. You gave us the power to bind and unbind, and now You can't take that away. So why have You come here to interfere with us?'"

Alyosha's brow furrowed deeper. "What does he mean by warnings?"

Ivan's smile faded slightly. "That's the heart of the old man's speech," he explained. "'Thewisespirit—thespirit of destruction— came to You in the wilderness,' the old man continues. 'They call it temptation in the Scriptures, but was it really temptation? Those questions he asked You—weren't they the truest questions ever posed? And what did You do? You rejected them. But those questions weren't just ordinary questions—they were profound truths.'"

Judge for Yourself who was right—You or the one who questioned You back then? Remember the first question; its meaning, in other words, was this: "You would go into the world, and You are going with empty hands, with some promise of freedom that men in their simplicity and their natural unruliness cannot even understand, that they fear and dread—for nothing has ever been more unbearable for a man and a human society than freedom. But do You see these stones in this dry and barren wilderness? Turn them into bread, and mankind will follow You like a flock of sheep, grateful and obedient, though always trembling, afraid You'll withdraw Your hand and deny them Your bread." But You didn't want to take man's freedom away, and You rejected the offer, thinking, what is freedom worth if obedience is bought with bread? You answered that man does not live by bread alone. But do You realize that for the sake of that earthly bread, the spirit of the earth will rise against You, will strive with You and defeat You, and all will follow him, crying, "Who can compare with this beast? He has given us fire from heaven!" Do You know that the ages will pass, and humanity will declare through their wise men that there is no crime, and therefore no sin—there is only hunger? "Feed men and then ask them to be virtuous!" That's what they'll write on the banner they'll raise against You, and with it, they will destroy Your temple. Where Your temple once stood, a new building will rise—a terrible Tower of Babel will be built again, and though, like the first one, it will not be finished, You could have stopped the new tower and shortened mankind's suffering by a thousand years. For they will come back to us after a thousand years of agony with their tower. They will seek us out again, hidden underground in the catacombs, for we will be persecuted and tortured once more. They will find us and cry, "Feed us, for those who promised us fire from heaven have not given it!" And then we shall finish building their tower, for the one who feeds them is the one who finishes the building. And we alone will feed them in Your name, falsely declaring that it is in Your name. Oh, they will never be able to feed themselves without us! No science will give them bread so long as they remain free. In the end, they will lay their freedom at our feet and say to us, "Make us your slaves, but feed us." They will finally understand that freedom and enough bread for all can never exist together, for they will never be able to share between them! They will also be convinced that they can never be free, for they are weak, vicious, worthless, and rebellious. You promised them the bread of Heaven, but I repeat again, can that compare with earthly bread in the eyes of the weak, sinful, and ignoble human race? And if, for the sake of the bread of Heaven, thousands shall follow You, what will happen to the millions and tens of thousands of millions who will not have the strength to give up earthly bread for the sake of the heavenly? Or do You care only for the tens of thousands of the great and strong, while the millions, as numerous as the sands of the sea, who are weak but love You, must exist only for the sake of the great and strong? No, we care for the weak too. They are sinful and rebellious, but in the end, they will also become obedient. They will marvel at us and see us as gods because we are ready to bear the freedom they have found so dreadful and to rule over them—so terrible it will seem to them to be free. But we will tell them we are Your servants and that we rule them in Your name. We will deceive them again, for we will not let You come back to us. That deception will be our suffering because we will be forced to lie.

This is the meaning of the first question in the wilderness, and this is what You rejected for the sake of that freedom You placed above all else. And yet, in that question lay hidden the great secret of this world. By choosing "bread," You would have satisfied the universal and everlasting craving of humanity—to find someone to worship. As long as man remains free, he will search endlessly and painfully for someone to worship. But man doesn't want to worship something uncertain; he wants to worship something that everyone can agree on. These poor creatures aren't just searching for something they can worship, but something that everyone will believe in and worship together. What they need is unity in their worship. This craving for a common object of worship is the greatest suffering for every man and for all humanity from the beginning of time. For the sake of this shared worship, they've killed each other with swords. They've set up gods and told each other, 'Put away your gods and worship ours, or we'll kill you and your gods!' And this will continue until the end of the world, even when the gods disappear from the earth. They will still bow down before idols just the same. You knew this secret of human nature, but You rejected the one unfailing banner that could have made all men bow down to You—the banner of earthly bread. You rejected it for the sake of freedom and the bread of Heaven. Look at what You did—all for the sake of freedom! I tell You, man is tormented by no greater anxiety than to find someone to give that gift of freedom to, that gift which he was so tragically born with. But only someone who can quiet their conscience can take their freedom. Bread alone would have given You an unfailing banner; give bread, and man will worship You, for nothing is more certain than bread. But if someone else takes hold of their conscience— oh! then they will throw away Your bread and follow the one who holds their conscience. In that, You were right. For man's secret isn't just about living, but about having something to live for. Without a clear idea of what his purpose is, man wouldn't even want to go on living. He'd rather destroy himself than stay on earth, even if he had plenty of bread. That's true. But what happened? Instead of taking men's freedom away, You made it even greater!

Did You forget that man prefers peace, and even death, over the freedom to choose between good and evil? Nothing is more tempting for man than freedom of conscience, but nothing causes him more suffering. Instead of giving man a solid foundation to rest his conscience on forever, You chose everything uncertain, mysterious, and unclear. You chose what was far beyond men's strength, as if You didn't love them at all—You, who came to give Your life for them! Instead of taking control of man's freedom, You increased it, and You burdened the spiritual kingdom of mankind with its suffering forever. You wanted man's free love, for him to follow You freely, drawn in by You and captivated by You. Instead of the rigid old law, man now has to freely decide for himself what's good and what's evil, with only Your image as his guide. But didn't You realize that in the end, he would reject even Your image and Your truth, overwhelmed by the heavy burden of free choice? In the end, they'll cry out that the truth is not in You, for You left them in greater confusion and suffering than ever before, laying on them so many difficult decisions and unsolvable problems.

So, in truth, You laid the foundation for the destruction of Your own kingdom, and no one is more to blame than You. But what were You offered? There are three powers, only three, that can hold people's consciences captive forever and make them happy—miracle, mystery, and authority. You rejected all three and set the example for others to do the same. When the wise and fearsome spirit set You on the pinnacle of the temple and said to You, 'If You are the Son of God, throw Yourself down, for it is written: the angels will catch You so You won't hurt Yourself, and You will know for sure that You are the Son of God, and prove how great Your faith in Your Father is.'"

But You refused and did not cast Yourself down. Oh, of course, You acted proudly and like God, but the weak, unruly race of men—are they gods? You knew then that by taking one step, by making one movement to cast Yourself down, You would be tempting God, losing all Your faith in Him, and would have been shattered on the very earth You came to save. And the wise spirit

that tempted You would have rejoiced. But I ask again, are there many like You? Could You believe for one moment that men, too, could face such a temptation? Is the nature of men such that they can reject miracles and, in the greatest moments of their lives, in the deepest, most painful spiritual struggles, cling only to the free verdict of their hearts? Oh, You knew that Your act would be written in books, passed down through time to the farthest corners of the earth, and You hoped that man, following You, would hold fast to God without asking for miracles. But You did not know that when man rejects miracles, he rejects God too; for man seeks not so much God as the miraculous. And since man cannot live without the miraculous, he will create new miracles for himself and worship witchcraft and sorcery, even if he is a hundred times a rebel, heretic, or unbeliever. You didn't come down from the Cross when they shouted to You, mocking and taunting, "Come down from the Cross and we will believe You are the One." You didn't come down because You would not enslave man through a miracle, and You wanted faith to be freely given, not based on miracles. You desired free love, not the shallow admiration of a slave in awe of overwhelming power. But You thought too highly of men, for they are slaves, of course, though rebellious by nature. Look around and judge: fifteen centuries have passed—look at them. Whom have You raised up to Yourself? I swear, man is weaker and baser by nature than You believed him to be! Can he, can he do what You did? By showing him so much respect, You stopped feeling for him because You asked too much from him— You, who loved him more than Yourself! If You had respected him less, You would have asked less of him. That would have been closer to true love, for his burden would have been lighter. He is weak and vile. What if he is now rebelling everywhere against our power and proud of his rebellion? It is the pride of a child or a schoolboy. They are like children, throwing a tantrum and locking the teacher out of the classroom. But their childish joy will come to an end; they will pay dearly for it. They will tear down temples and soak the earth in blood. But in the end, these foolish children will realize that, though they are rebels, they are powerless rebels, unable to maintain their own rebellion. Drenched in tears, they will finally understand that He who made them rebels must have done so as a cruel joke. In despair, they will say this, and their words will be a blasphemy that will make them even more miserable, for man's nature cannot bear blasphemy, and in the end, he always punishes himself for it. And so, unrest, confusion, and unhappiness—this is what mankind is left with after You endured so much for their freedom!

The great prophet tells in visions and symbols that he saw all those who took part in the first resurrection, and that there were twelve thousand from each tribe. But if there were so many, they must not have been men, but gods. They bore Your cross, they spent decades in the barren, hungry wilderness, living on locusts and roots—and You may well take pride in those children of freedom, of free love, of free and noble sacrifice for Your name. But remember, they were only a few thousand; what about the rest? How can the others, the weak ones, be blamed because they couldn't endure what the strong ones endured? How can the weak soul be blamed for not being able to accept such harsh gifts? Did You come only for the chosen, for the elect? If so, it's a mystery we cannot understand. And if it's a mystery, we also have the right to preach a mystery, and to teach them that it's not the free judgment of their hearts or love that matters, but a mystery that they must blindly follow, even against their conscience. So that is what we've done. We have corrected Your work and based it on miracle, mystery, and authority. And men were happy to be led like sheep again, relieved that the terrible burden that brought them so much suffering was lifted from their hearts at last.

Were we wrong to teach them this? Tell me! Did we not love mankind when we acknowledged their weakness, lovingly lightened their burden, and even allowed their weak nature to sin with our permission? Why have You come now to get in our way? Why do You look at me so silently and so deeply with Your gentle eyes? Be angry with me! I don't want Your love, for I do not love You. And what is the point of hiding anything from You? Don't I know to whom I am speaking? Everything I can say is already known to You. And is it for me to hide our secret from You? Perhaps You want to hear it from my lips. So listen, then. We are not with You, but with him—that is our secret. It's been eight centuries since we've been on his side, not Yours. Eight centuries ago, we took from him what You rejected with scorn, the last gift he offered You when he showed You all the kingdoms of the world. We took from him Rome and the sword of Caesar and declared ourselves the sole rulers of the earth, even though we have not yet completed our work. But whose fault is that? Oh, the work is just beginning, but it has begun. It will take a long time to finish, and the earth still has much to suffer, but we will triumph, and we will be Caesars. Then we will plan the universal happiness of man. But You could have taken the sword of Caesar even then. Why did You reject that final gift? If You had accepted the mighty spirit's last counsel, You would have accomplished everything man seeks on earth: someone to worship, someone to keep his conscience, and some way to unite everyone into a single, harmonious society. The desire for universal unity is the third and last anguish of man.

All of mankind has always longed to create a universal state. There have been many great nations with great histories, but the more developed they became, the more unhappy they were because they felt the craving for global unity more intensely than other people. Great conquerors, like Timur and Genghis Khan, swept across the earth like hurricanes, trying to subdue its people. They were simply the unconscious expression of this same desire for universal unity. If You had taken the world and Caesar's purple, You would have created a universal empire and given the world peace. Who else can rule over people if not the one who holds their conscience and their bread in his hands? We took Caesar's sword, and in taking it, we rejected You and followed him. Oh, there are still many ages to come filled with the confusion of free thought, science, and cannibalism. For in building their Tower of Babel without us, they will, of course, end up with cannibalism. But then the beast will crawl to us, licking our feet and covering them with blood and tears. We will sit upon the beast and raise the cup, and written on it will be the word "Mystery." And then, and only then, will man's reign of peace and happiness begin. You are proud of Your chosen ones, but You only have the chosen, while we give rest to everyone. And besides, how many of Your chosen, those mighty ones who could have become Your chosen, have grown weary of waiting for You, have given up their strength and heart to the other side, and have raised their free banner against You? You Yourself lifted that banner. But with us, everyone will be happy, and they will no longer rebel or destroy each other as they did under Your freedom. Oh, we will convince them that they will only be truly free when they surrender their freedom to us and submit to us. And will we be right, or will we be lying? They will believe we are right because they will remember the horrors of slavery and the chaos Your freedom brought them. Freedom, free thought, and science will lead them into such confusion, into such unsolvable mysteries, that some of them—the rebellious, fierce ones—will destroy themselves, while others—the weak and rebellious—will destroy each other. The rest, weak and miserable, will crawl to our feet and whine to us, 'Yes, you were right, you alone hold His secret, and we are coming back to you. Save us from ourselves!'

"Receiving bread from us, they will clearly understand that the bread we give them is actually the bread they made with their own hands, and that we give it to them without performing any miracle. They will see that we do not change stones into bread, but despite that, they will be even more grateful to receive it from us than for the bread itself! They will remember all too well how, in the past, without our guidance, even the bread they produced turned to stones in their hands. But now that they have returned to us, even the stones have turned into bread. They will deeply comprehend the value of complete submission. And until mankind learns this, they will remain unhappy. Now, who is to blame for their lack of understanding? Speak! Who scattered the flock and sent them wandering down unfamiliar paths? But the flock will gather again and submit once more, and this time, their submission will be permanent. Then we will grant them the peaceful, humble happiness that befits weak creatures like them by nature. Oh, we will finally convince them to abandon their pride, for You lifted them up too high and taught them to be proud. We will show them that they are weak, that they are nothing more than pitiful children, and that childlike happiness is the sweetest of all. They will become timid and frightened, always looking to us for protection, huddling close to us like baby chicks do with a hen. They will be amazed by our power and wisdom and will tremble in awe before us, taking pride in how mighty and intelligent we are for being able to tame such a wild and chaotic flock of millions. They will tremble before our wrath, their minds filled with fear and confusion, and they will cry easily like women and children. But just as easily, at a single sign from us, they will shift from tears to laughter, from sorrow to happiness, and from grief to innocent joy. Yes, we will keep them busy with work, but in their free time, we will make their lives as simple and joyful as a child's game, with songs and innocent dances. Oh, we will even allow them to sin, for they are weak and helpless, and they will love us like children because we permit them to indulge in sin. We will tell them that every sin they commit will be forgiven as long as they do it with our permission, and that we allow them to sin because we love them. And we will take on the burden of their sins ourselves, standing before God as the ones responsible for their misdeeds. And they will love us even more for this, for we will have become their saviors who have taken upon ourselves their sins in front of God.

They will have no secrets from us. We will control every aspect of their lives. We will allow or forbid them to live with their wives and mistresses, to have children or not—depending on whether they obey us or not—and they will gladly and willingly submit to our judgment. They will bring to us all the most painful secrets of their conscience, and we will have answers for all of them. They will be happy to believe our answers because those answers will relieve them of the terrible burden of making free decisions for themselves, sparing them from the agony and anxiety of their own conscience. And thus, all will be happy, all the millions of weak creatures—except for the hundred thousand who rule over them. For only we, we who guard the mystery and bear the responsibility of their sins, will be unhappy. There will be billions of contented children living without sin, and only a few hundred thousand of us who will suffer under the weight of knowing good and evil. They will die in peace, pass away quietly in Your name, and beyond the grave, they will find nothing but death. But we will keep the secret from them, and for the sake of their happiness, we will tempt them with the promise of heaven and eternity. Even if there were anything in the afterlife, it would certainly not be for such as them.

It is foretold that You will come again in victory, with Your chosen ones, the proud and strong. But we will say that, while Your chosen ones saved only themselves, we saved all of humanity. It is written that the harlot who sits upon the beast, holding the mystery in her hands, will be put to shame, and that the weak will rise up, tear her royal robes apart, and expose her repulsive body to the world. But I will stand before You then, and I will point to the billions of happy children, all of whom have known no sin. And we, who took their sins upon ourselves to ensure their happiness, will stand before You and say, 'Judge us if You can and if You dare.' Know this: I do not fear You. Know that I too have been in the wilderness. I too have lived on roots and locusts. I too cherished the freedom You bestowed upon mankind. I too strived to be among Your chosen ones, thirsting 'to make up the number' of the strong and powerful. But I woke up and refused to serve madness any longer. I turned back and joined those who corrected Your work. I left the proud and returned to the humble, for the sake of their happiness. What I tell You will come to pass, and our reign will be established. I repeat, tomorrow You will see that obedient flock—those who, at my command, will rush to heap burning coals around the pyre where I will burn You for coming to interfere with us. For if anyone has ever deserved to be burned, it is You. Tomorrow, I will burn You. Dixi."

Ivan paused. His voice had risen in excitement as he spoke, and now, having finished, he smiled suddenly. Alyosha had listened quietly the whole time. Near the end, he had become very emotional, and several times he looked like he was about to interrupt, but he restrained himself. Now, his words burst out.

"But... that's absurd!" he cried, his face turning red. "Your story actually praises Jesus instead of blaming Him, as you meant it to! And who would believe your view of freedom? Is that how you understand it? That's not the idea of freedom in the Orthodox Church... that's the idea of Rome, and not even all of Rome—just the worst of it! The Inquisitors, the Jesuits! And your Inquisitor is impossible. What are these 'sins of mankind' they take upon themselves? Who are these 'keepers of the mystery' who claim to take on some curse for the happiness of humanity? When have they ever been seen? People speak badly of the Jesuits, but they're nothing like what you describe! They're not that at all. They are simply the army of the Roman Church, seeking to dominate the world with the Pope as emperor. That's all they stand for—lust for power, for filthy earthly gain, for control over everything. There's no mystery or lofty sadness in it. It's all just about domination and creating a kind of universal slavery with them as the masters. They probably don't even believe in God! Your 'suffering Inquisitor' is pure fantasy."

"Calm down, calm down," Ivan laughed. "You say it's a fantasy? Very well, let it be a fantasy! Of course, it's a fantasy. But tell me, do you really think the Roman Catholic movement over the last few centuries has been nothing but a lust for power and earthly gain? Is that what Father Païssy teaches?"

"No, no, not at all! Father Païssy once said something that was a little like what you're saying... but it's definitely not the same, not at all the same," Alyosha quickly corrected himself.

"Aha! A valuable admission, even with your 'not at all the same.' Let me ask you this: do you really believe that the Jesuits and Inquisitors have united simply for material gain? Why couldn't there be one among them who was a martyr, burdened by sorrow, and who truly loved humanity? Imagine that among all those who desired nothing but wealth and power, there was just one person like my Inquisitor, a man who had eaten roots in the desert, a man who had struggled desperately to overcome his flesh and achieve freedom and perfection. But despite all his efforts, he still loved humanity deeply. Then suddenly, his eyes were opened, and he realized that it was no great moral triumph to attain freedom and perfection if, at the same time, millions of people had been created just to suffer. He saw that these poor, rebellious souls could never become giants capable of completing the tower, that they were not the kind of people the great idealist had dreamed of when he envisioned harmony. Seeing all this, he turned back and joined the 'clever people,' the ones who sought power. Isn't it possible that this could have happened?"

"Joined whom, what clever people?" cried Alyosha, completely caught up in the conversation. "They don't have any great cleverness, no mysteries, no secrets... Maybe all they have is atheism, that's their big secret. Your Inquisitor doesn't believe in God, that's his secret!"

"What if you're right! At last, you've figured it out. It's absolutely true, that's their whole secret. But don't you see how much suffering that must bring to a man like him, who spent his entire life in the desert but couldn't let go of his deep love for humanity? In his old age, he came to the conclusion that only the advice of the great, dreadful spirit could create any sort of livable world for these weak, chaotic, 'unfinished creatures, made as a joke.' So, realizing this, he understood that he had to follow the advice of the wise spirit—the spirit of death and destruction. And that meant accepting lies and deception and leading people knowingly toward death and destruction but deceiving them the entire time so that they wouldn't realize where they were headed. He wanted to make sure these poor blind souls would at least think they were happy along the way. And remember, the deception was done in the name of the One whose ideal the old man had believed in so passionately his entire life. Isn't that tragic? If just one man like him stood at the head of the whole movement 'driven by a lust for power for the sake of filthy gain,' wouldn't that alone be enough to turn it into a tragedy? In fact, just one such man at the top is enough to create the leading idea behind the Roman Church, with all its armies and Jesuits—the highest idea. I tell you honestly, I firmly believe there has always been at least one man like that leading the movement. Who knows, maybe there have been some among the Popes of Rome. Maybe the spirit of that cursed old man, who stubbornly loves humanity in his own twisted way, exists even now in many others like him. They're not there by chance but by agreement—a secret group formed long ago to guard the mystery, to protect it from the weak and the unhappy so they can be happy. Without a doubt, this is true, and it has to be this way. I even suspect that among the Freemasons, there's something similar at the core of their beliefs, which is why the Catholics hate the Freemasons so much. They see them as rivals who are breaking apart the unity of the idea. But it's so important that there be only one flock and one shepherd... But from how strongly I'm defending this idea, you'd think I was the author getting upset with your criticism. That's enough of this."

"Maybe you're a Mason yourself!" Alyosha suddenly blurted out. "You don't believe in God," he added sorrowfully. He thought he saw a hint of irony in his brother's expression. "How does your poem end?" he asked, looking down. "Or was that the end?"

"I meant to end it like this. When the Inquisitor finished speaking, he waited for his Prisoner to answer him. The silence weighed heavily on him. He saw that the Prisoner had listened intently the entire time, gazing gently at him but clearly not intending to reply. The old man longed for Him to say something, even if it was bitter or terrible. But instead, the Prisoner quietly approached the old man, and without a word, gently kissed him on his bloodless, aged lips. That was His only answer. The old man shuddered. His lips trembled. He went to the door, opened it, and said to Him, 'Go, and come no more... never, never come again!' And he let Him out into the dark streets of the city. The Prisoner left."

"And the old man?" asked Alyosha.

"The kiss burned in his heart, but the old man stuck to his beliefs." "And you agree with him, don't you?" Alyosha cried, his voice filled with sorrow.

Ivan laughed. "Why, it's all nonsense, Alyosha. It's just a foolish poem written by a foolish student who couldn't string together two lines of verse. Why do you take it so seriously? Do you really think I'm going to join the Jesuits and help them 'correct His work'? Good heavens, it's none of my business. I've told you before, all I want is to live until I'm thirty, and then... smash the cup to the ground!"

"But what about the little sticky leaves, the precious tombs, the blue sky, and the woman you love? How will you live? How will you love them?" Alyosha cried out, his heart aching. "With such hell in your heart and your head, how can you? No, that's exactly why you're going away—to join them. If not, you'll destroy yourself. You won't be able to endure it!"

"There's a strength that lets you endure everything," Ivan said with a cold smile.

"What strength?"

"The strength of the Karamazovs—the strength of Karamazov wickedness."

"To fall into depravity, to drown your soul in corruption, right?"

"Maybe even that... But I think I'll escape it until I'm thirty. And after that—"

"How will you escape it? With what will you escape it? Your ideas make it impossible."

"In the Karamazov way, of course."

"'Everything is lawful,' you mean? 'Everything is lawful,' is that it?"

Ivan frowned, and suddenly his face turned strangely pale. "Ah, you've latched onto yesterday's phrase— the one that so offended Miüsov and that Dmitri picked up on so clumsily," he said with a strange smile. "Yes, if you like, 'everything is lawful'—since it's been said, I won't deny it. And Mitya's version wasn't bad either."

Alyosha gazed at him silently.

"I thought that when I left here, at least I would still have you," Ivan said suddenly, his voice filled with unexpected emotion. "But now I see there's no place for me in your heart either, my dear hermit. The phrase 'everything is lawful'—I won't take it back. Will you push me away for that?"

Alyosha stood up, walked over to him, and gently kissed him on the lips.

"That's plagiarism," Ivan cried, laughing with delight. "You stole that from my poem! But thanks anyway. Come on, Alyosha, it's time for both of us to go."

They left, but when they reached the entrance of the restaurant, they stopped.

"Listen, Alyosha," Ivan began in a firm voice, "if I do end up loving the little sticky leaves, it will be because of you. It's enough for me to know that you're here, somewhere. That will keep me from losing my desire to live, at least for now. Is that enough for you? Take it as a declaration of love if you like. Now you go to the right, and I'll go to the left. And that's it. Enough. Even if I don't leave tomorrow, though I probably will, and we see each other again, don't bring this up again. I'm asking you, please, don't. And as for Dmitri, don't mention him to me either. It's all been said already, hasn't it? I'll make you a promise: when I turn thirty and decide to 'smash the cup,' wherever I am, I'll come to see you one last time, even if I have to come from America. You can count on it. It will be interesting to see what you're like by then. It's a serious promise. And who knows, maybe we really won't see each other for seven or ten years. Now, go to Father Seraphicus, he's dying. If he dies without you by his side, you'll blame me for keeping you. Goodbye, kiss me one more time. That's right, now go."

Ivan suddenly turned and walked away without looking back. It was just like how Dmitri had left Alyosha the day before, even though the circumstances were completely different. The strange similarity hit Alyosha like an arrow, in the midst of his sadness and confusion. He stood for a moment, watching his brother walk away. Then he noticed that Ivan was swaying as he walked and that his right shoulder seemed lower than his left. He had never noticed that before. But suddenly he turned too and hurried back toward the monastery. It was almost dark, and he felt a strange fear growing inside him—something new and unfamiliar, something he couldn't explain. The wind had picked up again, just like the evening before, and the ancient pine trees murmured gloomily around him as he entered the path to the hermitage. He almost ran. "Father Seraphicus— that's what Ivan called him. Where did that come from?" Alyosha wondered. "Ivan, poor Ivan... when will I see you again? Ah, there's the hermitage. Yes, yes, that's him— Father Seraphicus. He will save me from him, and forever!"

Later, Alyosha would wonder how he could have so completely forgotten about his brother Dmitri when he left Ivan. Only a few hours earlier that morning, he had made a firm decision to find Dmitri and not give up, even if it meant not returning to the monastery that night.

Chapter 6: For a while a Very Obscure One

And Ivan, after parting from Alyosha, went back to Fyodor Pavlovitch's house. But, strangely enough, he was overcome by an unbearable depression, which only grew stronger with each step he took towards the house. It wasn't unusual for him to feel depressed—what was strange was that Ivan couldn't have said what exactly was causing it. He had often been depressed before, and it was not surprising for him to feel this way at such a moment, when he had just cut ties with everything that had brought him here, and was preparing to embark on a new path and step into an unknown future. He would be alone again, just as he had always been, and though he had great hopes, and perhaps overly high expectations from life, he couldn't have explained what those hopes or expectations, or even his desires, truly were.

Yet at that moment, even though the anxiety of the new and unknown was certainly present in his heart, what was truly troubling him was something else. "Is it because I loathe my father's house?" he wondered. "Quite possibly; I am so sick of it, and even though this is the last time I'll cross that hateful threshold, I still despise it… No, that's not it either. Is it because I'm parting with Alyosha and the conversation I had with him? I've kept silent with the world for so many years and refused to speak, and then suddenly I blurt out a long rambling speech like that." It might indeed have been the youthful frustration of inexperience and vanity—the frustration of failing to express himself properly, especially with someone like Alyosha, on whom he had certainly been counting in his heart. Surely, that was part of it, that irritation—it must have been—but that wasn't it either. "I feel sick with depression, and yet I don't even know what I want. Perhaps it's better not to think about it."

Ivan tried "not to think," but even that was useless. What made his depression so aggravating and annoying was that it felt almost like something external—it seemed to have an outside source, as if it didn't fully belong to him. He was aware of this feeling. It was as if something or someone was there, like how something can catch your eye, and although you might be busy with work or conversation, and don't notice it for a while, it still irritates you in the back of your mind until you realize what it is. Often, it's something small and absurd—a handkerchief lying on the floor, a book out of place on the shelf—and once you fix it, the irritation disappears.

At last, feeling very frustrated and ill-tempered, Ivan reached the house, and then, about fifteen steps away from the garden gate, it suddenly dawned on him what had been bothering him all this time. Sitting on a bench by the gate was Smerdyakov, the valet, enjoying the cool evening air, and at the first glance at him, Ivan immediately understood that Smerdyakov was what had been troubling his mind, and that it was this man his soul loathed. Everything became clear in an instant. Earlier, when Alyosha had mentioned meeting Smerdyakov, Ivan had felt a sudden pang of gloom and disgust, which had stirred up a burst of anger in his heart. He had forgotten about Smerdyakov for a while during their conversation, but as soon as he parted from Alyosha and began walking home, that forgotten feeling had resurfaced. "Can it really be that such a wretched, miserable creature is capable of bothering me this much?" he wondered, his irritation unbearable.

It was true that lately, Ivan had developed a deep dislike for the man, especially over the last few days. In fact, this dislike had grown into something very close to hatred. This hatred was likely made worse by the fact that when Ivan first arrived in the area, he had felt quite the opposite. At first, he had taken a genuine interest in Smerdyakov and even found him to be somewhat unique. Ivan had encouraged Smerdyakov to talk to him, even though he had always sensed a certain incoherence, or rather, an uneasiness, in the man's mind. He could never quite figure out what was constantly troubling Smerdyakov's thoughts. They discussed philosophical questions, even pondering how there could be light on the first day when the sun, moon, and stars weren't created until the fourth day, and what that could mean. But Ivan soon realized that although Smerdyakov seemed to enjoy such discussions, these topics were secondary to something else entirely that was gnawing at him.

In one way or another, Smerdyakov began to reveal an immense vanity, a wounded vanity at that, and that's what Ivan didn't like. That was what first triggered his aversion. Later, when more problems arose in the house—especially when Grushenka entered the picture and there were scandals involving his brother Dmitri— they discussed those events too. But despite Smerdyakov's passionate interest in these matters, Ivan couldn't figure out what exactly Smerdyakov was hoping for. There was something odd about the man's desires—they were often illogical, and even when they became apparent, they were vague and scattered. Smerdyakov would ask indirect but obviously intentional questions, but he never explained what his ultimate goal was, and just when it seemed like he was about to reveal something important, he would fall silent or switch to a different topic.

What really irritated Ivan the most, and what cemented his dislike, was the strange, disturbing familiarity that Smerdyakov had begun to show toward him. It wasn't that he forgot his place or spoke disrespectfully—on the contrary, Smerdyakov always spoke with great politeness. But for some reason, he had clearly convinced himself that there was some kind of unspoken understanding between him and Ivan, a secret shared only by the two of them, which others wouldn't understand. He spoke in a tone that implied there was some sort of mutual agreement between them, some kind of compact that had been acknowledged, though it had never actually been discussed. For a long time, Ivan couldn't figure out the true cause of his growing dislike for Smerdyakov, but lately, he had begun to realize what it was.

Feeling disgusted and irritated, Ivan tried to walk past the gate without speaking or even glancing at Smerdyakov. But as he passed, Smerdyakov stood up from the bench, and just from that movement, Ivan immediately knew that Smerdyakov wanted to speak to him. Ivan stopped, though he hadn't meant to, and this sudden change of mind only made his anger flare up even more. He looked at Smerdyakov with a mixture of anger and disgust, taking in his sickly, pale face and the small curls on his forehead. Smerdyakov's left eye twitched, and he smiled slightly, as if to say, "You're not going to walk past without speaking, are you? You know we have something to discuss."

Ivan felt a tremor of rage. "Get out of my sight, you miserable idiot! What do I have to do with you?" he nearly shouted. But to his own astonishment, what came out of his mouth instead was, "Is my father still asleep, or has he woken up?"

He asked the question softly, almost meekly, surprising himself once more. And then, once again to his surprise, he sat down on the bench. For a brief moment, he felt an odd flash of fear—he would remember that later. Smerdyakov stood in front of him, his hands behind his back, gazing at him with a calm confidence, almost as if he were judging him.

"He's still asleep," he said slowly, making sure his words were deliberate, as if to silently imply, "You spoke first, not me." Then, after a moment, he added, "I'm surprised at you, sir," lowering his eyes in a way that seemed exaggerated, setting his right foot forward, and fiddling with the tip of his shiny boot. His movements appeared overly controlled, almost as though he was putting on a show, but why exactly was unclear. The air felt heavy with unspoken tension.

"What are you surprised about?" Ivan asked abruptly, his voice filled with irritation. He was struggling to keep his composure and suddenly realized, to his own dismay, that an intense curiosity was bubbling up inside him. Despite his disgust, he couldn't deny it: he had to know what Smerdyakov was getting at. No matter how hard he tried to shake it off, Ivan knew he wouldn't be able to leave without uncovering the rest of the conversation. Something in the pit of his stomach twisted with a need for answers, as though walking away now would leave something critical unresolved.

"Why don't you go to Tchermashnya, sir?" Smerdyakov asked, his eyes lifting suddenly with a smile that felt too familiar, almost inappropriate for the situation. His expression held a strange mix of knowing and amusement. "Why I smile, you must figure out for yourself if you're a smart man," his squinted left eye seemed to say, as though there were some secret Ivan wasn't in on yet, but ought to be.

"Why should I go to Tchermashnya?" Ivan asked, taken aback by the question. His surprise was genuine, as he had no idea what Smerdyakov was hinting at. He sensed there was more going on here than was being said directly, but the puzzle pieces weren't fitting together yet.

Smerdyakov paused again, leaving the air between them thick with silence.

"Fyodor Pavlovitch himself asked you to go," Smerdyakov finally responded, his tone slow and casual, as if the matter held no real importance. "I just gave you a secondary reason," he seemed to suggest, "just to say something," like he was throwing out explanations without any real weight to them.

"Damn you! Just say what you want already!" Ivan snapped, the sharpness in his voice cutting through the stillness. His patience had worn thin, and he could no longer hold back his anger. What began as an effort to remain calm had now turned into full-blown frustration. The words exploded out of him, his emotions shifting suddenly from restraint to outburst.

Smerdyakov pulled his right foot back to meet his left, straightening himself up. He still maintained the same serene expression, and that familiar, unnerving little smile remained on his face. It was as though he took some pleasure in Ivan's frustration, or perhaps he was just indifferent to it.

"Nothing significant—just talking for the sake of it," Smerdyakov said with a slight shrug, his tone light, as though he hadn't just stirred up tension in the conversation.

Another stretch of silence fell between them. They sat there, unspeaking, for nearly a full minute. Ivan was aware that he should have stood up, should have shown his anger more clearly. But something about Smerdyakov kept him in place. He could almost feel Smerdyakov waiting—watching—to see how he'd react, as if the man were testing him in some way, provoking him to see if Ivan would take the bait. At least, that's how it seemed to Ivan. The longer the silence stretched, the more palpable the tension became.

At last, Ivan began to move, intending to get up from his seat. But in that very moment, Smerdyakov seemed to seize the opportunity to speak, as though he'd been waiting for exactly this.

"I'm in a terrible situation, Ivan Fyodorovitch. I really don't know what to do," he said firmly, his voice clear and steady, though there was a sigh at the end that hinted at some deeper stress. His words were spoken with such resolve that Ivan found himself sitting back down, unable to ignore the seriousness in Smerdyakov's tone.

"They're both completely out of their minds—like children," Smerdyakov went on, as if what he had to say was urgent. "I mean your father and your brother Dmitri Fyodorovitch. It's about to start again soon: Fyodor Pavlovitch will wake up any minute and start pestering me every second, asking, 'Has she come yet? Why hasn't she come?' He'll keep at it until midnight, maybe even later. And if Agrafena Alexandrovna doesn't show up (and she probably doesn't plan to come at all), then tomorrow morning, he'll start all over again, 'Why didn't she come? When will she come?' He'll act like it's my fault she hasn't shown up. On the other hand, it's no better with Dmitri Fyodorovitch. As soon as the sun starts setting—or even earlier—your brother appears, carrying that gun of his. 'Watch out, you dirty cook! If she comes and you don't tell me, I'll kill you before anyone else does.' Then, once the night is over, in the morning, he starts tormenting me just like Fyodor Pavlovitch. 'Why hasn't she come? Will she come soon?' And he also seems to think it's my fault that his lady hasn't come. Every day, every hour, they're angrier and angrier. Sometimes I think I might kill myself out of sheer panic. I can't rely on them, sir. They're impossible."

"And why did you get involved in all this? Why start spying for Dmitri Fyodorovitch?" Ivan asked, his tone irritated and sharp. He couldn't understand why Smerdyakov had gotten tangled up in such a mess.

"How could I avoid it?" Smerdyakov replied, sounding almost defensive. "Honestly, I didn't get involved at all, if you want the truth. I kept my mouth shut from the beginning, not daring to say anything. But he forced me to be his servant. Ever since, he's been threatening me with the same thing over and over: 'I'll kill you, you scoundrel, if you miss her.' I'm absolutely sure, sir, that I'll have a long fit tomorrow."

"What do you mean by 'a long fit'?" Ivan asked, his curiosity piqued despite himself.

"A long fit—a seizure, sir—lasting hours, maybe even a whole day or two. Once, it lasted for three days. I fell out of the attic that time. The seizures stopped for a bit, then started again, and for three days, I was completely out of it. Fyodor Pavlovitch sent for the doctor, Herzenstube, and he put ice on my head and tried some other treatments. I could have died."

"But people say you can't predict epilepsy. How can you know you'll have a fit tomorrow?" Ivan inquired, his voice tinged with an irritated kind of curiosity.

"That's true. You can't predict it," Smerdyakov agreed.

"And yet you fell out of the attic that time," Ivan pointed out, his tone challenging.

"I go up to the attic every single day. I could fall from there again tomorrow. And if not from the attic, I might fall down the cellar stairs. I have to go into the cellar every day too, you know," Smerdyakov responded, his voice still calm and matter-of-fact, as though discussing something as trivial as the weather.

Ivan looked at him, his eyes narrowing as if trying to read the man's thoughts.

"You're talking nonsense, I can see that now, and I don't fully understand you," he said softly, though there was a distinct hint of menace in his voice. "Are you trying to tell me you plan to fake being sick for three days?"

Smerdyakov, who had been staring at the ground, toying with the toe of his boot again, placed his foot firmly on the ground, moved his left foot forward, and, grinning slightly, began to speak slowly, deliberately.

"If I could pretend to have a seizure—and it wouldn't be that hard for someone who's used to them—I would have every right to use that trick to save my life. Even if Agrafena Alexandrovna came while I was sick, Fyodor Pavlovitch wouldn't blame a man who's ill for not telling him. He'd be too ashamed to say anything."

"Damn it all!" Ivan exploded, his face twisting with anger, the intensity of his emotions flaring up. "Why are you always so terrified for your life? My brother Dmitri's threats are just empty words, nothing more. He's not going to kill you. It's not you he's after!"

"He'd kill me first, just like swatting a fly," Smerdyakov replied, his tone still unnervingly calm. "But even more than that, I'm afraid they'll take me for his accomplice when he does something crazy to his father."

"Why would they think you're involved?" Ivan asked, his curiosity deepening.

"They'll think I'm in on it because I told him about the signals," Smerdyakov said slowly, as though weighing each word carefully.

"What signals? What are you talking about? Speak clearly, damn it!" Ivan demanded, his patience completely worn out.

"I have to admit," Smerdyakov said, his voice calm and almost too composed, "that Fyodor Pavlovitch and I have a secret understanding about this. You may already know, or maybe you don't, but for the past few days, Fyodor Pavlovitch has been locking himself in every evening as soon as it gets dark. You've been going upstairs early each night lately, and yesterday you didn't come down at all, so you might not know how cautious he's been. Even if Grigory Vassilyevitch comes to his door, he won't open it unless he hears his voice. But Grigory doesn't come anymore, because I've been waiting on Fyodor Pavlovitch alone in his room. That's the arrangement he made after the whole mess with Agrafena Alexandrovna started. At night, I go out to the lodge by his orders, and I don't get to sleep until midnight. Instead, I stay on guard, walking around the yard, waiting for her. Lately, Fyodor Pavlovitch has been completely frantic, expecting her any minute. He says she's scared of Dmitri Fyodorovitch—Mitya, as he calls him—and that's why she'll sneak in late, through the back way, to see him. He tells me, 'Watch for her until midnight or later, and if she comes, knock at my door or at the window from the garden. First, knock twice, softly, then knock three more times, quicker. That way, I'll know she's here, and I'll let you in quietly.' He also gave me another signal in case something unexpected happens. First, two knocks, then a pause, and a third knock, louder. That way, he'll know something urgent is happening, and he'll let me in so I can talk to him. That's in case Agrafena Alexandrovna can't come herself but sends a message instead. Dmitri Fyodorovitch might come as well, so I'm supposed to let him know right away if he's near. His honor is absolutely terrified of Dmitri Fyodorovitch, so even if Agrafena Alexandrovna is locked inside with him, and Dmitri Fyodorovitch shows up, I'd have to signal him right away. The first set of five knocks means Agrafena Alexandrovna has arrived, and the second set of three knocks means there's something urgent. His honor has shown me the signals many times and explained them clearly. No one else knows about these signals except me and Fyodor Pavlovitch, so he'd open the door without hesitation, without making a sound (he's deathly afraid of making any noise). Well, now Dmitri Fyodorovitch knows those signals too."

"How does he know? Did you tell him? How did you dare to tell him?" Ivan asked, his voice rising in disbelief.

"I told him because I was scared. How could I keep it from him? Dmitri Fyodorovitch kept pressuring me every day, saying, 'You're lying to me, hiding something from me! I'll break both your legs!' So I told him about the secret signals to show him I was loyal, that I wasn't hiding anything from him, but telling him everything I knew."

"If you think he's going to use those signals to break in, don't let him."

"But what if I have one of my fits? How could I stop him from coming in, even if I wanted to? Especially knowing how desperate he is?"

"Damn it! How can you be so sure you're going to have a fit? Are you making fun of me?" Ivan asked, his frustration rising.

"How could I dare laugh at you? I'm not in any mood to laugh with all this fear hanging over me. I just feel it—I'm sure I'll have a fit. It's this fear that will bring it on."

"Damn it! If you do have a fit, Grigory will be there. Let Grigory know ahead of time. He'll make sure Dmitri doesn't get in."

"I wouldn't dare tell Grigory Vassilyevitch about the signals without orders from my master. Besides, Grigory Vassilyevitch has been sick since yesterday, and Marfa Ignatyevna is planning to give him some medicine tomorrow. They've already decided on it. It's a strange remedy of hers. Marfa Ignatyevna has a special mix she always uses. It's made from some kind of herb, and she always keeps it on hand. It's strong stuff. She rubs it on his back for half an hour, and it makes his skin all red and swollen. Then she gives him what's left in the bottle to drink, with a special prayer, though she doesn't drink it all. She always keeps a little for herself and drinks it too. Since neither of them drink alcohol, they fall asleep immediately and sleep deeply for a long time. When Grigory Vassilyevitch wakes up, he's completely fine, but Marfa Ignatyevna always gets a headache from it. So if she gives him the medicine tomorrow, neither of them will hear a thing if Dmitri Fyodorovitch tries to get in. They'll be sound asleep."

"What a load of nonsense! And all this just happens to be happening at the same time, like it's all been planned. You're going to have a fit, and they'll both be knocked out?" Ivan shouted. "You're not trying to arrange it this way, are you?" he suddenly accused, his face twisting with anger.

"How could I? And why would I, when it all depends on Dmitri Fyodorovitch and what he plans to do? If he decides to do something, he will. But if not, I won't be the one pushing him to attack his father."

"And why would he go to father secretly, especially if, as you say, Agrafena Alexandrovna isn't even going to show up?" Ivan pressed, his anger rising again. "You yourself have said she won't come, and I've been thinking this whole time that the old man's just imagining things. She won't come. So why would Dmitri sneak in if she's not going to be there? Speak up, I want to know what you're thinking!"

"You know why he'll come. What difference does my opinion make? He'll come because he's angry or maybe because he's suspicious about me being sick. He'll barge in just like he did yesterday, impatient to check the rooms and see if she slipped in while he wasn't looking. Plus, he knows Fyodor Pavlovitch has an envelope with three thousand roubles in it, tied with ribbon and sealed with three seals. It's addressed, 'To my angel Grushenka, if she comes,' and three days later he added, 'For my little chicken.' Who knows what that might drive him to do?"

"That's ridiculous!" Ivan yelled, almost losing control. "Dmitri won't come here just to steal money and kill my father for it. He might have killed him yesterday in a fit of rage over Grushenka, like the wild fool he is, but he's not a thief."

"He's in serious need of money right now, Ivan Fyodorovitch. You don't understand just how desperate he is," Smerdyakov explained calmly and clearly, his voice unsettling in its composure. "He considers that three thousand roubles his own. He told me so himself. 'My father still owes me exactly three thousand,' he said. Besides, think about it, Ivan Fyodorovitch—there's something else that's very likely. Agrafena Alexandrovna could force your father to marry her if she wants to. Fyodor Pavlovitch, I mean. If she wanted to, she could definitely make it happen. All I said is that she won't come tonight, but she might have other plans in mind— like becoming the mistress here. I know for a fact that her merchant friend, Samsonov, has been joking with her about it, saying it wouldn't be such a bad idea. And she's smart. She wouldn't marry a penniless man like Dmitri Fyodorovitch. So, Ivan Fyodorovitch, consider this: if she marries your father, neither Dmitri Fyodorovitch nor you or your brother Alexey Fyodorovitch will inherit a single rouble after your father's death. Agrafena Alexandrovna will take it all. But if your father were to die now, there'd be some forty thousand roubles left for sure, even for Dmitri Fyodorovitch, whom your father hates. He hasn't written a will yet, you see. Dmitri Fyodorovitch knows all this perfectly well."

Ivan's face suddenly showed a flash of shock. His skin turned a deep red.

"So why, then," he interrupted Smerdyakov, his voice sharp, "did you suggest I go to Tchermashnya? What did you mean by that? If I leave, you know what could happen here." He struggled to catch his breath.

"Exactly," Smerdyakov replied, his voice calm and reasonable, though his eyes were locked on Ivan, studying him closely.

"What do you mean, 'exactly'?" Ivan demanded, his eyes flashing with anger, barely able to control himself.

"I said it because I felt bad for you. If I were you, I would leave it all behind, instead of staying in such a difficult situation," Smerdyakov replied, his voice honest, his expression open, though Ivan's angry eyes bore into him. They both fell silent for a moment.

"You're an absolute idiot—and a complete scoundrel, too," Ivan snapped suddenly, standing up from the bench. He started to storm through the gate, but then stopped abruptly and turned back toward Smerdyakov. What happened next was unexpected. In a sudden burst of emotion, Ivan bit his lip, clenched his fists, and for a moment it seemed like he might attack Smerdyakov. Smerdyakov noticed this instantly and stepped back, startled. But the moment passed, and Ivan, silent and confused, turned toward the gate.

"I'm leaving for Moscow tomorrow, early in the morning, if you care to know. That's all!" he shouted angrily, surprising even himself with the outburst. Later, he would wonder why he had felt the need to tell Smerdyakov that.

"That's the best thing you could do," Smerdyakov responded, as if he had expected Ivan to say that. "Of course, you could always be telegraphed from Moscow if anything happens here."

Ivan paused again and then turned back to face Smerdyakov, his anger still simmering. But something had changed. Smerdyakov's casual demeanor was gone. His face now showed something different: attention, expectation, almost a timid eagerness. He looked as though he were waiting for Ivan to say more, his eyes full of questions he didn't dare ask aloud.

"And couldn't I be telegraphed from Tchermashnya too, if something happened?" Ivan suddenly shouted, his voice rising for no apparent reason.

"From Tchermashnya too… yes, you could be telegraphed," Smerdyakov muttered under his breath, almost in a whisper. He looked thrown off but kept his eyes locked on Ivan's.

"Then why are you so insistent on Tchermashnya being closer? Is it to save me some money on the fare, or is it just because it's not as far away?" Ivan demanded, his voice still loud, his anger bubbling to the surface.

"Exactly…" Smerdyakov muttered, his voice cracking slightly. He gave Ivan a weak, unpleasant smile and took a step back again. To his surprise, Ivan suddenly burst into laughter and walked through the gate, still laughing as he went. But anyone who saw his face at that moment would have known that his laughter was not coming from a place of joy. He himself couldn't have explained what he was feeling. He moved forward, walking like a man overtaken by nerves, his mind in turmoil.

Chapter 7: "It's Always Worth While Speaking to A Clever Man"

In the same nervous frenzy, Ivan spoke. When he saw Fyodor Pavlovitch in the drawing room as soon as he walked in, he shouted, waving his hands, "I'm going upstairs to my room, not to you. Goodbye!" He walked past, trying not to even glance at his father. Maybe the old man disgusted him too much at that moment, but this open show of hostility even surprised Fyodor Pavlovitch. The old man clearly had something he wanted to say right away and had come into the drawing room on purpose to meet him. When he received such a "friendly" greeting, he just stood still, watching his son go upstairs with a sarcastic look on his face until Ivan disappeared.

"What's wrong with him?" he immediately asked Smerdyakov, who had followed Ivan.

"He's angry about something. Who knows?" the servant mumbled evasively.

"Forget him! Let him be angry then. Bring the samovar and hurry up! Any news?"

Then came a series of questions, the same kind that Smerdyakov had just been complaining to Ivan about, all about the visitor Fyodor Pavlovitch was expecting. We'll skip over these questions. About half an hour later, the house was locked up, and the old man was pacing around the rooms, excited and waiting, thinking he'd hear the five knocks at any moment. Every now and then, he'd peek outside into the dark, but he saw nothing.

It was very late, but Ivan was still awake and thinking. He stayed up until two in the morning. We won't go into detail about his thoughts now, this isn't the time to delve into his mind—it will have its moment later. And even if we tried, it would be hard to describe them, because there were no clear thoughts in his head, just vague feelings mixed with intense excitement. He himself realized that he had lost his sense of direction. He was also bothered by all kinds of strange and almost shocking urges; for example, after midnight, he suddenly had a powerful and uncontrollable urge to go downstairs, open the door, go to the lodge, and beat Smerdyakov. But if someone had asked him why he wanted to do that, he wouldn't have been able to explain it clearly. Maybe it was because he despised the servant as someone who had insulted him more than anyone else in the world. On the other hand, more than once that night, he felt overwhelmed by an odd, humiliating kind of fear that seemed to freeze his body in place. His head throbbed, and he felt dizzy. A sense of hatred was growing inside him, as if he needed to take revenge on someone. He even found himself hating Alyosha when he remembered the conversation they had just had. At times, he hated himself intensely. He barely thought about Katerina Ivanovna and was shocked by this later, especially since he clearly remembered that when he had so bravely told her that he would leave for Moscow the next day, something inside him whispered, "That's nonsense, you're not going anywhere, and leaving will be much harder than you're pretending it will be."

Looking back on that night, Ivan remembered with disgust how he had suddenly gotten up from the couch, sneaked to the door as if he were afraid someone might see him, stepped out onto the stairs, and listened for sounds of Fyodor Pavlovitch moving around downstairs. He stood there for about five minutes, holding his breath and listening to his own heartbeat, all while feeling a strange sense of curiosity. And he couldn't explain why he did this or why he was listening. That action, for the rest of his life, he would call "shameful," and deep down, he thought of it as the lowest thing he had ever done. He didn't feel any hatred for Fyodor Pavlovitch at that moment. He was just extremely curious to know how his father was moving around down there, and what he was doing. He imagined Fyodor Pavlovitch peeking through the dark windows, pausing in the middle of the room, listening— listening for someone to knock. Twice that night, Ivan went out onto the stairs to listen like that.

Around two o'clock, when everything was quiet and even Fyodor Pavlovitch had gone to bed, Ivan finally lay down, determined to fall asleep right away, as he felt utterly exhausted. And he did fall asleep immediately, sleeping deeply without any dreams, but woke up early, at seven o'clock, when it was already light outside. Opening his eyes, he was surprised to feel incredibly energetic. He jumped out of bed and dressed quickly, then dragged out his trunk and started packing right away. His laundry had been returned the previous morning. Ivan couldn't help but smile at how everything seemed to be lining up perfectly for his sudden departure. And his departure really was sudden. Though Ivan had told Katerina Ivanovna, Alyosha, and Smerdyakov the day before that he would be leaving the next day, he remembered that he hadn't seriously thought about leaving when he went to bed. At the very least, he hadn't imagined that the first thing he would do in the morning was pack his things. Finally, his trunk and bag were ready. It was around nine o'clock when Marfa Ignatyevna came in with her usual question, "Where would you like your tea, sir, in your room or downstairs?" Ivan looked almost cheerful, but there was something hurried and scattered about his words and movements. He greeted his father warmly and even specifically asked about his health, though he didn't wait for the full answer. He announced that he was leaving for Moscow in an hour and this time for good, asking for horses to be arranged. His father heard the news without showing any surprise and, in a rather rude way, forgot to express any sadness about Ivan leaving. Instead, he suddenly got all flustered, remembering some important business of his own.

"What a guy! You didn't tell me yesterday! Never mind, we can still manage. Do me a big favor, my dear boy. On your way, go to Tchermashnya. All you need to do is turn left at the station in Volovya. It's only twelve more versts and you'll be in Tchermashnya."

"I'm sorry, I can't. It's eighty versts to the railway, and the train to Moscow leaves at seven o'clock tonight. I'll barely make it."

"You can catch it tomorrow or the day after. But today, go to Tchermashnya. It won't be too much trouble to help your father! If I didn't have something keeping me here, I would've gone myself long ago. But you see, it's not the right time for me to go now. I have two pieces of woodland there. The Maslovs, an old merchant and his son, are offering eight thousand for the timber. Last year, I almost sold it to someone else who would've paid twelve. Around here, you can't find anyone else to buy it. The Maslovs control everything. You have to take what they offer because no one dares to bid against them. But the priest in Ilyinskoe wrote me last Thursday, saying that a merchant named Gorstkin, a man I know, has shown up. What makes him valuable is that he's not from around here, so he's not afraid of the Maslovs. He's offering me eleven thousand for the woodland. Do you hear that? But he'll only be here for about a week, according to the priest, so you need to go right away and strike a deal with him."

"Well, then write to the priest. He'll take care of the deal."

"He can't handle it. He has no head for business. He's a real treasure; I'd trust him with twenty thousand roubles without even asking for a receipt. But when it comes to business, he's helpless—like a child, completely naive. Even a crow could fool him. And yet, would you believe it? He's such a learned man! But when it comes to dealing with people like Gorstkin, he's no match. This Gorstkin may look like a simple peasant in his blue kaftan, but don't let that fool you. He's a proper swindler, a crook through and through. That's what everyone says about him. He's also a liar. Sometimes, he tells such ridiculous lies that you have to wonder why he even bothers. A couple of years ago, he told me his wife had passed away and that he'd remarried. And do you know what? None of it was true! His first wife never died, she's still alive to this day, and they say she beats him up twice a week! So, what you have to figure out is whether he's telling the truth or just trying to cheat you when he says he's willing to buy the land and pay eleven thousand."

"I wouldn't be of any use in this situation. I don't have an eye for such things either."

"Wait, wait! Don't be so quick to dismiss it. You could still be of help, because I'll tell you exactly what to look for when dealing with Gorstkin. I've done plenty of business with him over the years, so I know all his tricks. Here's the thing: you've got to watch his beard. He has this nasty, thin red beard. If it starts shaking while he's talking and he gets angry, then you know he's serious—he's telling the truth and genuinely wants to make the deal. But if he strokes his beard with his left hand and grins while he's talking, then he's up to no good, and you know he's trying to cheat you. Don't waste your time watching his eyes; he's too clever for that. You won't see anything in them. But keep your eye on his beard. I'll write you a note to show him. He's called Gorstkin, but his real name is Lyagavy. Don't use his real name though—he'll be offended. If you manage to come to an agreement and see that everything checks out, send me a letter immediately. You only need to write one line: 'He's not lying.' That's it. Make sure you stick to the price of eleven thousand. You can come down a thousand if you must, but no more. Just think! There's a big difference between eight thousand and eleven thousand. It's practically like finding three thousand roubles lying in the street! It's not easy to find a buyer for that kind of property, and I really need the money. Just let me know if the deal's serious, and I'll make the time to come and finalize it. I'll find a way, somehow. But there's no point in me hurrying over there if it's just some nonsense that the priest thought up. So, will you go?"

"I really can't spare the time. You'll have to excuse me."

"Come on, can't you do this one thing for your father? I won't forget it, I promise. None of you have any heart, that's the truth of it. What's a day or two to you? What are you in such a hurry for, Venice? Your Venice will still be there in two days. I would've sent Alyosha, but what use would he be in this? I'm sending you because you're smart—you know that. Don't think I haven't noticed. You may not know anything about timber, but you've got a sharp eye, and that's what's needed. You just need to figure out if the man is serious or not. Trust me, just watch his beard—if it shakes, he's being honest."

"So, you're really forcing me to go to that cursed Tchermashnya yourself, then?" Ivan asked, with a bitter smile.

Fyodor Pavlovitch either didn't notice the bitterness or chose to ignore it, but he definitely caught the smile.

"So, you'll go, you'll go! I'll write the note for you right away." "I don't know yet if I'll go or not. I'll decide on the way."

"Nonsense! Decide now. Don't leave it up in the air, my dear boy! If you settle the deal, just send me a note. Give it to the priest, and he'll make sure it gets to me quickly. That's all you'll have to do. Then you can go to Venice. The priest will arrange horses for you to get back to the station at Volovya."

The old man was absolutely thrilled. He quickly wrote the note and sent for the horses. A light lunch was brought in, with some brandy. When Fyodor Pavlovitch was in a good mood, he usually became quite talkative, but today, he seemed to hold himself back. He didn't say a word about Dmitri, and he didn't seem particularly affected by Ivan's departure. In fact, it seemed like he didn't know what to say. Ivan noticed this, thinking to himself, "He's probably bored of me." Only when they stepped outside did Fyodor Pavlovitch begin to fuss a bit. He almost went to kiss Ivan goodbye, but Ivan quickly extended his hand, clearly avoiding the kiss. His father noticed this right away and awkwardly pulled back.

"Well, good luck to you! Good luck to you!" he repeated as he stood on the steps. "You'll come back to visit sometime, won't you? Be sure to come. I'll always be glad to see you. Well, God bless you!"

Ivan climbed into the carriage.

"Goodbye, Ivan! Don't be too hard on me!" his father called out one last time.

The entire household came out to see him off—Smerdyakov, Marfa, and Grigory. Ivan handed them each ten roubles. Once he was seated in the carriage, Smerdyakov climbed up to arrange the rug for him.

"You know, I'm going to Tchermashnya," Ivan said suddenly, as if the words slipped out on their own. Just like the day before, the statement seemed to come out of nowhere, and he laughed—a strange, nervous laugh. It was the kind of laugh that he would remember long after.

"It's true what they say: 'It's always worth talking to a clever man,'" Smerdyakov replied firmly, giving Ivan a meaningful look.

The carriage began to move. Ivan wasn't sure of anything, but as they rolled along, he eagerly looked around at the fields, the hills, and the trees. He even noticed a flock of geese flying high in the bright blue sky. All of a sudden, he felt a strange wave of happiness wash over him. He tried to strike up a conversation with the driver and found himself oddly interested in what the man was saying. But after a moment, he realized he hadn't really been paying attention at all. He fell silent again, but it was a peaceful kind of silence. The air was fresh and cool, and the sky was clear and bright. Thoughts of Alyosha and Katerina Ivanovna flitted through his mind, but he smiled softly and let those thoughts drift away. "There's plenty of time for all that," he thought. They soon reached the station, changed horses, and sped toward Volovya. "Why did Smerdyakov say it's always worth talking to a clever man? What was he getting at?" The thought suddenly tightened Ivan's chest. "And why did I even tell him I was going to Tchermashnya?" They soon arrived at Volovya Station. Ivan got out of the carriage, and the drivers gathered around, discussing the twelve verst journey to Tchermashnya. Ivan told them to harness the horses, but then, just as he was about to head inside, he stopped abruptly. He turned around, glanced toward the entrance, and then made up his mind.

"I'm not going to Tchermashnya after all. Can I still make it to the station in time for the seven o'clock train?"

"We can just make it, if we hurry. Should we get the carriage ready?"

"Yes, right away. Will any of you be going into town tomorrow?" "Mitri will, for sure."

"Great. Can you do me a favor, Mitri? Go to my father, Fyodor Pavlovitch Karamazov, and tell him I didn't go to Tchermashnya. Can you do that for me?"

"Of course, sir. I've known Fyodor Pavlovitch for years."

"Here's something for your trouble, because I doubt my father will give you anything for delivering the message," Ivan said with a light-hearted laugh.

"You can count on him not giving me a thing," Mitri laughed as well. "Thank you, sir. I'll make sure to pass along the message."

At seven o'clock, Ivan boarded the train for Moscow. "Goodbye to the past. I'm done with that old world forever. No more news, no more echoes from it. On to a new life, new places, and no looking back!" But instead of feeling joy or freedom, his heart was filled with an unbearable sense of sorrow, and a deep, aching pain that he had never known before. He thought all night long as the train sped along the tracks, and only when dawn broke as they neared Moscow did he stir from his thoughts.

"I'm a scoundrel," he whispered to himself.

Meanwhile, Fyodor Pavlovitch was feeling quite pleased with himself after seeing Ivan off. For the next two hours, he felt almost happy, sipping on brandy. But then, something happened that upset everyone in the house and quickly ruined his mood. Smerdyakov had gone down to the cellar for something and had fallen down the stairs. Luckily, Marfa Ignatyevna had been outside and heard him scream—a strange, familiar scream that she knew all too well as the sound of an epileptic fit. She didn't see him fall, but she knew what had happened the moment she heard that scream. It wasn't clear whether the fit caused him to fall or if the fall triggered the fit, but they found him at the bottom of the cellar steps, shaking and foaming at the mouth. At first, they feared he might have broken an arm or leg, but "God spared him," as Marfa Ignatyevna put it—he hadn't broken anything. Still, it wasn't easy to get him out of the cellar. They had to ask the neighbors for help. Fyodor Pavlovitch stayed there the whole time, clearly rattled and disturbed. Smerdyakov didn't regain consciousness, and though the convulsions stopped briefly, they started again, making everyone fear the worst. It reminded them of the time he had fallen from the attic a year ago. They remembered putting ice on his head back then. There was still some ice left in the cellar, so Marfa Ignatyevna brought it up. That evening, Fyodor Pavlovitch sent for Doctor Herzenstube, who arrived quickly. He was an old man, known for being the most careful and thorough doctor in the entire province. After examining Smerdyakov closely, he determined that the fit was severe and could have serious consequences. He wasn't sure what the outcome would be, but he promised to try something else by morning if the current treatments didn't work. Smerdyakov was moved to a room in the lodge, close to where Grigory and Marfa Ignatyevna stayed.

But that wasn't the end of Fyodor Pavlovitch's troubles that day. Marfa Ignatyevna had prepared dinner, but the soup, compared to Smerdyakov's cooking, was "no better than dishwater," and the chicken was so overcooked it was nearly impossible to chew. When Fyodor Pavlovitch complained, and rightly so, Marfa Ignatyevna shot back that the chicken was old to begin with, and that she had never been trained as a cook. To make matters worse, Grigory, who had been unwell for the last three days, was now completely bedridden with terrible back pain. Fyodor Pavlovitch finished his tea as quickly as he could and locked himself up in the house, alone. He was in a state of intense excitement and anticipation. That evening, he was almost certain that Grushenka would come. Earlier that morning, Smerdyakov had assured him that she had promised to come without fail. Fyodor Pavlovitch's heart pounded with excitement as he paced through his empty rooms, ears alert for any sign of her. He had to be ready. Dmitri might be lurking nearby, waiting for her to arrive. And when she knocked on the window (Smerdyakov had told him exactly where and how she would knock), he would need to open the door immediately. He couldn't let her linger in the hallway, not even for a second, in case—God forbid—she got scared and fled. Fyodor Pavlovitch had many thoughts racing through his mind, but never had his heart been so full of eager anticipation. This time, he was almost certain—she would come!

Book 6: The Russian Monk

Chapter 1: Father Zossima And His Visitors

When Alyosha entered his elder's cell, his heart heavy with worry, he was almost shocked by what he saw. Instead of finding a dying man, unconscious or barely alive as he had feared, he found him sitting up in his chair. Though the elder was weak and worn out, his face was bright and full of peace. He was surrounded by visitors, calmly and happily chatting with them. But the elder had only gotten out of bed about fifteen minutes before Alyosha arrived; the visitors had gathered earlier, waiting for him to wake. They had come because Father Païssy had confidently assured them that "the teacher would get up, and, as he had promised in the morning, would speak once more with those dear to his heart." Father Païssy believed every word of the elder's promise completely. Even if he had seen the elder unconscious, even if he had seen him take his last breath, if the elder had promised he would rise to say goodbye, Father Païssy would not have believed in his death. He would have still expected him to wake up and keep his promise. That morning, as Father Zossima lay down to rest, he had said to Father Païssy, "I will not die without the joy of one more conversation with you, dear to my heart. I will look on your face again and pour out my soul to you once more." The monks who had gathered for this likely final conversation with Father Zossima had been close to him for many years. There were four of them: Father Iosif, Father Païssy, Father Mihaïl—the warden of the hermitage—and Father Anfim.

Father Mihaïl was not very old and was not considered a particularly learned man. He was humble, strong-willed, and deeply faithful, with an austere appearance. Though he hid it well, there was a deep tenderness in him, almost as if he were embarrassed by it. The fourth monk, Father Anfim, was a very old and humble man from the poorest peasant background. He was almost illiterate and very quiet, rarely speaking to anyone. He was the humblest of the humble, looking as though he had been frightened by something great and beyond his understanding. Father Zossima had a deep affection for this timid man and always treated him with great respect, though he had spoken very little to him over the years, despite the many years they had spent wandering holy Russia together. That had been long ago, forty years earlier, when Father Zossima first became a monk in a small, poor monastery in Kostroma. Not long after, he had gone on a pilgrimage with Father Anfim to collect alms for their monastery.

All of them were gathered in the small bedroom, which was so cramped that it barely had space for the four monks to sit around Father Zossima, along with Porfiry, the novice, who stood nearby. Chairs had been brought in from the sitting room to make space for them. The room was beginning to darken, lit only by lamps and candles placed in front of the icons.

When Father Zossima saw Alyosha standing in the doorway, looking a little embarrassed, he smiled at him warmly and reached out his hand.

"Welcome, my quiet one, welcome, my dear," he said. "I knew you would come."

Alyosha stepped forward, bowed deeply before him, and began to weep. His heart was full, and his soul trembled with emotion. He felt like he needed to sob.

"Come now, don't weep for me yet," Father Zossima said with a smile, placing his right hand on Alyosha's head. "You see, I'm sitting here, talking. Who knows? Maybe I'll live another twenty years, like that dear woman from Vishegorye hoped yesterday. She came with her little Lizaveta in her arms. God bless the mother and the little girl Lizaveta," he said, crossing himself. "Porfiry, did you take her offering where I told you?"

He was referring to the sixty copecks that the kind-hearted woman had given him the day before, asking that it be given to someone poorer than herself. Such offerings were often made as a form of penance, given by those who had earned the money through hard work. The elder had sent Porfiry the night before to deliver the money to a widow whose house had recently burned down. The widow, left homeless, had been forced to beg for alms with her children. Porfiry quickly confirmed that he had given the money to the widow as instructed, telling her it came from "an unknown benefactress."

"Get up, my dear boy," Father Zossima said to Alyosha, "let me look at you. Have you been home? Have you seen your brother?" Alyosha found it strange that the elder asked so directly about one of his brothers—he wondered which one the elder meant. Perhaps the elder had sent him out yesterday and today for the sake of that brother specifically.

"I've seen one of my brothers," Alyosha replied. "I mean your elder brother, the one I bowed to."

"I saw him yesterday, but I couldn't find him today," Alyosha answered.

"Go find him quickly—tomorrow, go and find him right away. Drop everything else and make haste. You may still have time to stop something terrible from happening. Yesterday, I bowed to the great suffering that lies ahead for him."

Father Zossima suddenly became silent, as though deep in thought. His words sounded strange to Alyosha. Father Iosif, who had witnessed what had happened yesterday, exchanged a glance with Father Païssy. Alyosha could not hold back his question any longer.

"Father, teacher," he said, his voice full of emotion, "your words are too mysterious… what is this suffering you speak of that awaits him?"

"Do not ask me," Father Zossima replied quietly. "Yesterday, I saw something terrible in his eyes… it was as if his whole future was laid bare in them. I saw a look in his eyes that filled me with dread, as if I saw what fate awaited him. I've only seen such a look a few times in my life, but when I did, the person's fate unfolded just as that look had foretold. I sent you to him, Alexey, hoping that your brotherly face might help him. But everything, all our fates, are in the hands of the Lord. 'Unless a grain of wheat falls to the ground and dies, it remains alone; but if it dies, it bears much fruit.' Remember that. I've often blessed you in my heart, Alexey, without saying a word. Know that."

The elder smiled kindly at Alyosha and continued, "This is what I think about you—you will leave these walls, but you will live as a monk in the world. You will have many enemies, but even your enemies will love you. Life will bring you many hardships, but you will find happiness in them. You will bless life, and you will help others bless it too, which is the most important thing. Yes, that is your character."

Then, turning to the other monks, he added with a tender smile, "Fathers, I have never told even him why I hold his face so dear to me. But now, I will tell you all. His face has been a symbol to me—a sign and a prophecy. When I was a child, at the very beginning of my life, I had an older brother who died when he was seventeen, right in front of me. And over time, I became convinced that my brother had been sent to me as a guide, a sign from heaven. If he hadn't been in my life, I might never have become a monk, might never have taken this precious path. He was the one who appeared in my childhood, and now, at the end of my journey, he seems to have appeared again in Alexey. It is truly wonderful, fathers, that Alexey—though he doesn't look exactly like my brother—resembles him in spirit so much that I often feel as though he is my brother, returned to me at the end of my journey as a reminder and an inspiration. I have been amazed at how strange this dream of mine has been."

Turning to Porfiry, the novice, the elder said, "Porfiry, many times I've seen a look on your face that you were hurt, that you felt I loved Alexey more than you. Now you know why. But know this: I love you too, and many times I have grieved over your hurt feelings."

Then, addressing the group of monks again, Father Zossima said, "I would like to tell you more about that youth, my brother, for no one else in my life has been more precious or more meaningful to me. My heart is full of tenderness as I look back on my life at this moment, as though I am living it all over again."

I must mention that Father Zossima's last conversation with the friends who visited him on the final day of his life was partly written down. Alexey Fyodorovitch Karamazov wrote it down from memory some time after his elder's death. However, it is unclear whether this was just the conversation that took place at that moment or if he also added parts of earlier conversations he had with his teacher. In his account, it appears that Father Zossima's talk continues without interruption, as if he were telling his life story to his friends in the form of a continuous narrative. But there is no doubt, from other accounts, that the conversation that evening was more of a general discussion. Although Father Zossima was not interrupted much by his visitors, they also spoke, perhaps even shared something themselves. Moreover, it's unlikely that Father Zossima could have spoken non-stop, since at times he was out of breath, his voice weakened, and he even lay down to rest on his bed, though he did not fall asleep, and his visitors remained seated. Once or twice, the conversation was interrupted by Father Païssy reading from the Gospel. It's worth noting that none of the visitors suspected that he would die that night, as after his deep sleep during the day, Father Zossima seemed to have regained some strength, which allowed him to continue this lengthy conversation. It was as though his love for his friends gave him a sudden surge of energy—but it only lasted a short while, as his life ended soon after… but more about that later. I'll add now that I chose to stick to the version told by Alexey Fyodorovitch Karamazov. It's shorter and less exhausting, though, as I've said before, Alexey incorporated parts from previous conversations.

Notes from the Life of the Deceased Priest and Monk, Elder Zossima, as recorded by Alexey Fyodorovitch Karamazov.

Biographical Notes

Father Zossima's Brother

Dear fathers and teachers, I was born in a distant northern province, in the town of V. My father was a nobleman by birth, but he wasn't of much significance or rank. He passed away when I was only two years old, so I don't remember him at all. He left my mother a small wooden house and a modest inheritance, enough to ensure that she and her children lived comfortably. There were two of us—my older brother Markel and I. Markel was eight years older than me. He had a quick temper but a kind heart and never spoke sarcastically. He was unusually quiet, especially at home with our mother, me, and the servants. He did well in school but didn't get along with his classmates, though he never argued with them — at least that's what my mother told me. Six months before his death, when he was seventeen, he made friends with a political exile who had been banished from Moscow to our town for his radical views. The man lived alone and was an accomplished scholar who had earned distinction in philosophy at the university. For some reason, he took a liking to Markel and invited him to visit. My brother spent entire evenings with him that winter, until the exile was called back to Petersburg at his own request, thanks to his influential friends.

It was the start of Lent, and my brother refused to fast. He was disrespectful and mocked it. "That's all foolishness, there's no God," he said, shocking my mother, the servants, and me—even though I was only nine years old, I was horrified by his words. We had four servants, all of them serfs. I remember my mother selling one of them, the cook Afimya, who was elderly and lame, for sixty paper rubles, and hiring a free servant in her place.

In the sixth week of Lent, my brother, who had never been particularly strong and was prone to illness, became ill. He was tall, thin, and delicate, but very pleasant to look at. He must have caught a cold because the doctor soon told my mother privately that it was advanced tuberculosis and that he wouldn't survive the spring. My mother cried but tried not to let my brother know the severity of his condition. She begged him to go to church, confess, and take the sacrament while he was still able to walk. This made him angry, and he said something blasphemous about the church. He grew thoughtful, though; he quickly realized that he was seriously ill, which is why our mother was urging him to confess. For some time, he had known he wasn't well and had even casually mentioned at dinner a year earlier, "I won't be with you for long, I may not last the year," which now seemed like a prediction.

Three days passed, and Holy Week began. On Tuesday morning, my brother started going to church. "I'm only doing this for your sake, mother, to please and comfort you," he said. My mother cried with joy and sorrow. "His end must be near," she thought, "if he's changing so much." But he didn't go to church for long. Soon, he was confined to bed, and he had to confess and take the sacrament at home.

It was a late Easter, and the days were bright, warm, and full of fresh spring air. I remember how he coughed all night and slept poorly, but in the mornings, he would get dressed and try to sit up in a chair. That's how I remember him—sweet and gentle, always smiling, his face glowing and full of joy despite his illness. A remarkable transformation had come over him, and his spirit seemed to be completely renewed. Our old nurse would come in and say, "Let me light the lamp in front of the holy icon, my dear." In the past, he wouldn't have allowed it and would even blow it out.

"Light it, light it," he said now, "I was so wrong to stop you before. You are praying when you light the lamp, and I am praying when I feel joy watching you. So, in a way, we are both praying to the same God."

Those words seemed strange to us, and my mother would go to her room to cry. But when she returned to his room, she wiped her eyes and tried to look cheerful. "Mother, don't cry," he would say.

"I still have a long time left to live, a long time to enjoy life with you. Life is beautiful and full of joy."

"My dear boy, how can you talk about joy when you cough so terribly at night, as though you're tearing yourself apart?"

"Please don't cry, mother," he would reply. "Life is paradise, and we are all in paradise, but we just don't see it. If we could only see it, we would have heaven on earth tomorrow."

Everyone was amazed at his words. He spoke so confidently and with such certainty. We were all deeply moved and wept. Friends came to visit. "Dear friends," he would say to them, "what have I done to deserve your love? How can you love someone like me? And why didn't I realize this before? How didn't I appreciate it?"

When the servants came in to take care of him, he would constantly say, "Dear, kind people, why are you doing so much for me? Do I deserve all this attention? If it were God's will for me to live, I would serve you all, for we should all serve one another."

My mother would shake her head as she listened. "My dear, it's your illness making you talk this way."

"Mother, my sweet, my dear mother," he would say (he had started using such strange, affectionate words at this time), "my little heart, believe me, we are all responsible for everyone else. I don't know how to explain it, but I feel it deeply, even painfully. And how did we not realize this before? How did we keep living, getting angry, and not understanding?"

Every day, he became sweeter, more full of love and joy. When the doctor, an old German named Eisenschmidt, came to see him:

"Well, doctor, do I have another day left in this world?" my brother would ask jokingly.

"You still have many days left," the doctor would reply. "Many months and years as well."

"Months and years!" he would exclaim. "Why count the days? One day is enough for a person to experience complete happiness. My dear ones, why do we argue, try to outdo each other, and hold grudges? Let's go straight to the garden, walk and play there, love each other, appreciate one another, and glorify life."

"Your son doesn't have much time," the doctor told my mother as she walked him to the door. "The illness is affecting his brain."

The windows of his room looked out into the garden, and our garden was a shady one, full of old trees that were starting to bud. The first birds of spring were hopping around in the branches, chirping and singing by the windows. And as he watched them, he suddenly began asking for their forgiveness too: "Birds of heaven, happy birds, forgive me, for I have sinned against you as well." None of us could understand this at the time, but he cried tears of joy. "Yes," he said, "there was such a great glory of God all around me: the birds, the trees, the meadows, the sky. But I lived in shame, dishonored it all, and didn't notice the beauty and glory."

"You take too many sins upon yourself," my mother would say, crying.

"Mother, my dear, I'm crying out of joy, not sadness. I can't explain it to you, but I feel like humbling myself before them because I don't know how to love them enough. If I have sinned against everyone, then everyone forgives me too, and that's heaven. Am I not in heaven right now?"

And there were many more things he said that I don't remember. I recall once going into his room when no one else was there. It was a bright evening, the sun was setting, and the whole room was filled with light. He called me over, and I walked up to him. He placed his hands on my shoulders and looked into my face, tenderly, lovingly; he didn't speak for a moment, just looked at me like that.

"Well," he said, "run along and play now, enjoy life for me too."

I left then and ran off to play. Many times later in my life, I would remember—even with tears—how he told me to enjoy life for him as well. There were many other wonderful and beautiful things he said, though we didn't fully understand them at the time. He died in the third week after Easter. He was fully aware, although he could no longer speak. Until his last hour, he remained unchanged. He looked happy, his eyes sparkled, and he searched for us with his gaze, smiling and gesturing to us. People in town even talked about his death. I was deeply affected by everything at the time, though not overwhelmingly so, even though I cried a lot at his funeral. I was young, a child, but a lasting impression, a hidden feeling of it all, stayed in my heart, ready to rise and respond when the time came. And indeed, that's how it happened.

I was left alone with my mother. Her friends began advising her to send me to Petersburg, like many parents did. "You only have one son now," they said, "and you have a decent income. You might deprive him of a successful future if you keep him here." They suggested that I be sent to the Cadet Corps in Petersburg, so I could later join the Imperial Guard. My mother hesitated for a long time, as it was terrible to part with her only child, but eventually, she made up her mind, though not without many tears, believing she was doing it for my happiness. She brought me to Petersburg and placed me in the Cadet Corps, and I never saw her again. She too died three years later. She spent those three years mourning and grieving for both of us.

From my childhood home, I carry nothing but precious memories, as there are no memories more valuable than those from one's early childhood home. That is almost always true if there is any love and harmony in the family at all. Even in a bad home, if the heart knows how to find what is precious, memories can remain. Along with my memories of home, I also cherish my memories of the Bible, which I was eager to read as a child. I had a book of Bible stories with excellent illustrations, called A Hundred and Four Stories from the Old and New Testament, and I learned to read from it. I still have it on my shelf today, keeping it as a treasured relic from the past. But even before I learned to read, I remember first feeling moved by devotion when I was eight years old. My mother took me to mass alone (I don't remember where my brother was at the time) on the Monday before Easter. It was a beautiful day, and I remember, as if I could see it now, how the incense rose from the censer and gently floated upwards, blending in waves with the sunlight streaming through the little window in the dome. The sight stirred something in me, and for the first time, I consciously felt God's word in my heart. A young man came out into the center of the church, carrying a large book—so big that I thought he could hardly carry it. He placed it on the reading desk, opened it, and began reading. For the first time, I understood something being read in God's house. In the land of Uz, there lived a man who was righteous and God-fearing, and he was very wealthy, with many camels, sheep, and donkeys. He loved his children very much and prayed for them, saying, "It may be that my sons have sinned during their feasting." Then the devil came before the Lord, along with the sons of God, and told the Lord that he had traveled all over the earth. "Have you considered my servant Job?" God asked him. And God proudly pointed to His great and holy servant. But the devil laughed at God's words. "Give him over to me, and you'll see that your servant will curse you and complain." And God allowed the devil to test the righteous man He loved so much. The devil struck down his children, his cattle, and scattered all his wealth, as suddenly as a lightning bolt from heaven. And Job tore his clothes, fell to the ground, and cried out, "I came into this world naked from my mother's womb, and I will return naked to the earth. The Lord gave, and the Lord has taken away. Blessed be the name of the Lord forever."

Fathers and teachers, forgive my tears now, for all my childhood comes back to me, and I breathe now as I did then, with the heart of an eight-year-old child, and I feel the same awe, wonder, and joy. At that time, the camels captured my imagination, and Satan, who spoke to God like that, and God who gave His servant up to be tested, and His servant crying out: "Blessed be Your name, even though You punish me." And then the soft, sweet singing in the church: "Let my prayer rise up before You," and again the incense from the priest's censer, the kneeling, and the prayer. Ever since then—and only yesterday I read it again—I have never been able to read that sacred story without tears. How much greatness, mystery, and depth are in it! Later, I heard people mock and criticize, proud voices saying, "How could God give up His most beloved saint for the devil's amusement, take his children away, cover him with painful sores so that he had to scrape his skin with a broken piece of pottery—and all for the sake of showing off to the devil! 'Look what My saint can suffer for My sake.'" But the greatness of it lies in the fact that it is a mystery—that the temporary show of this world and the eternal truth come together in it. In the face of earthly truth, eternal truth is fulfilled. The Creator, just like He did on the first days of creation when He ended each day with praise, saying, "It is good, what I have made," looks at Job and once again praises His creation. And Job, praising the Lord, serves not only God but all of His creation, for generations and generations, and forever, because he was meant to do that. Good heavens, what a book it is, and what lessons are in it! What a book the Bible is, what a miracle, what strength it gives to people! It's like a mold that shapes the world, humans, and human nature—everything is there, and there's a law for everything for all time. And what mysteries are solved and revealed! God restores Job, gives him wealth again. Many years pass, and he has more children, and he loves them. But how could he love those new children when the first ones were gone, when he had lost them? Remembering them, how could he be fully happy with his new children, no matter how much he loved them? But he could, he could. It's one of the great mysteries of human life that old sorrow gradually turns into gentle, quiet joy. The calmness of old age replaces the wild energy of youth. I bless the rising sun every day, and, as before, my heart sings to greet it, but now I love even more the sunset, its long, slanting rays, and the soft, tender, gentle memories that come with it—the dear images from all of my long, happy life—and over all of it is the Divine Truth, softening, reconciling, forgiving! My life is ending, I know that well, but with each day that passes, I feel how my earthly life is connected to a new, infinite, unknown life—the one that is coming closer. This nearness makes my soul tremble with joy, my mind glow, and my heart weep with happiness.

Friends and teachers, I have heard more than once, and lately more often, that priests—especially village priests—are complaining everywhere about their small income and their difficult situation. They even say it plainly in print—I've read it myself—that they can't teach the Scriptures to people because of how little they have to live on. And if Lutherans and heretics come and lead their flock astray, they let them do it because they have so little to survive on. May the Lord provide more for them, as their complaint is just. But truly, I say, if anyone is to blame, half the fault is ours. Yes, he may not have much time; yes, he may truly say that he is overwhelmed with work and services, but still, it's not all the time—he can find an hour each week to remember God. He doesn't work every day of the year. Let him gather people around him once a week, for an hour in the evening, if only the children at first—the fathers will hear about it and start coming too. There's no need to build special halls for this. Let him invite them into his own home. They won't ruin his cottage; they'll only be there for one hour. Let him open that book and start reading, without using big words or talking down to them, but gently and kindly, glad that he's reading to them and that they are listening attentively. He should love the words himself and only stop occasionally to explain parts that the peasants might not understand. Don't worry—they'll understand everything. The heart of a faithful person understands it all! Let him read to them about Abraham and Sarah, about Isaac and Rebecca, about how Jacob went to Laban and wrestled with the Lord in his dream and said, "This place is holy"—and he will touch the devout heart of the peasant. Let him especially read to the children about how Joseph's brothers sold him, the tender boy, the dreamer and prophet, into slavery, and then told their father that a wild animal had eaten him, showing him Joseph's bloodstained clothes. Let him read how the brothers later went to Egypt to get grain, and how Joseph, now a great ruler, didn't reveal his identity at first, accused them, and kept his brother Benjamin, all out of love: "I love you, and because I love you, I cause you pain." For he remembered all his life how they had sold him to merchants in the hot desert by the well, and how he had cried and begged his brothers not to sell him into slavery in a foreign land. And when he saw them again after many years, he loved them even more, but out of love, he tormented them. At last, unable to bear the pain in his heart, he left them, threw himself on his bed, and cried. Then, wiping away his tears, he went back to them full of joy and said, "Brothers, I am your brother Joseph!" Let him continue reading to them about how happy old Jacob was when he learned that his beloved son was still alive, how he traveled to Egypt, leaving his own country, and how he died in a foreign land, giving his great prophecy that had been hidden in his humble and gentle heart all his life—that from his descendants, from Judah, would come the great hope of the world, the Messiah and Savior.

Fathers and teachers, forgive me and don't be upset that, like a little child, I've been talking about things you already know well and could explain to me a hundred times better. I only speak from joy, and forgive my tears because I love the Bible. Let the priest of God weep too, and be sure that the hearts of his listeners will respond with emotion. Only a small seed is needed—plant it in the heart of a peasant, and it won't die; it will live in his soul all his life, hidden in his darkness and sin like a bright spot, like a powerful reminder. There's no need for much teaching or explanation; he will understand it all simply. Do you think the peasants can't understand? Try reading them the moving story of the beautiful Esther and the proud Vashti, or the miraculous story of Jonah in the whale. Don't forget the parables of Our Lord either, especially from the Gospel of St. Luke (that's what I did), and also the story of St. Paul's conversion from the Acts of the Apostles (you must not leave that out), and from the Lives of the Saints, for instance, the life of Alexey, the Man of God, and, greatest of all, the story of the happy martyr and the seer of God, Mary of Egypt—and with these simple stories, you will reach their hearts. Just give one hour a week to it, despite your poverty—just one little hour. And you will see for yourselves that our people are kind and grateful and will repay you a hundred times over. Remembering their priest's kindness and the moving words they heard from him, they will willingly help him with his fields and his home, and will respect him even more—so much so that it will improve his worldly situation too. The idea is so simple that sometimes one is afraid to say it, in case others laugh, and yet it's so true! Someone who doesn't believe in God won't believe in God's people either. But if someone believes in God's people, he will see His Holiness, even if he didn't believe in it before. Only the people and their future spiritual power will convert our atheists, who have separated themselves from their roots.

And what good are Christ's words if we don't set an example? The people are lost without God's Word, because their souls thirst for the Word and for all that is good.

When I was young, nearly forty years ago, I traveled all over Russia with Father Anfim, collecting money for our monastery. One night, we stayed by the bank of a large river with some fishermen. A handsome young peasant, about eighteen years old, joined us; he had to hurry back the next morning to pull a merchant's barge along the bank. I noticed him looking straight ahead with clear and gentle eyes. It was a warm, calm July night, and a cool mist was rising from the wide river. We could hear the splash of a fish, the birds were quiet, everything was still and beautiful, everything was praying to God. Only the boy and I were awake, and we talked about the beauty of God's world and its great mystery. Every blade of grass, every insect, ant, and golden bee—they all know their path, even though they don't have intelligence. They bear witness to God's mystery and continually fulfill it. I could see the boy's heart was moved. He told me that he loved the forest and the birds that lived there. He was a bird-catcher and knew the sound of each bird and could call them. "There's nothing better than being in the forest," he said, "although everything is good."

"Truly," I said to him, "everything is good and beautiful, because all is truth. Look," I said, "at the horse, that large animal so close to man, or the humble, thoughtful ox, which feeds him and works for him. Look at their faces—what gentleness, what devotion to man, who often beats them without mercy. What kindness, what trust, and what beauty! It's touching to know that there's no sin in them because everything except man is sinless, and Christ has been with them before us."

"Why?" asked the boy, "Is Christ with them too?"

"It must be so," I said, "because the Word is for everyone. All creation and every creature, every leaf, is reaching for the Word, singing glory to God, weeping to Christ, and unknowingly fulfilling this through the mystery of their sinless lives. Look," I said, "in the forest, the fierce and frightening bear roams, and yet he is innocent too." And I told him how once a bear came to a great saint who was living in a tiny cell in the woods. The saint took pity on the bear, went up to him without fear, and gave him a piece of bread. "Go along," said the saint, "Christ be with you," and the wild animal walked away quietly and gently, causing no harm. The boy was delighted that the bear had left without hurting the saint, and that Christ was with him too. "Ah," he said, "how wonderful that is, how good and beautiful all of God's work is!" He sat there, quietly thinking, and I could see he understood. He fell asleep beside me, sleeping lightly and sinlessly. May God bless the young! And as I fell asleep, I prayed for him. Lord, send peace and light to Your people!

Chapter 2: The Duel

I spent a long time—almost eight years—at the military cadet school in Petersburg, and in the novelty of my surroundings there, many of my childhood impressions became fainter, although I forgot nothing. I picked up so many new habits and opinions that I transformed into a cruel, ridiculous, almost wild creature. I did manage to acquire a surface polish of courtesy and social manners, along with the French language.

But all of us, myself included, regarded the soldiers in our service as nothing more than animals. I was perhaps worse than the others in that regard because I was so much more impressionable than my companions. By the time we left the school as officers, we were all ready to lay down our lives for the honor of the regiment, yet not one of us understood the true meaning of honor, and if anyone had, they would have been the first to mock it. Drunkenness, debauchery, and devilry were almost what we prided ourselves on. I don't mean to say we were bad by nature—all those young men were good fellows—but they behaved badly, and I was the worst of all. What made it worse for me was that I had come into my inheritance, so I threw myself into a life of pleasure and plunged headlong into the reckless abandon of youth.

I was fond of reading, yet it was strange that the Bible was the one book I never opened during that time, even though I always carried it with me. I was never separated from it; in truth, I was saving that book "for the day and the hour, for the month and the year," though I wasn't aware of it.

After four years of living like this, I happened to be in the town of K., where our regiment was stationed at the time. We found the people there to be hospitable, wealthy, and fond of entertainment. I was well received everywhere, as I had a lively nature and was known to be rich, which always helps in the world. Then something happened that marked the beginning of everything.

I developed a strong attachment to a beautiful and intelligent young woman, noble in both character and spirit. She was the daughter of respected, well-off people of influence and status. They always gave me a warm and friendly welcome. I imagined that the young woman looked at me with favor, and the thought of that set my heart on fire. Later on, I fully realized that perhaps I wasn't as passionately in love with her as I thought, but rather I admired her mind and character, which I couldn't help but notice. However, at the time, my selfishness stopped me from proposing to her. I was unwilling to give up the temptations of my free and licentious bachelor life at the height of my youth, especially with my pockets full of money. I did hint at my feelings, though I delayed making any decisive move for a while. Then, suddenly, we were ordered away for two months to another district.

When I returned after two months, I found that the young woman had already married a wealthy neighboring landowner, a very kind man, still young, although older than I was, connected to the best society in Petersburg, which I was not, and highly educated, which I also was not. I was so stunned by this unexpected turn of events that I was utterly bewildered. The worst part was that, as I learned later, the young landowner had been engaged to her for quite some time. I had even met him many times at her house, but my own vanity had blinded me, and I noticed nothing. That humiliated me more than anything; almost everyone knew, while I was completely unaware. I was filled with a sudden, uncontrollable rage. My face flushed as I remembered how many times I had been on the verge of declaring my love to her, and since she had never tried to stop me or warn me, I concluded that she must have been laughing at me the whole time. Later, of course, I realized she hadn't been laughing at me at all. In fact, she had always managed to turn my attempts at flirtation into a joke and change the subject. But at that moment, I was incapable of thinking clearly and was consumed by a burning desire for revenge. I'm amazed now when I recall how foreign my feelings of anger and revenge were to my usual nature. I have always been of a mild temperament, and it's difficult for me to stay angry at anyone for long, so I had to work myself up artificially, and in the end, I became both disgusting and absurd.

I waited for my chance and managed to insult my "rival" in front of a large gathering. I insulted him over something completely unrelated, mocking his opinion on a significant public event—it was the year 1826—and people said my mockery was sharp and effective. I forced him to demand an explanation, and I behaved so rudely that he accepted my challenge to a duel, despite the great difference in rank between us, as I was younger, insignificant, and of lower status. I later found out that it was jealousy on his part that made him accept the challenge; he had been somewhat jealous of me regarding his wife even before their marriage. Now he feared that if he allowed me to insult him and refused the duel, and if she found out, she might lose respect for him and doubt her love. I quickly found a second in a comrade, an ensign from our regiment. In those days, though duels were harshly punished, dueling was still a popular fashion among officers—so deeply rooted can a brutal tradition become.

It was late June, and our duel was set for seven o'clock the next morning on the outskirts of town. Then, something happened that truly marked the turning point in my life. That evening, when I returned home in a savage and brutal mood, I lashed out at my servant Afanasy and struck him twice in the face with all my strength, so hard that his face was covered in blood. He hadn't been in my service for long, and although I had struck him before, I had never hit him with such cruelty. Believe me, even though it's been forty years, I still remember it with shame and regret. I went to bed and slept for about three hours. When I woke up, the day was beginning. I got up—I didn't want to sleep anymore— and went to the window. I opened it, and it looked out onto the garden. I saw the sun rising; it was warm and beautiful, and the birds were singing.

"What is this feeling?" I thought. "I feel something vile and shameful inside me. Is it because I'm about to shed blood? No," I thought, "that's not it. Am I afraid of death, afraid of being killed? No, that's not it either." And then, all at once, I understood what it was: it was because I had beaten Afanasy the night before! The memory came back to me vividly, as if it were happening again. I saw him standing before me while I hit him in the face. He stood there stiffly, his arms at his sides, his head held high, and his eyes fixed on me, as if he were standing at attention. He staggered with every blow, but he didn't even raise his hands to protect himself. That's what a man had been reduced to, and I was the man who had struck another human being! What a crime! It felt like a sharp knife had pierced my heart. I stood there as if frozen, while the sun shone, the leaves rustled joyfully, and the birds sang their praises to God. I covered my face with my hands, fell onto my bed, and broke into tears. And then, I remembered my brother Markel and what he had said on his deathbed to his servants: "My dear ones, why do you serve me? Why do you love me? Am I really worthy of your service?"

"Yes, am I worthy of it?" the thought flashed through my mind. "What makes me worthy of another man— a fellow human being, made in the image of God—serving me?" For the first time in my life, that question forced itself upon me. My brother had said, "Mother, my little heart, in truth, we are each responsible for everyone, for all. It's just that people don't know it. If they did, the world would become a paradise at once."

"God, can that be false too?" I thought as I cried. "Maybe I truly am more responsible than anyone, more of a sinner than all men in the world." And suddenly, the whole truth came to me, clear as day. What was I about to do? I was going to kill a good, smart, and noble man, who had done me no wrong. By taking away his wife's happiness, I would be torturing and killing her too. I lay there in my bed, my face buried in the pillow, not caring about how much time was passing. Suddenly, my second, the ensign, came in with the pistols to get me.

"Ah," he said, "good thing you're up already, it's time to go, let's go!"

I didn't know what to do and rushed around, unsure. Still, we headed out to the carriage.

"Wait here a minute," I said to him. "I'll be right back; I forgot my purse."

I ran back alone, straight to Afanasy's little room.

"Afanasy," I said, "yesterday I hit you twice in the face. Forgive me," I said.

He looked startled, as if scared, and stared at me. I realized that wasn't enough. Right then and there, still in my full officer's uniform, I dropped to my knees and bowed my head to the ground.

"Forgive me," I said.

He was completely shocked.

"Your honor… sir, what are you doing? Am I worth that?"

And he broke into tears just as I had done earlier. He covered his face with his hands, turned to the window, and shook as he sobbed. I rushed back to my comrade and jumped into the carriage.

"Ready," I shouted. "Have you ever seen a conqueror?" I asked him. "There's one right here in front of you."

I was overjoyed, laughing and talking the whole way, though I can't remember about what.

He looked at me. "Well, brother, you're a brave one. I see you'll keep the honor of the uniform."

We arrived at the meeting place, and they were already waiting for us. We stood twelve paces apart; he had the first shot. I stood there happily, looking him straight in the eye. I didn't even blink—I looked at him with love, knowing what I would do. His shot barely grazed my cheek and ear.

"Thank God," I shouted, "no one's been killed!" I grabbed my pistol, turned around, and threw it far into the woods. "That's where you belong!" I yelled.

I turned to my opponent.

"Forgive me, young fool that I am," I said, "for insulting you without reason and forcing you to fire at me. I'm ten times worse than you, maybe more. Tell that to the person you care about most."

As soon as I said that, all three of them shouted at me. "Honestly," my opponent said, annoyed, "if you didn't want to fight, why didn't you just leave me alone?"

"Yesterday I was a fool, today I know better," I answered cheerfully.

"You might be right about yesterday, but as for today, it's hard to agree with you," he said.

"Bravo!" I shouted, clapping my hands. "You're right about that too! I deserve that!"

"Are you going to shoot, or not?" he asked.

"No, I won't," I said. "If you want, you can fire at me again, but it would be better if you didn't."

The seconds, especially mine, started shouting too: "Are you really going to disgrace the regiment like this, standing here facing your opponent and asking for his forgiveness? If I'd known this!"

I stood facing them all, no longer laughing.

"Gentlemen," I said, "is it really so strange these days to find someone who can admit his own foolishness and publicly apologize for his wrongdoing?"

"But not in a duel!" my second shouted again.

"That's what's so strange," I said. "I should have admitted my fault as soon as we got here, before he fired a shot, before leading him into such a serious and deadly sin. But we've made our lives so ridiculous that doing something like that would've been impossible. He wouldn't have believed me unless I had stood there, faced his shot from twelve paces away, and only then could my words mean anything. If I had spoken earlier, he would've thought, 'He's a coward. The sight of the pistols scared him; no point in listening to him.'"

I suddenly spoke from the heart: "Gentlemen, look around at God's gifts—the clear sky, the fresh air, the soft grass, the birds.

Nature is beautiful and without sin, and we, only we, are sinful and foolish. We don't realize that life is heaven. If we only understood that, life would be fulfilled in all its beauty, and we would embrace each other and weep."

I wanted to say more, but I couldn't. My voice broke from the sweetness and joy I felt, and there was such happiness in my heart like I had never known before.

"All of this is reasonable and educational," said my opponent, "and in any case, you are quite the original person."

"You can laugh," I said, laughing too, "but later, you'll agree with me."

"Oh, I'm ready to agree with you right now," he said. "Will you shake hands? I believe you're sincere."

"No," I replied, "not now. Later, when I've become more worthy and earned your respect, then we'll shake hands, and you'll be doing the right thing."

We went back, and my second scolded me the whole way, while I kept kissing him. All my comrades heard about what had happened right away and gathered together that same day to pass judgment on me.

"He's disgraced the uniform," they said. "He should resign his commission."

Some defended me. "He faced the shot," they said.

"Yes, but he was afraid of the second shot and begged for forgiveness."

"If he had been afraid of being shot, he would've fired his pistol first before asking for forgiveness, but he threw his loaded gun into the woods. No, there's something different about this, something original."

I enjoyed listening to them and watching them talk. "My dear friends and comrades," I said, "don't worry about me resigning. I've already done it. I sent in my papers this morning, and as soon as I'm discharged, I'm going to a monastery. That's why I'm leaving the regiment."

When I said this, everyone burst into laughter.

"You should have told us that from the start; now everything makes sense, we can't judge a monk!" they exclaimed.

Their laughter was uncontrollable, but it wasn't mocking or scornful—it was warm, kind, and joyful. Instantly, their entire attitude toward me shifted. They all became friendly, even those who had been the harshest in their judgment. For the whole month before my discharge came through, they couldn't seem to say enough good things about me. Everywhere I went, they greeted me with smiles. "Ah, our monk!" they would tease, and they each had some kind words to say. Some of them even tried to talk me out of it, feeling a strange mix of sympathy and confusion: "What are you doing to yourself?" they would ask.

"No," they would insist, "he's a brave fellow. He stood up and faced the fire and could have fired his own pistol, but he had a dream the night before, a sign that he should become a monk, and that's why he did it."

It wasn't just my comrades in the regiment who treated me this way. The town's society, which had been kind to me but not especially attentive before, now seemed to take a new interest in me. All of a sudden, people who had barely noticed me before started inviting me everywhere. They laughed at me, it's true, but it was always in a good-natured way. They liked me, despite my odd behavior. I should mention that, even though the duel was openly discussed and everyone knew about it, the authorities decided to turn a blind eye. This was largely because my opponent was related to our general, and since no one had been harmed and I had resigned my commission, they treated the whole affair as a bit of a joke.

Afterward, I started to speak openly and without fear, not minding the laughter that sometimes followed my words. Their laughter never felt cruel; it was always lighthearted. These conversations often happened in the evenings, in the company of ladies. The women, in particular, seemed to enjoy listening to me, and they often encouraged the men to pay attention to what I was saying as well.

"But how can I possibly be responsible for everyone?" someone would laugh and ask me, amused by my ideas. "How could I be responsible for you, for instance?"

"You might not realize it," I would reply calmly, "but that's because for so long, the world has been following a completely different path. We have accepted the most outrageous lies as truth and demanded that others believe those same lies. I've acted with sincerity for the first time in my life, and yet you all treat me like a madman. You're friendly toward me, it's true, but at the same time, you laugh at me."

"But how could we not be friendly toward you?" my hostess would say, laughing kindly. The room would often be filled with people, all of them listening. Then, unexpectedly, the young woman for whom the duel had been fought—the very woman I had once believed would become my wife—stood up. I hadn't even noticed her come into the room. She got up slowly and walked over to me. She held out her hand with a serious expression on her face. "Let me tell you something," she said quietly, "I'm the first person here not to laugh at you. In fact, I thank you with all my heart for what you did, and I respect you deeply for your actions."

Her husband followed closely behind her, and soon the others gathered around as well, almost as if they were about to embrace me. My heart swelled with joy at that moment. But among all the people who came up to me, my attention was especially drawn to a middle-aged man who approached me after the others. I knew who he was, at least by name, but I had never spoken with him before that night.

This man had been a government official in the town for many years. He held a prominent position, was widely respected, and was quite wealthy. He had a reputation for being charitable, regularly donating large sums to the local orphanage and poorhouse. What people didn't know until after his death was that he had also been secretly helping many others, performing acts of kindness that were only discovered much later. He was about fifty years old, with a serious, almost stern appearance, and he wasn't the type to engage in casual conversation. He had been married for about ten years, and his wife, who was still quite young, had given him three children.

The next evening, while I was sitting alone in my room, my door suddenly opened, and this same gentleman walked in.

I should mention that I was no longer living in my old quarters by that time. After resigning from the military, I had moved into a small room rented from an elderly widow, the wife of a former government clerk. Her servant took care of me because, after the duel, I had sent Afanasy back to the regiment. I couldn't bear to face him after our last encounter. It's strange how easily a man of the world can feel embarrassed by his own good deeds.

"I've been listening to you speak in various homes over the past few days," my visitor began, "and I've been very interested in what you've said. I wanted to finally meet you in person so that we could talk more privately. May I ask, dear sir, for the pleasure of your company?"

"With the greatest pleasure," I replied, "and I consider it an honor." I said this with sincerity, though I admit I felt a bit uneasy. This man had made a strong impression on me from the moment he entered the room. While others had listened to me politely, no one had approached me with the same level of seriousness and focus that this man had. And now, here he was, visiting me in my own room. He sat down.

"You are clearly a man of great strength," he said, "because you had the courage to stand by the truth, even when it meant risking the scorn and contempt of everyone around you."

"Your praise might be more than I deserve," I responded humbly. "No, it's not too much," he answered firmly. "Believe me, acting in such a way is far more difficult than you might realize. That's what impressed me, and it's the reason I've come to speak with you," he continued. "Please, if you don't mind my curiosity, tell me exactly what you felt when you decided to ask for forgiveness during the duel. Don't think my question is frivolous; in fact, I have my own reasons for asking, which I may explain to you later, if it's God's will that we get to know each other better."

As he spoke, I kept my eyes fixed on his face, and something in his expression made me feel an immediate and complete sense of trust in him. At the same time, I was filled with curiosity, for I sensed that he had some deep, hidden secret.

"You're asking what I felt at the moment I asked my opponent for forgiveness," I said slowly, "but I think it's better if I tell you everything, from the beginning, something I haven't told anyone else yet." Then I told him the whole story, starting with what had happened between Afanasy and me, and how I had bowed down to the ground before him. "From that, you can understand," I concluded, "that by the time of the duel, it wasn't so difficult for me to take the next step. I had already started down that path when I was at home. Once I had taken that first step, continuing along it wasn't difficult at all—it was actually a source of deep joy and happiness for me."

I liked the way he looked at me as he listened. His eyes were filled with genuine interest, and after I finished speaking, he said, "Everything you've told me is extremely fascinating. I will come to see you again, and again."

And from that day on, he began visiting me almost every evening. Our bond could have deepened even more, had he spoken about himself. Yet, he hardly ever said anything about his own life; instead, he always seemed more interested in mine, constantly asking me about my thoughts, feelings, and experiences. Despite his silence about his own life, I found myself growing more and more fond of him. I spoke to him with complete honesty, sharing everything about my inner world, thinking, "Why should I need to know his secrets? I can already see clearly that he's a good man. Besides, he's much older and more serious than I am, and yet he comes to visit me—a younger man—and treats me as an equal." It felt reassuring, and I learned many valuable things from him, as he was a man with a noble and expansive mind.

"Life is heaven," he said to me one day, quite suddenly, "I've been thinking about that for a long time." Then, just as unexpectedly, he added, "In fact, I think about nothing else." His face lit up with a gentle smile as he looked directly at me. "I believe in it more than you do, and I will explain why soon."

I listened carefully, sensing that he was holding back something important, something he wanted to share.

"Heaven," he continued, "is hidden within all of us—it's here inside me right now. And if I truly will it, I could see it tomorrow and for the rest of my life."

I looked at him, studying his face closely. He spoke with deep emotion, and his gaze was intense, almost as though he were asking me a question, seeking something in my own understanding.

"And that we are all responsible for each other, not just for our own sins—you were absolutely right in thinking that," he said. "It's amazing how you grasped the full meaning of it right away. The truth is, once people truly understand this, the Kingdom of Heaven will no longer be a distant dream for them, but a reality—a living, breathing reality."

"But when?" I cried out, almost in despair. "When will this happen? Will it ever happen? Or is it just a dream we have, nothing more than an illusion?"

"So, you don't believe it," he said, a little surprised. "You speak of it, but you don't truly believe in it yourself. Believe me, this dream—what you call a dream—will come true, without question. It will happen, but not right now, because every process has its own time, its own laws. It's a spiritual and psychological transformation that must take place. In order to change the world, to recreate it from the ground up, people must first change themselves. Until we become brothers to one another in the truest sense, brotherhood will never come into being. No amount of scientific knowledge or shared interests will ever teach people to divide wealth and privileges equally and fairly. People will always feel as though they're getting less than others, and they will continue to envy, complain, and fight among themselves. You ask when it will happen—it will come, but first, we must pass through a period of isolation."

"What do you mean by isolation?" I asked, intrigued.

"I mean the kind of isolation that is everywhere now," he explained, "especially in our time. It hasn't fully developed yet, but it's spreading. Everyone is striving to keep their individuality separate, isolated. People want to secure as much fulfillment for themselves as they can, but in doing so, they destroy themselves. Instead of finding real fulfillment, they fall into complete loneliness. The world today is fragmented; humanity has broken down into countless isolated pieces. Everyone is living in their own little world, apart from everyone else. People keep their distance, hoarding what they have, hiding it from others, and in the end, they drive others away and are driven away themselves. Someone might amass wealth and think, 'Now I'm strong, now I'm safe,' but they are mad, for they do not understand that the more they gather, the more powerless they become. They become trapped in their fear of losing what they've gained, living in constant anxiety. They have taught themselves to rely on no one but themselves, cutting themselves off from the rest of humanity. They no longer believe in the help of others, or in the power of human solidarity. These days, people mock the idea that real security and strength lie in community and togetherness, rather than in individual effort. But this destructive individualism will eventually come to an end. People will suddenly realize how unnatural their separation from one another truly is. When that moment comes, it will be a great awakening, and people will marvel at how they lived in darkness for so long without seeing the light. And then, the sign of the Son of Man will appear in the heavens... But until that day, we must keep the banner of brotherhood flying high. Even if a man stands alone, even if his actions seem foolish or mad, he must set an example. He must try to pull others out of their isolation and inspire them toward acts of brotherly love. This is the only way to ensure that the great idea of unity does not die."

Evenings passed in such powerful and moving conversations. I found myself retreating more and more from society, visiting my neighbors much less frequently than before. Besides, my popularity had already begun to fade. I say this without bitterness—they still liked me and treated me kindly—but there's no denying that social fashion has a great influence. The more time I spent with my mysterious visitor, the more I admired him. Not only did I respect his intelligence and wisdom, but I also began to sense that he was preparing for something significant, perhaps a great deed. I think he appreciated that I didn't pry into his secret or try to discover it with subtle hints. He must have felt that I trusted him, and maybe that's why he kept coming back. Still, after some time, it became clear that he wanted to tell me something. It had become especially obvious about a month after he began visiting me regularly.

"Do you know," he said to me one evening, "that people in town are very curious about us? They wonder why I come to see you so often. But let them wonder, for soon, everything will be made clear."

Sometimes, a strange restlessness would overcome him, and almost always, on such occasions, he would stand up suddenly and leave without explanation. There were moments when he would look at me with such intensity that I thought, "He's about to say something important." But then, unexpectedly, he would change the subject and start talking about something ordinary, something trivial. He often complained of headaches, too.

One day, after we had been talking passionately for quite some time, I noticed that his face had grown pale, and his expression had changed drastically. He stared at me with a look I had never seen before.

"What's the matter?" I asked, alarmed. "Are you feeling ill?" He had been complaining of a headache earlier, but this seemed different.

"I... do you know..." he began slowly, "I killed someone."

He said this, and then smiled, but his face was as white as chalk. "Why is he smiling?" I thought to myself, even before I fully processed what he had just said. My own face must have gone pale, too.

"What are you saying?" I cried out in shock.

"See," he said, still smiling that eerie smile, "how difficult it was for me to say those first words? Now that I've said them, I feel like I've taken the first step, and now I can continue."

For a long time, I couldn't believe him. Even at that moment, I wasn't sure if I believed what he had just told me. But after he came to visit me for three days in a row and told me everything in detail, I had no choice but to believe him. It filled me with deep sorrow and disbelief. His crime was horrific.

Fourteen years earlier, he had murdered a wealthy, beautiful young widow who owned a large estate in our town. He had fallen madly in love with her, confessed his feelings, and asked her to marry him. But she had already given her heart to another man, an officer of noble birth and high rank in the military, who was away at the front but expected to return soon. She rejected his proposal and begged him not to visit her anymore. After he stopped visiting, he used his knowledge of her house to break in at night through the garden, risking discovery. But, as often happens, crimes committed with boldness sometimes succeed in ways that quieter ones do not.

He entered the attic through the skylight and went down the ladder, knowing that the door at the bottom was often left unlocked due to the servants' carelessness. He hoped it would be the same that night, and it was. In the dark, he made his way to her bedroom, where a light was still burning. By chance, both of her maids had gone to a birthday party nearby without asking for permission. The other servants were either asleep in their quarters or the kitchen downstairs. His passion flared up when he saw her sleeping, but then, filled with a jealous rage, his heart hardened, and, like a man who had lost his mind, he plunged a knife into her heart. She didn't even have time to scream. With a devilish and twisted cunning, he then carefully planned it so the blame would fall on the servants. He was vile enough to take her purse, open her chest with the keys from under her pillow, and steal a few things in a way that would make it look like a careless servant had done it. He left important documents behind but took only some money, larger pieces of gold, and a few personal items as keepsakes—though those details came later. After committing this terrible crime, he left the same way he came.

The next day, when the alarm was raised, no one even thought to suspect him. No one ever did. No one knew about his love for her because he had always been reserved and kept to himself. He didn't have a single friend with whom he shared his feelings. To most people, he was just an acquaintance of the murdered woman— one who hadn't even visited her in the two weeks leading up to her death. A serf of hers named Pyotr was immediately suspected, and all the evidence seemed to point to him. The woman had made it clear to Pyotr that she intended to send him off as a conscript, since he had no family and his behavior had been unacceptable. People had even overheard him drunkenly threatening her life at a tavern. Two days before the murder, he ran away, and no one knew where he had gone. The day after the murder, Pyotr was found passed out drunk on the road leading out of town, with a knife in his pocket and blood on his right hand. He claimed that his nose had been bleeding, but no one believed him. The maids admitted they had gone to the party, leaving the street door unlocked until they returned. With these and other details that surfaced, suspicion fell heavily on the innocent servant.

Pyotr was arrested and put on trial for the murder. But a week after his arrest, he fell ill with a fever and died in the hospital without ever regaining consciousness. And so, the case was closed. The judges, the authorities, and everyone in town remained convinced that the servant had committed the crime. After that, the real punishment began.

My mysterious visitor, who had become my friend, told me that at first, his conscience didn't trouble him at all. He was miserable for a long time, but not because of the crime itself. His misery came from the regret of having killed the woman he loved, from the fact that she was gone forever, and from the knowledge that in killing her, he had killed the love he had for her. His passion still burned within him, but the fact that he had taken an innocent life barely crossed his mind. The idea that she could have become someone else's wife was unbearable to him, and for a long time, he convinced himself that he couldn't have acted any differently.

He was briefly worried when the servant was arrested, but once Pyotr died, his mind was at ease. He told himself that the man's death wasn't caused by the arrest or the shock of being accused, but by the chill he caught after spending a night drunk on the damp ground when he ran away. The theft of money and valuables didn't weigh heavily on his conscience either because he reasoned that he hadn't stolen for personal gain but to divert suspicion. The amount he had taken was small, and not long after the murder, he donated all of it—and much more—to support a local almshouse. He did this deliberately to ease his conscience about the theft, and for a long time, he truly felt at peace. He told me this himself. He threw himself into his work, volunteering for challenging and laborious duties that kept him occupied for two years. He was a man of strong will and nearly managed to forget the past. When it did come to mind, he tried to push the thoughts away. He also became deeply involved in charitable work, establishing and supporting many institutions in town. He contributed in both Moscow and Petersburg and was even elected to philanthropic societies in both cities.

But eventually, the weight of the past became too much for him to bear. He tried to distract himself by courting an intelligent and kind young woman, and they soon married. He hoped that his new life and his commitment to his wife and children would help him escape from his haunting memories. But the exact opposite happened. From the first month of his marriage, he was plagued by the thought: "My wife loves me, but what would she think if she knew?" When she told him she was expecting their first child, he felt troubled. "I'm giving life," he thought, "but I've also taken life." As their children were born, he struggled with his role as a father. "How can I love them, teach them, and raise them to be virtuous when I've taken a life?" He adored his children—they were bright and full of promise—but he couldn't look at their innocent faces without feeling unworthy.

Soon, the memory of the blood he had shed, the young life he had destroyed, began to haunt him. It was as if the blood cried out for justice. He started having terrible nightmares, but being a strong- willed man, he endured his suffering in silence, telling himself, "I will make up for everything through this private torment." But even that hope was in vain. The longer he carried the burden, the more unbearable it became.

He was highly respected in society for his charitable work and active involvement in the community. But the more he was respected, the more unbearable his inner torment grew. He confessed to me that he even considered taking his own life. But another idea began to take hold of him—a thought that initially seemed impossible, something he could hardly imagine. Yet, over time, it gripped him so strongly that he couldn't shake it off. He began to dream of standing up, walking out into the world, and publicly confessing that he had committed murder. For three years, this idea tormented him, appearing to him in different forms. Eventually, he came to believe that if he confessed his crime, he would finally heal his soul and find peace. But this belief terrified him. How could he ever follow through with such a confession? And then, something happened during my duel.

"Looking at you, I've made up my mind," he said. I stared at him, stunned.

"Is it possible," I asked, clasping my hands together, "that such a small event could lead to such a huge decision?"

"My decision has been building for the last three years," he replied. "Your story only gave the final push. Watching you, I felt ashamed and envious." He said this almost angrily.

"But no one will believe you," I pointed out. "It's been fourteen years since it happened."

"I have proof—solid proof. I will show it," he said. Then I cried and kissed him.

"Tell me just one thing," he said, like it all depended on me, "my wife, my kids! My wife could die from grief. Even though my kids won't lose their status or property, they'll be the children of a convict forever! What kind of memory will they have of me in their hearts?"

I didn't say anything.

"And to leave them, to never see them again? It's forever, you know, forever!"

I sat still and quietly prayed. I got up eventually, feeling scared. "Well?" He looked at me.

"Go," I said. "Confess. Everything passes, but the truth remains. When your kids grow up, they'll understand how noble your decision was."

That time he left like he'd finally made up his mind. But for more than two weeks after that, he came to me every evening, still getting ready, still unable to take that final step. It made my heart ache. One day he would come determined, saying passionately:

"I know I'll feel like I'm in heaven the moment I confess. I've been in hell for 14 years. I want to suffer. I'll accept my punishment and start living again. You can go through life doing wrong, but you can't undo it. Now, I can't even love my neighbor or my own children. Dear God, maybe my kids will understand what my punishment has cost me and won't judge me! God isn't about power, but truth."

"Everyone will understand your sacrifice," I said. "Maybe not right away, but they will later. You've served a higher truth, not an earthly one."

He'd leave comforted, but the next day, he'd come back, bitter, pale, and sarcastic.

"Every time I come, you look at me like you're thinking, 'He still hasn't confessed!' Wait a little, don't judge me too harshly. It's not as easy as you think. Maybe I won't do it at all. You won't report me, will you?"

Far from being curious about him, I was too scared to look at him at all. I was sick with worry and my heart was heavy with sorrow. I couldn't sleep at night.

"I just came from my wife," he said. "Do you know what 'wife' means? When I left, my kids called after me, 'Goodbye, Dad, come back soon to read The Children's Magazine with us.' No, you don't understand that! No one can truly understand someone else's pain."

His eyes were shining, his lips trembling. Suddenly, he slammed his fist on the table, making everything on it shake. It was the first time he'd ever done that; he was usually such a gentle person.

"But do I have to?" he shouted. "Should I? No one else was punished, no one was sent to Siberia in my place. The man died of fever. I've already paid for the blood I shed with my suffering. And they won't believe me, they won't believe my proof. Do I have to confess? Do I really have to? I'm willing to suffer for the rest of my life for the blood I spilled, as long as my wife and kids are spared. Is it fair to drag them down with me? Maybe we're wrong. What's the right thing to do? Will people understand it, will they respect it?"

"Good Lord!" I thought. "He's worried about what people will think at a time like this!" I felt so sorry for him then that I would've shared his fate if it would've given him peace. I saw that he was on the edge. I was horrified, realizing deep inside what this decision meant.

"Decide my fate!" he cried again.

"Go and confess," I whispered. My voice was weak, but I said it firmly. I picked up the New Testament from the table, the Russian version, and showed him the Gospel of St. John, chapter 12, verse 24: "Truly, truly, I say to you, unless a grain of wheat falls into the earth and dies, it remains alone; but if it dies, it bears much fruit."

I had just read that verse when he came in. He read it.

"That's true," he said, but smiled bitterly. "It's terrifying, the things you find in those books," he said after a pause. "It's easy for you to push them on people. And who wrote them? Could men have written this?"

"The Holy Spirit wrote them," I said.

"It's easy for you to preach," he smiled again, this time almost with hatred.

I took the book again, opened it to another spot, and showed him Hebrews, chapter 10, verse 31. He read: "It is a fearful thing to fall into the hands of the living God."

He read it and threw the book down. He was trembling all over.

"That's a terrifying verse," he said. "No denying you've picked out good ones." He got up from his chair. "Well!" he said, "Goodbye,

maybe I won't come back… we'll meet in heaven. I've spent 14 years 'in the hands of the living God.' That's how I should think of these 14 years. Tomorrow, I'll beg those hands to let me go."

I wanted to hug him and kiss him, but I didn't dare. His face was twisted and dark. He left.

"Good God," I thought, "what is he about to face?" I dropped to my knees before the icon and prayed for him, for the Holy Mother of God, our quick protector and helper, to watch over him. I prayed for half an hour, weeping, and it was late, about midnight. Suddenly, I heard the door open, and he came in again. I was surprised.

"Where have you been?" I asked him.

"I think I forgot something… maybe my handkerchief… Even if I didn't forget anything, can I stay a little longer?"

He sat down. I stood over him. "Sit down too," he said.

I sat down. We stayed like that for a couple of minutes. He looked at me intensely and suddenly smiled—I remember that. Then he stood up, hugged me warmly, and kissed me.

"Remember how I came back a second time," he said. "Do you hear me? Remember it!"

And he left.

"Tomorrow," I thought.

And so it happened. I didn't know that evening that the next day was his birthday. I hadn't been out for the past few days, so I had no way of hearing about it from anyone. On his birthday, he always had a big gathering, and everyone in town would attend. It was the same this time. After dinner, he walked to the center of the room with a paper in his hand—a formal confession to the head of his department, who was present. He read it aloud to everyone. The confession gave a full account of the crime in every detail.

"I cut myself off from people like a monster. God has punished me," he said as he finished. "I want to suffer for my sin!"

Then he took out and laid on the table all the things he had been holding on to for fourteen years, things he thought would prove his crime: the jewels he stole from the murdered woman to cover his tracks, a cross and a locket he took from her neck with her fiancé's portrait inside, her notebook, and two letters. One letter was from her fiancé, telling her he would be with her soon, and the other was her unfinished reply, which she had planned to send the next day. He had taken both letters—why? Why did he keep them for fourteen years instead of destroying the evidence?

This is what happened: everyone was shocked and horrified, but no one believed him. They thought he had gone mad, though they listened with great curiosity. A few days later, people in every household had agreed that the poor man had lost his mind. The authorities couldn't ignore the case, but they soon dropped it. Even though the trinkets and letters made them think, they decided that even if the items were real, it wouldn't be enough to convict him. After all, the woman could have given him those things as a friend or asked him to keep them for her. But I later heard that the woman's friends and family confirmed the items were real, and there was no doubt about it. Still, nothing came of it.

Five days later, the whole town heard that he had fallen ill, and his life was in danger. I couldn't explain what kind of illness it was; they said it had to do with his heart. But it became known that his wife had asked the doctors to check his mental state as well, and they concluded that he was indeed insane. I didn't tell anyone anything, even though people came running to question me. But when I wanted to visit him, I wasn't allowed to for a long time, especially not by his wife.

"It's your fault he's sick," she told me. "He was always gloomy, but over the last year, people noticed that he had become unusually agitated and acted strangely, and now you've destroyed him. Your preaching brought him to this. He spent the whole last month with you."

Not only his wife but the whole town turned against me, blaming me. "It's all your doing," they said. I stayed silent, but deep down, I was happy because I saw God's mercy at work for this man who had turned against himself and punished himself. I couldn't believe that he was really insane.

Finally, they let me see him because he insisted on saying goodbye to me. When I went in to see him, I realized immediately that not only his days but his hours were numbered. He was weak and pale, his hands trembled, and he struggled to breathe, but his face was full of tenderness and peace.

"It's done!" he said. "I've been wanting to see you for a long time. Why didn't you come?"

I didn't tell him that they had forbidden me from seeing him. "God has had mercy on me and is calling me to Him. I know I'm dying, but for the first time in years, I feel joy and peace. From the

moment I confessed, I felt heaven in my heart. Now I can dare to love my children and kiss them. Neither my wife nor the judges, nor anyone else believed my confession. My children will never believe it either. I see this as God's mercy to them. I'll die, and my name will stay untarnished for them. Now I feel God near, and my heart rejoices like I'm in Heaven… I've done my duty."

He couldn't talk anymore, he was gasping for breath. He squeezed my hand warmly, looking at me with deep emotion. We didn't speak for long because his wife kept peeking in at us. But he found time to whisper to me:

"Do you remember how I came back to you that second time, at midnight? I told you to remember it. Do you know why I came back? I came to kill you!"

I was startled.

"I left your house that night and wandered the streets, fighting with myself. Suddenly, I hated you so much I could hardly stand it. I thought, 'Now he's the only thing standing in my way, and he's my judge. I can't avoid my punishment tomorrow because he knows everything.' It wasn't that I was afraid you'd tell anyone—I never thought of that. But I couldn't bear the thought of facing you if I didn't confess. Even if you were at the other end of the earth, but still alive, it would've been unbearable to know you were out there, judging me. I hated you like you were to blame for everything, like it was all your fault. I came back to you, remembering you had a dagger on your table. I sat down and asked you to sit too, and for a full minute, I thought about it. If I had killed you, I would've been ruined by that murder, even if I hadn't confessed the other. But I didn't think about that at all in the moment. I just hated you and wanted to take revenge on you for everything. But the Lord defeated the devil in my heart. But let me tell you, you were never closer to death."

A week later, he died. The whole town followed him to his grave. The head priest gave a heartfelt speech. Everyone mourned his tragic illness that had cut his life short. But after the funeral, the entire town turned against me, and people even refused to speak to me. At first, only a few believed his confession, but later more people came to believe his story. They came to see me, eager to question me because people love to witness the downfall of someone righteous. But I said nothing, and shortly after that, I left town. Five months later, by God's grace, I entered the safe and blessed path, praising the unseen hand that had guided me so clearly to it. But to this day, in my prayers, I remember the servant of God, Mihail, who suffered so much.

Chapter 3: Conversations And Exhortations of Father Zossima

Fathers and teachers, what is a monk? Nowadays, in the educated world, the word is said by some with mockery, and

by others as an insult, and this scorn for monks is growing. It is true, alas, it is true, that there are many lazy, gluttonous, immoral, and arrogant beggars among monks. Educated people point to these: "You are idle, useless members of society; you live off the labor of others; you are shameless beggars." Yet, how many gentle and humble monks there are, yearning for solitude and sincere prayer in peace! These monks are less noticed or overlooked completely. And how surprised people would be if I said that perhaps from these gentle monks, who long for peaceful prayer, the salvation of Russia might once again come! For they are truly being prepared in peace and quiet "for the day and the hour, the month and the year." Meanwhile, in their solitude, they keep the image of Christ pure and undefiled, in the truth of God, as it was in the days of the early Fathers, the Apostles, and the martyrs. And when the time comes, they will reveal it to the unstable creeds of the world. This is a profound idea. That star will rise in the East.

This is my view of the monk. Is it wrong? Is it too proud? Look at the worldly people and all those who elevate themselves above the people of God. Hasn't God's image and His truth been distorted in them? They have science; but in science, there is only what can be sensed. The spiritual world, the higher aspect of human existence, is entirely rejected, dismissed with a sense of triumph, even with hatred. The world has declared the reign of freedom, especially in recent times, but what do we see in their freedom? Nothing but slavery and self-destruction! For the world says:

"You have desires, so satisfy them, for you have the same rights as the wealthiest and most powerful. Don't fear satisfying them, and even multiply your desires." This is the modern world's teaching. They see this as freedom. And what follows from this multiplication of desires? In the rich, it leads to isolation and spiritual death; in the poor, it leads to envy and violence, for while they are given rights, they are not shown the means of fulfilling their needs. They claim that the world is becoming more united, more bound together in brotherly harmony, as it conquers distance and sends thoughts flying through the air.

But don't put your faith in such a bond of unity. By interpreting freedom as the increase and quick satisfaction of desires, people distort their own nature, fostering many senseless and foolish desires, habits, and ridiculous fantasies. They live only for mutual envy, for luxury and showing off. Having dinners, visits, carriages, rank, and servants is seen as necessary, for which life, honor, and human feeling are sacrificed, and people even commit suicide if they can't satisfy these needs. The same thing is happening among those who are not wealthy, as the poor drown their unsatisfied desires and envy in alcohol. But soon, they will drink blood instead of wine; they are being led in that direction. I ask you, is such a person free? I once knew a "champion of freedom" who told me that when he was deprived of tobacco in prison, he was so miserable without it that he almost betrayed his cause just to get tobacco again! And this man claimed, "I am fighting for the cause of humanity."

How can such a person fight? What is he capable of? He may be able to carry out some quick action, but he can't hold on for long. And it's no surprise that instead of gaining freedom, they've fallen into slavery. Instead of serving the cause of brotherly love and the unity of humanity, they've fallen, as my mysterious visitor and teacher once told me in my youth, into division and isolation. And so, the idea of serving humanity, of brotherly love and the solidarity of mankind, is slowly dying out in the world, and sometimes this idea is even mocked. Because how can a person break free from their habits? What will become of them if they are slaves to the countless desires they have created for themselves? They are isolated, and what concern do they have for the rest of humanity? While they've accumulated more material things, joy in the world has decreased.

The monastic way is entirely different. Obedience, fasting, and prayer are often laughed at, yet only through these can true freedom be found. I cut off my excess and unnecessary desires, I discipline my proud and wild will, and with God's help, I achieve spiritual freedom and with it, spiritual joy. Who is better able to grasp a great idea and serve it—the wealthy person in isolation or the one who has freed himself from the tyranny of material things and habits? The monk is criticized for his solitude: "You've hidden yourself away in a monastery for your own salvation and forgotten about serving humanity!" But we'll see who truly works for brotherly love. It's not us who are isolated, but them, though they don't realize it. In the past, leaders of the people came from among us, and why shouldn't that happen again? These same humble monks will rise up and go out to work for the greater cause. The salvation of Russia will come from the people, and the Russian monk has always been with the people. We are isolated only if the people are isolated. The people believe as we do, and an atheist reformer will never succeed in Russia, no matter how sincere or talented they are. Remember that! The people will confront the atheist and defeat him, and Russia will remain united and Orthodox. Care for the peasant and guard his heart. Keep educating him quietly. That is your duty as monks because the peasant carries God in his heart.

Of course, I'm not denying that there is sin among the peasants. The fire of corruption is spreading rapidly, working its way from the top down. The spirit of isolation is affecting the people too. Moneylenders and those who exploit the community are rising up. Merchants are becoming more eager for rank, trying to show they are cultured, though they have no real culture, and in their pursuit, they despise their old traditions and are even ashamed of their ancestral faith. They visit princes, though they are only peasants corrupted by wealth. The peasants are sinking into drunkenness and can't break free. And how cruel they are to their wives, even to their children—this all comes from drunkenness! I've seen children as young as nine in factories, frail, bent, and already corrupted. The stuffy workshop, the noise of machinery, working all day long, the foul language, and the drinking—is this what a child needs? No, a child needs sunlight, play, good examples around him, and at least a little love. This must stop, monks—no more tormenting of children! Rise up and preach this, quickly!

But God will save Russia, for although the peasants are corrupted and cannot break their sinful habits, they know that these sins are cursed by God and that they are doing wrong. So, our people still believe in righteousness, have faith in God, and shed tears of devotion.

It's different with the upper classes. They, following science, want to base justice only on reason and no longer on Christ, as before, and they have already declared that there is no crime and no sin. And that makes sense because, without God, what meaning does crime have? In Europe, the people are rising up violently against the rich, and their leaders tell them their anger is just. But their anger is cursed because it is cruel. Still, God will save Russia, as He has done many times before. Salvation will come from the people, from their faith and humility.

Fathers and teachers, watch over the faith of the people, and this vision will not be a dream. I have always been struck by the dignity of our great people, their true and appropriate dignity. I have seen it myself, and I can testify to it. I have seen it and marveled at it, despite the degraded sins and the poor, pitiful conditions of our peasants. They are not servile, and even after two centuries of serfdom, they are free in spirit and manner, without being arrogant, vengeful, or envious. They think, "You are rich and noble, you are clever and talented— well, good for you. I respect you, but I know that I, too, am a person. By respecting you without envy, I show my own dignity as a human being."

If they don't say this out loud (because they don't know how yet), this is how they act. I have seen it myself; I know it for a fact. And would you believe it, the poorer our Russian peasant is, the more evident this quiet goodness is. For the rich among them are often already corrupted, and much of this is due to our neglect and lack of care. But God will save His people, for Russia is great in her humility. I dream of a future where even the most corrupt of our rich people will feel ashamed of their wealth in front of the poor. And the poor, seeing this humility, will understand and give way, responding with kindness to this honorable shame. Believe me, this is how it will end—things are moving in that direction. True equality is found only in the spiritual dignity of people, and this will only be understood here. If we are brothers, we will have true fraternity. But until then, they will never agree on how to divide wealth. We preserve the image of Christ, and it will shine forth like a precious diamond to the whole world. So may it be, so may it be!

Fathers and teachers, something touching once happened to me. During my travels, I met my old orderly, Afanasy, in the town of K. It had been eight years since we had parted. He happened to see me in the marketplace, recognized me, and ran up to me, overjoyed. He nearly pounced on me, saying, "Master dear, is it really you? Is it really you I see?" He took me home with him.

He was no longer in the army; he was married and had two little children. He and his wife earned their living as vendors in the marketplace. His home was poor but bright and clean. He made me sit down, prepared the samovar, and sent for his wife, treating my visit as if it were a special holiday. He brought me his children and said, "Bless them, Father."

"Is it for me to bless them? I am only a humble monk. I will pray for them. And for you, Afanasy Pavlovitch, I have prayed every day since that day, because everything came from you," I said. And I explained it to him as best I could. And what do you think? The man kept looking at me and could not believe that I, his former master, an officer, was now standing in front of him like this, in this appearance and position; it brought him to tears.

"Why are you crying?" I said. "It would be better to rejoice for me, my dear friend, whom I will never forget, because my path is one of joy and happiness." He didn't say much, but he kept sighing and shaking his head at me with tenderness.

"What has become of your fortune?" he asked.

"I gave it to the monastery," I replied. "We live together and share everything."

After we had tea, I was about to say goodbye, and suddenly he brought out half a rouble as a gift to the monastery, and another half-rouble I saw him quickly pushing into my hand: "That is for you during your travels, it may help you, Father."

I accepted his half-rouble, bowed to him and his wife, and left, feeling happy. And as I walked, I thought: "Now we are both here, him at home, and me on the road, probably both sighing and shaking our heads, but still smiling happily in our hearts, remembering how God made it possible for us to meet."

I have never seen him again since then. I was once his master, and he was my servant, but now, when we exchanged a loving kiss with soft hearts, there was a great human bond between us. I have thought about it a lot, and now this is what I believe: Is it really so impossible to imagine that this grand and simple-hearted unity could one day spread to all the Russian people? I believe it will happen, and that the time is near.

And about servants, I will add this: When I was young, I often used to get angry with servants; "the cook had made the food too hot, the servant hadn't brushed my clothes." But what taught me to see things differently was something my dear brother had once said when I was a child: "Do I deserve it, that someone else should serve me, being commanded around by me in their poverty and lack of understanding?" At the time, I was amazed that such simple and obvious thoughts were so slow to come to our minds.

It is impossible to imagine that there will be no servants in the world, but you should act in a way that makes your servant feel freer in spirit, even more so than if they were not a servant. And why shouldn't I be a servant to my servant, and even let them see it, without any pride on my part or mistrust on theirs? Why can't my servant be like one of my own family members, so that I can bring them into my home and feel joy in doing so? Even now this is possible, but in the future, it will lead to the great unity of mankind, when no one will want to seek out servants for themselves, or try to turn others into servants as they do now, but instead, they will desire with all their heart to serve others, as the Gospel teaches us.

And can it really be a dream that, in the end, people will find joy only in doing good and merciful acts, and not in the cruel pleasures that they enjoy now, like overeating, sinful behavior, showing off, boasting, and being envious of one another? I firmly believe it is not a dream, and that the time is close. People laugh and ask: "When will that time come? Does it even seem like it's coming?" But I believe that with Christ's help, we will achieve this great thing. And think about it—how many ideas have appeared on earth throughout history that seemed unthinkable just ten years before they came? Yet when their destined time came, they appeared and spread across the whole world. It will be the same for us, and our people will shine in the world, and all men will say: "The stone which the builders rejected has become the cornerstone of the building."

And we can ask those who laugh at us: If our hope is just a dream, when will you build your ideal world and bring justice using only your intellect, without Christ? If they say that they are the ones moving toward unity, only the most simple-minded among them believe it, and one can't help but marvel at such simplicity. In fact, they have more ridiculous dreams than we do. They aim for justice, but by rejecting Christ, they will end up flooding the world with blood, because blood calls for more blood, and whoever lives by the sword will die by the sword. Without Christ's promise, they would kill each other until only two men remained on earth. And even those last two men wouldn't be able to hold back their pride, and one would kill the other and then himself. That is what would happen if it weren't for Christ's promise that, for the sake of the humble and meek, the days will be shortened.

When I was still an officer after my duel, I spoke about servants in general company, and I remember everyone was shocked by what I said. "What!" they asked, "Are we supposed to make our servants sit on the sofa and offer them tea?" And I answered, "Why not, at least sometimes?" Everyone laughed. Their question was silly, and my answer wasn't very clear, but the idea behind it was somewhat true.

Young man, don't forget to pray. Every time you pray, if your prayer is sincere, there will be new meaning and new feeling in it, which will give you new strength, and you will see that prayer teaches you. Also, remember, every day and whenever you can, say to yourself, "Lord, have mercy on all who stand before You today." Every hour, every minute, thousands of people leave this life, and their souls stand before God. And how many of them die alone, unknown, sad that no one is mourning them, or even knows if they lived or not! And yet, from the other side of the world, your prayer for their peace may reach God, even though you didn't know them, and they didn't know you. How touching it must be for a soul standing in fear before God to feel, in that moment, that someone else on earth is praying for them, that another human being is showing love for them! And God will look more kindly on both of you, for if you had so much compassion for that soul, how much more will God have, since He is far more loving and merciful than you! And He will forgive them because of your prayer.

Brothers, don't be afraid of people's sins. Love people, even when they sin, because that reflects Divine Love, and that is the highest love on earth. Love all of God's creation, every part of it, down to the smallest grain of sand. Love every leaf, every ray of God's light. Love the animals, love the plants, love everything. If you love everything, you will see the divine mystery in things. Once you see it, you will start to understand it better every day.

And eventually, you will come to love the whole world with a love that includes everything.

Love the animals: God gave them the beginnings of thought and joy without worry. Don't ruin it, don't hurt them, don't take away their happiness, don't go against God's purpose. Humans, don't think you are superior to animals; they are without sin, and yet, with all your greatness, you defile the earth with your presence, leaving behind the mess of your wrongdoing—sadly, this is true of almost every one of us!

Love children especially, because they are also innocent like angels. They live to soften and purify our hearts, and it's almost as if they guide us. Woe to the person who harms a child! Father Anfim taught me to love children. He was a kind, quiet man, and during our travels, he would often use the small coins we were given to buy sweets and cakes for the children. He couldn't pass a child without feeling deeply moved. That was just the kind of person he was."

At some thoughts, one stands puzzled, especially when seeing the sins of others, and wonders whether to use force or humble love. Always choose humble love. If you make that choice once and for all, you might conquer the whole world. Humble love is incredibly strong, stronger than anything else, and nothing else compares to it.

Every day and every hour, every minute, pay attention to yourself and examine if your behavior is proper. You walk past a child, and you walk past him with a spiteful attitude, speaking harsh words, your heart filled with anger; you might not have noticed the child, but he has seen you, and your ugly, improper image may stay in his innocent heart. You don't realize it, but you may have planted a bad seed in him, and it may grow, and all of this because you didn't show careful, active love in yourself. Brothers, love is a teacher, but you must learn how to acquire it, for it is difficult to gain, it comes at a high price, and it is only obtained slowly, through long and hard work. We must love not just occasionally, for a brief moment, but always. Everyone can love sometimes, even wicked people can.

My brother asked the birds to forgive him; that may sound foolish, but it was right; because everything is like an ocean, everything is flowing and connected; a touch in one place causes movement on the other side of the world. It may seem silly to ask birds for forgiveness, but birds would be happier at your side—a little happier, at least—and children and all animals, if you were a kinder and nobler person than you are now. Everything is like an ocean, I tell you. Then you would pray to the birds as well, filled with an all-encompassing love, in a kind of ecstasy, and pray that they too will forgive your sins. Cherish this feeling, no matter how senseless it may seem to others.

My friends, pray to God for joy. Be joyful like children, like the birds of the air. And don't let the sins of others confuse or discourage you in your efforts. Don't be afraid that their sins will wear down your work and prevent it from being finished. Don't say, "Sin is powerful, evil is powerful, the wicked world is powerful, and we are weak and helpless, and this evil world is wearing us down and stopping our good work from being done." Flee from those thoughts, my children! There is only one path to salvation, and that is to make yourself responsible for everyone's sins. That's the truth, you know, my friends, because as soon as you honestly make yourself responsible for everything and everyone, you will immediately see that it is truly so, and that you are to blame for everyone and everything. But if you blame your own laziness and weakness on others, you will end up sharing the pride of Satan and complaining against God.

As for Satan's pride, this is what I think: it is hard for us on earth to truly understand it, and that's why it's so easy to fall into the same error and share in it, even thinking we are doing something great and noble. Indeed, many of the strongest feelings and drives in our nature are things we can't fully understand while on earth. Don't let that be an obstacle, and don't think it excuses anything you do. For the Eternal Judge asks you to understand only what you can, not what you can't. You will see that yourself later, for you will see everything clearly then and will not argue with it. On earth, we are lost, in a way, and if it weren't for the precious image of Christ in front of us, we would be ruined and completely lost, just as the human race was before the flood. Much is hidden from us here, but to make up for it, we've been given a special, mystical sense of our living connection with the other world, the higher heavenly world, and the roots of our thoughts and feelings are not here but in other worlds. That's why philosophers say that we can't fully understand the true reality of things on earth.

God took seeds from different worlds and sowed them on this earth, and His garden grew, and everything that could grow did grow. But what grows only stays alive because of its connection with other mysterious worlds. If that connection weakens or is destroyed in you, the heavenly part of you will wither and die.

Then, you will become indifferent to life and may even come to hate it. That is what I believe.

Remember especially that you cannot judge anyone. No one can judge a criminal until they recognize that they are just as much of a criminal as the person standing before them, and that they, perhaps, are even more to blame for the crime. Once they understand that, then they will be able to judge. Though that may sound strange, it is true. If I had been righteous myself, perhaps there wouldn't have been a criminal standing before me. If you can take upon yourself the crime of the criminal your heart is judging, take it upon yourself immediately, suffer for him, and let him go without any blame. And even if the law makes you his judge, act in the same way as much as possible, for he will leave and condemn himself more harshly than you ever could. If, after your kindness, he leaves untouched and mocks you, don't let that be a stumbling block to you. It means his time hasn't come yet, but it will come eventually. And if it doesn't, no matter; if not him, then someone else will understand and suffer, and judge and condemn himself, and the truth will be fulfilled. Believe that, believe it without any doubt, because that is where all the hope and faith of the saints lies.

Work without stopping. If, as you are about to fall asleep at night, you remember, "I haven't done what I should have done," get up immediately and do it. If the people around you are angry and hard-hearted and won't listen to you, fall down before them and ask for their forgiveness, because in truth, you are to blame for their unwillingness to hear you. And if you can't speak to them because of their bitterness, serve them silently and humbly, never losing hope. If everyone abandons you and even drives you away by force, when you are left alone, fall to the ground and kiss it. Water the earth with your tears, and it will bear fruit even if no one has seen or heard you in your solitude. Believe until the end, even if everyone else strays and you are the only one left faithful; still, bring your offering and praise God in your loneliness. And if two of you are gathered together, then that is an entire world, a world filled with living love. Embrace each other tenderly and thank God, for if His truth is fulfilled in just the two of you, then it is enough.

If you sin and feel sorrow so deep it almost leads to despair because of your sins or a sudden wrongdoing, still rejoice for others. Rejoice for the righteous person, rejoice that if you have sinned, he is righteous and has not sinned.

If the wrongdoing of others fills you with anger and overwhelming sadness, even to the point where you desire revenge on the wrongdoers, avoid that feeling above all else. Go right away and seek suffering for yourself, as if you were the one guilty of the wrong. Accept that suffering and carry it, and your heart will find comfort. You will understand that you too are guilty because you could have been a light to the wrongdoers, even if just one sinless person, but you were not. If you had been a light, you would have lit the way for others too, and perhaps the wrongdoer would have been saved by your light from his sin. And even if your light was shining but they weren't saved by it, stay strong and don't doubt the power of the heavenly light. Believe that if they weren't saved, they will be saved in the future. And if they aren't saved, their children will be, because your light will not die even after you are gone. The righteous person leaves, but his light remains. People are often saved after the death of their savior. They reject their prophets and kill them, but then they honor and love their martyrs, the ones they killed. You are working for everyone, for the future. Don't seek rewards, because your reward is already great on this earth: the spiritual joy that only comes to the righteous person. Don't fear the powerful or the mighty, but be wise and always calm. Know your limits, know the right time, and study these things. When you are alone, pray. Love to throw yourself down on the earth and kiss it. Kiss the earth and love it with a never-ending, consuming love. Love all people, love everything. Seek that joy and ecstasy. Water the earth with your tears of joy, and love those tears. Don't be ashamed of that joy, treasure it, because it is a gift from God, and it is a great gift; it is not given to many but only to a chosen few.

Fathers and teachers, I often think, "What is hell?" I believe it is the suffering of being unable to love. Once, in all of eternity, beyond all time and space, a spiritual being was given, when he came to earth, the power to say, "I am and I love." Just once, and only once, he was granted a moment of active, living love, and for that reason, he was given life on earth, along with time and seasons. That fortunate creature rejected the precious gift, did not value it, did not love it, scorned it, and remained cold-hearted. Such a person, having left the earth, sees Abraham's bosom and talks with Abraham, as we are told in the parable of the rich man and Lazarus, and he beholds heaven and can ascend to the Lord. But that is precisely his torment—to rise to the Lord without ever having loved, to approach those who have loved while having despised their love. For he now clearly understands and says to himself, "Now I have understanding, and though I now thirst to love, there can be nothing great, no sacrifice in my love, for my earthly life is over, and Abraham will not come with even a drop of living water (which is the gift of earthly active life) to cool the burning thirst of spiritual love that consumes me now, though I disregarded it on earth. There is no more life for me, and there will be no more time! Though I would now gladly give my life for others, it is impossible, for the life that could have been sacrificed for love is now past, and now a great gulf is fixed between that life and this existence."

They speak of hellfire in a material sense. I do not delve into that mystery, and I avoid it. But I think that if there were material fire, they would be glad of it, for I imagine that in the agony of the body, their even greater spiritual agony might be forgotten for a moment. Moreover, that spiritual agony cannot be taken away from them, for that suffering is not outside them, but within them. And if it could be taken away from them, I think it would make them even more miserable. For even if the righteous in paradise forgave them, seeing their torment, and in their boundless love called them up to heaven, it would only intensify their suffering, for it would awaken in them an even stronger, flaming thirst for a love that is now impossible—active, thankful love. In the humility of my heart, I imagine, however, that the very realization of this impossibility might, in the end, bring them some comfort. For by accepting the love of the righteous along with the impossibility of returning it, through this submission and the humility that comes with it, they will at last attain, in a sense, something resembling that active love which they rejected in life, something like its outward expression... I regret, my friends and brothers, that I cannot express this clearly. But woe to those who have taken their own lives on earth, woe to the suicides! I believe that no one can be more miserable than they are. We are told that it is a sin to pray for them, and outwardly the Church seems to turn away from them, but in my deepest heart, I believe we may still pray for them. Love can never be an offense to Christ. For such as these, I have prayed secretly all my life, I confess this, fathers and teachers, and even now I pray for them every day.

Oh, there are some who remain proud and fierce even in hell, despite their certain knowledge and vision of the absolute truth; there are some terrifying souls who have completely given themselves over to Satan and his proud spirit. For such people, hell is a choice, and it is always consuming; they are tormented by their own will. They have cursed themselves, cursing God and cursing life. They live off their vengeful pride, like a starving man in the desert sucking the blood from his own body. But they are never satisfied, and they refuse forgiveness, they curse the God who calls them. They cannot look upon the living God without hatred, and they cry out that the God of life should be destroyed, that God should destroy Himself and all His creation. And they will burn forever in the fire of their own wrath, longing for death and annihilation. But they will not reach death...

Here, Alexey Fyodorovitch Karamazov's manuscript ends. I must repeat that it is incomplete and fragmentary. For example, the biographical details cover only Father Zossima's early youth. His teachings and ideas are scattered, clearly spoken on different occasions. His words from the last hours of his life have not been kept separate from the rest, but their general meaning can be understood from what we have in Alexey Fyodorovitch's manuscript.

The elder's death came unexpectedly in the end. Although those who gathered around him that last evening realized that his death was near, it was still hard to imagine it would come so suddenly. On the contrary, as I have already noted, his friends, seeing him that night so cheerful and talkative, were convinced that his condition had at least temporarily improved. Even five minutes before his death, they later said with surprise, it was impossible to foresee it. He suddenly felt a sharp pain in his chest, turned pale, and pressed his hands to his heart. Everyone rose from their seats and rushed to him. But though he was suffering, he still looked at them with a smile, slowly sank from his chair onto his knees, then bowed his face to the ground, stretched out his arms, and as if in joyful ecstasy, praying and kissing the ground, quietly and joyfully gave up his soul to God.

The news of his death quickly spread through the hermitage and reached the monastery. His closest friends, and those whose duty required it, began preparing his body according to the ancient rites, and all the monks gathered in the church. Before dawn, the news of his death had reached the town. By morning, everyone in town was talking about it, and crowds of people were making their way from the town to the monastery. But this will be discussed in the next book. I will only add here that before a day had passed, something occurred— so unexpected, so strange, so unsettling and confusing to both the monks and the townspeople—that even after all these years, that day of suspense is still vividly remembered in the town.

Part 3

Book 7: Alyosha

Chapter 1: The Breath of Corruption

The body of Father Zossima was prepared for burial according to the established ritual. As is well known, the bodies of monks and hermits who have died are not washed. In the words of the Church Ritual: "If one of the monks departs in the Lord, the monk designated (that is, whose office it is) shall wipe the body with warm water, making first the sign of the cross with a sponge on the forehead of the deceased, on the chest, on the hands and feet, and on the knees, and that is sufficient." All of this was done by Father Païssy, who then dressed the deceased in his monastic garb and wrapped him in his cloak, which was, as custom dictated, slightly slit to allow it to be folded about him in the form of a cross. On his head, he placed a hood with an eight-pointed cross. The hood was left open, and the dead man's face was covered with black gauze. In his hands, they placed an icon of the Savior. Towards morning, he was placed in the coffin that had been made ready long before. It was decided to leave the coffin in the cell all day, in the larger room where the elder used to receive his visitors and fellow monks. As the deceased was a priest and monk of the strictest rule, the Gospel, not the Psalter, had to be read over his body by monks in holy orders. The reading was begun by Father Iosif immediately after the requiem service. Later, Father Païssy wanted to read the Gospel all day and night over his dead friend, but for the present, both he and the Father Superintendent of the Hermitage were very busy and preoccupied, for something extraordinary, an unheard-of, even "improper" excitement and impatient expectation had begun to spread among the monks, the visitors from the monastery hostels, and the crowds of people coming from the town. And as time went on, this became more and more evident. Both the Superintendent and Father Païssy did everything they could to calm the general commotion and agitation.

When daylight fully came, some people began bringing their sick, in most cases children, with them from the town—as if they had been waiting for this moment, fully convinced that the dead elder's remains had the power to heal, and that this would be immediately revealed, in accordance with their faith. It was only then that it became clear how unquestionably everyone in the town had accepted Father Zossima during his lifetime as a great saint. And those who came were not only from the lower classes.

This intense expectation from the believers, displayed with such haste, such openness, even with impatience and almost insistence, struck Father Païssy as inappropriate. Although he had long anticipated something like this, the actual expression of this feeling was far beyond what he had expected. When he came across any of the monks showing this excitement, Father Païssy began to rebuke them. "Such immediate expectation of something extraordinary," he said, "shows a lightness of spirit, acceptable to worldly people but unworthy of us."

But little attention was given to him, and Father Païssy noticed this with unease. Yet, even he himself (if the whole truth must be told), secretly, deep in his own heart, held almost the same hopes, though he was angry at the overly impatient expectation around him, seeing it as frivolous and vain. Still, it was especially unpleasant for him to encounter certain individuals whose presence filled him with great anxiety. In the crowd gathered in the dead man's cell, he noticed with inward discomfort (for which he immediately scolded himself) the presence of Rakitin and the monk from Obdorsk, who was still staying in the monastery. For some reason, Father Païssy suddenly became suspicious of both of them—though, in fact, he could have had the same feelings about others.

The monk from Obdorsk was particularly noticeable in the excited crowd. He was everywhere—asking questions, listening, whispering on all sides with a strange, secretive look. His expression showed the greatest impatience and even a kind of irritation.

As for Rakitin, it later became clear that he had come to the hermitage so early at the special request of Madame Hohlakov. As soon as that good-hearted but somewhat foolish woman—who could not have been admitted to the hermitage herself—woke up and heard about Father Zossima's death, she was overcome with such intense curiosity that she immediately sent Rakitin to the hermitage to carefully observe everything and send her written updates every half hour on "everything that was happening." She thought of Rakitin as a very religious and devout young man. He was especially clever at figuring people out and playing whatever role he thought would please them most if he saw any advantage in it for himself.

It was a bright, clear day, and many of the visitors were gathered around the tombs, which were numerous, especially near the church and scattered around different parts of the hermitage. As he walked around the hermitage, Father Païssy suddenly remembered Alyosha and realized that he hadn't seen him for quite some time—not since the previous night. And as soon as he thought of him, he saw him sitting in the farthest corner of the hermitage garden, on the tombstone of a monk who had long ago been famous for his saintliness. Alyosha was sitting with his back to the hermitage and his face towards the wall, as if hiding behind the tombstone. When Father Païssy approached him, he saw that Alyosha was quietly but deeply crying, with his face buried in his hands, his whole body trembling with sobs. Father Païssy stood over him for a moment.

"Enough, my dear son, enough, dear," he said softly at last, with feeling. "Why are you crying? Rejoice and do not weep. Don't you know that this is the greatest of his days? Just think where he is now, at this very moment!"

Alyosha glanced at him, uncovering his face, which was swollen from crying like a child's, but immediately turned away without saying a word and hid his face in his hands again.

"Perhaps it is good," said Father Païssy thoughtfully. "Weep if you must—Christ has sent you these tears."

"Your tears will be a comfort to your spirit and will bring joy to your dear heart," he added to himself as he walked away from Alyosha, thinking of him with affection. He moved away quickly, however, for he felt that if he stayed longer, he might begin to cry himself.

Meanwhile, time was passing; the monastery services and the requiems for the dead proceeded according to their proper schedule. Father Païssy once again took over for Father Iosif by the coffin and continued reading the Gospel. But before three o'clock in the afternoon, something occurred, something I alluded to at the end of the last book, something so unexpected by all of us and so opposite to everyone's hopes that, I must say again, this trivial incident has been remembered in detail to this day in our town and the surrounding area. Personally, I find it almost unpleasant to recall this event, which caused such frivolous excitement and became such a stumbling block for many, though in truth it was the most natural and insignificant thing. I would certainly have left it out of the story if it had not had such a profound effect on the heart and soul of the central figure—although he is still to fully become the hero of this story—Alyosha. This event marked a crisis and turning point in his spiritual growth, shaking his understanding, but ultimately strengthening it for the rest of his life and giving it a clear direction.

And now, to continue the story. When they placed Father Zossima's body in the coffin before dawn and moved it to the front room, someone casually suggested opening the windows. However, this suggestion went unanswered and was almost entirely ignored. Some of those present might have inwardly taken note of it, but they dismissed the thought, believing that anticipating decay from the body of such a saint was absurd, something that would provoke pity (if not a smile) for the lack of faith and the foolishness it showed. For everyone expected something completely different.

And then, soon after noon, signs of something unusual began to appear. At first, these signs were silently noticed by those who entered and left the room, with each person apparently afraid to express what was on their mind. But by three o'clock, the signs had become so obvious and undeniable that the news quickly spread among the monks and visitors in the hermitage, then rapidly reached the monastery, where it left all the monks astonished, and before long, the word had reached the town, exciting everyone— believers and nonbelievers alike. The nonbelievers rejoiced, and even some of the believers were happier than the nonbelievers because, as the elder himself had said in one of his teachings, "people love to see the fall and disgrace of the righteous."

The fact was that a smell of decomposition had begun to emanate from the coffin, growing stronger and more obvious, and by three o'clock it was unmistakable. In the entire history of our monastery, no such scandal had ever been recalled, and under no other circumstances could such a scandal have been possible, as the disorder that immediately broke out after this discovery among the monks themselves. Even years later, some of the more sensible monks looked back in amazement and horror, remembering how far the scandal had gone. For in the past, other monks of very holy lives had died—God-fearing old men whose saintliness was universally acknowledged—yet from their simple coffins, too, the odor of decay had come, as naturally happens with all bodies, but this had caused no scandal, nor even the slightest excitement.

Of course, there had been saints in the monastery whose relics, according to tradition, had shown no signs of decay. This fact was regarded by the monks as deeply moving and mysterious, and the tradition was cherished as something blessed and miraculous, a promise by God's grace of even greater glory to come from their tombs in the future.

One such saint, whose memory was particularly cherished, was an old monk named Job, who had died seventy years before at the age of one hundred and five. He had been a renowned ascetic, strict in fasting and silence, and his tomb was shown to all visitors with great reverence, accompanied by hints of great hopes connected to it. (It was the very tomb on which Father Païssy had found Alyosha sitting that morning.) Another cherished memory in the monastery was that of the famous Father Varsonofy, who had only recently passed away and had been the elder before Father Zossima. He was revered during his lifetime as a "crazy saint" by all the pilgrims who visited the monastery. There was a tradition that both of these monks had lain in their coffins as though still alive, showing no signs of decay, and that their faces had shone with a holy light. Some people even claimed that a sweet fragrance had come from their bodies.

Yet, despite these inspiring memories, it is difficult to explain the foolishness, absurdity, and malice that were displayed around the coffin of Father Zossima. In my opinion, several different factors were at work at the same time, one of which was the deep-rooted hostility to the institution of elders, viewed by some as a harmful new practice, a hostility that lay hidden in the hearts of many of the monks. Even more powerful was the jealousy of the elder's saintliness, which had become so firmly established during his lifetime that it was almost forbidden to question it. Although the late elder had won many hearts, more through love than through miracles, and had gathered around him a large number of devoted followers, this only increased the jealousy of others, leading to bitter enemies, both inside the monastery and in the world outside it. He had harmed no one, but still, people asked, "Why do they think he's so saintly?" That simple question, repeated often enough, eventually gave rise to intense and unshakable hatred of him. That, I believe, is why many people were quietly pleased by the smell of decomposition that came so soon—after all, not even a full day had passed since his death. At the same time, there were some among his former followers who felt personally offended and almost humiliated by this incident. This is what happened.

As soon as signs of decay began to appear, the expressions on the monks' faces revealed their inner thoughts as they entered the cell. They would go in, stay for a short time, and then hurry out to confirm the news to the other monks waiting outside. Some of these monks shook their heads sadly, but others didn't even bother to hide the satisfaction that gleamed openly in their eyes. And now, no one scolded them for it, and no one raised their voice in protest, which was surprising, considering that most of the monks had been devoted to the elder. But it seemed that, in this case, God had allowed the minority to take control for a while.

Visitors from outside, especially those from the educated class, also began to enter the cell with the same curiosity. Very few peasants went into the cell, although many were gathered at the gates of the hermitage. After three o'clock, the number of worldly visitors increased significantly, no doubt because of the shocking news.

People were drawn there who otherwise would not have come that day and had no intention of coming, and among them were some people of high social standing. But outward decorum was still maintained, and Father Païssy, with a stern expression, continued reading the Gospel aloud in a clear, firm voice, seemingly unaware of what was happening around him, though in fact, he had noticed something unusual long before. But finally, even he couldn't ignore the murmurs that had begun quietly but were growing louder and more confident. "It shows that God's judgment is not like man's," Father Païssy heard someone say suddenly. The first to say these words aloud was a layman, an elderly town official known for his deep religious devotion. But he was only repeating what the monks had been whispering among themselves for some time. They had long ago formed this conclusion, and the worst part was that a kind of triumphant satisfaction with this conclusion became more and more obvious with each passing moment. Soon, they began to abandon even the appearance of respect, and it almost seemed as though they felt entitled to do so.

"And why did this happen?" some of the monks asked, at first pretending to be regretful. "He was small, and his flesh had wasted away—what was there to decay?"

"It must be a sign from heaven," others quickly added, and this opinion was immediately accepted without protest. They also pointed out that if the decay had been natural, as it happens with any ordinary sinner, it would have shown itself later, after at least twenty-four hours. But this premature decay was "beyond nature," and so it was clear to them that God's hand was at work. It was meant as a sign. This conclusion seemed impossible to refute.

Gentle Father Iosif, the librarian, who had been a great admirer of the dead man, tried to respond to some of those speaking ill of him. He explained that "this is not understood the same way everywhere," and that the idea of saints' bodies remaining uncorrupted was not an official doctrine of the Orthodox Church, but just a belief. Even in the most Orthodox places, like Mount Athos, the smell of decay was not seen as a scandal. There, the most important sign of a saint's glorification wasn't that the body remained intact, but rather the color of the bones after years of being buried in the earth. "If the bones are yellow like wax, that's the great sign that the Lord has glorified the saint. If they're black, it means that God has not deemed them worthy of such honor. That's what they believe at Athos, a sacred place where Orthodox teachings have been preserved in their purest form," Father Iosif said in conclusion.

But his words had little effect and even provoked some mocking replies. "That's just pedantry and new ideas—there's no point listening to it," the monks decided. "We stick to the old teachings; there are so many new ideas these days, are we supposed to follow all of them?" others added. "We've had just as many holy fathers as they have. They live under the Turks over there, they've forgotten everything. Their beliefs have long been corrupted, and they don't even have church bells," added the most sarcastic among them.

Father Iosif walked away, deeply saddened, especially because he had voiced his opinion without much confidence, almost as if he didn't fully believe in it himself. He could already see, with great distress, that something very improper was starting and that there were clear signs of disobedience. Gradually, all the sensible monks, like Father Iosif, were reduced to silence. And it happened that all those who had loved the elder and had faithfully accepted the institution of eldership suddenly felt terribly discouraged, exchanging anxious glances when they encountered one another. Meanwhile, those who had been against the idea of elders from the start, considering it a dangerous innovation, now proudly held their heads high. "There was no smell of decay from the late elder Varsonofy, only a sweet fragrance," they maliciously pointed out. "But he gained that honor not because he was an elder, but because he was a truly holy man."

After this, a flood of criticism and even blame was directed toward Father Zossima. "His teachings were wrong; he said life is full of joy and not a valley of tears," some of the more unreasonable monks claimed. "He followed modern ideas, he didn't even believe in literal fire in hell," added others, even more unreasonable. "He wasn't strict with fasting, he allowed himself sweets, and he ate cherry jam with his tea—ladies used to send it to him. Is it right for a monk to drink tea?" some of the envious monks muttered. "He was full of pride," the most spiteful declared viciously. "He thought of himself as a saint and accepted it when people knelt before him." "He abused the sacrament of confession," the fiercest opponents of eldership whispered maliciously. Among these critics were some of the oldest monks, known for their devotion and strict asceticism, who had remained silent during Father Zossima's lifetime but now, suddenly, found their voices. This was alarming because their words held great influence over the younger monks who were still uncertain in their beliefs. The monk from Obdorsk listened attentively to all of this, sighing deeply and nodding his head. "Yes, it seems Father Ferapont was right in his judgment yesterday," he thought, and just at that moment, Father Ferapont himself appeared, as though to add to the confusion.

I've already mentioned that Father Ferapont rarely left his wooden hut near the beehives. He was seldom seen even at church, and his absence was overlooked because of his reputed madness, and he wasn't held to the same rules as the others. But in truth, they didn't really have a choice. It would have been a mistake to try and enforce the usual rules on such a great ascetic, who prayed day and night (even falling asleep on his knees). If they had tried, the other monks would have said, "He's holier than all of us, and he follows a much stricter rule than we do. If he doesn't come to church, it's because he knows when he should; he has his own rule." To avoid stirring up these sinful murmurs, they left Father Ferapont in peace.

As everyone knew, Father Ferapont especially disliked Father Zossima. Now, word had reached him in his hut that "God's judgment is different from man's" and that something had happened that was "beyond nature." It's likely that the monk from Obdorsk, who had visited him the evening before and left the cell terrified, was one of the first to rush to him with the news.

I've mentioned earlier that although Father Païssy, standing firm and steady as he read the Gospel by the coffin, couldn't hear or see what was happening outside the cell, he had already sensed most of it in his heart, for he knew the men around him well. He wasn't disturbed by it and calmly waited to see what would happen next, observing with insight for the outcome of all this excitement.

Suddenly, a loud commotion erupted in the hallway, openly defying proper conduct. The door was thrown open, and Father Ferapont appeared in the doorway. Behind him, a crowd of monks and people from the town could be seen. They didn't enter the cell but stood at the bottom of the steps, waiting to see what Father Ferapont would say or do. Despite their audacity, they still felt a certain fear, sensing that he hadn't come for no reason. Standing in the doorway, Father Ferapont raised his arms, and under his right arm, the curious little eyes of the monk from Obdorsk peered in. He alone, driven by intense curiosity, couldn't resist running up the steps after Father Ferapont. The others, on the other hand, stepped back in sudden alarm when the door was noisily thrown open. Holding his hands high, Father Ferapont suddenly shouted:

"Out! Out, I cast you out!" He then turned in all directions, making the sign of the cross toward each of the four walls and corners of the cell, one by one. Everyone who had accompanied Father Ferapont understood what he was doing. They knew he always did this wherever he went and that he wouldn't sit down or say a word until he had driven out the evil spirits.

"Satan, go away! Satan, go away!" he repeated with each sign of the cross. "Out, I cast you out!" he roared again.

He wore a rough robe, tied with a rope. His bare chest, covered with gray hair, was visible beneath his rough shirt. His feet were bare. As soon as he began waving his arms, the heavy chains he wore under his robe could be heard clanking.

Father Païssy paused in his reading, stepped forward, and stood in front of him, waiting.

"What have you come for, worthy Father? Why are you disturbing the order here? Why are you disrupting the peace of the brothers?" he asked at last, looking at him sternly.

"Why have I come? You ask why? What kind of faith do you have?" Father Ferapont shouted crazily. "I've come to cast out your visitors—the unclean devils. I've come to see how many of them have gathered here while I've been away. I want to sweep them all out with a birch broom."

"You cast out the evil spirit, but maybe you are serving him yourself," Father Païssy said bravely. "And who can say of themselves 'I am holy'? Can you, Father?"

"I am unclean, not holy. I wouldn't sit in a chair and have people bow down to me like an idol," Father Ferapont thundered. "People today are destroying the true faith. That dead man, your saint," he said, turning to the crowd and pointing to the coffin, "didn't believe in devils. He gave medicine to drive them away. And now devils are as common as spiders in the corners. And now he himself has started to stink. That's a great sign from God."

The event he referred to was this: One of the monks had been tormented by nightmares and later, even in waking moments, he saw visions of evil spirits. When he told Father Zossima in complete fear, the elder advised him to keep praying and to fast strictly. But when that didn't help, he advised him, while continuing prayer and fasting, to take a special medicine. Many people were shocked when they heard this and shook their heads in disapproval—especially Father Ferapont, who had been informed of this "strange" advice by some of the more critical monks.

"Go away, Father!" Father Païssy said in a firm voice. "It is not for humans to judge, but for God. Maybe we're seeing a 'sign' that neither you, nor I, nor anyone else can understand. Go, Father, and stop troubling the flock!" he said firmly again.

"He didn't keep the fasts according to the rules, and that's why this sign has come. That's clear, and it's wrong to hide it," Father Ferapont, driven by a zeal that went beyond reason, refused to calm down. "He was tempted by sweets, women brought them to him in their pockets. He sipped tea, worshipped his belly, filled it with sweet things, and filled his mind with proud thoughts... And that's why he's being shamed..."

"You speak carelessly, Father," Father Païssy raised his voice as well. "I admire your fasting and discipline, but you speak recklessly, like some immature youth, fickle and childish. Leave now, Father, I command you!" Father Païssy said loudly in conclusion.

"I will go," said Ferapont, seeming slightly taken aback but still bitter. "You scholars! You're so clever, you look down on my humility. I came here with little knowledge, and now I've forgotten what little I knew. God Himself has protected me in my weakness from your cunning ways."

Father Païssy stood over him, waiting firmly. Father Ferapont paused, then suddenly rested his cheek in his hand with a downcast look and, in a sing-song voice, gazing at the coffin of the dead elder, he said, "Tomorrow, they'll sing 'Our Helper and Defender' over him—a beautiful hymn. But over me, when I die, all they'll sing is 'What earthly joy'—a little song," he added tearfully. "You are proud and puffed up. This place is full of vanity!" he suddenly shouted like a madman, and with a wave of his hand, he turned quickly and went down the steps. The crowd waiting below shifted uncertainly; some followed him immediately while others lingered, as the cell was still open. Father Païssy, following Father Ferapont onto the steps, stood watching him. But the excited old fanatic wasn't entirely silenced. Walking about twenty steps away, he suddenly turned towards the setting sun, raised both his arms, and, as though struck down, fell to the ground with a loud cry.

"My God has conquered! Christ has conquered the setting sun!" he screamed frantically, stretching his hands towards the sun, then falling face down on the ground, sobbing like a child, his body shaking with tears and his arms spread out on the ground. Immediately, people rushed towards him; there were cries and sympathetic sobs... A sort of frenzy seemed to take hold of everyone.

"This is the true saint! This is the holy man!" some cried out, losing their fear. "He should be an elder," others added spitefully.

"He wouldn't become an elder... he'd refuse... he wouldn't be part of that cursed innovation... he wouldn't join their foolishness," other voices chimed in immediately. It's hard to say how far this might have gone, but at that moment, the bell rang, calling everyone to service. They all started crossing themselves at once. Father Ferapont also got up, crossed himself, and walked back to his cell without looking back, still muttering incoherent exclamations. A few followed him, but most dispersed quickly, hurrying to the service. Father Païssy let Father Iosif take his place reading and went down. The wild cries of fanatics hadn't shaken him, but a strange melancholy suddenly filled his heart for some unknown reason. He stood still and wondered, "Why am I so sad, almost depressed?" and then realized, to his own surprise, that his sudden sadness came from a very small and specific cause. In the crowd at the entrance to the cell, he had noticed Alyosha, and he remembered feeling a sharp pang in his heart when he saw him. "Can that boy mean so much to me now?" he asked himself, amazed.

At that moment, Alyosha passed by him, hurrying away, but not towards the church. Their eyes met. Alyosha quickly looked away and lowered his gaze, and from the boy's expression alone, Father Païssy could tell that a great change was happening within him at that moment.

"Have you, too, fallen into temptation?" cried Father Païssy. "Can you be one of those who lack faith?" he added sorrowfully.

Alyosha stood still and looked vaguely at Father Païssy, but quickly turned his eyes away again and stared at the ground. He stood sideways, never turning fully to face Father Païssy, who was watching him intently.

"Where are you going? The bell is calling us to the service," he asked again, but Alyosha didn't answer.

"Are you leaving the hermitage? What, without asking for permission or a blessing?"

Alyosha suddenly gave a bitter smile, cast a strange, very strange, look at the Father to whom his former guide, the once-sovereign of his heart and mind, his beloved elder, had entrusted him as he lay dying. Then, still without saying a word, Alyosha waved his hand dismissively, as if no longer caring to be respectful, and with rapid steps walked towards the gates, leaving the hermitage behind.

"You will return!" murmured Father Païssy, watching him walk away with a sorrowful look of surprise.

Chapter 2: A Critical Moment

Father Païssy was certainly right when he thought that his "dear boy" would return again. In fact, he may have had some insight into the true meaning of Alyosha's spiritual state. However, I must honestly admit that it would be very difficult for me to provide a clear explanation of that strange, uncertain moment in the life of the young man I care for so much. To Father Païssy's sorrowful question, "Are you also among those of little faith?" I could, of course, confidently answer for Alyosha, "No, he is not among them. Quite the opposite." In truth, all his suffering was because he had great faith. But still, the suffering was there, and it was so intense that even long afterward, Alyosha remembered that sorrowful day as one of the bitterest and most decisive days of his life.

If someone were to ask, "Could all of his grief and turmoil really have been caused by the fact that his elder's body had shown signs of premature decomposition, instead of performing miracles right away?" I must answer directly, "Yes, it certainly was." However, I would ask the reader not to be too quick to laugh at my young hero's pure heart. I do not intend to excuse him or justify his innocent faith by saying that it was due to his youth, his lack of education, or any such reason. In fact, I have great respect for the qualities of his heart. Undoubtedly, a more cautious young man, whose feelings were more restrained, whose love was lukewarm, and whose mind was too sensible for his age—such a young man, I admit, might have avoided what happened to my hero. But in certain cases, it is truly more admirable to be swept away by a feeling, no matter how irrational, when it stems from deep love, than to remain unmoved. And this is especially true for young people, for a young man who is always reasonable is to be doubted, and is, in my opinion, of little value!

"But," some reasonable people might exclaim, "not every young man can believe in such superstitions, and your hero is no model for others." To this, I would reply again, "Yes, my hero had faith, a faith that was holy and steadfast, but even so, I am not going to apologize for him."

Although I declared earlier—and perhaps too hastily—that I would not explain or justify my hero, I realize now that some explanation is necessary to understand the rest of my story. So let me say this: It was not a question of miracles. There was no shallow or impatient expectation of miracles in Alyosha's mind. At that time, Alyosha did not need miracles to affirm some preconceived idea—oh, no, not at all. What he saw above all was one figure— the figure of his beloved elder, the figure of that holy man whom he revered with such devotion. The fact is, all the love that had been hidden in Alyosha's pure heart for everyone and everything had, for the past year, been concentrated—and perhaps too much so—on one person: his beloved elder. It is true that this person had, for so long, been accepted by Alyosha as his ideal, that all his youthful energy and strength had been drawn to that ideal, even to the point of forgetting "everyone and everything else" for the moment. Later, Alyosha remembered how, on that terrible day, he had completely forgotten his brother Dmitri, though he had been so anxious about him the day before. He had also forgotten to take the two hundred rubles to Ilusha's father, though he had intended to do so warmly the previous evening. But again, it was not miracles that Alyosha needed, but only "justice," a higher justice, which, in his view, had been deeply offended by the blow that had so suddenly and cruelly struck his heart.

And what if this "justice," as Alyosha saw it, naturally took the form of miracles, expected to be performed by the ashes of his beloved teacher? Why not? After all, everyone in the monastery shared the same thoughts and hopes, even those whose intelligence Alyosha deeply respected, like Father Païssy. So, without any doubts, Alyosha's dreams naturally took the same shape as everyone else's. A whole year of life in the monastery had formed the habit of this expectation in his heart. But what Alyosha truly thirsted for was justice, not miracles.

And now, the man who Alyosha believed should have been exalted above everyone else in the world was, instead, suddenly disgraced and humiliated! Why? Who had judged him? Who had passed this decree? These were the questions that tormented Alyosha's innocent heart. He could not endure, without feeling deep shame and even anger, that the holiest of holy men had been subjected to the jeering and mocking of a crowd that was so far beneath him. Even if there had been no miracles, even if there had been nothing extraordinary to justify his hopes, why such disgrace? Why such humiliation? Why this premature decay, "beyond nature," as the spiteful monks said? Why this "sign from heaven," which they celebrated along with Father Ferapont, and why did they think they had the right to celebrate it? Where was the hand of Providence? Why did Providence seem to hide its face "at the most critical moment" (as Alyosha saw it), as if surrendering to the blind, pitiless laws of nature?

This is why Alyosha's heart was breaking, and of course, as I have already said, the most painful part of it was that the person he loved more than anything else in the world was being shamed and humiliated! Perhaps this sorrow was irrational, but I will say again—and I am ready to admit that this feeling may be hard to defend— that I am glad my hero was not too reasonable at that moment. After all, a reasonable man will always return to reason in time, but if love does not triumph in a young man's heart at such an exceptional moment, when will it?

I must also mention something strange that surfaced in Alyosha's mind at this fatal and confusing moment. It was the troubling impression left by his conversation with Ivan, which now kept haunting Alyosha's thoughts. This was not because his deep, fundamental faith in God had been shaken—no, Alyosha still loved and believed in his God steadfastly, even though, in his heart, he was murmuring against Him. But this vague, troubling impression from his conversation with Ivan the day before suddenly rose again within him, forcing its way into his thoughts.

By the time dusk was falling, Rakitin, who was walking through the pine grove between the hermitage and the monastery, suddenly saw Alyosha lying face down on the ground under a tree, motionless, as if asleep. Rakitin walked over and called his name.

"You here, Alexey? Could it be—" he started to ask, but stopped. He had meant to say, "Could it be that you've come to this?"

Alyosha didn't look at him, but from a slight movement, Rakitin could immediately tell that he heard and understood him.

"What's going on?" he continued, but the surprise on his face slowly turned into a smile that grew more and more mocking. "I've been looking for you for the last two hours. You just disappeared. What are you up to? What kind of nonsense is this? You could at least look at me…"

Alyosha lifted his head, sat up, and leaned against the tree. He wasn't crying, but his face showed signs of pain and irritation. He still didn't look at Rakitin, keeping his eyes turned away to the side.

"Do you know your face has changed? There's no sign of that famous gentleness. Are you mad at someone? Did somebody hurt you?"

"Leave me alone," Alyosha said suddenly, with a tired wave of his hand, still not looking at him.

"Oh ho! So that's how it is! You can snap at people just like everyone else. That's quite a fall from your angelic state. I must say, Alyosha, you've surprised me, you know that? I mean it. I haven't been surprised by anything here in a long time. I always thought you were smarter than this…"

Alyosha finally looked at him, but it was a vague look, like he barely understood what Rakitin was saying.

"Are you really so upset just because your elder started to stink? Don't tell me you seriously thought he was going to perform miracles?" Rakitin said, genuinely surprised again.

"I believed, I believe, I want to believe, and I will believe. What more do you want?" Alyosha replied irritably.

"Nothing at all, my friend. Come on! Not even a thirteen-year- old kid believes that stuff anymore. But here you are… So now you're mad at God, rebelling against Him because He didn't give out miracles and honors? Oh, you people are something else!"

Alyosha stared at Rakitin for a long time with half-closed eyes, but it wasn't anger directed at Rakitin.

"I'm not rebelling against God; I just don't accept His world," Alyosha said suddenly, forcing a smile.

"What do you mean, you don't accept the world?" Rakitin thought for a moment. "What kind of nonsense is that?"

Alyosha didn't answer.

"Come on, enough of this. Let's get down to business. Have you eaten anything today?"

"I don't remember… I think I have."

"You need something to eat, judging by how you look. It's sad to see you like this. I heard you didn't sleep last night either, and you had that meeting in there, followed by all this commotion. You've probably only had a bit of holy bread. I've got some sausage in my pocket; I brought it just in case. But you don't eat sausage, do you?"

"Give me some."

"What?! You're really going for it now! This is practically a rebellion! Well, we might as well make the most of it. Come to my place… I wouldn't mind a bit of vodka myself. I'm exhausted. Vodka might be too much for you… or would you like some?"

210

"Give me some vodka too."

"Wow! You're full of surprises today!" Rakitin said, staring at him in amazement. "Well, whether it's vodka or sausage, this is quite the moment. Let's go."

Alyosha got up silently and followed Rakitin.

"If your brother Ivan could see this—he'd be shocked! Oh, by the way, did you know Ivan left for Moscow this morning?"

"Yes," Alyosha answered dully, and suddenly the image of his brother Dmitri flashed in his mind. But only for a moment, and even though it reminded him of something urgent, some duty or terrible obligation, it didn't leave any lasting impression on him. The thought faded from his mind and was forgotten almost instantly. But later on, Alyosha would remember this moment.

"Your brother Ivan once said I was 'a useless liberal with no talents at all.' And once, even you couldn't resist hinting that I was 'dishonorable.' Well! I'd love to see what your talents and sense of honor will do for you now." Rakitin muttered the last part quietly to himself.

"Hey!" he said out loud, "let's take the path past the monastery, straight into town. Hmm! I should probably stop by Madame Hohlakov's on the way. Just imagine, I wrote her about everything that happened, and would you believe it? She replied right away in pencil (she's obsessed with writing notes) that 'she never expected such behavior from a man as respected as Father Zossima.' Those were her exact words: 'behavior.' She's angry too. You people are a strange bunch!" he suddenly stopped and grabbed Alyosha by the shoulder to stop him as well.

"Do you know, Alyosha," Rakitin said, peering into his eyes with a new idea forming in his mind. Though he laughed on the outside, he was clearly afraid to say this thought out loud, still struggling to believe the unexpected mood Alyosha was in. "Alyosha, do you know where we should go?" he finally said, sounding nervous but excited.

"I don't care... wherever you want," Alyosha replied calmly. "Let's go see Grushenka. What do you say? Will you come?"

Rakitin finally asked, trembling with anticipation.

"Let's go see Grushenka," Alyosha said calmly, without hesitation. This immediate and calm response shocked Rakitin so much that he almost stepped back.

"Well! I never!" he cried in amazement, but grabbing Alyosha's arm, he led him along the path, still worried that Alyosha might change his mind.

They walked in silence, and Rakitin was too nervous to talk.

"And just imagine how happy she'll be, how thrilled!" he mumbled, then fell silent again. And it wasn't really to make Grushenka happy that Rakitin was taking Alyosha to her. He was a practical man and never did anything without expecting some kind of gain. He had two motives here: one was the malicious satisfaction of seeing "the downfall of a righteous man," watching Alyosha fall "from saint to sinner," which he was already gleefully imagining. And the second was some material gain for himself, which we'll discuss later.

"So, the moment of truth has arrived," Rakitin thought to himself with spiteful delight. "And we'll strike while the iron is hot, because this is exactly what we've been waiting for."

Chapter 3: An Onion

Grushenka lived in the busiest part of town, near the cathedral square, in a small wooden lodge located in the courtyard of the house belonging to the widow Morozov. The house itself was a large, two-story stone building, old and very unattractive. The widow lived a quiet and secluded life with her two unmarried nieces, who were also elderly women. She had no need to rent out her lodge, but it was well known that she had taken Grushenka as a lodger four years earlier solely to please her relative, the merchant Samsonov, who was known to be Grushenka's protector. People said that the jealous old man placed his "favorite" with the widow Morozov so that the old woman could keep a close watch on Grushenka's behavior. However, this sharp eye soon proved unnecessary, and eventually, the widow Morozov rarely saw Grushenka and did not bother to supervise her at all.

It is true that four years had passed since the old man had brought the slim, delicate, shy, timid, dreamy, and sad girl of eighteen from the provincial capital, and much had happened since then. Little was known about Grushenka's past in the town, and what was known was vague. In the last four years, despite many people becoming interested in the beautiful young woman Grushenka had become, no further details of her history were learned. Rumor had it that she had been betrayed at the age of seventeen by someone—some sort of officer—and shortly after, abandoned by him. The officer left, got married, and Grushenka was left behind, in disgrace and poverty. However, it was said that although Samsonov had rescued her from poverty, Grushenka came from a respectable family of the clerical class and that she was the daughter of a deacon or someone like that.

Now, after four years, the sensitive, wounded, and pitiful little orphan had turned into a plump, rosy beauty of the classic Russian type, a woman of bold and determined character, proud and even insolent. She had a good business sense, was careful with money, and had, through both fair and questionable means, managed to accumulate a small fortune. There was only one point on which everyone agreed. Grushenka was not easily approached, and except for her elderly protector, there had not been a single man who could boast of her favors during those four years. This was a well-known fact, especially as many men had tried to gain her favor in the last two years. All their efforts had been in vain, and some of these suitors had been forced to retreat in an undignified and even comical way, owing to the firm and ironic resistance they met from the strong-willed young woman. It was also known that Grushenka, especially recently, had begun to engage in what people called "speculation," and she had shown particular skill in this area, to the point where many people began saying she was no better than a Jew. This did not mean that she lent money with interest, but it was known, for example, that for some time she had, in partnership with old Karamazov, actually invested in purchasing bad debts for a fraction of their nominal value and then profited ten times over from them.

The old widower Samsonov, a man of considerable wealth, was stingy and ruthless. He dominated his grown sons, but over the last year, during which he had been ill and had lost the use of his swollen legs, he had fallen more and more under the influence of his protégée. At first, he had kept her under strict control and in humble conditions—"on Lenten fare," as people joked at the time. However, Grushenka had succeeded in gaining her freedom and, at the same time, established a firm belief in her loyalty in the old man. Though he could no longer live without her (especially in the last two years of his life), he did not leave her a large fortune, and he would not have been moved to do so, even if she had threatened to leave him. Nevertheless, he did give her a small sum of money, and when it became known, it was a surprise to everyone.

"You're a clever girl," he told her when he gave her eight thousand rubles, "and you'll have to take care of yourself. But let me tell you, aside from your usual yearly allowance, you won't get another kopeck from me as long as I'm alive, and you won't get anything in my will either."

He kept his word. When he died, he left everything to his sons, whom he had treated like servants their whole lives, along with their wives and children. Grushenka wasn't even mentioned in the will. All of this became known later. Samsonov, however, had helped Grushenka by giving her advice to increase her capital and providing her with business opportunities.

When Fyodor Pavlovitch first became involved with Grushenka through a speculative deal, he ended up, to his own surprise, falling madly in love with her. Old Samsonov, seriously ill as he was, found this highly amusing. Remarkably, throughout their entire acquaintance, Grushenka had always been completely open with the old man, and he seemed to be the only person in the world with whom she was so honest. Recently, however, when Dmitri had also entered the picture with his own love for Grushenka, the old man stopped laughing. In fact, he gave her some very serious advice.

"If you have to choose between the father and the son, it would be better to choose the old man—but only if you make sure the old scoundrel marries you and settles some money on you beforehand. But leave the captain alone, you'll get nothing from him."

These were the very words of the old libertine, who already felt his death approaching and who indeed died five months later.

I should also note, in passing, that although many people in town were aware of the absurd and grotesque rivalry between the Karamazovs—father and son—over Grushenka, very few actually understood her attitude toward either of them. Even Grushenka's two servants (after the catastrophe that we will discuss later) testified in court that she had only received Dmitri Fyodorovitch out of fear because "he threatened to kill her." These servants were an elderly cook, who was almost deaf and had come from Grushenka's old home, and her granddaughter, a sharp young woman of twenty, who acted as her maid. Grushenka lived quite frugally, and her surroundings were far from luxurious. Her lodge consisted of three rooms, all furnished with old mahogany furniture in the style of the 1820s that belonged to her landlady.

It was already dark when Rakitin and Alyosha entered Grushenka's rooms, but no lights were on. Grushenka was lying in the drawing room on a large, hard, old-fashioned sofa with a mahogany back. The sofa's leather covering was worn and torn. She had two white down pillows from her bed under her head. She lay stretched out on her back, not moving, with her hands behind her head. She was dressed as if she was expecting someone, wearing a black silk dress and a delicate lace scarf on her head, which looked very flattering. A lace shawl was thrown over her shoulders, fastened with a large gold brooch. She definitely seemed to be waiting for someone. She looked impatient and tired, her face pale, and her lips and eyes heated, as she restlessly tapped the arm of the sofa with the tip of her right foot. The arrival of Rakitin and Alyosha caused a stir. From the hallway, they could hear Grushenka jump up from the sofa and call out in a startled voice, "Who's there?" But the maid met the guests and quickly called back to her mistress.

"It's not him, just some other visitors."

"What's going on?" Rakitin muttered, leading Alyosha into the drawing room.

Grushenka was standing by the sofa, still looking alarmed. A thick strand of her dark brown hair had slipped from the lace covering and fallen over her right shoulder, but she didn't notice it or fix it until she had looked at her visitors and recognized them.

"Oh, it's you, Rakitin? You really scared me. Who have you brought with you? Oh my goodness, you've brought him!" she exclaimed, recognizing Alyosha.

"Get us some candles!" Rakitin said with the casual attitude of someone who felt comfortable giving orders in the house.

"Candles... yes, of course, candles... Fenya, get a candle for him. Well, you've picked quite a moment to bring him here!" she said again, nodding toward Alyosha, and turning to the mirror to quickly fix her hair with both hands. She seemed a little irritated.

"Haven't I managed to please you?" Rakitin asked, sounding almost offended.

"You just startled me, Rakitin, that's all," Grushenka smiled, turning to Alyosha. "Don't be afraid of me, dear Alyosha, you can't imagine how happy I am to see you, my unexpected guest. But you gave me a fright, Rakitin. I thought it was Mitya barging in. You see, I tricked him just now. I made him promise to trust me, and I told him a lie. I told him I was going to spend the evening with my old man, Kuzma Kuzmitch, and that I'd be there late, counting his money. I spend one evening every week with him, helping with his accounts. We lock ourselves in, and he counts using those beads, while I write everything down in the book. I'm the only one he trusts. Mitya believes I'm there now, but I came back here and have been sitting here, locked in, waiting for some news. How did Fenya let you in? Fenya, Fenya, go out to the gate and see if the captain is around! He might be hiding and spying on me. I'm really scared."

"There's no one out there, Agrafena Alexandrovna, I just checked. I keep peeking through the crack in the door, but I'm scared myself," Fenya replied.

"Are the shutters closed, Fenya? We need to pull the curtains too—that's better!" She drew the heavy curtains herself. "If Mitya sees a light, he'll burst in right away. I'm really afraid of your brother today, Alyosha."

Grushenka spoke aloud, and even though she was frightened, she seemed happy about something.

"Why are you so scared of Mitya today?" Rakitin asked. "I thought you weren't afraid of him, that you could twist him around your little finger."

"I'm waiting for some news, some important news, and I don't want Mitya here at all. And I know he didn't believe me when I said I'd be at Kuzma Kuzmitch's all night. I bet he's hiding now, watching me from behind Fyodor Pavlovitch's house in the garden. If he's there, at least he won't come here, which is even better! But I really did go to Kuzma Kuzmitch's, and Mitya took me there. I told him I'd be there until midnight, and I asked him to come pick me up at midnight. He left, and I sat with Kuzma Kuzmitch for about ten minutes, but then I came back here. Ugh, I was scared, running back, hoping not to bump into him."

"And why are you all dressed up? What's with that fancy cap you're wearing?" Rakitin asked.

"You sure are curious, Rakitin! I told you, I'm expecting a message. If it comes, I'll be off, and you won't see me again. That's why I'm dressed up, to be ready."

"And where are you going?"

"If you know too much, you'll get old too soon."

"Well, you're in high spirits! I've never seen you like this before. You look like you're dressed for a ball," Rakitin said, eyeing her from head to toe.

"What do you know about balls?" "And what do you know about them?"

"I've seen a ball. Two years ago, Kuzma Kuzmitch's son got married, and I watched from the gallery. Do you think I want to talk to you, Rakitin, when I have a prince like this standing here? Such a guest! Alyosha, my dear boy, I look at you and can hardly believe my eyes. Good heavens, could you have really come to see me? Honestly, I never thought you'd come. I didn't expect you to visit me, ever. Although it's not the best time, I'm so happy to see you. Sit down on the sofa, yes, right there, my shining young moon. I still can't believe it... Eh, Rakitin, if only you had brought him yesterday or the day before! But I'm glad anyway. Maybe it's even better that he came now, at this moment, and not the day before yesterday."

She cheerfully sat down next to Alyosha on the sofa, looking at him with real delight. And she truly was happy—she hadn't been lying when she said so. Her eyes were bright, and her lips curled into a warm, kind smile. Alyosha hadn't expected to see such a gentle expression on her face. He had barely known her until the day before, and after witnessing the cruel trick she played on Katerina Ivanovna, he had formed a troubling image of her. But now, to his surprise, she was completely different from what he had imagined. Though he was weighed down by his own grief, Alyosha couldn't help but look at her closely. Her entire demeanor had changed for the better—there was hardly any trace of the over-the-top sweetness or seductive movements that had unsettled him before. Now, she was simple and good-natured, her gestures quick and straightforward, though clearly excited.

"Everything is happening today!" she went on, talking excitedly. "And why I'm so happy to see you, Alyosha, I don't even know! If you asked me, I couldn't tell you."

"Oh, come on, you know why you're happy," Rakitin said with a smirk. "You've been pestering me to bring him. You must've had a reason."

"I had another reason before, but not anymore. That's done with. This isn't the time for that. You know, I'm feeling so generous right now. You should sit down too, Rakitin. Why are you still standing? Oh, you've already sat down? Of course, there's no way Rakitin would forget to look after himself. Look, Alyosha, he's sitting there across from us, pretending to be offended because I didn't ask him to sit first. Ugh, Rakitin's always so touchy!" Grushenka laughed. "Don't be mad, Rakitin. I'm in a good mood today. Why do you look so sad, Alyosha? Are you afraid of me?" She leaned in, peeking into his eyes playfully.

"He's upset. His elder didn't get his promotion," Rakitin said with a booming voice.

"What promotion?"

"His elder's body smells bad."

"What? That's just mean! You're trying to say something nasty. Stop it, you fool! Let me sit on your lap, Alyosha, like this." She suddenly leaped forward, laughing, and sat on his knee like a little kitten, wrapping her right arm around his neck. "I'll cheer you up, my sweet boy. Really, will you let me sit here? You won't be mad? If you want me to move, just say so."

Alyosha stayed silent. He sat frozen, hearing her words, "If you tell me, I'll get off," but didn't respond. But unlike what Rakitin, who was watching him bitterly from his corner, might have thought, there was no improper feeling in Alyosha's heart. His deep sorrow overpowered any other emotion, and had he been able to think clearly at that moment, he would have realized that his grief was like a shield, protecting him from any temptation. Despite his overwhelming sadness, Alyosha couldn't help but notice something strange. This woman, who had once terrified him, now didn't scare him at all. Instead of fear, he felt a pure and intense interest in her—a feeling completely free of the fear he had once had.

"You've been talking nonsense long enough," Rakitin broke in. "You should bring us some champagne. You owe me some, remember?"

"Yes, I do! Alyosha, did you know I promised him champagne if he brought you? I'll drink some too! Fenya, Fenya, bring the bottle Mitya left! Hurry! Even though I'm usually so stingy, I'll share a bottle—though not for you, Rakitin, you're just a toadstool. But he's a falcon! And even though my heart is full of other things, I'll drink with you. I'm in the mood for a little fun."

"But what's going on with you? What's this message you're waiting for? Or is it a secret?" Rakitin asked curiously, doing his best to ignore how often she was brushing him off.

"Oh, it's no secret, and you already know about it," Grushenka said, suddenly sounding anxious. She turned her head toward Rakitin and shifted a little away from Alyosha, though she still had her arm around his neck. "My officer is coming, Rakitin. He's finally coming."

"I heard he was coming, but is he really that close?"

"He's in Mokroe now. He's supposed to send a messenger from there. That's what he wrote in the letter I got today. I'm expecting the messenger any minute."

"No way! Why is he in Mokroe?"

"That's a long story. I've told you enough."

"Mitya's going to be up to something when he finds out! Does he know yet?"

"Know? Of course not. If he knew, there would be a murder. But I'm not afraid of that anymore, not even his knife. Stop reminding me of Dmitri Fyodorovitch, Rakitin. He's bruised my heart, and I don't want to think about that right now. I want to focus on Alyosha here. I want to look at Alyosha... Smile at me, dear. Cheer up, smile at my silliness, at my happiness. Ah, he's smiling! He's smiling! He looks at me so kindly. You know, Alyosha, I've been thinking all this time that you were mad at me because of the other day, because of that young lady. I was awful, that's true. But it's actually a good thing it happened that way. It was terrible, but in a way, it was for the best." Grushenka smiled dreamily, and a hint of something cruel flickered in her smile. "Mitya told me she screamed that I 'should be whipped.' I really did insult her horribly. She wanted to make a conquest of me, win me over with her chocolates. No, it's good it ended like that." She smiled again. "But I'm still afraid you might be angry."

"Yes, that's actually true," Rakitin chimed in, sounding genuinely surprised. "Alyosha, she's really scared of you, like you're some harmless little bird."

"He's harmless to you, Rakitin, because you have no conscience, that's why! You see, I love him with all my heart, that's how it is! Alyosha, do you believe I love you with all my soul?"

"Ah, you shameless woman! She's confessing her love to you, Alyosha!"

"Well, so what if I am? I love him!"

"And what about your officer? And that precious message from Mokroe?"

"That's completely different."

"That's just how women think!"

"Don't make me mad, Rakitin," Grushenka interrupted him, her voice full of heat. "This is something different. I love Alyosha in a different way. It's true, Alyosha, I had sneaky intentions towards you before. I'm a horrible, violent person. But sometimes, I've looked at you like you're my conscience. I've kept thinking, 'How could someone like him not despise someone as horrible as me?' I thought that just two days ago, when I ran home from that young lady's house. I've thought of you like that for a long time, Alyosha, and Mitya knows. I've talked to him about it. Mitya understands. Can you believe it, I sometimes look at you and feel so ashamed of myself. And how, or when, I started thinking of you this way, I can't remember."

Fenya came in, bringing a tray with an uncorked bottle and three glasses of champagne, setting it down on the table.

"Here's the champagne!" Rakitin exclaimed. "You're excited, Agrafena Alexandrovna, and not yourself. Once you've had a glass of champagne, you'll be ready to dance. Eh, they didn't even do that right," he added, looking at the bottle. "The old woman poured it out in the kitchen, and now the bottle's warm and uncorked. Oh well, I'll have some anyway." He walked over to the table, took a glass, downed it in one gulp, and poured himself another.

"You don't come across champagne often," he said, licking his lips. "Now, Alyosha, grab a glass, show us what you can do! What should we drink to? The gates of paradise? Go on, Grushenka, you drink to the gates of paradise, too."

"What gates of paradise?" she asked, taking a glass. Alyosha took his, tasted it, and put it back.

"No, I'd better not," he said softly, with a gentle smile. "And you bragged!" Rakitin teased.

"Well, if that's the case, I won't either," Grushenka joined in, "I really don't want any. You can drink the whole bottle yourself, Rakitin. If Alyosha drinks, then I will."

"What touching sentimentality!" Rakitin mocked, "and she's sitting on his knee too! He's got something to grieve about, but what's your excuse? He's rebelling against God and is ready to eat sausage."

"How's that?" she asked.

"His elder passed away today, Father Zossima, the saint."

"So Father Zossima is dead?" Grushenka gasped. "Oh my God, I didn't know!" She crossed herself quickly. "Goodness, what have I been doing, sitting on his knee like this at such a moment!" She immediately jumped off his knee and sat down on the sofa.

Alyosha gave her a long, wondering look, and a light seemed to brighten his face.

"Rakitin," he said suddenly, in a firm and loud voice, "don't mock me for rebelling against God. I don't want to be angry with you, so you should be kinder, too. I've lost a treasure, something you've never had, and you can't judge me now. You should look at her— see how she feels for me? I came here looking for something wicked, drawn to evil because I was feeling evil myself, but I found a true sister, I found a treasure—a loving heart. She pitied me just now.... Agrafena Alexandrovna, I'm talking about you. You've lifted my soul from the depths."

Alyosha's lips were trembling, and he was trying to catch his breath.

"She saved you, did she?" Rakitin sneered spitefully. "And she meant to trap you, don't you realize?"

"Wait, Rakitin." Grushenka jumped up. "Quiet, both of you. I'll tell you everything. Alyosha, your words make me feel ashamed because I'm bad and not good—that's what I am. And you, Rakitin, shut up, because you're lying. I had the low idea of trapping him, but now you're lying, things are different now. And don't let me hear another word from you, Rakitin."

Grushenka said all of this with deep emotion.

"They're both crazy," Rakitin said, looking at them in astonishment. "I feel like I'm in a madhouse. They're both so emotional they'll start crying any minute."

"I am going to cry, I will," Grushenka repeated. "He called me his sister, and I'll never forget that. But listen, Rakitin, even though I'm bad, I once gave away an onion."

"An onion? You really are crazy."

Rakitin was baffled by their excitement. He was offended and annoyed, though he should have realized that both of them were going through a spiritual crisis, the kind that doesn't happen often in life. But even though Rakitin was highly sensitive about anything related to himself, he was completely blind to the emotions and feelings of others—partly because of his youth, and partly because of his deep self-centeredness.

"You see, Alyosha," Grushenka turned to him with a nervous laugh. "I was bragging when I told Rakitin I gave away an onion, but I'm not bragging to you. It's just a story, but it's a nice one. I heard it when I was a child from Matryona, my cook, who's still with me. It goes like this: Once upon a time, there was a peasant woman, and she was very wicked. When she died, she didn't leave behind a single good deed. The devils grabbed her and threw her into the lake of fire. But her guardian angel stood there, trying to think of one good deed she had done to tell God. 'She once pulled up an onion in her garden,' the angel said, 'and gave it to a beggar woman.' And God replied, 'Take that onion, hold it out to her, and if she grabs hold, pull her out. If the onion holds, she can come to paradise, but if it breaks, she has to stay in the lake.' So the angel hurried to the woman, held out the onion, and said, 'Grab on, and I'll pull you out.' He began to pull her out gently. He had just about pulled her all the way out when the other sinners in the lake saw what was happening and grabbed onto her so they could be pulled out too. But she was a wicked woman, and she started kicking them away. 'I'm the one being pulled out, not you! It's my onion, not yours.' And the moment she said that, the onion broke, and she fell back into the lake, where she's still burning. The angel cried and walked away. That's the story, Alyosha; I know it by heart because I am that wicked woman. I bragged to Rakitin that I gave away an onion, but to you, I'll admit: I've only ever given away one onion in my whole life—that's the only good thing I've ever done. So don't praise me, Alyosha, don't think I'm good. I'm bad, I'm a wicked woman, and when you praise me, it makes me feel ashamed. Oh, I have to confess everything. Listen, Alyosha. I was so desperate to get you here that I promised Rakitin twenty-five roubles if he would bring you to me. Wait, Rakitin!"

She hurried over to the table, opened a drawer, pulled out a purse, and took out a twenty-five-rouble note.

"What nonsense!" cried Rakitin, visibly uncomfortable.

"Take it, Rakitin. I owe it to you, and I know you won't refuse it—you asked for it yourself." And she threw the note at him.

"As if I'd refuse it," Rakitin said, obviously embarrassed but trying to act casual. "It'll come in handy. Fools exist for wise men to take advantage of."

"And now, be quiet, Rakitin. What I'm about to say isn't for you. Sit over there in that corner and keep quiet. You don't like us, so just stay silent."

"What should I like you for?" Rakitin growled, not hiding his irritation. He stuffed the twenty-five rouble note into his pocket, feeling embarrassed that Alyosha had seen it. He had planned to get the money later, without Alyosha knowing, and now, feeling ashamed, he grew angrier. Until that moment, he had tried not to argue too much with Grushenka, despite her snubbing, since he still hoped to get something out of her. But now he was mad too.

"People love others for a reason, but what have either of you done for me?"

"You should love people without needing a reason, like Alyosha does."

"How does he love you? What has he done to show it, that you make such a big deal about it?"

Grushenka was standing in the middle of the room. Her voice was full of passion, and there was a hysterical tone to it.

"Hush, Rakitin, you know nothing about us! And don't you dare talk to me like that again. How dare you speak to me so boldly! Sit in that corner and be quiet, like you're my servant! And now, Alyosha, I'll tell you the whole truth, so you can see what a wretch I really am! I'm not talking to Rakitin, but to you. I wanted to ruin you, Alyosha, that's the honest truth; I really did. I wanted it so badly that I paid Rakitin to bring you here. And why did I want to do that? You didn't know anything about it, Alyosha. You avoided me, and when you passed by, you wouldn't even look at me. I've looked at you a hundred times before today; I asked everyone about you. Your face stuck in my heart. 'He despises me,' I thought. 'He won't even glance at me.' And it bothered me so much that I wondered why I was so scared of a boy. I'll trap him and laugh at him. I was full of anger and spite. Can you believe it? Nobody here would even dare think about coming to Agrafena Alexandrovna with any bad intentions. Old Kuzma is the only man I have any dealings with here; I was basically sold to him. The devil brought us together, but there's been no one else. But when I looked at you, I thought, I'll trap him and laugh at him. You see how mean I am, and yet you called me your sister! And now the man who hurt me is back; I'm sitting here waiting for a message from him. Do you know what that man was to me? Five years ago, when Kuzma brought me here, I would lock myself away so no one could see or hear me. I was a silly, young girl; I used to sit here crying. I would lie awake all night, thinking, 'Where is he now, the man who wronged me? He's probably laughing with some other woman.' If only I could see him again, I thought, I'd get my revenge! At night, I would cry into my pillow in the dark, tormenting myself on purpose, enjoying my anger. 'I'll get my revenge, I'll get my revenge!' I would scream in the dark. And when I thought about how I might never do anything to him, that he was probably laughing at me or had forgotten about me completely, I would throw myself on the floor, crying helplessly, shaking until dawn. In the morning, I would get up more bitter than ever, ready to tear the world apart. And what do you think happened? I started saving money. I grew harder, put on weight—did I grow wiser, you ask? No, nobody sees it, nobody knows it, but when night falls, sometimes I still lie there like I did five years ago, clenching my teeth, crying through the night, thinking, 'I'll get my revenge!' Do you hear? Now you understand me. A month ago, I got a letter—he was coming, he was a widower, and he wanted to see me. I couldn't breathe. Then I thought, 'If he comes and calls for me, I'll go crawling back to him like a whipped dog.' I couldn't believe it. Am I really that low? Will I run back to him or not? And I've been so furious with myself all month that I'm even worse now than I was five years ago. Do you see now, Alyosha, what a hateful and vengeful person I am? I've told you the whole truth! I used Mitya to stop myself from running back to the other man. Quiet, Rakitin, this isn't for you to judge me. I'm not talking to you. Before you came in, I was lying here, waiting, thinking about my entire future, and you'll never know what was in my heart. Yes, Alyosha, tell your lady not to be angry with me for what happened the other day.... Nobody in the world knows what I'm going through, and no one ever will.... Maybe I'll even take a knife with me today. I can't decide…"

At this dramatic moment, Grushenka broke down. She covered her face with her hands, threw herself onto the sofa pillows, and sobbed like a child.

Alyosha stood up and walked over to Rakitin.

"Misha," he said, "don't be angry. She hurt you, but don't hold a grudge. You heard what she said, right? You can't ask too much from people; you have to be merciful."

Alyosha said this instinctively, feeling like he had to speak, and he turned to Rakitin. If Rakitin hadn't been there, Alyosha would've said it to the air. But Rakitin looked at him with a mocking smile, and Alyosha stopped.

"You're all charged up from your elder's teachings last night, and now you have to preach to me, huh, Alexey, man of God?" Rakitin sneered with hatred.

"Don't laugh, Rakitin, don't smile, don't speak ill of the dead—he was the best man in the world!" Alyosha cried, his voice trembling with tears. "I didn't speak to you as a judge, but as the lowest of the low. What am I compared to her? I came here ready to ruin myself, and I thought, 'Who cares?' in my cowardice. But her, after five years of suffering, just one word spoken from the heart, and she forgets everything, forgives everything, and cries. The man who hurt her is back, he sends for her, and she forgives him instantly, rushes to meet him with joy, and she won't even take a knife with her. She won't! No, I'm not like that. I don't know about you, Misha, but I'm not like that. It's a lesson to me. She's more loving than we are. Have you ever heard her talk like this before, about what she's just told us? No, you haven't. If you had, you would've understood her long ago.... And the person who was insulted the other day should forgive her too! She will, once she knows. And she'll find out. This soul isn't at peace yet, we have to be gentle with it. There might be a treasure in that soul."

Alyosha stopped speaking, his breath catching in his throat. Despite his bad mood, Rakitin stared at him in surprise. He had never expected such a passionate outburst from the usually calm Alyosha.

"She's found someone to defend her! What, are you in love with her? Agrafena Alexandrovna, our monk's really fallen for you; you've won him over!" Rakitin said with a nasty laugh.

Grushenka lifted her head from the pillow, her tear-streaked face shining with a tender smile as she looked at Alyosha.

"Leave him alone, Alyosha, my cherub; you see what he's like, he's not someone you should talk to. Mihail Osipovitch," she turned to Rakitin, "I was going to apologize for being rude to you, but now I don't want to. Alyosha, come here, sit next to me." She waved him over with a happy smile. "That's right, sit here. Tell me," she shook his hand and looked into his face, smiling, "tell me, do I love that man or not? The man who wronged me, do I love him or not? Before you came, I was lying here in the dark, asking myself that. Decide for me, Alyosha; the time has come, and I'll do what you say. Should I forgive him or not?"

"You've already forgiven him," Alyosha said, smiling.

"Yes, I really have forgiven him," Grushenka murmured, lost in thought. "What a pathetic heart I have! To my pathetic heart!" She grabbed a glass from the table, gulped it down, raised it in the air, and smashed it on the floor. The glass shattered with a loud crash. A cruel edge appeared in her smile.

"Or maybe I haven't forgiven him," she said with a threatening tone, lowering her eyes to the floor as if talking to herself. "Maybe my heart is just getting ready to forgive. I'll wrestle with my heart. You see, Alyosha, I've grown to love my tears over these five years... Maybe I only love my anger, not him..."

"Well, I wouldn't want to be in his shoes," Rakitin hissed. "Well, you won't be, Rakitin. You'll never be in his shoes. You're fit to clean my shoes, Rakitin, that's where you belong. You'll never get a woman like me... and maybe he won't either..."

"Won't he? Then why are you all dressed up like that?" Rakitin sneered.

"Don't mock me for dressing up, Rakitin, you don't know what's in my heart! If I wanted to, I could rip off these clothes right now, this very minute," she cried in a ringing voice. "You don't know what this is for, Rakitin! Maybe when I see him, I'll say, 'Have you ever seen me look like this before?' He left me as a sick, crying 17-year-old girl. I'll sit by him, charm him, and rile him up. 'Do you see me now?' I'll say to him; 'Well, that's all you get, my dear, there's many a slip 'twixt the cup and the lip!' Maybe that's why I'm dressed up, Rakitin." Grushenka finished with a bitter laugh. "I'm full of anger, Alyosha. I'll tear off my clothes,

I'll destroy my beauty, I'll burn my face, slash it with a knife, and become a beggar. If I feel like it, I won't go anywhere now, to see anyone. If I feel like it, I'll give Kuzma back everything he's ever given me tomorrow, all his money, and I'll go work as a cleaner for the rest of my life. You think I wouldn't do it, Rakitin, that I wouldn't dare? I would, I would, I could do it right now, just don't push me... and I'll tell him to go to hell, I'll laugh in his face, and he'll never see me again!"

She screamed the last words hysterically, then collapsed again, burying her face in the pillow, shaking with sobs.

Rakitin stood up.

"It's time to go," he said. "It's late; we'll get locked out of the monastery."

Grushenka jumped up.

"You're not leaving, Alyosha, are you?" she cried, full of sorrow. "What are you doing to me? You've stirred up all my feelings, tortured me, and now you're going to leave me to face this night alone!"

"He can't stay with you all night! But if he wants to, he can! I'll go alone," Rakitin sneered sarcastically.

"Shut up, you snake!" Grushenka snapped at him. "You've never said the things to me that he has."

"What did he say that's so special?" Rakitin asked irritably.

"I can't say, I don't know. I don't even know what he said. It went straight to my heart... He's the first person, the only one who has ever felt sorry for me. That's what it is. Why didn't you come sooner, you angel?" She suddenly fell to her knees before him in a frenzy. "I've been waiting all my life for someone like you. I knew someone like you would come and forgive me. I always believed that, no matter how awful I am, someone would truly love me, not just with some dirty kind of love!"

"What have I done for you?" Alyosha asked, bending over her with a tender smile and gently holding her hands. "I only gave you an onion, nothing more than a little onion. That's all!"

He was so moved that he was on the verge of tears himself. At that moment, there was a sudden noise in the hallway. Someone had come in. Grushenka jumped up, looking scared. Fenya ran into the room, out of breath and excited.

"Mistress, mistress darling! A messenger just arrived," she shouted, breathless and full of joy. "A carriage from Mokroe, driven by Timofey, with three horses. They're getting fresh horses ready now… A letter, here's a letter, mistress."

She waved the letter in the air as she talked. Grushenka snatched it from her hand and rushed to the candle. It was just a short note, a few lines. She read it in an instant.

"He's called for me," she whispered, her face pale and twisted, with a sad smile. "He's whistling for me, telling me to crawl back like a dog."

But she only hesitated for a second. Suddenly, her face flushed, her cheeks glowing.

"I'm going!" she cried. "Five years of my life! Goodbye! Goodbye, Alyosha, my fate is sealed. Go, go, all of you, I don't want to see you again! Grushenka is off to start a new life… Don't hold a grudge against me either, Rakitin. I might be going to my death! Ugh, I feel like I'm drunk!"

She suddenly rushed out of the room and into her bedroom.

"Well, she's not thinking about us anymore!" Rakitin grumbled. "Let's go, or we'll hear more of her screaming. I'm tired of all these tears and cries."

Alyosha let Rakitin lead him out without a word. In the yard, a covered cart was waiting. The horses had been unhitched, and men were running around with lanterns. Three fresh horses were being led through the open gate. But as Alyosha and Rakitin reached the bottom of the steps, Grushenka's bedroom window suddenly opened, and she called out to Alyosha in a clear voice.

"Alyosha, give my greetings to your brother Mitya and tell him not to hold a grudge against me, even though I've brought him so much pain. And tell him this in my own words: 'Grushenka has fallen for a scoundrel, not for you, noble heart.' And also tell him that Grushenka only loved him for one hour, just one short hour, and that he should remember that hour for the rest of his life—tell him, 'Grushenka tells you to!'"

She ended with a voice full of sobs. The window slammed shut.

"Hm, hm!" Rakitin grumbled, laughing. "She ruins your brother's life and then tells him to remember it forever! What cruelty!"

Alyosha didn't reply. It was as if he hadn't heard. He walked quickly beside Rakitin as if in a terrible rush, lost in thought, moving mechanically. Rakitin felt a sharp sting, like he'd been hit in an old wound. He had expected something very different when he brought Grushenka and Alyosha together. What had actually happened was nothing like what he had imagined.

"He's a Pole, you know, that officer of hers," he began again, trying to control himself. "But he's not really an officer anymore. He worked in customs somewhere in Siberia, near the Chinese border. Some pathetic little Pole, I'm sure. Lost his job, they say. He probably heard that Grushenka's saved up some money, so now he's come crawling back—that's the whole mystery."

Again, Alyosha didn't seem to hear him. Rakitin couldn't hold back anymore.

"So, you've saved the sinner?" he laughed bitterly. "Did you guide the Magdalene back to the right path? Did you drive out her seven demons? Looks like the miracle you were hoping for just happened!"

"Quiet, Rakitin," Alyosha replied, his heart aching.

"So, you look down on me now because of those twenty-five roubles? You think I sold out my friend? But you're not Christ, and I'm not Judas."

"Oh, Rakitin, I promise, I had forgotten all about it," Alyosha cried. "You're the one reminding me now…."

But that was too much for Rakitin.

"Curse you all!" he suddenly shouted. "Why did I ever bother with you? I don't want anything to do with you from now on. Go your own way, there's your road!"

And with that, he abruptly turned down another street, leaving Alyosha alone in the dark. Alyosha left the town and walked across the fields to the monastery.

Chapter 4: Cana of Galilee

It was very late, according to the monastery's schedule, when Alyosha returned to the hermitage; the doorkeeper let him in through a special entrance. It was already nine o'clock—the hour for rest and calm after such an agitated day for everyone. Alyosha carefully opened the door and entered the elder's cell where his coffin now stood. No one was in the cell except for Father Païssy, who was reading the Gospel alone over the coffin, and the young novice Porfiry, who, exhausted from the previous night's conversation and the disturbing events of the day, was sleeping deeply on the floor of the other room. Though Father Païssy heard Alyosha enter, he did not even look in his direction.

Alyosha turned to the right from the door to the corner, fell on his knees, and began to pray.

His soul was overflowing with mixed feelings; no single sensation stood out distinctly; rather, one drove out another in a slow, continuous cycle. Yet, there was a sweetness in his heart, and, strangely, Alyosha was not surprised by it. Again, he saw the coffin in front of him, holding the hidden, lifeless figure so dear to him, but the weeping and sharp sorrow he had felt that morning no longer ached in his soul. As soon as he entered, he knelt before the coffin, just as if it were a holy shrine, but joy, yes, joy, was glowing in his mind and heart. The single window of the cell was open, and the air was fresh and cool. "So, the smell must have gotten stronger, if they opened the window," Alyosha thought. But even this thought, about the smell of decay, which had seemed so terrible and humiliating a few hours earlier, no longer made him feel sad or indignant. He began praying quietly, but soon noticed that he was praying almost mechanically. Thoughts drifted through his soul, flashing like stars, only to disappear again immediately, making room for others. Yet, there was a sense of wholeness in his soul—something steadfast and comforting—and he was aware of it within himself. At times, he would begin praying with great fervor, wishing to pour out all his gratitude and love.

But as soon as he started to pray, he would suddenly find himself thinking of something else, drifting into thought, forgetting both his prayer and what had interrupted it. He began to listen to what Father Païssy was reading, but slowly, worn out with exhaustion, he began to doze off.

"And on the third day there was a wedding in Cana of Galilee," Father Païssy read. "And the mother of Jesus was there. Jesus and His disciples had also been invited to the wedding."

"A wedding? What's that?... A wedding!" the word swirled in Alyosha's mind. "There's happiness for her, too... She's gone to the feast... No, she hasn't taken the knife... That was just a dramatic phrase... Well... dramatic phrases should be forgiven, they should be. They give comfort... Without them, sorrow would be too heavy for people to bear. Rakitin has gone off to the back alley. As long as Rakitin broods over his wrongs, he'll always take the back alley... But the high road... The road is wide and straight, and bright as crystal, with the sun at the end of it... Ah!... What's being read?"

"And when they wanted wine, the mother of Jesus said to Him, 'They have no wine,'" Alyosha heard.

"Ah, yes, I didn't want to miss that part, I love that passage: it's Cana of Galilee, the first miracle... Ah, that miracle! That sweet miracle! Christ didn't come to the sadness of men, but to their joy. His first miracle was to bring gladness to people... 'He who loves mankind also loves their joy'... He kept repeating that, it was one of His main ideas... 'There's no life without joy,' Mitya says... Yes, Mitya... 'Everything true and good is always full of forgiveness,' he used to say that too..."

"Jesus said to her, 'Woman, what does this have to do with you and Me? My time has not yet come.' His mother said to the servants, 'Whatever He tells you to do, do it.'"

"Do it... Joy, the joy of some poor, very poor, people... Of course, they were poor if they didn't have enough wine even at a wedding... Historians write that the people around Lake Gennesaret were some of the poorest imaginable... And another great heart, His Mother, knew that He didn't come just to make that great and terrible sacrifice. She knew that His heart was open, even to the simple, humble celebrations of some unknown, unimportant people who had warmly invited Him to their poor wedding. 'My time has not yet come,' He said to her, probably with a gentle smile. (He must have smiled kindly at her.) And was He really here on earth just to make sure there was enough wine at poor people's weddings? And yet, He went and did as she asked... Ah, he's reading again..."

"Jesus said to them, 'Fill the waterpots with water.' And they filled them up to the brim. And He said, 'Now draw some out and take it to the master of the feast.' And they took it. When the master tasted the water that had been turned into wine, he did not know where it came from, but the servants who had drawn the water knew. The master called the bridegroom over and said, 'Every man serves the good wine first, and when people have drunk freely, then the cheap wine. But you have saved the best wine until now.'"

"But what's this? What's this? Why is the room getting wider?... Ah, yes... It's the wedding, of course... Here are the guests, the young couple, the joyful crowd... Where's the wise master of the feast? But wait, who's that? Who? The walls are moving back... Who's rising from the great table? What!... He's here too? But he's in the coffin... and yet he's here too. He has stood up, he sees me, he's coming towards me... God!"

Yes, he was coming towards him. That little, thin old man, with tiny wrinkles on his face, joyful and softly laughing. There was no coffin now, and he was dressed just as he had been yesterday, sitting with them when the visitors gathered around him. His face was uncovered, his eyes were shining. How was this possible? He, too, had been called to the feast. He, too, was at the wedding in Cana of Galilee.

"Yes, my dear, I've been called too. I've been invited," he heard a gentle voice saying over him. "Why are you hiding here? Come and join us."

It was his voice, Father Zossima's voice. It must be him, since he was calling to him!

The elder took Alyosha's hand and lifted him to his feet.

"We are rejoicing," the little, thin old man went on. "We are drinking the new wine, the wine of great new joy. Do you see how many guests there are? Here are the bride and groom, here is the wise master of the feast, tasting the new wine. Why are you surprised to see me? I gave an onion to a beggar, so I'm here too. And many others here have given nothing more than an onion—just one little onion. What are all our deeds? And you, my gentle one, you, my kind boy, you, too, knew how to give a starving woman an onion today. Begin your work, dear one, begin it, gentle one... Do you see our Sun, do you see Him?"

"I'm afraid... I don't dare look," Alyosha whispered.

"Do not fear Him. He is awe-inspiring in His greatness, overwhelming in His glory, but endlessly merciful. He became like us out of love and is rejoicing with us. He is turning the water into wine so the joy of the guests won't be cut short. He is expecting new guests, calling them constantly, forever... There, they are bringing more wine. Do you see? They are bringing the vessels..."

Something lit up in Alyosha's heart, something filled it until it hurt, and tears of joy welled up from deep within him. He stretched out his hands, let out a cry, and woke up.

Once again, there was the coffin, the open window, and the soft, solemn, and clear reading of the Gospel. But Alyosha wasn't really paying attention to the reading. Strangely, he had fallen asleep on his knees, but now he found himself standing. Suddenly, as if pulled forward, he took three quick, strong steps straight to the coffin. His shoulder brushed against Father Païssy, but he didn't notice. Father Païssy briefly lifted his eyes from the book he was reading but quickly looked back down when he saw something unusual happening with the boy. Alyosha stared for half a minute at the coffin, at the still, lifeless figure inside it, covered and motionless, with the icon on his chest and the peaked cap with the octagonal cross on his head. He had just been hearing the voice of this man, and the sound of that voice still echoed in his ears. He was listening, still expecting to hear more, but suddenly he turned sharply and walked out of the cell.

He didn't pause on the steps either; instead, he hurried down them. His soul, full of overflowing joy, longed for freedom, for space, for the wide-open air. The vast sky above him, filled with soft, shining stars, stretched out endlessly. The Milky Way flowed in two pale streams from the top of the sky down to the horizon. The fresh, still, quiet night wrapped itself around the earth. The white towers and golden domes of the cathedral shone against the deep blue sky. The beautiful autumn flowers in the garden beds around the house were quietly resting until morning. The silence of the earth seemed to melt into the silence of the heavens. The mystery of the earth became one with the mystery of the stars.

Alyosha stood there, gazing, and suddenly threw himself down onto the ground. He didn't know why he felt the need to embrace it. He couldn't have explained why he so desperately wanted to kiss the earth, to kiss it all over. But he kissed it, crying, sobbing, and soaking it with his tears. He made a passionate vow to love it, to love it forever and ever. "Water the earth with the tears of your joy, and love those tears," echoed in his soul.

What was he crying for?

Oh! In his joy, he was crying even for the stars, shining down on him from the endless reaches of space, and "he wasn't ashamed of that joy." It was as if there were invisible threads connecting his soul to all those countless worlds of God, and his soul trembled as it touched those other worlds. He longed to forgive everyone for everything and to beg for forgiveness. Not for himself, but for all people, for all and for everything. "And others are praying for me too," echoed again in his soul. But with every passing second, he felt more clearly, almost physically, that something strong and unshakable, as solid as the sky above, had entered into his soul. It was as if a great idea had taken control of his mind, and it was going to stay with him for all his life, forever and ever. He had fallen to the earth as a weak boy, but he rose up as a determined champion, and he knew and felt it all at once, right in the middle of his joy. Alyosha would never, ever forget that moment for the rest of his life.

"Someone visited my soul in that hour," he would say later, fully believing in the truth of his words.

Three days later, he left the monastery, following the instructions of his elder, who had told him to "go out into the world."

Book 8: Mitya

Chapter 1: Kuzma Samsonov

But Dmitri, to whom Grushenka, rushing off to start a new life, had left her last words, asking him to remember the hour of her love forever, knew nothing about what had happened to her. At that very moment, he was in a state of feverish agitation and activity. For the last two days, his mind had been in such a wild state that he could have easily fallen ill with brain fever, as he said himself later. Alyosha had been unable to find him the day before, and Ivan hadn't managed to meet him at the tavern on the same day. The people at his lodging, following his instructions, kept his movements hidden.

During those two days, Dmitri had been running all over the place, "fighting his fate and trying to save himself," as he explained afterward. For a few hours, he had even left town for some urgent business, though it was painful for him to be away from Grushenka even for a moment. Later, all of this was explained in detail and supported by documents, but for now, we will only focus on the most important events of those two terrible days that came just before the dreadful catastrophe that hit him so suddenly.

Although Grushenka had indeed loved him for an hour, genuinely and sincerely, she also sometimes tortured him cruelly and without mercy. The worst part was that he never knew what she intended to do. He couldn't win her over by force or kindness—she wouldn't give in to anything. He knew very well that she would only get angry and turn away from him completely if he tried, and he already understood this. Dmitri suspected, quite accurately, that Grushenka was going through her own inner struggle. He sensed she was deeply unsure of herself, trying to make a decision but unable to do so. That's why, with a sinking heart, he guessed— correctly, though painfully—that at times, she must simply hate him and his intense love. And that was likely true. But Dmitri couldn't understand what was troubling Grushenka so much. For him, the whole agonizing issue was between him and Fyodor Pavlovitch.

Here, it's important to mention one fact: Dmitri firmly believed that Fyodor Pavlovitch had either already offered or would offer Grushenka marriage. He didn't believe for a second that the old man thought he could win her over with just three thousand roubles. Dmitri had come to this conclusion based on his knowledge of Grushenka's character. This is why, at times, he believed that all of Grushenka's uncertainty stemmed from her not knowing which of them—him or Fyodor Pavlovitch—would be better for her.

Strangely, during those days, Dmitri never thought about the return of the "officer," the man who had played such a destructive role in Grushenka's life and whose arrival she was anxiously awaiting. It's true that lately Grushenka hadn't mentioned him much. Still, Dmitri was well aware of the letter she had received from this man a month ago because she had told him about it herself. He even knew part of what the letter said. In a moment of anger, Grushenka had shown Dmitri the letter, but to her surprise, he didn't take it very seriously. It's hard to say why. Maybe, overwhelmed by the horrifying struggle he was having with his own father over Grushenka, Dmitri simply couldn't imagine anything worse happening—at least, not for the time being. He didn't believe that a suitor who had disappeared for five years would suddenly show up again, let alone that he would arrive soon. Besides, the "officer's" first letter, which Dmitri had seen, had only vaguely mentioned the possibility of him coming back. The letter was filled with sentimental, high-flown language and didn't seem serious. However, it's important to note that Grushenka had hidden the last lines of the letter from Dmitri, which mentioned the officer's return more clearly. Dmitri also remembered noticing a certain proud disdain on Grushenka's face when she read the letter from Siberia. She didn't tell him anything more about her interactions with the officer, and over time, Dmitri had completely forgotten about the man's existence.

He felt that no matter what happened next, his final confrontation with Fyodor Pavlovitch was coming soon, and it had to be settled before anything else. With a heavy heart, he waited anxiously for Grushenka to make her decision, always believing it would come suddenly, in a moment of impulse. He imagined she would suddenly say to him, "Take me, I'm yours forever," and that would be it. He would grab her and take her away immediately to the ends of the earth. Yes, he would take her far, far away—to the farthest corner of Russia, if not the world—then he would marry her, and they would live together in secret, so that no one would know anything about them, anywhere. Then, a new life would begin right away!

He feverishly dreamed of this new, better, and "virtuous" life ("It must, it must be virtuous!"). He longed for this change, this renewal. The filthy, muddy pit he had sunk into by his own choice disgusted him, and like many men in such situations, he believed that a change of scenery would solve everything. If only it weren't for these people, if only it weren't for these circumstances, if only he could get away from this cursed place, then he could be completely transformed, starting fresh on a new path. That's what he believed, and that's what he longed for.

But all of this depended on one condition: Grushenka's decision. There was another possibility, a darker and more terrible one. She might suddenly say, "Go away. I've made a deal with Fyodor Pavlovitch. I'm going to marry him, and I don't need you." And then... but then... Dmitri didn't know what would happen next. Even up until the last moment, he didn't know. To his credit, he hadn't planned anything. He had no specific intentions, no crime in mind. He was simply watching, waiting in agony, while hoping for the best possible outcome. He tried to push away any other thoughts. But as he waited for that happy outcome, a new and pressing worry appeared—a problem he couldn't ignore.

If Grushenka were to say, "I'm yours; take me away," how could he do it? Where would he find the money to take her away? At that moment, all financial support from Fyodor Pavlovitch, which had been flowing steadily for years, had suddenly stopped. Grushenka had money, of course, but Dmitri felt an intense and strange pride about this. He wanted to take her away and start their new life with his own money, not hers. The idea of taking her money filled him with disgust. I won't dwell on this or analyze it too much here, but that's how Dmitri felt at the time. This feeling may have come, in part, from the guilt he carried for taking Katerina Ivanovna's money dishonestly. "I've already been a scoundrel to one of them, and I'll just be a scoundrel again to the other," he thought. "And when Grushenka finds out, she won't want someone as low as me."

So where would he find the money? Where could he get the funds he needed? Without the money, everything would fall apart, and nothing could be done—"and all because I didn't have the money. Oh, the shame of it!"

To get ahead of the story: maybe Dmitri did know where to get the money, maybe he even knew where it was at that very moment. I won't say more about this now, as it will become clear later. But his main problem, though I'll explain it vaguely, was that to get the money he thought of, to have the right to take it, he first had to return the three thousand roubles he owed Katerina Ivanovna. If he didn't, "I'm just a common thief, a scoundrel, and I refuse to start a new life as a scoundrel," Dmitri decided. So, he made up his mind to do whatever it took to return that three thousand to Katerina Ivanovna, and that would come first.

The final stage of this decision only happened during the last few hours, after his most recent talk with Alyosha two days earlier, on the road, on the evening when Grushenka had insulted Katerina Ivanovna. After Alyosha told him what had happened, Dmitri admitted that he was a scoundrel and told Alyosha to tell Katerina Ivanovna that, if it would make her feel any better. After parting from his brother that night, Dmitri, in his frantic state, felt that it would be better "to kill and rob someone than fail to pay my debt to Katya. I'd rather everyone think I'm a murderer and thief, I'd rather go to Siberia, than have Katya say that I tricked her, stole her money, and used it to run away with Grushenka and start a new life! I can't do that!" So, Dmitri made up his mind, grinding his teeth, and at times he thought his brain would break under the pressure. But still, he kept going.

Strangely enough, even though it seemed like he had no hope— what chance did he have to raise that much money with nothing to his name?—he kept hoping, right until the end, that he would somehow find that three thousand roubles. He believed that the money would somehow come to him, like it might fall from the sky. This is how people like Dmitri think—people who have never had to earn money themselves, but who have only spent whatever came to them by inheritance or other lucky circumstances, without any effort on their part. His thoughts were a wild mess of fantasies right after he said goodbye to Alyosha two days ago, and his mind became tangled in confusion. That's how he ended up deciding on an outrageous plan. Maybe, for people like Dmitri, when they're in situations like this, the most impossible ideas are the first ones that come to mind, and they seem the most practical.

He suddenly decided to go to Samsonov, the merchant who had been Grushenka's protector, and propose a "business plan" to him, hoping to get all the money he needed from Samsonov right away. Dmitri had no doubts about the value of his plan— not even a little—and was only unsure about how Samsonov would react to it if he thought about it from any perspective other than a business one. Although Dmitri knew Samsonov by sight, they weren't acquaintances, and they had never spoken. But for some strange reason, Dmitri had long believed that the old man, who was near death, wouldn't object to Grushenka securing a respectable life and marrying a reliable man. Not only did Dmitri believe that Samsonov wouldn't object, but he also thought this was exactly what Samsonov wanted, and if the opportunity arose, he would be willing to help. Dmitri had picked up from some rumor—or maybe from something Grushenka said—that the old man would probably prefer him over Fyodor Pavlovitch as Grushenka's husband.

Many of the readers of my story might think that Dmitri showed a lot of insensitivity and lack of tact by counting on this kind of help, and by being ready to take his bride, so to speak, from the hands of her protector. I'll just point out that Dmitri saw Grushenka's past as something completely over. He looked at it with great pity and was determined, with all the passion of his love, that once Grushenka told him she loved him and would marry him, it would mean a new beginning for both of them—a new Grushenka and a new Dmitri, free from every vice. They would forgive each other, and they would start their lives fresh. As for Kuzma Samsonov, Dmitri thought of him as someone who had played an important role in Grushenka's distant past, even though she had never loved him. To Dmitri, Samsonov was now a figure of the past, completely irrelevant, as good as gone. In fact, Dmitri barely thought of Samsonov as a real person at all, because everyone in town knew that the old man was just a broken shell, whose relationship with Grushenka had long ago changed into something more like a father-daughter bond.

In any case, there was a lot of naivety on Dmitri's part in all of this, because despite all his faults, he was a very simple-hearted man. This simplicity was clear in how he seriously believed that old Kuzma, being close to death, must truly regret his past relationship with Grushenka, and that there was no one in the world more devoted to her and more eager to protect her than this now-harmless old man.

After his conversation with Alyosha at the crossroads, Dmitri barely slept that night. By ten o'clock the next morning, he was already at Samsonov's house, asking the servant to announce him. It was a large, dark, two-story house with a lodge and outbuildings. Samsonov's two married sons lived on the lower floor with their families, along with his elderly sister and his unmarried daughter. In the lodge, two of Samsonov's clerks lived, and one of them had a large family too. Both the lodge and the lower floor were overcrowded, but the old man kept the upper floor to himself. He wouldn't even let his daughter live up there with him, though she had to take care of him, and despite her asthma, she was forced to run upstairs to him at certain times or whenever he called for her.

The upper floor of the house had several large rooms, all furnished in an old-fashioned merchant style. There were long rows of heavy mahogany chairs lined up along the walls, glass chandeliers covered with shades, and gloomy mirrors hanging everywhere. These rooms were never used and always empty. The old man lived in just one room, a small, out-of-the-way bedroom, where an elderly servant woman with a headscarf and a young boy attended to him. The boy would often sit on a chest in the hallway. The old man could barely walk because his legs were swollen, and he was only occasionally lifted from his leather armchair. When he was moved, the old woman would help him walk up and down the room once or twice. He rarely spoke, even to her, and always seemed grumpy.

When the old man was told that the "captain" had arrived, he immediately refused to see him. But Mitya was persistent and sent his name up again. Samsonov questioned the boy in detail, asking what Mitya looked like, whether he was drunk, and if he seemed likely to cause trouble. The boy reported that Mitya was sober but refused to leave. The old man once again declined to meet him. Then, as Mitya had expected, he took out a pencil and paper, wrote a clear message that said, "Regarding important business concerning Agrafena Alexandrovna," and sent it to the old man.

After thinking it over for a moment, Samsonov told the boy to bring Mitya to the drawing room. He also sent the old servant woman downstairs to fetch his younger son and tell him to come upstairs immediately. This son was a tall man, over six feet, with incredible physical strength. He was clean-shaven and dressed in modern European clothes, unlike his father, who still wore a traditional kaftan and beard. The younger son arrived without saying a word because the entire family was terrified of the old man. Samsonov hadn't called his son because he feared Mitya (he wasn't a man easily scared), but because he wanted a witness in case something happened. Supported by his son and the young boy, the old man finally shuffled into the drawing room. It's likely he was very curious about Mitya.

The drawing room where Mitya waited was a vast, gloomy space that made people feel uneasy. It had two rows of windows, marble walls, and three enormous chandeliers with glass shades. Mitya sat nervously on a small chair near the entrance, waiting anxiously to learn his fate. When the old man appeared in the doorway, seventy feet away, Mitya jumped to his feet. He walked quickly toward the old man with his long military stride. Mitya was dressed sharply, wearing a frock coat, a round hat, and black gloves in his hands, just as he had been three days earlier during the family meeting with his father and brothers. The old man stood tall and stiff, waiting for Mitya to approach, and Mitya could feel that Samsonov was sizing him up as he walked closer. He was also struck by Samsonov's swollen face, especially his thick lower lip, which hung down like a bun.

The old man silently motioned Mitya to sit in a low chair by the sofa. Leaning on his son's arm, he groaned with effort as he lowered himself onto the sofa opposite Mitya. Watching his painful movements, Mitya immediately felt guilty and acutely aware of his own insignificance in front of this dignified man he had come to disturb.

"What do you want from me, sir?" the old man asked, speaking slowly, clearly, and sternly, but with politeness, once he was seated.

Mitya jumped, startled, then sat back down. He began speaking right away in a loud, frantic rush, waving his hands and practically in a state of desperation. It was obvious that he was a man cornered, on the edge of ruin, clinging to the last chance he had. Samsonov likely understood all of this immediately, though his face remained cold and still like a statue.

"Honored sir, Kuzma Kuzmitch, you've likely heard about my disagreements with my father, Fyodor Pavlovitch Karamazov, who stole my inheritance from my mother... the whole town has been gossiping about it... because people here love to talk about things they shouldn't... and maybe you've also heard about it from Grushenka... I mean, from Agrafena Alexandrovna... Agrafena Alexandrovna, the lady I respect and hold in the highest regard..."

Mitya trailed off, stumbling over his words from the very beginning. We won't repeat his entire speech word for word but will summarize its main points. Three months earlier, Mitya had—intentionally, he emphasized this word—consulted a lawyer in the province's main town. "A distinguished lawyer, Kuzma Kuzmitch, Pavel Pavlovitch Korneplodov. You might have heard of him? He's a man of great intellect, a mind like a statesman... he knows you, too... spoke of you very highly..." Mitya stumbled again, but he quickly skipped over these parts and pushed forward.

This lawyer, Korneplodov, after thoroughly questioning Mitya and examining the documents Mitya had brought with him (Mitya mentioned the documents vaguely, hurrying past the subject), concluded that Mitya had grounds to sue over the village of Tchermashnya, which should have come to Mitya from his mother's inheritance. The lawyer believed this could outsmart Mitya's father, Fyodor Pavlovitch. "There are still some doors open, and justice could find a way," the lawyer had said. Mitya could expect an additional sum of six or even seven thousand roubles from his father, since the village was worth at least twenty-five thousand, maybe even twenty-eight thousand roubles, "thirty thousand, Kuzma Kuzmitch! And can you believe it, I didn't even get seventeen thousand from that heartless man!" So, Mitya had put the matter aside for the moment, not knowing enough about the law. But when he arrived in town, he was taken by surprise by a counterclaim filed against him (here, Mitya lost track of his thoughts again but quickly jumped ahead), "So, Kuzma Kuzmitch, I'm asking if you, as a noble and generous man, would take on my case against that terrible man and give me an advance of just three thousand roubles?... You see, you wouldn't lose anything. On my honor, I swear that. In fact, you might even gain six or seven thousand instead of just three." Above all, Mitya needed the deal to be settled that very day.

"I'll make the deal with you at a notary's office, or however it's done... I'm ready to do whatever's needed... I'll hand over all the documents... sign anything you want... we could draw up the agreement right away... and if possible, pay me the three thousand by tomorrow morning. You're the wealthiest man in this town, so you could save me... you'd be saving me, and I mean saving me for something good, something honorable... because I have the most honorable feelings toward a certain person, whom you know and care about like a father. That's why I came to you. I wouldn't have come otherwise. And, honestly, this is a struggle involving three people in this situation—it's fate, Kuzma Kuzmitch, and fate is a terrible thing! It's a tragedy, Kuzma Kuzmitch! And since you've been out of it for so long, now it's a tug-of-war between two. I'm probably saying this poorly, but I'm not a writer. You see, on one side there's me, and on the other, that monster. You have to choose. It's either me or him. The fate of three lives and the happiness of two people are in your hands. Forgive me, I'm not saying this well, but I know you understand... I can see from your wise eyes that you understand... and if you don't, well, I'm doomed... so you see!"

Mitya finished his clumsy speech with those words, "so you see!" and, jumping up from his seat, waited for a response to his desperate offer. As soon as he finished speaking, he suddenly realized that it had all fallen flat and that, worst of all, he had been talking complete nonsense.

"How strange," Mitya thought in despair. "On the way here, everything made sense, and now it's all just nonsense." All this was going through his mind while the old man sat still, watching him with cold, icy eyes. After a moment of silence, Samsonov finally spoke, his voice firm and frostily final.

"Sorry, we don't deal with that kind of business." Mitya suddenly felt his legs weakening beneath him.

"What am I to do now, Kuzma Kuzmitch?" he muttered with a pale smile. "I suppose it's all over for me—what do you think?"

"Sorry..."

Mitya stood still, staring, without moving. Suddenly, he noticed a slight movement in the old man's face. He was startled.

"You see, sir, we don't handle business like that," said the old man slowly. "There's the court and the lawyers—it's a real misery. But if you like, I can suggest someone for you to approach."

"Heavens! Who is it? You're my savior, Kuzma Kuzmitch," stammered Mitya.

"He doesn't live here, and he's not in town right now. He's a peasant, deals in timber. His name is Lyagavy. He's been negotiating with Fyodor Pavlovitch for the last year over your woodland at Tchermashnya. They can't agree on the price— maybe you've heard? Well, he's back now and staying with the priest at Ilyinskoe, about twelve versts from the Volovya station. He wrote to me about the deal too, asking for advice. Fyodor Pavlovitch plans to see him himself. So, if you could get to him first and make him the same offer you've made me, he might be interested—"

"A brilliant idea!" Mitya interrupted, full of excitement. "He's exactly the man, it would suit him perfectly. He's haggling over the price, and here he'd have all the documents proving he owns the property. Ha ha ha!"

And Mitya burst into his short, strange laugh, which startled Samsonov.

"How can I ever thank you, Kuzma Kuzmitch?" cried Mitya, overflowing with gratitude.

"Don't mention it," said Samsonov, nodding his head.

"But you don't understand—you've saved me. It was a lucky instinct that brought me to you. Now, off to this priest!"

"No need for thanks."

"I'll rush there immediately. I hope I haven't exhausted you. I'll never forget this. That's a promise from a true Russian, Kuzma Kuzmitch, a real R-r-russian!"

"Indeed."

Mitya grabbed his hand to shake it but caught a flash of something malicious in the old man's eyes. He withdrew his hand quickly but immediately scolded himself for being suspicious.

"He's just tired," Mitya thought.

"For her sake! For her sake, Kuzma Kuzmitch! You understand this is for her," he shouted, his voice echoing through the room. He bowed, turned abruptly, and walked to the door with long strides without looking back. He was trembling with excitement.

"Everything was on the verge of ruin, and my guardian angel saved me," he thought to himself. If a businessman like Samsonov (such a respectable old man, and with such dignity!) had suggested this idea, then… then success was certain. He would rush off immediately. "I'll be back by tonight, the deal will be done, and it's over. Could the old man have been mocking me?" Mitya wondered as he hurried back to his lodgings. Of course, he couldn't imagine anything other than that the advice was sound "from such an experienced businessman" who clearly understood this Lyagavy (what an odd name!). Or—had the old man been laughing at him?

Alas, the second possibility was true. Long afterward, when the disaster had happened, old Samsonov himself admitted, laughing, that he had tricked the "captain." He was a cold, spiteful, and sarcastic man, prone to strong dislikes. Whether it was Mitya's frantic expression or the ridiculous confidence of this "reckless spendthrift," thinking that Samsonov could be fooled by such an absurd story, or perhaps his jealousy over Grushenka, on whose behalf this "good-for-nothing" had rushed in to ask for money, I can't say. But at the moment when Mitya stood before him, his legs shaking beneath him, desperately crying that he was ruined, the old man looked at him with bitter hatred and decided to make a fool of him.

After Mitya had left, Kuzma Kuzmitch, white with rage, turned to his son and ordered him to make sure that beggar never set foot near him again, never even allowed into the yard, or else he would—

He didn't finish his threat, but even his son, who had seen him furious many times before, was terrified. For a full hour afterward, the old man trembled with anger, and by the evening, his condition worsened, and he had to send for the doctor.

Chapter 2: Lyagavy

So, he had to travel as fast as possible, but he didn't have the money for horses. All he had was forty kopecks— just forty kopecks left after all those years of living well! But at home, he had an old silver watch that hadn't worked in a long time. He grabbed it and took it to a Jewish watchmaker who had a shop in the marketplace. The Jew gave him six roubles for it.

"And I wasn't expecting that!" Mitya exclaimed excitedly. (He was still caught up in his excitement.) He took the six roubles and ran back home. When he got there, he borrowed three roubles from the people he lived with. They liked him so much that they were happy to lend it to him, even though it was all they had. In his excitement, Mitya told them right away that his fate would be decided that day, and in his haste, he explained the whole plan he had presented to Samsonov, what Samsonov had decided, his own hopes for the future, and everything else. The people already knew many of Mitya's secrets, so they saw him as a gentleman who wasn't too proud and almost one of them. After collecting the nine roubles, Mitya ordered horses to take him to the Volovya station. This is how it was remembered and recorded later that "at noon, the day before everything happened, Mitya didn't have a penny, had sold his watch for money, and had borrowed three roubles from his landlord, all in front of witnesses."

I mention this detail now because it will be important later.

Even though Mitya was glowing with joy, thinking that he was finally going to solve all his problems, he was still worried as he got closer to the Volovya station. He kept thinking about what Grushenka might be doing while he was away. What if today was the day she decided to go to Fyodor Pavlovitch? That's why he hadn't told her he was leaving, and why he told his landlady not to tell anyone where he'd gone if they asked about him.

"I have to get back tonight," he repeated to himself as he bounced along in the cart. "I'll probably have to bring this Lyagavy back with me... to draw up the paperwork." That's what Mitya was thinking, his heart racing, but unfortunately, things didn't go as planned.

First, he was late because the shortcut he took from the Volovya station turned out to be eighteen versts, not twelve. Second, when he arrived in Ilyinskoe, the priest wasn't home—he had gone to a nearby village. Mitya, now riding the same tired horses, went after him, and by the time he found him, it was nearly dark.

The priest, a small, kind-looking man, told him right away that while Lyagavy had been staying with him at first, he was now at Suhoy Possyolok, spending the night in a forester's cottage because he was also buying timber there. When Mitya begged him to take him to Lyagavy immediately and "save him," the priest, after hesitating a bit, agreed to take him to Suhoy Possyolok, his curiosity clearly piqued. Unfortunately, he suggested they walk, saying it wasn't "much over" a verst. Mitya quickly agreed and marched off with his long strides, so fast that the poor priest had to almost run to keep up with him. The priest was a cautious man, though he wasn't old.

Mitya immediately began talking nervously, explaining his plans and asking for advice about Lyagavy. The priest listened closely but didn't offer much advice. He responded to Mitya's questions with phrases like, "I don't know," "I can't say," and "How can I tell?" When Mitya began talking about his fight with his father over the inheritance, the priest grew visibly uncomfortable, since he was somewhat dependent on Fyodor Pavlovitch. However, he did ask, surprised, why Mitya called the peasant trader Lyagavy instead of Gorstkin. The priest explained that while the man's real name was Lyagavy, he never went by that name and would be greatly offended if Mitya called him that. "You must call him Gorstkin, or you won't get anywhere with him—he won't even listen to you," the priest warned.

Mitya was briefly surprised and explained that Samsonov had called him Lyagavy. When the priest heard that, he dropped the subject, though he probably should have voiced his suspicion that if Samsonov had sent Mitya to the peasant calling him Lyagavy, there might have been something fishy going on, and perhaps Samsonov had been making fun of him. But Mitya had no time to dwell on such small details. He hurried along, only realizing when they finally reached Suhoy Possyolok that they had walked not one verst, nor even one and a half, but at least three. This irritated him, but he held it in.

They entered the cottage. The forester lived in one half of the hut, while Gorstkin was staying in the better room on the other side of the hallway. They went into that room and lit a tallow candle. The hut was incredibly hot. On the table sat a samovar that had gone out, a tray with cups, an empty rum bottle, a half-full bottle of vodka, and some leftover crusts of wheat bread. The man they had come to see was lying stretched out on the bench, using his coat as a pillow, snoring loudly. Mitya stood there, unsure of what to do.

"Of course, I have to wake him up. My business is urgent. I've come in such a rush, and I need to get back today," he said, obviously stressed. But the priest and the forester remained silent, not offering any advice. Mitya went up and tried to wake him himself, shaking him vigorously, but the man didn't wake up.

"He's drunk," Mitya concluded. "Good Lord! What am I supposed to do? What can I do?" Impatient, he started pulling on the man's arms and legs, shaking his head, and trying to lift him up to sit on the bench. But even after all his effort, all he got were some incoherent grumbles and curses from the drunk man.

"No, you'd better wait a while," the priest finally said. "He's clearly not in a fit state to talk."

"He's been drinking all day," added the forester.

"Heavens!" Mitya cried out. "If only you knew how important this is to me and how desperate I am!"

"No, you should really wait until morning," the priest repeated.

"Until morning? That's impossible!"

In his desperation, Mitya was about to try waking the man again but stopped, realizing it would be useless. The priest said nothing more, and the sleepy forester looked sullen.

"What terrible tragedies life creates for people," Mitya said, completely defeated. Sweat was pouring down his face. The priest seized the opportunity to calmly point out that even if Mitya managed to wake the man, he would still be too drunk to have any useful conversation. "Your business is important," he said, "so you'd be better off waiting until morning." With a sigh of despair, Mitya agreed.

"Father, I'll stay here with the candle and wait for the right moment. As soon as he wakes, I'll start talking. I'll pay you for the candle," Mitya said to the forester, "and for the night's lodging, too; remember my name, Dmitri Karamazov. But Father, I don't know what we'll do with you. Where will you sleep?"

"No, I'm going home. I'll take the forester's horse and get home," the priest said, pointing to the forester. "Now, I'll say goodbye. I wish you success."

With that, it was settled. The priest rode off on the forester's horse, happy to leave, though he shook his head, wondering whether he should tell his benefactor, Fyodor Pavlovitch, about this strange incident tomorrow, "or he might hear about it later, get angry, and stop helping me."

The forester, scratching himself, returned to his room without saying a word, and Mitya sat on the bench to "wait for the right moment," as he called it. A heavy sense of depression settled over him like a thick fog. Intense, deep depression! He sat there, thinking, but couldn't come to any conclusion. The candle flickered dimly, and a cricket chirped. The room felt unbearably stuffy from the heat. Suddenly, Mitya imagined the garden, the path behind the garden, the door of his father's house opening mysteriously, and Grushenka running inside. He jumped up from the bench.

"It's a tragedy!" he growled, clenching his teeth. Mechanically, he walked over to the sleeping man and stared at his face. The man was a middle-aged peasant with a long face, curly blond hair, and a thin reddish beard. He was wearing a blue cotton shirt and a black waistcoat, with the chain of a silver watch peeking out of the pocket. Mitya looked at his face with intense hatred, and for some reason, the curly hair especially irritated him.

What felt unbearably humiliating to Mitya was that, after abandoning such important matters and making so many sacrifices, he now found himself, completely exhausted, standing over this idiot—someone upon whom his entire future depended—while the man snored away as if nothing was wrong, as if he'd come from a different planet entirely.

"Oh, the irony of fate!" Mitya cried out, losing his temper. He threw himself into waking the drunk peasant again, this time with fury. He shook him, shoved him, and even gave him a few blows. But after five minutes of useless effort, Mitya slumped back down on the bench, overwhelmed by hopeless frustration.

"Idiot! Idiot!" he yelled. "And how shameful this all is!" Something made him say it out loud. His head started pounding painfully. He wondered if he should just give up and leave altogether. "No, I'll wait until tomorrow now," he decided. "I'll stay just to prove a point. What else can I do? Besides, I have no way to leave. How could I even get out of here now? This whole thing is ridiculous!"

But the pain in his head only grew worse. He sat motionless, and before he realized it, he dozed off, falling asleep right there on the bench. It felt like he had been asleep for two hours or more when the pounding in his head became so intense that it woke him, almost making him scream. His temples throbbed, and the top of his head felt as if it would split open. It took a long moment for him to fully wake up and understand what was happening.

Then it hit him—the room was filled with smoke from the stove, and if he stayed there, he might suffocate. Meanwhile, the drunk peasant lay there snoring away. The candle was flickering, almost burnt out. In a panic, Mitya stumbled across the hall into the forester's room. The forester woke up instantly but, to Mitya's shock and irritation, showed little concern when he heard about the smoke. Still, the forester got up to take a look.

"He's going to die! And… what am I supposed to do then?" Mitya cried desperately.

They threw open the doors and windows, and cleared the chimney. Mitya fetched a bucket of water from the hall. He poured some on his own head first, then found a rag, soaked it, and laid it across the peasant's head. The forester still acted indifferent, and after opening the window, he muttered, "It'll be fine now," and went back to sleep, leaving Mitya with a lit lantern.

Mitya spent the next half-hour tending to the drunk peasant, wetting his head repeatedly. He made a firm decision not to sleep at all that night. But he was so utterly exhausted that, when he sat down to catch his breath, his eyes drifted shut, and without meaning to, he stretched out on the bench and fell into a deep sleep.

He woke up terribly late—around nine in the morning. Sunlight streamed through the two small windows of the hut. The curly-haired peasant sat on the bench, already dressed, with another samovar and another bottle in front of him. The bottle from yesterday was empty, and the new one was already more than halfway gone.

Mitya shot up, realizing at once that the wretched man was drunk again—completely and hopelessly drunk. He stared at him in disbelief. The peasant looked back, calm and smug, as if amused by Mitya's frustration. The sly, almost condescending look on his face was unbearable. Furious, Mitya rushed over to him.

"Look, excuse me… You've probably heard from the forester," Mitya began, struggling to stay composed. "I'm Lieutenant Dmitri Karamazov, the son of old Karamazov, the one selling the copse to you."

"That's a lie," the peasant said confidently.

"A lie? You know Fyodor Pavlovitch, don't you?"

"I don't know any Fyodor Pavlovitch," the peasant slurred, his words heavy with drink.

"You're negotiating with him about the copse! Please, try to focus! Father Pavel of Ilyinskoe brought me here. You wrote to Samsonov, and he sent me to you," Mitya said, out of breath.

"You're lying," Lyagavy muttered again. Mitya felt his legs go cold.

"For heaven's sake, this is no joke! Maybe you're drunk, but you can still talk and understand… Can't you? Or else I'm losing my mind!"

"You're just a painter!" Lyagavy shot back.

"I swear, I'm Karamazov—Dmitri Karamazov! I have a great offer for you—an excellent one about the copse!"

The peasant stroked his beard slowly, as if considering something important.

"No, you made a deal and now you've messed it up. You're just a scoundrel!"

"You're mistaken, I swear!" Mitya cried, wringing his hands in desperation.

The peasant kept stroking his beard, then suddenly narrowed his eyes with a cunning look.

"Show me the law that allows crooks like you! You're a scoundrel, plain and simple. Do you get that?"

Mitya stepped back in disbelief, feeling as if something had just hit him in the head. Later, he would describe it as if a light had suddenly flicked on in his mind—a moment of clarity. "How could I, an intelligent person, fall for something so stupid?" he thought, stunned. "I wasted almost twenty-four hours running in circles around this drunk fool, soaking his head like an idiot."

"This man is completely drunk—beyond help. He'll just keep drinking for days. What's the point of staying here? And what if Samsonov sent me here on purpose? What if… what if she… Oh, God, what have I done?"

The peasant kept grinning at him. If it had been any other time, Mitya might have attacked him in rage, but now he felt too weak, like a child. Without a word, he slowly went to the bench, put on his overcoat, and left the hut.

There was no sign of the forester in the next room. The place was empty. Mitya took fifty kopecks from his pocket and placed the coins on the table to cover his stay, the candle, and any trouble he had caused.

When he stepped outside, the forest surrounded him on all sides. He wandered off without knowing which way to go—whether to the right or the left. The night before, rushing there with the priest, he hadn't noticed the path. He felt no anger toward anyone, not even Samsonov. He just walked along the narrow forest trail, aimless and lost, barely aware of where he was going. He was so drained—physically and emotionally—that even a child could have knocked him over.

Somehow, he made it out of the forest, and endless fields stretched before him, bare after the harvest.

"What despair! What emptiness!" he repeated, striding forward without direction.

He was saved when he came across an old merchant riding through the countryside in a rented trap. When Mitya caught up to him, he asked for directions, and it turned out the merchant was also headed to Volovya. After a brief conversation, Mitya climbed into the trap. Three hours later, they arrived.

As soon as they reached Volovya, Mitya ordered fresh horses to take him to the town. It hit him then just how hungry he was. While the horses were being prepared, they made him an omelet. He devoured it instantly, along with a large piece of bread and a sausage, and downed three glasses of vodka.

With food in his stomach, his spirits lifted, and his heart felt lighter. He urged the driver to hurry, filled with sudden determination. A new and "unchangeable" plan took shape in his mind: he would get that cursed money by the end of the day, no matter what.

"To think—just think—a man's entire life ruined over a lousy three thousand!" he said bitterly. "I'll put an end to this today."

If it weren't for the constant worry about Grushenka—what might have happened to her, a fear that haunted him every moment—he might have even felt happy again. But the thought of her pierced his heart like a knife with every step.

At last, they arrived in town, and Mitya immediately ran off to find Grushenka.

Chapter 3: Gold Mines

This was the visit from Mitya that Grushenka had described to Rakitin with such fear. At the time, she was anxiously waiting for the "message" and had been relieved that Mitya hadn't come by that day or the day before. She hoped, "Please God, let him not come before I've left," but then, all of a sudden, he burst in on her. The rest of what happened, we already know. To get rid of him, she immediately suggested that he accompany her to Samsonov's, saying she absolutely needed to go "to settle his accounts." When Mitya agreed right away, she said goodbye to him at the gate, making him promise to return at midnight to take her home. Mitya was pleased with the plan, too. If she stayed at Samsonov's, it meant she couldn't visit Fyodor Pavlovitch— unless she had lied to him, Mitya thought. But based on what he saw, he believed she was telling the truth.

Mitya was the type of jealous man who, whenever the woman he loved was out of sight, would instantly start imagining all kinds of terrible things—wondering how she might be betraying him. But even when he was heartbroken and convinced she had been unfaithful, he would run back to her. And at the first sight of her playful, affectionate smile, all his fears would vanish. He would forget his suspicions, overcome with shame at his jealousy, and feel joyful again.

After leaving Grushenka at the gate, Mitya hurried home. He still had so much to do that day, but at least the heavy weight on his heart had been lifted.

"Now I just need to hurry and ask Smerdyakov whether anything happened last night—whether, by any chance, she went to Fyodor Pavlovitch. Ugh!" This thought raced through his mind.

But before Mitya could even reach his lodging, jealousy already surged up again in his restless heart.

Jealousy! "Othello wasn't jealous; he was trusting," Pushkin once said. That line alone shows the great insight of our poet. Othello's soul shattered because his ideal of love had been destroyed, but he never resorted to spying or sneaking around. On the contrary, Othello was trusting by nature. It took a lot of effort to push him to believe he had been deceived. But a truly jealous man is not like that. There is no limit to how far jealousy can drag a person, making them sink to disgraceful behavior without the slightest sense of guilt. And yet, jealousy isn't limited to petty or vulgar souls. Even a person with noble intentions—someone whose love is sincere and selfless—can stoop to bribing the lowest people, hiding under tables, and spying in shameful ways.

Othello wasn't incapable of forgiving betrayal; he simply couldn't make himself accept that it had happened in the first place. His soul was as pure as a child's, free from malice. But a deeply jealous man is entirely different. It's hard to imagine what a jealous man can tolerate, what he can excuse, and what he can forgive. In fact, jealous men are often the quickest to forgive, and all women know this. A jealous man can forgive shocking things—though not without a heated confrontation first. He might even forgive an affair, with undeniable proof—kisses, embraces, and all—so long as he believes it was the "last time." All he needs is to be convinced that the rival will disappear forever or that he himself will take the woman far away, somewhere the rival can never find her. But even that peace lasts only briefly. Even if the rival vanishes, the jealous man will soon invent another one to be jealous of. It makes one wonder what value there could be in a love that needs such constant guarding. But the jealous man never thinks of that.

And yet, among these jealous men are those with noble hearts. Even when they hide in cupboards, eavesdropping and spying, they feel no guilt at the time. They are fully aware of the shameful depths to which they've fallen, but they don't care.

The moment Mitya saw Grushenka, all his jealousy melted away. For that brief moment, he became trusting and generous, and even felt disgusted with himself for having such unworthy thoughts. This showed that his love for her wasn't purely physical—it wasn't just about the "curve of her body," as he had told Alyosha. But as soon as Grushenka was out of sight, suspicion crept back into his mind. He began doubting her again, and this time, he felt no shame about it.

And so, jealousy returned. Mitya knew he had to act quickly. His first task was to secure at least a small loan of money to get by for now. His nine rubles had almost entirely been spent on his recent trip, and as everyone knows, it's impossible to do anything without money. Fortunately, Mitya had already thought of a solution while riding in the cart earlier. He had a pair of fine dueling pistols in a case. He hadn't pawned them yet because they were his most treasured possession. But now, it seemed like the only choice.

At the "Metropolis" tavern, Mitya had gotten to know a young official some time ago and found out that this wealthy bachelor was obsessed with weapons. The man enjoyed collecting pistols, revolvers, and daggers, hanging them on his walls, and proudly showing them to his friends. He prided himself on his collection and had become something of an expert on how revolvers worked. Without pausing to think, Mitya went straight to him and offered to pawn his pistols for ten rubles. The official, thrilled with the offer, tried hard to persuade Mitya to sell the pistols outright, but Mitya wouldn't agree. In the end, the young man gave him the ten rubles and insisted that he would never charge him interest. They parted on good terms.

Mitya was in a rush. He took the back way toward Fyodor Pavlovitch's house, heading for the garden arbor to find Smerdyakov as quickly as he could. This much is certain: three or four hours before a particular event— an event I'll mention later— Mitya had no money at all and pawned a valuable possession for just ten rubles. Yet, three hours later, he would have thousands. But I'm getting ahead of the story.

Mitya learned from Marya Kondratyevna, a woman who lived near Fyodor Pavlovitch, that Smerdyakov was seriously ill. She told him about how Smerdyakov had fallen into the cellar, had a seizure, and needed a visit from the doctor, which left Fyodor Pavlovitch deeply worried. Mitya also learned, with some surprise, that his brother Ivan had left for Moscow that morning.

"So he must have passed through Volovya before me," Mitya thought. But Smerdyakov's illness troubled him even more. "What am I supposed to do now? Who will keep watch for me? Who will bring me news?" These thoughts raced through his mind.

He questioned the women eagerly, trying to find out if they had seen anything unusual the night before. They quickly realized what he wanted to know and assured him that nothing strange had happened. No one had come by; Ivan Fyodorovitch had spent the night there as usual, and everything had been perfectly normal. Mitya thought about it and realized that he would have to keep watch himself that day. But where? Should he wait at Fyodor Pavlovitch's house or by Samsonov's gate? In the end, he decided he would have to keep an eye on both places. In the meantime...

The problem was that he needed to follow through with the new plan he had come up with during his trip back. He was certain it would succeed, but there was no time to waste. Mitya decided he could only spare one hour for it. "In an hour, I'll know everything, and it'll all be settled. Then I'll go to Samsonov's, find out if Grushenka is there, come back here and wait until eleven, and finally head to Samsonov's again to bring her home." That was his plan.

He hurried back to his lodging, washed up, combed his hair, brushed his clothes, got dressed, and went straight to Madame Hohlakov's house. His hopes were pinned on her. His plan was to borrow three thousand rubles from her. And what's more, Mitya was suddenly convinced that she wouldn't refuse him. You might wonder why, if he was so confident, he hadn't gone to her first. Why go to Samsonov, someone he barely knew and had nothing in common with, instead of Madame Hohlakov, someone closer to his social circle?

The truth was, Mitya didn't know Madame Hohlakov well. In fact, he hadn't seen her in over a month, and she had never liked him. From the very beginning, she had disliked him because he was engaged to Katerina Ivanovna. For reasons of her own, Madame Hohlakov had decided that Katerina should break off the engagement and marry Ivan instead, as she thought Ivan was charming, refined, and well-mannered. She couldn't stand Mitya's behavior. He had even mocked her once, saying she was as lively as she was uncultured.

But while riding in the cart that morning, Mitya came up with what he thought was a brilliant idea: "If she's so desperate for me to leave Katerina Ivanovna" (and he knew how obsessed she was with that idea), "why wouldn't she give me three thousand rubles just to make it happen? These spoiled rich women will do anything to get what they want. And besides, she's very wealthy," Mitya thought to himself.

The plan he had in mind was the same as before: he would offer his share of Tchermashnya. But this time, it wasn't about profit, as it had been with Samsonov. He wasn't trying to tempt Madame Hohlakov with the chance to make six or seven thousand rubles. Instead, he would offer his rights to the land as collateral for the loan. As he thought it over, Mitya grew more and more excited about the plan. That was how he always was—he would throw himself into every new idea with wild enthusiasm.

Yet, as he climbed the steps to Madame Hohlakov's house, a chill ran down his spine. In that moment, he realized with cold clarity that this was his last chance. If this plan failed, he would have no other options. Nothing would be left for him except to "rob someone or kill someone for the three thousand rubles."

It was half-past seven when he rang the bell.

At first, it seemed as though fortune was on his side. The moment he was announced, he was admitted without delay. "It's as if she's been waiting for me," Mitya thought. When he was shown into the drawing room, Madame Hohlakov herself hurried in to greet him.

"I knew you would come! I was expecting you!" she exclaimed. "Even though I had no real reason to think you'd visit me, I just knew you would! Isn't that amazing, Dmitri Fyodorovitch? I was certain all morning that you would show up."

"That's remarkable, madam," Mitya said, sinking into a chair, "but I've come to see you about something extremely important... Something very urgent for me... And I need to act quickly—"

"I know you've come on urgent business, Dmitri Fyodorovitch. This isn't just a hunch or some kind of miracle—I've moved beyond believing in those things (have you heard about Father Zossima?). No, this is pure logic. After everything that happened with Katerina Ivanovna, it was inevitable that you'd come to me. It's like math—it couldn't have happened any other way."

"This is real life, madam. But please, allow me to explain—"

"Yes, real life! I believe in realism now. I've had enough of miracles. Oh, and did you hear that Father Zossima passed away?"

"No, madam, this is the first I've heard of it," Mitya said, feeling

surprised. The image of Alyosha immediately came to his mind. "Yes, last night. Can you imagine—"

"Madam," Mitya interrupted, "the only thing I can imagine right now is that I'm in a desperate situation. If you don't help me, everything will collapse, including me. Forgive me if I sound blunt, but I'm at my breaking point—"

"I know, I know you're desperate. That's obvious. Whatever you say, I already know it. I've been thinking about your fate for a long time, Dmitri Fyodorovitch. I've been watching over you and analyzing everything... Believe me, I'm an expert in matters of the soul."

"If that's true, madam, then I'm certainly an experienced patient," Mitya said, doing his best to stay polite. "And if you've really been watching over me, I hope you'll help me now that I'm in ruin. Please, just let me explain my plan—and what I need from you. I've come here today—"

"There's no need to explain your plan. That part isn't important. As for helping you, you're not the first person I've helped, Dmitri Fyodorovitch. Have you heard of my cousin, Madame Belmesov? Her husband was in terrible trouble—'ruined,' as you put it so well. I advised him to start breeding horses, and now he's doing just fine. Do you know anything about horse breeding, Dmitri Fyodorovitch?"

"Not the slightest, madam! Not the slightest!" Mitya cried, unable to contain his impatience. He jumped up from his seat, desperate. "Please, madam, I beg you to listen to me. Just give me two minutes to explain everything. I'm running out of time!" His voice was frantic as he tried to stop her from talking again. "I've come to you in absolute despair, begging for a loan of three thousand rubles. It'll be a loan with proper security—trustworthy guarantees! Just let me explain—"

"You can tell me all that later," Madame Hohlakov said, raising a hand to silence him. "Whatever you want to say, I already know it. You need three thousand rubles, but I can give you far more— much more. I will save you, Dmitri Fyodorovitch, but you must listen to me."

Mitya jumped up again from his seat. "Madam, will you really do this?" he cried with deep emotion. "Oh God, you've saved me! You've saved me from a violent death, from a bullet... I'll be forever grateful—"

"I will give you more, so much more than three thousand!" Madame Hohlakov exclaimed, smiling brightly as she watched Mitya's excitement.

"More? But I don't need that much. I only need the three thousand to solve everything, and I can promise you my endless gratitude for it. I have a plan—"

"Enough, Dmitri Fyodorovich," Madame Hohlakov interrupted, with the calm satisfaction of someone being generous. "I've promised to save you, and I will. Just like I saved Belmesov. What do you think about the gold mines, Dmitri Fyodorovich?"

"The gold mines, madam? I haven't thought much about them."

"Well, I've thought about them for you. Thought about them over and over again. I've been watching you for the past month. A hundred times as you've walked by, I've said to myself: 'There's a man of energy who should be at the gold mines.' I've studied how you walk and I've decided: that's a man who would find gold."

"From the way I walk, madam?" Mitya said, smiling.

"Yes, from your walk. You don't deny that a person's character can be seen in how they walk, do you, Dmitri Fyodorovich? Science supports this idea. I'm all about science and realism now. After everything with Father Zossima, which really upset me, starting today, I'm a realist. I want to dedicate myself to practical things. I'm healed. 'Enough!' as Turgenev says."

"But, madam, the three thousand you generously offered to lend me—"

"It's yours, Dmitri Fyodorovich," Madame Hohlakov quickly said. "The money is practically in your pocket. Not three thousand, but three million in no time at all. I'm giving you the idea: you will find gold mines, make millions, return as a successful man, and lead us all to better things. Are we just going to leave everything to the Jews? You'll create institutions and businesses of all kinds. You'll help the poor, and they will be so grateful to you. This is the age of railroads, Dmitri Fyodorovich. You'll become famous and be needed by the Department of Finance, which is struggling right now. The falling value of the ruble keeps me up at night, Dmitri Fyodorovich; people don't realize that about me—"

"Madam, madam!" Dmitri interrupted with a sense of dread. "I might follow your advice, your very wise advice... I might go to the gold mines... I'll come see you again about it, many times, but for now, that three thousand you so kindly... that would free me, and if you could give it to me today... you see, I don't have a minute to waste today—"

"Enough, Dmitri Fyodorovich, enough!" Madame Hohlakov said firmly. "The real question is, will you go to the gold mines or not? Have you made up your mind? Yes or no?"

"I'll go, madam, later... I'll go wherever you want... but right now—"

"Wait!" Madame Hohlakov shouted. She jumped up and rushed to a beautiful desk with lots of little drawers. She frantically pulled open drawer after drawer, looking for something with great urgency.

"The three thousand," Mitya thought, his heart nearly stopping. "Right away... no paperwork or formalities... doing it like a true lady! She's wonderful, if only she didn't talk so much!"

"Here!" Madame Hohlakov shouted, hurrying back to Mitya, clearly pleased. "Here's what I was looking for!"

It was a tiny silver icon on a string, like the ones worn under a person's clothes with a cross.

"This is from Kiev, Dmitri Fyodorovich," she said reverently. "From the relics of Saint Varvara. Let me put it around your neck myself, and with it, I dedicate you to a new life, a new path."

And she really did put the string around his neck, carefully arranging it. Feeling very awkward, Mitya bent down to help, and finally, they managed to get it under his tie and collar and down inside his shirt, resting against his chest.

"Now you're ready to go," Madame Hohlakov declared, sitting down proudly in her chair again.

"Madam, I'm so moved. I don't know how to thank you for such kindness, but... If you only knew how precious time is for me right now... That money, the sum I'll owe to your generosity... Oh, madam, since you're being so kind and generous to me," Mitya suddenly burst out, "let me confess to you... though you probably already know... that I'm in love with someone here. I've been unfaithful to Katya... Katerina Ivanovna, I mean. I've treated her terribly, dishonorably, but I've fallen in love with someone else... a woman you, madam, probably despise because you know everything, but I can't leave her, no matter what, and that's why the three thousand is so important right now—"

"Forget everything, Dmitri Fyodorovich," Madame Hohlakov cut him off sharply. "Forget everything, especially women. The gold mines are your future, and women don't belong there. When you come back rich and famous, then you'll find the woman of your dreams in the highest circles of society. She'll be modern, educated, and full of new ideas. By then, the women's movement will have advanced, and the 'new woman' will have appeared."

"Madam, that's not what I'm talking about," Mitya pleaded, clasping his hands.

"Yes, it is, Dmitri Fyodorovich. It's exactly what you need, even if you don't realize it. I'm not against the women's movement, Dmitri Fyodorovich. The growth of women's rights, even political freedom for women in the near future—that's my ideal. I have a daughter myself, Dmitri Fyodorovich; people don't know that about me. I once wrote a letter to the writer Shtchedrin about it. He's taught me so much about women's role in society. Last year, I sent him an anonymous note that said, 'I embrace and kiss you, my teacher, for your work on modern women. Keep going.' And I signed it 'A Mother.' I thought about signing it 'A Modern Mother,' but I decided to stick with just 'Mother.' It has more moral beauty. And the word 'modern' might have reminded him of 'The Contemporary,' which is a painful memory because of censorship... Oh my God, what's the matter?"

"Madam!" Mitya cried, jumping up at last, clasping his hands in front of her in helpless desperation. "You'll make me cry if you keep delaying the kindness you promised—"

"Oh, go ahead and cry, Dmitri Fyodorovich, cry! It's a noble emotion... Such a bright future lies ahead for you! Your tears will ease your heart, and later you'll return full of joy. You'll rush back to see me from Siberia just to share your happiness with me—"

"But madam!" Mitya suddenly cried out. "For the last time, I beg you, tell me, can I have the money you promised today? If not, when can I come back for it?"

"What money, Dmitri Fyodorovich?"

"The three thousand you promised me... that you so kindly—"

"Three thousand? Roubles? Oh no, I don't have three thousand," Madame Hohlakov said calmly, with a serene look of surprise. Mitya stood there, completely shocked.

"But you just said... you said... you said it was as good as in my hands—"

"Oh no, you misunderstood me, Dmitri Fyodorovitch. In that case, you misunderstood what I said. I was talking about the gold mines. Yes, I remember, I promised you more, much more than three thousand, but I was speaking about the gold mines."

"But the money? The three thousand?" Mitya said awkwardly, struggling to understand.

"Oh, if you're talking about money, I don't have any. I don't have a single penny, Dmitri Fyodorovitch. I've been quarreling with my steward about it, and I just borrowed five hundred roubles from Miüsov myself. No, no, I have no money. And you know, Dmitri Fyodorovitch, even if I had the money, I wouldn't give it to you. First of all, I never lend money. Lending money only makes you lose friends. And I wouldn't give it to you, in particular. I wouldn't give it to you because I like you and want to save you, because all you need is the gold mines, the gold mines, the gold mines!"

"Oh, the devil!" Mitya roared, slamming his fist down on the table with all his strength.

"Aie! Aie!" cried Madame Hohlakov in alarm, rushing to the other side of the room.

Mitya spat on the ground and stormed out of the room, out of the house, into the street, into the darkness! He walked like a man possessed, hitting his chest, right where he had hit himself two days before in front of Alyosha, the last time he had seen him, in the dark, on the road. What those blows to his chest meant, and why he did it, was a secret for now, a secret that no one else knew and that he hadn't even told Alyosha. But that secret was more than just disgrace; it meant total ruin, and even suicide. That was what he had decided if he didn't get the three thousand roubles to pay his debt to Katerina Ivanovna and remove the shame that weighed on his conscience. All of this will be explained to the reader later, but for now, with his last hope gone, this man, who appeared so strong, broke down, crying like a child just a few steps from Madame Hohlakov's house. He kept walking, unaware of where he was going, wiping his tears away with his fist. As he walked, he suddenly stumbled into someone. He heard a sharp cry from an old woman he had almost knocked over.

"Good Lord, you nearly killed me! Why don't you look where you're going, you reckless fool?"

"Why, it's you!" Mitya exclaimed, recognizing the old woman in the dark. It was the old servant who worked for Samsonov, someone Mitya had paid particular attention to the day before.

"And who are you, sir?" the old woman asked in a completely different voice. "I don't recognize you in the dark."

"You work for Kuzma Kuzmitch, don't you? You're a servant there?"

"Yes, sir. I was just running out to Prohoritch's... but I don't know you now."

"Tell me, is Agrafena Alexandrovna there now?" Mitya asked, his voice full of anxiousness. "I saw her go into the house earlier."

"She was there, sir. She stayed for a little while and then left again."

"What? She left?" Mitya cried in disbelief. "When did she leave?"

"Right after she arrived. She stayed just a minute. She told Kuzma Kuzmitch a funny story that made him laugh, and then she ran off."

"You're lying, damn you!" Mitya roared in anger.

"Aie! Aie!" screamed the old woman, but Mitya had already disappeared.

He ran as fast as he could to the house where Grushenka lived. At that very moment, Grushenka was already on her way to Mokroe. She had left no more than fifteen minutes before.

Fenya was sitting in the kitchen with her grandmother, the old cook Matryona, when Mitya suddenly rushed in. Fenya screamed the moment she saw him.

"You're screaming?" Mitya bellowed. "Where is she?"

But before the terrified Fenya could answer, Mitya collapsed at her feet.

"Fenya, for the love of Christ, tell me, where is she?"

"I don't know, Dmitri Fyodorovitch, I swear I don't know. You could kill me, but I still wouldn't be able to tell you," Fenya cried desperately. "You left with her not too long ago—"

"She came back!"

"No, she didn't! I swear to God, she didn't come back."

"You're lying!" Mitya shouted. "I can see from your terror that you know where she is."

He rushed out of the house. Fenya, frightened but relieved to have gotten off so easily, knew that it was only because Mitya was in such a hurry. Otherwise, she might not have been so lucky. But as he ran out, he did something that surprised both Fenya and old Matryona. On the table stood a brass mortar, with a pestle inside it, a small brass pestle about six inches long. Mitya had already opened the door with one hand when, with the other, he grabbed the pestle and slipped it into his side pocket.

"Oh, Lord! He's going to kill someone!" cried Fenya, raising her hands in horror.

Chapter 4: In The Dark

Where was he running? "Where could she be except at Fyodor Pavlovitch's? She must have gone straight to him

from Samsonov's, it's clear now. The whole plot, the whole trick is obvious." It all rushed through his mind like a whirlwind. He didn't run to Marya Kondratyevna's. "There's no need to go there... not the slightest need... I must not raise any alarm... they would run and tell right away. Marya Kondratyevna is obviously part of the plan, Smerdyakov too, him as well, they've all been bribed!"

He quickly made a new plan: he ran a long way around Fyodor Pavlovitch's house, crossed the lane, ran down Dmitrovsky Street, then over the little bridge, and came to the empty alley in the back. It was deserted and quiet, with a low fence on one side from a neighbor's garden and a strong, tall fence surrounding Fyodor Pavlovitch's yard on the other. He picked a spot, apparently the very place where, according to stories, Lizaveta had once climbed over. "If she could get over it," he thought, not knowing why, "then surely I can." And indeed, he jumped up, caught the top of the fence, and pulled himself over, sitting on it. From the fence, he could see the bathhouse in the garden, and he could also see the lit windows of the house.

"Yes, the old man's room is lit up. She's in there!" he thought as he jumped down into the garden. Even though he knew Grigory was sick, and Smerdyakov too probably, and that no one would hear him, he instinctively hid himself, standing still to listen. But it was completely silent all around him, as if on purpose, not even a breath of wind.

"And nothing but whispering silence," for some reason, this line popped into his mind. "I hope no one heard me jump the fence! I don't think so." After standing still for a minute, he crept slowly over the grass in the garden, carefully avoiding the trees and bushes. He moved quietly, step by step, listening to his own footsteps. It took him five minutes to reach the lit window. He remembered that just below the window, there were several thick bushes of elder and whitebeam. He had carefully checked to see if the door from the house into the garden was shut while passing, and it was. Finally, he reached the bushes and hid behind them, holding his breath. "I need to wait now," he thought, "to calm them down if they heard me. I can't cough or sneeze."

He waited for two minutes. His heart was pounding so hard that it felt like he could barely breathe. "No, I can't stand this pounding in my chest," he thought. "I can't wait any longer." He was hiding behind a bush in the shadows, with the light from the window shining on the front part of the bush.

"How red the whitebeam berries are," he muttered, not knowing why. Softly and silently, step by step, he crept up to the window, rising on his tiptoes. All of Fyodor Pavlovitch's bedroom was visible to him. It wasn't a big room and was divided in two by a red screen, which Fyodor Pavlovitch always called "Chinese." The word "Chinese" flashed in Mitya's mind. "And behind that screen is Grushenka," thought Mitya. He began watching Fyodor Pavlovitch, who was wearing a new striped silk robe that Mitya had never seen before, along with a silk cord tied around his waist. He had on a clean, fancy shirt of fine linen with gold buttons peeking out from under the robe's collar. On his head, Fyodor Pavlovitch had the same red bandage that Alyosha had seen.

"He's all dressed up," thought Mitya.

His father was standing by the window, lost in thought. Suddenly, he jerked his head up, listened for a moment, and hearing nothing, walked to the table. He poured himself half a glass of brandy from the decanter and drank it quickly. Then he sighed deeply, stood still for a second, and then casually walked to the mirror on the wall. He lifted the red bandage on his forehead with his right hand and began examining the bruises and scars that had not yet faded.

"He's alone," thought Mitya. "He must be alone."

Fyodor Pavlovitch moved away from the mirror and suddenly turned toward the window, looking out. Mitya quickly slipped back into the shadows.

"She could be behind the screen. Maybe she's asleep by now," he thought with a painful pang in his heart. Fyodor Pavlovitch moved away from the window. "He's looking for her outside. So, she's not there. Why would he be staring into the dark? He's desperate with impatience." Mitya moved back again and began watching through the window once more. The old man had sat down at the table, clearly disappointed. Finally, he leaned his elbow on the table and rested his right cheek in his hand. Mitya watched him closely.

"He's alone, he's alone!" he repeated again to himself. "If she were here, his face would look different."

Strangely enough, a sharp, irrational irritation grew in his heart because she wasn't there. "It's not that she's not here," he told himself, "but that I can't be sure whether she is or not." Mitya would later recall that his mind was exceptionally clear at that moment, that he noticed everything down to the smallest detail and missed nothing. But with every passing second, a deep sense of uncertainty and helplessness was growing in his heart. "Is she here or not?" The angry doubt filled him up, and suddenly, he made a decision. He reached out and softly knocked on the window frame. He knocked the signal that the old man had agreed on with Smerdyakov—two slow knocks and then three quicker ones, the signal that meant "Grushenka is here!"

The old man jumped, lifted his head quickly, and sprang up. He rushed to the window. Mitya instantly moved back into the shadows. Fyodor Pavlovitch opened the window and stuck his entire head out.

"Grushenka, is that you? Is it you?" he whispered nervously, his voice shaking. "Where are you, my angel, where are you?" He was out of breath and extremely anxious.

"He's alone," Mitya confirmed to himself.

"Where are you?" the old man called again. He leaned out further, sticking his head out up to his shoulders, and looked in all directions, left and right. "Come here, I have a little present for you. Come, I'll show you..."

"He means the three thousand," Mitya thought.

"But where are you? Are you at the door? I'll open it right now."

The old man was almost climbing out of the window, trying to peer into the darkness toward the garden door. In just a second, he would've definitely run out to open the door without waiting for Grushenka's answer.

Mitya looked at him from the side without moving. The old man's profile, which he hated so much, his hanging Adam's apple, his hooked nose, and his lips that smiled in greedy anticipation, were all brightly lit by the slanting lamplight coming from the room to the left. A terrible surge of hatred suddenly filled Mitya's heart: "There he was, his rival, the man who had tormented him and ruined his life!" It was that sudden, furious, revengeful anger he had spoken of, as if he had predicted it, to Alyosha four days ago in the arbor, when, in response to Alyosha's question, "How can you say you'll kill our father?" he had said, "I don't know, I don't know. Maybe I won't kill him, maybe I will. I'm afraid he'll suddenly become so disgusting to me at that moment. I hate his double chin, his nose, his eyes, his shameless grin. I feel a personal hatred. That's what I'm afraid of, that it will be too much for me."

This personal hatred was becoming unbearable. Mitya was losing control of himself. Suddenly, he pulled the brass pestle out of his pocket.

"God was watching over me then," Mitya would later say. At that very moment, Grigory woke up from his sickbed. Earlier that evening, he had gone through the treatment that Smerdyakov had described to Ivan. He had rubbed himself all over with vodka mixed with a secret, very strong concoction, then drank the rest of it while his wife repeated a certain prayer over him, and then he went to bed. Marfa Ignatyevna had tasted the drink as well, and, not being used to strong alcohol, was sleeping deeply beside her husband.

But Grigory woke up in the night, suddenly. After thinking for a moment, even though he immediately felt a sharp pain in his back, he sat up in bed. He thought for another moment, then got up and dressed quickly. Maybe his conscience bothered him at the idea of sleeping while the house was left unguarded "in such dangerous times." Smerdyakov was lying motionless in the next room, exhausted from his seizure. Marfa Ignatyevna didn't move. "That drink was too much for her," Grigory thought as he glanced at her. Groaning, he went out onto the steps. He probably only meant to look out from the steps since he could barely walk because of the pain in his back and his right leg. But he suddenly remembered that he hadn't locked the small gate to the garden that evening. Grigory was a punctual and precise man, always following the same routine for years. Limping and grimacing in pain, he went down the steps and headed toward the garden. Yes, the gate was wide open. Without thinking, he stepped into the garden. Maybe he thought he saw something, or heard a sound, but when he glanced to the left, he noticed that his master's window was open. No one was looking out of it.

"Why is it open? It's not summer anymore," Grigory thought. And at that very moment, he saw something strange in the garden ahead of him. Forty steps away, it looked like someone was running in the dark, a shadow moving quickly.

"Good Lord!" cried Grigory, forgetting the pain in his back, and he hurried to cut off the running figure. He took a shortcut— clearly, he knew the garden better—and the figure ran toward the bathhouse, then went behind it and headed for the garden fence. Grigory followed closely, not letting the figure out of his sight, running and forgetting everything else. He reached the fence just as the person was climbing over it. Grigory shouted, overwhelmed with emotion, grabbed him, and clutched his leg with both hands.

Yes, his instincts had been right. He recognized him. It was him, the "monster," the "parricide."

"Parricide!" the old man screamed so loudly that the whole neighborhood could hear, but he didn't have time to yell more. He fell to the ground as if struck by lightning.

Mitya jumped back into the garden and bent over the fallen man. He still had the brass pestle in his hand, and without thinking, he threw it into the grass. It landed two steps away from Grigory, not in the grass but on the path, in plain sight. For a few seconds, he stared at the old man lying on the ground. Grigory's head was covered in blood. Mitya reached out his hand and began to feel it. He would remember later that he had been desperate to know if he had broken the old man's skull or just knocked him out with the pestle. But the blood was pouring out horribly, and soon Mitya's fingers were soaked with the hot stream. He remembered taking a clean white handkerchief out of his pocket, the one he had brought for his visit to Madame Hohlakov, and pressing it to the old man's head, trying senselessly to wipe the blood from his face and temples. But the handkerchief was immediately soaked with blood.

"Good heavens! Why am I doing this?" Mitya thought, suddenly coming to his senses. "If I broke his skull, how can I tell now? And what does it even matter now?" he added hopelessly. "If I killed him, then I killed him... You've had your misfortune, old man, and there you must lie!" he said aloud. Then, turning toward the fence, he climbed over it into the lane and started running— the blood-soaked handkerchief clenched in his right hand. As he ran, he shoved it into the back pocket of his coat. He ran as fast as he could, and the few people he passed in the dark streets would later remember seeing a man running that night. He flew back toward Widow Morozov's house.

After Mitya had left the house earlier that evening, Fenya had rushed to the head porter, Nazar Ivanovitch, begging him, for the love of Christ, "not to let the captain back in tonight or tomorrow." Nazar Ivanovitch had promised, but then his mistress had sent for him suddenly, and on his way upstairs, he ran into his nephew, a twenty-year-old boy who had recently come from the countryside. Nazar told him to take his place but forgot to mention "the captain." So when Mitya came running up to the gate and knocked, the boy recognized him right away since Mitya had tipped him several times before. He immediately opened the gate and let him in with a friendly smile, saying, "Agrafena Alexandrovna isn't home right now, you know."

"Where is she, Prohor?" Mitya asked, stopping in his tracks. "She left two hours ago with Timofey for Mokroe."

"What for?" Mitya cried out.

"I don't know. Something about an officer. Someone invited her, and they sent horses to fetch her."

Mitya didn't wait. He ran off like a madman to find Fenya.

Chapter 5: A Sudden Resolution

She was sitting in the kitchen with her grandmother; they were both just about to go to bed. Trusting in Nazar Ivanovitch, they hadn't locked the door. Mitya rushed in, grabbed Fenya by the throat, and shouted, "Tell me right now! Where is she? Who is she with at Mokroe?" He roared with fury. Both women screamed.

"I'll tell you! I'll tell you everything, Dmitri Fyodorovitch, darling, I won't hide anything," Fenya stammered, terrified. "She went to Mokroe, to see her officer."

"What officer?" Mitya shouted.

"Her officer, the same one she used to know, the one who abandoned her five years ago," Fenya babbled as quickly as she could.

Mitya released her throat. He stood there, pale as death, unable to speak, but his eyes showed that he understood everything. He realized it all from her very first word, understanding the entire situation. Poor Fenya was too terrified at that moment to notice if he understood or not. She remained sitting on the trunk where she had been when he ran into the room, trembling all over, holding her hands out in front of her as if trying to protect herself. She seemed frozen in that position. Her wide, frightened eyes were fixed on him without blinking. To make things worse, both of his hands were smeared with blood. While running, he must have wiped his forehead with them, spreading blood across his forehead and right cheek. Fenya was on the verge of hysterics. The old cook had jumped up and was staring at him like a madwoman, nearly fainting from terror.

Mitya stood still for a moment, then mechanically sat down in a chair next to Fenya. He didn't think about what he was doing but seemed to be in shock, frozen. But everything was as clear as day: that officer—he knew about him. He had known everything. He had heard it from Grushenka herself, had known that a letter from him had arrived a month ago. So, for a whole month, all of this had been going on behind his back, and he hadn't even thought about it! But how could he have forgotten about this officer so easily, after hearing about him? That question now stood in front of him like something monstrous, and he looked at this monstrous thing with horror, growing colder with fear.

But suddenly, as gently as a kind child, he began speaking to Fenya, as if he had completely forgotten how he had just frightened and hurt her. He started questioning her with great precision, which was surprising given his current state. Although Fenya kept glancing at his blood-stained hands in fear, she quickly and eagerly answered every question, wanting to tell him everything. Little by little, she explained the details of the day, almost as if she enjoyed helping him, eager to be of service. She described everything: the visit from Rakitin and Alyosha, how she, Fenya, had been keeping watch, how her mistress had left, and how she had called out to Alyosha from the window, asking him to give Mitya her message: "to remember forever how she had loved him for an hour."

When Mitya heard this, he suddenly smiled, and a flush of color appeared on his pale cheeks. At the same moment, Fenya, no longer afraid to ask questions, said, "Look at your hands, Dmitri Fyodorovitch. They're covered in blood!"

"Yes," Mitya answered absently. He looked at his hands for a moment, then immediately forgot about them and Fenya's question.

He fell silent again. Twenty minutes had passed since he had rushed in. His initial terror had passed, but clearly, a new and firm resolve had taken hold of him. He suddenly stood up, smiling dreamily.

"What happened to you, sir?" asked Fenya, pointing to his hands again. She spoke softly, almost with compassion, as if she now felt close to him in his grief. Mitya looked at his hands again.

"That's blood, Fenya," he said, looking at her with a strange expression. "That's human blood, and my God, why was it shed? But... Fenya, there's a fence here" (he looked at her like he was giving her a riddle), "a tall fence, frightening to look at. But tomorrow, at dawn, when the sun rises, Mitya will jump over that fence. You don't understand what fence, Fenya, but don't worry.... You'll understand tomorrow when you hear about it... and now, goodbye. I won't stand in her way. I'll step aside, I know how to step aside. Live your life, my joy You loved me for an hour, so remember Mityenka Karamazov forever. . . She always called me Mityenka, do you remember?"

And with those words, he suddenly walked out of the kitchen. Fenya was almost more frightened by his sudden departure than she had been when he had burst in and grabbed her.

Just ten minutes later, Dmitri went to see Pyotr Ilyitch Perhotin, the young official to whom he had pawned his pistols. It was already half-past eight, and Pyotr Ilyitch had finished his evening tea and had just put his coat on again to go to the "Metropolis" to play billiards. Mitya caught him just as he was leaving.

Seeing Mitya's face smeared with blood, the young man cried out in surprise.

"Good heavens! What's happened to you?"

"I've come for my pistols," Mitya said, "and I've brought the money. Thanks very much. I'm in a hurry, Pyotr Ilyitch, so please be quick."

Pyotr Ilyitch became more and more shocked. He suddenly noticed the bundle of banknotes in Mitya's hand, and even stranger, Mitya was holding the money in a very odd way: he had the notes in his right hand, held out in front of him as if showing them off. Perhotin's servant boy, who had met Mitya in the hallway, later said that Mitya had entered the house in the same way, with the money held out in his hand, so he must have been carrying it like that as he walked through the streets. The notes were all brightly colored hundred-rouble bills, and the fingers holding them were stained with blood.

When Pyotr Ilyitch was later asked about the amount of money, he said it was hard to judge at a glance, but it looked like two thousand, maybe three thousand roubles—it was a large, "fat" bundle of cash. "Dmitri Fyodorovitch," he later testified, "didn't seem like himself. He wasn't drunk, but he seemed almost like he was in a state of exaltation, lost to everything around him, yet at the same time focused, like he was searching for something but couldn't make a decision. He was in a great hurry, answering abruptly and strangely, and at times he even seemed cheerful."

"But what's wrong with you? What happened?" cried Pyotr Ilyitch, staring at his guest in shock. "Why are you covered in blood? Did you fall? Look at yourself!"

He grabbed Mitya by the elbow and led him to a mirror. Seeing his bloodstained face, Mitya started and scowled angrily.

"Damn it! That's just what I needed," he muttered furiously. He quickly shifted the bundle of notes from his right hand to his left and impulsively pulled out his handkerchief. But the handkerchief was soaked with blood too—it was the same one he had used to wipe Grigory's face. There wasn't a clean spot left on it; it had already dried stiff and couldn't be opened up. Mitya threw it angrily to the floor.

"Damn it!" he said. "Don't you have some kind of rag... to wipe my face?"

"So you're just stained, not hurt? You should wash up," said Pyotr Ilyitch. "There's a washstand here. I'll pour some water."

"A washstand? Sure, but where do I put this?" Mitya said, looking strangely confused as he pointed to the bundle of hundred-rouble notes, as if waiting for Pyotr Ilyitch to decide what he should do with his own money.

"Put it in your pocket, or leave it on the table here. It won't disappear."

"In my pocket? Yes, in my pocket. All right.... But wait, this is nonsense," he suddenly said, as if snapping out of a daze. "Let's settle the matter with the pistols first. Give them back to me. Here's your money... because I really need them... and I don't have a minute, not a single minute to waste."

He pulled out the top note from the bundle and held it out to Pyotr Ilyitch.

"But I won't have enough change. Don't you have something smaller?"

"No," said Mitya, glancing again at the bundle. As if not trusting himself, he shuffled through the top few bills.

"No, they're all the same," he added, looking again at Pyotr Ilyitch with a questioning expression.

"How did you get so much money?" Pyotr Ilyitch asked. "Wait, I'll send my boy to Plotnikov's—they close late—maybe they can break it. Misha!" he called into the hallway.

"Plotnikov's shop, great!" Mitya exclaimed, as if struck by an idea. Turning to the boy who came in, he said, "Misha, go to Plotnikov's and tell them Dmitri Fyodorovitch sends his regards and will be there soon.... But listen, tell them to have champagne—three dozen bottles—ready before I arrive, and packed like last time for Mokroe. I took four dozen bottles then," he added, addressing Pyotr Ilyitch suddenly. "They know all about it. Don't worry about it, Misha," he turned back to the boy. "Wait, listen; tell them to add cheese, Strasbourg pies, smoked fish, ham, caviar, and everything else they've got, up to a hundred roubles, or a hundred and twenty, like last time. And don't forget dessert—sweets, pears, watermelons, two or three or four—no, just one melon's enough, and chocolate, candy, toffee, fondants; everything I bought for Mokroe last time, about three hundred roubles' worth with the champagne... just like that again. And remember, Misha, is your name Misha? It is, right?" He turned to Pyotr Ilyitch again.

"Hold on," Pyotr Ilyitch interrupted, watching him with concern, "you'd better go yourself and explain it. He's going to get it all mixed up."

"He will, I see it! Oh, Misha, I was going to kiss you for this errand.   If you don't mess it up, there's ten roubles for you, so hurry! Champagne is the most important, but get brandy too, and red and white wine, just like before. They know what I got then."

"But wait!" Pyotr Ilyitch interrupted again, sounding impatient. "Let him just go change the money and tell them not to close, and you can go give the rest of the orders yourself. Give him your note. Off you go, Misha! Hurry up!"

It seemed like Pyotr Ilyitch was rushing Misha out on purpose since the boy was standing there with his mouth wide open, staring in shock at Mitya's blood-covered face and trembling, blood-stained hands holding the notes.

"All right, come wash up," said Pyotr Ilyitch firmly. "Put the money on the table or in your pocket. That's it, come along. But take off your coat."

As he helped Mitya take off his coat, he cried out again:

"Look, your coat's covered in blood, too!"

"That... it's not the coat. It's just a little on the sleeve. And that's only where the handkerchief was. It must've soaked through. I must've sat on the handkerchief at Fenya's, and the blood went through," Mitya explained, with a childlike innocence that was shocking. Pyotr Ilyitch frowned as he listened.

"Well, you must've gotten into something; you must've fought someone," he muttered.

They began washing up. Pyotr Ilyitch held the pitcher and poured the water. Mitya, in a desperate rush, barely soaped his hands (which were shaking, something Pyotr Ilyitch remembered later). But Pyotr Ilyitch insisted he soap them thoroughly and scrub more. The young official seemed to gain more and more control over Mitya as time went on. It's worth noting that he was a man of strong character.

"Look, your nails aren't clean. Now scrub your face; here, on your temples, by your ear.... Are you going out in that shirt? Where are you going? Look, the cuff of your right sleeve is covered in blood."

"Yeah, it's all bloody," Mitya said, glancing at his shirt cuff.

"Then change your shirt."

"I don't have time. You see, I'll..." Mitya continued, with the same trusting tone, drying his face and hands on the towel and putting his coat back on. "I'll just roll up the cuff. It won't show under the coat... see?"

"Now tell me, what have you been up to? Have you been fighting with someone? Were you at a tavern again, like before? Did you beat up that captain again?" Pyotr Ilyitch asked, sounding reproachful. "Who did you beat this time... or did you kill someone?"

"Nonsense!" said Mitya. "Why 'nonsense'?"

"Don't worry about it," Mitya suddenly laughed. "I knocked down an old woman in the marketplace just now."

"Knocked down? An old woman?"

"An old man!" Mitya shouted, looking straight at Pyotr Ilyitch, laughing and raising his voice like Pyotr was hard of hearing.

"Good grief! An old woman, an old man. Did you kill someone?"

"We made up. We had a fight—and then we made up. It was in a place I know. We parted as friends. He's an idiot. He's forgiven me.... By now, he's definitely forgiven me... unless he's gotten up, in which case, he hasn't forgiven me"—Mitya suddenly winked—"but forget about him, you know, I say, Pyotr Ilyitch, forget him! Don't think about him! I don't care right now!" Mitya blurted out, decisively.

"Why do you keep picking fights with everyone? Just like you did with that captain over nothing. You've been fighting, and now you're off on a spree—that's typical of you! Three dozen bottles of champagne—what do you need all that for?"

"Bravo! Now give me the pistols. Honestly, I don't have time right now. I'd like to sit and chat with you, my friend, but I really can't. And it's too late for talking anyway. Where's my money? Where did I put it?" Mitya cried, patting his pockets frantically.

"You put it on the table... yourself. Here it is. Did you forget? Money's like dirt or water to you, isn't it? Here are your pistols. It's funny, at six o'clock you pawned them for ten roubles, and now you've got thousands—two or three, I'd guess."

"Three, definitely," Mitya laughed, stuffing the notes into the side pocket of his trousers.

"You'll lose them like that. Did you find a gold mine?"

"The mines? The gold mines?" Mitya shouted at the top of his voice and burst into laughter. "Would you like to go to the mines,

Perhotin? There's a lady I know who'll give you three thousand roubles if you go. She did it for me—she's really into gold mines. You know Madame Hohlakov?"

"I don't know her, but I've heard of her and seen her around. Did she really give you three thousand? Are you serious?" Pyotr Ilyitch asked, looking at him suspiciously.

"As soon as the sun rises tomorrow, as soon as Phœbus, ever young, flies up into the sky, praising and glorifying God, go to Madame Hohlakov and ask her if she gave me that three thousand. Go ahead, find out."

"I don't know what kind of relationship you two have... but since you say it so confidently, I guess she did give it to you. You've got the money in your hands, but instead of going to Siberia, you're spending it all... where are you really headed now, huh?"

"To Mokroe."

"To Mokroe? But it's nighttime!"

"Once the lad had everything, now the lad has nothing," Mitya suddenly cried out.

"What do you mean 'nothing'? You've got thousands!"

"I'm not talking about money. Forget the money! I'm talking about women.

Fickle is the heart of woman, Treacherous and full of vice; I agree with Ulysses—that's what he says."

"I don't understand you!" "Am I drunk?"

"Not drunk, but worse."

"I'm drunk in spirit, Pyotr Ilyitch, drunk in spirit! But enough about that."

"What are you doing? Are you loading the pistol?" "Yes, I'm loading the pistol."

Mitya opened the pistol case, took out the powder horn, carefully poured in the charge, and then took the bullet. Before loading it, he held it up to the candle, staring at it between two fingers.

"Why are you looking at the bullet?" asked Pyotr Ilyitch, watching him with concern.

"Oh, just a thought. If you were going to put that bullet into your

brain, would you look at it first or not?"

"Why look at it?"

"It's going into my brain, so it's interesting to see what it looks like. But that's just foolishness, a moment of foolishness. Anyway, it's done now," he added, loading the bullet and packing it in with the ramrod. "Pyotr Ilyitch, my friend, this is all nonsense, such nonsense, and if only you knew how much nonsense! Now, give me a piece of paper."

"Here's some paper."

"No, a clean piece, writing paper. That's better."

Taking a pen from the table, Mitya quickly scribbled two lines, folded the paper in four, and tucked it into his waistcoat pocket. Then he locked the pistols in the case and held it in his hand. He looked at Pyotr Ilyitch with a slow, thoughtful smile.

"Now, let's go."

"Where are we going? No, wait a minute... are you thinking of putting that bullet in your brain or something?" Pyotr Ilyitch asked, worried.

"I was just joking about the bullet! I want to live. I love life! You can be sure of that. I love golden-haired Phœbus and his warm light... dear Pyotr Ilyitch, do you know what it means to step aside?"

"What do you mean by 'stepping aside'?"

"To make way. To make way for someone you care about and for someone you hate. And to let the one you hate become dear to you—that's what stepping aside means! To tell them, 'God bless you, go on, live your life,' while I—"

"While you—?"

"That's enough, let's go."

"Honestly, I'm thinking of telling someone to stop you from going," said Pyotr Ilyitch, watching him closely. "What are you going to Mokroe for?"

"There's a woman there, a woman. That's all you need to know. Now stop asking questions."

"Listen, even though you're a wild one, I've always liked you... but I'm worried about you."

"Thanks, old friend. You call me wild. Wild! That's what I always say. Wild! Oh wait, here's Misha! I almost forgot about him."

Misha rushed in, out of breath, with a handful of change and reported that everyone at Plotnikov's was busy. "They're packing up the bottles, the fish, and the tea. Everything will be ready soon," he said. Mitya grabbed ten roubles and handed them to Pyotr Ilyitch, then threw another ten-rouble note to Misha.

"Don't do that!" shouted Pyotr Ilyitch. "I won't allow that kind of thing here. It's a bad habit. Put your money away. Save it for tomorrow—you'll probably need to borrow from me again soon. Why do you keep stuffing those notes in your side pocket? You're going to lose them!"

"I say, my dear fellow, let's go to Mokroe together." "What should I go for?"

"I say, let's open a bottle at once, and drink to life! I want to drink, and especially to drink with you. I've never drunk with you, have I?"

"Very well, we can go to the 'Metropolis.' I was just going there."

"I haven't time for that. Let's drink at the Plotnikovs', in the back room. Shall I ask you a riddle?"

"Ask away."

Mitya took the piece of paper out of his waistcoat pocket, unfolded it, and showed it. In a large, distinct hand was written: "I punish myself for my whole life, my whole life I punish!"

"I will certainly speak to someone, I'll go at once," said Pyotr Ilyitch, after reading the paper.

"You won't have time, dear boy, come and have a drink. March!"

Plotnikov's shop was at the corner of the street, next door but one to Pyotr Ilyitch's. It was the largest grocery shop in our town, and by no means a bad one, belonging to some rich merchants. They kept everything that could be found in a Petersburg shop: groceries of all sorts, wines "bottled by the brothers Eliseyev," fruits, cigars, tea, coffee, sugar, and so on. There were three shop assistants and two errand boys always employed. Though our part of the country had grown poorer, the landowners had left, and trade had worsened, yet the grocery stores flourished as before, every year with increasing prosperity; there were always plenty of purchasers for their goods.

They were awaiting Mitya with impatience in the shop. They vividly remembered how three or four weeks ago, he had bought wine and goods of all sorts to the value of several hundred roubles, paid for in cash (they would never have let him have anything on credit, of course). They remembered that then, as now, he had a bundle of hundred-rouble notes in his hand and had scattered them at random, without bargaining, without reflecting, or caring to reflect what use so much wine and provisions would be to him. The story was told all over town that, driving off then with Grushenka to Mokroe, he had "spent three thousand in one night and the following day, and had come back from the spree without a penny." He had picked up a whole troop of gypsies (encamped in our neighborhood at the time), who for two days got money without limit from him while he was drunk and drank expensive wine without restraint. People used to tell, laughing at Mitya, how he had given champagne to grimy-handed peasants, and feasted the village women and girls on sweets and Strasburg pies. Though to laugh at Mitya to his face was rather a risky thing to do, there was much laughter behind his back, especially in the tavern, at his own public confession that all he had gotten from Grushenka by this "escapade" was "permission to kiss her foot, and that was the most she had allowed him."

By the time Mitya and Pyotr Ilyitch reached the shop, they found a cart with three horses harnessed abreast, with bells, and Andrey, the driver, ready and waiting for Mitya at the entrance. In the shop, they had almost finished packing one box of provisions and were only waiting for Mitya's arrival to nail it down and put it in the cart. Pyotr Ilyitch was astounded.

"Where did this cart come from in such a hurry?" he asked Mitya.

"I met Andrey as I ran to you, and told him to drive straight here to the shop. There's no time to lose. Last time I drove with Timofey, but Timofey now has gone on ahead with the witch. Will we be very late, Andrey?"

"They'll only get there an hour at most before us, not even that maybe. I got Timofey ready to start. I know how he'll drive. Their pace won't match ours, Dmitri Fyodorovitch. How could it be? They won't get there an hour earlier!" Andrey, a lanky, red-haired, middle-aged driver, wearing a full-skirted coat, and with a kaftan on his arm, replied warmly.

"Fifty roubles for vodka if we're only an hour behind them."

"I warrant the time, Dmitri Fyodorovitch. Eh, they won't be half an hour before us, let alone an hour."

Though Mitya bustled about seeing after things, he gave his orders strangely, as if disconnectedly, and incoherently. He would start a sentence and forget the end of it. Pyotr Ilyitch found himself obliged to step in and help.

"Four hundred roubles' worth, not less than four hundred roubles' worth, just as it was then," commanded Mitya. "Four dozen champagne, not a bottle less."

"What do you want with so much? What's it for? Wait!" cried Pyotr Ilyitch. "What's this box? What's in it? Surely there isn't four hundred roubles' worth here?"

The shop assistants began explaining politely that the first box contained only half a dozen bottles of champagne and only "the most essential items," such as savory snacks, sweets, toffee, etc. But the bulk of the goods ordered would be packed and sent off, as on the previous occasion, in a special cart with three horses traveling at full speed, so that it would arrive not more than an hour later than Dmitri Fyodorovitch himself.

"Not more than an hour! Not more than an hour! And pack in more toffee and fondants. The girls there are so fond of it," Mitya insisted heatedly.

"The fondants are all right. But what do you want with four dozen bottles of champagne? One would be enough," said Pyotr Ilyitch, almost angrily. He began bargaining, asking for a bill of the goods, and refused to be satisfied. But he only succeeded in saving a hundred roubles. In the end, it was agreed that only three hundred roubles' worth should be sent.

"Well, you may go to the devil!" cried Pyotr Ilyitch, on second thoughts. "What's it to do with me? Throw away your money, since it's cost you nothing."

"This way, my economist, this way, don't be angry." Mitya drew him into a room at the back of the shop. "They'll give us a bottle here directly. We'll taste it. Oh, Pyotr Ilyitch, come along with me, for you're a nice fellow, the sort I like."

Mitya sat down on a wicker chair before a little table covered with a dirty dinner napkin. Pyotr Ilyitch sat down opposite, and the champagne soon appeared. Oysters were even suggested to the gentlemen: "First-class oysters, the last lot in."

"To hell with the oysters. I don't eat them. And we don't need anything," cried Pyotr Ilyitch, almost angrily.

"There's no time for oysters," said Mitya. "And I'm not hungry. Do you know, friend," he said suddenly, with feeling, "I never have liked all this chaos."

"Who does like it? Three dozen bottles of champagne for peasants, upon my word, that's enough to make anyone angry!"

"That's not what I mean. I'm talking about a higher kind of order. There's no order in me, no higher purpose. But... that's all over. There's no need to grieve about it. It's too late, damn it! My whole life has been disorder, and I need to set it right. Is that a joke, eh?"

"You're raving, not making jokes!"

"Glory be to God in Heaven, Glory be to God in me..."

"That verse came from my heart once. It's not really a verse, but more like a tear... I made it up myself... not while I was pulling the captain's beard, though."

"Why do you bring him up all of a sudden?"

"Why do I bring him up? Foolishness! Everything comes to an end; everything gets balanced out. That's all there is to it."

"You know, I keep thinking about your pistols."

"That's nonsense, too! Drink, and stop being fanciful. I love life. I've loved it too much, shamefully much. Enough! Let's drink to life, dear friend. What can be more precious than life? Nothing! To life, and to one queen of queens!"

"Let's drink to life and to your queen, too, if you like."

They each drank a glass. Although Mitya was excited and lively, there was a hint of melancholy in him, as if some heavy, overwhelming worry was pressing down on him.

"Misha... here comes your Misha! Misha, come here, my boy, drink this glass to Phœbus, the golden-haired, of tomorrow's dawn."

"What are you giving him that for?" cried Pyotr Ilyitch, irritably. "Yes, yes, let me! I want to!"

"E—ech!"

Misha emptied the glass, bowed, and ran out.

"He'll remember it later," Mitya remarked. "Women... I love women! What are they? The queens of creation! My heart feels heavy, Pyotr Ilyitch. Do you remember Hamlet? 'I am very sorry, good Horatio! Alas, poor Yorick!' Maybe I'm Yorick now, and later just a skull."

Pyotr Ilyitch listened in silence. Mitya, too, was silent for a while.

"What dog is that you've got here?" he asked the shop assistant casually, noticing a pretty little lapdog with dark eyes sitting in the corner.

"It belongs to Varvara Alexyevna, the mistress," the clerk answered. "She brought it here and forgot it. It needs to be taken back to her."

"I saw one like it... in the regiment..." murmured Mitya dreamily, "only that one had a broken hind leg... By the way, Pyotr Ilyitch, I wanted to ask you: have you ever stolen anything in your life?"

"What kind of question is that?"

"Oh, I didn't mean anything serious. Like, from someone's pocket. I don't mean government money; everyone steals that, and I'm sure you do too…"

"Go to hell."

"I'm talking about other people's money. Stealing straight out of a pocket? From a purse, maybe?"

"I once stole twenty copecks from my mother when I was nine years old. I took it off the table in secret and held onto it tightly."

"Well, and what happened?"

"Oh, nothing. I kept it for three days, then I felt ashamed, confessed, and gave it back."

"And what happened next?"

"Of course, I got whipped. But why are you asking? Have you stolen something?"

"I have," said Mitya, winking slyly.

"What did you steal?" Pyotr Ilyitch asked curiously.

"I stole twenty copecks from my mother when I was nine years old, and gave it back three days later."

As he said this, Mitya suddenly stood up.

"Dmitri Fyodorovitch, are we leaving now?" Andrey called from the door of the shop.

"Are you ready? We're coming!" Mitya started. "Just a few more words—Andrey, give him a glass of vodka before we start. And give him some brandy too! That box," he pointed to the one with the pistols, "put it under my seat. Goodbye, Pyotr Ilyitch, don't hold anything against me."

"But you're coming back tomorrow?" "Of course."

"Will you settle the bill now?" called the clerk, hurrying forward.

"Oh, yes, the bill. Right." Mitya pulled out the bundle of notes from his pocket again, picked out three hundred roubles, threw them on the counter, and ran out of the shop quickly. Everyone followed him out, bowing and wishing him good luck. Andrey, coughing from the brandy he had just swallowed, jumped up onto the box. But Mitya had barely taken his seat when, to his surprise, he saw Fenya in front of him. She came running, panting, clasped her hands together, and fell at his feet.

"Dmitri Fyodorovitch, dear Dmitri Fyodorovitch, please don't harm my mistress. It was me who told you everything… and don't kill him, please! He came first, and he's hers now! He's going to marry Agrafena Alexandrovna. That's why he came back from Siberia. Please, Dmitri Fyodorovitch, don't take another man's life!"

"Tut-tut-tut! So that's it, huh? You're off to cause trouble!" muttered Pyotr Ilyitch. "Now it's all clear, as clear as day. Dmitri Fyodorovitch, give me your pistols right now if you plan on acting like a real man," he shouted to Mitya. "Do you hear me, Dmitri?"

"The pistols? Wait, brother, I'll throw them into the pool on the way," Mitya answered. "Fenya, get up. Don't kneel to me. Mitya won't hurt anyone. The fool won't hurt anyone again. But, Fenya," he shouted, having taken his seat, "I hurt you earlier, so forgive me. Have pity on me. Forgive a scoundrel… But it doesn't matter if you don't. It's all the same now. Now then, Andrey, let's go! Full speed!"

Andrey whipped up the horses, and the bells began ringing. "Goodbye, Pyotr Ilyitch! My last tear is for you!"

"He's not drunk, but he's babbling like a madman," Pyotr Ilyitch thought as he watched Mitya leave. He had half a mind to stay and make sure the remaining wines and provisions were packed properly, knowing they might cheat Mitya. But, suddenly irritated with himself, he cursed, turned away, and went to the tavern to play billiards.

"He's a fool, though he's a good guy," he muttered as he walked. "I've heard about that officer, Grushenka's old flame. Well, if he's come back... And those pistols! Damn it all! I'm not his babysitter! Let them do whatever they want. It'll come to nothing. They'll drink and fight, fight and make up. They're not the kind of people to really do anything serious. What does he mean by 'I'm stepping aside, I'm punishing myself?' It'll come to nothing! He's shouted things like that a thousand times, drunk, in the taverns. But now he's not drunk. 'Drunk in spirit'—they love their fancy phrases, these fools. Am I his nurse? He must have been fighting; his face was all bloody. With who? I'll find out at the 'Metropolis.' And that handkerchief soaked in blood... It's still on my floor... Damn it!"

He reached the tavern in a foul mood and quickly got involved in a game. The game lifted his spirits. He played a second game, and then, suddenly, he started telling one of his partners that Dmitri Karamazov had come into some money again—about three thousand roubles—and had gone off to Mokroe to spend it with Grushenka. This news caught the attention of his listeners. They all started talking about it, not laughing, but with a strange seriousness. They stopped playing.

"Three thousand? But where could he have gotten three thousand?"

Questions started flying. The story of Madame Hohlakov's gift was met with skepticism.

"Hasn't he robbed his old father? That's the real question." "Three thousand? There's something odd about that."

"He said in front of everyone that he'd kill his father. We all heard him. And he mentioned three thousand..."

Pyotr Ilyitch listened, growing short and abrupt in his answers. Though he had intended to mention the blood on Mitya's face and hands, he suddenly didn't feel like bringing it up anymore.

They started a third game, and gradually, the conversation about Mitya faded. But by the end of the third game, Pyotr Ilyitch no longer felt like playing. He set down his cue, skipped the supper he had planned, and left the tavern. When he reached the market square, he stopped, confused by his own thoughts. He realized that what he really wanted was to go to Fyodor Pavlovitch's place and see if anything had happened there. "Over some ridiculous nonsense, as it's bound to turn out, am I really going to wake everyone up and make a scene? Damn it, is it my job to look after them?"

In a bad mood, he started heading home, but then he suddenly remembered Fenya. "Damn it all! I should've questioned her earlier," he thought angrily. "I would've found out everything." The urge to talk to her and get some answers became so strong that when he was halfway home, he abruptly turned around and headed toward Grushenka's place. When he reached the gate, he knocked. The sound of his knock in the quiet night sobered him a bit, making him feel even more annoyed. No one answered; everyone in the house was asleep.

"And here I am about to cause a fuss," he thought, feeling frustrated. But instead of leaving, he knocked harder, making a racket in the silent street.

"If they won't come, I'll wake them up, I swear!" he muttered with each knock, fuming at himself, but continuing to pound harder on the gate.

Chapter 6: "I Am Coming, Too!"

But Dmitri Fyodorovitch was speeding along the road. It was a little more than twenty versts to Mokroe, but Andrey's three horses galloped at such a pace that the distance might be covered in an hour and a quarter. The swift motion revived Mitya. The air was fresh and cool, and there were big stars shining in the sky. It was the very night, and perhaps the very hour, in which Alyosha fell on the earth, and rapturously swore to love it forever and ever.

All was confusion, confusion, in Mitya's soul, but although many things were goading his heart, at that moment his whole being was yearning for her, his queen, to whom he was flying to look on her for the last time. One thing I can say for certain: his heart did not waver for one instant. I shall perhaps not be believed when I say that this jealous lover felt not the slightest jealousy of this new rival, who seemed to have sprung out of the earth. If any other had appeared on the scene, he would have been jealous at once, and would perhaps have stained his fierce hands with blood again. But as he flew through the night, he felt no envy, no hostility even, for the man who had been her first lover It is true he had not yet seen him.

"Here there was no room for dispute: it was her right and his; this was her first love which, after five years, she had not forgotten; so she had loved him only for those five years, and I, how do I come in? What right have I? Step aside, Mitya, and make way! What am I now? Now everything is over apart from the officer—even if he had not appeared, everything would be over..."

These words would roughly have expressed his feelings, if he had been capable of reasoning. But he could not reason at that moment. His present plan of action had arisen without reasoning. At Fenya's first words, it had sprung from feeling and been adopted in a flash, with all its consequences. And yet, in spite of his resolution, there was confusion in his soul, an agonizing confusion: his resolution did not give him peace. There was so much behind that tortured him. And it seemed strange to him, at moments, to think that he had written his own sentence of death with pen and paper: "I punish myself," and the paper was lying there in his pocket, ready; the pistol was loaded; he had already resolved how, next morning, he would meet the first warm ray of "golden-haired Phœbus."

And yet he could not be quit of the past, of all that he had left behind and that tortured him. He felt that miserably, and the thought of it sank into his heart with despair. There was one moment when he felt an impulse to stop Andrey, to jump out of the cart, to pull out his loaded pistol, and to make an end of everything without waiting for the dawn. But that moment flew by like a spark. The horses galloped on, "devouring space," and as he drew near his goal, again the thought of her, of her alone, took more and more complete possession of his soul, chasing away the fearful images that had been haunting it. Oh, how he longed to look upon her, if only for a moment, if only from a distance!

"She's now with him," he thought, "now I shall see what she looks like with him, her first love, and that's all I want." Never had this woman, who was such a fateful influence in his life, aroused such love in his breast, such new and unknown feeling, surprising even to himself, a feeling tender to devoutness, to self- effacement before her! "I will efface myself!" he said, in a rush of almost hysterical ecstasy.

They had been galloping nearly an hour. Mitya was silent, and though Andrey was, as a rule, a talkative peasant, he did not utter a word either. He seemed afraid to talk; he only whipped up smartly his three lean, but mettlesome, bay horses. Suddenly Mitya cried out in horrible anxiety:

"Andrey! What if they're asleep?"

This thought fell upon him like a blow. It had not occurred to him before.

"It may well be that they're gone to bed by now, Dmitri Fyodorovitch."

Mitya frowned as though in pain. Yes, indeed... he was rushing there... with such feelings... while they were asleep... she was asleep, perhaps, there too.... An angry feeling surged up in his heart.

"Drive on, Andrey! Whip them up! Look alive!" he cried, beside himself.

"But maybe they're not in bed!" Andrey went on after a pause. "Timofey said there were a lot of them there—"

"At the station?"

"Not at the posting-station, but at Plastunov's, at the inn, where they let out horses, too."

"I know. So you say there are a lot of them? How's that? Who are they?" cried Mitya, greatly dismayed at this unexpected news.

"Well, Timofey was saying they're all gentlefolk. Two from our town—who they are I can't say—and there are two others, strangers, maybe more besides. I didn't ask particularly. They've set to playing cards, so Timofey said."

"Cards?"

"So, maybe they're not in bed if they're at cards. It's most likely not more than eleven."

"Quicker, Andrey! Quicker!" Mitya cried again, nervously.

"May I ask you something, sir?" said Andrey, after a pause. "Only I'm afraid of angering you, sir."

"What is it?"

"Why, Fenya threw herself at your feet just now and begged you not to harm her mistress, and someone else, too... so you see, sir— It's I am taking you there... forgive me, sir, it's my conscience... maybe it's stupid of me to speak of it—"

Mitya suddenly seized him by the shoulders from behind. "Are you a driver?" he asked frantically.

"Yes, sir."

"Then you know that one has to make way. What would you say to a driver who wouldn't make way for anyone, but would just drive on and crush people? No, a driver mustn't run over people. One can't run over a man. One can't spoil people's lives. And if you have spoiled a life—punish yourself. If only you've spoiled, if only you've ruined anyone's life—punish yourself and go away."

These phrases burst from Mitya almost hysterically. Though Andrey was surprised at him, he kept up the conversation.

"That's right, Dmitri Fyodorovitch, you're quite right. One mustn't crush or torment a man, or any kind of creature, for every creature is created by God. Take a horse, for instance, for some folks, even among us drivers, drive anyhow. Nothing will restrain them; they just force it along."

"To hell?" Mitya interrupted, and went off into his abrupt, short laugh. "Andrey, simple soul," he seized him by the shoulders again, "tell me, will Dmitri Fyodorovitch Karamazov go to hell, or not, what do you think?"

"I don't know, darling, it depends on you, for you are. you see, sir, when the Son of God was nailed on the Cross and died, He went straight down to hell from the Cross and set free all sinners that were in agony. And the devil groaned, because he thought that he would get no more sinners in hell. And God said to him, then, 'Don't groan, for you shall have all the mighty of the earth, the rulers, the chief judges, and the rich men, and shall be filled up as you have been in all the ages till I come again.' Those were His very words..."

"A peasant legend! Capital! Whip up the left, Andrey!"

"So, you see, sir, who it is hell's for," said Andrey, whipping up the left horse, "but you're like a little child... that's how we look on you... and though you're hasty-tempered, sir, yet God will forgive you for your kind heart."

"And you, do you forgive me, Andrey?"

"What should I forgive you for, sir? You've never done me any harm."

"No, for everyone, for everyone, will you, right here on the road, forgive me on behalf of all? Speak, simple peasant heart!"

"Oh, sir! I'm afraid to drive you, your words are so strange."

But Mitya didn't hear him. He was frantically praying and muttering to himself.

"Lord, receive me with all my sins, and don't condemn me. Let me pass by Your judgment... do not condemn me, for I have condemned myself. Don't condemn me, because I love You, O Lord. I'm a wretch, but I love You. If You send me to hell, I will love You there, too, and I'll cry out from there that I love You forever and ever... but let me love until the end... just for five more hours here... until the first light of Your day... because I love the queen of my soul... I love her and I cannot help loving her. You see my whole heart... I will rush to her, fall before her, and say, 'You are right to leave me. Farewell, forget your victim... don't worry about me!'"

"Mokroe!" cried Andrey, pointing ahead with his whip.

Through the pale darkness of the night, a solid mass of buildings appeared, as if dropped in the vast plain. The village of Mokroe had two thousand people, but at that hour, everyone was asleep, with only a few lights twinkling here and there.

"Drive on, Andrey, I'm coming!" Mitya exclaimed feverishly.

"They're not asleep," Andrey said again, pointing with his whip to the Plastunovs' inn, at the entrance of the village. The six windows facing the street were all brightly lit.

"They're not asleep," Mitya repeated joyfully. "Faster, Andrey! Gallop! Drive up with a dash! Let the bells ring! Let everyone know that I have arrived. I'm coming! I'm coming, too!"

Andrey lashed his tired horses into a gallop, driving with speed and pulling up the steaming, panting horses at the high steps of the inn.

Mitya jumped out of the cart just as the innkeeper, on his way to bed, peeked out, curious to see who had arrived.

"Trifon Borissovitch, is that you?"

The innkeeper bent down, looked closely, then ran down the steps and rushed up to Mitya with eager delight.

"Dmitri Fyodorovitch, your honor! Is it really you?"

Trifon Borissovitch was a stocky, healthy peasant, of medium height, with a rather fat face. His expression was severe and strict, especially with the peasants of Mokroe, but he could quickly turn obsequious when he sensed it was in his interest. He dressed in traditional Russian style, with a shirt buttoning down one side, and a full-skirted coat. He had saved a good sum of money but constantly dreamed of improving his position. Most of the local peasants owed him money, and many were deeply in his debt. He also rented and bought land from nearby landowners, using peasants to work the land as payment for their debts, which they could never seem to repay. He was a widower with four grown-up daughters. One was already a widow and lived at the inn with her two children, his grandchildren, working for him like a maid. Another daughter was married to a low-level official, and in one of the rooms of the inn, among family photographs, there was a miniature picture of this official in his uniform with epaulettes. The two younger daughters wore fashionable dresses on holidays, tight-fitting with long trains, but the next morning, they'd be up at dawn, sweeping the rooms with a birch broom, emptying slops, and cleaning after the guests.

Despite having saved thousands of roubles, Trifon Borissovitch loved to take advantage of a drunken guest. Remembering how a month ago he had made two, maybe three hundred roubles in just 24 hours from Dmitri's escapade with Grushenka, he greeted him now with eager anticipation, sensing more profit.

"Dmitri Fyodorovitch, dear sir, we see you again!"

"Wait, Trifon Borissovitch," Mitya began, "first and most important, where is she?"

"Agrafena Alexandrovna?" The innkeeper understood immediately, looking sharply at Mitya. "She's here, too..."

"With who? With who?"

"Some strangers. One is an official, a Pole, judging from his accent. He sent horses for her from here. There's another with him, maybe a friend or fellow traveler, hard to tell. They're dressed like civilians."

"Well, are they feasting? Do they have money?"

"Not much of a feast. Nothing grand, Dmitri Fyodorovitch." "Nothing grand? Who else is with them?"

"Two gentlemen from town. They've just returned from Tcherny and are staying here. One is a young gentleman, probably a relative of Mr. Miüsov, but I've forgotten his name... and the other, you might know him, a man called Maximov. He says he's been on a pilgrimage to the town monastery. He's traveling with the young relative of Mr. Miüsov."

"Is that all?" "Yes."

"Wait, listen, Trifon Borissovitch. Tell me the most important thing: how is she? How is she doing?"

"She just arrived. She's sitting with them." "Is she happy? Is she laughing?"

"No, I don't think she's laughing much. She's sitting quietly, a bit down. She's combing the young gentleman's hair."

"The Pole—the officer?"

"No, not the Pole. He's not young, and he's not an officer. It's the young gentleman who's related to Mr. Miüsov... I forgot his name."

"Kalganov."

"That's it, Kalganov!"

"All right. I'll see for myself. Are they playing cards?"

"They were, but they've stopped. Now they're having tea. The official gentleman asked for some liqueurs."

"Wait, Trifon Borissovitch, my good man, I'll check for myself. Now, tell me one more thing: are the gypsies here?"

"You can't have the gypsies now, Dmitri Fyodorovitch. The authorities sent them away. But we've got some Jews who play the cymbals and fiddle in the village. We could send for them; they'd come."

"Send for them! Definitely send for them!" Mitya shouted. "And gather the girls like you did last time—Marya, especially, and Stepanida and Arina. Two hundred roubles for a chorus!"

"For that kind of money, I could wake up the whole village, even though they're probably asleep by now. Are the peasants or the girls worth it, Dmitri Fyodorovitch? Spending that much on such rude and rough people! What's the point of giving a peasant a cigar to smoke? They just stink! And the girls are dirty. Besides, I can wake my own daughters for free, without needing to spend that much. They just went to bed, but I'll wake them up and have them sing for you. You gave champagne to the peasants last time, remember? E-eh!"

Even though Trifon Borissovitch acted like he felt sorry for Mitya, he had hidden six bottles of champagne the last time, and he also picked up a hundred-rouble note from under the table, which he kept for himself.

"Trifon Borissovitch, last time I was here, I threw around more than a thousand. Do you remember?"

"I remember. You really did throw it around. You must have left behind three thousand."

"Well, I'm back to do it all over again, you see?"

He pulled out his roll of cash and waved it in front of the innkeeper's face.

"Now, listen and remember. In an hour, the wine will arrive, along with snacks, pies, and sweets—bring everything up right away. The box that Andrey has—bring that up too. Open it and start serving the champagne immediately. And we need the girls, especially Marya."

He turned to the cart and pulled out the box of pistols.

"Andrey, let's settle up. Here's fifteen roubles for the drive, and fifty for the vodka... for your speed and loyalty. Remember Karamazov!"

"I'm scared, sir," Andrey stammered. "Give me five more roubles, but no more than that. Trifon Borissovitch, be my witness. Forgive me for saying something stupid…"

"What are you afraid of?" Mitya asked, studying him. "Well, get lost if you feel that way!" he shouted, tossing five roubles at him. "Now, Trifon Borissovitch, take me inside quietly so I can see them first without them seeing me. Where are they? In the blue room?"

Trifon Borissovitch looked worried but quickly did as Mitya asked. He led him through the hallway and went into the first large room next to where the guests were sitting. He turned off the light, then snuck Mitya into the corner of the room where he could watch without being seen. But Mitya didn't need to look for long. In fact, he didn't even see the others—he only saw her. His heart pounded, and everything went dark before his eyes.

She was sitting sideways at the table in a low chair. Next to her, on the sofa, was the handsome young man Kalganov. She was holding his hand and seemed to be laughing, while Kalganov, looking annoyed and not paying attention to her, was talking loudly to Maximov, who sat across from Grushenka at the table. Maximov was laughing hard at something. Another stranger was sitting on the sofa, and someone else sat in a chair nearby. The man on the sofa was slouching, smoking a pipe. Mitya noticed he was short, broad-faced, and looked angry about something. The other stranger struck Mitya as extremely tall, but he couldn't see much more. His breath caught. He couldn't stand it for another minute. He put the pistol case on a chest, and with his heart racing and feeling cold all over, he walked straight into the blue room to face everyone.

"Aie!" Grushenka screamed, noticing him first.

Chapter 7: The First and Rightful Lover

Mitya walked quickly up to the table with long, fast steps. "Gentlemen," he said loudly, almost shouting and stuttering

a little, "I ... I'm fine! Don't worry!" he exclaimed. "I—there's nothing wrong," he added, turning suddenly to Grushenka, who had moved back in her chair towards Kalganov, and grabbed his hand tightly. "I ... I'm coming, too. I'll stay here until morning. Gentlemen, can I stay with you until morning? Just until morning, for the last time, in this room?"

He finished speaking and looked at the fat little man sitting on the couch with a pipe. The man took his pipe out of his mouth and said in a serious tone, "Sir, we're having a private gathering. There are other rooms."

"Wait, it's you, Dmitri Fyodorovitch! What's going on?" Kalganov said suddenly. "Come sit with us. How have you been?"

"Good to see you, dear ... and special friend, I've always had a lot of respect for you," Mitya responded eagerly, quickly reaching his hand across the table.

"Ow! You're squeezing so hard! You almost broke my fingers," laughed Kalganov.

"He always squeezes like that, always," Grushenka added cheerfully with a shy smile, feeling suddenly reassured by Mitya's calm appearance. She was watching him closely, still a bit nervous. Something about him grabbed her attention, and she hadn't expected him to come in and talk like this at such a moment.

"Good evening," said Maximov politely from the left. Mitya rushed over to him as well.

"Good evening. You're here too! I'm glad you're here too! Gentlemen, gentlemen, I—" (He turned back to the Polish man with the pipe, clearly thinking he was the most important person in the room.) "I rushed over here.... I wanted to spend my last day, my last hour in this room, in this exact room ... where I, too, worshipped ... my queen. Forgive me, sir," he shouted wildly,

"I rushed here and made a vow— Oh, don't worry, this is my last night! Let's drink to our understanding. They'll bring the wine right away.... I brought this with me." (He pulled out a bundle of notes from his pocket.) "Let me, sir! I want music, singing, a celebration, like before. But the worm, the unnecessary worm, will go away, and there'll be no more of him. I'll celebrate my day of joy on my last night."

He was almost choking with emotion. He had so much to say, but all that came out were strange exclamations. The Pole stared at him, at the bundle of notes in his hand, then looked at Grushenka, clearly confused.

"If my sovereign lady allows—" he began.

"What does 'sovereign' mean? Like a queen or something?" Grushenka interrupted. "I can't help laughing at how you talk. Sit down, Mitya, what are you saying? Don't scare us, please. You won't scare us, will you? If not, I'm happy to see you ..."

"Me, scare you?" Mitya cried, throwing his hands up. "Oh, ignore me, carry on, I won't bother you!..."

Then, out of nowhere, he surprised everyone, and probably even himself, by throwing himself into a chair and bursting into tears, turning his head toward the wall while hugging the back of the chair tightly as if holding onto it for dear life.

"Come on, come on, what's wrong with you!" Grushenka scolded him. "That's just like you—every time you come to see me, you start talking, and I can never understand what you mean. You cried like this before, and now you're crying again! It's embarrassing! Why are you crying? What do you even have to cry about?" she added mysteriously, with a bit of annoyance in her voice.

"I ... I'm not crying.... Well, good evening!" He turned back around in his chair and suddenly started laughing, but not his usual quick, awkward laugh—it was a long, shaky, almost silent, nervous laugh.

"Well, here you go again.... Come on, cheer up, cheer up!" Grushenka said, trying to comfort him. "I'm really happy you're here, really happy, Mitya, do you hear me? I'm really happy! I want him to stay with us," she said firmly, speaking to everyone but clearly directing her words at the man sitting on the couch. "I want it, I want it! And if he leaves, I'm leaving too!" she added with a fierce look in her eyes.

"What my queen commands is law!" said the Pole, gallantly kissing Grushenka's hand. "Sir, please join us," he added politely, looking at Mitya.

Mitya was about to jump up and deliver another speech, but the words didn't come.

"Let's drink, sir," he blurted out instead. Everyone laughed.

"Oh my goodness! I thought he was going to start up again!" Grushenka exclaimed nervously. "Do you hear me, Mitya," she continued insistently, "don't get all worked up, but it's good you brought champagne. I want some myself, and I can't stand liqueurs. And the best part is that you're here. We were so bored.... You've come for a party again, haven't you? But put your money away. Where did you get so much?"

Mitya had been holding the crumpled bundle of notes the whole time, and everyone, especially the Poles, had been staring at it. Embarrassed, he quickly shoved them into his pocket. He blushed. Just then, the innkeeper came in with an uncorked bottle of champagne and glasses on a tray. Mitya grabbed the bottle, but he was so flustered that he didn't know what to do with it. Kalganov took it from him and poured out the champagne.

"Another! Another bottle!" Mitya called to the innkeeper, and, forgetting to clink glasses with the Pole he had so seriously invited to drink with him, he drank his glass all at once without waiting for anyone else. His whole expression suddenly changed. The serious and dramatic look he had when he entered disappeared completely, and he now looked gentle, almost childlike. He seemed shy and happy, smiling nervously at everyone, like a guilty dog that had done something wrong, been punished, and then forgiven. He seemed to have forgotten everything and was looking around at everyone with a cheerful, innocent smile. He kept laughing and moved his chair closer to Grushenka. Slowly, he started to get a sense of the two Poles, though he hadn't fully figured them out yet.

The Pole on the couch caught his attention with his dignified attitude, his Polish accent, and especially his pipe. "Well, what's wrong with that? It's good that he's smoking a pipe," Mitya thought. The Pole's round, middle-aged face, with its tiny nose and two thin, pointed, dyed mustaches, didn't raise any suspicions in Mitya. He wasn't even bothered by the Pole's ridiculous wig from Siberia, with silly love-locks combed over his temples. "I guess it's fine if he's wearing a wig," Mitya thought happily. The younger Pole, who was staring at everyone with an arrogant and defiant look and silently listening to the conversation, only impressed Mitya with his great height, which stood in sharp contrast to the Pole on the couch. "If he stood up, he'd be about six-foot-three," the thought flashed through Mitya's mind. He also figured that this Pole must be the other's friend, like his "bodyguard," and probably the tall Pole was at the beck and call of the little Pole with the pipe. But Mitya thought this was perfectly fine and not worth questioning. In his mood of dog-like submission, all feelings of competition had disappeared.

Mitya didn't quite understand Grushenka's mood or the hidden meaning in some of her words. All he could feel, with his heart racing, was that she was being kind to him, she had forgiven him, and she made him sit next to her. He was overjoyed, watching her sip from her glass of champagne. But the silence in the room seemed to catch his attention, and he looked around at everyone with curious eyes.

"Why are we just sitting here, gentlemen? Why don't we do something?" his eyes seemed to ask with a smile.

"He keeps talking nonsense, and we were all laughing," Kalganov suddenly said, as if he knew what Mitya was thinking, pointing at Maximov.

Mitya immediately looked at Kalganov, then at Maximov.

"He's talking nonsense?" Mitya laughed, his short, wooden laugh, suddenly excited about something—"ha ha!"

"Yes, can you believe it? He insists that all our cavalry officers in the 1820s married Polish women. Isn't that complete nonsense?" "Polish women?" Mitya repeated, completely thrilled.

Kalganov knew how Mitya felt about Grushenka and had guessed about the Polish man too, but he wasn't really interested in that. What caught his attention was Maximov. He had come here with Maximov by chance and was meeting the Poles at the inn for the first time. He had met Grushenka before, had even visited her once with someone else, but she hadn't liked him. Now, however, she was looking at him kindly. Before Mitya arrived, she had been paying a lot of attention to him, but he didn't seem to care much. He was a young man, not yet twenty, dressed like a fashionable gentleman, with a handsome, pale face and thick, beautiful blond hair. His pale blue eyes sometimes held a deep and intelligent look, far beyond his years, although at times he acted and spoke just like a child and wasn't embarrassed by it, even when he knew it himself. He was usually very strong-willed, sometimes even moody, though he was always friendly. Occasionally, his face had a stubborn look, like he was thinking hard about something else. Sometimes he seemed lazy and uninterested, but other times he would get excited, even about things that didn't seem very important.

"Can you believe it, I've been taking him around with me for the past four days," Kalganov continued lazily, dragging out his words, but naturally, without trying to sound different. "Ever since your brother, remember, pushed him out of the carriage and sent him flying. That's when I started paying attention to him. I took him to the country, but he keeps talking so much nonsense that I'm embarrassed to be with him. I'm bringing him back."

"The gentleman hasn't seen Polish ladies and is talking about things he doesn't understand," said the Pole with the pipe, addressing Maximov.

He spoke Russian quite well, much better than he pretended. Whenever he used Russian words, he always gave them a Polish twist.

"But I was married to a Polish lady myself," Maximov chuckled. "But were you in the cavalry? You were talking about cavalry officers. Were you a cavalry officer?" Kalganov quickly added.

"Was he really a cavalry officer? Ha ha!" Mitya cried, listening eagerly and looking at each person as they spoke, as if he wasn't sure what strange thing he might hear next.

"No, you see," Maximov turned to Mitya. "What I meant is that those pretty Polish ladies ... when they danced the mazurka with our Uhlans ... when one of them dances the mazurka with a Uhlan, she jumps onto his knee like a kitten ... a little white one ... and the father and mother just watch and let it happen. They let it happen and the next day, the Uhlan comes and offers her his hand.... That's how it goes he offers her his hand, he he!" Maximov finished, giggling.

"The man is a fool!" the tall Pole sitting in the chair growled suddenly and crossed one leg over the other. Mitya's eyes were drawn to his large, greasy boot, with its thick, dirty sole. Both Poles' clothes looked rather grimy.

"Well, now he's calling him a fool! What's he so mad about?" Grushenka asked, suddenly annoyed.

"Pani Agrippina, the man here saw only servant girls in Poland, not real ladies," the Pole with the pipe said to Grushenka.

"You can believe that," the tall Pole added with a sneer.

"What does it matter? Let him talk! People talk; it makes things more lively," Grushenka said irritably.

"I'm not stopping them, pani," said the Pole with the wig, giving Grushenka a long look. Then, returning to his dignified silence, he puffed on his pipe again.

"No, no. The Polish gentleman is right," Kalganov got excited again, as if this was an important matter. "He's never been to Poland, so how can he talk about it? I suppose you weren't married in Poland, were you?"

"No, in the Province of Smolensk. But a Uhlan brought my wife over from Poland, with her mother and aunt and another relative. He brought them straight from Poland and handed her over to me. He was a lieutenant in our regiment, a very nice young man. At first, he wanted to marry her himself. But he didn't because she turned out to be lame."

"So you married a lame woman?" Kalganov shouted.

"Yes. They both tricked me a little at the time and kept it hidden. I thought she was hopping around for fun.... I thought she was excited to marry me."

"So happy she was going to marry you!" Kalganov shouted in his high-pitched, childish voice.

"Yes, so happy. But it turned out to be something else. After we got married, on our wedding night, she told me the truth and asked for forgiveness. She said, 'When I was a little girl, I jumped over a puddle and hurt my leg.' He he!"

Kalganov burst out laughing, nearly falling onto the couch. Grushenka laughed too. Mitya felt like he was on top of the world.

"You know, it's true! He's not lying this time," Kalganov said, turning to Mitya. "And did you know he's been married twice?

He's talking about his first wife. But his second wife, do you know, ran away, and she's still alive."

"Really?" Mitya said, turning quickly to Maximov with a look of complete shock.

"Yes, she ran away. I had the misfortune of experiencing that," Maximov admitted quietly. "She left with some other man. What's worse, she had already transferred all my property into her name before she left. 'You're an educated man,' she said to me. 'You'll find a way to support yourself.' That's how she settled things. A wise bishop once told me, 'One of your wives was lame, but the other was too quick on her feet.' He he!"

"Listen, listen!" Kalganov cried, bubbling with laughter. "Even if he's lying—and he often does—he's just doing it to entertain us. There's no harm in that, right? You know, sometimes I like him. He's really low-class, but that's just who he is, don't you think? Some people are low because they're selfish, but he's just naturally like that. Would you believe he actually claims (he argued about it all day yesterday) that Gogol wrote Dead Souls about him? Do you remember the landowner named Maximov in the book, who got beaten by Nozdryov? He was charged, if you remember, 'for beating landowner Maximov while drunk.' Would you believe it, he says he was that Maximov, and that he got beaten! But can that be true? Tchitchikov made his journey at the very latest in the early 1820s, so the dates don't even match. He couldn't have been beaten then, could he?"

It was hard to tell why Kalganov was so excited, but it was clear that he really was. Mitya didn't argue and just followed his lead.

"Well, what if they did beat him up?" Mitya said, laughing.

"It wasn't exactly that they beat me up, but what I'm saying is—" Maximov cut in.

"What do you mean? Either they beat you or they didn't."

"What time is it, sir?" the Pole with the pipe asked his tall friend, looking bored. The tall one just shrugged, not having a watch.

"Why not let people talk? Just because you're bored doesn't mean other people shouldn't talk," Grushenka snapped at him, clearly looking for a reason to pick a fight. For the first time, something seemed to click in Mitya's mind. The Pole responded with irritation this time.

"Miss, I didn't say anything. I'm not stopping them."

"All right then. Come on, tell us your story," Grushenka said to Maximov. "Why is everyone so quiet?"

"There's not much to tell, it's all pretty silly," Maximov replied, sounding pleased with himself and acting a bit fancy. "Besides, all that in Gogol is just symbolism. He gave the characters meaningful names. Nozdryov was really named Nosov, and Kuvshinikov had a different name too—he was called Shkvornev. Fenardi was really Fenardi, but he wasn't Italian, he was Russian. And Mamsel Fenardi was a pretty girl with lovely little legs in tights. She wore a short, sparkly skirt and spun around, but not for four hours—only for four minutes. Everyone was enchanted by her..."

But why did they beat you up?" Kalganov interrupted. "For Piron!" Maximov answered.

"Piron? What Piron?" Mitya asked.

"The famous French writer, Piron. We were all drinking—there was a big group of us at the tavern during the fair. They had invited me, and I started quoting some witty lines. 'Is that you, Boileau? What a funny outfit!' And Boileau says he's going to a masquerade—that means the baths—he he! They didn't like that, so I quickly told them another sarcastic one that all educated people know:

Yes, Sappho and Phaon are we!
But one grief is weighing on me.
You don't know your way to the sea!

They got even more offended and started insulting me. And as bad luck would have it, I tried to fix things by telling them a cultured story about Piron—how he wasn't accepted into the French Academy and wrote his own funny epitaph:

Ci-gît Piron qui ne fut rien,
Pas même académicien.

That's when they grabbed me and beat me up." "But why? Why did they do that?"

"For my education. People can beat you up for anything,"

Maximov finished, in a short and serious way.

"Okay, enough! That's all so dumb, I don't want to hear any more. I thought it would be funny," Grushenka suddenly interrupted.

Mitya stopped laughing right away. The tall Pole got up, looking bored and out of place, and started pacing back and forth across the room, with his hands behind his back.

"Oh, he can't sit still," Grushenka said, glaring at him with contempt. Mitya started to feel uneasy. He noticed that the other Pole on the couch was also looking at him with an annoyed expression.

"Gentlemen!" Mitya suddenly shouted, "Let's have a drink! And you too, sir! Let's drink."

He quickly pulled three glasses toward him and filled them with champagne.

"To Poland, gentlemen! I drink to your Poland!" Mitya cried.

"I'd be honored, sir," said the Pole on the couch with a dignified tone, accepting his glass.

"And the other gentleman—what's his name? Drink, my good sir, take your glass!" Mitya urged.

"Pan Vrublevsky," the Pole on the couch added.

Pan Vrublevsky came over to the table, swaying slightly as he walked.

"To Poland, gentlemen!" Mitya shouted, raising his glass. "Hurrah!"

All three of them drank. Mitya grabbed the bottle and poured more champagne into the glasses.

"Now, let's drink to Russia, gentlemen! Let's all be brothers!" "Pour some for us," Grushenka said. "I'll drink to Russia too!" "So will I," Kalganov added.

"I will too... to Russia, the old grandmother!" Maximov giggled.

"All of us! Let's all drink!" Mitya shouted. "Trifon Borissovitch, bring more bottles!"

The other three bottles Mitya had brought were placed on the table. Mitya filled the glasses again.

"To Russia! Hurrah!" he shouted. Everyone drank, except the Poles, but Grushenka finished her entire glass in one go. The Poles didn't touch their glasses.

"What's going on, gentlemen?" Mitya asked. "Aren't you going to drink?"

Pan Vrublevsky lifted his glass and said loudly, "To Russia, as she was before 1772."

"Well, that's more like it!" the other Pole cheered, and they both drained their glasses at once.

"You're fools, both of you," Mitya suddenly blurted out.

"Sir!" both Poles shouted angrily, jumping up like two roosters. Pan Vrublevsky was especially furious.

"How can a man not love his own country?" he yelled.

"Stop it! No fighting! I won't allow any fighting!" Grushenka shouted, stomping her foot on the floor. Her face was flushed, and her eyes were glowing. The champagne she had just drunk was clearly affecting her. Mitya was terrified.

"Gentlemen, forgive me! It's my fault, I'm sorry. Vrublevsky, sir, I'm sorry."

"Shut up, you idiot! Sit down, you fool!" Grushenka scolded, clearly annoyed.

Everyone sat down, and the room fell silent. They all looked at each other, saying nothing.

"Gentlemen, it was all my fault," Mitya began again, still unable to understand what Grushenka had said. "Come on, why are we sitting here? What should we do for fun?"

"Ugh, it's not fun at all," Kalganov muttered lazily.

"Let's play faro again, like before," Maximov suddenly giggled. "Faro? Excellent!" Mitya shouted. "If the gentlemen agree—"

"It's late, gentlemen," the Pole on the sofa responded, sounding reluctant.

"That's true," Pan Vrublevsky agreed.

"Late? What do you mean by 'late'?" Grushenka asked.

"Late, miss! I mean it's a late hour," the Pole on the sofa explained.

"They always say it's late. They can never do anything!" Grushenka nearly shouted in frustration. "They're boring themselves, so they want everyone else to be bored too. Before you came, Mitya, they were quiet and kept looking down their noses at me."

"My goddess!" the Pole on the sofa cried. "I see you don't like me, and that's why I'm gloomy. But I'm ready, sir," he added, turning to Mitya.

"Let's start, gentlemen," Mitya agreed, pulling out his notes and placing two hundred-rouble bills on the table. "I want to lose a lot of money to you. Take your cards. Let's make the bank."

"We'll get cards from the landlord, sir," said the smaller Pole, seriously.

"That's the best way," Pan Vrublevsky chimed in.

"From the landlord? Good idea. Let's get them. Cards!" Mitya called to the landlord.

The landlord brought in a fresh, unopened pack of cards and told Mitya that the girls were getting ready and that the musicians would probably arrive soon, but the cart with the supplies hadn't come yet. Mitya jumped up from the table and ran into the next room to give orders, but only three girls had arrived, and Marya wasn't there. He didn't even know what orders to give or why he'd rushed out. He just told them to take out the gifts for the girls—the sweets, the toffee, and the fondants. "And vodka for Andrey, vodka for Andrey!" he shouted quickly. "I was rude to Andrey!"

Suddenly, Maximov, who had followed him, tapped him on the shoulder.

"Give me five roubles," he whispered to Mitya. "I want to bet on faro too, he he!" "Perfect! Here, take ten!"

Once again, Mitya pulled out all the notes from his pocket and handed Maximov one for ten roubles. "And if you lose that, come back, come back again."

"Thanks!" Maximov whispered happily and hurried back. Mitya returned, apologizing for the delay. The Poles had already sat down and opened the pack of cards. They seemed much friendlier now, almost warm. The Pole on the sofa had lit another pipe and was getting ready to deal, looking very serious.

"Take your seats, gentlemen," Pan Vrublevsky said.

"I'm not playing anymore," Kalganov said. "I've already lost fifty roubles to them."

"The gentleman had no luck earlier. Maybe this time he will," said the Pole on the sofa, looking at him.

"How much is in the bank? To match?" Mitya asked.

"That depends, sir. Maybe a hundred, maybe two hundred, as much as you want to bet."

"A million!" Mitya joked.

"Have you heard of Pan Podvysotsky?" asked the Pole. "Who's Podvysotsky?"

"In Warsaw, there was a bank, and anyone could bet against it. Podvysotsky came in, saw a thousand gold pieces, and bet against the bank. The banker asked, 'Sir Podvysotsky, are you putting down the gold, or should we trust your honor?' 'My honor, sir,' said Podvysotsky. 'Even better,' said the banker. He threw the dice, and Podvysotsky won. 'Take it, sir,' said the banker, opening the drawer and giving him a million. 'Take it, sir, it's yours.' There was a million in the bank. 'I didn't know that,' said Podvysotsky. 'Sir Podvysotsky,' said the banker, 'you trusted your honor, and we trusted ours.' Podvysotsky took the million."

"That's not true," Kalganov said.

"Sir Kalganov, in polite society, one doesn't say such things."

"As if a Polish gambler would give away a million!" Mitya exclaimed, but then quickly corrected himself. "Forgive me, sir, that was my fault. He would, he would give away a million for honor, for Polish honor. See, I speak Polish! Ha ha! Here, I bet ten roubles, the jack leads."

"And I'll bet a rouble on the queen, the queen of hearts, the lovely lady," Maximov laughed, pulling out his queen and, as if trying to hide it, moved closer and quickly crossed himself under the table. Mitya won, and so did Maximov's rouble.

"A corner!" Mitya yelled.

"I'll bet another rouble, just a small one," Maximov muttered, delighted at his win.

"Lost!" Mitya shouted. "Double on the seven!" The seven was trumped.

"Stop!" Kalganov suddenly shouted.

"Double! Double!" Mitya kept doubling his bets, and each time, the Poles trumped his cards. The smaller bets kept winning.

"On the double!" Mitya shouted angrily.

"You've lost two hundred, sir. Will you bet another hundred?" the Pole on the sofa asked.

"What? Already lost two hundred? Then another two hundred! All on doubles!"

Mitya pulled more money from his pocket and was about to place two hundred roubles on the queen when Kalganov covered the money with his hand.

"That's enough!" Kalganov shouted.

"What's wrong?" Mitya asked, staring at him.

"That's enough! I don't want you to keep playing. Stop!" "Why?"

"Because I said so. That's why. I won't let you keep playing." Mitya looked at him, confused.

"Give it up, Mitya. Maybe he's right. You've already lost a lot," Grushenka said with a strange tone in her voice. Both Poles stood up, clearly offended.

"Are you joking, sir?" the shorter man asked, glaring at Kalganov. "How dare you!" Pan Vrublevsky growled at Kalganov.

"Don't you dare shout like that," Grushenka snapped. "Ah, you idiots!"

Mitya looked at each of them in turn. But then something about Grushenka's expression caught his attention, and at that moment, a strange new thought popped into his mind.

"Miss Agrippina," the small Pole began, red with anger, when Mitya suddenly stepped up to him and clapped him on the shoulder.

"My dear sir, I need to have a word with you." "What do you want?"

"In the next room. I've got something to tell you. Something good, very good. You'll want to hear it."

The smaller man hesitated and looked nervously at Mitya but agreed, on the condition that Pan Vrublevsky came along too.

"The bodyguard? Let him come. I want him, too. I need him!" Mitya shouted. "Let's go, gentlemen!"

"Where are you going?" Grushenka asked, sounding worried. "We'll be back in a moment," Mitya replied.

There was a boldness in his eyes, and his face looked different than when he had first come in an hour earlier. He didn't lead the Poles into the large room where the girls were gathering and the table was being set. Instead, he took them to the bedroom on the right, where the trunks and packages were kept, and there were two large beds with stacks of pillows on each. A small candle was burning on a simple wooden table in the corner. Mitya and the smaller Pole sat down at the table, facing each other, while the large Vrublevsky stood nearby with his hands behind his back. The Poles looked serious, but it was clear they were curious.

"What can I do for you, sir?" asked the small Pole in a soft voice.

"Well, here's the deal, sir, I won't keep you long. I've got some money for you," Mitya said, pulling out his notes. "How about three thousand? Take it and go on your way."

The Pole stared at Mitya with wide eyes, trying to read his face.

"Three thousand, sir?" He glanced at Vrublevsky.

"Yes, three thousand! Listen, sir, you seem like a smart man. Take three thousand and get out of here, and take Vrublevsky with you—do you hear me? Right now, this minute, and forever. You understand that, sir? Forever. Here's the door, just walk out. Got a coat or something? I'll bring it to you. The horses will be ready soon, and then—goodbye!"

Mitya waited for a response, confident that the deal was done.

The Pole's face showed sudden determination. "And the money, sir?"

"The money? I'll give you five hundred right now for the trip, as the first payment, and two thousand five hundred tomorrow in town. I swear on my honor, I'll get it no matter what!" Mitya said passionately.

The Poles exchanged glances again. The short man's face grew darker.

"Seven hundred, not five hundred. Right now, cash," Mitya added, sensing something was wrong. "What's the matter, sir? Don't you trust me? I can't give you all three thousand right away. If I do, you might come back to her tomorrow... Besides, I don't have the full amount with me. It's in town, at my place," Mitya stammered, feeling his confidence slip with every word. "I swear, the money's there, hidden."

The short Pole's expression suddenly changed to one of pride.

"What are you saying?" he asked with a sneer. "Shame on you!"

He spat on the floor. Pan Vrublevsky spat as well.

"You're doing that, sir," Mitya said, realizing in despair that the deal was falling apart, "because you think you can get more from Grushenka? You're just a couple of cowards, that's what you are!"

"This is a serious insult!" The little Pole's face turned as red as a crab, and he stormed out of the room, not wanting to hear another word. Vrublevsky followed, and Mitya trailed after them, confused and ashamed. He was afraid of Grushenka, afraid the Pole would start shouting. And that's exactly what happened. The Pole marched into the room and dramatically threw himself in front of Grushenka.

"Miss Agrippina, I've been insulted!" he cried. But Grushenka suddenly lost her temper, as though he had hit a nerve.

"Speak Russian! Speak Russian!" she yelled. "Not another word of Polish! You used to speak Russian. You didn't forget it in five years."

Her face was red with anger. "Miss Agrippina—"

"My name's Agrafena, Grushenka! Speak Russian or I won't listen!"

The Pole was shocked and, with great dignity, began speaking in broken Russian.

"Miss Agrafena, I came here to forget the past and forgive it, to leave all that's happened behind—"

"Forgive me? You came here to forgive me?" Grushenka interrupted, jumping up from her seat.

"Yes, miss, I'm not a coward, I'm generous. But I was shocked to see your lovers. Mr. Mitya offered me three thousand in the other room to leave. I spat in his face."

"What? He offered you money for me?" Grushenka cried

hysterically. "Is that true, Mitya? How dare you? Am I for sale?"

"Sir! Sir!" Mitya yelled. "She's pure and honest, and I've never been her lover! That's a lie!"

"How dare you defend me to him?" Grushenka shrieked. "It wasn't virtue that kept me pure, and I wasn't afraid of Kuzma! It was so I could hold my head high when I saw him and call him a scoundrel. And he actually refused the money?"

"He took it! He took it!" Mitya shouted. "He just wanted the whole three thousand right away, but I only had seven hundred."

"I see! He heard I had money and came here to marry me!"

"Miss Agrippina!" the little Pole cried out. "I'm a knight, a nobleman, not a fool. I came here to make you my wife, and I find you've become someone different, twisted and shameless."

"Oh, go back where you came from! I'll tell them to throw you out, and they will!" Grushenka screamed, furious. "I've been such a fool, miserable for five years! And it wasn't even for him, it was my own anger that made me suffer. And this isn't even him! Was he like this? He could've been his father! Where did you get that wig from? He was a falcon, and you're just a goose. He used to laugh and sing to me... And I've been crying for five years, like a pathetic fool!"

She collapsed into her chair and covered her face with her hands. At that moment, the chorus from Mokroe started singing a lively dance song in the next room.

"A real Sodom!" Vrublevsky shouted suddenly. "Landlord, send these shameless women away!"

The landlord, who had been peeking through the door, curious about the shouting and guessing that his guests were fighting, entered the room.

"What's all the yelling about? Do you want to tear your throat out?" he said, addressing Vrublevsky rudely.

"Animal!" Vrublevsky bellowed.

"Animal? What kind of cards were you playing with just now? I gave you a pack, and you hid it. You were playing with marked cards! I could send you to Siberia for cheating, you know that? It's just as bad as using fake money."

And walking over to the sofa, he stuck his fingers between the back and the cushion and pulled out an unopened pack of cards.

"Here's my unopened pack!" he held it up and showed it to everyone in the room. "I saw him from where I was standing! He took my pack and swapped it with his—you're a cheat, not a gentleman!"

"And I saw him switch a card twice!" Kalganov shouted.

"How shameful! How shameful!" Grushenka cried, clasping her hands and blushing with real embarrassment. "Dear Lord, has it come to this?"

"I thought so, too!" Mitya added. But before he could finish, Vrublevsky, his face red with confusion and fury, shook his fist at Grushenka and yelled:

"You filthy woman!"

Mitya immediately lunged at him, grabbed him with both hands, lifted him into the air, and in a flash carried him into the room they had just come from.

"I threw him on the floor in there," Mitya said as he came back, still gasping from excitement. "He's fighting back, that scoundrel! But don't worry, he won't be coming back in here..."

He closed one side of the folding doors and held the other open, calling out to the smaller Pole:

"Sir, would you kindly leave as well?"

"My dear Dmitri Fyodorovitch," Trifon Borissovitch spoke up, "you should make them give you back the money you lost. It's practically been stolen from you."

"I don't want my fifty roubles back," Kalganov said suddenly.

"I don't want my two hundred either," Mitya yelled. "I wouldn't take it back for anything! Let him keep it as a parting gift."

"Good for you, Mitya! You're a real hero!" Grushenka cried, her voice filled with fierce anger.

The little Pole, red with rage but still trying to hold onto his dignity, made his way toward the door. He stopped suddenly and, turning to Grushenka, said:

"Miss, if you want to come with me, come. If not, goodbye."

Swelling with self-importance, he marched to the door. This was a man who thought highly of himself; even after everything that had happened, he still believed Grushenka might marry him. Mitya slammed the door behind him.

"Lock it," Kalganov said. But the lock clicked from the other side—they had locked it from the inside.

"That's perfect!" Grushenka said coldly. "Serves them right!"

Chapter 8: Delirium

Wthat followed was almost like a wild party, where everyone was welcome. Grushenka was the first to ask for wine.

"I want to drink. I want to get really drunk, like we did before. Do you remember, Mitya? Do you remember how we became friends here last time?"

Mitya himself was almost out of his mind with excitement, feeling like his happiness was close. But Grushenka kept sending him away from her.

"Go have fun. Tell them to dance, to have a good time, like before! Remember, 'let the stove and cottage dance'?" she kept shouting. She was extremely excited, and Mitya rushed to do what she asked. The group of singers was in the next room. The room they had been in before was too small, and it was divided by cotton curtains. Behind the curtains was a huge bed with a soft mattress and a pile of pillows. The four rooms for guests had beds in them, too. Grushenka sat down near the door, and Mitya placed a comfortable chair for her. She had sat in the same spot the last time, watching the dancing and singing. All the girls who had come had been there that time, too. The Jewish band with fiddles and zithers had arrived, and at last, the long-awaited cart showed up with the wine and food.

Mitya hurried around. All sorts of people began to show up to watch, peasants and their wives who had been woken up, drawn by the promise of another amazing party like the one from a month before. Mitya recognized their faces, greeting and hugging everyone he knew. He opened bottles and poured wine for everyone who came by. The girls were especially eager for champagne. The men preferred rum, brandy, and most of all, hot punch. Mitya had chocolate made for the girls and ordered that three samovars should be kept boiling all night so people could help themselves to tea and punch.

Things soon turned into a ridiculous mess, but Mitya thrived in that kind of chaos, and the crazier it got, the better he felt. If the peasants had asked him for money right then, he would've pulled out his notes and handed them over without a second thought. This was probably why the landlord, Trifon Borissovitch, kept hanging around Mitya to look out for him. He seemed to have given up on going to bed that night but only had a small glass of punch and made sure to keep an eye on Mitya's spending in his own way. He jumped in at just the right moments, politely reminding Mitya not to give away cigars, Rhine wine, or—most importantly— money to the peasants, as he had done before. He was also outraged that the peasant girls were drinking liqueur and eating sweets.

"They're a bunch of freeloaders, Dmitri Fyodorovitch," he said. "I'd give them all a good kick, and they'd take it as an honor— that's all they're worth!"

Mitya remembered Andrey again and ordered more punch to be sent to him. "I was rude to him earlier," he repeated in a softer voice. Kalganov didn't feel like drinking at first and wasn't interested in the girls' singing. But after a couple of glasses of champagne, he became extremely cheerful, wandering around the room, laughing, complimenting the music and the songs, and admiring everyone and everything. Maximov, completely drunk and happy, never left his side. Grushenka was getting drunk too. Pointing at Kalganov, she said to Mitya:

"What a sweet, charming boy he is!"

Mitya, delighted, ran over to kiss Kalganov and Maximov. His hopes were high. Grushenka hadn't said anything specific yet, and it seemed like she was avoiding it on purpose. But she kept glancing at him with loving, passionate eyes. Finally, she suddenly grabbed his hand and pulled him toward her. She was sitting in a low chair by the door.

"How did you end up here just now, huh? Did you walk in?... You scared me. So you really wanted to give me to him, didn't you? Did you really want to?"

"I didn't want to ruin your happiness!" Mitya stammered joyfully. But she didn't need his answer.

"Well, go have fun..." she sent him away again. "Don't cry, I'll call you back again."

He ran off, and she listened to the singing and watched the dancing, though her eyes followed him wherever he went. But in another fifteen minutes, she called him again, and once more, he rushed back to her.

"Come sit by me. Tell me, how did you find out about me coming here yesterday? Who told you first?"

Mitya began telling her the whole story, but it came out disjointed, rambling, and full of excitement. He spoke strangely, frowning often and stopping suddenly.

"What are you frowning about?" she asked.

"Nothing... I left someone sick behind. I'd give ten years of my life to know he'd get better, to know he's okay!"

"Well, don't worry about him if he's sick. So you planned to shoot yourself tomorrow! What a silly boy! Why would you do that? I like reckless guys like you," she said, slurring her words a bit. "So you'd do anything for me, huh? Did you really plan to shoot yourself tomorrow, you fool? No, wait a little. Tomorrow I might have something to say to you... I won't say it today, but tomorrow. You'd like it to be today? No, I don't want to today. Now, go on, go have fun."

Once, however, she called him over, looking puzzled and uneasy.

"Why are you sad? I can tell you're sad... Yes, I see it," she added, looking closely into his eyes. "Even though you're kissing the peasants and shouting, I can see it. No, cheer up. I'm happy, so you should be happy too... I love someone here. Guess who it is. Ah, look, my boy has fallen asleep, poor thing, he's drunk."

She meant Kalganov. He had, in fact, fallen asleep for a moment on the sofa, drunk. But it wasn't just the alcohol making him sleepy; he suddenly felt down, or as he put it, "bored." The girls' songs, which had become more vulgar as the drinking went on, had depressed him. The dances were no better. Two girls dressed up as bears, while a lively girl named Stepanida, holding a stick, played the role of their trainer and started to "perform" with them.

"Come on, Marya, move or you'll get the stick!"

The girls dressed as bears were rolling on the floor in the most ridiculous way, making the crowd of men and women burst into laughter.

"Well, let them have their fun!" said Grushenka, with a delighted look on her face. "When people get a chance to enjoy themselves, why shouldn't they be happy?"

Kalganov looked like he had been covered in dirt.

"This is disgusting, all this peasant nonsense," he muttered, walking away. "It's the kind of thing they do when it stays light all night in summer."

He especially hated one of the new songs that had a lively tune. It was about a gentleman who tried to win over the girls to see if they would love him:

The master came to try the girls:
Would they love him, would they not?
But the girls could not love the master:
He would beat me cruelly,

And such love won't do for me.

Then a gypsy came along and tried his luck:

The gypsy came to try the girls:
Would they love him, would they not?
But they couldn't love the gypsy either:
He would be a thief, I fear,
And would cause me many tears.

More men came to try, including a soldier:

The soldier came to try the girls:
Would they love him, would they not?

But the soldier was turned away with two rude lines that got a huge laugh from the audience.

The song ended with a merchant:
The merchant came to try the girls:
Would they love him, would they not?
And it turns out the girls love him because:
The merchant will make gold for me,
And his queen I'll gladly be.

Kalganov was furious.

"That song is brand new!" he said aloud. "Who writes this garbage for them? They might as well have had a railway worker or a Jew try his luck with the girls—they'd win for sure."

He felt insulted by the whole thing, declared that he was bored, and sat down on the sofa, immediately falling asleep. His handsome face looked pale as it rested on the cushion.

"Look how pretty he is," said Grushenka, pulling Mitya over to see. "I was combing his hair just now; it's so soft, like flax, and really thick."

Leaning over him tenderly, she kissed Kalganov on the forehead. Kalganov instantly opened his eyes, looked at her, stood up, and anxiously asked where Maximov was.

"So that's who you want," Grushenka laughed. "Stay with me for a minute. Mitya, go find his Maximov."

Maximov, it seemed, couldn't keep away from the girls. He kept running off to pour himself more liqueur and had already had two cups of chocolate. His face was red, his nose was even redder, and his eyes were watery and sweet. He rushed up, announcing that he was going to dance the "sabotière."

"They taught me all the fancy, upper-class dances when I was little."

"Go with him, Mitya, and I'll watch him dance from here," said Grushenka.

"No, no, I want to see it too," Kalganov exclaimed, pushing away Grushenka's suggestion to sit with him. They all went to watch Maximov dance. But no one seemed impressed except Mitya. The dance was just a series of skips and hops, where Maximov kicked his feet up and slapped the soles of his shoes with every jump. Kalganov didn't enjoy it at all, but Mitya kissed the dancer.

"Thanks. You must be tired. What are you looking for here? Want some sweets? A cigar?"

"A cigarette."

"Want something to drink?"

"I'll have a liqueur. Got any chocolates?"

"Yes, there's a bunch on the table. Take one, my dear friend." "I like the ones with vanilla... good for older folks. He he!" "No, we don't have any of those."

Maximov leaned in to whisper in Mitya's ear. "That girl, little Marya, he he! How about you help me get friendly with her?"

"So that's what you're after! No, no, that won't work!" "I wouldn't harm anyone," Maximov muttered sadly.

"All right, all right. They're just here to dance and sing, you know. But hang on... enjoy the food and drinks for now. Do you need any money?"

"Maybe later," Maximov smiled. "All right, all right..."

Mitya's head was burning. He went outside to the wooden balcony that wrapped around the building, overlooking the courtyard. The fresh air cleared his head a little. He stood alone in a dark corner and suddenly grabbed his head with both hands. His jumbled thoughts started to come together, his feelings merged, and all of a sudden, he had a terrible, awful realization. "If I'm going to shoot myself, why not now?" the thought crossed his mind. "Why not go get the pistols, bring them here, and end it all in this dark, filthy corner?"

He stood there, thinking about it for almost a minute. A few hours ago, when he had rushed over here, he had been running from the shame of what he had done, the theft, and the blood... the blood! But still, it had been easier then. Back then, everything seemed over: he had lost her, let her go. She was gone from his life— oh, in that moment, dying had felt easier, almost like something he had to do, because what reason did he have to stay alive?

But now? Was it the same as before? Now, one fear, one terrifying thought had disappeared: that original lover, that haunting figure was gone, leaving nothing behind. The terrifying ghost had become something small, even ridiculous, locked away in the bedroom. It would never return. She was ashamed, and from the look in her eyes, he could see who she truly loved. Now, everything he needed for happiness was right in front of him… yet he couldn't go on living, he just couldn't. "Oh, God! Bring back the man I knocked down by the fence! Let this awful burden be lifted from me! Lord, you've worked miracles for sinners like me before! But what if the old man is still alive? Oh, if that were true, I could wipe away the shame of what I've done. I'd return the money, I'd find a way to give it back… Then nothing but the guilt would remain in my heart forever! But no, no—those dreams are impossible and cowardly! Oh, curse it all!"

Still, there was a tiny glimmer of hope in his darkness. He jumped up and ran back to the room—to her, his queen forever! Wasn't one moment of her love worth more than anything else, even if it meant disgrace for the rest of his life? This wild thought grabbed his heart. "To her, only to her—to see her, to hear her, to forget everything, even just for this night, for one hour, for a single moment!" Just as he turned from the balcony and headed down the hallway, he ran into the landlord, Trifon Borissovitch. Mitya thought he looked worried, and wondered if he had come looking for him.

"What's up, Trifon Borissovitch? Are you looking for me?"

"No, sir," the landlord seemed uneasy. "Why would I be looking for you? Where have you been?"

"Why do you look so serious? You're not upset, are you? Don't worry, you'll be able to get some sleep soon. What time is it?"

"It's almost three o'clock, or just past it." "We'll stop soon. We'll stop."

"Don't worry about it, sir. Go on as long as you want."

"What's wrong with him?" Mitya wondered for a second, but he rushed back to the room where the girls were dancing. But she wasn't there. She wasn't in the blue room either; only Kalganov was there, still asleep on the sofa. Mitya peeked behind the curtain—there she was. She was sitting in the corner on a trunk, bent forward with her head and arms resting on the bed next to her, crying bitterly and trying hard to stifle her sobs. When she saw Mitya, she motioned for him to come over, and when he did, she grabbed his hand tightly.

"Mitya, Mitya, I loved him, you know. I've loved him for five years, all that time! Did I love him, or was it just my own anger? No, it was him, him! It's a lie that I loved my anger more than him. Mitya, I was only seventeen then; he was so kind to me, so happy. He used to sing to me… or at least that's what it felt like to a silly girl like me. But now, oh God, he's not the same man anymore. Even his face has changed; he's a completely different person. I wouldn't have recognized him. I came here with Timofey, thinking the whole time about how I would meet him, what I would say, how we would look at each other. My heart felt weak, and then suddenly it was like he dumped a bucket of dirty water on me. He talked to me like I was a child, so serious and formal. I was speechless. At first, I thought he was too embarrassed to talk in front of that big Pole. I just sat there staring at him, wondering why I couldn't say a word. It must have been his wife who ruined him. You know he left me to marry her. She's the one who changed him. Mitya, it's so humiliating! Oh, Mitya, I'm ashamed, ashamed for the rest of my life. Curse it, curse those five years!"

She started crying again but clung tightly to Mitya's hand and wouldn't let go.

"Mitya, darling, stay, don't leave. I need to say something," she whispered, suddenly lifting her tear-stained face to him. "Tell me, who is it that I love? I love someone here. Who is it? That's what you need to tell me."

A smile spread across her swollen, tear-streaked face, and her eyes sparkled in the dim light.

"A falcon flew in, and my heart sank. 'Fool! That's the one you love!' That's what my heart told me the moment you walked in. Everything seemed brighter when you entered. 'What's he afraid of?' I wondered.

Because you were scared—you couldn't even speak. But it wasn't them you were afraid of—how could you be afraid of anyone? It was me. You were only afraid of me, I thought. So, Fenya told you, you little fool, that I had called out to Alyosha from the window and said I had loved Mityenka for an hour, and now I was going to love... someone else. Mitya, Mitya, how could I have been so stupid to think I could love anyone else after you? Do you forgive me, Mitya? Do you forgive me or not? Do you love me? Do you love me?"

She jumped up and grabbed him by the shoulders. Mitya, overwhelmed with joy, stared into her eyes, at her tearful face, at her smile, and suddenly pulled her close, kissing her passionately.

"Will you forgive me for tormenting you? I did it out of spite. I tormented everyone out of spite. I drove that old man crazy out of spite... Do you remember the time you drank at my house and smashed the wine glass? I remembered that, and today I smashed a glass and drank 'to my rotten heart.' Mitya, my falcon, why won't you kiss me? You kissed me once, and now you just stand there and stare. Why are you listening to me? Kiss me, kiss me hard, that's right. If you love me, then love me! I'll be your slave now, your slave forever. It's sweet to be a slave. Kiss me! Beat me, hurt me, do whatever you want with me... I deserve to suffer. But wait, stop, I don't want that..."

Suddenly, she pushed him away. "Go on, Mitya, I'll come and drink some wine. I want to get drunk, I'm going to drink and dance; I have to, I have to!"

She broke free from his arms and disappeared behind the curtain. Mitya followed her like a man in a daze.

"Yes, come what may—whatever happens now, I'd give the whole world for just one minute," he thought. Grushenka did, in fact, drink a whole glass of champagne in one gulp and quickly became tipsy. She sat back in the chair with a blissful smile on her face. Her cheeks were glowing, her lips were hot, and her sparkling eyes were teary with emotion. There was something intensely passionate in her gaze. Even Kalganov felt a twinge of something in his heart and went up to her.

"Did you feel me kiss you while you were asleep?" she slurred. "I'm drunk now, that's what it is... Aren't you drunk, too? And why isn't Mitya drinking? Why aren't you drinking, Mitya? I'm drunk, and you're not drinking..."

"I'm drunk! I'm drunk on you... and now I'll get drunk on wine, too."

He drank another glass, and—strangely—this glass made him completely drunk. All of a sudden, he was intoxicated, though he had been perfectly sober up until then. He remembered that clearly. From that moment on, everything swirled around him, as if he were in a fever dream. He walked, laughed, talked to everyone, without knowing what he was saying or doing. Only one intense, burning feeling stayed with him, like a "red-hot coal in his heart," as he would later describe it. He went up to her, sat beside her, stared at her, listened to her. She was talking a lot now, calling everyone over to her, beckoning to the girls from the chorus. Whenever a girl came close, Grushenka would either kiss her or make the sign of the cross over her. In the next moment, she looked as if she might burst into tears. She was highly amused by the "little old man," as she called Maximov. He kept running up to kiss her hands, "every little finger," and finally, he danced another dance to an old song he sang himself. He danced energetically to the refrain:

The little pig says, "Oink, oink, oink!"
The little calf says, "Moo, moo, moo!"
The little duck says, "Quack, quack, quack!"
The little goose says, "Honk, honk, honk!"
The hen struts through the porch,
"Cluck, cluck, cluck," she'll say,
"Cluck, cluck, cluck," she'll say!

"Give him something, Mitya," said Grushenka. "Give him a gift, he's poor, you know. Oh, the poor, the ones who've been insulted... You know, Mitya, I'm going to become a nun. No, really, one day I will. Alyosha said something to me today that I'll never forget... Yes. But today, let's dance. Tomorrow I'll go to the convent, but today we'll dance. I want to have fun today, good people, and why not? God will forgive us. If I were God, I'd forgive everyone: 'My dear sinners, from now on, I forgive you.' I'll beg for forgiveness: 'Forgive me, good people, a foolish woman.' I'm a beast, that's what I am. But I want to pray. I gave a little onion. As wicked as I've been, I want to pray. Mitya, let them dance, don't stop them. Everyone in the world is good. Everyone, even the worst of them. The world is a wonderful place. Even though we're bad, the world is good. We're good and bad, good and bad... Come on, tell me, I have a question for you: Why am I so good? You know I'm good. I'm very good... Come on, why am I so good?"

Grushenka babbled on, getting more and more drunk. Finally, she announced that she was going to dance, too. She stood up, swaying.

"Mitya, don't give me any more wine—if I ask, don't give it to me. Wine doesn't bring peace. Everything is spinning, the stove, and everything around me. I want to dance. Let everyone see how I dance... let them see how beautifully I dance…"

She really meant it. She pulled out a white handkerchief from her pocket and held one corner in her right hand to wave it while she danced. Mitya ran around excitedly. The girls got quiet, ready to start singing as soon as she gave the signal. Maximov, hearing that Grushenka wanted to dance, squealed with joy and began skipping around in front of her, singing:

"With legs so slim and sides so trim,
And its little tail curled tight."

But Grushenka waved her handkerchief at him and shooed him away.

"Shh! Mitya, why aren't they coming? Let everyone come and watch. Call in those who were locked up... Why did you lock them up? Tell them I'm going to dance. Let them watch, too."

Mitya, drunk and stumbling, swaggered over to the locked door

and began banging on it with his fist, calling out to the Poles.

"Hey, you... Podvysotskys! Come on, she's going to dance. She's calling you."

"Lajdak!" one of the Poles yelled from the other side. "You're the lajdak! You're just a little scoundrel."

"Stop mocking Poland," Kalganov said seriously. He was also drunk.

"Relax, boy! If I call him a scoundrel, it doesn't mean I'm calling all of Poland that. One lajdak doesn't represent all of Poland. Calm down, my sweet boy, eat a candy."

"Ah, what guys! As if they weren't even men. Why won't they be friends?" Grushenka said, stepping forward to dance. The chorus began to sing, "Ah, my porch, my new porch!" Grushenka threw her head back, half-opened her lips, smiled, waved her handkerchief, and then, suddenly, she wobbled and stood still in the middle of the room, looking confused.

"I'm weak…" she said softly, "Forgive me... I'm weak, I can't... I'm sorry."

She bowed to the singers and then began bowing to everyone around.

"I'm sorry… Forgive me…"

"The lady's been drinking. The pretty lady has had too much to drink," people murmured.

"The lady is drunk," Maximov giggled, explaining to the girls.

"Mitya, take me away… take me," Grushenka said weakly. Mitya rushed over, scooped her up in his arms, and carried her through the curtains.

"Well, I guess it's time for me to leave," Kalganov thought as he walked out of the blue room, closing the door behind him. But the wild party in the other room kept going and got even louder. Mitya gently laid Grushenka on the bed and kissed her lips.

"Don't touch me…" she whispered, pleading. "Don't touch me until I'm yours… I told you I'm yours, but not yet… spare me… with them here, so close, it's not right. He's here. It's filthy here…"

"I'll obey you! I won't even think of it… I worship you!" Mitya mumbled. "Yes, it's horrible here, disgusting."

Still holding her in his arms, Mitya sank to his knees beside the bed.

"I know you're rough, but you're generous," Grushenka said with difficulty. "We need to be honorable… from now on, let's be good, not like animals… Take me away, far away. Do you hear? I don't want to stay here, let's go far, far away…"

"Yes, yes, we must!" Mitya said, squeezing her tightly. "I'll take you, and we'll run away… Oh, I'd give anything to know what really happened with that blood."

"What blood?" Grushenka asked, confused.

"Nothing," Mitya muttered through his teeth. "Grusha, you want to be good, but I'm a thief. I stole money from Katya… It's a disgrace!"

"From Katya? That young woman? No, you didn't steal it. Give it back to her, take it from me… Why make a fuss? Now everything I have is yours. Money doesn't matter. We'll waste it anyway… People like us always waste money. But we should go work the land. I want to dig the earth with my own hands. We need to work, do you hear? Alyosha said so. I won't be your mistress, I'll be faithful to you, I'll be your slave, I'll work for you. We'll go to her together and beg her to forgive us, and then we'll leave. And if she doesn't forgive us, we'll leave anyway. Give her the money and love me… Don't love her… don't love her anymore. If you do, I'll strangle her… I'll poke out her eyes with a needle…"

"I love you. I only love you. I'll love you even in Siberia…"

"Siberia? Fine, Siberia it is, I don't care… We'll work… there's snow in Siberia… I love riding through the snow… and we'll need bells… Can you hear that? There's a bell ringing. Where is it? There are people coming… now it's stopped."

She closed her eyes, exhausted, and dozed off for a moment. There really had been a distant sound of a bell, but it had stopped. Mitya rested his head on her chest. He didn't notice that the bell had stopped ringing or that the singing and shouting had died down. The house was completely silent now. Grushenka opened her eyes.

"What's wrong? Was I asleep? Yes… a bell… I was dreaming about riding through the snow with bells, and I fell asleep. I was with someone I loved, with you. We were far away, and I was holding you and kissing you, snuggling close to you. It was cold, and the snow sparkled… You know how snow glitters at night when the moon is shining. It felt like I wasn't even on earth. Then I woke up, and my love is right next to me. How sweet it is…"

"Right next to you," Mitya whispered, kissing her dress, her chest, her hands. Then, suddenly, he had a strange thought: it seemed like she wasn't looking at him, but staring straight ahead, over his head, with an intense, almost fearful look. A look of surprise, even alarm, appeared on her face.

"Mitya, who is that watching us?" she whispered.

Mitya turned around and saw that someone had, in fact, parted the curtains and seemed to be watching them. And it wasn't just one person, it seemed like there were more.

He jumped up and quickly walked over to the intruder.

"Come with us, come here," said a voice, not loud, but firm and commanding.

Mitya stepped through the curtain and froze. The room was full of people, but not the ones who had been there before. A sudden shiver ran down his spine. He recognized them all immediately. That tall, stocky old man in the overcoat and cap with the badge—that was the police captain, Mihail Makarovitch. And that well-dressed, pale man with polished boots—that was the deputy prosecutor. "He owns a watch worth 400 rubles; he showed it to me." And the short young man in glasses... Mitya couldn't remember his name, but he knew him, had seen him before: he was the investigator, from the law school, who had only recently come to town. And there was the police inspector, Mavriky Mavrikyevitch, a man Mitya knew well. And those men with the brass badges—why were they here? And those other two... peasants... And over by the door stood Kalganov and Trifon Borissovitch.

"Gentlemen! What's this all about?" Mitya started to ask, but then, as if he couldn't help himself, he suddenly shouted at the top of his lungs:

"I un-der-stand!"

The young man in glasses stepped forward and, with a serious but hurried tone, said:

"We need to... in short, I ask you to come over here, to the sofa. It's absolutely necessary for you to explain."

"The old man!" Mitya cried out in a panic. "The old man and his blood!... I understand."

He collapsed into a chair as if struck down.

"You understand? He understands! Monster! Murderer! Your father's blood is crying out against you!" the police captain suddenly shouted, stepping up to Mitya. His face was red with rage, and he was trembling all over.

"This can't be!" cried the young man in glasses. "Mihail Makarovitch, you can't act like this!... Please let me speak. I never expected this kind of behavior from you..."

"This is madness, gentlemen, absolute madness!" the police captain yelled. "Look at him: drunk, at this hour, with a disreputable woman, with his father's blood on his hands... It's madness!"

"I urge you, Mihail Makarovitch, to control yourself," the prosecutor whispered urgently to the police captain, "or I will have to—" but the lawyer in glasses cut him off. He turned to Mitya and, in a loud, dignified voice, said:

"Former Lieutenant Karamazov, I must inform you that you are being charged with the murder of your father, Fyodor Pavlovitch Karamazov, committed earlier this evening..."

He said something else, and the prosecutor added a few words, but though Mitya heard them, he couldn't make sense of what they were saying. He stared at them all, wide-eyed and in shock.

Book 9: The Preliminary Investigation

Chapter 1: The Beginning of Perhotin's Official Career

Pyotr Ilyitch Perhotin, who had been left knocking at the solid locked gates of the widow Morozov's house, finally managed to make himself heard. Fenya, still shaken from the fright she had experienced two hours earlier and too upset to go to bed, was almost driven to hysterics when she heard the furious knocking at the gate.

Even though she had seen him leave, she thought that it must be Dmitri Fyodorovitch knocking again, as no one else would knock so aggressively. She ran to the house porter, who had already woken up and gone to the gate, begging him not to open it. But after questioning Pyotr Ilyitch and learning that he wanted to see Fenya on very "important business," the porter finally decided to open the gate.

Pyotr Ilyitch was allowed into Fenya's kitchen, but the girl asked for the house porter to stay with them "because she had a bad feeling." He began questioning her and immediately learned the most important fact: when Dmitri Fyodorovitch had run out to look for Grushenka, he had grabbed a pestle from the mortar. When he returned, the pestle was gone, and his hands were smeared with blood.

"And the blood was just pouring out, dripping from him, dripping!" Fenya kept exclaiming. This awful detail was entirely a product of her upset imagination. However, although it wasn't "dripping," Pyotr Ilyitch had seen Dmitri's hands covered in blood and had helped wash them. Furthermore, the question he had to answer now wasn't how fast the blood had dried, but where Dmitri Fyodorovitch had gone with the pestle— more precisely, whether it had really been to Fyodor Pavlovitch's, and how he could find out for sure. Pyotr Ilyitch kept returning to this point, and although he didn't uncover anything definite, he left with a firm belief that Dmitri Fyodorovitch could have gone nowhere but to his father's house, and that something must have happened there.

"And when he came back," Fenya added excitedly, "I told him everything, and then I started asking him, 'Why do you have blood on your hands, Dmitri Fyodorovitch?' And he said it was human blood, and that he had just killed someone. He confessed everything to me, and then he ran off like a madman. I sat down and thought, where's he run off to now, like a madman? He'll go to Mokroe, I thought, and kill my mistress there. I ran out to beg him not to kill her. I was running to his lodgings, but as I passed by Plotnikov's shop, I saw him just getting ready to leave, and there was no blood on his hands then." (Fenya had noticed this and remembered it.) Fenya's old grandmother confirmed as much as she could. After asking a few more questions, Pyotr Ilyitch left the house even more troubled and uneasy than when he had entered it.

The most straightforward and easiest thing for him to do would have been to go straight to Fyodor Pavlovitch's to find out if anything had happened there, and if so, what exactly. Then, he could go to the police captain as he had intended to do if something had happened. But the night was dark, Fyodor Pavlovitch's gates were strong, and he would have to knock again. He barely knew Fyodor Pavlovitch, and what if, after all that knocking, they opened the gates and nothing had happened? Fyodor Pavlovitch, in his mocking way, would tell the whole town how some stranger named Perhotin had broken in on him at midnight, asking if someone had killed him. It would cause a scandal. And Pyotr Ilyitch feared scandal more than anything in the world.

Yet, his feeling of unease was so strong that, although he cursed himself and stomped his foot in frustration, he didn't head to Fyodor Pavlovitch's but went to Madame Hohlakov's instead. He decided that if she denied having given Dmitri Fyodorovitch the three thousand rubles, he would go straight to the police captain, but if she admitted it, he would go home and let the matter rest until the morning.

It's clear, of course, that going to Madame Hohlakov's house at eleven o'clock at night, a fashionable lady he didn't even know, and possibly waking her up to ask her an unbelievable question, was more likely to cause a scandal than going to Fyodor Pavlovitch's. But that's how it is sometimes, especially in situations like this, when even the calmest and most reasonable people make strange decisions. At this moment, Pyotr Ilyitch was anything but calm. He would remember for the rest of his life how a growing sense of dread took hold of him, becoming more painful, driving him on against his own will. Even so, as he walked to the lady's house, he cursed himself the whole way but kept repeating through clenched teeth, "I'm going to get to the bottom of this, I will!"

It was exactly eleven o'clock when he arrived at Madame Hohlakov's house. He was let into the yard quickly, but when he asked if the lady was still awake, the porter could only tell him that she was usually in bed by that time.

"Ask upstairs. If she wants to see you, she will. If she doesn't, she won't."

Pyotr Ilyitch went upstairs, but things weren't so easy there. The footman didn't want to give his name to the lady, but after a while, a maid was called. Pyotr Ilyitch politely but firmly asked her to tell the lady that an official named Perhotin, from town, was there on very urgent business, and if it weren't of the utmost importance, he wouldn't have dared to come. "Tell her exactly that, in those words," he insisted.

The maid left, and Pyotr waited in the hallway. Madame Hohlakov was already in her bedroom, though not yet asleep. She had been feeling uneasy since Mitya's visit and had a sense that she wouldn't get through the night without one of the headaches that always followed such stressful events. She was surprised when the maid told her about the visitor, but despite her curiosity, she irritably refused to see him. The unexpected visit from an "official living in town" at such an hour piqued her curiosity, but she didn't want to give in.

But Pyotr Ilyitch was as stubborn as a mule. He begged the maid to take another message, saying:

"He has come on business of the greatest importance, and Madame Hohlakov may regret it later if she refuses to see him now."

The maid, staring at him in amazement, went back to deliver his message again. Madame Hohlakov was deeply intrigued. She paused for a moment to think, asked what he looked like, and learned that he was "very well-dressed, young, and extremely polite." It's worth noting, as an aside, that Pyotr Ilyitch was a rather handsome young man and quite aware of this fact. Madame Hohlakov decided to see him. She was still in her dressing gown and slippers, but she hastily threw a black shawl over her shoulders. "The official" was invited into the drawing room, the same room where Mitya had been received earlier. The lady walked into the room to greet her guest with a stern and questioning expression, and without inviting him to sit down, immediately began with the question:

"What do you want?"

"I have dared to disturb you, madam, over a matter concerning our common acquaintance, Dmitri Fyodorovitch Karamazov," Perhotin began.

But as soon as he uttered the name, the lady's face showed signs of extreme irritation. She nearly screamed and interrupted him, full of anger:

"How much longer must I endure that horrible man's nonsense?" she shrieked, her voice full of hysteria. "How dare you, sir! How could you presume to disturb a lady, a stranger to you, in her own house at such an hour!... And to come barging in here to talk about a man who just earlier today was here in this very room, threatening to murder me, and then stormed out in a way no decent person would. Let me tell you, sir, I intend to file a complaint against you! I will not let this go! Leave at once... I'm a mother... I... I—"

"Murder! So he tried to murder you too?" asked Perhotin quickly.

"What? Has he killed someone else?" Madame Hohlakov impulsively asked, her voice rising.

"If you'll just listen, madam, for a moment, I can explain everything in a few words," Perhotin replied firmly. "At five o'clock this afternoon, Dmitri Fyodorovitch borrowed ten roubles from me, and I know for a fact that he had no other money. But by nine o'clock, he came to see me with a bundle of hundred-rouble notes, somewhere around two or three thousand roubles. His hands and face were covered in blood, and he looked like he had lost his mind. When I asked him where he got so much money, he told me that he had just received it from you, that you had given him three thousand roubles so he could go to the gold mines...."

Madame Hohlakov's face showed a mix of intense and painful emotions.

"My God! He must have killed his own father!" she cried, clasping her hands together. "I never gave him any money, never! Oh, run, run!... Don't say another word! Save the old man... run to his father... run quickly!"

"Excuse me, madam, so you didn't give him any money? You're absolutely sure that you didn't give him anything?" Perhotin asked cautiously.

"No, I didn't! I didn't give him anything! I refused because I knew he wouldn't value it properly. He stormed out in a fit of rage, stomping his feet. He even lunged at me, but I managed to get away... And let me tell you, as I'm not trying to hide anything from you now, he actually spat at me! Can you imagine that? But why are we standing here? Ah, please sit down."

"Excuse me, I..."

"Or better yet, run, run immediately! You need to save that poor old man from an awful death!"

"But what if he's already killed him?" Perhotin asked, his voice full of concern.

"Oh heavens, yes! Then what are we to do now? What do you think we should do now?" she asked frantically.

By now, she had made Pyotr Ilyitch sit down, and she sat across from him. Briefly, but clearly, Pyotr Ilyitch explained what had happened, at least the parts he had seen firsthand. He also told her about his visit to Fenya and mentioned the pestle. All of these details deeply affected the already distressed lady, who kept gasping and covering her face with her hands.

"Can you believe it, I foresaw all of this! I have this unique ability, where whatever I imagine comes true. And I've always looked at that awful man and thought, 'That man will end up murdering me.' And now it's happened... or rather, it would have happened if he hadn't murdered his own father instead. God's hand must have saved me! And what's more, I'm certain he was ashamed to murder me because, right here, in this room, I placed the holy ikon of Saint Varvara around his neck. And to think how close I was to death at that moment! I walked right up to him, and he bowed his neck to me! You know, Pyotr Ilyitch (I believe that's your name?), I'm not one to believe in miracles, but this ikon and what happened to me just now—it has shaken me to my core. I'm ready to believe in anything now. Have you heard about Father Zossima? Oh, but I'm rambling... And imagine, with the ikon around his neck, he spat at me. But still, at least he only spat, he didn't kill me, and. he stormed out! But what should we do now? What must we do?" she asked in desperation.

Pyotr Ilyitch stood up and told her that he was going straight to the police captain to report everything and let him decide what to do.

"Oh, he's an excellent man, truly excellent! Mihail Makarovitch, I know him well. Of course, you're absolutely right to go to him. You've thought of everything so well! I would never have been able to come up with that!" Madame Hohlakov exclaimed, still sitting.

"Especially since I know the police captain personally," added Pyotr Ilyitch, who was now standing and clearly eager to leave the emotional lady, who kept talking without allowing him to say goodbye and depart.

"And please, do come back and tell me what you find out, what happens, what they uncover... how they'll try him... and what he'll be sentenced to. Tell me, we don't have the death penalty, do we? But do come back, even if it's three in the morning, four, or half-past four... Tell them to wake me up if I'm asleep... But oh, I won't sleep! Wait, should I come with you?"

"N-no. But if you could write a quick note, just three lines, in your own hand, stating that you didn't give Dmitri Fyodorovitch any money, it could be helpful... in case it's needed," suggested Pyotr Ilyitch.

"Of course!" Madame Hohlakov eagerly rushed to her desk. "You know, I'm amazed by your cleverness and how well you've handled all of this. Are you in government service here? I'm so pleased to think you are!"

As she spoke, she quickly scribbled the following note on half a sheet of paper:

I have never in my life lent that unfortunate man, Dmitri Fyodorovitch Karamazov (for despite everything, he is unfortunate), three thousand roubles today. I have never given him money, never. I swear by all that is holy!

K. HOHLAKOV.

"Here's the note!" she quickly turned to Pyotr Ilyitch. "Go, save him. What a noble thing you're doing!" And she made the sign of the cross over him three times. She rushed out to see him off as he walked down the hallway.

"How thankful I am to you! You can't imagine how grateful I am that you came to me first. How is it that we haven't met before? I would be so honored to have you visit my house again in the future. It's wonderful that you live here! Such precision! Such practical skills! They must really value you; they must see how capable you are. If there's anything I can do for you, believe me... oh, how I love young people! I'm just in love with young people! The younger generation is the only support for our suffering country. Our only hope... Oh, go, go!"

But Pyotr Ilyitch had already hurried off, or else she might not have let him leave so quickly. Yet, despite being caught up in such an unpleasant situation, Madame Hohlakov had left a somewhat positive impression on him, which eased his mind a little. As they say, different people have different tastes. "She's really not that old," he thought, feeling somewhat amused. "Actually, I would have mistaken her for her daughter."

As for Madame Hohlakov, she was absolutely charmed by the young man. "Such intelligence! Such precision! In such a young man! In today's world! And all that combined with such good manners and appearance! People always say that today's youth are good for nothing, but here's an example to prove them wrong!" And so, she completely forgot about the "terrible situation," and it wasn't until she was getting into bed that she suddenly remembered "how close to death she had been." She gasped, "Oh, it's awful, just awful!" But then she quickly fell into a deep, peaceful sleep.

I wouldn't have focused on these seemingly trivial and unrelated details, except for the fact that this strange meeting between the young official and the not-so-old widow ended up being the starting point for that precise and practical young man's entire career. His story is still remembered with astonishment in our town, and perhaps I will have more to say about it when I finish this long account of the Brothers Karamazov.

Chapter 2: The Alarm

Our police captain, Mihail Makarovitch Makarov, was a retired lieutenant-colonel, a widower, and an excellent man. He had only joined us three years ago but had already earned widespread respect, mostly because he "knew how to keep society together." He was never without visitors, and he couldn't bear being without company. Someone was always dining with him; he never sat down to a meal alone. He hosted dinners regularly, sometimes for the most unexpected reasons. Although the meals weren't fancy, there was always plenty to go around. The fish pies were outstanding, and while the wine wasn't the best, there was always more than enough of it.

The first room his guests entered was a well-equipped billiard room, with pictures of English racehorses in black frames on the walls—an essential decoration for any bachelor's billiard room. Every evening, there were card games at his house, even if it was just one table. Occasionally, the whole society of our town, including mothers and young women, gathered at his place to dance. Though Mihail Makarovitch was a widower, he

282

didn't live alone. His widowed daughter lived with him, along with her two grown-up, unmarried daughters, who had already completed their education. They were cheerful and good-looking, and though everyone knew they wouldn't have dowries, they still attracted all the fashionable young men to their grandfather's house.

Mihail Makarovitch wasn't particularly good at his job, but he didn't do it any worse than most people in similar positions. To be blunt, he wasn't a well-educated man. He didn't always understand the limits of his authority and sometimes made noticeable mistakes when interpreting the new reforms. It wasn't because he was unintelligent, but rather because he didn't take the time to carefully study them. He was always in too much of a hurry to dive into the details. "I have the heart of a soldier, not a civilian," he often said about himself. He hadn't even grasped the core principles behind the reforms involving the emancipation of the serfs. Instead, he absorbed bits and pieces of it gradually, through experience. Ironically, he was also a landowner himself.

Pyotr Ilyitch was certain he would find some of Mihail Makarovitch's guests there that evening, but he wasn't sure exactly who. As it turned out, the prosecutor and Varvinsky, our district doctor, were playing whist at the police captain's house. Varvinsky was a young man who had recently come from Petersburg after earning a brilliant degree at the Academy of Medicine. Ippolit Kirillovitch, the prosecutor—though technically the deputy prosecutor, we all just called him "the prosecutor"—was a rather peculiar man. He was about thirty-five, a bit sickly, and married to a plump, childless wife. He had both intelligence and a kind heart, but he was also vain and easily irritated. His biggest flaw was that he thought more highly of himself than his abilities justified, which left him constantly restless.

He had a particular interest in psychology and enjoyed studying human behavior, especially the minds of criminals and their motives. He felt unappreciated in his position, convinced that he had enemies in high places who were holding him back. During his darker moods, he even considered leaving his post to become a defense lawyer in criminal cases. The sudden emergence of the Karamazov case affected him deeply. "This case will be talked about all over Russia," he thought. But I'm getting ahead of myself.

Nikolay Parfenovitch Nelyudov, a young investigating lawyer who had arrived from Petersburg just two months earlier, was sitting in the next room with the young ladies. Later, people would comment on how strange it was that so many important figures happened to gather at the police captain's house on the very night of the crime, as if by some plan. But it had all happened naturally, by chance.

Ippolit Kirillovitch's wife had been suffering from a toothache for two days, so he had come to the captain's house to escape her groans. The doctor, being the kind of man who couldn't imagine spending an evening without playing cards, was naturally there as well. As for Nikolay Parfenovitch, he had been planning to stop by for several days. He had come with the playful intention of surprising Olga Mihailovna, the eldest granddaughter, by showing that he knew her secret—it was her birthday, but she had kept it quiet to avoid throwing a dance. He expected to have a lot of fun teasing her with jokes about her age, her secrecy, and her attempts to avoid celebration. Nikolay Parfenovitch was known for his mischievous charm, earning him the nickname "the naughty man" among the ladies, which he happily embraced.

Despite his playful nature, he was well-mannered, came from a respectable family, and knew how to behave properly. Though he lived for pleasure, his jokes were always tasteful. He was short and delicate in appearance, with slender white fingers that always wore several large, sparkling rings. Yet when it came to his work, he became very serious, fully aware of the importance of his duties. He had a knack for confusing peasants during interrogations, leaving them bewildered, if not impressed.

Pyotr Ilyitch was shocked when he entered the police captain's house. It was clear that everyone already knew what had happened. They had dropped their cards and were standing, talking excitedly. Even Nikolay Parfenovitch had rushed in from the other room, looking serious and ready for action. Pyotr Ilyitch was met with the shocking news that old Fyodor Pavlovitch had been murdered that evening in his own home, and that he had also been robbed.

The news had reached them in an unusual way. Marfa Ignatyevna, the wife of old Grigory—who had been knocked unconscious near the fence—had taken a sleeping draught and was in a deep sleep. She might have slept through the night if not for a sudden, terrifying scream from Smerdyakov, who was in the next room. His screams always preceded his epileptic fits, and no matter how often Marfa heard them, she could never get used to the sound.

She jumped out of bed, half-asleep, and ran to Smerdyakov's room, but the room was dark, and all she could hear was the sound of him gasping and struggling to breathe. She panicked and screamed, intending to call her husband, but then she realized that Grigory wasn't in bed beside her. She groped around the mattress, but it was empty.

"He must have gone outside," she thought in confusion. She went to the steps and called out to him, but there was no reply. Then she heard faint groaning coming from the garden. She listened carefully, and the sound came again—it was definitely coming from the garden.

"Oh no! Just like what happened with Lizaveta Smerdyashchaya!" Marfa thought in horror. She cautiously made her way down the steps and saw that the gate to the garden was open.

"He must be out there," she thought anxiously. She approached the gate, and just then, she heard Grigory calling her name: "Marfa! Marfa!" His voice was weak and filled with pain.

"Lord, keep us safe from harm!" Marfa Ignatyevna whispered as she ran toward the voice—and that's how she found Grigory. But instead of being by the fence where he had been struck down, he was lying about twenty paces away. Later, it was discovered that after regaining consciousness, he had managed to crawl that far, likely losing consciousness several times along the way. Marfa noticed immediately that he was covered in blood and began screaming at the top of her lungs. Grigory was mumbling incoherently, "He killed... killed his father... Why scream, foolish woman... go, get someone..."

But Marfa kept screaming. Seeing that the window to her master's room was open and a candle was burning inside, she ran to it, calling out to Fyodor Pavlovitch. However, when she peered through the window, what she saw made her blood run cold. Fyodor Pavlovitch was lying on his back, motionless, on the floor. His light-colored robe and white shirt were soaked with blood. The candle on the table cast a bright light over the pool of blood and Fyodor Pavlovitch's lifeless face. Horrified, Marfa dashed away from the window, ran out of the garden, unlatched the big gate, and took off by the back path to her neighbor, Marya Kondratyevna.

Both Marya and her daughter were asleep, but they were jolted awake by Marfa's frantic banging on the shutters and her desperate screams. Through her incoherent cries, Marfa managed to tell them what had happened and begged for their help. It just so happened that Foma, a wandering acquaintance, was spending the night with them. They woke him immediately, and all three of them ran toward the crime scene.

On the way, Marya Kondratyevna recalled that around eight o'clock that night, she had heard a horrifying scream from their garden. That scream, she now realized, must have been Grigory's shout of "Parricide!" when he grabbed Mitya's leg. "Someone cried out once and then fell silent," Marya explained as they hurried along. When they reached the spot where Grigory lay, the two women, with Foma's help, carried him back to the lodge.

They lit a candle and saw that Smerdyakov was in no better condition than before. He was convulsing violently, his eyes twisted in a squint, and foam dribbled from his mouth. They sprinkled Grigory's forehead with a mixture of water and vinegar, which revived him almost immediately. His first question was, "Is the master dead?"

Without delay, Foma and the two women ran to Fyodor Pavlovitch's house. This time, they noticed not only that the window was open but also that the garden door stood wide open, even though Fyodor Pavlovitch had made it a habit to lock himself inside every night for the past week, not even allowing Grigory in under any circumstances. Afraid that something terrible might happen if they went inside, they hesitated. Returning to Grigory, the old man instructed them to go straight to the police captain. Marya Kondratyevna ran ahead to sound the alarm. She reached the captain's house only five minutes before Pyotr Ilyitch arrived, so his account was no longer just speculation but a confirmation of what everyone already suspected about the identity of the murderer—a theory that, deep down, Pyotr Ilyitch had refused to believe until that moment.

It was decided that they needed to act quickly. The town's deputy police inspector was ordered to gather four witnesses and go directly to Fyodor Pavlovitch's house to conduct an official investigation on the spot. The district doctor, who was new to his job and very enthusiastic, insisted on accompanying the police captain, the prosecutor, and the investigating lawyer.

Fyodor Pavlovitch was found dead, with his skull smashed. The murder weapon was believed to be the same one used to strike Grigory. They found the weapon quickly—a heavy brass pestle— lying in plain sight on the garden path near the fence. Inside the house, the room where Fyodor Pavlovitch's body lay showed no signs of a struggle. However, behind a screen near the bed, they discovered a large, thick envelope on the floor. The envelope bore the inscription, "A gift of three thousand rubles for my angel, Grushenka, if she agrees to come." Below that, Fyodor Pavlovitch had added, "For my little chicken."

The envelope, sealed with three red wax seals, had been torn open, and the money was missing. Nearby, they found a piece of narrow pink ribbon, which had once tied the envelope shut.

One detail from Pyotr Ilyitch's account made a strong impression on both the prosecutor and the investigating lawyer: Mitya had told Pyotr that he intended to shoot himself before dawn. Mitya had spoken openly about this plan, loading his pistols in front of Pyotr, writing a letter, and placing it in his pocket. When Pyotr, still unwilling to believe him, threatened to tell someone and stop him, Mitya had grinned and replied, "You'll be too late." This meant they had to hurry to Mokroe and catch the criminal before he followed through on his plan to kill himself.

"That makes sense, absolutely!" the prosecutor said excitedly. "That's exactly how madmen like him behave: 'I'll kill myself tomorrow, so tonight I'll have one last celebration!'"

The news about Mitya buying wine and provisions only fueled the prosecutor's excitement. "Do you remember the case of that man who killed the merchant Olsufyev?" the prosecutor asked. "He stole fifteen hundred rubles, got his hair curled right afterward, and then, without even hiding the money, carried it openly to the brothels."

However, their investigation at Fyodor Pavlovitch's house took time. The search, inquiries, and necessary paperwork delayed their departure by two hours. Before setting out, they sent the rural police officer, Mavriky Mavrikyevitch Schmertsov, ahead to Mokroe. He had come to town that morning to collect his pay. His instructions were clear: when he reached Mokroe, he was to avoid raising any alarm, keep a close eye on the suspect until the authorities arrived, and gather witnesses for the arrest.

Mavriky Mavrikyevitch followed his instructions, keeping his mission a secret. He only confided in an old acquaintance, Trifon Borissovitch, giving him a hint of the situation. He spoke to Trifon just before Mitya showed up on the balcony, looking for the landlord in the dark. Trifon's change in expression and tone told Mavriky that something was going on. Still, neither Mitya nor anyone else knew that they were being watched.

Trifon Borissovitch had taken Mitya's box of pistols and put it somewhere safe. Shortly before sunrise, at around four o'clock, the officials—the police captain, prosecutor, and investigating lawyer—arrived in two carriages, each drawn by three horses. The doctor stayed behind to perform a post-mortem on Fyodor Pavlovitch's body the next day. However, the doctor's main interest was in Smerdyakov's condition.

"Fits this severe, lasting for a full twenty-four hours, are extremely rare and of great interest to medical science," the doctor eagerly told his companions as they were leaving. They laughed and congratulated him on his unexpected "discovery." The prosecutor and investigating lawyer clearly remembered the doctor saying that Smerdyakov was unlikely to survive the night.

Now that we've covered these important details, let's return to the point where we left off in our story.

Chapter 3: The Sufferings of A Soul, The First Ordeal

And so, Mitya sat there, staring wildly at the people around him, unable to understand what they were saying to him. Suddenly, he stood up, raised his hands, and shouted aloud, "I'm not guilty! I didn't shed that blood! I'm not guilty of my father's blood... I intended to kill him, but I didn't! I'm not guilty. It wasn't me."

But before he had even finished speaking, Grushenka burst out from behind the curtain and threw herself at the police captain's feet. "It's my fault! It's my wickedness!" she cried, her voice breaking with emotion, tears streaming down her face. She reached out with her clasped hands toward the others. "He did it because of me! I tortured him and drove him to it! I tormented that poor old man, too—the one who is dead—and it's all because of my wickedness. I am the one to blame! It's my fault—mine first, mine most, all my fault!"

"Yes! It's your fault! You are the real criminal! You witch, you harlot! It's all your fault!" the police captain shouted, raising his hand threateningly toward her. But he was quickly stopped. The prosecutor grabbed him firmly and cried, "This is completely out of order, Mihail Makarovitch! You're interfering with the investigation... you're undermining the case..." He could barely catch his breath.

"Follow the proper procedure! Stick to the procedure!" cried Nikolay Parfenovitch, who was just as agitated. "If not, this will be completely impossible!"

"Judge us together!" Grushenka cried desperately, still kneeling on the floor. "Punish us together! I'll go with him, even if it's to death!"

"Grusha, my love, my life, my everything!" Mitya dropped to his knees beside her, wrapping his arms around her tightly. "Don't believe her!" he cried. "She's innocent! She hasn't spilled anyone's blood! She's done nothing wrong!"

Later, Mitya remembered that several men had pulled him away from her by force and led her out of the room. When he came to his senses, he found himself sitting at the table. The guards with metal plates stood beside and behind him. Across from him, on the other side of the table, sat the investigating lawyer, Nikolay Parfenovitch, who kept urging him to drink water from a glass on the table. "It will help you feel better. It will calm you. Just stay calm. Don't be afraid," he said, speaking very politely.

Mitya later recalled that he became strangely fascinated by the lawyer's large rings—one with an amethyst and another with a bright yellow, transparent stone that gleamed brilliantly. Long afterward, Mitya would remember with amazement how those rings had captivated his attention through all the terrible hours of interrogation, making it impossible for him to tear his eyes away from them, even though they had nothing to do with his situation.

On Mitya's left side, where Maximov had been sitting earlier in the evening, the prosecutor now sat. To his right, where Grushenka had been, sat a rosy-cheeked young man in a worn hunting jacket, with ink and paper before him. This was the lawyer's secretary, who had accompanied him. The police captain stood by the window at the far end of the room, next to Kalganov, who was seated there quietly.

"Drink some water," the lawyer softly urged again for the tenth time.

"I've already had some, gentlemen," Mitya replied. "But come on, gentlemen, crush me, punish me, decide my fate!" His eyes were wide and filled with desperation as he stared directly at the lawyer.

"So you are now formally stating that you are not guilty of the murder of your father, Fyodor Pavlovitch?" the lawyer asked, gently but insistently.

"I'm not guilty. I am guilty of another old man's blood, but not my father's. And I grieve for that! I killed that old man—I knocked him down. But now I have to answer for another crime—a terrible crime—that I didn't commit. It's an unbearable accusation, gentlemen. But who killed my father? If not me, then who? It's incredible, impossible to believe."

"Yes, who could have killed him?" the lawyer began to say, but the prosecutor, Ippolit Kirillovitch, glanced at him and interrupted to address Mitya directly.

"You don't need to worry about the old servant, Grigory Vassilyevitch. He's alive. He's going to survive, despite the severe blows you gave him, as both you and he confirmed. According to the doctor, there's no doubt that he will live."

"He's alive? He's really alive?" Mitya exclaimed, raising his hands in joy. His face lit up with happiness. "Thank You, Lord, for this miracle! You've answered my prayer! I prayed all night!" He crossed himself three times, almost out of breath from the excitement.

The prosecutor continued, "Grigory has given us crucial evidence about you—" but before he could finish, Mitya suddenly jumped to his feet.

"Wait! Just one minute, gentlemen, for God's sake! I need to see her—just for a moment!"

"Sorry, but that's impossible right now!" Nikolay Parfenovitch almost shouted, jumping to his feet as well. The guards seized Mitya, but he sat back down on his own.

"What a shame," Mitya said mournfully. "I only wanted one minute with her! I just wanted to tell her that the burden on my heart is gone—that the blood I carried all night has been lifted. I'm not a murderer anymore! She is my fiancée!" His eyes shone with reverence as he looked around at them. "Oh, thank you, gentlemen! In this one moment, you've given me new life, a new heart! That old man—Grigory—he carried me in his arms when I was a little boy, abandoned by everyone. He washed me in the tub. He was like a father to me!"

The lawyer started to speak. "And so you—" but Mitya interrupted.

"Please, gentlemen! Just one more moment," Mitya begged, leaning forward on the table and covering his face with his hands. "Let me think—just let me breathe for a moment. This is too much... overwhelming. A man isn't a drum, gentlemen!"

"Drink a little more water," Nikolay Parfenovitch murmured softly.

Mitya took his hands away from his face and laughed. His eyes looked sure of himself, and in an instant, he seemed like a different person. His whole posture changed, as if he were suddenly on equal footing with the men around him, as though they were old acquaintances who had met the day before at some friendly gathering. It's worth mentioning that, when Mitya first started visiting the police captain's house, he had been warmly welcomed. But recently, especially over the past month, Mitya had barely visited. When the captain met him on the street, Mitya noticed that the man would frown and only bow to him out of politeness. He knew the prosecutor less well, although he had occasionally visited the prosecutor's nervous and somewhat imaginative wife, not really knowing why. She always greeted him warmly and, for some reason, had taken an interest in him right up to the very end. As for the investigating lawyer, Mitya hadn't had the chance to get to know him well, though they had talked twice before—each time about women.

"You're a talented lawyer, Nikolay Parfenovitch!" Mitya said with a cheerful laugh. "But I can help you now. Gentlemen, I feel like a new man! And please, don't take offense if I speak plainly with you. I'll be honest— I'm a bit drunk." He gave a playful grin. "I think I had the pleasure of meeting you, Nikolay Parfenovitch, at my relative Miusov's. But gentlemen, I know I'm not your equal here. I understand exactly what kind of position I'm in. There's a terrible suspicion hanging over me, especially if Grigory has testified against me. It's awful, just awful! But let's get to it, gentlemen. I'm ready! Let's get this over with quickly because—listen!—I know I'm innocent, so we can clear this up right now. Can't we? Can't we?"

Mitya spoke quickly and with enthusiasm, as though he genuinely believed these men were his closest friends.

"For now, we'll note that you deny the charge against you," said Nikolay Parfenovitch, speaking carefully as he leaned toward the secretary and quietly dictated what to write down.

"You want to write that down? Fine, write it down! I agree, gentlemen. But—wait, wait! Write this, too. I admit I'm guilty of disorderly behavior. I admit I used violence against an old man. And there's something else I carry in my heart that I feel guilty about—but that part you don't need to write down," Mitya added suddenly, turning toward the secretary. "That's personal—it's my private life and has nothing to do with you." He paused for a moment, then continued, "But as for the murder of my father—no! I'm not guilty! That's a ridiculous idea. It's completely absurd! I'll prove it to you, and you'll see it for yourselves. You'll laugh at how crazy the whole thing sounds!"

"Please stay calm, Dmitri Fyodorovich," the lawyer said, trying to steady Mitya with his composed tone. "Before we continue, I'd like to confirm something, if you don't mind. Is it true that you disliked your father, Fyodor Pavlovitch, and that you often argued with him? A moment ago, you even said, 'I wanted to kill him. I didn't kill him, but I wanted to.'"

"Did I really say that?" Mitya asked, as if surprised by his own words. "Ah, yes... I suppose I did, gentlemen. Sadly, it's true. I did want to kill him. I wanted to many times... It's tragic, really. Tragic!"

"So, you admit you wanted to kill him?" the lawyer asked. "Would you explain what drove you to feel such hatred toward your father?"

"What's there to explain, gentlemen?" Mitya said with a shrug, lowering his gaze. "I've never hidden my feelings. Everyone in town knows how I felt—ask anyone in the tavern. I even talked about it in Father Zossima's cell. And on the same day, in the evening, I nearly killed my father. I beat him, and I swore in front of witnesses that I'd come back to finish him off. A thousand witnesses could tell you the same thing! I've been shouting it for the past month, telling anyone who would listen. The facts speak for themselves. But feelings... feelings are a different matter." Mitya frowned, then added, "I don't think you have the right to question me about my feelings. I know you're just doing your job, but this is personal—deeply personal. But since I've been so open about my feelings before, talking to everyone in the tavern, I won't hide them now."

Mitya leaned forward, his voice more serious. "I understand that the facts don't look good for me. I told everyone I wanted to kill him, and now, suddenly, he's dead. So naturally, people think I must be the killer! I get that, gentlemen. It makes sense. Even I'm shocked—if I didn't do it, then who did? That's what I want to know. I need to know!" He slammed his hand down on the table. "Where was he killed? How was he killed? What was used to kill him? Tell me!"

"We found him in his study," the prosecutor said. "He was lying on his back, and his head had been smashed in."

"Horrible!" Mitya shuddered and covered his face with one hand, resting his elbows on the table.

"We'll continue," Nikolay Parfenovitch interjected calmly. "You've mentioned that jealousy played a part in your hatred toward your father. Is that correct?"

"Yes, jealousy. But it wasn't just jealousy," Mitya admitted. "There were also disagreements over money, right?"

"Yes, over money, too."

"There was a dispute about three thousand rubles, if I remember correctly, which you claimed as part of your inheritance?"

"Three thousand? It was more than that—much more!" Mitya exclaimed passionately. "It was over six thousand, maybe even ten! I told everyone that—I shouted it to them! But in the end, I decided to let it go and settle for three thousand. I desperately needed that money. And those three thousand rubles—those exact bills—were the ones I knew he kept under his pillow for Grushenka. To me, that money felt stolen—stolen from me! I saw it as mine, as my rightful property."

The prosecutor exchanged a quick glance with the investigating lawyer and gave him a subtle wink.

"We'll come back to that later," the lawyer said smoothly. "For now, we'll note that you considered that money to be your own."

"Write it down, go ahead. I know that this is just another fact that makes me look guilty, but I'm not afraid of the truth, and I'll say it even if it's against me. Do you understand?" Mitya said, suddenly looking gloomy and tired. "You think I'm a different kind of person than I really am. But I want you to know that you're dealing with a man of honor—real honor. Even though I've done a lot of shameful things, deep down I've always been, and still am, honorable at heart. That's the truth. I don't even know how to explain it properly. This sense of honor has made me miserable my whole life. It's like I've been chasing it, like Diogenes with his lantern, looking for something I could never quite reach. And yet, despite all that, I've done terrible things—like the rest of us, gentlemen... no, worse than the rest. Just me, only me!" His forehead tightened in pain. "My head is killing me."

He paused, gathering his thoughts. "You see, gentlemen, I couldn't stand the sight of him. There was something vile about him—something disrespectful, trampling over everything sacred, something sneering and disgusting. He was hateful. But now that he's dead, I feel... different."

"What do you mean?" one of the men asked.

"I don't feel exactly different. I just wish I hadn't hated him so much."

"Do you feel sorry now?"

"No, not exactly sorry. Don't write that down. I'm not a good man myself, not admirable in any way, so I had no right to judge him as repulsive. That's what I mean. Write that down if you want."

As Mitya said this, his mood darkened further, and he grew more gloomy as the questioning continued.

At that moment, something unexpected happened. Even though Grushenka had been taken to another room, it wasn't far from where the interrogation was happening. She had only been moved to the next room over, beyond the large hall where the dancing and feasting had taken place. It was a small room with one window. Grushenka sat there with only Maximov by her side. He was miserable and scared, clinging to her like a frightened child. At the door stood one of the guards with a metal plate on his chest. Grushenka had been crying quietly, but suddenly, her emotions overwhelmed her. She jumped to her feet, threw her arms into the air, and with a loud, heart-wrenching cry, burst out of the room toward Mitya. Her movement was so sudden that the guard didn't have time to stop her.

Hearing her cry, Mitya trembled, sprang to his feet, and rushed toward her with a shout, unaware of what he was doing. But they weren't allowed to meet. Several men grabbed Mitya by the arms, struggling to hold him back as he tried to break free. It took three or four men to restrain him. At the same time, Grushenka was also seized. Mitya saw her reaching out to him, her arms stretched wide, crying out as they dragged her away.

When the commotion ended, Mitya found himself back in his chair, sitting across from the investigating lawyer. "What do you want from her? Why are you torturing her? She hasn't done anything—nothing at all!" he shouted angrily.

The lawyers tried to calm him down, and about ten minutes passed in this way. Finally, Mihail Makarovitch, who had been out of the room, came back in, looking flustered. He addressed the prosecutor in an excited voice. "She's been moved downstairs. May I say something to this poor man? Just a word, in your presence?"

"Of course, Mihail Makarovitch," the lawyer replied. "We have no reason to object."

Mihail Makarovitch turned to Mitya, his face full of warmth, almost like a father. "Listen, Dmitri Fyodorovich, my dear boy. I took your Agrafena Alexandrovna downstairs myself and left her with the landlord's daughters. Old Maximov is with her, too, watching over her. I calmed her down, do you hear? I made sure she understood that you need to focus on defending yourself. I told her not to upset you or make you lose your head, or else you might say something wrong. She's a sensible girl, you know— kind-hearted. She even wanted to kiss my old hands, begging me to help you. She asked me to come tell you not to worry about her. And now I must go back and tell her that you're calm and not upset. So, you need to stay calm, do you understand? I was wrong to be harsh with her earlier—she really is a gentle soul, a Christian woman, and not to blame for anything. So, what should I tell her, Dmitri Fyodorovich? Will you stay calm?"

The police captain spoke more freely than was appropriate, but he had been deeply moved by Grushenka's suffering, and tears welled up in his eyes. Mitya jumped up and rushed toward him. "Please forgive me, gentlemen! Let me thank him! Mihail Makarovitch, you have the heart of an angel. Thank you for looking after her. I promise, I'll stay calm. I'll be cheerful, even! Tell her I'm fine— happy, even. I'll be laughing soon, knowing she has someone like you to watch over her. I'll get through all of this, and once I'm free, I'll be with her. She'll see! Tell her to wait for me."

Turning toward the lawyers, Mitya added eagerly, "Gentlemen, I'll tell you everything now—my whole soul. We'll get this over with, and we'll laugh about it when it's done, won't we? But let me tell you one thing. That woman is the queen of my heart. She's everything to me! She is my light, my holy one. And if only you knew! Did you hear her cry out, 'I'll go to death with you'? And what have I done to deserve that? I'm nothing—a poor, ugly man. How could she love someone like me? She's ready to follow me into exile, and yet, what have I ever done for her? Just now, she fell at your feet for my sake! And she's so proud—and innocent! How can I not love her with everything I have? How could I not run to her just now? Please forgive me, gentlemen. But now— now I feel at peace."

Mitya sank back into his chair, covering his face with his hands, and began to weep. But they were tears of happiness. He quickly regained control of himself. The police captain looked pleased, and even the lawyers seemed satisfied. They could tell that the interrogation had entered a new phase.

When the police captain left, Mitya's spirits lifted noticeably. "Now, gentlemen," he said brightly, "I'm entirely at your disposal. If it weren't for these little details, we'd have this sorted out in no time. But here we are, stuck on the details again. I'm ready to cooperate, but we need to trust each other—both ways. Without trust, we'll never finish this. Let's get to business, gentlemen, real business. Don't poke around in my soul or bother me with trivialities. Just ask me about the facts—what matters—and I'll give you the answers you need right away. Forget the details!"

And with that, the questioning resumed.

Chapter 4: The Second Ordeal

"You don't know how much we appreciate your willingness to answer, Dmitri Fyodorovich," said Nikolay Parfenovitch enthusiastically, his short-sighted light gray eyes gleaming with satisfaction as he took off his spectacles. "And you've made an excellent point about mutual trust. Without it, it's nearly impossible to manage cases like this, especially if the accused truly intends to defend himself and has the means to do so. On our end, we'll do everything we can, as you can see from how we've been conducting the investigation. Don't you agree, Ippolit Kirillovitch?" He turned toward the prosecutor.

"Of course," replied the prosecutor, though his tone was cooler compared to Nikolay Parfenovitch's excitement.

It's worth noting here that Nikolay Parfenovitch, who had recently arrived in our town, held a great deal of respect for Ippolit Kirillovitch from the start. In fact, he had become almost like a close friend to the prosecutor. Nikolay Parfenovitch was probably the only person who believed completely in Ippolit Kirillovitch's talents as both a psychologist and an orator, as well as in the validity of the grievances he held about being overlooked in his career. He had even heard of the prosecutor's reputation while in Petersburg. On the other hand, young Nikolay Parfenovitch seemed to be the only person whom the "underappreciated" prosecutor truly liked. During their journey to Mokroe, they had reached a full understanding about how they would handle the case. Now, seated at the table, the sharp-eyed younger lawyer closely followed every word, glance, or slight gesture from his senior colleague, interpreting them instantly.

"Gentlemen, let me tell you my story without stopping me with little questions, and I'll explain everything to you in no time," Mitya said eagerly.

"Excellent! Thank you. But before we begin, may I ask about another matter of interest? I'm referring to the ten rubles you borrowed yesterday around five o'clock, using your pistols as security with Pyotr Ilyitch Perhotin," Nikolay Parfenovitch asked politely.

"Yes, I pledged them for ten rubles. That's it. As soon as I got back to town, I pawned them," Mitya answered.

"So, you returned to town? That means you had been away?"

"Yes. I traveled forty versts out into the countryside. Didn't you know that?"

The prosecutor and Nikolay Parfenovitch exchanged a brief glance.

"Maybe it would be helpful if you started by telling us everything you did yesterday, step by step, from the morning onward," the prosecutor suggested. "Please include when you left town, why you left, and when you came back—all the relevant details."

"You should've asked me that from the start!" Mitya said with a laugh. "If you'd like, we don't even need to start with yesterday— we can go back to the day before. That way, everything will make sense. I'll tell you why I left, where I went, and what happened along the way. The day before yesterday, I visited a merchant in town named Samsonov to borrow three thousand rubles. I needed it urgently—it was an unexpected situation."

"Why exactly three thousand rubles?" the prosecutor asked politely.

"Oh, come on, gentlemen! Do we really need to get into the details of why it had to be that much and not more or less? If we go down that road, this conversation will turn into a three-volume novel, and then you'll want an epilogue too!" Mitya said, with a good- natured but impatient smile, eager to explain the main points.

"Gentlemen," he added quickly, "please don't get annoyed with me. I truly respect you, and I know you're just doing your job. And believe me, I'm sober now. But even if I were drunk, it wouldn't matter—I'm one of those people who somehow become wiser when drunk! Ha! But I know jokes aren't appropriate right now. I have to maintain my dignity, and I understand that I'm not your equal in this situation. I know that right now, I'm in the position of a criminal, and it's your job to watch me carefully. I'm not expecting any pats on the back after what I did to Grigory. You'll probably sentence me to six months or maybe a year in a house of correction. I don't know exactly what punishment I'll get, but it won't strip me of my rank, will it?"

He paused, his smile fading a little. "But, seriously, the way you're questioning me could confuse even God Himself. 'How did you walk? Where did you step? When exactly did you step, and what did you step on?' If you keep asking questions like that, I'll get so mixed up that everything will end up being used against me. And what will be the point of that? It won't help anyone. Even if I sound like I'm rambling now, just let me finish. You're honorable men, and I trust you'll forgive me if I'm a bit rough around the edges. But please, don't follow that usual method— starting with minor things like what time I woke up, what I ate, and where I spat, only to suddenly hit me with, 'Who did you kill? Who did you rob?' Ha! That trick might work on peasants, but it won't work on me. I know how these things go—I've been in the service too. Ha ha ha! You're not mad at me, are you, gentlemen? You'll forgive me for being a bit bold?"

Mitya smiled warmly, his good-natured personality shining through. "Come on, it's just Mitya Karamazov talking here. You'll forgive me, won't you? It would be inexcusable for a sensible man, but for someone like me—well, you can let it slide, can't you? Ha ha!"

Nikolay Parfenovitch laughed along with him, unable to resist Mitya's charm. The prosecutor, however, remained serious, his sharp eyes fixed on Mitya, watching his every movement, every expression, every twitch in his face.

"That's how we've treated you from the start," said Nikolay Parfenovitch with a smile. "We didn't try to trip you up with silly questions about how you spent your morning or what you had for breakfast. We began with the most important matters right away."

"I understand. I noticed it and appreciated it, and I'm even more grateful now for your kindness, which is truly remarkable and worthy of noble hearts. We are all gentlemen here, and everything between us should be based on mutual trust, the way it is among educated, well-bred people with a shared sense of honor. At this moment in my life, when my honor is being attacked, allow me to see you as my best friends. I hope you don't mind me saying that?"

"Not at all. You put it perfectly, Dmitri Fyodorovich," Nikolay Parfenovitch replied approvingly.

"And let's not waste any more time on tricky little questions!" Mitya exclaimed with enthusiasm. "There's no telling where that could lead us, right?"

"I'll take your sensible advice," the prosecutor said, addressing Mitya. "But I'm not withdrawing my question. It's important for us to understand exactly why you needed that amount— specifically three thousand rubles."

"Why I needed it? Oh, for this and that... Well, it was to pay off a debt."

"A debt to whom?"

"That's something I refuse to answer, gentlemen. Not because I can't or because I'm afraid—it's a small, unimportant matter. But I won't answer because it's a matter of principle. It's part of my private life, and I won't let anyone invade that. It has nothing to do with the case, and anything unrelated to the case is my business. All I'll say is that I wanted to pay off a debt of honor. As for who the debt was to, I won't say."

"Allow me to make a note of that," the prosecutor said.

"Go ahead. Write down that I won't say. Write that I consider it dishonorable to say. Go ahead and write that down if you have nothing better to do with your time."

"Let me remind you, sir," the prosecutor began, his tone stern and formal, "that you have every right to refuse to answer any question. We are not allowed to force you to answer if you choose not to. That is your personal right. However, it's also our duty to inform you that refusing to provide certain information could harm your case. Now, please continue."

"I'm not angry, gentlemen... I'm not..." Mitya muttered awkwardly. "Anyway, about Samsonov, the man I went to see..."

We won't repeat the details Mitya shared here since the reader is already familiar with them. Mitya was eager to tell everything, not leaving out a single detail, but he also wanted to get through it quickly. Since his testimony was being written down, the lawyers had to stop him frequently to keep things clear, which irritated him. Still, he went along with it, though not without a few good-natured outbursts. "Gentlemen, you'd drive an angel mad with this!" he exclaimed once. "It's no good trying to provoke me."

Despite his frustration, Mitya remained in relatively good spirits, at least for a while. He explained how Samsonov had tricked him two days earlier—a fact he had now fully realized. The lawyers were surprised to hear about Mitya selling his watch for six rubles to pay for his journey, and this detail caught their attention. To Mitya's annoyance, they made a note of it, seeing it as proof that he was nearly out of money at the time. As the questioning went on, Mitya became more irritable.

After describing his trip to see Lyagavy, the night spent in the stuffy hut, and other events, he began talking about his return to town. Without much prompting, he gave a detailed account of the jealousy that had tormented him over Grushenka.

The lawyers listened attentively, focusing especially on the fact that Mitya had hidden at Marya Kondratyevna's house behind Fyodor Pavlovitch's garden to spy on Grushenka. They also asked questions about Smerdyakov's involvement in feeding him information. These points seemed to interest them greatly, and they made sure to write everything down.

Mitya spoke passionately about his jealousy, going into great detail. Although he felt ashamed to expose his deepest emotions, he forced himself to be honest. The cold, scrutinizing way the prosecutor and investigating lawyer stared at him made him uneasy.

"That young lawyer, Nikolay Parfenovitch, the one I was joking with about women just a few days ago— and that pale, sickly prosecutor—why am I telling them all this?" Mitya thought bitterly. "It's humiliating. I should stay calm. Be patient. Keep quiet." These thoughts raced through his mind, but he managed to pull himself together and keep going.

When he reached the part of his story about visiting Madame Hohlakov, his spirits lifted a bit. He even tried to share a funny anecdote about her, though it had nothing to do with the case. However, the lawyer politely interrupted and asked him to stick to the relevant facts.

Finally, Mitya got to the point where he described his despair after leaving Madame Hohlakov's house. He confessed that he had been so desperate for the three thousand rubles that he even considered killing someone to get it. The lawyers immediately noted this down as evidence that he had intended to commit murder. Mitya didn't argue—he let them write it down without protest.

He continued until he reached the part of his story where he discovered that Grushenka had deceived him. She had returned from Samsonov's much earlier than she had said she would, though she'd promised to stay until midnight.

"If I didn't kill Fenya right then, gentlemen, it was only because I didn't have the time," Mitya blurted out suddenly. The lawyers carefully wrote down this disturbing remark, too.

Mitya waited quietly while they made their notes, then began explaining how he had run into his father's garden. At that moment, the investigating lawyer stopped him and reached for the large portfolio sitting beside him on the sofa. He opened it and pulled out the brass pestle.

"Do you recognize this?" the lawyer asked, holding it up for Mitya to see.

"Oh, yes," Mitya said with a dark chuckle. "Of course I recognize it. Let me have a look at it… Oh, never mind!"

"You forgot to mention it earlier," the lawyer pointed out.

"Damn it all, I didn't mean to hide it from you. Do you think I could've managed without it? It just slipped my mind."

"Please tell us exactly how you came to take the pestle with you." "Of course, gentlemen. I'll tell you."

Mitya then explained how he grabbed the pestle and ran off.

"But why did you take a weapon like that? What were you planning to do with it?"

"What plan? There was no plan. I just picked it up and ran." "Why would you do that if you didn't have a reason?"

Mitya's temper flared. He glared intensely at the young lawyer and gave a dark, bitter smile. Shame started to settle in—he regretted being so honest about his jealousy with these men.

"To hell with the pestle!" he snapped suddenly. "But still—"

"Oh, I took it to scare off dogs… or because it was dark… or just in case something happened."

"Do you normally carry a weapon when you go out at night, since you're afraid of the dark?"

"Damn it, gentlemen! It's impossible to talk to you!" Mitya shouted, his patience snapping. Turning to the secretary, his face red with fury, he barked, "Write this down right now: 'I grabbed the pestle to kill my father, Fyodor Pavlovitch, by smashing his head with it!' There, are you happy now? Does that answer your questions?" He stared at them with defiance, his voice dripping with sarcasm.

"We understand that you made that statement out of frustration with our questions," the prosecutor replied coolly. "You may think these questions are trivial, but they are actually very important."

"Gentlemen! Yes, I took the pestle. Why do people grab things at moments like that? I don't know! I just picked it up and ran. That's all. Now let's move on—or I swear I won't say another word."

Mitya rested his elbows on the table and propped his head in his hands. He turned away from the lawyers, staring at the wall as he fought off a wave of nausea. For a moment, he felt a powerful urge to get up and announce that he wouldn't answer anything more, even if they threatened to hang him.

"Listen, gentlemen," he said finally, struggling to keep control of himself. "When I sit here, answering your questions, it reminds me of a dream I often have. It's always the same. In the dream, someone is chasing me— someone I'm terrified of. It's night, and I try to hide somewhere, behind a door or inside a cupboard. But the worst part is, he always knows exactly where I'm hiding. He just pretends not to know, dragging it out to enjoy my fear. And that's exactly what you're doing to me right now. It feels just like that dream."

"Is that really the kind of dream you have?" the prosecutor asked.

"Yes, it is. Don't you want to write that down?" Mitya asked, his smile twisting bitterly.

"No, there's no need to write it down. But you do seem to have some unusual dreams."

"This isn't about dreams, gentlemen! This is real life! I'm the wolf, and you're the hunters. Go on, hunt me down!" Mitya shouted.

"There's no need for comparisons like that," Nikolay Parfenovitch said gently.

"Yes, there is!" Mitya shot back, though it was clear the outburst had lightened his mood. He grew more relaxed with each word. "You might not trust a criminal or a man under interrogation, but you have to believe in an honorable heart! I swear to you, I am speaking from the heart—and that is something you have no right to doubt." His voice softened, and he spoke as if quoting from a prayer:

"Be silent, heart.

Be patient, humble, hold thy peace."

He paused, his tone suddenly turning gloomy. "So, shall I go on?" "If you'd be so kind," Nikolay Parfenovitch responded.

Chapter 5: The Third Ordeal

Though Mitya spoke with a sullen tone, it was clear he was doing his best not to forget a single detail. He explained how he had jumped over the fence into his father's garden, how he approached the window, and everything that had happened while he stood beneath it. He described his emotions clearly and precisely, especially the torment he felt as he desperately tried to figure out whether Grushenka was inside with his father.

Strangely, though, the two lawyers now seemed cold and distant. They asked very few questions and listened with an odd sense of reserve. Mitya couldn't read anything from their faces.

"They're angry and offended," he thought bitterly. "Well, let them be."

When he described how he finally decided to give his father the "signal" to make him believe Grushenka had arrived and open the window, the lawyers barely reacted to the word "signal." It was as if they didn't understand its meaning at all, and Mitya noticed this.

At last, he got to the moment when his father leaned out the window, and hatred flared up inside him. He pulled the pestle from his pocket—but then, as if on purpose, he stopped telling the story. He sat quietly, gazing at the wall, aware that both lawyers were watching him closely.

"Well?" the investigating lawyer prompted. "You pulled out the weapon, and… what happened next?"

"What next? Well, I killed him, of course. I hit him on the head and cracked his skull. That's the story, right? Isn't that what you think happened?"

Mitya's eyes flashed with sudden anger, and all the rage he had tried to contain surged to the surface.

"Our story?" Nikolay Parfenovitch repeated calmly. "And what's your story?"

Mitya lowered his eyes and sat in silence for a long time.

"My story, gentlemen? Here's how it really happened," he began softly. "I don't know if it was someone's tears, or my mother praying to God, or maybe a good angel kissed me in that moment, but the devil inside me was defeated. I ran away from the window and headed toward the fence. My father saw me for the first time then. He cried out in alarm and jumped back from the window. I remember that clearly. I ran through the garden toward the fence… and that's where Grigory caught me while I was sitting on top of it."

Mitya finally lifted his eyes and looked at the lawyers. They stared back at him, their faces completely calm and expressionless. A wave of anger and indignation surged through him.

"You're laughing at me right now, aren't you?" Mitya suddenly exclaimed.

"What makes you think that?" Nikolay Parfenovitch asked.

"You don't believe a single word I've said—that's why! I get it, of course. We've come to the crucial part of the story. The old man is lying there with his skull smashed, and after I've told you all about how I wanted to kill him, and how I grabbed the pestle, suddenly I run away from the window. Sounds like fiction, right? Pure fantasy. Like you're supposed to take my word for it. Ha! You're all just making fun of me."

He twisted in his chair, making it creak loudly under his weight.

"Tell me," the prosecutor asked, ignoring Mitya's outburst, "did you notice if the door to the garden was open when you ran from the window?"

"No, it wasn't open." "Are you sure?"

"It was shut. And who could have opened it? Bah, the door... wait!" Mitya suddenly paused, as if something had just occurred to him. "Did you find the door open?"

"Yes, it was open."

"But who could've opened it if you didn't do it yourselves?" Mitya asked, astonished.

"The door was wide open. The murderer must have entered through that door, committed the crime, and left the same way," the prosecutor said slowly, emphasizing every word as if carving them into stone. "It's perfectly clear. The murder took place inside the room, not through the window. The position of the body and the rest of the evidence prove that beyond any doubt."

Mitya sat there, stunned.

"That's impossible!" he cried, completely bewildered. "I... I didn't go inside. I swear to you, the door was closed the entire time I was in the garden. When I left the garden, it was still shut. I only stood at the window. I saw him through the glass, that's it. That's all! I remember everything perfectly. And even if I didn't remember, it wouldn't matter—no one knew the signal except me, Smerdyakov, and my father. He wouldn't have opened the door for anyone else without that signal."

"What signal?" the prosecutor asked, suddenly eager, his calm demeanor slipping. His voice betrayed his excitement, almost trembling with the possibility that this new piece of information might unlock something crucial.

"So you didn't know about the signals?" Mitya smirked, his expression both mocking and triumphant. "What if I refuse to tell you? Who could you ask? No one else knew about them—just me, my father, and Smerdyakov. That's all. Even Heaven knew, but Heaven won't tell you, either. But this is good—this little detail could change everything for you." He laughed darkly. "Fine, I'll tell you. You probably have some ridiculous theory brewing in your heads. But you don't understand who you're dealing with. I'm not like most prisoners. I'll tell you things that only hurt me because I'm a man of honor. And you... well, you're not."

The prosecutor swallowed the insult without comment. His eagerness to learn more was too great for him to react. Trembling with impatience, he leaned forward, ready to hear the rest.

Mitya described the signals in full detail. He explained how his father had come up with the idea for Smerdyakov, tapping out the signals on the table to demonstrate what each one meant. When Nikolay Parfenovitch asked whether Mitya had used the signal for "Grushenka has come" when he tapped at the window, Mitya confirmed that he had.

"There you go," Mitya said bitterly. "Now you can build your theory. Go ahead."

He turned away from them again, his contempt clear.

"So, no one knew about these signals except your father, Smerdyakov, and you?" Nikolay Parfenovitch asked again, just to confirm.

"Yes. Just us—and Heaven, of course. Write down 'Heaven.' You might need God's help yourselves someday."

The lawyers were already writing everything down. As they did, the prosecutor's expression suddenly changed, as if a new idea had just struck him.

"But if Smerdyakov knew the signals," the prosecutor said slowly, "and you insist that you're not responsible for your father's death, isn't it possible that Smerdyakov used the signal himself to get your father to open the door and then... committed the murder?"

Mitya stared at the prosecutor with deep contempt and simmering hatred. His gaze was so intense that it made the prosecutor blink.

"You've got it all figured out now, haven't you?" Mitya sneered. "You think I'd jump on that idea, grab hold of it, and start shouting, 'It was Smerdyakov! He's the murderer!' Admit it—that's exactly what you were hoping for. Go on, admit it, and I'll continue."

The prosecutor said nothing. He just waited.

"Well, you're wrong. I'm not going to shout that Smerdyakov did it," Mitya said firmly.

"You don't even suspect him?" the prosecutor asked. "Do you suspect him?" Mitya shot back.

"He's under suspicion, yes."

Mitya stared down at the floor, his expression darkening.

"Honestly," he said, his voice low and serious, "I've been thinking about Smerdyakov from the very beginning. From the moment I rushed out and started shouting that I was innocent, he was on my mind. I couldn't stop thinking about him. Even now, I can't get him out of my head. Just now, I almost thought it might be him... but no. It's not him. It can't be. It's not Smerdyakov."

"Is there anyone else you suspect?" Nikolay Parfenovitch asked carefully.

"I don't know who it could be—whether it's the hand of Heaven or the Devil—but it's not Smerdyakov," Mitya answered firmly.

"And why are you so sure it isn't him?"

"Because I just know. Smerdyakov is pathetic—a coward through and through. Not just a coward—he's cowardice itself, walking on two legs. The man has the heart of a chicken. Whenever he talked to me, he'd tremble in fear, convinced I might kill him, even though I never even raised my hand. He once dropped to his knees and cried, kissing my boots, literally begging me, 'Please, don't frighten me!' Can you believe that? I even offered him money! He's a sickly, weak, epileptic fool—a child could beat him. He has no character at all. No, it's not him. Besides, Smerdyakov doesn't care about money. He wouldn't even accept the gifts I tried to give him. And what reason would he have to kill my father? Why would he? Honestly, he might even be my father's illegitimate son. Did you know that?"

"We've heard the rumor. But you're also his son, yet you told everyone you wanted to murder him," the prosecutor pointed out.

"That's a cheap shot! A low blow! And it's unfair, because I'm the one who told you that myself!" Mitya shouted, growing angrier. "I didn't just say I wanted to kill him—I admitted I almost did it! I went out of my way to tell you that, but here's what you don't get: I didn't do it! My guardian angel stopped me—that's the part you ignore. I didn't kill him! I didn't kill him! Do you hear me?"

Mitya's voice was hoarse with emotion. This was the most upset he had been during the entire interrogation.

"So, what did Smerdyakov say to you, gentlemen? Can I ask that?" Mitya added after a pause.

"You're allowed to ask anything related to the case," the prosecutor replied coldly. "We are required to answer your questions. We found Smerdyakov unconscious in his bed, suffering from an extreme epileptic fit. The doctor told us he might have had as many as ten seizures in a row. The doctor also said that Smerdyakov might not survive the night."

"If that's true, then the devil himself must have killed him," Mitya muttered suddenly, as if he had been wrestling with the thought of whether Smerdyakov could have done it.

"We'll come back to this later," Nikolay Parfenovitch said. "Would you like to continue your statement now?"

Mitya asked for a break, which was granted. After resting, he resumed his story, but it was clear he was emotionally drained. He seemed defeated, embarrassed, and deeply shaken. The prosecutor made things worse by interrupting frequently with irritating questions about small details, as if trying to provoke him on purpose.

Mitya had just described how, while sitting on the fence, he had struck Grigory on the head with the pestle as the old man clung to his leg. He explained how he jumped down to check on Grigory, only for the prosecutor to stop him with another question.

"Can you explain exactly how you were sitting on the wall?" the prosecutor asked.

Mitya looked surprised. "I was sitting like this—astride, with one leg on each side of the wall."

"And the pestle?"

"I had it in my hand."

"Not in your pocket? Are you sure about that? And was the blow you gave him a hard one?"

"It must have been hard. Why are you asking me this?"

"Would you mind sitting on the chair the same way you were on the wall? Show us exactly how you swung your arm and in what direction."

"You're mocking me, aren't you?" Mitya asked, glaring at the prosecutor. But the prosecutor didn't react.

Frustrated, Mitya sat astride on the chair and swung his arm to demonstrate. "This is how I hit him! That's how I knocked him down! What more do you want?"

"Thank you. Now, tell us why you jumped down. What were you trying to do?"

"Damn it… I jumped down to check on him. I don't even know why!"

"Even though you were so upset and in a hurry to escape?"

"Yes, even though I was upset and trying to get away."

"Were you trying to help him?"

"Help him? Maybe. I don't know."

"You don't know? Then you weren't fully aware of what you were doing?"

"No, I knew exactly what I was doing! I jumped down to see if he was alive. I wiped his face with my handkerchief."

"We saw your handkerchief. Were you hoping to wake him up?"

"I don't know what I was hoping for. I just wanted to see if he was still alive."

"Ah, so you wanted to be sure?"

"Yes, I wanted to be sure."

"And what did you do after that?"

"I'm not a doctor. I couldn't tell if he was alive or not. I thought I'd killed him, so I ran away. And now, it turns out he's alive."

"Good," the prosecutor said calmly. "That's all I needed to know. Please, continue."

Mitya never thought to tell them—though he remembered it— that he had jumped down out of pity. As he stood over Grigory's unconscious body, he had even whispered, "Poor old man... you've come to harm, and there's nothing I can do for you. You'll have to lie here."

The prosecutor could only come to one conclusion: Mitya had jumped down "in that moment of panic and excitement just to make sure the only witness to his crime was dead." This meant, the prosecutor thought, that Mitya must have been someone with remarkable strength, calmness, and foresight, even in such a heated moment. He felt satisfied with the outcome: "I've pushed the nervous man with small questions, and he's said more than he meant to."

With difficulty, Mitya continued his story. But this time, Nikolay Parfenovitch interrupted him right away.

"Why did you run to the servant, Fedosya Markovna, with your hands and, it seems, even your face covered in blood?"

"I didn't even notice the blood at the time," Mitya replied.

"That's very possible. It does happen," the prosecutor agreed, exchanging a glance with Nikolay Parfenovitch.

"I really didn't notice it. You're right about that," Mitya added quickly.

Then the conversation turned to Mitya's sudden decision to "step aside" and let others find happiness. But this time, he didn't want to open up about Grushenka, "the queen of his soul." He hated the idea of talking about her to these cold men, whom he described as "clinging to him like bugs." So, when they pressed him with more questions, he gave brief, abrupt answers.

"I decided to kill myself. What else was there to live for? That question was staring me right in the face. Her first love had returned—the one who hurt her but had come back after five years to make things right and offer her marriage. I knew it was over for me. And behind me, I had nothing but disgrace—and Grigory's blood. What was left for me? So, I went to get my pistols, load them, and put a bullet in my brain the next morning."

"And you threw a grand feast the night before?" the prosecutor asked.

"Yes, a grand feast. Damn it, gentlemen, hurry up and get this over with! I was going to shoot myself not far from here, just beyond the village, at five in the morning. I even wrote a note—at Perhotin's place when I loaded my pistols. Here's the letter. Read it! I'm not explaining it just for you," he added bitterly, pulling the letter from his waistcoat pocket and tossing it onto the table.

The lawyers read the letter with interest and added it to the case documents.

"And you didn't think to wash your hands at Perhotin's house? You weren't worried about arousing suspicion?" one of the lawyers asked.

"Suspicion? I didn't care about suspicion. I'd have come here and shot myself at five, no matter what. You wouldn't have had time to stop me. If it hadn't been for what happened to my father, you wouldn't even know about any of this, and you wouldn't have shown up here. It's all the devil's doing. He killed my father, and it's thanks to him you found out so fast. How did you manage to get here so quickly? It's unbelievable—like a dream."

"Mr. Perhotin told us that when you arrived at his house, your hands were covered in blood. And you had money—lots of it—a whole bundle of hundred-rouble notes. His servant boy saw it too."

"That's true," Mitya admitted. "I remember that."

"Well, here's a little question for you," Nikolay Parfenovitch said softly, his voice cautious. "Can you tell us where you got all that money so suddenly? After all, we know from the timeline that you didn't go home."

The prosecutor frowned at the directness of the question but didn't interrupt.

"No, I didn't go home," Mitya replied calmly, though he kept his eyes on the floor.

"Then let me ask again," Nikolay Parfenovitch continued, carefully pressing the point. "Where did you get such a large sum of money, especially since earlier that same day—"

"I was desperate for ten roubles and had to pawn my pistols at Perhotin's. Then I went to Madame Hohlakov to ask for three thousand roubles, which she wouldn't lend me, and so on. You know all of that already," Mitya interrupted sharply. "Yes, I needed money badly. And suddenly I have thousands! That's what's bothering you now, isn't it? You're both worried, thinking, 'What if he doesn't tell us where he got it?' Well, you guessed right—I'm not going to tell you. You'll never know," he said, his words sharp and deliberate.

The lawyers fell silent for a moment.

"You have to understand, Mr. Karamazov, that it's essential for us to know," Nikolay Parfenovitch said gently.

"I understand that perfectly. But I still won't tell you."

The prosecutor stepped in again, reminding Mitya that he had every right to remain silent if he thought it would help his case. However, he warned that refusing to answer could harm his defense, especially in a case as serious as this one.

"And so on, and so on, gentlemen. I've heard this speech before," Mitya said, cutting him off impatiently. "I know how serious this is. I know this is the key moment. And still, I'm not telling you anything."

"This isn't our problem—it's yours," Nikolay Parfenovitch said nervously. "You're the one hurting yourself by staying silent."

"You see, gentlemen, all joking aside," Mitya began, lifting his eyes and looking seriously at them, "I knew from the start that this is where we'd hit a dead end. At first, when I started giving my statement, everything still felt distant and unclear. I thought we could build some trust between us, but now I realize that trust is impossible. We were bound to reach this cursed point sooner or later, and here we are. It's over. But I don't blame you. You can't take me at my word, and I understand that."

He fell into a gloomy silence.

"Without abandoning your decision to remain silent on the key issue, couldn't you at least give us a hint about your motives?" asked Nikolay Parfenovitch carefully. "What is it that makes you refuse to answer, especially when you're in so much danger?"

Mitya gave a sad, almost dreamy smile. "I'm kinder than you think, gentlemen. I'll give you that hint, even though you don't deserve it. I won't tell you where I got the money because it would stain my honor. If I told you the truth, it would disgrace me more than if I had murdered and robbed my father. That's why I can't say. It's about saving my dignity. What, are you going to write that down?"

"Yes, we'll write it down," Nikolay Parfenovitch murmured.

"You shouldn't write that," Mitya said with scorn. "I told you that out of kindness—I didn't have to tell you anything. I gave you that as a gift, and now you're pouncing on it. Fine, write whatever you want. I'm not afraid of you. I can still hold my head high."

"Can't you tell us what kind of disgrace you're trying to avoid?" Nikolay Parfenovitch ventured.

The prosecutor frowned, displeased.

"No. It's over. Don't bother. I've already dirtied myself enough by talking to you. None of you are worth more of my time." Mitya's tone was sharp and final.

Nikolay Parfenovitch decided not to push further, but from the look in the prosecutor's eyes, it was clear that he hadn't given up hope.

"Can you at least tell us how much money you had with you when you went to Mr. Perhotin's? How many roubles exactly?"

"I can't tell you that."

"You mentioned to Mr. Perhotin that you received three thousand from Madame Hohlakov, didn't you?"

"Maybe I did. Enough questions, gentlemen. I won't say how much I had."

"Can you tell us what you did after you arrived here?" "Ask anyone around here. But I'll tell you, if you insist."

Mitya went on to give a brief account of his actions, but we won't repeat it here. He spoke flatly, without emotion, leaving out any mention of his love or despair. He explained that he had given up on the idea of suicide because of "new developments," but he didn't go into details. This time, the lawyers didn't press him much—it was clear they found nothing significant in his story.

"We'll confirm everything during the witness interviews, which will take place with you present," said Nikolay Parfenovitch. "Now, please place everything you have with you on the table, especially any money you still have."

"My money? Of course, I understand. I'm surprised you didn't ask earlier. Not that I could have gone anywhere—I've been right here the whole time. Here's my money—count it. Take it all. I think that's everything."

Mitya emptied his pockets, even pulling out two twenty-copeck coins from his waistcoat pocket. The lawyers counted everything, totaling eight hundred and thirty-six roubles and forty copecks.

"Is that all?" asked the investigator. "Yes."

"You mentioned earlier that you spent three hundred roubles at Plotnikov's, gave Perhotin ten, and twenty to your driver. You also lost two hundred here, correct?"

Nikolay Parfenovitch added it all up, with Mitya's help, making sure not to miss a single coin.

"With this eight hundred roubles, you must have had around fifteen hundred to start with," Nikolay Parfenovitch concluded.

"Sounds about right," Mitya replied curtly.

"But others claim you had more," Nikolay Parfenovitch said. "Let them say what they want."

"But you also said so yourself." "Yes, I did."

"We'll compare this with the statements of other witnesses. Don't worry about the money—it will be kept safe and returned to you at the end of this process, provided it's proven to be legally yours."

Nikolay Parfenovitch stood up suddenly, his tone becoming more formal. "Now, I must inform you that we are required to conduct a thorough search of your clothing and all your belongings."

"Of course, gentlemen. I'll empty all my pockets."

He began turning out his pockets, pulling out everything he had. "You'll also need to remove your clothes," said the investigator. "What? Undress? Damn it! Can't you search me without that?" "No, Dmitri Fyodorovitch, you need to take off your clothes."

"As you wish," Mitya muttered grimly. "But let's do it behind the curtains. Who will be conducting the search?"

"Behind the curtains, of course," Nikolay Parfenovitch confirmed with a solemn nod. His small face looked unusually serious.

Chapter 6: The Prosecutor Catches Mitya

Something completely unexpected happened next, shocking Mitya. He couldn't have imagined, not even a moment before, that anyone would treat him like this—especially him, Mitya Karamazov. What made it worse was how humiliating it felt, and how the others acted with scorn and superiority. It was one thing to take off his coat, but they told him to undress further. Not asked—ordered. He knew that much for sure. Out of pride and disdain, he obeyed without arguing. Several peasants stayed on their side of the curtain with the lawyers. "They're here in case they need to use force," Mitya thought, "or maybe for some other reason."

"Do I have to take off my shirt, too?" Mitya asked sharply, but Nikolay Parfenovitch didn't respond. He was too focused, working with the prosecutor to examine Mitya's coat, trousers, waistcoat, and cap. They both seemed deeply interested in what they were finding. "They don't even pretend to be polite," Mitya thought bitterly.

"I'm asking again—do I have to take off my shirt or not?" he snapped, more irritated this time.

"Don't worry; we'll tell you what's needed," Nikolay Parfenovitch replied, his tone firm, which Mitya found infuriating.

Meanwhile, the lawyers whispered to each other. They discovered a large, stiff, dried bloodstain on the back of the coat, near the left side. There were also bloodstains on the trousers. In front of the peasant witnesses, Nikolay Parfenovitch ran his fingers along the collar, cuffs, and seams of Mitya's clothes, clearly searching for something—money, Mitya assumed. He didn't even try to hide his suspicion that Mitya might have sewn the money into the fabric.

"He's treating me like some petty thief, not an officer," Mitya muttered to himself. The investigators exchanged their thoughts freely, without any concern for how it looked. The secretary, who was also behind the curtain, pointed to Mitya's cap as they handled it.

"Remember that case with Gridyenko, the clerk?" the secretary remarked. "He got drunk last summer and claimed he lost the office's payroll. They found the money sewn into the lining of his cap—rolled-up hundred-rouble notes hidden in the seams."

Both lawyers remembered the case well. They set Mitya's cap aside, deciding they would inspect all his clothes more thoroughly later.

"Excuse me," Nikolay Parfenovitch said suddenly, noticing the right cuff of Mitya's shirt was turned inward and stained with blood. "What's this? Blood?"

"Yes," Mitya said shortly.

"Whose blood? And why is the cuff turned inside?"

Mitya explained that his sleeve got stained while tending to Grigory and that he had rolled it up when washing his hands at Perhotin's house.

"You'll need to take off your shirt too. It's important evidence,"

Nikolay Parfenovitch instructed.

Mitya's face flushed red with anger. "What, do you want me completely naked?" he shouted.

"Don't worry—we'll arrange something. For now, take off your socks."

"You've got to be kidding! Is this really necessary?" Mitya's eyes burned with fury.

"This is no joke," Nikolay Parfenovitch said sternly.

"Well, fine then!" Mitya grumbled. He sat on the bed and began pulling off his socks, feeling incredibly humiliated. Being the only one undressed while everyone else stood clothed made him feel ashamed, as if he was somehow lesser than them. A strange thought came to him: "When everyone is undressed, it's not so bad, but being the only one stripped down feels degrading." It reminded him of a recurring nightmare he'd had—finding himself in a humiliating situation where he was exposed and vulnerable.

Taking off his socks was particularly painful for Mitya. They were filthy, as were his underclothes, and now everyone could see. To make things worse, he hated his feet—especially the crooked nail on his right big toe, which had always embarrassed him. Now everyone would see it, and that thought filled him with shame. His embarrassment made him act more defiantly. He yanked off his shirt and threw it down.

"Do you want to check anything else? If you're not too ashamed to look," he said bitterly.

"No, there's no need for now."

"So, am I just supposed to sit here naked?" Mitya growled.

"For now, yes. You can wrap yourself in the quilt from the bed," Nikolay Parfenovitch said calmly. "I'll take care of this."

The investigators laid out all of Mitya's belongings for the witnesses to see and wrote up the search report. At last, Nikolay Parfenovitch and the prosecutor left the room, taking Mitya's clothes with them. Now Mitya was alone with the silent peasants, who never took their eyes off him. He wrapped the quilt around himself, but he still felt cold. His bare feet stuck out, and no matter how he adjusted the quilt, he couldn't cover them properly.

"It's taking him forever," Mitya thought bitterly. "That bastard thinks I'm nothing more than a dog." His teeth clenched in frustration. "And that prosecutor—he couldn't even stand to be in the same room with me once I was naked. It disgusted him."

Mitya had expected that his clothes would be searched and returned. But when Nikolay Parfenovitch finally returned, a peasant followed him, carrying a different set of clothes.

"Here are some clothes for you," Nikolay Parfenovitch said cheerfully, clearly satisfied with his solution. "Mr. Kalganov kindly lent these for the occasion, along with a clean shirt. Luckily, he had them in his trunk. You can keep your socks and underclothes."

Mitya flew into a rage.

"I won't wear someone else's clothes!" he shouted angrily. "Give me my own!"

"That's not possible."

"Give me my own! Damn Kalganov and his clothes too!"

It took a long time to calm him down, but they managed somehow. They explained that his clothes, stained with blood, had to be kept as evidence and that they legally couldn't give them back to him yet, considering how the case might turn out. Finally, Mitya understood. He fell silent, scowling, and quickly put on the new clothes. As he got dressed, he commented bitterly that these clothes were much nicer than his old ones, but it annoyed him to benefit from the situation. The coat, however, was so tight it felt ridiculous.

"What now? Are you dressing me up like a fool for your entertainment?" he asked bitterly.

They told him he was overreacting and reminded him that Kalganov was only slightly taller than he was, so the trousers might just be a bit long. But the coat really did fit too tightly in the shoulders.

"Damn it! I can barely button it," Mitya grumbled. "Tell Kalganov I didn't ask for his clothes, and it's not my fault they've dressed me like a clown."

"He understands," said Nikolay Parfenovitch awkwardly. "He's not upset about lending you his clothes, only about this whole situation."

"Who cares about his feelings?" Mitya muttered. "So, what now? Do I just sit here?"

They asked him to return to the other room. Mitya walked in with a scowl, avoiding eye contact with everyone. Dressed in another man's clothes, he felt humiliated, even in front of the peasants and Trifon Borissovitch, who briefly appeared in the doorway, then vanished. "He came just to see me looking like this," Mitya thought bitterly. He sat in the same chair as before, overwhelmed by a strange, dreamlike feeling, as though he were losing his mind.

"So what now? Are you going to flog me? Is that all that's left for you to do?" he sneered, glaring at the prosecutor. He refused to acknowledge Nikolay Parfenovitch, as if it was beneath him to speak to the man.

"He made sure to inspect my socks and turn them inside out, just to humiliate me in front of everyone. What a scoundrel," Mitya thought angrily.

"Well, we'll move on to questioning the witnesses now," Nikolay Parfenovitch said, answering Mitya's sarcastic remark as if it were a serious question.

"Yes," the prosecutor agreed, as though lost in thought.

"We've tried to help you, Dmitri Fyodorovitch," Nikolay Parfenovitch continued, "but since you've refused to tell us where you got the money—"

"What kind of stone is in your ring?" Mitya interrupted suddenly, as if waking from a daze. He pointed to one of the three large rings on Nikolay Parfenovitch's hand.

"This? My ring?" Nikolay Parfenovitch asked, surprised.

"Yes, that one, on your middle finger, with the little veins in it. What kind of stone is it?" Mitya asked like an irritated child.

"It's a smoky topaz," Nikolay Parfenovitch answered with a smile. "Would you like to take a closer look? I can take it off."

"No! Don't take it off!" Mitya shouted suddenly, as if angry with himself. "There's no need. Damn it all! Gentlemen, you've polluted my heart! Do you think if I were guilty of killing my father, I'd try to hide it from you? Do you think I'd lie and cover it up? That's not who I am! If I were guilty, I wouldn't have waited for you to come or for the sunrise—I would have shot myself long ago! I've learned more about myself in this cursed night than I could've learned in twenty years. And do you really believe I'd sit here talking like this if I had murdered my father? Could I look at you like this, move and speak like this, knowing I'd done such a thing? I've been tortured all night just thinking I might have killed Grigory by accident—not because I feared punishment, but because of the shame. And you want me to be honest with people like you? Blind fools who see nothing and believe in nothing. And now you expect me to tell you some other disgraceful secret, thinking it will save me? No! I'd rather go to Siberia! The man who opened that door, the one who went into my father's room—he's the one who killed him, he's the one who robbed him. And I swear to you, it wasn't me! That's all I can say, and it's enough. Just leave me alone. Send me to exile, punish me, but don't question me anymore. Call your witnesses!"

Mitya's sudden outburst left the room in stunned silence. He seemed determined not to say another word. The prosecutor, watching him closely the entire time, finally spoke in a calm, measured tone, as though the conversation had taken a perfectly ordinary turn.

"Regarding the open door you mentioned earlier," the prosecutor began, "we have some new evidence, which may be important for both you and us. Grigory, the man you wounded, gave us a clear and detailed statement after he regained consciousness. He said that when he stepped out onto the porch and heard a noise in the garden, he decided to enter through the small gate, which was standing open. Before he saw you running in the dark from the window, just as you described, he noticed the door to the house was wide open. That's the same door you've insisted was shut the entire time you were in the garden."

Mitya jumped from his chair, halfway through the prosecutor's explanation.

"Nonsense!" he shouted furiously. "That's a lie! He couldn't have seen the door open—it was shut! He's lying!"

"I have to tell you that Grigory stands by his statement. He's been questioned several times, and he hasn't wavered," the prosecutor replied calmly.

"Yes," Nikolay Parfenovitch added eagerly. "We've questioned him several times, and he's been consistent."

"It's a lie! Either he's lying to frame me, or he imagined it because he was delirious from the injury," Mitya insisted, still shouting. "He must have imagined it when he came to. He's raving!"

"But he noticed the open door before he was hurt—right when he entered the garden from the lodge," the prosecutor clarified.

"It's not true! It can't be true! He's framing me out of spite! He couldn't have seen it open—I didn't come through that door!" Mitya gasped, desperate to convince them.

The prosecutor turned to Nikolay Parfenovitch and said firmly, "Show it to him."

"Do you recognize this object?" asked Nikolay Parfenovitch as he placed a large, thick envelope on the table. The envelope had three intact seals but was slit open and empty. Mitya stared at it, wide-eyed.

"That... that must be my father's envelope, the one with the three thousand roubles! And if it says, 'For my little chicken' on it— yes, it's three thousand! Do you see? Three thousand! Do you see?" he shouted.

"We see it, of course," one of the men replied. "But we didn't find the money inside. It was empty and lying on the floor by the bed, behind the screen."

Mitya stood frozen, stunned. Then suddenly, he shouted at the top of his voice, "It was Smerdyakov! He's the one who killed him! He robbed him! No one else knew where the old man hid that envelope—it had to be Smerdyakov! It's obvious now!"

"But you knew about the envelope too," the prosecutor pointed out calmly. "You knew it was under your father's pillow."

"I didn't know that! I never saw it! This is the first time I've laid eyes on it. I only heard about it from Smerdyakov... He was the only one who knew where it was hidden. I swear I didn't know!" Mitya gasped for breath, overwhelmed.

"But you told us yourself that the envelope was under the pillow," the prosecutor continued. "You specifically said it was there, so how could you not have known?"

"We have it written down," confirmed Nikolay Parfenovitch.

"That's absurd! I had no idea it was there! Maybe it wasn't even under the pillow—it was just a wild guess! What does Smerdyakov say? Have you asked him? That's what matters! I only said it was under the pillow without thinking, and now you—oh, you know how people say things they don't mean! No one knew except Smerdyakov—only him, no one else! He didn't even tell me where it was! But it had to be him—he killed my father, I know it! It's as clear as day!" Mitya cried frantically, his words becoming more disjointed as he grew more agitated. "You have to understand—arrest him right now! He must have killed him when I ran off and while Grigory was unconscious. That's the only way it makes sense. He used the signal, and my father let him in. No one but Smerdyakov knew the signal! Without it, Father wouldn't have opened the door."

"But you're forgetting," the prosecutor interjected smoothly, still calm but with a hint of triumph in his voice, "there was no need for a signal if the door was already open when you were in the garden."

"The door... the door," Mitya mumbled, staring helplessly at the prosecutor. He slumped back into his chair, stunned and silent.

"Yes, the door. This is a nightmare! God is against me!" he whispered, staring blankly in disbelief.

"You see," the prosecutor continued with measured calm, "you can judge for yourself, Dmitri Fyodorovitch. On one hand, we have the fact of the open door, which you ran through. This fact weighs heavily against you. On the other hand, we have your stubborn silence about the source of the money that was suddenly in your hands, just hours after you were so desperate that you pawned your pistols for ten roubles. Considering these facts, what are we supposed to believe? What can we trust? Don't accuse us of being cynical or cold-hearted. Try to understand our position."

Mitya was trembling, visibly shaken. His face grew pale.

"Fine!" he cried suddenly. "I'll tell you my secret. I'll tell you where I got the money! I'll confess everything, even if it means disgrace. I don't want to blame myself or you later."

"Believe me, Dmitri Fyodorovitch," Nikolay Parfenovitch added warmly, almost as if trying to comfort him, "a complete and honest confession right now could greatly improve your situation later—perhaps even—"

The prosecutor gave Nikolay Parfenovitch a discreet nudge under the table, cutting him off just in time. Mitya didn't seem to notice.

Chapter 7: Mitya's Great Secret. Received With Hisses

Gentlemen," Mitya began, still visibly agitated, "I want to make a full confession: that money was mine." The lawyers' faces fell; this was not at all what they had expected.

"What do you mean?" Nikolay Parfenovitch stammered. "Didn't you say yourself that at five o'clock that same day—"

"To hell with five o'clock and my own confession!" Mitya snapped. "That's got nothing to do with it now! The money was mine—well, not really mine—I mean, I stole it! Fifteen hundred roubles, and I had it on me all the time, the whole time..."

"But where did you get it?"

"I took it from around my neck. It was sewn up in a rag and tied around my neck. I've been wearing it there for a month—God help me—shame and disgrace!"

"And who did you... take it from?"

"You mean steal it? Yes, fine, I stole it! At least, that's how it feels. If you want to be polite, call it appropriation. But it's theft, plain and simple. And last night, I finally stole it for good."

"Last night? But didn't you say you've had it for a month?"

"Yes, I did. But it wasn't my father's. It wasn't from him, so don't get excited. I stole it from her. Let me tell you, and don't interrupt—it's not easy to say this, you know. A month ago, Katerina Ivanovna—my former fiancée—sent for me. You know her, don't you?"

"Yes, of course."

"I thought so. She's noble, the noblest woman alive. But she's despised me for a long time, with good reason—good reason!"

"Katerina Ivanovna?" Nikolay Parfenovitch repeated in disbelief, while the prosecutor raised his eyebrows in surprise.

"Don't say her name lightly! I'm a scoundrel for even bringing her into this. I knew she hated me... from the very beginning. Even that first night at my lodging... but never mind that. You don't deserve to know those things. I'll only tell you this: a month ago, she gave me three thousand roubles to send to her sister and another relative in Moscow—like she couldn't have sent it herself! And that's when everything fell apart for me. You see, by then I'd already fallen in love with someone else—Grushenka. She's sitting downstairs now."

He exhaled sharply, as if the memory was too much. "I took Grushenka here to Mokroe and blew through half of that cursed three thousand in two days. But I kept the other half on me, sewn into that rag around my neck. Yesterday, I finally spent it. What's left of it—eight hundred roubles—is in your hands now, Nikolay Parfenovitch. That's what's left of the fifteen hundred."

"Wait a minute," one of the lawyers interjected.

"But when you were here a month ago, didn't you spend the entire three thousand? Everyone says you did."

"Who says that? Who counted the money? I didn't let anyone count it."

"But you told people yourself that you spent three thousand."

"Yes, I told the whole town. Everyone in Mokroe thought it was three thousand. But it wasn't—it was fifteen hundred. The other fifteen hundred I kept, sewn into that rag around my neck. That's the money I used yesterday."

"This is... astonishing," murmured Nikolay Parfenovitch.

"Tell me," the prosecutor leaned in, "did you tell anyone else about this—the fifteen hundred you kept?"

"No. No one."

"No one at all?"

"No one. Absolutely no one."

"And why did you keep it a secret? What made you hide it?"

The prosecutor's voice was calm, though he couldn't hide his disbelief. "You just told us your disgraceful secret—but in reality, taking the three thousand wasn't as bad as it could have been. Yes, it was reckless, but it wasn't unforgivable. Even if it was dishonorable, it wasn't truly disgraceful. In fact, people have been gossiping about the money you took from Katerina Ivanovna for some time now. It wasn't a secret. Mihail Makarovitch heard the rumors, too. So why did you keep the fifteen hundred such a painful secret, as if it was some horrible burden? Why would you rather go to Siberia than confess it?"

The prosecutor's irritation started to show. He spoke more quickly now, as though venting his frustration. "It's not about the fifteen hundred, is it? The real shame is that you separated it from the rest."

"Yes," Mitya said firmly. "That's what's disgraceful."

"Why?" the prosecutor pressed, now clearly annoyed. "What's so shameful about setting aside half of the money? What's worse— taking the whole amount or deciding to keep part of it for yourself? And why did you do it, anyway? What was the point? Can you explain that to us?"

"Oh, gentlemen, the whole point is in the purpose!" Mitya cried out. "I set that money aside because I was vile—because I was calculating. And being calculating in a situation like that is vile. That vileness went on for an entire month."

"I don't understand," one lawyer said.

"I'm not surprised, but let me make it clearer. Maybe it really is confusing. Look, listen closely to what I'm saying. I took three thousand roubles that were entrusted to me in good faith. Then I spent it—wasted it all. Say I blew the whole amount. The next morning, I'd have to go to Katya and tell her, 'I wasted your three thousand roubles.' Would that be right? No, that would be shameful. It would make me a coward and a fool, with no self- control—like a wild animal. But at least I wouldn't be a thief, right? Not a real thief. I would've spent it, but I wouldn't have stolen it. Now let's look at another option."

He paused, trying to focus his thoughts. "Now imagine I only spent fifteen hundred—half of it. The next day, I go to her and say, 'Katya, here's fifteen hundred. I'm a disgraceful fool, an unreliable scoundrel, and I wasted the other half. I'll probably waste this half too, so you'd better hold on to it to keep me from more temptation.' What happens then? Yes, I'd still be a fool and a scoundrel, but not a thief. Not entirely, at least. If I'd kept half, that means I still planned to pay back what I spent. She would know that I was going to do my best to make things right. She would see that I'd work until I repaid every kopeck. In that case, you could call me a scoundrel, but not a thief. Not a thief!"

The prosecutor gave a cold smile. "I understand the difference, but it's strange that you think it's so important."

"It is important! Every man might be a scoundrel—maybe we all are—but not every man can be a thief. Being a thief takes a special kind of villainy. Look, maybe I can't explain it properly, but in my heart, I know that a thief is worse than a scoundrel. Much worse. I carried that money around my neck for an entire month. Every day, I thought to myself, 'Tomorrow, I'll give it back.' But I couldn't do it. Every single day, I told myself, 'Just give it back,' but I never could. And that's the real disgrace— don't you see?"

"Yes, I see. That much is clear," the prosecutor admitted. "I won't argue with you about that. But let's leave these subtle distinctions aside and get to the main point. The real question is: why did you split the money in half? What was your plan for the fifteen hundred you set aside? What were you going to do with it?"

"Yes! That's exactly it!" Mitya exclaimed, hitting his forehead with his palm. "Forgive me for rambling, but I need you to understand. The motive is the key—it's the most shameful part of all! It was all because of my father, the old man. He wouldn't leave Grushenka alone, and I was jealous. I thought she was torn between the two of us. Every day, I imagined that she might finally choose me, that she'd say, 'I love you, not him. Take me away to the other side of the world.' But what if that moment came, and I only had forty copecks in my pocket? What could I do? I'd be helpless."

He sighed heavily. "I didn't know her then. I didn't understand her. I thought she wanted money—that she'd never forgive me for being poor. So, like a fool, I counted out half of the three thousand, sewed it into a bag, and tied it around my neck. I thought, 'If the time comes, I'll have something to take her away with.' I did that before I even got drunk. Then, with the other half, I went and drank myself silly. That's the truth. That's the whole disgraceful truth. Do you understand now?"

The two lawyers laughed.

"I'd say it was smart of you to save some of the money," Nikolay Parfenovitch chuckled. "At least you didn't waste it all."

"No! You don't get it," Mitya shouted, his voice full of frustration. "I stole it! That's what matters. And the fact that you don't see that horrifies me! Every day that I carried that fifteen hundred around my neck, I told myself, 'You're a thief, you're a thief.' That's why I've been so angry this whole month. That's why I got into fights at the tavern. That's why I attacked my father. I knew I was a thief. I couldn't even tell my brother Alyosha about it. I felt too ashamed—like a criminal, like a pickpocket."

He leaned forward, his eyes burning. "But do you know what kept me going? Every day, I thought, 'I can still fix this. I can still take the money to Katya and tell her the truth. If I do that, I won't be a thief.' That hope was the only thing keeping me sane. And then yesterday—yesterday, on the way from Fenya's to Perhotin's— I finally made up my mind. I tore that cursed bag off my neck and spent the money. That was the moment I became a real thief. That was the moment I ruined myself forever."

He dropped his head into his hands. "When I spent that money, I destroyed the only chance I had left. I wanted to go to Katya and say, 'I'm a scoundrel, but I'm not a thief.' But now I'll never be able to say that. Do you understand now? Do you get it?"

"What made you decide to do it yesterday?" Nikolay Parfenovitch asked quietly.

"Why? It's ridiculous to even ask," Mitya shouted. "I had already decided to die at five this morning, at dawn. I thought it didn't matter if I died a thief or an honorable man. But now I see—it does matter. It makes a difference. Believe me, gentlemen, what tortured me the most last night wasn't the thought that I killed the old servant or the fear of Siberia, just when my love was finally being returned, and heaven seemed open to me again. That did torment me, yes, but not as much as the awful realization that I had torn that cursed money from my neck, spent it, and become a true thief! Oh, gentlemen, I tell you with a bleeding heart, I've learned a lot during this night. I've learned that it's not just impossible to live like a scoundrel—it's impossible to die as one. No, a person must die with honor."

Mitya's face was pale, his features exhausted and hollow, despite the intensity of his emotions.

"I'm starting to understand you, Dmitri Fyodorovitch," the prosecutor said slowly, his voice soft and almost sympathetic. "But, if you'll allow me to say so, I believe this is a matter of nerves. Your nerves are completely frayed, that's all. And why, for example, did you put yourself through all this misery for a whole month? Why not just give the fifteen hundred roubles back to the lady who gave it to you? Why not explain things to her? Considering the desperate position you were in, as you've described, why not follow a simpler course—confess your mistake to her honestly and ask her to lend you the money? With her generous heart, she surely wouldn't have refused to help, especially if you had offered some security, like the kind you promised Samsonov or Madame Hohlakov. I assume you still consider that security worth something?"

Mitya's face flushed with anger. "Surely you don't think I could stoop that low?" he asked, glaring at the prosecutor. "You can't be serious!"

"I am serious," the prosecutor replied calmly, though he looked surprised by Mitya's reaction. "Why do you think I'm not?"

"Oh, how vile that would've been!" Mitya cried, raising his voice. "Gentlemen, do you even understand what you're suggesting? You're tormenting me! Fine, I'll tell you everything—all the vile things I've thought and done—just to shame you! You'll be shocked at how low a man can sink when driven by conflicting passions. Do you want to know? I'll admit it: I had already considered the very plan you suggested, prosecutor. Yes, I've had that thought in my mind all month. I was so low, I almost carried it out. I nearly went to Katya to beg her for the money. Yes, I was vile enough to think of that. But imagine—going to her, confessing my betrayal, and asking for money so I could use it to run away with her rival, the woman who hated and insulted her. To beg Katya for money so I could betray her! What kind of monster would that make me?"

"I didn't think about jealousy," the prosecutor replied carefully. "Or at least, not quite in the way you've described. But I can see now that there's some truth in what you say."

"That would've been the most disgusting thing imaginable!" Mitya slammed his fist on the table. "It would've been vile beyond words! And, yes, she probably would've given me the money—oh, she absolutely would have! She would've done it just to humiliate me, to get her revenge. She has a fierce, fiery spirit. She would've handed me the money just to show her scorn, to prove how little I meant to her. And I—I would've taken it! Yes, I would have taken it! And then, for the rest of my life… Oh, God, forgive me, gentlemen. I'm shouting because that thought has been eating away at me. It was just two days ago, when I was dealing with Lyagavy, and again yesterday—all day yesterday— that I couldn't stop thinking about it."

"Until what happened?" Nikolay Parfenovitch asked eagerly, though Mitya didn't seem to hear him.

"I've made a terrible confession," Mitya said, his voice low and full of despair. "You should at least appreciate it. You ought to respect it. If my confession means nothing to you—if it doesn't move you at all— then you have no respect for me. And if that's the case, I'll die of shame for confessing it to men like you. I swear, I'll shoot myself! I can already tell you don't believe me. What, are you really going to write all this down?"

"Yes, we need to," Nikolay Parfenovitch replied, looking slightly surprised. "What you just said—that you were seriously considering going to Katerina Ivanovna to ask for the money— it's very important. It could have a major impact on this case, and especially on your situation."

"Have some decency, gentlemen!" Mitya cried out, throwing up his hands. "Don't write that down—please! Have some shame! I've torn my heart open for you, and now you're poking at the wounds! Oh, my God!"

He buried his face in his hands, overwhelmed with anguish.

"Calm yourself, Dmitri Fyodorovitch," the prosecutor said gently. "Everything we write down will be read back to you later. If you disagree with anything, we'll change it. But I have to ask you one more time—are you absolutely certain that no one else knew about the money you sewed up? It's hard to believe that no one knew."

I am carefully translating "The Complete Collection of Works" by Fyodor Dostoevsky into contemporary English to make it easily readable for everyone. This is the original English version of one of the passages: "No one, no one, I told you so before, or you've not understood anything! Let me alone!"

"Very well, this matter is bound to be explained, and there's plenty of time for it, but meantime, consider; we have perhaps a dozen witnesses that you yourself spread it abroad, and even shouted almost everywhere about the three thousand you'd spent here; three thousand, not fifteen hundred. And now, too, when you got hold of the money you had yesterday, you gave many people to understand that you had brought three thousand with you."

"You've got not dozens, but hundreds of witnesses, two hundred witnesses, two hundred have heard it, thousands have heard it!" cried Mitya.

"Well, you see, all bear witness to it. And the word all means something."

"It means nothing. I talked rot, and every one began repeating it." "But what need had you to 'talk rot,' as you call it?"

"The devil knows. From bravado perhaps ... at having wasted so much money.... To try and forget that money I had sewn up, perhaps ... yes, that was why ... damn it ... how often will you ask me that question? Well, I told a fib, and that was the end of it, once I'd said it, I didn't care to correct it. What does a man tell lies for sometimes?"

"That's very difficult to decide, Dmitri Fyodorovitch, what makes a man tell lies," observed the prosecutor impressively. "Tell me, though, was that 'amulet,' as you call it, on your neck, a big thing?"

"No, not big."

"How big, for instance?"

"If you fold a hundred⬚rouble note in half, that would be the size."

"You'd better show us the remains of it. You must have them somewhere."

"Damnation, what nonsense! I don't know where they are."

"But excuse me: where and when did you take it off your neck? According to your own evidence you didn't go home."

"When I was going from Fenya's to Perhotin's, on the way I tore it off my neck and took out the money."

"In the dark?"

"What should I want a light for? I did it with my fingers in one minute."

"Without scissors, in the street?"

"In the market⬚place I think it was. Why scissors? It was an old rag. It was torn in a minute." "Where did you put it afterwards?" "I dropped it there."

"Where was it, exactly?"

"In the market⬚place, in the market⬚place! The devil knows whereabouts. What do you want to know for?"

"That's extremely important, Dmitri Fyodorovitch. It would be material evidence in your favor. How is it you don't understand that? Who helped you to sew it up a month ago?"

"No one helped me. I did it myself." "Can you sew?"

"A soldier has to know how to sew. No knowledge was needed to do that."

"Where did you get the material, that is, the rag in which you sewed the money?"

"Are you laughing at me?"

"Not at all. And we are in no mood for laughing, Dmitri Fyodorovitch."

"I don't know where I got the rag from—somewhere, I suppose." "I should have thought you couldn't have forgotten it?"

"Upon my word, I don't remember. I might have torn a bit off my linen."

"That's very interesting. We might find in your lodgings to⬚morrow the shirt or whatever it is from which you tore the rag. What sort of rag was it, cloth or linen?"

"Goodness only knows what it was. Wait a bit.   I believe I didn't tear it off anything. It was a bit of calico. I believe I sewed it up in a cap of my landlady's."

"In your landlady's cap?"

"Yes. I took it from her."

"How did you get it?"

"You see, I remember once taking a cap for a rag, perhaps to wipe my pen on. I took it without asking, because it was a worthless rag. I tore it up, and I took the notes and sewed them up in it. I believe it was in that very rag I sewed them. An old piece of calico, washed a thousand times."

"And you remember that for certain now?"

"I don't know whether for certain. I think it was in the cap. But, hang it, what does it matter?"

"In that case your landlady will remember that the thing was lost?"

"No, she won't, she didn't miss it. It was an old rag, I tell you, an old rag not worth a farthing."

"And where did you get the needle and thread?"

"I'll stop now. I won't say any more. Enough of it!" said Mitya, losing his temper at last.

"It's strange that you should have so completely forgotten where you threw the pieces in the market-place."

"Give orders for the market-place to be swept to-morrow, and perhaps you'll find it," said Mitya, sneering. "Enough, gentlemen, enough!" he decided, in an exhausted voice. "I see you don't believe me! Not for a moment! It's my fault, not yours. I ought not to have been so ready. Why, why did I degrade myself by confessing my secret to you? It's a joke to you. I see that from your eyes. You led me on to it, prosecutor? Sing a hymn of triumph if you can. Damn you, you torturers!"

He bent his head, and hid his face in his hands. The lawyers were silent. A minute later he raised his head and looked at them almost vacantly. His face now expressed complete, hopeless despair, and he sat mute and passive as though hardly conscious of what was happening. In the meantime they had to finish what they were about. They had immediately to begin examining the witnesses.

It was by now eight o'clock in the morning. The lights had been extinguished long ago. Mihail Makarovitch and Kalganov, who had been continually in and out of the room all the while the interrogation had been going on, had now both gone out again. The lawyers, too, looked very tired. It was a wretched morning, the whole sky was overcast, and the rain streamed down in bucketfuls. Mitya gazed blankly out of the window.

"May I look out of the window?" he asked Nikolay Parfenovitch, suddenly.

"Oh, as much as you like," the latter replied.

Mitya got up and went to the window The rain lashed against its

little greenish panes. He could see the muddy road just below the house, and farther away, in the rain and mist, a row of poor, black, dismal huts, looking even blacker and poorer in the rain. Mitya thought of "Phœbus the golden-haired," and how he had meant to shoot himself at his first ray. "Perhaps it would be even better on a morning like this," he thought with a smile, and suddenly, flinging his hand downwards, he turned to his "torturers."

"Gentlemen," he cried, "I see that I am lost! But she? Tell me about her, I beseech you. Surely she need not be ruined with me? She's innocent, you know, she was out of her mind when she cried last night 'It's all my fault!' She's done nothing, nothing! I've been grieving over her all night as I sat with you. Can't you, won't you tell me what you are going to do with her now?"

Can you rephrase this text into simpler English at an 8th-grade reading level? Please rewrite it and do not plagiarize. Do not give an answer, only give the translated text.

Make sure that the reading experience "flows", for example by not using the same words & sentence structures too often. Do not mention the "Parts" or the "chapters" if they're mentioned

Please format the text properly without separating lines between the passages and exactly in the same structure it was so I can easily copy/paste it entirely into the manuscript of the book. Remove the numbers of the subchapters inbetween the paragraphs

You must translate/rewrite everything exactly and not shorten it.

Please try to adjust my translation sentence-by-sentence and do not make it shorter!

Please adjust my translation sentence-by-sentence in English and do not make it shorter!

So do not skip translating any sentence line-by-line in English and do not make the translation shorter.

"You can set your mind quite at rest on that score, Dmitri Fyodorovich," the prosecutor responded immediately, with obvious eagerness. "So far, we have no reason to take any action regarding the lady you are so concerned about. I trust that the situation will remain the same as the case progresses... On the contrary, we will do everything within our power to handle that matter. You can set your mind completely at ease."

"Gentlemen, I thank you. I knew from the start that you were honest, straightforward people, despite everything. You've lifted a huge burden from my heart... So, what are we to do now? I'm ready."

"Well, we need to hurry. We must move on to questioning the witnesses without delay. This must be done in your presence, so—"

"Shouldn't we have some tea first?" Nikolay Parfenovitch interrupted, "I think we've earned it!"

They agreed that if the tea was already prepared downstairs (Mihail Makarovitch had probably gone down to fetch it), they would drink a glass and then "keep going," postponing their proper breakfast until a more convenient time. The tea was indeed ready downstairs and was soon brought up. At first, Mitya refused the glass that Nikolay Parfenovitch politely offered him, but afterward, he asked for it himself and drank it eagerly. He appeared to be surprisingly exhausted. Given his extraordinary physical strength, one would think that a night of heavy drinking, even with intense emotions, would have little effect on him. However, he felt as though he could barely keep his head up, and from time to time, everything around him seemed to shift and sway before his eyes. "A little more and I'll start raving," he thought to himself.

Chapter 8: The Evidence of The Witnesses the Babe

The examination of the witnesses began. However, we will not continue our story in as much detail as before. Thus, we will not dwell on how Nikolay Parfenovitch emphasized to each witness called that they must provide their testimony truthfully and in good conscience, and that later they would be required to repeat their testimony under oath. Nor will we elaborate on how each witness was asked to sign the official record of their testimony, and so on. We will only note that the main focus of the questioning was the matter of the three thousand roubles. That is, whether Mitya had spent three thousand or fifteen hundred roubles here at Mokroe during his first visit a month earlier, and again whether he had spent three thousand or fifteen hundred roubles yesterday. Unfortunately, all the testimony given by each witness turned out to be against Mitya. Not a single witness supported him, and some witnesses introduced new, almost devastating, facts that contradicted Mitya's version of events.

The first witness examined was Trifon Borissovitch. He was not in the least bit intimidated as he stood before the lawyers. On the contrary, he had an air of stern and angry indignation toward the accused, which gave him an appearance of honesty and personal dignity. He spoke little, with restraint, waited to be questioned, and answered each question with precision and deliberation. He firmly and without hesitation testified that the amount spent a month earlier could not have been less than three thousand roubles, and that all the local peasants would confirm that they had heard Mitya himself mention the sum of three thousand roubles. "What a lot of money he threw away on the gypsy girls alone! He must have spent a thousand on them alone."

"I don't believe I gave them even five hundred," was Mitya's gloomy response to this. "It's a pity I didn't count the money at the time, but I was drunk. "

Mitya was sitting sideways, his back to the curtains. He listened gloomily, with a melancholy and exhausted expression, as if to say:

"Oh, say whatever you want. It doesn't matter now."

"More than a thousand went to them, Dmitri Fyodorovitch," Trifon Borissovitch retorted firmly. "You threw the money around carelessly, and they picked it up. They were a gang of thieves, horse-stealers; they've been driven away from here, or else they might have testified themselves about how much they got from you. I saw the money in your hands with my own eyes—I didn't count it, you wouldn't let me, that's true enough—but judging by the look of it, I'd say it was far more than fifteen hundred roubles. fifteen hundred, indeed! We've seen money before, we can estimate amounts. "

As for the amount spent yesterday, he stated that Dmitri Fyodorovitch had told him as soon as he arrived that he had brought three thousand roubles with him.

"Now, really, Trifon Borissovitch?" Mitya replied. "Surely I didn't declare so confidently that I'd brought three thousand?"

"You did say so, Dmitri Fyodorovitch. You said it in front of Andrey. Andrey is still here; send for him. And in the hall, when you were treating the choir, you shouted outright that you'd leave your sixth thousand here—meaning with what you had spent before, we understand. Stepan and Semyon heard it, and Pyotr Fomitch Kalganov was standing next to you at the time. Maybe he'll remember it. "

The mention of the "sixth" thousand made a remarkable impression on the two lawyers. They were thrilled with this new way of reckoning: three and three made six, three thousand then and three thousand now made six; that was clear.

They questioned all the peasants suggested by Trifon Borissovitch—Stepan and Semyon, the driver Andrey, and Kalganov. The peasants and the driver confirmed Trifon Borissovitch's testimony without hesitation. They recorded with special care Andrey's account of the conversation he had with Mitya on the road: " 'Where,' he says, 'am I, Dmitri Fyodorovitch, going—to heaven or to hell? And will I be forgiven in the next world or not?'"

The psychologically astute Ippolit Kirillovitch listened to this with a sly smile and concluded by recommending that these remarks about where Dmitri Fyodorovitch might go should be "included in the case."

When Kalganov was called in, he entered reluctantly, frowning and in a bad mood, and he spoke to the lawyers as though he had never seen them before in his life, even though they were people he had been meeting every day for a long time. He began by saying that "he knew nothing about it and didn't want to." But it turned out that he had indeed heard about the "sixth" thousand, and he admitted that he had been standing nearby at the time. As for how much money Mitya had in his hands, he said he "didn't know." He insisted that the Poles had cheated at cards. When asked repeatedly, he stated that after the Poles had been thrown out, Mitya's relationship with Agrafena Alexandrovna had definitely improved, and that she had said she loved him. He spoke of Agrafena Alexandrovna with restraint and respect, as though she were a lady of high society, and did not once refer to her as Grushenka. Despite the young man's obvious reluctance to give testimony, Ippolit Kirillovitch questioned him at length, and it was only from him that the prosecutor learned all the details of what could be called Mitya's "romantic episode" that night. Mitya did not interrupt Kalganov once. Finally, they let the young man go, and he left the room with open indignation.

The Poles were also questioned. Although they had gone to bed in their room, they had not slept all night, and when the police officers arrived, they quickly got dressed, knowing they would surely be summoned. They gave their testimony with dignity, though not without some uneasiness. The little Pole turned out to be a retired twelfth-class official who had worked in Siberia as a veterinary surgeon. His name was Mussyalovitch. Pan Vrublevsky turned out to be an uncertified dentist. Though Nikolay Parfenovitch asked them questions upon their entrance, they both directed their answers to Mihail Makarovitch, who was standing off to the side, mistakenly assuming that he was the most important person in the room and in command, addressing him as "Pan Colonel" at every turn. Only after several corrections from Mihail Makarovitch himself did they realize they were supposed to address their answers to Nikolay Parfenovitch. It turned out that they could speak Russian quite well, aside from a slight accent in some words. Pan Mussyalovitch spoke proudly and warmly about his past and present relationship with Grushenka, which immediately infuriated Mitya, who declared that he would not allow the "scoundrel" to speak like that in his presence! Pan Mussyalovitch quickly pointed out the word "scoundrel" and requested that it be noted in the official record. Mitya seethed with anger.

"He's a scoundrel! A scoundrel! You can write that down. And write down too that, even after the protocol, I still declare that he's a scoundrel!" he shouted.

Although Nikolay Parfenovitch did add this to the record, he handled the situation with great tact. After sharply reprimanding Mitya, he quickly moved on from the romantic parts of the case and focused on what was truly important. One piece of evidence given by the Poles particularly interested the lawyers: in that very room, Mitya had tried to buy off Pan Mussyalovitch, offering him three thousand roubles to give up his claims, with seven hundred paid immediately and the rest—two thousand three hundred—to be paid the next day in town. Mitya had sworn at the time that he didn't have the whole amount with him at Mokroe, but that his money was in town. Mitya protested hotly, saying he hadn't promised to pay the rest in town the next day. But Pan Vrublevsky confirmed the claim, and Mitya, after thinking for a moment, admitted with a frown that it must have been as the Poles said. He had been excited at the time and might have said it.

The prosecutor jumped on this evidence eagerly. It seemed to suggest to the prosecution (and they built a deduction around it) that part of the three thousand roubles Mitya had received could still be hidden somewhere in town or possibly even here in Mokroe. This would explain the puzzling fact that only eight hundred roubles had been found in Mitya's possession, which had previously been the one small point in Mitya's favor. Now, even that small point had fallen apart. When the prosecutor asked Mitya where he would have gotten the remaining two thousand three hundred roubles, since he had denied having more than fifteen hundred, Mitya confidently replied that he had intended to give the "little fellow" not money, but a formal deed transferring his rights to the village of Tchermashnya, the same rights he had already offered to Samsonov and Madame Hohlakov. The prosecutor smiled at the "innocence of this excuse."

"And do you really think he would have accepted such a deed in place of two thousand three hundred roubles in cash?"

"He certainly would have," Mitya declared passionately. "Look, he might have squeezed not just two thousand, but four or six thousand out of it. He could have had his lawyers—Poles and Jews—go after it and possibly gotten not just three thousand, but the whole property from the old man."

Pan Mussyalovitch's testimony was, of course, written down in full detail. Then the Poles were dismissed. The matter of cheating at cards was barely touched upon. Nikolay Parfenovitch was already satisfied with them and didn't want to bother them with minor details, especially since it was just a foolish drunken argument over cards. There had been enough drinking and disorder that night anyway... So the two hundred roubles remained in the Poles' pockets.

Next, old Maximov was called. He came in nervously, shuffling with small steps, looking messy and downcast. He had been hiding with Grushenka downstairs this whole time, sitting silently beside her, occasionally bursting into tears and wiping his eyes with a blue checkered handkerchief, as Mihail Makarovitch later described. Grushenka had even tried to comfort and calm him. The old man immediately confessed that he had done wrong, that he had borrowed "ten roubles in my poverty" from Dmitri Fyodorovitch, and that he was willing to repay it. When Nikolay Parfenovitch asked him directly if he had noticed how much money Dmitri Fyodorovitch had in his hand—since Maximov must have seen it clearly when he took the note—Maximov firmly stated that there had been twenty thousand roubles.

"Have you ever seen as much as twenty thousand before?" Nikolay Parfenovitch asked with a smile.

"Of course I have, not twenty, but seven thousand, when my wife mortgaged my small property. She only let me see it from a distance, showing off to me. It was a thick bundle of rainbow- colored notes. And Dmitri Fyodorovitch's money was rainbow- colored, too. "

Maximov wasn't kept long. Finally, it was Grushenka's turn. Nikolay Parfenovitch was clearly nervous about how Mitya might react to her presence, and he whispered a few words of caution to him, but Mitya bowed his head silently, signaling that he wouldn't make a scene. Mihail Makarovitch personally escorted Grushenka in. She walked in with a stern, serious expression, looking calm and almost composed, and sat down quietly in the chair that Nikolay Parfenovitch offered her. She was very pale, wrapped tightly in her luxurious black shawl as though she were cold. She was suffering from a slight feverish chill—the first sign of the long illness that followed that night. Her serious demeanor, direct gaze, and quiet manner made a positive impression on everyone. Even Nikolay Parfenovitch was a bit "charmed." He later admitted, when talking about it afterward, that only then did he realize "how beautiful the woman was," though he had seen her several times before. He had always thought of her as a "provincial courtesan." "She has the manners of the best society," he said enthusiastically while gossiping with a group of ladies. But this remark was met with outrage from the ladies, who immediately scolded him for being "naughty," much to his amusement.

As she entered the room, Grushenka only glanced at Mitya for a moment, who watched her anxiously. But her calm expression quickly reassured him. After the usual initial questions and warnings, Nikolay Parfenovitch, hesitating slightly but remaining polite, asked her what kind of relationship she had with the retired lieutenant, Dmitri Fyodorovitch Karamazov. Grushenka answered firmly and calmly:

"He was an acquaintance. He visited me as a friend during the past month." In response to further questions, she explained honestly and openly that while she had occasionally found him attractive, she had not loved him. She said she had won over both Mitya and his old father "out of spite," and that she knew Mitya had been jealous of Fyodor Pavlovitch and others. But she had only found that amusing. She never intended to go to Fyodor Pavlovitch, she had just been laughing at him. "I wasn't thinking about either of them at all this past month. I was waiting for another man who had wronged me. But I don't think it's necessary for you to ask me about that, and I won't answer, because that's my own business."

Nikolay Parfenovitch immediately followed this hint and shifted the focus back to the serious part of the case—the question of the three thousand roubles. Grushenka confirmed that three thousand roubles had indeed been spent during the first party at Mokroe, and though she hadn't counted the money herself, she had heard the amount from Dmitri Fyodorovitch.

"Did he tell you that when you were alone, or in front of others? Or did you hear him say it to others while you were there?" the prosecutor asked immediately.

Grushenka replied that she had heard him say it in front of other people and also when they were alone.

"Did he say it to you alone once or several times?" the prosecutor asked, learning that Mitya had told Grushenka the amount several times.

Ippolit Kirillovitch was very pleased with this testimony. Further questioning revealed that Grushenka also knew where the money had come from—that Dmitri Fyodorovitch had gotten it from Katerina Ivanovna.

"And did you never hear that the money spent a month ago wasn't three thousand, but less, and that Dmitri Fyodorovitch had saved half that amount for himself?"

"No, I never heard that," Grushenka replied.

It was further explained that, on the contrary, Mitya often told her that he didn't have a single coin.

"He kept hoping to get some money from his father," Grushenka added.

"Did he ever say to you—maybe casually or in anger—that he was planning to harm his father?" Nikolay Parfenovitch asked suddenly.

"Ah, yes, he did say that," Grushenka sighed. "Did he say it once or more than once?"

"He mentioned it several times, always when he was angry." "And did you believe he would really do it?"

"No, I never believed it," she answered firmly. "I trusted his good heart."

"Gentlemen, let me say one word to Agrafena Alexandrovna, in your presence," Mitya called out suddenly.

"You may speak," agreed Nikolay Parfenovitch.

Mitya stood up. "Agrafena Alexandrovna, trust in God and trust me. I did not kill my father!"

Mitya sat down again. Grushenka stood up, crossed herself before the icon, and said, her voice trembling with emotion, "Thank You, Lord." Then, still standing, she turned to Nikolay Parfenovitch and said, "Believe him! I know him. He might joke or act stubbornly, but he would never lie against his conscience. He's telling the truth, and you can believe it."

"Thank you, Agrafena Alexandrovna. Your words give me strength," Mitya replied in a shaky voice.

Regarding the money spent the day before, Grushenka said she didn't know the exact amount. However, she had heard Mitya tell several people that he had three thousand roubles with him. When asked where he got the money, she explained that he had told her he had "stolen" it from Katerina Ivanovna. She had responded that it wasn't really stolen, but that he needed to return it the next day.

The prosecutor pressed further, asking if the money Mitya had referred to was the amount spent yesterday or the money used a month ago. Grushenka answered that he was referring to the money spent a month ago, and that was how she had understood him.

Grushenka was finally allowed to leave. Nikolay Parfenovitch, perhaps moved by her presence, told her she could return to town immediately and offered to help with transportation or even an escort if she wished.

"I appreciate your kindness," Grushenka said with a polite bow. "But I'll go back to town with this old gentleman. While I'm waiting, I'd like to stay downstairs and hear what you decide about Dmitri Fyodorovitch."

She left the room. Mitya seemed momentarily calm, even cheerful, but the feeling didn't last. He was becoming increasingly exhausted, his eyes heavy with fatigue. Finally, the witness testimonies were complete, and the lawyers began reviewing the final report.

Mitya stood, moved to the corner by the curtain, lay down on a large chest covered with a rug, and instantly fell asleep.

In his sleep, he had a strange dream, one that felt entirely disconnected from his surroundings.

He was traveling through the snowy plains of the steppe, where he had once been stationed long ago. A peasant was driving him in a cart pulled by two horses through the cold, wet snow. It was early November, and the snowflakes melted the moment they touched the ground. The peasant driving the cart was about fifty, with a fair, long beard, and wore a simple gray smock. They passed a nearby village where the blackened remains of huts stood, half- burned, with charred beams poking out of the ruins.

As they drove through, Mitya saw a line of peasant women standing along the road. They were all thin, pale, with brownish faces, as if starved. One woman at the edge of the line stood out— she was tall and gaunt, with a long, bony face. Though she looked forty, she might have been only twenty. She held a small baby in her arms, and the baby was crying. Her breasts looked dry, as if she had no milk left to feed the child. The baby stretched out its bare little arms, its tiny fists blue with cold, still crying.

"Why are they crying? Why are they crying?" Mitya asked as they sped past.

"It's the baby," the driver said. "The baby's crying."

Mitya was struck by how tenderly the peasant called it "the baby," and he liked the simple kindness in that word.

"But why is it crying?" Mitya asked again, confused. "Why are its little arms bare? Why don't they wrap it in something warm?"

"The baby is cold. Its clothes are frozen—they can't keep it warm."

"But why? Why is it like that?" Mitya kept asking, as if he couldn't grasp the situation.

"They're poor people. Their houses burned down. They have no bread. They're begging because they've lost everything."

"No, no," Mitya said, still not understanding. "Why do those poor mothers stand there like that? Why are people poor? Why is the baby poor? Why is the steppe so barren? Why don't they hug each other and sing joyful songs? Why do they look so dark with sadness? Why can't they feed the baby?"

Though he knew his questions made no sense, Mitya felt he had to ask them. He felt an overwhelming wave of pity rising in his heart, stronger than anything he had ever felt before. He wanted to cry. He wanted to do something, anything, to help these people, so that the baby wouldn't cry anymore, so that the weary mother wouldn't suffer, so that no one would have to cry again, ever. And he wanted to do it immediately, without hesitation, with all the reckless urgency that came naturally to him as a Karamazov.

"And I'll go with you. I'll stay with you for the rest of my life. I won't leave you," he suddenly heard Grushenka's voice, soft and full of emotion, close beside him.

His heart filled with warmth, and he felt a powerful longing to live—really live—and to move forward towards the light that seemed to call to him. He wanted to go, to keep going, without stopping, towards that new, bright light, and to hurry, to hurry, right now!

"What? Where?" he exclaimed, waking suddenly and sitting up on the chest, as if he had just come out of a deep trance, a bright smile spreading across his face.

Nikolay Parfenovitch stood beside him, asking if he wanted to hear the final report read aloud before signing it. Mitya guessed he must have been asleep for over an hour, though he wasn't sure.

Then, something odd struck him: there was a pillow under his

head, though it hadn't been there when he first lay down.

"Who put this pillow under my head? Who was so kind?" Mitya asked, his voice filled with unexpected gratitude, almost on the verge of tears, as if someone had done him a great kindness.

He never found out who it was—perhaps one of the peasants, or maybe Nikolay Parfenovitch's young assistant. Whoever it was, the simple act touched him deeply, and he felt his whole soul tremble with emotion.

He stood, went over to the table, and said, "I'll sign whatever you need."

"I had a wonderful dream, gentlemen," Mitya said, his voice carrying a strange tone, as if something new and joyful had awakened within him.

Chapter 9: They Carry Mitya Away

When the protocol was signed, Nikolay Parfenovitch turned to the prisoner with a serious expression and read the official "Committal." It stated that on such-and-such a year, on such a day, and in such a place, the investigating lawyer of the district court had examined Dmitri Fyodorovitch Karamazov, accused of various crimes (each one carefully listed). It further explained that although the accused did not plead guilty, he had offered no defense, while the witnesses and other circumstances testified against him. Following certain articles of the law, it was decided that to prevent Dmitri from escaping judgment, he was to be held in such-and-such prison. A copy of this decision was to be sent to the deputy prosecutor.

In short, Mitya was told that from this moment on, he was a prisoner, and he would be taken to the town and locked up in an unpleasant place. Mitya listened closely and only shrugged his shoulders.

"Well, gentlemen, I don't blame you. I'm ready... I understand you don't have a choice."

Nikolay Parfenovitch gently informed him that he would be escorted immediately by the rural police officer, Mavriky Mavrikyevitch, who happened to be nearby.

"Wait," Mitya interrupted suddenly. Overcome by emotion, he turned to everyone in the room and said:

"Gentlemen, we're all cruel, we're all monsters, we all make people weep—mothers and little babies too—but of all of us, let it be clear right now, I am the lowest. I've sworn to change, but every day I've done the same horrible things. I understand now that people like me need a blow from destiny to catch them like a trap and force them to change. I never would have changed on my own! But the thunderbolt has struck, and I accept the torture of accusation and my public shame. I want to suffer, and through suffering, I hope to be purified. Maybe I will be purified, gentlemen? But listen, for the last time, I am not guilty of my father's blood. I accept punishment not because I killed him, but because I meant to kill him, and maybe I really could have done it. Still, I plan to fight you. I warn you now—I'll fight this out to the end, and then God will decide. Goodbye, gentlemen. Don't be angry with me for yelling at you during the questioning. Oh, I was such a fool then... In another minute, I'll be a prisoner, but now, for the last time, as a free man, Dmitri Karamazov offers you his hand. In saying goodbye to you, I say goodbye to all men."

His voice trembled, and he held out his hand, but Nikolay Parfenovitch, who was standing closest, suddenly pulled his hands behind his back, almost nervously. Mitya noticed immediately and let his hand drop.

"The investigation isn't over yet," Nikolay Parfenovitch muttered, a bit embarrassed. "We'll continue in town, and I, for one, of course, wish you all the best... in your defense. Actually, Dmitri Fyodorovitch, I've always thought of you as more unfortunate than guilty. And if I may speak for everyone here, we all see you as, deep down, an honorable man—just one who has been carried away by certain passions."

By the time he finished, Nikolay Parfenovitch's small figure looked almost dignified. Mitya had the strange thought that in another minute, this "boy" would take his arm, lead him aside, and start talking about girls again. But many irrelevant and strange thoughts pass through a prisoner's mind, even when he's being led to his fate.

"Gentlemen, you're good people, you're kind. May I see her one last time to say goodbye?" Mitya asked.

"Certainly, but considering... it must be done with—" "Oh, well, if that's how it has to be, then so be it!"

Grushenka was brought in, but the farewell was brief and few words were exchanged. It didn't satisfy Nikolay Parfenovitch. Grushenka bowed deeply to Mitya.

"I've told you I am yours, and I will be yours. I will follow you forever, wherever they send you. Farewell. You are innocent, though you've ruined yourself."

Her lips trembled, and tears streamed down her face.

"Forgive me, Grusha, for my love, for ruining you with it too."

Mitya wanted to say more, but he stopped and left. Immediately, he was surrounded by the men assigned to keep watch over him. At the bottom of the steps, where he had arrived so boldly the day before with Andrey's three horses, two carts were waiting. Mavriky Mavrikyevitch, a sturdy, thickset man with a wrinkled face, was upset about something, some unexpected problem. He was shouting angrily and asked Mitya to get into the cart with excessive gruffness.

"When I bought him drinks at the tavern, he had a very different face," Mitya thought as he climbed in. A crowd had gathered at the gate—peasants, women, and drivers. Trifon Borissovitch also came down the steps. Everyone stared at Mitya.

"Forgive me, good people!" Mitya suddenly shouted from the cart.

"Forgive us too!" he heard two or three voices call back. "Goodbye to you, too, Trifon Borissovitch!"

But Trifon Borissovitch didn't even turn around. He was too busy, shouting and fussing over some problem. Apparently, the second cart, which was supposed to carry two constables along with Mavriky Mavrikyevitch, wasn't ready yet. The peasant driver who had been assigned to the second cart was putting on his coat, insisting that it wasn't his turn to go but Akim's. But Akim was nowhere to be found. People ran to look for him, while the peasant continued to argue, asking them to wait.

"You see how our peasants are, Mavriky Mavrikyevitch? They have no shame!" Trifon Borissovitch exclaimed. "Akim gave you twenty-five copecks two days ago, and you drank it all, and now you're making a fuss. I'm amazed at your patience with these peasants, Mavriky Mavrikyevitch, truly amazed."

"But why do we need a second cart?" Mitya asked. "Let's just go with one, Mavriky Mavrikyevitch. I won't cause any trouble. I won't run away from you, old fellow. Why do we need an escort?"

"I'll ask you to watch your language, sir, if no one has ever taught you how. I'm not your 'old fellow,' and you can save your advice for another time!" Mavriky Mavrikyevitch snapped, clearly eager to take out his frustration.

Mitya fell silent, his face flushing with embarrassment. A moment later, he felt cold. The rain had stopped, but the sky was still overcast, and a cold wind was blowing straight into his face.

"I've caught a chill," Mitya thought, shivering.

Finally, Mavriky Mavrikyevitch climbed into the cart, sitting down heavily and squeezing Mitya into the corner without seeming to notice. It was clear he was in a bad mood and disliked the task assigned to him.

"Goodbye, Trifon Borissovitch!" Mitya shouted again, though he realized that this time, he hadn't called out from kindness but from anger.

But Trifon Borissovitch stood with his hands behind his back, glaring at Mitya with a stern, angry expression. He didn't respond.

"Goodbye, Dmitri Fyodorovitch, goodbye!" came Kalganov's voice all of a sudden. He rushed up to the cart and held out his hand to Mitya. He wasn't wearing his cap.

Mitya managed to grab and squeeze his hand.

"Goodbye, dear friend! I'll never forget your kindness," he said warmly.

But the cart started moving, and their hands were pulled apart. The bell began to ring as Mitya was driven away.

Kalganov ran back inside, sat in a corner, hid his face in his hands, and began to cry. He cried for a long time, like a little boy, though he was a young man of twenty. He believed almost without a doubt in Mitya's guilt.

"What kind of people are we? What can humans be after this?" he muttered incoherently, sinking into deep despair. At that moment, he didn't want to live anymore.

"Is it worth it? Is life worth it?" the young man cried in his grief.

Part 4

Book 10: The Boys

Chapter 1: Kolya Krassotkin

It was the beginning of November. There had been a hard frost, about eleven degrees Réaumur, with no snow, but a light, dry snow had fallen on the frozen ground during the night, and a sharp, dry wind was blowing it along the bleak streets of our town, especially around the market square. It was a dull morning, but the snow had stopped.

Not far from the market square, near Plotnikov's shop, there stood a small house, very clean both inside and out. It belonged to Madame Krassotkin, the widow of a former provincial secretary, who had been dead for fourteen years. His widow, still an attractive woman of thirty-two, was living in her neat little house on her private means. She lived quietly and respectably, with a gentle but fairly cheerful disposition. She had been about eighteen when her husband died, and they had only been married for a year when he passed away, leaving her with a newborn son. From the day of his death, she had devoted herself completely to the upbringing of her only child, her son Kolya. Though she had loved him passionately for those fourteen years, he had caused her far more worry and anxiety than happiness. She spent every day in fear, trembling and fainting with terror that he might fall ill, catch a cold, do something naughty, climb on a chair and fall, and so on and so on.

When Kolya started school, his mother threw herself into studying all his subjects with him, hoping to help him with his lessons and go through them together. She rushed to make friends with the teachers and their wives, and even tried to get close to Kolya's schoolmates, fawning over them in the hope of protecting Kolya from being teased, laughed at, or beaten by them. She went so far that the boys actually started mocking him because of her and teasing him for being a "mama's boy."

But Kolya could stand up for himself. He was a determined boy, "incredibly strong," as the rumor went around in his class, and this rumor soon proved true. He was quick, strong-willed, and bold, with an adventurous spirit. He did well in his studies, and there was talk at school that he was even better at arithmetic and world history than the teacher, Dardanelov. Although he looked down on others, he was a good friend and didn't act superior. He accepted the respect of his schoolmates as his due, but he was still friendly with them. Most importantly, he knew where to draw the line. He could control himself when needed, and with the teachers, he never crossed that invisible line where a prank turns into a serious violation of discipline. But he loved mischief just as much as the youngest boys in school, not because he wanted to cause trouble, but because he enjoyed creating a stir, inventing something clever, something that would stand out and get attention. He was extremely proud of himself.

He even knew how to make his mother give in to him; he was almost tyrannical in his control over her. She had been giving in to him for years. The one thing she could not bear was the thought that her son didn't love her much. She constantly feared that Kolya was "unfeeling" toward her, and at times, she would break down into hysterical tears, accusing him of being cold-hearted. Kolya disliked this, and the more she demanded affection, the more he seemed to avoid it. Yet it wasn't intentional on his part, but simply his nature—it was part of his character. His mother was wrong; he cared about her deeply. He just disliked what he called "sappy sentimentality," as he put it in his schoolboy way.

There was a bookcase in their house with a few books that had belonged to his father. Kolya loved reading and had already gone through several of them on his own. His mother didn't mind this and only sometimes wondered at seeing him stand for hours by the bookcase, deeply absorbed in a book, instead of playing outside. This was how Kolya ended up reading some things that were not quite suitable for his age.

Although Kolya usually knew where to draw the line in his mischief, recently he had started pulling pranks that seriously worried his mother. It's true that there was nothing malicious in what he did, but his wild, reckless behavior frightened her.

That summer, during the July holidays, Kolya and his mother went to another district, forty-five miles away, to visit a distant relative, whose husband worked as an official at the railway station (the same station from which, a month later, Ivan Fyodorovitch Karamazov would depart for Moscow). While there, Kolya took it upon himself to study every detail about the railways, knowing he could impress his schoolmates with his newfound knowledge when he returned home. However, there were other boys in the area, and Kolya quickly became friends with them. Some of these boys lived near the station, while others were from the surrounding area. There were six or seven boys in total, all between twelve and fifteen years old, and two of them came from Kolya's town. The boys began playing together, and after a few days, they made a foolish bet. Kolya, who was almost the youngest of the group and was looked down upon because of his age, was driven by pride or reckless bravery to bet two roubles that he could lie down between the rails at night as the eleven o'clock train passed over him, and stay there without moving. The boys had checked beforehand and confirmed that it was possible to lie flat enough between the rails for the train to pass over without touching you, but lying there was no joke. Kolya insisted he would do it. At first, the others laughed at him, calling him a liar and a show-off, which only pushed him further. What hurt his pride most was that the fifteen-year-olds looked down on him, treating him as a little kid who wasn't good enough to join their group, which was an insult he couldn't stand.

So, they made plans to meet that evening, half a mile from the station, where the train would have gained full speed after leaving. The boys gathered. It was a pitch-dark night with no moon. At the appointed time, Kolya lay down between the rails. The five other boys who had taken the bet hid in the bushes by the tracks, their hearts pounding with excitement that soon turned into fear and regret. Eventually, they heard the distant rumble of the train leaving the station. Two red lights appeared out of the darkness, and the train roared as it rushed toward them.

"Run! Get off the tracks!" the boys shouted to Kolya from the bushes, their voices full of terror. But it was too late—the train sped past. The boys rushed over to Kolya. He lay still, unmoving. They began pulling at him, trying to lift him up. Suddenly, he stood and walked away without a word. Later, he explained that he had pretended to be unconscious just to scare them, but much later, he admitted to his mother that he had actually lost consciousness. This was how his reputation as a "daredevil" was established forever. He returned to the station pale as a ghost. The next day, he had a slight fever, but he was in high spirits and very pleased with himself. The incident didn't become widely known right away, but when they returned to town, word spread through the school, and even the teachers heard about it. Kolya's mother hurried to beg the teachers on his behalf, and in the end, Dardanelov, a respected and influential teacher, intervened on his behalf, and the matter was quietly dropped.

Dardanelov was a middle-aged bachelor who had been deeply in love with Madame Krassotkin for many years. About a year earlier, he had nervously, and with great respect, asked her to marry him. But she had firmly refused, feeling that accepting his proposal would be a betrayal of her son. However, Dardanelov had some reason to believe, from subtle signs, that he wasn't completely disliked by the charming, though very modest and tender-hearted widow. After Kolya's daring stunt on the railway, things seemed to change, and Dardanelov was given a small glimmer of hope. It was a faint hope, but for someone as pure and delicate as Dardanelov, it was enough to make him happy for the time being.

He was fond of Kolya, although he thought it beneath him to try to win the boy over. In class, he was strict with him. Kolya, in turn, kept his distance. He always did his lessons perfectly and was second in his class. He remained reserved with Dardanelov, and the whole class believed that Kolya knew so much about history that he could outsmart Dardanelov. Kolya had once asked him, "Who founded Troy?" to which Dardanelov gave a vague answer about the migration of peoples and the myths surrounding that ancient time. But he didn't answer the question of who exactly founded Troy, and for some reason, he even seemed to think the question was silly. Nevertheless, the boys were convinced that Dardanelov didn't know who founded Troy. Kolya had read about the founders of Troy in a book by Smaragdov, one of the books from his father's collection. All the boys became curious about the answer to the question of who had founded Troy, but Kolya refused to tell them, and his reputation for knowledge remained intact.

After the incident on the railway, Kolya's attitude toward his mother changed somewhat. When Anna Fyodorovna (Madame Krassotkin) learned of her son's dangerous prank, she nearly lost her mind with fear. She had terrible hysterical fits that lasted on and off for several days. Finally, Kolya, seriously worried, promised on his honor that he would never pull such a prank again. He swore on his knees before the holy image and swore on his father's memory, at his mother's request. The "manly" Kolya burst into tears like a six-year-old boy. That entire day, mother and son kept rushing into each other's arms, sobbing. By the next day, Kolya was as "unfeeling" as ever, but he had become quieter, more modest, sterner, and more thoughtful.

Six weeks later, it's true, he got into another scrape, which even reached the ears of the Justice of the Peace. But this incident was entirely different—it was amusing and foolish, and Kolya wasn't even the ringleader. He was only indirectly involved. But more about that later. His mother continued to worry and tremble with fear, but the more anxious she became, the more hope Dardanelov had. It's worth noting that Kolya knew perfectly well what Dardanelov felt for his mother and, of course, deeply despised him for it. He had been so tactless in the past that he had even shown this contempt in front of his mother, hinting that he knew what Dardanelov was after. But since the railway incident, Kolya had changed his behavior in this respect too. He no longer made any remarks about it and even began speaking more respectfully of Dardanelov in front of his mother. The sensitive Madame Krassotkin noticed this change and was endlessly grateful. However, if a visitor mentioned Dardanelov in Kolya's presence, his mother would blush like a rose. At such moments, Kolya would either stare out the window with a scowl, inspect his boots, or call out angrily for "Perezvon," the large, shaggy, mangy dog he had found about a month before. He had brought the dog home and kept it indoors secretly, never showing it to his schoolmates. He bullied the poor dog terribly, teaching it all sorts of tricks, so much so that the dog howled whenever Kolya was away at school. When Kolya returned, the dog would whine with excitement, dash around like a lunatic, and show off all the tricks Kolya had taught him—pretending to be dead, begging, lying on the ground, and so on. The dog did all this without waiting for commands, simply out of the eagerness of its overjoyed heart.

By the way, I've forgotten to mention that Kolya Krassotkin was the boy stabbed with a penknife by Captain Snegiryov's son, Ilusha, who had been defending his father when the schoolboys mocked him and called him the nickname "wisp of tow."

Chapter 2: Children

On that cold, snowy, and windy November day, Kolya Krassotkin was at home. It was Sunday, so there was no school. The clock had just struck eleven, and he was eager to leave the house for what he considered very urgent business. However, he was left alone in charge, as all the adults were away due to an unexpected event. Madame Krassotkin had rented two small rooms, separated from the main part of the house by a hallway, to a doctor's wife, who lived there with her two young children. The doctor's wife, who was the same age as Madame Krassotkin, had become a close friend. Her husband, the doctor, had left a year ago, traveling first to Orenburg, then to Tashkent, and she hadn't heard from him for six months. Without Madame Krassotkin's friendship to comfort her, the poor woman would have been overwhelmed by her loneliness.

Adding to her troubles, her only servant, Katerina, had suddenly announced the night before that she was about to give birth. This came as a complete surprise to everyone, as no one had noticed her condition earlier. The doctor's wife, shocked but quick to act, decided to take Katerina to a midwife's place in town. She valued

Katerina greatly, so she stayed with her overnight to help. By morning, Madame Krassotkin was busy assisting her friend and seeking help for the unexpected situation.

With both women away, and the Krassotkins' servant, Agafya, off at the market, Kolya was left to watch over the house and look after the doctor's children. Kolya wasn't worried about the responsibility—he liked being in charge—and he had his dog Perezvon by his side. Perezvon had been told to stay perfectly still under the bench in the hall. Every time Kolya passed through the hall, Perezvon would tap his tail twice on the floor, hoping for a signal to move. But Kolya gave him a stern look, and the dog, understanding, would remain motionless, waiting patiently for the command to come.

The only thing bothering Kolya was having to watch the two children. Although he thought little of Katerina's sudden situation, he was fond of the kids. Earlier, he had given them a picture book to keep them occupied. The older child, Nastya, was eight and could read, while her seven-year-old brother, Kostya, enjoyed listening to her. Kolya could have entertained them in other ways—playing soldiers with them or sending them to hide all over the house. He had done so before, and there had even been rumors at school that Kolya played "horses" with the children at home, pretending to be a horse with his head tilted to the side. When his classmates teased him about it, Kolya defended himself, saying it was silly to play horses with boys his age, but doing it for the younger kids was different since he liked them. He insisted no one had the right to criticize his feelings for the children.

But today, Kolya was preoccupied. He had something important on his mind, almost like a secret mission. Time was passing, and Agafya hadn't come back from the market yet. Kolya kept opening the door to the children's room to check on them. Every time he looked in, the kids grinned at him, hoping he would stay and play. But Kolya, too distracted, didn't join them.

When the clock struck eleven, Kolya made up his mind. If Agafya didn't return in the next ten minutes, he would leave without waiting for her. He decided he would make the children promise to behave while he was gone—not to get scared, not to climb on anything dangerous, and not to cry. With that plan in mind, he put on his winter coat, which had a warm fur collar, and slung his satchel over his shoulder. Ignoring his mother's constant warnings to wear galoshes in cold weather, Kolya gave the galoshes a dismissive glance and went out in just his boots.

Perezvon, sensing that Kolya was leaving, wagged his tail enthusiastically. The dog's whole body trembled with excitement, and he let out a small, eager whine. But Kolya saw this excitement as a lack of discipline. He kept Perezvon waiting under the bench a little longer. Only after Kolya opened the door did he give a sharp whistle, releasing the dog. Perezvon sprang up joyfully, bounding ahead with excitement.

Kolya paused at the door to check on the children one last time. They were still sitting at the table, but instead of reading, they were having a lively argument. The children often debated important matters, and since Nastya was older, she usually won. If Kostya couldn't convince her, he would appeal to Kolya, whose opinion they both trusted completely.

Kolya stood in the hallway, listening to their conversation with amusement. Seeing him there made the children argue even more enthusiastically.

"I'll never believe that old women find babies in cabbage patches," Nastya declared firmly. "It's winter, so there aren't any cabbages. How could they bring Katerina a baby?"

Kolya smirked quietly, amused by her logic.

"Maybe they only bring babies to married people," Nastya added thoughtfully.

Kostya stared at her, trying to make sense of it. "Nastya, that doesn't make sense," he said calmly. "How could Katerina have a baby if she isn't married?"

Nastya, annoyed by his questioning, snapped back. "You don't know anything! Maybe she has a husband, but he's in prison, so now she has a baby."

Kostya frowned, thinking it over. "Is her husband really in prison?" he asked seriously.

Nastya, forgetting her earlier theory, quickly changed her mind. "No, you're right—she doesn't have a husband. But she's been thinking about getting married so much that she ended up with a baby instead."

Kostya nodded, satisfied. "Well, maybe. But you didn't say that before, so how was I supposed to know?"

Kolya finally stepped into the room, smiling. "You two are something else," he said, shaking his head.

"And Perezvon's with you!" Kostya shouted excitedly, snapping his fingers to call the dog.

Kolya looked at them seriously. "Listen, kids, I've got a bit of a problem, and I need your help. Agafya must've broken her leg or something since she hasn't come back yet. I really have to go out. Will you let me?"

The children exchanged anxious glances. Although they adored Kolya, the thought of being left alone made them uneasy.

"You'll behave, right?" Kolya asked. "You won't climb on the cupboards and hurt yourselves? You won't get scared and cry?"

Their cheerful faces turned worried.

"But," Kolya added with a mischievous grin, "if you promise to behave, I'll show you something really cool when I get back—a little cannon that shoots real gunpowder."

The children's faces immediately brightened with excitement.

"Show us the cannon!" Kostya begged eagerly, his eyes sparkling with anticipation.

Krassotkin reached into his satchel and pulled out a little bronze cannon, placing it on the table.

"Ah, you just had to ask! Look, it's on wheels." He rolled the toy along the table. "And it can actually be fired. You can load it with shot and fire it."

"Can it really kill someone?" asked Kostya.

"It can kill anyone, you just have to aim it right," Krassotkin explained as he showed where to put the powder and where to roll in the shot, pointing to a tiny hole like a touch-hole, and told them that it kicked back when it was fired.

The children listened with wide eyes. The fact that the cannon kicked back really excited them.

"Do you have any powder?" Nastya asked.

"Yes," he replied.

"Show us the powder too," she said with a pleading smile.

Krassotkin reached into his satchel again and pulled out a small flask that held a bit of real gunpowder. He also had some shot wrapped in a piece of paper. He uncorked the flask and poured a little powder into his palm.

"You have to be careful there's no fire around, or it could blow up and kill us all," Krassotkin warned them dramatically.

The children stared at the powder, both scared and thrilled. But Kostya seemed more interested in the shot.

"Does the shot burn?" he asked.

"No, it doesn't."

"Can I have a little shot?" he asked, almost begging.

"I'll give you some, but don't show it to your mother until I come back. She'll think it's gunpowder, and she'll get so scared she'll punish you."

"Our mother never punishes us," Nastya quickly pointed out.

"I know, I just said that to make it sound good. But don't ever lie to your mother, except for this one time, until I get back. So, can I go now, kids? You won't be scared and cry while I'm gone?"

"We will cry," Kostya said, already on the verge of tears.

"We'll cry, we'll definitely cry," Nastya added quickly, sounding nervous.

"Oh, children, how dangerous your young years are! I guess there's no choice. I'll have to stay with you, even though time is ticking away. Time is passing, oh dear!"

"Make Perezvon pretend to be dead!" Kostya begged.

"There's no way around it; we'll have to call on Perezvon. Ici, Perezvon." Kolya began giving the dog commands, and Perezvon eagerly performed all his tricks.

Perezvon was a scruffy dog, medium-sized, with a coat that was a sort of grayish-lilac color. He was blind in one eye, and his other ear was torn. The dog whined and jumped, stood on his hind legs, and even lay down on his back with his paws in the air, stiff like he was dead. While the dog performed his last trick, the door opened, and Agafya, Madame Krassotkin's servant, appeared. She was a stout woman of forty, her face marked with smallpox, and she held a bag full of groceries in one hand. Standing in the doorway with the bag raised, she watched the dog's performance. Even though Kolya had been waiting for her to return, he didn't stop the show, and only when Perezvon had played dead for the usual time did Kolya whistle to him. The dog leaped up joyfully, happy to have completed his duty.

"Just imagine, a dog!" Agafya said, shaking her head. "Why are you late, woman?" Kolya asked sternly. "Woman? You little brat!" she shot back.

"Brat?"

"Yes, brat. What's it to you if I'm late? If I am, I have a good reason for it," Agafya muttered as she started working near the stove, but without any real anger. She seemed to enjoy the playful argument with her spirited young master.

"Listen here, you silly woman," Kolya said, standing up from the sofa. "Can you swear by everything you hold dear and something else besides, that you'll keep a close watch on the kids while I'm gone? I'm going out."

"And why should I swear?" Agafya laughed. "I'll look after them just fine without that."

"No, you must swear on your eternal salvation. Otherwise, I won't go."

"Well, then don't go. What do I care? It's cold out anyway—stay home."

"Kids," Kolya said, turning to them, "this woman will stay with you until I come back or until your mother gets home, because she should have been back by now. She'll give you lunch, too. Right, Agafya?"

"That I can do," she agreed.

"Goodbye, kids. I'm leaving with my mind at ease. And you, granny," he added in a low, serious tone as he passed Agafya, "please be kind to their young hearts and don't fill their heads with old wives' tales about Katerina. Ici, Perezvon!"

"Get out of here!" Agafya retorted, now genuinely annoyed. "You ridiculous boy! You deserve a good whipping for talking like that, that's what you need!"

Chapter 3: The Schoolboy

But Kolya didn't hear her. At last, he could go out. As he stepped out of the gate, he glanced around, shrugged his shoulders, and said, "It's freezing." He walked straight down the street and turned right toward the marketplace. When he reached the second-to-last house before the marketplace, he stopped at the gate, pulled a whistle from his pocket, and blew it as loudly as he could, like he was giving a signal. He didn't have to wait more than a minute before a rosy-cheeked boy, about eleven years old and dressed in a warm, neat, and even fashionable coat, came rushing out to meet him. This was Smurov, a boy in the preparatory class, two years behind Kolya Krassotkin, and the son of a well-off official. His parents had apparently forbidden him from hanging out with Krassotkin, who was known for being a bit of a troublemaker, so Smurov had clearly sneaked out on the sly.

If you remember, Smurov was one of the boys who had thrown stones at Ilusha two months earlier. He was also the one who told Alyosha Karamazov about the whole thing.

"I've been waiting for you for the past hour, Krassotkin," Smurov said calmly, and the two boys walked toward the marketplace.

"I got held up," Kolya said. "I was delayed by some things. Are you going to get in trouble for coming along with me?"

"Trouble? I never get in trouble! Do you have Perezvon with you?"

"Yes," Kolya answered. "You're bringing him along?" "Yes."

"Oh! If only it were Zhutchka!"

"That's not possible. Zhutchka doesn't exist anymore. He's lost in the fog of the past."

"Wait—what if we did this?" Smurov suddenly stopped walking. "Ilusha said Zhutchka was a scruffy, grayish dog, kind of like Perezvon. What if we told him Perezvon is Zhutchka? He might believe it."

"Lying is bad, kid, no matter the reason. And just to be clear— you didn't tell anyone I'm coming, did you?"

"Of course not! I know what I'm doing. But Perezvon won't really cheer Ilusha up," Smurov said with a sigh. "You know his dad—the captain, the one they call 'the wisp of tow'? He said he'd bring Ilusha a real mastiff puppy today, one with a black nose. He thinks it'll help, but I'm not so sure."

"How's Ilusha doing?"

"He's doing really bad. I think he's got consumption. He's still aware of things, but his breathing is awful. The other day, he wanted to put on his boots and walk around the room. He tried to stand, but he couldn't. He said, 'I told you, Dad, these boots were no good! I could never walk right in them.' He thinks it's the boots making him weak, but really, it's just his body failing him. I don't think he'll last another week. Herzenstube is taking care of him now. They've got plenty of money again—lots of it."

"They're all crooks."

"Who are?"

"Doctors. All of them. As a group and as individuals. I don't believe in medicine. It's a waste of time. I'm going to figure it all out one day. But what's with all this emotional stuff? Is the whole class visiting him?"

"Not the whole class—just ten of us go every day. It's nothing big."

"What I don't understand is what Alexey Karamazov is doing in all of this. His brother's trial starts tomorrow or the next day for something really serious, yet he has time to get all wrapped up in this sentimental stuff with a bunch of kids."

"There's nothing sentimental about it. You're going to see Ilusha yourself, aren't you?"

"'Making it up with him'? What a ridiculous way to say it. And no one gets to question what I do."

"Ilusha's going to be so happy to see you. He has no idea you're coming. Why wouldn't you visit him all this time?" Smurov asked, suddenly full of emotion.

"My dear boy, that's my business, not yours. I'm going now because I want to, but you all went because Karamazov dragged you along. That's the difference. And who says I'm going to make it up with him at all? What a silly way to put it."

"It wasn't Karamazov who made us go. We went on our own, though we did go with him at first. And there was nothing silly about it. One boy went, then another. His dad was really happy to see us. If Ilusha dies, his father will lose his mind. He knows Ilusha is dying, but he's barely holding it together. If Ilusha dies, he'll either go mad or hang himself. He wasn't all there to begin with, but he's a decent man. We made a mistake, blaming him before. It's that thug who beat him up—that's who's really to blame."

"Karamazov is still a mystery to me," Kolya said thoughtfully. "I could have gotten to know him a long time ago, but I like to keep my pride intact sometimes. Besides, I have a theory about him that I need to work through."

Kolya fell silent, and Smurov stopped talking too. Smurov admired Kolya and would never think of himself as his equal. He was very curious about Kolya's sudden decision to visit Ilusha— it seemed like there must be a deeper reason behind it.

They crossed the marketplace, which was busy with wagons carrying goods from the countryside and many live chickens. Women were selling bread, fabric, and thread from stalls. These Sunday markets were called "fairs" in the town, and there were many such fairs throughout the year.

Perezvon ran around excitedly, sniffing everywhere. He checked out one spot, then another, and greeted other dogs with careful sniffs, following the usual dog rules.

"I like watching stuff like this," Kolya said suddenly. "Have you noticed how dogs always sniff each other when they meet? It's like a law of nature."

"Yeah, it's kind of funny," Smurov said.

"No, it's not funny. You're wrong. There's nothing funny in nature, even if people with their biases think it is. If dogs could think and judge us the way we judge them, they'd probably find us even more ridiculous. There's far more nonsense in the way people act than in animals. That's Rakitin's idea, and it's a brilliant one. I'm a Socialist, Smurov."

"What's a Socialist?" Smurov asked.

"It means everyone's equal, and we all share everything. There's no marriage, and people can follow any religion and laws they like. You're too young to understand it now. Anyway, it's freezing out here."

"Yeah, twelve degrees below zero. My dad checked the thermometer just before I came."

"Have you noticed, Smurov, that in the middle of winter, even when it's fifteen or eighteen degrees below freezing, it doesn't feel as cold as it does now, at the start of winter, when it suddenly drops to twelve degrees? Especially when there's not much snow. It's because people aren't used to it yet. Everything is about habit— everything, even social and political relationships. Habit is what drives everything."

Kolya pointed toward a tall peasant with a friendly face, wearing a long sheepskin coat. The man was standing by his wagon, clapping his hands, which were covered by shapeless leather gloves, trying to warm them. His long, light-colored beard was frozen white with frost.

"That peasant's beard is frozen!" Kolya called out loudly, making sure the man could hear him.

"A lot of people's beards are frozen," the peasant answered calmly, his words deliberate.

"Don't provoke him," Smurov said softly.

"It's fine; he won't mind. He's a good guy. Goodbye, Matvey!"

"Goodbye."

"Is your name Matvey?"

"Yes. Didn't you know?"

"No, I guessed."

"Really? You must be a schoolboy, huh?"

"Yep."

"I bet they whip you at school, don't they?" "Not much—just sometimes."

"Does it hurt?"

"Yeah, it does."

"What a life!" the peasant sighed deeply, as if the weight of the world rested on his heart.

"Goodbye, Matvey."

"Goodbye. You're a good kid, you are." The boys continued on their way.

"That was a nice peasant," Kolya said to Smurov. "I like talking to peasants. I always try to be fair to them."

"Why did you lie and say we get whipped?" Smurov asked. "I had to say that to make him feel better."

"What do you mean?"

"See, Smurov, I don't like being asked the same thing twice. I expect people to understand me the first time. Some things just don't need explaining. In a peasant's mind, schoolboys get whipped—it's what makes them schoolboys. If I told him we weren't whipped, it would've disappointed him. But you don't get that. You have to know how to talk to peasants."

"Just don't mess with them, okay? I don't want you getting in trouble again, like you did with that goose."

"So you're scared?"

"Don't laugh, Kolya. Of course I'm scared. My dad would be furious. He told me I'm not allowed to hang out with you."

"Relax, nothing bad will happen this time. Hey, Natasha!" Kolya shouted at a market woman selling goods from one of the stalls.

"My name's not Natasha! It's Marya," the woman shouted back, looking annoyed.

"I'm glad it's Marya. Goodbye!"

"Oh, you little rascal!" the woman exclaimed. "A brat like you, causing trouble!"

"I'm in a hurry. I can't stay now. Tell me next Sunday," Kolya called, waving his hand at her like she was the one bothering him.

"Tell you what? You're the one who started it, you cheeky monkey! I didn't even say anything!" Marya shouted after him. "You deserve a good whipping, you impudent little scamp!"

The other market women burst into laughter around her. Suddenly, a young man came charging out of the nearby arcade of shops, his face twisted with anger. He wasn't from the town—he had dark curly hair, a pale face pockmarked from smallpox, and wore a long blue coat with a peaked cap. He looked like a clerk for a merchant and was clearly agitated, shaking his fist at Kolya.

"I know you!" he shouted furiously. "I know you!"

Kolya stared at him, trying to place him. He had been in so many arguments and fights on the street that he couldn't remember them all.

"You do?" Kolya asked sarcastically.

"I know you! I know you!" the man repeated, almost foolishly. "Good for you. Anyway, I have to go. Goodbye!"

"You're causing trouble again, aren't you?" the man shouted. "Back at your old tricks! I know it—I know you're up to something!"

"That's none of your business, buddy," Kolya said, stopping to size him up.

"Not my business?"

"Nope, not your business."

"Then whose business is it?"

"It's Trifon Nikititch's business, not yours."

"Who's Trifon Nikititch?" the man asked, blinking in confusion but still seething with anger.

Kolya looked at him seriously.

"Have you been to the Church of the Ascension?" Kolya asked, his voice suddenly stern.

"The Church of the Ascension? No, why would I?" the man answered, caught off guard.

"Do you know Sabaneyev?" Kolya pressed, speaking even more firmly.

"Sabaneyev? No, never heard of him."

"Then you can go to the devil," Kolya snapped, abruptly ending the conversation. He turned sharply and strode away, as if the man wasn't worth any more of his time.

"Wait—hey! What Sabaneyev?" the man shouted after him, still angry and confused. "What did he say?" He turned to the women at the stalls, hoping for some kind of explanation.

The women laughed.

"You never know what that kid's up to," one of them said. "What Sabaneyev is he talking about?" the man asked again, flustered and still waving his fist.

"He must mean the Sabaneyev who used to work for the Kuzmitchovs," one of the women suggested.

The man looked at her wildly.

"The one who worked for the Kuzmitchovs?" another woman added. "But his name wasn't Trifon—it was Kuzma. So it can't be the same person. The boy said Trifon Nikititch."

"His name isn't Trifon, and it's not Sabaneyev either. It's Tchizhov—Alexey Ivanitch Tchizhov," a third woman said gravely, speaking for the first time.

"That's right, it's Tchizhov," another woman confirmed with a nod.

The man stared at them, utterly bewildered.

"But what did he mean? What was he asking about?" he cried in frustration. " 'Do you know Sabaneyev?' he asked. Who on earth is Sabaneyev?"

"You're a fool," one of the women said. "It's not Sabaneyev—it's Tchizhov, Alexey Ivanitch Tchizhov."

"Who's this Tchizhov, then? Tell me if you know!"

"He's that tall, sniveling guy who used to sit in the marketplace during the summer."

"And what does your Tchizhov have to do with me, eh?" the young man asked in frustration.

"How should I know?" another woman chimed in. "You're the one making a fuss about him. If you're yelling about Tchizhov, you must know what you want with him. He talked to you, not us, you fool. Don't you really know him?"

"Know who?" "Tchizhov."

"To hell with Tchizhov—and with you too! I'll teach him a lesson, I swear. He was laughing at me!"

"You, teach Tchizhov a lesson? More likely he'll teach you one! You're a fool, that's what you are."

"Not Tchizhov, not Tchizhov, you nasty, meddling woman! I mean the boy! I'll give him a thrashing! Catch him—he was laughing at me!"

The woman burst into laughter, but by then Kolya was already far ahead, striding away with a victorious air. Smurov walked beside him, glancing back nervously at the group still shouting in the distance. Despite his unease, he felt excited, though part of him worried about getting in trouble while hanging out with Kolya.

"What Sabaneyev were you talking about?" Smurov asked, already guessing Kolya's answer.

"How should I know?" Kolya smirked. "They'll be going on about it all day now. I like stirring up idiots from every part of society. Look at that other fool—see that peasant over there? They say, 'There's no one dumber than a dumb Frenchman,' but a dumb Russian shows it all over his face just as much. Can't you see it on that peasant's face?"

"Leave him alone, Kolya. Let's just keep going."

"Nothing's going to stop me now that I've started. Hey, good morning, peasant!"

A sturdy peasant with a round, simple face and a grizzled beard looked up as he walked by. He seemed a little drunk.

"Good morning—if you're not making fun of me," the peasant replied slowly.

"And what if I am?" Kolya laughed.

"A joke's a joke. Go ahead and laugh if you want. No harm in that," the peasant said with a shrug.

"I'm sorry, brother. I was just joking."

"Well, may God forgive you!"

"Do you forgive me too?"

"I forgive you. Go on now."

"You seem like a clever guy."

"I'm cleverer than you," the peasant replied, his expression serious.

"I doubt that," Kolya said, a little caught off guard.

"It's true, though."

"Maybe you're right."

"I am, brother."

"Goodbye, peasant!"

"Goodbye!"

"There are all kinds of peasants," Kolya said to Smurov after a brief pause. "How was I supposed to know I ran into a smart one? I'm always willing to admit when a peasant is intelligent."

In the distance, the cathedral clock struck half-past eleven. The boys picked up their pace, walking quickly and in near silence until they reached Captain Snegiryov's house. It was a long walk, but they covered it without stopping. Twenty steps from the house, Kolya halted and told Smurov to go on ahead and ask Karamazov to come outside.

"I just need to check things out first," Kolya explained.

"Why make him come out?" Smurov protested. "Just go inside. They'll be really happy to see you. Why stand around talking in the cold?"

"I have my reasons for meeting him outside," Kolya snapped in the bossy tone he liked to use with younger boys. Smurov didn't argue further and ran off to do what Kolya asked.

Chapter 4: The Lost Dog

Kolya leaned against the fence, trying to look confident while waiting for Alyosha to appear. He had wanted to meet him for a long time. The other boys had told him a lot about Alyosha, but Kolya had always acted like he didn't care and even criticized what he'd heard. Secretly, though, he really wanted to get to know Alyosha. There was something about what the boys had said that made Alyosha seem kind and appealing. This moment felt important to Kolya—he had to make a good first impression and show his independence. "Otherwise, he'll just think of me as a thirteen-year-old kid, like the others. What do those boys mean to him, anyway? I'll ask him once I get to know him. Too bad I'm so short. Tuzikov is younger than me, and he's already half a head taller. But at least I have a smart face. I know I'm ugly, but I've got a clever face. I better not be too friendly right away. If I throw myself at him, he might think... Ugh! How awful if he thought that!"

These thoughts ran through Kolya's mind as he tried hard to look self-assured. What bothered him most was not how "ugly" he thought he was but how short he was. At home, he had made a pencil mark on the wall a year ago to measure his height and had been checking against it every two months, hoping to see some progress. But, unfortunately, he was growing very slowly, which sometimes made him feel hopeless. In truth, Kolya wasn't ugly at all. His face was actually quite nice, with fair, pale skin and some freckles. His lively gray eyes had a bold look, and they often lit up with emotion. His cheekbones were a bit high, and his lips were small, very red, and not very full. His nose was small and turned up a little. "A real pug nose, just like a pug's," he would mutter to himself whenever he looked in the mirror. It always annoyed him when he saw it. Sometimes he even doubted that his face looked clever. But it's important to note that he didn't obsess over his appearance all the time. In fact, as upsetting as those moments in front of the mirror could be, Kolya would soon forget about them, throwing himself completely into "real life," as he liked to call it.

Alyosha came out quickly and walked straight toward Kolya, clearly happy to see him. Before Alyosha even reached him, Kolya could tell how pleased he looked. "Is he really that happy to see me?" Kolya wondered, feeling pleased himself. It's worth noting that Alyosha looked very different from the last time we saw him. He no longer wore a cassock but instead had on a well- tailored coat and a soft, round hat. His hair was cut short, and the new look suited him well, making him appear quite handsome. Alyosha's kind face always had a warm, cheerful expression, but his smile had a calm and gentle quality to it.

To Kolya's surprise, Alyosha came outside without an overcoat, clearly having rushed out. He immediately reached out his hand to Kolya.

"Here you are at last! We've all been so eager to see you!"

"There were reasons for the delay, which I'll explain soon. But I'm happy to meet you. I've wanted to for a long time, and I've heard a lot about you," Kolya said, slightly out of breath.

"We were bound to meet eventually. I've heard a lot about you, too, though you took your time getting here."

"So, how are things going?"

"Ilusha is very sick. He's definitely dying."

"That's terrible! You have to admit, Karamazov, that medicine is useless," Kolya said passionately.

"Ilusha has talked about you a lot—so many times, even in his sleep when he's delirious. It's clear that you meant a great deal to him before... well, before the incident with the knife. There's also another reason..." Alyosha paused and glanced at the dog beside Kolya. "Is that your dog?"

"Yes, this is Perezvon."

"Not Zhutchka?" Alyosha asked, his eyes full of sympathy. "Is Zhutchka gone for good?"

"I know you would all like it to be Zhutchka. I've heard all about it," Kolya said with a mysterious smile. "Listen, Karamazov, I'll tell you everything. That's why I came and asked you to come out here—so I could explain the whole thing to you before we go in," he began with excitement. "You see, Karamazov, Ilusha joined the preparatory class last spring. You know what that class is like—it's just a group of little kids. They started teasing Ilusha right away. I'm two grades above them, so I stayed out of it, just watching from a distance. I noticed right away that Ilusha was small and weak, but he wouldn't back down. He fought back against them, and I saw the pride in his eyes. He had a fire in him. I like kids like that. But the other boys teased him even more because of it.

"The worst part was that he was terribly dressed—his pants were too short, and his boots had holes in them. The boys mocked him for that, and I just can't stand bullying like that. So I stepped in and gave the bullies a good beating. And guess what? They still adore me, Karamazov!" Kolya said with a bit of pride. "I've always liked kids. In fact, I have two baby chickens at home right now— that's part of why I was late today. Anyway, after that, the kids stopped picking on Ilusha, and I took him under my wing. I knew he was proud, and he stayed that way, but over time, he became completely devoted to me. It was like I was his hero. He followed all my orders, did whatever I told him to do, and even tried to copy me. Between classes, he'd always come straight to me, and we'd spend time together. We even hung out on Sundays. People like to joke about older boys being friends with younger ones, but that's just prejudice. If I enjoy his company, why shouldn't I be friends with him? I'm teaching him, helping him grow. Why shouldn't I do that if I like him? You're doing the same thing with those younger boys, Karamazov. I can see you want to influence them, help them, and make a difference in their lives. Honestly, hearing about that side of you made me want to meet you even more.

"Now, here's the problem. I noticed that Ilusha was starting to get soft—too sentimental. And I can't stand that kind of weak sentimentality. I've hated it ever since I was a kid. But Ilusha was a contradiction. He was proud, yet completely devoted to me. But out of nowhere, his eyes would flash with anger, and he'd argue with me or get mad. Sometimes, I'd say certain things just to see how he'd react. And I could tell it wasn't the ideas he had a problem with—it was more like he was rebelling against me personally because I wasn't affectionate

335

enough with him. So, to teach him a lesson, I acted even colder the more affectionate he became. I did it on purpose because I wanted to toughen him up, to shape his character and help him grow into a man. I think you get what I mean.

"Then, for three days, I noticed something was really bothering him. It wasn't just my coldness—there was something else, something bigger. I tried to figure out what was going on. Eventually, I found out that he had been hanging out with Smerdyakov, your father's servant, before your father died. Smerdyakov taught Ilusha a cruel trick. He told him to stick a pin inside a piece of bread and throw it to a stray dog—one of those hungry dogs that eat anything without thinking. Then he told Ilusha to watch what happened. So, Ilusha tried it. He threw the bread to Zhutchka—the scruffy dog that everyone's been talking about. The poor dog was always starving because no one ever fed it, even though it barked all the time. Do you like that kind of barking, Karamazov? I can't stand it. Anyway, Zhutchka grabbed the bread, swallowed it, and then started squealing in pain. It spun around in circles and ran off, still squealing, until it disappeared.

"Ilusha told me the whole story himself. He was crying so hard, hugging me, shaking all over. He kept saying, 'He ran away squealing.' The memory of it haunted him. I could see how much guilt he felt. I took it seriously. I knew I needed to teach him a lesson—not just for this, but for other things, too. So I pretended to be angrier than I really was. I told him, 'What you did was disgusting. You're a scoundrel. I won't tell anyone, but I can't be friends with you for a while. I need to think about whether I should stay friends with you or cut you off for good.' I told him I'd send Smurov—that's the boy who came with me today, he always helps me out—with my decision. Ilusha was heartbroken. Honestly, I felt like I'd gone too far, but I thought it was the right thing to do at the time.

"A couple of days later, I sent Smurov to tell him I wouldn't speak to him again. That's how we punish each other in school— by refusing to talk, as if the other person doesn't exist. I only meant to ignore him for a few days, just to see if he felt sorry. Then I planned to forgive him. But guess what happened? When Smurov gave him my message, Ilusha's eyes filled with rage. He told Smurov, 'Tell Krassotkin I'll throw bread with pins to every dog I see—every single one!' So I thought, 'Okay, we need to cool this temper of his.' After that, I started treating him with contempt. Whenever I saw him, I'd either ignore him or give him a sarcastic smile.

"Then that incident with his father happened. You remember that, right? Ilusha was already upset, and the other boys saw that I had cut him off. So they started bullying him again, calling him 'wisp of tow' and picking fights with him. He got into a lot of fights with them, and I feel bad about that now. I think they even gave him a really bad beating once. One day, Ilusha couldn't take it anymore. As the kids were leaving school, he attacked them. I was standing nearby, watching. I swear I wasn't laughing—I actually felt sorry for him. I was just about to step in and help him when he looked at me. I don't know what he thought, but he suddenly pulled out a penknife, ran at me, and stabbed me in the leg. Right here, in my right thigh. I didn't move. Honestly, Karamazov, I can be brave when I need to be. I just stood there, looking at him like, 'Is this how you repay me? Go ahead, stab me again if you want—I'm ready.' But he didn't stab me again. He got scared, dropped the knife, burst into tears, and ran away.

"I didn't tell on him, of course, and I made sure the other boys kept quiet so the teachers wouldn't find out. I didn't even tell my mother until the wound had healed. It was just a scratch anyway. Then I heard that on the same day, Ilusha threw stones at someone and bit your finger. Now you can see how upset he was. I should have gone to visit him when he got sick, but I didn't. I regret that now. I had my reasons, though. Anyway, that's the whole story. But honestly, I think I handled things badly."

"Oh, what a shame!" Alyosha said, his voice full of emotion. "If only I had known what was going on between you two, I would've come to you long ago and asked you to visit him with me. When he had a fever, he kept talking about you in his delirium. I didn't realize how much you meant to him. And you still haven't found the dog? His father and the boys have searched the whole town for it. Since he got sick, I've heard him say three times, with tears in his eyes, 'It's because I killed Zhutchka that I'm sick. God is punishing me.' He can't stop thinking that. I believe that if we found the dog alive, it might even cure him. We've all been counting on you to help us."

"Why did you think I could find the dog?" Kolya asked, his curiosity piqued. "Why me, of all people?"

"There was talk that you were searching for the dog and would bring it once you found it. Smurov mentioned something like that. We've all been trying to convince Ilusha that the dog is still alive, that people have seen it. The boys even brought him a live hare, but he just gave a faint smile and told them to set it free in the fields. So that's what we did. His father just got back and brought him a mastiff puppy, hoping it would cheer him up, but I think it's only made things worse."

"Tell me, Karamazov, what do you think of his father? I know him, but how do you see him—a clown, a fool?"

"Oh no, some people with deep feelings act like fools as a way of coping. Their clownish behavior is a bitter form of irony against people they can't confront honestly, because they've spent years being humiliated and afraid. Believe me, Krassotkin, that kind of clowning can be incredibly tragic. His whole life is wrapped up in Ilusha now. If Ilusha dies, I think he'll either go insane from grief or take his own life. I really believe that, just from how he seems right now."

"I understand, Karamazov. I see that you really understand people," Kolya said with genuine feeling. "And when I saw you with a dog, I thought you might be bringing Zhutchka."

"Just wait, Karamazov, we might still find Zhutchka. But this dog here is Perezvon. I'll take him in now— maybe he'll make Ilusha happier than the mastiff puppy. Hang on a second, Karamazov; you'll see what I mean soon. But look at me, keeping you out here in the cold!" Kolya exclaimed suddenly. "You don't even have an overcoat! I'm such a selfish person. But then again, aren't we all selfish, Karamazov?"

"Don't worry about it. It's cold, but I don't get sick easily. Let's go inside. By the way, what's your full name? I know you're called Kolya, but what else?"

"Nikolay—Nikolay Ivanovitch Krassotkin, or as they put it on official documents, 'Krassotkin, son of Ivan.' " Kolya chuckled for some reason, then suddenly added, "Though I really hate my name, Nikolay."

"Why do you hate it?"

"It's so boring and ordinary."

"You're thirteen, right?" Alyosha asked.

"No, fourteen—or almost. I'll be fourteen in two weeks. I'll admit something to you, Karamazov, since this is our first real conversation. I hate it when people ask how old I am. And there's this awful rumor going around about me—that I played robbers with the younger boys last week. It's true that I played with them, but saying I did it for fun is just slander. I'm sure you've heard the story. The real reason I played with them was because they couldn't come up with anything to do on their own. But people always twist things. This town is full of gossip, I can tell you."

"But even if you did play for fun, what's wrong with that?"

"Come on, Karamazov! For fun? Do you play horse like a little kid?"

"Look at it this way," Alyosha said with a smile. "Grown-ups go to the theater to watch plays about heroes, robbers, or battles. Isn't that the same thing, just in a different form? When young people play soldiers or robbers, it's like an early form of art. These games come from the natural creativity young people have. And sometimes, their games are even better than theater because they get to act things out themselves instead of just watching actors. It's only natural."

"Is that what you think? Is that really your view?" Kolya looked at Alyosha intently. "That's an interesting way to look at it. When I get home, I'll think more about that. To be honest, I hoped I could learn something from you. That's why I came—to learn from you, Karamazov," Kolya said, his voice filled with sudden emotion.

"And I hope to learn from you, too," Alyosha replied, smiling warmly and shaking Kolya's hand.

Kolya felt a deep sense of satisfaction. What pleased him the most was that Alyosha treated him as an equal, speaking to him like a grown-up.

"I've got something to show you, Karamazov. It's like a little performance," Kolya said with a nervous laugh. "That's part of why I came."

"Let's stop by the house on the left first. All the boys leave their coats in there—it's too small and warm inside the other room for everyone to keep their coats on."

"Oh, I'm only going in for a minute. I'll keep my coat on. Perezvon will wait here in the hallway and play dead. Ici, Perezvon, lie down and be dead! Look—see how perfectly dead he is?" Kolya laughed. "I'll go in first and scout things out. When the time's right, I'll whistle, and you'll see—he'll come running in like crazy. But Smurov has to make sure the door is open at just the right moment. I'll take care of everything—you'll see."

Chapter 5: By Ilusha's Bedside

The room where Captain Snegiryov's family lived was already familiar to the reader. At that moment, it was small and crowded with visitors. Several boys were sitting with Ilusha, and even though they were all, like Smurov, ready to deny that Alyosha was the one who had brought them there and helped them make peace with Ilusha, that was indeed the truth. Alyosha had skillfully led them to Ilusha one by one, without showing any "sheepish sentimentality," making it seem casual and unplanned. This was a great comfort to Ilusha during his illness. He was deeply moved by the almost tender affection and sympathy shown to him by the boys, who had once been his enemies. The only one missing was Krassotkin, and his absence weighed heavily on Ilusha's heart. Perhaps the most painful of all his bitter memories was the time he had stabbed Krassotkin, who had once been his friend and protector. Clever little Smurov, the first to make peace with Ilusha, believed that was the case. But when Smurov hinted to Krassotkin that Alyosha wanted to visit him to discuss something, Krassotkin cut him off, telling Smurov to let "Karamazov" know that he knew best what to do, didn't need anyone's advice, and that if he decided to visit Ilusha, he would do so on his own terms for his own reasons.

This happened two weeks before that Sunday. That's why Alyosha hadn't gone to see him as he had intended. But while waiting, he sent Smurov to him twice more. Each time, Krassotkin met him with a short, impatient refusal, telling Alyosha not to bother him again and warning that if he came himself, Krassotkin wouldn't visit Ilusha at all. Even up to the very last day, Smurov didn't know that Kolya planned to visit Ilusha that morning. Only the evening before, as he said goodbye to Smurov, Kolya abruptly told him to wait for him at home the next morning because he would take him to the Snegiryovs'. However, he warned Smurov not to say a word about it, as he wanted to show up casually. Smurov obeyed. Smurov's belief that Kolya would bring back the lost dog was based on a comment Kolya had made about how "they must be idiots if they couldn't find the dog, assuming it was alive." When Smurov timidly hinted about the dog, Krassotkin flew into a rage. "I'm not stupid enough to go searching the town for other people's dogs when I've got one of my own! And how can you think a dog could survive after swallowing a pin? That's just sheepish sentimentality!"

For the last two weeks, Ilusha hadn't left his little bed beneath the icons in the corner of the room. He hadn't been to school since the day he met Alyosha and bit his finger. He fell ill that very same day, though for a month afterward, he was sometimes able to get up and walk around the room and hallway. But lately, he had grown so weak that he couldn't move without his father's help. His father was deeply worried about him. He even stopped drinking and was nearly out of his mind with fear that his son might die. Often, after helping

Ilusha walk around the room and putting him back in bed, he would rush to a dark corner in the hallway, press his head against the wall, and weep violently, stifling his sobs so Ilusha wouldn't hear.

When he returned to the room, he usually tried to entertain and comfort his precious boy, telling him funny stories or mimicking comic people he had met. He even imitated the howls and cries of animals. But Ilusha couldn't stand to see his father acting foolish. Though the boy tried not to show it, it broke his heart to see his father becoming an object of ridicule, and he was constantly haunted by the memory of the "wisp of tow" and that "terrible day."

Nina, Ilusha's gentle, crippled sister, also disliked her father's clownish behavior (Varvara had gone to Petersburg some time ago to study at the university). But their half-imbecile mother found it amusing and laughed heartily whenever her husband started acting silly. It was the only thing that could cheer her up; the rest of the time, she complained that everyone had forgotten her, that no one respected her anymore, and that she was being slighted. But in recent days, she had changed. She started watching Ilusha in his bed with a thoughtful expression. She was quieter and more reserved, and when she cried, it was quietly, so no one could hear. The captain noticed this change with sad bewilderment. At first, the boys' visits only annoyed her, but over time, their cheerful chatter and stories began to entertain her, and eventually, she became fond of them. If the boys had stopped coming, she would have been lonely without them. She laughed and clapped her hands when they told stories or played games. She even called a few of them over to kiss them. She especially liked Smurov.

As for the captain, having the children around to cheer up Ilusha filled him with joy from the start. He even began to hope that the boys' company would lift Ilusha's spirits and help him recover. Despite his fears for Ilusha, he hadn't, until recently, doubted for a moment that his son would ultimately recover.

He treated the boys with great respect and took care of them as best as he could, even allowing them to ride on his back like a horse. However, Ilusha didn't like this game, so it was stopped. The captain began buying small treats for the boys, like gingerbread and nuts, and he served them tea and made sandwiches for them. It should be noted that he had plenty of money during this time. As Alyosha had predicted, he had taken the two hundred rubles from Katerina Ivanovna. After learning more about the family's situation and Ilusha's illness, Katerina Ivanovna visited them herself, got to know the family, and managed to win over the half-imbecile mother. Since then, she had generously helped them, and the captain, terrified by the thought that his son might be dying, swallowed his pride and accepted her assistance.

During this time, Doctor Herzenstube, who had been called in by Katerina Ivanovna, visited every other day, though his visits did little good, and he dosed the sick boy relentlessly. However, that Sunday morning, a new doctor was expected, one who had come from Moscow with a great reputation. Katerina Ivanovna had sent for him at great expense, though not specifically for Ilusha, but for another reason, which will be explained later. Since the doctor was already there, she asked him to see Ilusha as well, and the captain had been told to expect him. He had no idea that Kolya Krassotkin would be coming, even though he had longed for a visit from the boy, knowing how much Ilusha missed him.

At the moment Kolya Krassotkin opened the door and entered the room, the captain and the boys were gathered around Ilusha's bed, looking at a tiny mastiff puppy. The puppy had been born just the day before, though the captain had arranged for it a week ago, hoping it would cheer up Ilusha, who was still heartbroken over the loss of Zhutchka, the dog he believed to be dead. Ilusha had been told three days earlier that he would be given a special puppy—not just any puppy, but a pedigree mastiff, which was supposed to make him feel better. Trying to be polite, Ilusha pretended to be pleased with the gift. But both his father and the boys could tell that the puppy only reminded him of the dog he had lost.

The puppy lay quietly beside Ilusha, moving weakly, while Ilusha stroked it gently with his thin, pale hand. It was clear that he liked the little dog, but it wasn't Zhutchka. If he could have both Zhutchka and the puppy, then he would have been truly happy.

"Krassotkin!" one of the boys shouted suddenly, being the first to notice him enter.

Kolya's arrival caused a stir among the boys, and they quickly moved aside to give him space by Ilusha's bed. The captain rushed over to greet him.

"Please, come in! You're very welcome!" the captain said eagerly. "Ilusha, Mr. Krassotkin has come to see you!"

Kolya shook hands with the captain briefly, then, showing his understanding of proper manners, he first turned to the captain's wife, who was sitting in her chair. She was in a bad mood, grumbling that the boys were blocking her view of Ilusha's bed and the new puppy. With great politeness, Kolya gave her a small bow, scraping his foot, then made a similar bow to Nina, as she was the only other lady in the room. His respectful behavior left a good impression on the captain's wife, who was not in her right mind.

"There, you can tell right away that this young man has been raised properly," she exclaimed, throwing up her hands. "Unlike the others—they just pile in one after the other!"

"What do you mean, mama, 'one on top of another'?" the captain asked gently, though he was a bit concerned by her words.

"They come in riding on each other's shoulders, prancing into a decent family's home like that! Strange sort of visitors!"

"But who came in like that, mama?"

"Why, that boy rode in on the back of the other, and the other on someone else's!"

By this time, Kolya was already standing by Ilusha's bedside. Ilusha turned even paler when he saw him. He tried to raise himself up and stared hard at Kolya. It had been two months since Kolya had seen Ilusha, and he was shocked by how much his friend had changed. He never imagined Ilusha would look so thin and pale, with large, feverish eyes and fragile hands. He could hear the boy's labored breathing and noticed how dry his lips were. Feeling overwhelmed, Kolya stepped closer, held out his hand, and said softly, "Well, old man... how are you?" But his voice faltered, and he struggled to keep his composure. The corners of his mouth twitched, and he couldn't manage the relaxed tone he had intended.

Ilusha gave him a weak, sorrowful smile, still unable to speak. Moved by emotion, Kolya reached out and gently brushed Ilusha's hair with his hand.

"Never mind," Kolya whispered, trying to comfort him, though he wasn't entirely sure why he said it. They sat in silence for a moment.

"So, you've got a new puppy?" Kolya said suddenly, trying to sound casual.

"Y-yes," Ilusha whispered in reply, gasping for air.

"A black nose—that means it'll be a fierce dog, good for guarding the house," Kolya said with forced seriousness, pretending to care only about the puppy's features. But inside, he was struggling to hold back tears. No matter how hard he tried, he could feel his emotions getting the best of him. "When it grows up, you'll probably need to keep it chained up," he added.

"It'll be huge!" one of the boys exclaimed.

"Of course it will," another boy chimed in. "A mastiff! A big one!"

"It'll be as big as a calf!" shouted several boys at once.

"Yes, as big as a real calf," the captain added enthusiastically. "I picked this breed on purpose. It's one of the fiercest kinds. Its parents are enormous and fierce—they stand this high from the floor." He raised his hand to demonstrate. "Come, sit here by Ilusha's bed, or take a seat on the bench. You're welcome here— we've been hoping you'd come for a long time. Did you come with Alexey Fyodorovitch?"

Kolya sat down on the edge of Ilusha's bed, near the boy's feet. Although he had probably planned what he wanted to say on his way over, he suddenly found himself at a loss for words.

"No... I came with Perezvon. I have a dog now—his name is Perezvon. It's a Slavonic name. He's waiting outside. If I whistle, he'll come running in. I brought him here to show you." Then, as if struck by a sudden thought, Kolya asked, "Do you remember Zhutchka, old man?"

Ilusha's face trembled, and he looked at Kolya with a pained expression. Alyosha, standing by the door, frowned and made a quick gesture to Kolya, signaling him not to mention Zhutchka. But Kolya either didn't notice or chose to ignore him.

"Where... is Zhutchka?" Ilusha asked in a broken voice.

"Oh, well, my boy, your Zhutchka is lost and gone," Kolya said lightly.

Ilusha didn't say anything, but his gaze remained fixed on Kolya. Alyosha tried again to catch Kolya's eye, silently begging him to stop, but Kolya turned away, pretending not to see him.

"It must have run off and died somewhere. A dog wouldn't survive after eating something like that," Kolya said, his voice calm but strained. "But I've got a dog, Perezvon... A Slavonic name. I brought him here just for you."

"I don't want him," Ilusha whispered suddenly.

"No, no, you really need to see him. He'll cheer you up. I brought him on purpose. He's a shaggy dog, just like Zhutchka. Please, madam, may I call him in?" Kolya asked Madame Snegiryov, his voice unusually excited.

"I don't want him! I don't want him!" Ilusha cried, his voice breaking with sorrow. His eyes shone with a look of deep reproach.

"You'd better wait," the captain murmured, rising from the chest where he had been sitting. "Another time, perhaps..." But Kolya couldn't be stopped.

"Open the door!" he called urgently to Smurov. As soon as the door was open, Kolya blew his whistle, and Perezvon came bounding into the room.

"Jump, Perezvon! Beg! Beg!" Kolya shouted, leaping to his feet. The dog stood up on its hind legs beside Ilusha's bed, just as Kolya had trained it.

What happened next took everyone by surprise. Ilusha jolted forward, staring at the dog with wide, trembling eyes, as if holding his breath.

"It's... Zhutchka!" Ilusha suddenly cried out, his voice filled with both joy and pain.

"And who did you think it was?" Kolya shouted back, his voice ringing with excitement. He bent down, scooped up Perezvon, and held the dog out to Ilusha, his face beaming with happiness.

"Look, old man, see? He's blind in one eye, and his left ear is torn—just like you described to me. That's how I knew it was him. I found him right away. He didn't belong to anyone!" Kolya explained eagerly, turning from the captain to his wife, to Alyosha, and then back to Ilusha. "He used to hang out in the Fedotovs' backyard, but they didn't feed him. He was just a stray dog that ran away from a village... but I found him. And see, old man? There's no way he could have swallowed what you gave him. If he had, he would've died. He must have spit it out, which is why he's still alive. You didn't actually see him swallow it, right? The pin must have pricked his tongue—that's why he squealed. He ran off squealing, and you thought he'd swallowed it. But it was just because the inside of a dog's mouth is so sensitive—more sensitive than ours!" Kolya exclaimed, his face glowing with excitement.

Ilusha stared at him, pale as a sheet, his mouth slightly open, with his large eyes wide and fixed on Kolya. If Kolya had known how dangerous this moment might be for Ilusha's health, he never would have played such a trick. But Kolya had no idea. Alyosha, however, seemed to sense the risk. The captain, on the other hand, was as joyful as a child.

"Zhutchka! It's Zhutchka!" the captain cried out in delight. "Ilusha, look—it's Zhutchka! Your Zhutchka!" He turned to his wife, almost in tears. "Mamma, look—it's Zhutchka!"

"I never guessed!" Smurov exclaimed regretfully. "Bravo,

Krassotkin! I knew he'd find the dog, and here he is!" "Here he is!" another boy echoed happily. "Krassotkin is the best!" one boy shouted.

"He's the best! The best!" the other boys cheered, clapping their hands.

"Wait, wait," Kolya shouted above the noise. "Let me tell you how it all happened—that's the most important part! I found him and took him home right away. I hid him there and didn't show him to anyone until today. Only Smurov knew about him for the past two weeks, but I told him the dog's name was Perezvon, so he wouldn't guess. And during that time, I taught him a bunch of tricks! You wouldn't believe how many tricks he knows now. I wanted to bring you a well-trained dog, old man, so you'd see how amazing your Zhutchka is now!"

"Do you have any meat? I'll show you a trick that will make you laugh until it hurts!" Kolya asked eagerly.

The captain immediately ran across the hall to the landlady, where their cooking was done. Meanwhile, Kolya, not wanting to waste a second, shouted to Perezvon, "Dead!" The dog instantly rolled over onto his back, his four paws sticking up in the air. The boys burst into laughter. Ilusha gave a weak, pained smile, but it was his mother who seemed most delighted by the dog's performance. She laughed heartily, snapping her fingers and calling out, "Perezvon! Perezvon!"

"He won't get up, no matter what!" Kolya said triumphantly. "You can yell all you want, and he'll just stay there. But if I call him, he'll jump up right away. Ici, Perezvon!" Kolya called. The dog leaped to his feet, barking joyfully and wagging his tail.

The captain came rushing back, carrying a piece of cooked beef. "Is it hot?" Kolya asked, taking the meat with a businesslike air.

"Dogs don't like hot food. No, it's fine. Look, everyone! Look, Ilusha—why aren't you watching? I brought him for you!"

Kolya's next trick involved balancing the piece of meat on the dog's nose. Perezvon had to stay perfectly still, with the meat balanced on his nose, until Kolya gave the signal. Even if it took half an hour, the dog wasn't allowed to move a muscle. Kolya only made Perezvon wait a moment before shouting, "Paid for!" In an instant, the dog snapped the meat from his nose and devoured it. The boys cheered in amazement.

"Did you really stay away all this time just to train the dog?" Alyosha asked, a hint of gentle reproach in his voice.

"Yes!" Kolya answered cheerfully. "I wanted to show him to you at his best."

"Perezvon! Perezvon!" Ilusha called suddenly, snapping his thin fingers and beckoning to the dog.

"What is it? Let him up on the bed! Ici, Perezvon!" Kolya slapped the bed, and the dog immediately jumped up beside Ilusha. The boy threw his arms around Perezvon's head, and the dog licked his cheek eagerly. Ilusha nestled close, stretching out in the bed and burying his face in the dog's shaggy fur.

"Dear, dear!" the captain kept saying, overcome with emotion. Kolya sat back down on the edge of the bed.

"Ilusha, I've got another surprise for you. Remember that little cannon I told you about? You said you really wanted to see it. Well, I brought it!" Kolya pulled a small bronze cannon from his satchel, his hands trembling with excitement. He was so happy that he couldn't wait for the excitement over Perezvon to settle. "You're all happy now, so here's something to make you even happier!"

Kolya beamed with joy as he showed the cannon to everyone. "I've been wanting to give this to you for a long time, old man. It used to belong to Morozov—he got it from his brother, but it wasn't much use to him. I traded a book from my father's bookshelf for it. It was an old book—A Kinsman of Mahomet or Salutary Folly—a scandalous thing that was published in Moscow a hundred years ago, before censorship existed. Morozov liked stuff like that, so he was happy to trade with me."

Kolya held the little bronze cannon up for everyone to admire. Ilusha sat up slightly, one arm still wrapped around the dog, and gazed at the toy with shining eyes. The excitement in the room grew even more when Kolya announced that he had gunpowder and they could fire the cannon right away—if the ladies didn't mind, of course.

"Let me see it!" Ilusha's mother asked eagerly, holding out her hands. Kolya handed her the cannon, and she rolled it back and forth on her lap, delighted. Without fully understanding what she had agreed to, she gave them permission to fire it.

Kolya showed the boys the powder and the small shot. The captain, as a former military man, took charge of loading the cannon. He put a tiny amount of powder inside and suggested saving the shot for another time. They set the cannon on the floor, aiming it at an empty part of the room. Kolya added three grains of powder to the touch hole and struck a match.

There was a loud explosion. Ilusha's mother jumped in surprise but quickly burst out laughing. The boys were thrilled, cheering in triumph. But no one was more pleased than the captain, who couldn't take his eyes off Ilusha.

Kolya picked up the cannon and placed it in Ilusha's hands, along with the powder and shot. "This is for you, old man! I've been saving it just for you."

"Give it to me! No, give it to me!" Ilusha's mother suddenly cried out, her voice filled with childlike desperation. Her face showed a pitiful expression, as if she feared she might not get the toy.

Kolya hesitated, caught off guard by her sudden request. The captain fidgeted nervously.

"Mamma, it's yours—of course it's yours," he said gently. "But it's a gift for Ilusha. He'll let you play with it anytime. It'll belong to both of you—both of you."

"No! I don't want to share it! I want it all for myself, not Ilusha's!" she insisted, her voice trembling as if she were about to cry.

"Take it, mother, here, keep it!" Ilusha cried. "Krassotkin, may I give it to my mother?" He looked at Kolya with a pleading expression, as if worried Kolya might be offended if he gave the gift away.

"Of course you can," Kolya replied warmly. He took the cannon from Ilusha and handed it directly to Ilusha's mother with a polite bow. Overwhelmed with emotion, she began to cry.

"Ilusha, my darling! You're the one who really loves his mother!" she said tenderly, wheeling the cannon back and forth on her lap with childlike delight.

"Mamma, let me kiss your hand," the captain exclaimed, rushing over to her and pressing his lips to her hand.

"And I've never met such a delightful young man as this fine boy," Ilusha's mother said gratefully, pointing at Kolya.

"And I'll bring you all the powder you want, Ilusha. We've started making it ourselves now. Borovikov figured out the recipe—twenty-four parts saltpeter, ten parts sulfur, and six parts birchwood charcoal. You mix it all with water to make a paste, and then rub it through a tammy sieve—that's how it's done."

"Smurov told me about your powder," Ilusha said with interest, "but father says it's not real gunpowder."

"Not real?" Kolya blushed. "It burns, doesn't it? I don't know, of course..."

"No, no, I didn't mean it like that," the captain said quickly, looking guilty. "I only meant that real powder is usually made a bit differently. But that doesn't matter—it works just as well."

"I wouldn't know—you're the expert," Kolya admitted. "We tried some in a pomatum jar. It burned perfectly, leaving just a tiny bit of ash. But that was just the paste—if you sieve it, it's even better. But you know more about it than I do... Oh, did you hear what happened to Bulkin? His father whipped him because of our powder," Kolya said, turning to Ilusha.

"Yes, I heard," Ilusha replied, listening eagerly.

"We'd made a whole bottle of it, and Bulkin kept it hidden under his bed. His father found it, said it might explode, and gave him a beating on the spot. He even wanted to report me to the schoolmasters. Now Bulkin isn't allowed to hang out with me anymore. No one is, really. Even Smurov isn't supposed to spend time with me. I've got a bad reputation with everyone—they all say I'm 'a troublemaker,' " Kolya added with a scornful smile. "And it all started with that incident on the railway."

"Oh, yes, we heard about your stunt," the captain exclaimed. "How could you lie there on the tracks like that? Weren't you scared at all, lying under the train?" The captain was practically fawning over Kolya.

"Not really," Kolya answered carelessly. "But the thing that really ruined my reputation was that stupid goose," he said, turning to Ilusha. Despite his nonchalant tone, it was clear he was struggling to stay composed.

"I heard about the goose!" Ilusha said, lighting up with a smile. "They told me the story, but I didn't quite understand. Did they really take you to court over it?"

"It was such a ridiculous little thing, and they blew it way out of proportion, like they always do," Kolya began, pretending not to care. "I was walking through the marketplace one day, just when some geese were being brought in. I stopped to watch them, and this guy, who works as an errand boy for Plotnikov now, said to me, 'What are you staring at the geese for?' He was this clueless guy with a round face—must've been twenty or so. You know, I always take the side of the peasants. I like talking with them. Honestly, we've fallen behind the peasants—that's a fact. Are you laughing, Karamazov?" Kolya asked suspiciously.

"No, of course not. I'm listening," Alyosha answered kindly, putting Kolya at ease.

"Well, here's my theory, Karamazov," Kolya continued, brightening up. "I believe in the people. I like to give them credit where it's due. But I'm not in favor of spoiling them—that's essential. Anyway, about the goose. So I said to this fool, 'I'm wondering what the goose is thinking about.' He gave me a dumb look and asked, 'What does a goose think about?' So I pointed to a cart nearby. There was a sack of oats on it, and some oats were spilling out. The goose had stuck its neck under the wheel to eat them. 'See that?' I asked him. 'Now, if the cart moves forward, will it break the goose's neck?'

"'Of course it will,' he said, grinning like an idiot. "So I said, 'Well, let's try it, then.'

"And he agreed! It didn't take us long to set things up. He held the horse's bridle while I directed the goose. The cart owner wasn't paying attention—he was chatting with someone. The goose stuck its head right under the wheel to eat the oats. I gave the boy a wink, and he tugged the bridle. Crack—the goose's neck snapped in two.

"Just our luck, the peasants saw the whole thing. They kicked up a huge fuss. 'You did it on purpose!' they shouted. 'No, we didn't!' I said. 'Yes, you did!' And before we knew it, they were dragging us off to the justice of the peace.

"They brought the goose along with us, too. The boy was terrified— he started crying like a little kid. The farmer kept yelling that you could kill as many geese as you liked that way. There were witnesses, of course. The justice settled it right away—the farmer was to be paid a ruble for the goose, and the boy got to keep the goose. The justice warned him not to pull any more stunts like that. And the poor boy just kept sobbing, 'It wasn't me! He made me do it!' pointing at me.

"I calmly told the justice that I hadn't 'made' anyone do anything—I'd only raised a hypothetical question. The justice smiled at that, but then he immediately frowned, embarrassed that he had found it funny. 'I ought to report you to your teachers,' he said, 'so you won't waste your time on silly ideas like that instead of studying.' He didn't actually report me, though—it was just a joke. But somehow, word got out, and it reached the schoolmasters. News travels fast, you know! The classical studies teacher, Kolbasnikov, was especially outraged. But Dardanelov helped me out of the mess again. Kolbasnikov's been grumpy with everyone ever since—like an old mule.

"By the way, did you know he just got married? He got a dowry of a thousand rubles, but his bride is supposed to be a real terror— ugly as can be." Kolya smirked. "The boys in the third class even wrote an epigram about it..."

"Astounding news has reached the class, Kolbasnikov has been an ass."

And so on, it's awfully funny—I'll bring it to you later," Kolya said with a smirk. "I don't have anything against Dardanelov, though. He's a smart guy, no doubt about it. I respect people like him, and not just because he stood up for me."

"But you totally put him in his place about the founders of Troy!" Smurov chimed in suddenly, beaming with pride. He was especially pleased by the goose story and eager to share this moment.

"Did you really take him down?" the captain asked, clearly trying to flatter Kolya. "On the topic of who founded Troy? We heard about it—Ilusha told me at the time."

"He knows everything, father, more than any of us!" Ilusha added, looking at Kolya with admiration. "He pretends like it's nothing, but he's top in every subject."

Ilusha gazed at Kolya with pure happiness.

"Oh, that Troy stuff is nonsense, really. A trivial matter. I don't consider it an important question," Kolya said, trying to sound humble but with a certain air of superiority. By now, he had regained his composure, though he still felt uneasy. He realized that in his excitement, he had talked about the goose incident with too little restraint. And Alyosha's quiet seriousness throughout the whole conversation made Kolya worry that perhaps Alyosha thought he was just showing off. The thought of Alyosha silently judging him began to gnaw at Kolya.

"I consider it a trivial matter," Kolya repeated firmly, as if trying to convince himself.

"I know who founded Troy," a quiet voice suddenly piped up, surprising everyone. It was a shy boy named Kartashov, about eleven years old, sitting near the door. Kolya looked at him with a mix of disbelief and slight irritation.

The truth was that the identity of Troy's founders had been a mystery to the entire class, only discoverable by reading Smaragdov, a book that only Kolya owned. Some time ago, when Kolya wasn't looking, Kartashov had sneaked a glance at the book and found the passage about Troy's founders. For weeks, he had been itching to reveal that he knew the answer but had been too scared of how Kolya might react. Finally, he couldn't hold back any longer.

"Well, who founded it?" Kolya asked with a haughty tone, narrowing his eyes. He could see from Kartashov's face that the boy really did know the answer, and Kolya had already decided how to handle the situation.

"Troy was founded by Teucer, Dardanus, Ilius, and Tros," Kartashov blurted out, immediately blushing deeply, so much that it was painful to watch. The other boys stared at him in shock for a full minute before all their eyes turned to Kolya, waiting to see his reaction. Kolya scanned the boy with disdainful calm.

"In what sense did they found it?" Kolya finally asked, condescendingly. "And what does it even mean to 'found' a city or a state? Do you think they each laid a brick?"

The boys burst into laughter. Kartashov's face turned from pink to crimson, and he went silent, on the verge of tears. Kolya let him stew in the discomfort for a moment.

"Before you talk about something as significant as the founding of a city, you need to understand what that means," Kolya lectured him in a stern voice. "But I don't give much importance to these old legends anyway, and I don't think much of universal history in general," he added carelessly, now addressing the whole group.

"Universal history?" the captain asked, looking slightly alarmed.

"Yes, universal history—it's just the study of mankind's endless foolishness, and nothing more. The only subjects worth respecting are mathematics and natural science," Kolya declared, clearly showing off as he stole a glance at Alyosha. Alyosha's was the only opinion that really mattered to him. But Alyosha remained silent, serious as ever. Kolya was growing increasingly irritated, thinking that perhaps Alyosha's silence was due to contempt.

"And the classical languages, too—they're pure madness, nothing else. You don't agree with me, Karamazov?" Kolya asked, now directly addressing Alyosha.

"I don't," Alyosha replied, with a faint smile.

"Studying the classics," Kolya continued, ignoring the dissent, "is just a method of control, a way to keep students busy with nonsense. That's the only reason Latin and Greek were introduced in schools—to dull the mind. Education was already boring, so what did they do to make it even more boring? They added Greek and Latin. That's my opinion, and I don't think I'll ever change it," Kolya finished abruptly, his face flushed with excitement.

"That's true," Smurov chimed in suddenly, his voice ringing with conviction. He had been listening intently.

"And yet, he's first in Latin," one of the boys said suddenly, pointing out the irony.

"Yes, father, he says that, but he's top in Latin," Ilusha echoed.

"What of it?" Kolya felt the need to defend himself, though the praise was sweet to him. "I'm working hard at Latin because I have to, because I promised my mother I would pass my exams. I believe that whatever you do, you should do it well. But in my heart, I have nothing but contempt for the classics and all the nonsense that goes with them. You don't agree, Karamazov?"

"Why call it nonsense?" Alyosha asked with another gentle smile.

"Well, all the classical authors have been translated into every language. So, the point isn't to study the classics themselves; it's just a method to dull our minds. What else could it be but a fraud?"

"Who taught you all this?" Alyosha asked, genuinely surprised for the first time.

"For starters, I'm perfectly capable of thinking for myself without being taught. Besides, our teacher, Kolbasnikov, said the same thing to the whole third class about the classics being translated."

"The doctor's here!" Nina suddenly called out, breaking her silence.

A carriage belonging to Madame Hohlakov pulled up at the gate. The captain, who had been waiting for the doctor all morning, rushed out to greet him. "Mamma" composed herself and assumed a dignified posture. Alyosha went over to Ilusha and began adjusting his pillows. Nina, sitting in her invalid chair, anxiously watched him tidy the bed. The boys hurriedly said their goodbyes, with some promising to return in the evening. Kolya called for Perezvon, and the dog jumped off the bed.

"I'm not leaving, I'm not leaving," Kolya said quickly to Ilusha. "I'll wait in the hallway and come back once the doctor is done. I'll bring Perezvon back too."

At that moment, the doctor arrived—a man with an important air, sporting long, dark whiskers and a clean-shaven chin, dressed in a heavy bearskin coat. As he stepped across the threshold, he paused, clearly taken aback, perhaps thinking he had entered the wrong house. "What's this? Where am I?" he muttered, not bothering to remove his coat or his peaked sealskin cap. The crowded, shabby room, with laundry hanging on a line in the corner, seemed to confuse him. The captain, bending nearly double, bowed repeatedly before him.

"It's here, sir, right here, sir," the captain muttered obsequiously. "You're in the right place. This is where you were coming…"

"Sne-gi-ryov?" the doctor bellowed pompously. "Mr. Snegiryov— is that you?"

"That's me, sir!" the captain replied eagerly.

"Ah!" The doctor surveyed the room with a look of distaste, then threw off his coat, revealing a grand decoration hanging around his neck. The captain caught the fur coat mid-air, and the doctor removed his cap.

"Where is the patient?" he asked with a tone of authority.

Chapter 6 – Precocity

"What do you think the doctor will say to him?" Kolya asked quickly. "He's got a pretty awful face, hasn't he? I really can't stand anything to do with medicine."

"Ilusha is dying. I'm certain of it," Alyosha answered softly, his voice filled with sorrow.

"Doctors are frauds! Medicine's a scam!" Kolya muttered angrily. Then, as if shifting gears, he added, "I'm glad to have met you, Karamazov. I've wanted to for a long time. It's just a shame we're meeting under such sad circumstances."

Kolya felt an urge to say something more heartfelt, but he hesitated, feeling awkward. Alyosha noticed his discomfort, smiled warmly, and gave his hand a reassuring squeeze.

"I've had a lot of respect for you for quite a while," Kolya mumbled, still unsure of himself. "I've heard people call you a mystic—because of the monastery and all that. But honestly, that didn't put me off. You'll grow out of it eventually. It always happens with people like you once they get in touch with real life."

"What do you mean by mystic? And what exactly do you think I need to be cured of?" Alyosha asked, puzzled.

"Oh, you know, the whole God thing," Kolya answered vaguely.

"Wait, do you not believe in God?" Alyosha asked, looking at him with curiosity.

"I don't have anything against God," Kolya said, starting to blush. "God is just a hypothesis, that's all. But... I think He's necessary— for order in the universe and all that. And if He didn't exist, we'd probably have to invent Him." Kolya's face flushed even deeper. Suddenly, he felt an uncomfortable suspicion that Alyosha might think he was trying to act smarter than he really was. "I don't care if he thinks I'm showing off," Kolya thought angrily, though the idea bothered him more than he liked to admit.

"I can't stand getting into these kinds of discussions," Kolya said abruptly, trying to close the subject. "But still, isn't it possible for someone who doesn't believe in God to love humanity? I mean, Voltaire didn't believe in God, and he cared about humanity, didn't he?" Kolya caught himself again and cursed inwardly: "Why do I keep going on like this?"

"Actually, Voltaire did believe in God—though not very seriously—and I don't think he had much love for humanity either," Alyosha replied quietly. His gentle, natural tone made it seem like he was speaking to an equal, or even someone older than himself. Kolya was struck by the way Alyosha gave his opinion so modestly, as if leaving the matter open for Kolya to decide.

"Have you read Voltaire?" Alyosha asked.

"Not really," Kolya admitted. "But I did read Candide—in an old Russian translation that was pretty bad and ridiculous." He winced again. "There I go, talking too much again!"

"And did you understand it?" Alyosha asked.

"Of course I did!" Kolya answered, a bit defensively. "Why wouldn't I? Sure, it's a bit nasty in parts, but I know it's a philosophical novel and that it's pushing a certain idea." Kolya was starting to get flustered. "I'm a Socialist, Karamazov—a real, committed Socialist," he declared suddenly, as if that explained everything.

"A Socialist?" Alyosha laughed kindly. "When did you have time to become one? I thought you were only thirteen."

Kolya winced at the mention of his age. "First of all, I'm not thirteen—I'll be fourteen in two weeks!" he snapped, blushing again. "And secondly, what does my age have to do with anything? The real question is about my beliefs, not how old I am."

"When you get older, you'll understand how age affects your beliefs," Alyosha said gently. "And I get the feeling that some of what you're saying isn't really your own idea."

Kolya cut him off hotly. "Come on, you just want everyone to follow orders and believe in mysticism. Admit it—the Christian religion has only ever been used to keep the poor and weak under control. Isn't that the truth?"

"I know exactly where you got that idea," Alyosha said, smiling. "Someone told you that, didn't they?"

"Why do you think someone told me? I can think for myself!" Kolya insisted indignantly. "I don't mind Christ, though. He was a kind, humane person. If He were alive today, He'd probably be a revolutionary—He might even play a leading role in the movement."

"Where did you get that idea from? Who's been feeding you nonsense like that?" Alyosha asked, half-laughing in disbelief.

"All right, all right! I've talked with Mr. Rakitin a few times—but Byelinsky said it too, you know."

"Byelinsky? I don't think he ever wrote that anywhere."

"Maybe not, but they say he said it," Kolya replied. "I heard it... somewhere, but never mind where."

"Have you actually read Byelinsky?" Alyosha asked.

"Not much. I only read the part about why Tatyana didn't run away with Onegin."

"You read that? Do you really understand it?" Alyosha asked, clearly amused.

"Come on, Karamazov! Don't treat me like I'm little Smurov," Kolya said with a grin, though he was clearly irritated. "And don't think I'm some kind of radical. I disagree with Rakitin about a lot of things. For example, even though I mentioned Tatyana, I don't support all this nonsense about women's emancipation. Women are meant to obey—it's just the way things are. Les femmes tricottent, as Napoleon said." Kolya smiled. "At least on that point, I completely agree with that so-called great man. And as for people running off to America, I think it's cowardly. Why run away when there's so much good you can do here? Now more than ever!"

"What do you mean? Has someone suggested that you go to America?" Alyosha asked, curious.

"Yes, someone did. But I refused," Kolya said, lowering his voice confidentially. "Don't tell anyone, Karamazov—this is just between us. I don't want to end up in the clutches of the secret police or taking lessons at the Chain Bridge prison.

'Long will you remember
The house at the Chain Bridge...'

Do you know that line? It's from a poem—pretty good, isn't it?" Kolya smiled nervously. "Why are you laughing? You don't think I'm lying, do you?" He cringed inwardly, worried Alyosha might figure out that he had only read one issue of The Bell from his father's bookshelf and nothing more.

"No, no—I'm not laughing. And I certainly don't think you're lying. Unfortunately, all of this sounds all too believable," Alyosha said with a sigh. "But tell me—have you read Pushkin? Eugene Onegin, perhaps? You mentioned Tatyana earlier."

"No, I haven't read it yet, but I want to read it. I have no prejudices, Karamazov; I want to hear both sides. Why do you ask?"

"Oh, no reason."

"Tell me, Karamazov, do you have an awful contempt for me?" Kolya asked suddenly, standing up straight as if he were a soldier at attention. "Please, tell me honestly, without beating around the bush."

"Contempt for you?" Alyosha replied, surprised. "Why would I? I'm only saddened that such a wonderful nature like yours is being led astray by all this nonsense before you've really begun your life."

"Don't worry about my nature," Kolya interrupted, sounding somewhat pleased with himself. "But it's true, I'm ridiculously sensitive, almost crudely so. You smiled just now, and I thought maybe—"

"Oh, my smile meant something entirely different. Let me tell you why I smiled. Not long ago, I read an article by a German who lived in Russia. He was criticizing our students and schoolboys today. He wrote, 'Show a Russian schoolboy a map of the stars, which he knows nothing about, and by the next day he'll return it with corrections.' No knowledge, just endless conceit—that's what he meant about Russian students."

"Yes, that's absolutely true!" Kolya laughed suddenly. "Bravo to the German! But he missed the good side, don't you think? Sure, there's conceit, which comes from youth and can be corrected if needed. But there's also an independent spirit, a boldness of thought and conviction, even from childhood, that's absent in those groveling before authority... like sausage-makers. Still, the German was right. Bravo to him! But Germans need to be strangled all the same. They're so good at science and learning, but they should still be strangled."

"Strangled? Why?" Alyosha asked with a smile.

"Well, maybe I'm talking nonsense. I admit, I get carried away sometimes, especially when I'm happy. I can't help but blurt out all kinds of foolish things. But I say, we've been chatting here for a while, and that doctor's taking an awfully long time. Maybe he's examining Ilusha's mother and poor Nina. I liked Nina, you know. As I was leaving, she whispered to me, 'Why didn't you come earlier?' And in such a reproachful voice! I think she's really sweet and a bit sad."

"Yes, yes! Well, you'll come by often now, and you'll get to know what she's really like. It will do you a lot of good to be around people like them—to learn to appreciate things you can only discover through knowing them," Alyosha said warmly. "That'll have a far greater effect on you than anything else."

"Oh, how I regret and blame myself for not coming sooner!" Kolya exclaimed, his voice full of bitterness.

"Yes, it's a shame. You saw how happy Ilusha was to see you, how much he had been waiting for you."

"Don't tell me that! It makes it worse! But I deserve it. My conceit, my selfish vanity, and my stupid stubbornness kept me from coming. I've struggled with it all my life, but I can never fully get rid of it. I see that now. I'm a beast in so many ways, Karamazov!"

"No, you have a lovely nature, even though it's been distorted. I understand why you've had such an influence on this sensitive, generous boy," Alyosha said sincerely.

"And you say that to me?" Kolya cried out. "Would you believe it? I've thought several times since I've been here that you despised me! If only you knew how much I value your opinion!"

"But are you really so sensitive? At your age? Just now, when you were telling your story, I could tell—you must be quite sensitive."

"You noticed that? You've got a keen eye! I bet it was when I was talking about the goose. That's when I felt sure you despised me for being so eager to show off. For a moment, I even hated you for it, and I started rambling like an idiot. And when I said that if there were no God, He'd have to be invented, I felt I was trying too hard to show off my knowledge—especially since I got that phrase from a book. But I swear, I wasn't trying to impress you out of vanity, even though I don't really know why. Maybe because I was so happy? Yes, I think it was because I was so happy... but it's disgraceful to gush like that just because you're pleased, I know that. Still, now I'm convinced you don't despise me. It was all in my head. Oh, Karamazov, I'm deeply unhappy. I imagine all sorts of things, like everyone's laughing at me, the whole world, and then I feel like turning everything upside down."

"And you end up worrying everyone around you," Alyosha said with a smile.

"Yes, I do, especially my mother. Karamazov, tell me, do I seem ridiculous to you right now?"

"Don't think about that at all!" Alyosha exclaimed. "And what does 'ridiculous' even mean? Isn't everyone always being or seeming ridiculous at some point? Even most clever people today are terrified of appearing ridiculous, and that makes them miserable. I'm just surprised you're feeling this way so early. But I've noticed it for a while now, and not just in you—children these days are starting to feel it, too. It's like a kind of madness. The devil has taken hold of this vanity and infected the whole generation. It's simply the devil," Alyosha added, without a hint of the smile Kolya expected to see. "You're like everyone else," he continued, "that is, like so many others. But you must not be like everybody else. That's the key."

"Even if everyone is like that?"

"Yes, even if everyone is like that. You should be the only one who isn't. And you're not like everyone else. You're not ashamed to admit your flaws or even say something ridiculous. Who does that these days? No one.

People don't even feel the need to criticize themselves anymore. Don't be like everyone else, even if you're the only one."

"Brilliant! I knew I wasn't wrong about you. You really know how to comfort someone. Oh, how I've longed to meet you, Karamazov! I've wanted this meeting for so long. Did you really think about me, too? You said just now that you thought about me."

"Yes, I've heard about you and thought of you... and if it's partly vanity that makes you ask, it doesn't matter."

"You know, Karamazov, this conversation has felt like a declaration of love," Kolya said bashfully, his voice softening. "That's not ridiculous, is it?"

"Not at all," Alyosha replied, smiling warmly. "And even if it were, it wouldn't matter, because it's a good thing."

"But you know, Karamazov, I think you're a little embarrassed right now. I can tell by your eyes," Kolya said, with a sly, happy smile.

"Why would I be embarrassed?" "Well, why are you blushing then?"

"It was you who made me blush," Alyosha laughed, and indeed, his face had turned slightly red. "Well, I am blushing a bit... I don't even know why," he added, sounding a little sheepish.

"Oh, I love you so much for that!" Kolya exclaimed, his voice filled with excitement. "I admire you even more because you're embarrassed—because you're just like me!" His cheeks flushed, and his eyes sparkled with joy.

"You know, Kolya," Alyosha said suddenly, as if compelled by something deeper, "I think you're going to have a hard time in life."

"I know, I know! You've already figured everything out!" Kolya agreed, nodding quickly, as if Alyosha had just confirmed what he already believed.

"But even so, you'll still love life in the end," Alyosha added, his voice warm and full of certainty.

"Exactly! Hurrah! You really are a prophet," Kolya cried, practically glowing. "We're going to get along so well, Karamazov! You know what makes me happiest? It's that you treat me like an equal. But we're not equals, not really—you're better than me. But that doesn't matter. I know we'll get along."

He leaned closer, almost conspiratorially. "Do you know? This whole last month, I kept thinking, 'Either we'll be best friends forever, or we'll be enemies until the day we die!'"

"And as you were thinking that, you were already fond of me," Alyosha said with a joyful laugh.

"I was! I liked you so much. I've been dreaming about meeting you, and now we're really talking. But how did you know all of this already?" Kolya shook his head in wonder. Then, as if suddenly remembering, his expression changed. "Oh! Here comes the doctor! Look at his face! What's he going to say?"

Chapter 7: Ilusha

The doctor came out of the room again, wrapped in his heavy fur coat with his cap still on. His expression was one of anger and disgust, as if he were afraid of getting dirty just by being there. He gave a quick, stern glance around the hallway, pausing briefly on Alyosha and Kolya. Alyosha waved to the coachman from the door, and the carriage that had brought the doctor rolled up to the entrance. The captain hurried after the doctor, bowing nervously, desperate for some final word from him. His face was full of fear, his eyes wide and pleading.

"Your Excellency, please… is it really hopeless?" he stammered, wringing his hands in despair. He stared at the doctor, as if hoping that a single word from him might somehow change Ilusha's fate.

"I'm not God. I can't do anything more," the doctor replied curtly, though with an air of professional importance.

"But… Your Excellency, will it be soon? Very soon?" the captain asked, his voice trembling with dread.

"You need to be prepared for anything," the doctor said firmly, emphasizing his words. With that, he turned toward the waiting carriage.

"For the love of Christ, Your Excellency!" the captain cried out, stopping the doctor again. "Isn't there anything—anything at all—that could save him?"

"It's out of my hands now," the doctor said impatiently. Then, after a brief pause, he added, "Well… if you could send him immediately, without any delay—" The words "without any delay" were spoken so sharply that the captain flinched. "—to Syracuse, the new climate might help…"

"Syracuse?" the captain repeated, not understanding.

"Syracuse is in Sicily," Kolya explained suddenly. The doctor glanced at him, surprised.

"Sicily, Your Excellency?" the captain stammered, gesturing helplessly at the room around them. "But… you've seen our situation here—our family, our home…"

"No, no. Sicily wouldn't be suitable for the whole family," the doctor said dismissively. "In the spring, send your daughter to the Caucasus for her health. Your wife should also go there for her rheumatism, and after that, she must be sent to Paris to see Dr. Lepelletier, a specialist. I can write a note to him for you, and perhaps that might make a difference—"

"Doctor, please! Look around you!" The captain spread his arms hopelessly, motioning to the bare wooden walls of the hallway.

"That's not my problem," the doctor replied with a thin, dismissive smile. "I've only told you what medical science suggests. As for anything beyond that… it's out of my hands."

"Don't be afraid, apothecary. My dog won't bite you," Kolya said loudly, noticing the doctor's wary glance at Perezvon, who stood by the doorway. His voice was sharp, deliberately using the word "apothecary" instead of "doctor" to offend him, as he later explained.

"What did you say?" the doctor snapped, looking at Kolya in disbelief. "Who is this?" he asked Alyosha, clearly annoyed.

"I'm Perezvon's owner. Don't worry about me," Kolya replied coolly.

"Perezvon?" the doctor repeated, confused.

"He hears the bell but can't tell where it's coming from," Kolya said with a smirk. "Goodbye—we'll see you in Syracuse!"

"Who is this? Who is this?" The doctor's anger flared.

"He's just a mischievous schoolboy," Alyosha said quickly, frowning at Kolya. "Ignore him, Doctor. Kolya, keep quiet!" Alyosha added, his voice firm. "Just ignore him," he repeated to the doctor, trying to keep things from escalating.

"What that boy needs is a good thrashing!" the doctor snapped, furious.

"And be careful, apothecary—Perezvon might bite!" Kolya said, his voice trembling with anger, though his face had gone pale. "Ici, Perezvon!" he called to the dog.

"Kolya, say one more word, and I won't have anything more to do with you," Alyosha warned sharply.

"There's only one person in the world who can tell Nikolay Krassotkin what to do—and that's him," Kolya said, pointing at Alyosha. "I obey him. Goodbye!"

With that, Kolya opened the door and walked quickly into the room where Ilusha lay. Perezvon followed close behind him.

The doctor stood frozen for a moment, staring at Alyosha as if he couldn't believe what had just happened. Then, muttering a curse under his breath, he stormed off toward the carriage. "This... this... I don't know what this is!" he exclaimed, still seething as he climbed into the carriage. The captain rushed after him to help him inside, bowing apologetically as the doctor settled into the seat.

Meanwhile, Alyosha followed Kolya into the room, where Ilusha was waiting for them. The sick boy was holding Kolya's hand tightly and calling out for his father. A moment later, the captain returned, his face pale and drawn.

"Father, Father, come closer..." Ilusha whispered, his voice trembling with excitement. But he couldn't finish his sentence. Instead, he threw his thin arms around both his father and Kolya, pulling them into a tight embrace. He held them close, clinging to them as if he would never let go.

The captain began to shake with silent sobs, his body trembling as he tried to hold back his tears. Kolya's chin quivered, and his lips trembled, but he stayed silent.

"Father... Father... I feel so sorry for you," Ilusha whispered, his voice filled with sorrow.

"Ilusha... my dear boy... the doctor said you'll get better. We'll all be happy... the doctor said..." the captain stammered, trying to smile through his tears.

"Father, I know what the doctor told you," Ilusha interrupted softly. "I saw it in your eyes."

Once again, he hugged them both as tightly as he could, burying his face in his father's shoulder.

"Don't cry, Father," Ilusha whispered. "And when I'm gone, find another boy—a good boy. Choose one from the others... call him Ilusha and love him the way you loved me."

"Stop it, old man! You're going to get better!" Kolya said suddenly, his voice rough with emotion, as if trying to convince himself as much as Ilusha.

"Just don't forget me, Father," Ilusha continued quietly. "Visit my grave... and bury me by the big stone where we used to walk. Come visit me there in the evenings with Krassotkin... and bring Perezvon. I'll be waiting for you... Father... Father..."

His voice faltered, and they all remained silent, holding one another in the embrace. Nina sat in her chair, quietly sobbing.

When "mamma" saw everyone else crying, she also broke down into tears.

"Ilusha! Ilusha!" she wailed.

Kolya suddenly pulled himself free from Ilusha's embrace. "Goodbye, old man! Mother's expecting me home for dinner," he said hurriedly. "What a shame I didn't tell her where I was going! She'll be worried sick... But I'll come back right after dinner, I promise! I'll stay with you the whole afternoon, the whole evening. I'll tell you all sorts of things! And I'll bring Perezvon. But I'll take him with me now—he'll start howling if I leave him here, and that will just bother you. Goodbye!"

Kolya dashed out into the hallway. He tried to keep himself from crying, but as soon as he reached the passage, the tears came. Alyosha found him there, quietly sobbing.

"Kolya, you must keep your promise and come back. He'll be so heartbroken if you don't," Alyosha said seriously.

"I will! I swear I will!" Kolya choked out between sobs, no longer trying to hide his tears. "Oh, how I hate myself for not coming sooner!"

At that moment, the captain burst out of the room and quickly shut the door behind him. His face was wild, his lips trembling. He stood before Kolya and Alyosha, flinging his arms up in a frantic gesture.

"I don't want a good boy! I don't want another boy!" he whispered hoarsely, clenching his teeth. "If I forget thee, O Jerusalem, let my tongue—" His voice cracked, and he broke off with a sob. He sank to his knees in front of the wooden bench, pressing his fists against his head. His sobs were pitiful and strange, as if he was trying with all his might to keep the sound from reaching the room.

Kolya bolted out into the street.

"Goodbye, Karamazov! You will come, won't you?" he called sharply, his voice tinged with anger.

"I'll definitely come this evening," Alyosha assured him.

"What was that about Jerusalem? What did he mean?" Kolya demanded.

"It's from the Bible," Alyosha explained. "'If I forget thee, O Jerusalem'—it means if I forget what's most precious to me, if I let anything replace it, then—"

"I get it. That's enough!" Kolya interrupted. "Don't forget—be sure to come!" He then called to the dog, "Ici, Perezvon!" in a fierce tone. With quick, determined strides, he headed home.

Book 11 Ivan

Chapter 1: At Grushenka's

Alyosha walked toward the cathedral square, heading to the widow Morozov's house to see Grushenka. Earlier that morning, she had sent Fenya with an urgent message, begging him to come. As Alyosha questioned Fenya, he learned that Grushenka had been especially distressed since the day before. Over the two months since Mitya's arrest, Alyosha had frequently visited Grushenka, partly from his own wish to see her and partly to deliver messages from Mitya. Three days after Mitya's arrest, Grushenka fell seriously ill, remaining bedridden for nearly five weeks. For one whole week, she had been completely unconscious.

Now she looked thinner, and her skin had taken on a slight pallor. Yet, despite the toll illness had taken on her, Alyosha found her more beautiful than before. When he visited, he liked to catch her gaze, noticing a newfound firmness and thoughtful determination in her expression. There was a subtle line between her brows, giving her face an air of focus, almost stern at first glance. The playful, frivolous nature that had once defined her seemed to have vanished completely.

What puzzled Alyosha was that, despite everything—Mitya's arrest, the uncertainty surrounding his trial, and her own illness— Grushenka hadn't lost her cheerful spirit. Her eyes, once proud, now held a softer glow, though occasionally that old flash of bitterness would reappear, sparked by a lingering thought that seemed stronger than ever. The root of that thought remained unchanged: Katerina Ivanovna. Even during her delirium, Grushenka had raved about her. Alyosha knew how deeply jealous Grushenka felt toward Katerina, even though Katerina had never once visited Mitya in prison, despite having every opportunity to do so.

This complicated the situation for Alyosha, as Grushenka confided in him more than anyone else, constantly seeking his advice. Yet, at times, he found himself at a loss for words, unsure of how to respond to her questions.

When Alyosha entered her apartment, he found her home, and from the way she leapt out of her chair to greet him, it was clear that she had been waiting impatiently. A deck of cards, laid out for a game of "fools," sat on the table. On the leather sofa across the room, a bed had been made, and Maximov lay half-reclining on it. The old man wore a dressing gown and a cotton nightcap, looking weak and frail, but with a blissful smile on his face.

Maximov had arrived with Grushenka two months earlier, drenched from rain and sleet, and simply never left. He had sat on the sofa that first day, cold and soaked, wearing a timid, pleading smile as though hoping for some kindness. Grushenka, overwhelmed by grief and fever, barely noticed him at first. But after half an hour, she happened to glance at him and saw his pitiful little laugh. Feeling a surge of compassion, she called Fenya and told her to bring him some food.

That entire day, Maximov stayed on the sofa, hardly moving. When evening fell and the shutters were closed, Fenya asked her, "Is the gentleman staying the night, mistress?"

"Yes, make him a bed on the sofa," Grushenka answered.

After asking him more questions, Grushenka learned that he had nowhere to go. "Mr. Kalganov, my benefactor, told me directly that he wouldn't have me back," Maximov explained miserably. "He gave me five roubles and sent me on my way."

"Well, God bless you. You'd better stay here, then," Grushenka said kindly, managing a sympathetic smile despite her own sorrow. That smile broke the old man's heart, and his lips quivered with grateful tears. And so, the homeless wanderer had stayed with her ever since, even during the worst of her illness. Fenya and her grandmother, the cook, didn't turn him out either; they continued feeding him and making his bed every night on the sofa.

Over time, Grushenka grew accustomed to him. After she regained enough strength to visit Mitya in prison, she would come home and talk to "Maximushka" about trivial things, using their conversations to distract herself from her worries. Maximov turned out to be a surprisingly good storyteller, and he became an essential presence in her life.

Aside from Alyosha, Grushenka saw few visitors. Alyosha didn't come every day, and even when he did, he never stayed for long. Meanwhile, the old merchant who had once cared for Grushenka lay gravely ill and passed away a week after Mitya's trial. Three weeks before his death, knowing the end was near, he gathered his family—his sons, their wives, and children—around him and asked them to stay by his side. From that moment, he instructed his servants to refuse entry to Grushenka. If she came to inquire after him, they were to tell her, "The master wishes you long life and happiness, and asks you to forget him." Still, Grushenka sent messages almost every day to check on him.

"You've finally come!" Grushenka cried out, throwing down the cards and rushing toward Alyosha. "Maximushka's been scaring me, saying you might not come! Oh, how I need you today! Sit down—what will you have? Coffee?"

"Yes, please," Alyosha answered as he sat down at the table. "I'm really hungry."

"That's good. Fenya! Coffee, now!" Grushenka called out. "It's been ready for you for ages. And bring some pies—hot ones, mind you!" Then, turning back to Alyosha, she added, "Would you believe it? We had a storm over those pies today. I took them to the prison for him, and do you know what he did? He threw them back at me! Refused to eat them. He even stomped on one! So I told him, 'Fine! I'll leave them with the warder. If you don't eat them by evening, then your spite is all you'll have!' And with that, I left. We fought again, of course. We always fight whenever I go."

Grushenka rattled off her story in one breath, her agitation clear. Maximov, looking uncomfortable, gave a nervous smile and stared down at the floor.

"What was the fight about this time?" Alyosha asked gently.

"Oh, it was the last thing I expected!" Grushenka exclaimed. "He's jealous—jealous of the Pole, of all people! 'Why do you keep him around?' he said. 'So you're keeping him now?' He's jealous all the time, morning, noon, and night! Would you believe it—he even got jealous of Kuzma last week!"

"But... he knew about the Pole before, didn't he?" Alyosha asked.

"Yes, he's known about him from the start, but today he suddenly lost his temper over it," Grushenka said, frustrated. "Honestly, I'm ashamed to repeat the things he said. Silly man! Rakitin was just going in when I left. Maybe he's the one stirring things up. What do you think?" she added carelessly.

"He's just in love with you—that's the real reason. And now, with everything going on, he's more on edge than ever."

"Of course, with the trial tomorrow, how could he not be?" she sighed. "I went to him today because I wanted to talk about what's coming. I'm terrified of what might happen. You say he's worried, but I'm even more anxious! And he's going on about the Pole? So foolish! At least he's not jealous of poor Maximushka yet."

"My wife used to get terribly jealous of me," Maximov chimed in.

"Jealous of you?" Grushenka laughed, despite her mood. "Of who, exactly?"

"The servant girls," Maximov replied sheepishly.

"Enough, Maximushka. I'm in no mood to laugh," Grushenka snapped, though a faint smile lingered. "And stop eyeing the pies. You won't get any. They aren't good for you. No vodka either. I might as well be running a charity house with all the care I have to give," she added with a chuckle.

"I don't deserve your kindness. I'm a worthless man," Maximov murmured, his voice quivering with emotion. "You'd do better to help people who are worth more."

"Oh, Maximushka, everyone's worth something," she said warmly. "And who's to say who's worth the most? If only that Pole weren't around, Alyosha! And now, of all times, he's decided to fall ill! I went to see him earlier, and just to spite Mitya, I'll send him some pies. I hadn't planned to, but since Mitya accused me of doing it anyway, I might as well! Oh, here comes Fenya with a letter. Yes, it's from the Poles—begging again, of course."

Pan Mussyalovitch's letter was long and full of flowery, grandiose language, asking Grushenka for a loan of three roubles. It even came with a signed receipt promising repayment within three months, signed by both Mussyalovitch and Vrublevsky. During her recent illness, Grushenka had received several letters like this from them, all filled with exaggerated politeness. At first, she hadn't been able to read them through—especially the first one, which was full of elaborate language and sealed with a large family crest. She'd given up halfway through, unable to make sense of it.

In the following days, more letters came, each one asking for less and less money. The original request of two thousand roubles dwindled to a hundred, then twenty-five, and finally just one rouble, with both men signing a receipt for it. Feeling pity for them, Grushenka had gone to their shabby lodging at dusk and found them living in miserable conditions—no food, no fuel, and deep in debt to their landlady. The money they'd taken from Mitya that night in Mokroe had long since vanished.

Despite their dire situation, the two Poles greeted her with pompous speeches and acted as if they were still important gentlemen. Amused by their arrogance, Grushenka gave them ten roubles and later told Mitya about it, laughing. Mitya hadn't been jealous at the time, but ever since, the Poles had latched onto her, sending her daily letters begging for more money, which she always sent in small amounts. But now, suddenly, Mitya had decided to be jealous.

"Like a fool, I stopped by the Pole's place earlier on my way to see Mitya," Grushenka explained quickly, almost as if confessing. "He's sick too, poor thing. And I told Mitya about it, thinking he'd laugh with me. 'Can you believe it?' I said. 'The Pole tried to serenade me with his guitar, hoping I'd be moved enough to marry him!' And what did Mitya do? He flew into a rage, of course! So now, I'm definitely sending them the pies. Fenya, is that little girl still waiting? Give her three roubles and pack up a dozen pies for her to take. And Alyosha," she added with a mischievous smile, "be sure to tell Mitya I sent the pies."

"I won't say a word," Alyosha replied, smiling.

"Oh, you think he's really upset about it?" Grushenka said bitterly. "He's only jealous on purpose. He doesn't care—he just likes having something to be jealous about."

"On purpose?" Alyosha repeated, puzzled.

"You're so naïve, Alyosha," Grushenka said with a sigh. "With all your cleverness, you don't understand. I'm not upset that he's jealous—it's flattering, really. I'd be hurt if he wasn't jealous at all. I have a fierce heart, you know. I can get jealous too. What bothers me is that he doesn't truly love me. That's what hurts. He's not jealous because he cares about me—he's just using it as an excuse to attack me and make it seem like everything is my fault.

"Today, he started praising Katerina Ivanovna right to my face. He told me all about how she hired a fancy lawyer and brought in a doctor from Moscow just for him. So, of course, he must love her! More shame on him for that! He's treated me so poorly, and now he's turning everything on me, saying, 'You were with your Pole before me, so you can't blame me for Katerina.' That's what he's really doing—putting the blame on me."

Grushenka couldn't finish. She buried her face in her handkerchief, her body shaking with sobs.

"Mitya doesn't love Katerina Ivanovna," Alyosha said firmly.

"Well, whether he loves her or not, I'll find out soon enough," Grushenka said, her voice filled with determination. She wiped her eyes, but her expression had changed—her face was no longer calm and kind but hardened and resentful.

"Enough of this nonsense," she said abruptly, straightening up. "That's not why I sent for you. Alyosha, darling, I'm so scared about tomorrow. What will happen? No one seems to care about it except me. Everyone is going about their day as if nothing is wrong. Are you even thinking about it? Tomorrow is the trial! How will it go? You know the valet did it—the valet killed him! What if they convict Mitya instead? Won't anyone stand up for him? They haven't even seriously questioned the valet, have they?"

"He's been thoroughly interrogated," Alyosha replied thoughtfully. "But no one believes he's the one. He's been very ill since that seizure—truly unwell."

"Oh, couldn't you talk to the lawyer yourself and tell him everything?" Grushenka pleaded. "They brought him all the way from Petersburg, and they say he's costing three thousand roubles!"

"We gathered that money together—Katerina Ivanovna, Ivan, and I. She paid two thousand herself for the doctor from Moscow. Fetyukovitch, the lawyer, would have charged even more, but since the case is so famous now, he agreed to take it for the publicity. It's in all the papers and journals. I spoke with him yesterday."

"And what did he say?" Grushenka asked eagerly.

"He listened but didn't say much. He told me he already has his own opinion, but he promised to consider everything I said."

"Consideration! Ah, they are crooks! They'll ruin him. And why did she send for the doctor?"

"They're trying to prove that Mitya's insane, that he didn't know what he was doing when it happened," Alyosha replied gently. "But Mitya won't accept that."

"Yes, but that would only be true if he had actually killed him!" Grushenka exclaimed. "He was mad at the time, completely mad, and that's my fault, the wretch that I am! But he didn't do it, of course he didn't! Yet everyone's against him—the whole town. Even Fenya's testimony makes him look guilty. And the people at the shop, and that official, and at the tavern—everyone heard him say things that made him look guilty. They're all, all against him."

"Yes, there's a lot of evidence piling up," Alyosha said grimly.

"And Grigory—Grigory Vassilyevitch—won't budge from his story that the door was open. He swears he saw it. No one can shake him. I even went to talk to him myself, but he's stubborn and rude about it."

"That's probably the strongest piece of evidence against Mitya," Alyosha admitted.

"And as for Mitya being mad, he certainly seems like it now," Grushenka continued, her voice filled with a strange anxiety. "Alyosha, I've been wanting to talk to you about this for a while. I visit him every day, and I just can't understand what he's saying. He talks and talks, but it doesn't make sense to me. I thought it was something too intellectual for me to grasp. But then he suddenly started talking about a baby. He said, 'Why is the baby poor? It's for that baby I'm going to Siberia now. I'm not a murderer, but I have to go to Siberia.' I couldn't figure out what he meant. What baby? I had no idea. But the way he said it—it made me cry. He cried, too, and then he kissed me and made the sign of the cross over me. What does it mean, Alyosha? What baby is he talking about?"

"It must be Rakitin. He's been visiting Mitya recently," Alyosha said with a faint smile. "Though, honestly, I don't think this is Rakitin's influence. I haven't seen Mitya myself lately, but I will today."

"No, it's not Rakitin. It's his brother, Ivan Fyodorovitch, who's upsetting him. It's his visits that are doing it," Grushenka began, then suddenly stopped. Alyosha looked at her in surprise.

"Ivan's been visiting him? Mitya told me himself that Ivan hadn't visited him even once."

"Oh no, I've said too much!" Grushenka exclaimed, clearly flustered and blushing. "Stay, Alyosha, don't tell anyone. Since I've already let it slip, I'll tell you everything—he's been to see Mitya twice. The first time was right after he arrived from Moscow, before I fell ill. The second time was a week ago. He made Mitya promise not to tell you or anyone about it. He came in secret."

Alyosha sat in deep thought, processing the news. It clearly struck him.

"Ivan hasn't talked to me about Mitya's case," Alyosha said slowly. "He's barely said anything to me in the past two months. And when I visit him, he seems annoyed that I came, so I haven't been to see him in the last three weeks. Hm ... if he visited a week ago ... Mitya has been different this past week."

"Yes, there's been a change," Grushenka agreed quickly. "They're hiding something, Alyosha. Mitya even told me there's a secret. He can't rest because of it. Before that, he was more cheerful, and he still is sometimes, but now he's so restless. He shakes his head, paces the room, and keeps pulling at his hair. I can tell something is eating at him."

"But you just said he's been cheerful."

"Yes, he's cheerful, but also anxious. He switches from being cheerful to irritated so quickly. And sometimes he laughs at the silliest things, like a little child, even with everything hanging over him."

"And did he really ask you not to tell me about Ivan? Did he say, 'Don't tell him'?"

"Yes, he did. He's most afraid of you finding out. He said it's a secret. Alyosha, please go see him, find out what this secret is, and come tell me," Grushenka begged urgently. "I can't stand not knowing. That's why I sent for you."

"You think the secret has something to do with you? If it were, I don't think he would have told you there was a secret."

"I don't know. Maybe he wants to tell me but doesn't dare to. He warned me that there's a secret, but won't say what it is."

"What do you think it is?"

"I think it's the end for me. That's what I think. They're plotting to get rid of me, all three of them—Mitya, Ivan, and Katerina. It's all Katerina's doing. She's everything I'm not, and he's warning me in advance. He's planning to leave me, that's the secret. A week ago, he told me that Ivan is in love with Katerina because he visits her so often. Is it true? Tell me, Alyosha, I need to know."

"I'll be honest. I don't think Ivan is in love with Katerina."

"Oh, I knew it! He's lying to me, that shameless liar! He's just jealous, trying to put the blame on me. But I'll show him! He even accused me of thinking he did it. He said that to me! How could he? Just wait until the trial. I'll expose everything then!"

And she began to cry again.

"Grushenka," Alyosha said softly as he stood up, "I can tell you two things for certain. First, Mitya loves you more than anyone in the world. Only you. I know it for sure. Second, I won't force the secret out of him, but if he tells me today, I'll let him know I've promised to tell you. Then I'll come to you right away. But I really don't think this secret has anything to do with Katerina. I'm certain it's about something else. Goodbye for now."

Alyosha shook her hand. Grushenka was still crying, but it seemed she was a little more at ease after sharing her fears. Alyosha felt bad leaving her like this, but he had many things to do.

Chapter 2: The Injured Foot

The first task Alyosha had to take care of was at Madame Hohlakov's house, and he hurried there to get it over with quickly, hoping not to be late for Mitya. Madame Hohlakov had been feeling unwell for the past three weeks; her foot had swollen for some unknown reason, and though she wasn't confined to her bed, she spent most of the day reclining on the couch in her boudoir, dressed elegantly in a way that was both casual and deliberate. Alyosha had once noticed, with innocent amusement, that despite her illness, she had become quite concerned with her appearance—wearing ribbons, top-knots, and loose wraps. He had an idea of why she might be dressing this way, but he brushed it off as a frivolous thought. In the past two months, the young official, Perhotin, had become a frequent visitor at her home.

Alyosha hadn't visited in four days, and he was eager to head straight to Lise, as she had sent a maid the previous day asking him to come for an "important matter." This message piqued Alyosha's interest. However, when the maid went to announce his arrival, Madame Hohlakov heard about it first and sent a request for him to visit her "just for a moment." Alyosha figured it was better to oblige; otherwise, she would send interruptions to Lise's room every few minutes while he was there.

He found Madame Hohlakov reclining on her couch, dressed more elaborately than usual and clearly in a state of nervous excitement. She greeted him with enthusiastic delight.

"It's been ages, ages, absolute ages since I've seen you! A whole week—can you imagine? Oh, but wait, it was only four days ago— Wednesday! And now you've come to see Lise, haven't you? You were planning to sneak in quietly, tiptoeing so I wouldn't hear."

She smiled warmly, almost teasing.

"My dear, dear Alexey Fyodorovitch, if you only knew how worried I am about her! But we'll talk about that later—though it is the most important thing. Yes, later. You know, since Father Zossima's passing—God rest his soul!" She crossed herself. "I see you as a monk now, even though you do look rather charming in that new suit of yours! Where did you find such a tailor in this town? No, no, we'll talk about that later, too. Forgive me for calling you Alyosha; an old woman like me may take such liberties." She smiled playfully. "But that can wait. The important thing is that I don't forget what I need to tell you. Remind me yourself if my thoughts get muddled! Just say, 'What's the important thing?'

"Ah, I don't even know what's most important anymore! Ever since Lise took back her promise—her childish promise—to marry you, it's all been a blur. Of course, you know it was just the playful fancy of a sick child who spent too long in a chair. Thank God she can walk now! That new doctor Katya sent from

Moscow—he came for your poor brother, who, tomorrow... But why even think of tomorrow? The very thought makes me feel like I'll die of curiosity! That doctor was here yesterday; he saw Lise. I paid him fifty roubles. But that's not the point! Why do I keep going off track? I feel so rushed, but I don't even know why! Everything is tangled in my head. I'm afraid you'll run away before I can tell you anything. Oh, dear! And we haven't even had coffee! Yulia! Glafira! Coffee!"

Alyosha quickly thanked her, saying he had already had coffee.

"Where?"

"At Agrafena Alexandrovna's."

"At her house?" Madame Hohlakov exclaimed, suddenly agitated. "That woman has ruined everything! I know nothing about it, of course, but they say she's become a saint. A bit late for that, don't you think? She should've done it earlier! What's the point now?"

She paused, regaining some composure. "Oh, Alexey Fyodorovitch, I'm all over the place today. This dreadful trial... I'm making arrangements to attend. I'll be carried in my chair; I can sit up, you know. I'll have people with me. And I'm a witness, too! How am I going to testify? What will I say? Do you have to take an oath?"

"Yes, but I don't think you'll be able to go," Alyosha said gently. "I can sit up!" she insisted, annoyed. "Ah, you're distracting me! This trial, it's barbaric! And now they're all going off to Siberia. Some are getting married. Everything is happening so fast—too fast! And in the end, there's only old age and death. That's all we have to look forward to." She sighed dramatically. "Well, so be it. I'm tired. And Katya—cette charmante personne— she's ruined all my hopes. Now she's following one of your brothers to Siberia, and the other will live in the nearest town, and they'll all drive each other mad! The scandal! It's in all the newspapers— from Moscow to Petersburg.

"Oh, and would you believe it?" She leaned in conspiratorially. "They even published a piece saying I was 'a dear friend' of your brother's! Can you imagine such gossip?"

"Impossible! Where did they print that?" Alyosha asked in disbelief.

"I'll show you! I found it yesterday. It's in the Petersburg Gossip! The paper just started coming out this year. I love reading gossip— though now it's come back to bite me. Here, look at this."

She pulled a crumpled newspaper from under her pillow and handed it to Alyosha.

It wasn't exactly that Madame Hohlakov was upset; rather, she seemed overwhelmed, as if everything in her mind was tangled. The newspaper paragraph was shocking, no doubt, but fortunately, she seemed too scattered to dwell on any one thing for too long and might switch topics in an instant, forgetting the paper altogether.

Alyosha knew well how the story of the Karamazov case had spread throughout Russia. He had seen some of the wild rumors about his brother, the Karamazovs, and even himself during those two months. Some were utterly absurd. One paper claimed he had gone into a monastery in horror at his brother's crime, becoming a monk. Another paper contradicted this, suggesting that he and Father Zossima had broken into the monastery's funds and fled.

The paragraph in Gossip was titled The Karamazov Case at Skotoprigonyevsk (a name Alyosha had tried to keep hidden). Though brief, it was cutting. No names were mentioned directly, but the insinuations were clear. It described the accused as a retired army captain—a swaggering, idle, and reactionary bully—who was entangled in various love affairs and particularly favored by certain "lonely women." One of these was a widow, desperate to appear younger despite having a grown daughter. The article hinted that just two hours before the crime, she had offered the accused three thousand roubles to elope with her to the gold mines. But, it claimed, instead of taking her offer, the criminal had preferred to murder his father and take the three thousand roubles himself rather than flee to Siberia with her. The piece ended with a burst of righteous anger over the crime of parricide and a lament about the recent abolition of serfdom.

Alyosha read the paragraph with interest, folded the paper, and handed it back to Madame Hohlakov.

"Well, that's clearly about me," she said quickly, moving right along. "Obviously, I'm the one they mean. Barely an hour before the crime, I did bring up the idea of the gold mines, and now they accuse me of using my so-called 'middle-aged charms'! The writer must have done that out of spite! May God forgive him for mentioning such things, just as I forgive him," she said with mock piety. Then, with a conspiratorial look, she added, "Do you know who wrote that? Your friend Rakitin!"

"Perhaps," Alyosha replied, though he didn't sound convinced. "I haven't heard anything about it."

"It was him—no 'perhaps' about it! You know I threw him out of my house, don't you?"

"I know you told him not to visit anymore, but I never heard the full story from you."

"Oh! Then he must have told you himself—probably slandered me to no end!"

"He does speak badly about you," Alyosha admitted, "but he speaks badly about everyone. As for why you cut ties with him, I haven't heard anything from him, either. I rarely see him these days. We're not exactly friends."

"Well, I'll tell you everything, then. There's no hiding it. I admit I might have been a little at fault—but just a little, mind you! Hardly anything. You see, my dear boy..." Madame Hohlakov leaned in slightly, her smile mysterious. "You must forgive me, Alyosha. I speak to you now as if you were my father, not my son. It's like confessing to Father Zossima, you see! I called you a monk earlier, didn't I? Well, that frivolous young man—your friend, Rakitin—would you believe it, he fell in love with me!"

Alyosha blinked in surprise, but Madame Hohlakov pressed on.

"I didn't realize it at first. About a month ago, he started visiting more often—almost every day! Of course, we were already acquainted, but suddenly it dawned on me what was happening. And just when I was starting to notice, that charming young official, Pyotr Ilyitch Perhotin, became a regular visitor. You've met him here many times. He's a wonderful young man, isn't he? So polite, so well-dressed. I adore young people like that—talented and modest, just like you. He could be a diplomat one day, mark my words. And after that dreadful day, it was he who saved me by coming late at night.

"But Rakitin—oh, he comes in with those dreadful boots and stretches them right out on my carpet! Then he starts hinting about his feelings! One day, as he was leaving, he squeezed my hand so hard that my foot started swelling almost immediately after. I'm sure of it!"

Madame Hohlakov shook her head in mock dismay.

"Rakitin didn't like Pyotr Ilyitch, not one bit. He was always making little remarks about him. I found it amusing, watching them interact. And then, one day, when I was feeling unwell and lying here alone, Rakitin arrived—imagine this!—with a poem he'd written about my swollen foot!"

She paused dramatically, trying to recall the verse. "It went something like this:

A captivating little foot..."

It started like that somehow. I can never remember poems. I've got it here. I'll show it to you later. But it's really charming— charming; and you know, it's not just about my foot, it had a good message too, a nice idea, though I've forgotten what it was. In fact, it was just the sort of thing to put in an album. So, of course, I thanked him, and he seemed quite flattered. I had barely finished thanking him when in walked Pyotr Ilyitch, and Rakitin's face turned dark. I could tell Pyotr Ilyitch was interrupting something, because I knew Rakitin wanted to say more after giving me the poem. I could sense it. But then Pyotr Ilyitch came in. I showed him the poem but didn't say who wrote it. I'm sure he figured it out, though, even though he won't admit it to this day and still claims he had no idea. But I know he says that on purpose. Pyotr Ilyitch started laughing right away and criticized the poem. 'Terrible doggerel,' he called it, 'some divinity student must have written it,' and with such passion, too! Then, instead of laughing, your friend got really mad. 'Oh dear!' I thought, 'they're going to fight!' 'I wrote it,' Rakitin said. 'I wrote it as a joke,' he added, 'because I think it's beneath me to write poetry But it's good poetry! They want to put up a statue to Pushkin for writing about women's feet, but I wrote with a moral purpose,' he said. 'And you,' he said, 'are just stuck in the past. You don't have any humane ideas. You're not enlightened by modern thinking, and you're just another bureaucrat who takes bribes!' Then I started screaming and begging them to stop. And you know, Pyotr Ilyitch is no coward. He immediately became very polite, looked at Rakitin with a sarcastic expression, listened to him, and apologized. 'I had no idea,' he said. 'I wouldn't have said what I did if I'd known. I would have praised it. Poets are so sensitive,' he said. In short, he mocked Rakitin while keeping a gentlemanly tone. He later explained to me that he had been sarcastic the whole time. I thought he was being sincere. But as I lay here, just like I am now in front of you, I wondered, 'Should I throw Rakitin out for shouting so rudely at a guest in my house, or not?' Would you believe it? I lay here, closed my eyes, and couldn't decide if it was the right thing to do or not. One part of me said, 'Speak up,' while the other said, 'No, don't say anything.' And as soon as the second voice said that, I cried out and fainted. Of course, it caused a big fuss. I suddenly got up and said to Rakitin, 'I hate to say it, but I don't want to see you in my house again.' So I threw him out. Oh, Alexey Fyodorovitch, I know I was wrong. I was just acting. I wasn't really mad at him at all, but I suddenly thought—it was that thought that did it—that it would make such a dramatic scene. But believe me, it was still genuine. I really cried about it for several days afterward, and then, suddenly, one afternoon I forgot all about it. So it's been two weeks since he's been here, and I've been wondering if he would ever come back. I was even thinking about it yesterday, and then, last night, I saw that article in Gossip. I read it and was shocked. Who could have written it? It must have been him. He went home, sat down, wrote it right away, sent it in, and they published it. It was two weeks ago, you see. But, Alyosha, it's terrible how much I keep talking without getting to the point. Oh! The words just come out on their own!"

"It's really important that I see my brother today," Alyosha said softly.

"Of course, of course! You've brought me back to what I was thinking. Listen, what is an aberration?"

"What aberration?" Alyosha asked, confused.

"You know, in legal terms. An aberration where everything you do can be forgiven. No matter what, you'll be acquitted right away."

"What are you talking about?"

"I'll explain. This Katya … oh, she's such a delightful girl, but I can never figure out who she's in love with. She visited me not too long ago, but I couldn't get anything out of her. Especially now, she only talks to me about surface-level things. She's always going on about my health and nothing else. And the way she talks to me now! I finally just said to myself, 'Well, whatever. I don't care anymore.' Oh yes, I was talking about aberration. So, this doctor has arrived. You know about him, right? Of course, you do—he's the one who diagnoses madness. You requested him, no, wait—it wasn't you, it was Katya. It's all Katya's doing. So, you see, a person can be perfectly sane, but suddenly experience an aberration. They can be aware of what they're doing and still be in a state of aberration. And there's no doubt Dmitri Fyodorovitch was in such a state. They discovered aberration when they reformed the court system. It's one of the benefits of the new legal system. The doctor came and questioned me about that night, asking about the gold mines. 'How did he seem to you then?' the doctor asked me. He must have been in a state of aberration. He burst in yelling, 'Money, money, three thousand! Give me three thousand!' And then he left and immediately went and committed the murder. 'I don't want to kill him,' he said, and then he went and killed him. That's why they'll acquit him—because he fought against it, but still did it."

"But he didn't murder him," Alyosha interrupted, his voice sharp with anxiety.

"Yes, I know, it was Grigory who killed him."

"Grigory?" Alyosha gasped.

"Yes, yes! It was Grigory. He got knocked down by Dmitri

Fyodorovitch, but then he got up, saw the door open, went in, and killed Fyodor Pavlovitch."

"But why? Why would he?"

"He was in a state of aberration. When he recovered from the blow Dmitri gave him, he was in that state and went and did it. As for him denying it, he probably doesn't even remember. Still, it would be better—much better—if Dmitri did it. That's how it had to happen, though I keep saying it was Grigory. It was definitely Dmitri Fyodorovitch, and that's better, much better! Oh, not better that a son killed his father—I'm not saying that. Children should honor their parents, but it would still be better if it were Dmitri. That way, you wouldn't have anything to grieve over. He did it while he was unconscious—or rather, while he was conscious but didn't know what he was doing. They'll acquit him, and it'll show how humane our reformed courts are. I didn't know about any of this before, but they say it's been like this for a while. When I heard about it yesterday, I wanted to send for you right away. And if they acquit him, he should come straight from court to dinner at my place. I'll invite all my friends, and we'll drink to the reformed courts. I'm sure he wouldn't be dangerous, and I'll have plenty of people there in case anything happens. He could even become a justice of the peace in another town, since people who've been through trouble themselves make the best judges. And besides, who isn't suffering from aberration nowadays? You, me, all of us—we're all in that state. There are so many examples. A man could be singing a song, get annoyed at something, grab a pistol, and shoot the first person he sees, and no one would hold it against him. I read about it recently, and all the doctors agree. The doctors are always agreeing—they'll agree to anything. My Lise is in a state of aberration too. She made me cry yesterday, and the day before, and today I suddenly realized it's all due to aberration. Oh, Lise upsets me so! I'm starting to think she's really gone mad. Why did she send for you? Did she send for you, or did you come on your own?"

"Yes, she sent for me, and I'm about to go see her," Alyosha said firmly, standing up.

"Oh, my dear Alexey Fyodorovitch, this might be the most important thing of all," Madame Hohlakov cried, suddenly bursting into tears. "God knows I trust Lise to you completely, and it doesn't matter that she called for you secretly without telling me. But I can't trust Ivan Fyodorovitch with her in the same way, even though I still consider him one of the most honorable young men. But imagine—he came to see Lise, and I had no idea!"

"What? When?" Alyosha asked, surprised. He stayed on his feet, listening closely.

"I'll tell you, though I'm not even sure why I asked you to come now. Ivan Fyodorovitch has been here twice since he returned from Moscow. The first time, it was just a friendly visit to see me. The second time, he came because Katya was here. I never expected him to visit often, knowing how much he has to deal with—what with everything going on, your father's terrible death and all. But then I found out he came again—not to see me, but to visit Lise. That was six days ago. He stayed only five minutes and left, and I didn't even hear about it until three days later—from Glafira, no less. You can imagine how shocked I was!

"So I sent for Lise immediately, and do you know what she did? She just laughed and said, 'He thought you were asleep, so he came to ask how you were.' I guess that's what happened. But oh, Lise! She worries me so much! Can you believe that just four days ago—right after you last visited her—she had a hysterical fit? Screaming and crying! Why do I never have hysterics, I wonder? Then she had another fit the next day, and again the day after that, and yesterday too!

"And yesterday, during one of those fits, she suddenly shouted, 'I hate Ivan Fyodorovitch! I don't want him in the house ever again!' I was completely speechless. I asked her, 'How could I refuse to see such an excellent young man? A man with such knowledge and misfortune?' After all, this whole situation is such a tragedy, isn't it? But instead of calming down, she burst out laughing—rudely, too! At first, I thought I had cheered her up, that maybe the fits would stop. I was even relieved because I had already decided to stop seeing Ivan Fyodorovitch myself—his unannounced visits have been strange, and I planned to ask him about them. But early this morning, Lise threw another tantrum. She got angry at Yulia and—can you believe it?—she slapped her right across the face! That's unthinkable! I've always treated my servants with the utmost respect. And just an hour later, she was on her knees, kissing Yulia's feet, begging for forgiveness!

"Then she sent me a message saying she wasn't coming to see me at all anymore, that she never wanted to see me again. But when I managed to drag myself to her room, she rushed to me, crying and kissing me—and then, just as suddenly, she pushed me out of the room without saying a word! I don't know what's going on with her.

"Alexey Fyodorovitch, I have no one else to turn to. All my hopes rest on you. Please, I beg you—go to Lise, talk to her, and find out what's troubling her. You're the only one who can. And after you speak with her, come back and tell me. If you don't, it will be the death of me. I mean it—it will kill me if this keeps up! I've been patient, but if I lose my patience, who knows what awful thing might happen! Oh dear, Pyotr Ilyitch!" Madame Hohlakov suddenly exclaimed, her face lighting up as Perhotin entered the room. "You're late, so late! Well, sit down, please. Tell us what the lawyer said. What's the news? Where are you going, Alexey Fyodorovitch?"

"To Lise," Alyosha answered quickly.

"Oh yes! Please, don't forget what I asked! This is a matter of life and death!" she called after him.

"I won't forget, if I can," Alyosha muttered as he hurried to leave.

"No, you mustn't say 'if you can'! I'll die if you don't come back!" Madame Hohlakov cried out, but Alyosha was already out the door.

Chapter 3: A Little Demon

When Alyosha entered Lise's room, he found her half- reclining in her invalid chair, the one used when she couldn't walk. She didn't get up to greet him, but her sharp, intense eyes stayed locked on his face. Her gaze was feverish, and her face was pale and slightly yellow. Alyosha was stunned at how much she had changed in just three days. She looked thinner, her long, thin fingers resting motionless on her dress. She didn't offer her hand, so Alyosha gently touched her fingers before sitting down across from her in silence.

"I know you're rushing to get to the prison," Lise said bluntly. "And I bet Mama kept you forever, talking about me and Yulia."

"How did you know that?" Alyosha asked, surprised.

"I was listening. Why are you staring at me? I listen because I want to—what's wrong with that? I'm not apologizing."

"Are you upset about something?"

"No, I'm actually really happy. I've been thinking, for about the thirtieth time, how lucky I am that I refused to marry you. You would make a terrible husband. If I married you, I could send you off with a note for the man I loved after you, and you'd deliver it without a second thought and even bring back his reply. Even if you were forty, you'd still run errands like that for me."

She suddenly laughed, and Alyosha gave her a gentle smile.

"There's something sharp-tongued but also honest about you," he said.

"I'm only honest with you because I don't feel ashamed around you. And I don't want to feel ashamed with you, Alyosha—just with you. But do you know what? I don't respect you. I care about you, but I don't respect you. If I did, I wouldn't be able to talk to you like this."

"No, you wouldn't," Alyosha agreed.

"But do you believe I really feel no shame with you?" "No, I don't believe it."

Lise laughed nervously, speaking quickly. "I sent your brother Dmitri some sweets in prison. You know, Alyosha, you're actually kind of good-looking. I think I'll love you even more for letting me not love you."

"Why did you call me here today, Lise?" Alyosha asked gently.

"I wanted to tell you something I've been wishing for. I wish someone would marry me, then hurt me—lie to me, cheat on me, and leave me. I don't want to be happy."

"You're craving disorder?" Alyosha asked softly.

"Yes. I want chaos. Sometimes I feel like setting fire to the house—sneaking around and lighting it up. They'd try to put it out, but it would keep burning, and I'd just stand there knowing it was me. Silly, right? But I can't help it. I feel so bored."

She waved her hand as if dismissing everything with disgust. "That's what comes from a life of comfort," Alyosha said quietly. "So it's better to be poor?"

"Yes, it is better."

"That's something your monk taught you. But it's nonsense. Let me stay rich while everyone else is poor. I'll eat sweets and drink cream, and I won't share with anyone. Oh, don't even try to say anything," she warned, shaking her hand at him before he could open his mouth. "I already know what you're going to say. I've heard it all before, and it's boring. If I ever became poor, I'd just kill someone. And who knows—maybe I'll do it even if I stay rich. Why not? But you know what? I'd like to work in the fields. I'll marry you, and you can become a real peasant. We'll raise a colt together—what do you think?"

Alyosha smiled. "Do you know Kalganov?" "Yes," he replied.

"He's always daydreaming. He says life is better in dreams because real life is dull. But even he'll get married soon—he's already tried flirting with me. Can you spin tops?"

"Yes, I can."

"Well, he's like a spinning top himself. He wants to be wound up and whipped to keep spinning. If I marry him, I'll keep him spinning forever. You aren't embarrassed to be here with me, are you?"

"No," Alyosha answered.

"You must be angry that I don't talk about holy things. But I don't want to be holy. What's the punishment for the worst sin in the next life? You must know."

"God will judge you," Alyosha said quietly, watching her closely.

"Good. That's exactly what I want—to be judged. I'd stand there, and they'd scold me, and I'd just laugh in their faces. I really do want to set the house on fire, Alyosha—our house. You still don't believe me?"

"Why not? There are kids as young as twelve who feel like setting things on fire. And some actually do. It's like a kind of sickness."

"No, no, that's not it at all. There may be kids like that, but that's not what I mean."

"You're confusing good with bad," Alyosha said. "It's just a passing phase, maybe part of your illness."

"No, you despise me! I can tell. It's not an illness. I don't want to do good. I want to do bad things."

"But why?" Alyosha asked softly.

"Because I want to destroy everything. Oh, how wonderful it would be if everything were ruined! Sometimes I think about doing all kinds of terrible things, slowly and in secret, until everyone finds out. And when they do, they'll all point at me, and I'll just stand there, staring back at them. That would feel amazing. Why do you think that would feel so good, Alyosha?"

"I don't know," Alyosha admitted. "Maybe it's just the urge to destroy something good—or like you said, to set something on fire. It happens sometimes."

"It's not just talk. I will do it."

"I believe you," Alyosha said quietly.

"Oh, how I love you for saying you believe me. And you're not lying, not even a little. But do you think I'm saying all this just to annoy you?"

"No, I don't think that... though maybe there's a little bit of that in it, too."

"There is a little. I can never lie to you," she said with a strange fire in her eyes.

What struck Alyosha most was her seriousness. There wasn't a trace of humor or joking on her face now, even though she used to be full of fun and laughter, even in her most serious moments.

"Sometimes people love crime," Alyosha said thoughtfully.

"Yes, yes! You've said exactly what I think. People love crime— everyone loves crime. They love it all the time, not just in certain moments. You know, it's like people have made a pact to lie about it, and they've been lying about it ever since. They all claim to hate evil, but deep down, they love it."

"And are you still reading those nasty books?"

"Yes, I am. Mama reads them and hides them under her pillow, and I steal them."

"Aren't you ashamed of destroying yourself?"

"I want to destroy myself. There's a boy here who laid down between train tracks as the train passed. Lucky guy! Listen, your brother is on trial for killing his father, and everyone loves that he killed his father."

"Loves that he killed his father?"

"Yes, loves it. Everyone loves it! They all say it's horrible, but secretly, they love it. I, for one, love it."

"There's some truth in what you say about everyone," Alyosha said softly.

"Oh, the ideas you have!" Lise shrieked in delight. "And you're a monk! You wouldn't believe how much I respect you, Alyosha, for never lying. Oh, I must tell you about this funny dream I had. Sometimes I dream of devils. It's night, I'm in my room with a candle, and suddenly there are devils everywhere—in the corners, under the table, and they open the doors. There's a crowd of them behind the doors, trying to come in and grab me. They're just about to catch me when I make the sign of the cross, and they all pull back. They don't leave completely, though. They stay in the corners, watching and waiting. And then I get this horrible urge to curse God out loud, and when I do, the devils come rushing back, thrilled, and grab me again. But then I cross myself again, and they pull back. It's so much fun, it takes my breath away."

"I've had the same dream," Alyosha said suddenly.

"Really?" Lise asked in surprise. "Alyosha, don't joke—that's really important. Can two people have the same dream?"

"It seems like they can."

"Alyosha, I'm telling you, that's really important," Lise said, sounding amazed. "It's not just the dream—it's that we both had the same dream. You never lie to me, so don't lie now. Is it true? Are you not joking?"

"It's true."

Lise was deeply impressed and stayed silent for half a minute.

"Alyosha, come see me more often," she said suddenly, her voice pleading.

"I'll come see you as long as I live," Alyosha replied firmly.

"You're the only person I can talk to, you know," Lise continued. "I talk to no one but you and myself. Just you, in the whole world. And I talk to you even more easily than I talk to myself. And I'm not even a little bit ashamed in front of you. Alyosha, why am I not ashamed with you at all? Alyosha, is it true that at Easter, the Jews steal a child and kill it?"

"I don't know."

"There's a book here that talks about a trial of a Jew who took a four-year-old child, cut off all his fingers, and crucified him on a wall. He nailed him to it, and later, at the trial, he said the child died soon—within four hours. 'Soon,' he said! The child moaned the whole time, and he just stood there watching. Isn't that nice?"

"Nice?"

"Yes, nice. Sometimes I imagine that it was me who crucified him. The child would be hanging there, moaning, and I'd sit opposite, eating pineapple compote. I love pineapple compote. Do you like it?"

Alyosha looked at her in silence. Her pale, sallow face suddenly twisted, and her eyes burned with intensity.

"You know, when I first read about that Jew, I sobbed all night. I couldn't stop imagining how the little boy cried and moaned. A four-year-old understands things, you know. And all the while, I couldn't stop thinking about pineapple compote. In the morning, I wrote to someone, asking them to come see me. They came, and I told them all about the child and the pineapple compote— everything. And I said it was nice. He laughed and agreed that it was nice. Then he got up and left after five minutes. Do you think he despised me? Tell me, Alyosha—did he despise me?"

She sat up on the couch, her eyes flashing.

"Did you send for that person?" Alyosha asked, concerned.

"Yes, I did."

"Did you write him a letter?" "Yes."

"Just to ask about that, about the child?"

"No, not about that. But when he came, I asked him about it right away. He answered, laughed, and left."

"That person acted honorably," Alyosha said quietly. "But did he despise me? Did he laugh at me?"

"No. Maybe he believes in the pineapple compote himself. He's very sick right now, too, Lise."

"Yes, he does believe in it," Lise said, her eyes blazing.

"He doesn't despise anyone," Alyosha continued. "But he doesn't believe in anyone, either. If he doesn't believe in people, then of course he despises them."

"So, he despises me?"

"You, too."

"Good," Lise said through clenched teeth. "When he left, laughing, I realized it was nice to be despised. The child with the cut-off fingers is nice, and being despised is nice, too."

Lise laughed right in Alyosha's face—a feverish, malicious laugh. "Alyosha, do you know what I want?" she suddenly gasped.

"Alyosha, save me!" She jumped off the couch, grabbed his hands

with both of hers, and clung to him desperately. "Save me!" she almost groaned. "Is there anyone in the world I could have told all this to? I told you the truth—the truth! I'm going to kill myself because I hate everything! I don't want to live, I hate it all, every bit of it!" She stared at him wildly. "Alyosha, why don't you love me? Not even a little?"

"But I do love you!" Alyosha answered warmly.

"Will you cry for me if I die?" she asked. "Yes."

"Not because I won't be your wife, just for me, just cry for me?" "Yes."

"Thank you. That's all I want—your tears. Everyone else can punish me, trample me into the ground, every one of them—all of them! I don't love anyone. Do you hear? Not a single person! I hate him! Go, Alyosha, you need to go to your brother." She tore herself away from him suddenly.

"How can I leave you like this?" Alyosha asked, almost in alarm.

"Go to your brother! They'll close the prison soon—go! Here's your hat. Tell Mitya I send my love. Now go, go!" She pushed him toward the door almost forcefully.

Alyosha looked at her with a pained expression. As he reached the door, he noticed a small folded letter in his hand. It was tightly sealed. He glanced at it and immediately saw the address: To Ivan Fyodorovitch Karamazov. He looked back at Lise, puzzled. Her face had become cold and stern, almost threatening.

"You have to give it to him!" she demanded, trembling with intensity. "Today—right away—or I'll poison myself! That's why I called you here."

Before he could respond, she slammed the door shut. Alyosha heard the bolt click behind him. He tucked the letter into his pocket and hurried downstairs, completely forgetting about Madame Hohlakov in his rush.

As soon as Alyosha left, Lise unbolted the door, opened it just enough to slide a finger into the crack, and then slammed it hard, pinching her finger painfully. Ten seconds later, she released her throbbing hand and walked slowly to her chair. She sat upright, staring intently at her injured finger, watching the blood ooze from beneath the nail. Her lips quivered as she whispered rapidly to herself:

"I am a wretch, a wretch, a wretch, a wretch!"

Chapter 4: A Hymn and A Secret

It was already late (November days are short) when Alyosha rang the bell at the prison gate. The daylight was starting to fade. He knew, however, that he wouldn't have any trouble getting inside. In their small town, things worked just like everywhere else. At first, after the preliminary investigation had concluded, only a few close relatives or certain individuals could visit Mitya, and only after going through the required formalities. But over time, though the formal rules weren't officially loosened, some visitors—like Alyosha, Grushenka, and Rakitin—were treated more leniently. Their meetings with Mitya were often allowed to be private conversations.

The police captain, Mihail Mihailovitch, had taken a liking to Grushenka, especially after what had happened in Mokroe. His initial harsh opinion of her had softened once he learned the full story. Even though he remained convinced of Mitya's guilt, his attitude toward him began to shift after Mitya was imprisoned. "He might be a man with a good heart," the captain thought, "just someone who was ruined by drinking and a wild life." His earlier horror turned to pity.

As for Alyosha, the captain had always been fond of him. He had known him for a long time. Rakitin, too, had been visiting Mitya frequently. He was familiar with the captain's daughters—whom the captain jokingly called his "young ladies"—and spent a lot of time at their house. Rakitin also gave lessons to the children of the prison superintendent. The superintendent, though strict in his duties, was a kind man who had long-standing respect for Alyosha and enjoyed talking to him—especially about spiritual matters. Though the superintendent considered himself quite knowledgeable, even a philosopher, he admired Alyosha and was drawn to him. He had also become interested in studying the Apocryphal Gospels and would often discuss them with Alyosha and the monks at the monastery.

Because of all this, Alyosha was always welcomed at the prison. Even if he came late, the superintendent would make sure everything went smoothly. Everyone there, including the lowest guard, was used to seeing him. Even the sentry at the gate didn't trouble him since the officials trusted him.

When Mitya was called from his cell, he usually came downstairs to the designated visitor's room. As Alyosha entered, he saw that Rakitin was just leaving. Mitya was laughing loudly, clearly enjoying himself, while Rakitin, in contrast, looked irritated. Rakitin wasn't pleased to see Alyosha and only gave him a stiff, reluctant nod. He frowned, avoiding eye contact, while buttoning up his heavy coat with its fur trim and searching for his umbrella.

"I'd better not forget anything," Rakitin muttered, just to fill the silence.

"Careful you don't take anything that's not yours," Mitya joked, laughing at his own remark.

Rakitin's face turned red with anger. "You'd better tell that to your own family—those slave-drivers!" he snapped, trembling with rage.

"Hey, I was just joking!" Mitya exclaimed. "What's wrong with him?" he added, turning to Alyosha as Rakitin stormed out. "He was sitting here, laughing and chatting a minute ago, and now he flies off the handle like that. Did you see how he didn't even say goodbye to you? Have you two had a falling out or something? Anyway, why are you so late? I've been waiting for you all day— not just waiting, but thirsting for you to come!"

"Why does Rakitin come here so often? Are you two close now?" Alyosha asked, nodding toward the door Rakitin had just slammed behind him.

"Close with Rakitin? No, not really. Do you think I'd be close with someone like that? He thinks I'm a scoundrel. The problem with people like him is that they can't take a joke. Their souls are as dry as these prison walls were when I first got here. But I'll admit—he's a clever guy. Very clever. Well, Alyosha, it's all over for me now."

He sat down on the bench and motioned for Alyosha to sit beside him.

"Yes, the trial is tomorrow. Are you really feeling hopeless about it, brother?" Alyosha asked, a worried note in his voice.

"What are you talking about?" Mitya asked, looking at him with confusion. "Oh, you mean the trial? Damn it! I wasn't even talking about that. The trial doesn't matter. When I said it was all over for me, I wasn't talking about the trial."

"Then what did you mean?" Alyosha asked, puzzled.

"Just ideas, brother. Ethics and all that nonsense!" Mitya sighed. "Ethics?" Alyosha repeated, confused.

"Yes! Ethics—is that supposed to be some kind of science?"

"Well, yes, I guess it is a kind of science... but I can't explain exactly what kind," Alyosha admitted.

"Rakitin knows all about that stuff," Mitya muttered bitterly. "He's not going to become a monk, you know. He's headed to Petersburg, where he plans to dabble in philosophy and criticism. Who knows? He might even make a name for himself. These types always do—they know how to play the game. Damn ethics! I'm finished, Alyosha. I am done for, and you, my man of God, are the only one I truly love. It tears my heart just to look at you. By the way, do you know who Karl Bernard is?"

"Karl Bernard?" Alyosha repeated, bewildered.

"No, wait—I got it wrong. Claude Bernard! What was he? A chemist or something?"

"I've heard of him, but I don't know much about him," Alyosha admitted. "I think he was some sort of scholar."

"Well, forget him!" Mitya swore. "He's probably just another scoundrel. They're all scoundrels! And Rakitin will get ahead just like the rest of them. He's another Bernard, that one. Ugh, these Bernards are everywhere!"

Alyosha leaned closer. "What's really bothering you, Mitya?" he asked firmly.

"He wants to write an article about me, about my case, to kick off his literary career. That's why he keeps coming. He even told me himself," Mitya said with a wry smile. "He's trying to prove some theory, saying things like, 'He couldn't help killing his father. It's society's fault, a product of his environment.' He told me he'd even sprinkle in a bit of Socialism for flair. But I don't care. Let him write whatever he wants. He can't stand Ivan, you know. Hates him, actually. And he's not too fond of you either. But I let him stay around because, well, he's clever. Just full of himself, though. I told him earlier, 'The Karamazovs aren't scoundrels; we're philosophers. All true Russians are philosophers. But you, with all your studying, you're not a philosopher.

You're just low.' He laughed, all smug. So I said to him, 'De ideabus non est disputandum.' Pretty good, right? I'm playing the classic now!" Mitya laughed abruptly.

"But what did you mean earlier when you said it's all over for you?" Alyosha asked.

"Ah, that." Mitya paused, rubbing his temples. "It's hard to explain... It's just that... I think I'm sad about losing God. That's what it is."

"Losing God? What do you mean?" Alyosha leaned closer.

"Well, imagine this. Inside our brains, we have nerves, right? These little nerve endings, like tiny tails, are always twitching. I look at something with my eyes, and those tails start twitching. And when they twitch, an image pops into my mind. But it doesn't happen instantly. There's always a tiny delay—a second or two. And that's how I see and think, not because I have a soul or anything. It's just nerves doing their thing. Rakitin explained it all to me yesterday. Isn't that amazing? This is science! There's a new kind of man coming, Alyosha, and it's all thanks to science... but still, I'm sad about losing God."

"At least you feel sorry about it," Alyosha said gently.

"Yes, but it's all chemistry now, brother! Chemistry is taking over, and even God can't stop it. Rakitin hates God—hates Him with a passion. But he hides it, of course. They all do. They lie about it. 'Would you preach this in your articles?' I asked him. He just laughed and said, 'If I wrote that openly, they'd never publish me.' Then I asked him, 'What happens to people without God or the promise of eternal life? Can they do whatever they want?' And do you know what he said? 'A clever man always finds a way. But you? You messed up. You killed someone, and now you're rotting in prison.' He said that to my face! What a pig! I used to kick people like that out the door, but now I just listen. The worst part is, he makes sense sometimes. He's a good writer, too. He read me part of an article last week. I even copied down a few lines. Wait, here."

Mitya pulled a crumpled piece of paper from his pocket and read: "'In order to determine this question, it is above all essential to put one's personality in contradiction to one's reality.' What do you think that means?"

"I have no idea," Alyosha admitted, intrigued but puzzled.

"Me neither! It's nonsense. But these intellectuals love that kind of stuff. 'Everyone writes like this now,' Rakitin told me. 'It's all because of the environment.' He even writes poetry! Did you know that?"

"Yes, I heard about it."

"He wrote a poem about Madame Hohlakov's foot. Can you believe that? I've got it right here. I'll read it to you. But there's more to the story. Three weeks ago, he started bragging to me, saying, 'You ruined yourself over a measly three thousand, but I'm going to marry a widow and get my hands on one hundred and fifty thousand.' He said he was courting Madame Hohlakov. 'She wasn't very bright when she was young, and now that she's older, she's lost what little sense she had,' he told me. 'But she's sentimental, and that's how I'll win her. Once I marry her, I'll take her to Petersburg and start a newspaper.' And the way he talked, it wasn't about her at all—it was all about the money. Every day, he'd come here and say, 'She's coming around.' Then, all of a sudden, she kicked him out, and Perhotin took his place. I could kiss that old fool for getting rid of him!" Mitya chuckled.

"And this is the poem he wrote to try to win her over. Can you imagine? He even said, 'It's the first time I've lowered myself to write poetry, but it's for a good cause.' He claimed that once he got the money, he'd do something useful for society. That's how they justify everything! He even said his poem was better than anything Pushkin wrote, because his had a message. Here, listen to this nonsense:

A captivating little foot,
Though swollen and red and tender!

The doctors come and plasters put,
But still they cannot mend her.
Yet, 'tis not for her foot I dread—
A theme for Pushkin's muse more fit—
It's not her foot, it is her head:
I tremble for her loss of wit!
For as her foot swells, strange to say,
Her intellect is on the wane—
Oh, for some remedy I pray
That may restore both foot and brain!

"Can you believe that?" Mitya laughed bitterly. "What a pig! But he really thought it was clever. And wasn't he furious when she kicked him out! He was gnashing his teeth!"

"He's already getting his revenge," Alyosha said quietly. "He wrote that awful paragraph about her in Gossip."

"I knew it was him!" Mitya growled, frowning. "He's been spreading those nasty rumors—about Grushenka, too. And Katya... Hm." He paced the room, looking troubled.

"Brother, I can't stay much longer," Alyosha said softly after a moment. "Tomorrow is a big day—the trial. God's judgment will come to pass. And here you are, talking about poetry and who knows what else..."

Mitya interrupted passionately, "No, don't be surprised by me. Do you expect me to keep talking about that filthy creature? The murderer? I've said enough about him. I don't want to talk anymore about that disgusting son of Stinking Lizaveta! God will take care of him—just wait and see. Enough!"

He walked over to Alyosha, full of emotion, and kissed him. His eyes shone with intensity.

"Rakitin would never understand what I'm about to say," Mitya began, his voice shaking with excitement, "but you will. That's why I've been longing for you, waiting to talk. There's so much I've kept inside these peeling walls, things I've never said out loud because the moment never seemed right. But now, I can't wait any longer—I need to pour out my heart to you. Brother, these past two months, I've discovered someone new inside me. It's like a new man has come to life within me, a man I never knew was there. And if it weren't for this disaster—this blow from heaven—I might never have found him. But now, I'm afraid—so afraid—that I'll lose him."

Mitya's voice trembled, and he clutched Alyosha's hand. "I'm not afraid of breaking rocks in the mines for twenty years— that's nothing. What scares me is that this new man inside me will vanish. Even in the mines, deep underground, I might find another convict or murderer with a human heart buried inside him, and I could reach him. I could thaw his frozen heart, even if it takes years, and maybe, from the depths of his suffering, a noble soul might rise—a hero, an angel! There are so many like that, hundreds of them, and it's our fault they ended up there. That's why I dreamed of that poor baby. 'Why is the baby poor?' That question was a sign, Alyosha. I must go to the mines for that baby, because we're all responsible—for every child, every person. Whether they're small children or grown men, they're all babes. Someone has to take the blame. I didn't kill Father, but I will accept the punishment. I've realized that now, here, in these peeling walls."

Mitya's eyes burned as he spoke. "Down there in the mines, we'll be in chains. There won't be freedom, but in the midst of our suffering, we'll find joy again. We can't live without joy, Alyosha, just as God Himself can't exist without it. Joy is His greatest gift to us. In our deepest sorrow, we'll rise to joy. That's the miracle of it! Man was made for joy, Alyosha. What would I do underground without God? It's impossible to survive there without Him—it's even harder than surviving without Him up here. If they drive God out of the world, we'll hide Him underground. And we men, buried in the earth, will sing hymns to Him from the depths of the mines. We'll sing to God with joy in our hearts. I love Him!"

Mitya was gasping for breath, his lips quivering as tears rolled down his cheeks.

"Life is full—there's life even underground," he said with passion. "You wouldn't believe how much I want to live now. I have this overwhelming thirst for existence and awareness, even here, in these peeling walls. Rakitin doesn't understand any of that. All he cares about is money and comfort. But I've missed you, Alyosha. And as for suffering—let it come! I'm not afraid anymore, even if the suffering is beyond anything I can imagine. I could endure anything, just to be able to say to myself every moment, 'I exist.' Even in agony, I'll know I exist. Even if I'm tortured, even if I sit on a pillar alone for years, I'll still know, 'I exist.' I'll see the sun, and even if I don't see it, I'll know it's there. That alone will be enough."

Alyosha listened quietly, his heart aching for his brother.

"These thoughts, these philosophies—they're driving me mad," Mitya went on, pacing the room restlessly. "And Ivan—"

"What about Ivan?" Alyosha interrupted, but Mitya didn't seem to hear.

"Before, none of this ever troubled me. But now I see that these doubts have always been there, buried deep inside me. Maybe that's why I used to drink and fight—to drown them out, to keep them silent. But Ivan... Ivan isn't like Rakitin. Ivan has something real inside him, something deep and dangerous. Ivan is like a sphinx—he's always silent, always holding everything inside. And it's God who troubles me the most, Alyosha. What if God doesn't exist? What if Rakitin is right? What if God is just an idea we made up? If God isn't real, then man is the ruler of the world, of the universe. Isn't that magnificent? But without God, how can man be good? That's the real question. Who will we love if there is no God? Who will we thank? Who will we sing to?"

Mitya shook his head bitterly. "Rakitin says we can love humanity without God. But only a fool could believe that. Without God, men will just do whatever benefits them. I told Rakitin, 'Without God, you'll raise the price of meat if it suits you.' That shut him up. But tell me, Alyosha—what is goodness, really? Isn't it different for everyone? What's good for me might not be good for someone in China. So isn't goodness just relative? That question has been driving me mad. How do people go on living without thinking about this?"

Alyosha tried to speak, but Mitya pressed on, "And Ivan—he has no God, only an idea. And that's worse. He's silent, and I think he's hiding something. Maybe he's even a Freemason—I asked him, but he wouldn't answer. I wanted to understand him, to drink from his soul, but he wouldn't let me. Only once did he say something."

"What did he say?" Alyosha asked quickly.

Mitya's expression darkened. "I asked him, 'If there's no God, then everything is allowed, right?' And he said, 'Our father was a pig, but his ideas were right.' That's worse than anything Rakitin has ever said."

Alyosha nodded slowly, a deep sadness in his heart. "When did Ivan visit you?"

"I'll tell you everything later," Mitya promised. "After the trial, when it's all over, we'll talk. I have something huge to tell you— something I need you to judge. But not now. Let's leave it for later."

Mitya paused, his expression shifting again. "You keep talking about the trial tomorrow, but do you know something, Alyosha? I don't even care about it anymore."

"Have you spoken with your lawyer?" Alyosha asked.

"What's the point of the lawyer? I told him everything. He's just a smooth-talking, soft city guy—a real Bernard! But would you believe it, he doesn't believe me. He actually thinks I did it. I can tell by the way he looks at me. So, I asked him, 'If you think I'm guilty, why are you even defending me?' Damn them all! They even brought in a doctor to say I'm insane. But I won't have that! Katerina Ivanovna wants to do her duty to the very end, no matter how hard it is!" Mitya gave a bitter smile. "That woman! She knows I called her a woman of 'great wrath' back at Mokroe, and they told her I said it. The evidence against me keeps building up, like grains of sand. Grigory is still sticking to his story. He's honest, but he's a fool. Rakitin says a lot of people are only honest because they're fools. Grigory's my enemy now. And you know, some people make better enemies than friends—like Katerina Ivanovna. I'm scared she's going to tell the whole court about how she bowed down after I gave her that four thousand rubles. She'll pay it back, every last bit. I don't even want her sacrifice— it'll only humiliate me at the trial. How am I supposed to bear it? Alyosha, could you go to her and ask her not to say anything about that in court? Can't you try? But, damn it, what does it matter? I'll get through it somehow. I don't pity her—it's her own fault. She deserves what's coming. I have my own story to tell."

Mitya gave another bitter smile. "But Grusha, oh Grusha! God, why does she have to suffer so much?" He suddenly broke into tears. "She's killing me, Alyosha. The thought of her is tearing me apart. It's killing me. She was just here with me."

"She told me she was really upset with you today," Alyosha said softly.

"I know," Mitya muttered. "It was my stupid temper—jealousy. I felt bad and kissed her when she was leaving, but I didn't ask her to forgive me."

"Why not?" Alyosha asked, startled.

Suddenly, Mitya laughed, almost cheerfully. "Oh, my dear boy, may God save you from ever asking a woman you love for forgiveness! Especially one you truly love, no matter how much you've messed up. Women are impossible to understand! I know them well enough. If you admit you're wrong and say, 'I'm sorry, please forgive me,' she'll bury you under a mountain of complaints! She won't just forgive you—oh no! She'll bring up things that never even happened, remind you of every mistake, and make up new ones. And only after dragging you through all that will she forgive you. Even the best of them do it! They're all like that, these angels we can't live without. Believe me, every decent man ought to be under a woman's thumb. That's not just some theory—it's how I feel. It's no shame for a man—not even for a hero, not even for a Caesar! But remember what I'm telling you, brother. Never, ever beg for forgiveness. You have to find another way to make things right. I worship Grusha, Alyosha—I worship her. But she doesn't see it. She still thinks I don't love her enough. And so she tortures me with her love. What she did before was nothing—just those curves of hers driving me mad.

But now I've taken her whole soul into mine, and through her, I've become a better man. Will they let us marry? If they don't, I'll die of jealousy. I imagine the worst every day. What did she say to you about me?"

Alyosha repeated everything Grushenka had said. Mitya listened carefully, making him repeat parts, and seemed pleased by what he heard.

"So, she's not mad at me for being jealous?" he asked eagerly. "She's a real woman! 'I've got a fierce heart too,' she said. Ah, I love those fierce hearts, even though I can't stand it when anyone's jealous of me. I hate it! We'll probably fight about it, but I'll still love her, love her endlessly. Will they let convicts get married? That's the real question. I can't live without her…"

Mitya paced the room, frowning deeply. The light was fading, and shadows began to fill the room. Suddenly, his expression grew troubled. "She thinks there's a secret, a plot against her with Katya involved? No, no, my dear Grusha, you've got it all wrong. That's not what's going on. Alyosha, my brother, I'll tell you the real secret."

He glanced around quickly, then leaned in close to Alyosha, speaking in a low, urgent whisper. No one else could hear them— the old guard was dozing in the corner, and the soldiers outside were too far away.

"I have to tell you everything," Mitya whispered. "I was going to wait, but I can't decide anything without you. You're everything to me. I say Ivan is superior, but maybe it's you who's really superior. This is a matter of conscience—a higher conscience. It's too important for me to figure out on my own, and I've been waiting to talk to you about it. But don't decide anything yet. We have to wait until after the verdict. Once that's done, you'll decide my fate. Not now. Just listen for now. I'll tell you the main idea without the details. Stay quiet—no questions, no reactions. Can you do that? Oh, but what will I do if your eyes give me away? I'm afraid I'll see your answer just by looking at you. I can't bear it!"

Mitya's eyes sparkled with fear and hope. "Ivan thinks I should escape. Everything's planned out. I could run away to America with Grusha. You know I can't live without her. What if they don't let her come with me to Siberia? Do they even allow convicts to marry? Ivan thinks they won't. And if Grusha isn't with me, what's the point? I'd just smash my own skull with a hammer! But then, what about my conscience? I'd be running away from suffering. If I ignore this chance, am I rejecting a sign from above? Ivan says I'd be more useful in America, but what about the hymn we were supposed to sing from the depths? America is just vanity—and probably full of crooks too. I'd be running from my cross. That's why I'm telling you, Alyosha—only you can understand this. No one else would. People would think I'm mad or foolish. Ivan understands the hymn, but he won't talk about it. He doesn't believe in it."

Mitya's voice grew desperate. "Don't say anything, Alyosha! I can see your answer in your eyes already. Please, don't decide yet—just wait until after the trial! I need Grusha. I can't live without her."

Mitya held Alyosha by the shoulders, his fevered eyes locked on his brother's. "They won't let convicts marry, will they?" he whispered, almost pleading.

Alyosha, deeply moved and surprised, took a moment before replying. "Tell me—does Ivan really want you to escape? Was it his idea?"

"Yes, it was his idea, and he's serious about it," Mitya answered. "He didn't visit me at first, but when he finally did a week ago, he jumped right into it. He's determined. He didn't ask me—he ordered me to escape. He assumes I'll do as he says, even though I showed him my heart, just like I'm showing it to you. I told him about the hymn too. But he's got everything figured out—every detail. He says it's just a matter of money. Ten thousand rubles for the escape, and another twenty thousand to get me to America."

"And he told you not to tell me?" Alyosha asked quietly.

"Don't tell anyone, especially not you," Mitya whispered urgently. "He's afraid you'll stand in front of me like my conscience. Promise you won't tell him I told you. No matter what, don't let him know."

"You're right," Alyosha answered softly. "It's impossible to decide anything before the trial. After the trial, you'll make your decision. You'll find that new man inside you, and he'll know what to do."

"A new man—or maybe just another Bernard, making choices like a Bernard," Mitya muttered with a bitter grin. "I think I might be nothing more than a lousy Bernard myself."

"But, brother, don't you have any hope of being found innocent?" Alyosha asked.

Mitya shrugged nervously and shook his head. "Alyosha, dear, you need to go now," he said suddenly, his voice filled with urgency. "I hear the superintendent calling from the yard. He'll be here any moment. We're late—it's not allowed. Quick, hug me! Kiss me! Give me a blessing—cross me for the burden I'll have to carry tomorrow."

They embraced tightly, kissing each other on the cheek.

"Ivan," Mitya added abruptly, "thinks I should escape. But, deep down, I think he really believes I did it."

A sad smile flickered on his lips.

"Have you asked him if he believes it?" Alyosha inquired gently.

"No, I couldn't. I wanted to, but I didn't have the courage. I saw it in his eyes, though." Mitya let out a heavy breath. "Goodbye, Alyosha."

They kissed again, quickly and urgently, and Alyosha started to leave. But just as he reached the door, Mitya called him back.

"Wait! Face me!" Mitya ordered. Alyosha turned, and Mitya grabbed him by the shoulders, holding him firmly. In the dim light, his face looked frighteningly pale, and his lips trembled. His wide, anxious eyes locked onto Alyosha's.

"Alyosha, tell me the truth. Tell me like you're standing before God. Do you think I did it? Do you, deep down, believe I killed him? Don't lie—tell me the truth!"

Alyosha felt his heart twist painfully, as if a knife had pierced it. The room seemed to sway around him. "What are you saying?" he stammered, almost helplessly.

"The whole truth, Alyosha! No lies!" Mitya cried desperately.

Alyosha's voice trembled as he answered, "I've never believed, not for a second, that you were the one who killed him!" His hand shot up instinctively, as if swearing before God that he was speaking the truth.

Mitya's face changed completely—joy and relief washed over him like a warm light.

"Thank you," Mitya whispered, slowly releasing a breath like a man waking from a nightmare. "You've given me new life. Would you believe me if I told you I was too afraid to ask you this until now? Even you... I was afraid to ask. But now, I feel ready for tomorrow. God bless you, brother! Go now—and love Ivan."

Those were Mitya's parting words. Alyosha left the room in tears, shaken to his core. Mitya's doubt and mistrust—even toward him, Alyosha—had revealed a deep well of sorrow and despair in his brother's heart. Alyosha was overwhelmed with compassion, feeling his heart tear painfully in two.

"Love Ivan," he remembered Mitya saying. He was already on his way to see Ivan and had wanted to see him all day. He realized now that he was just as worried about Ivan as he was about Mitya—maybe even more.

Chapter 5: Not You, Not You!

On the way to Ivan, Alyosha had to pass the house where Katerina Ivanovna lived. He noticed lights in the windows and suddenly decided to go inside. He hadn't seen Katerina for over a week, but now it occurred to him that Ivan might be there with her, especially on the eve of such an important day. As he rang the bell and climbed the dimly lit staircase, illuminated only by a Chinese lantern, he saw a man coming down. As they crossed paths, Alyosha recognized him—it was Ivan. So, Ivan had just come from Katerina's.

"Oh, it's you," Ivan said flatly. "Well, goodbye. Are you going to see her?" "Yes."

"I wouldn't, if I were you. She's upset, and you'll only make things worse."

Just then, a door swung open above, and a voice called down urgently.

"No, no! Alexey Fyodorovitch, have you been with him?"

"Yes, I just came from him."

"Did he send any message for me? Come up, Alyosha! And you, Ivan Fyodorovitch, you must come back. Do you hear me? You must come back!"

Katerina's voice had such a commanding tone that, after a moment of hesitation, Ivan turned and followed Alyosha back upstairs.

"She was eavesdropping," Ivan muttered bitterly to himself, but Alyosha heard him.

"Forgive me for keeping my coat on," Ivan said as they entered the drawing room. "I'm not sitting down. I won't stay long."

"Sit down, Alexey Fyodorovitch," Katerina said, though she remained standing. She looked much the same as before, though her dark eyes gleamed with something ominous. Alyosha would later recall that she seemed especially beautiful at that moment.

"What did he ask you to tell me?"

"Just one thing," Alyosha answered, meeting her gaze. "He asked you to spare yourself and not bring up what happened between you two during your first meeting... in that other town."

"Oh, you mean when I bowed down to the ground for that money?" Katerina laughed bitterly. "So, is he worried about me or about himself? Who does he want me to protect—me or him? Tell me, Alexey Fyodorovitch!"

Alyosha studied her, trying to understand what she meant.

"Both you and him," he said quietly.

"Well, I'm glad to hear it," she replied with a sharp tone, her cheeks suddenly flushing.

"You don't know me yet, Alexey Fyodorovitch," she said with a threatening edge. "And to be honest, I don't know myself either. Maybe after my testimony tomorrow, you'll want to trample me underfoot."

"You'll testify with honor," Alyosha assured her. "That's all that matters."

"Women aren't always honorable," she sneered. "Just an hour ago, I thought I couldn't even touch that man—as if he were some kind of vile creature. But no, he's still a human being to me! But tell me—did he do it? Is he really the murderer?" she demanded suddenly, turning to Ivan with a desperate, almost hysterical tone.

Alyosha immediately realized that she had already asked Ivan this question—probably just before he arrived, and not for the first time. It seemed like she had asked it a hundred times, and it always ended in an argument.

"I went to see Smerdyakov... It was you—you convinced me that he killed Fyodor Pavlovitch. You're the only one I believed!" she continued, still directing her words at Ivan. Ivan gave her a strained smile, but Alyosha was startled by the unusual closeness in their interaction.

"That's enough for now," Ivan said abruptly, cutting the conversation short. "I'm leaving. I'll come back tomorrow." He turned and walked out of the room, heading quickly down the stairs.

Without a second thought, Katerina grabbed Alyosha's hands in a firm grip.

"Follow him! Don't leave him alone for a second!" she whispered urgently. "He's not well—don't you see? He's mad! The doctor told me it's a nervous fever. Go after him, quickly!"

Alyosha leapt to his feet and rushed after Ivan, who was already about fifty paces ahead.

"What do you want?" Ivan asked, spinning around as Alyosha caught up with him. "She sent you to chase after me, didn't she? She thinks I'm mad. I know exactly what's going on," he added irritably.

"She may be wrong, but she's right that you're unwell," Alyosha replied gently. "I could see it in your face just now. You don't look well at all, Ivan."

Ivan kept walking, and Alyosha stayed close beside him.

"Do you know, Alexey Fyodorovitch," Ivan began in a calm voice, with no trace of irritation, "do you know how people go mad?"

"No, I don't. I suppose it happens differently for everyone."

"Do you think someone can realize they're going mad?" Ivan asked, his tone curious, as if he were genuinely interested in the answer.

"I don't think you can see yourself clearly when it happens," Alyosha answered, puzzled by the question.

Ivan stopped walking and stood in silence for a moment.

"If you want to talk to me, change the subject," Ivan suddenly said.

"Oh, I almost forgot. I have a letter for you," Alyosha said timidly, pulling Lise's note from his pocket and handing it to Ivan. They were standing under a streetlight. Ivan recognized the handwriting immediately.

"Ah, from that little devil!" he laughed maliciously, and without opening it, he tore the envelope into pieces and scattered them in the wind. "She's not even sixteen yet and already offering herself," he said with contempt, continuing down the street.

"What do you mean, offering herself?" Alyosha exclaimed. "Like women of the street offer themselves, of course."

"How can you say that, Ivan? How can you?" Alyosha cried out, his voice full of pain. "She's just a child! You're insulting a child! She's sick, very sick, maybe even on the verge of insanity. I thought you might say something that could help her."

"You'll hear nothing from me. If she's a child, I'm not her nurse. Leave it alone, Alexey. I'm not even thinking about her."

They were quiet for a moment.

"She'll probably spend the whole night praying to the Mother of God, asking for guidance on what to do tomorrow at the trial," Ivan said sharply.

"You mean Katerina Ivanovna?" Alyosha asked.

"Yes. She's wondering whether she should save Mitya or destroy him. She'll pray for some kind of divine answer because she can't make up her own mind. She sees me as her caretaker too. She wants me to sing her lullabies."

"Katerina Ivanovna loves you, brother," Alyosha said softly. "Maybe, but I'm not very interested in her," Ivan replied coldly. "She's suffering. Why do you give her false hope sometimes?"

Alyosha asked, almost apologetically. "I know you've given her hope. Please forgive me for asking."

"I can't deal with her the way I should—by ending things completely and telling her it's over," Ivan said irritably. "I have to wait until the verdict is out. If I break things off now, she'll take revenge by destroying that scoundrel tomorrow at the trial because she hates him. She lies to herself, telling herself she doesn't hate him. But if I don't end things, she'll hold back, knowing that I want him to be saved. I wish that damned verdict would just come!"

The words "murderer" and "monster" echoed painfully in Alyosha's heart.

"But how could she ruin Mitya? What kind of evidence could she give?" Alyosha asked, trying to understand Ivan's words.

"You don't know? She has a letter in Mitya's own handwriting that proves he killed Fyodor Pavlovitch."

"That's impossible!" Alyosha cried out. "Why? I've read it myself," Ivan said.

"There can't be such a letter!" Alyosha repeated firmly. "There can't be, because Mitya isn't the murderer. He didn't kill Father. He didn't!"

Ivan stopped abruptly.

"Then who did, according to you?" he asked coldly, with a hint of sarcasm in his voice.

"You know who," Alyosha said quietly, his voice filled with emotion.

"Who? Are you talking about that ridiculous story about the epileptic, Smerdyakov?"

Alyosha suddenly felt himself trembling all over. "You know who," he whispered, barely able to speak.

"Who? Who?" Ivan shouted, losing his composure. All his restraint was gone.

"I only know one thing," Alyosha continued, still speaking softly but with conviction. "It wasn't you who killed Father."

"'Not me'? What do you mean by that?" Ivan was taken aback. "It wasn't you who killed Father, not you," Alyosha repeated, his voice firm.

There was silence for half a minute.

"I know I didn't. Are you out of your mind?" Ivan said, his smile pale and twisted. His eyes were fixed on Alyosha. They were both standing still under the streetlight.

"No, Ivan. You've told yourself many times that you're the murderer," Alyosha said.

"When did I ever say that? I was in Moscow! When have I said that?" Ivan stammered.

"You've said it to yourself many times over these two terrible months," Alyosha went on, his voice still calm but filled with a strange certainty, as though he was obeying a command beyond his control. "You've blamed yourself. You've told yourself that you're the murderer, but you're wrong. You didn't do it. You're not the murderer. Do you hear me? It wasn't you. God has sent me to tell you this."

The silence between them stretched on for what felt like an eternity. They stood there, staring into each other's eyes, both pale. Suddenly, Ivan began to tremble and grabbed Alyosha's shoulder.

"You've been in my room!" he whispered hoarsely. "You were there when he came. Admit it—did you see him?"

"Who do you mean—Mitya?" Alyosha asked, confused.

"Not him, damn the monster!" Ivan shouted, nearly out of control. "Don't you know that he visits me? How do you know about him? Tell me!"

"Who are you talking about? I don't know who you mean," Alyosha stammered, growing alarmed.

"Yes, you do know... how could you not?" Ivan suddenly stopped himself. He stood still, thinking for a moment, then a strange grin twisted his lips.

"Brother," Alyosha began again, his voice shaking, "I'm telling you this because I know you'll believe me. I swear to you, it wasn't you. You hear me? God has put it in my heart to tell you this, even if you end up hating me for it."

But by now, Ivan had regained his composure.

"Alexey Fyodorovitch," he said with a cold smile, "I can't stand prophets and epileptics—especially ones sent by God—and you know that. From this moment on, we are done. I break all ties with you, probably forever. I suggest you take your leave right here. This is your way back to your lodgings, too. And make sure you don't come to me again today. Do you understand?"

He turned and walked away, his steps firm, without looking back.

"Brother!" Alyosha called after him. "If anything happens to you today, come to me before anyone else!"

Ivan gave no reply. Alyosha stayed beneath the lamppost at the crossroads, watching until his brother disappeared into the darkness. Then, slowly, he turned and started walking home. Both Alyosha and Ivan rented rooms in town; neither of them wanted to stay in their father's empty house. Alyosha had taken a modest room in the home of a working-class family. Ivan lived farther away, in a spacious but simple lodge that was part of a larger, well-kept house owned by the widow of an official. However, the only person attending to Ivan was an old woman—deaf, frail, and plagued with rheumatism—who went to bed at six in the evening and woke at six in the morning. Lately, Ivan had grown indifferent to comfort and preferred solitude. He handled all his own tasks and rarely ventured beyond the one room he occupied, leaving the rest of the lodge untouched.

When Ivan arrived at the gate of the house, his hand rested on the bell, but he didn't ring it. A surge of anger swept over him, making him tremble. Cursing under his breath, he pulled his hand away from the bell and turned abruptly. He strode off in the opposite direction, walking quickly through the cold night.

He covered a mile and a half before reaching a small, weather-worn wooden house—more of a hut, leaning slightly to one side. This was where Marya Kondratyevna, the woman who used to visit Fyodor Pavlovitch's kitchen for soup and listen to Smerdyakov sing and play the guitar, now lived with her mother. She had sold their old house and moved here after his death. Smerdyakov, weak and gravely ill, had been staying with them since Fyodor Pavlovitch's murder. It was to him that Ivan was now heading, compelled by a sudden, unshakable urge.

Chapter 6: The First Interview with Smerdyakov

This was the third time Ivan had visited Smerdyakov since returning from Moscow. The first time he saw him and spoke with him was on the very day he had arrived. Then, he had visited him once more, a fortnight later. But his visits had stopped after that second one, and now, more than a month had passed without him seeing or hearing much about Smerdyakov.

Ivan had returned five days after his father's death, meaning he wasn't present for the funeral, which had taken place the day before he came back. His delay was caused by Alyosha, who, not knowing Ivan's Moscow address, had to ask Katerina Ivanovna to send him a telegram. But she, not knowing Ivan's address either, had to telegraph her sister and aunt, counting on Ivan going to see them when he arrived in Moscow. Ivan, however, didn't go to them until four days after his arrival. When he finally received the telegram, he had left immediately to return to the town. Alyosha was the first to meet him, and Ivan was greatly surprised when, contrary to what everyone in town believed, Alyosha refused to suspect Mitya and instead openly accused Smerdyakov of being the murderer.

After hearing the details from the police captain and the prosecutor and learning of the charges and Mitya's arrest, Ivan became even more surprised by Alyosha's stance. He chalked it up to Alyosha's intense brotherly love and sympathy for Mitya, whom he knew Alyosha loved deeply.

Let's pause for a moment to examine Ivan's own feelings toward his brother Dmitri (Mitya). Ivan didn't just dislike Mitya; he had, at best, fleeting moments of pity for him, but even that pity was mixed with great contempt, almost repulsion. Mitya's entire personality, even his appearance, was deeply off-putting to Ivan. He was particularly resentful of Katerina Ivanovna's love for his brother. Yet despite all this, Ivan still went to see Mitya on the first day of his return. That meeting did nothing to shake Ivan's belief in his brother's guilt; in fact, it only strengthened it. He found Mitya in an agitated state, nervously excited. Mitya had talked a lot, but he was incoherent and distracted. He used harsh language, repeatedly accusing Smerdyakov and seemed utterly confused. The majority of what he said revolved around the three thousand rubles that he claimed their father had stolen from him.

"The money was mine, it was my money," Mitya kept insisting. "Even if I had stolen it, I had the right to it."

Mitya barely challenged the evidence against him. When he did try to defend himself, he did so in a scattered and absurd way. He didn't seem to want to defend himself to Ivan or anyone else. On the contrary, he seemed angry and proud in the face of the charges. He would flare up in rage and lash out at everyone around him. He even laughed off Grigory's testimony about the open door, declaring, "the devil opened it," but he couldn't offer any reasonable explanation. He even managed to offend Ivan during their meeting by sharply telling him that someone like Ivan, who believes "everything is allowed," had no right to question him. In short, their meeting was far from friendly.

After that encounter with Mitya, Ivan went to see Smerdyakov for the first time. During his train journey from Moscow, Ivan kept thinking about his last conversation with Smerdyakov, which had taken place on the evening before Ivan left town. Several things about that conversation had struck him as strange and suspicious. However, when Ivan gave his statement to the investigating lawyer, he hadn't mentioned this conversation yet. He planned to hold off until after speaking with Smerdyakov again, who was now in the hospital.

Doctors Herzenstube and Varvinsky, whom Ivan had met at the hospital, had assured him that Smerdyakov's epileptic attack had been genuine. They were even surprised that Ivan had asked if it could have been faked on the day of the murder. The doctors explained that Smerdyakov's seizure had been severe, with repeated fits that put his life in danger. Only now, after treatment, were they confident that he would survive. However, Dr. Herzenstube warned that Smerdyakov's mental state might remain affected for a long time, possibly even permanently. When Ivan asked, with growing impatience, if that meant Smerdyakov had gone mad, the doctors clarified that he wasn't fully insane, but there were noticeable abnormalities in his behavior. Ivan decided he needed to see these abnormalities for himself.

At the hospital, Ivan was allowed to see Smerdyakov right away. He found him lying on a low bed in a small ward. There was only one other bed in the room, occupied by a dying tradesman swollen with dropsy, so there would be no disturbance to their conversation. When Smerdyakov saw Ivan, he gave him a brief, nervous grin—or at least Ivan thought he did—but that nervousness quickly passed. Ivan was struck by how calm and composed Smerdyakov seemed for the rest of the time. From the first glance, Ivan could tell that Smerdyakov was seriously ill. He looked frail, spoke slowly, and seemed to have difficulty moving his tongue. He was much thinner and paler than before. Throughout their twenty-minute conversation, Smerdyakov kept complaining about a persistent headache and pain all over his body. His thin, gaunt face seemed to have shrunk, and his disheveled hair stuck up in a thin tuft in front. However, despite his frailty, the sly look in his left eye—the one that often seemed to be hiding something—remained unchanged. Ivan was reminded of how Smerdyakov always enjoyed talking to "clever people."

Ivan sat down on a stool by the bed. Smerdyakov, with some effort, shifted his position slightly, but he didn't speak first. He stayed silent and didn't seem particularly interested in the conversation.

"Can you talk to me?" Ivan asked. "I won't take much of your time."

"Yes, I can," mumbled Smerdyakov weakly. "How long have you been back, sir?" he added, almost as if trying to encourage Ivan, like he was nervous.

"I just got here today... to see the mess you've made." Smerdyakov sighed.

"Why are you sighing? You knew this would happen," Ivan said sharply.

Smerdyakov was quiet for a while.

"How could I not know? It was obvious from the start. But how could I know it would end up like this?"

"What do you mean by 'end up like this'? Stop avoiding the question! You predicted that you'd have a fit, even down to the exact spot in the cellar. You said so yourself."

"Have you told the investigators about that yet?" Smerdyakov asked calmly.

Ivan felt a surge of anger.

"No, I haven't yet, but I certainly will. You owe me some explanations, and I won't let you play games with me!"

"Why would I play games with you when I trust you like I trust God Himself?" Smerdyakov replied in the same calm tone, only briefly closing his eyes.

"First of all," Ivan began, "I know epileptic fits can't be predicted in advance. I've checked. Don't try to fool me. You can't know exactly when a fit will happen, nor where. How did you know you'd fall down the cellar stairs during a fit unless you faked it?"

"I had to go to the cellar several times a day," Smerdyakov said slowly. "I fell from the attic just like that a year ago. It's true, you can't predict the exact moment of a fit, but you can sense when one's coming."

"But you predicted the exact time!"

"In regard to my epilepsy, sir, it's better if you ask the doctors here. You can ask them whether my fit was real or fake; there's no point in me saying more about it."

"And what about the cellar? How could you have known beforehand about falling in the cellar?"

"You're still stuck on that cellar!" Smerdyakov sighed. "When I was going down there, I was filled with fear and doubt. What scared me most was losing your trust and being left without anyone in the world to defend me. I went down the stairs thinking, 'It'll happen now; the fit will strike me down right here. Will I fall?' And because I was so scared, the spasm hit—just like it always does—and I collapsed. I told Dr. Herzenstube and Nikolay Parfenovitch, the investigator, everything about that night—how I was afraid and mentioned the cellar to you. It's all in the official records. Dr. Varvinsky told them the fit was triggered by the fear itself, the fear of having one. That's when it struck. So, they've written it down exactly like that—it was caused simply by fear."

He finished speaking with a heavy breath, like the effort had worn him out.

"So, you've already told them everything in your statement?" Ivan asked, surprised. He had intended to scare Smerdyakov by threatening to repeat their conversation, only to find out it had already been reported.

"Why would I be afraid? Let them record the truth," Smerdyakov replied firmly.

"And did you tell them every single word of what we talked about at the gate?"

"Not every word, no."

"And did you admit that you can fake seizures, like you bragged to me?"

"No, I didn't mention that part."

"Why did you send me to Tchermashnya then?" Ivan demanded.

"I was worried you'd go to Moscow instead; Tchermashnya is closer," Smerdyakov answered calmly.

"You're lying! You told me to leave because you wanted me to avoid trouble."

"That was just my way of looking out for you, sir," Smerdyakov said smoothly. "I knew things might go badly at home, and I wanted to spare you from it. But, truthfully, I was also thinking of myself. I hoped you would stay close by, and if anything happened, you could protect your father."

"You could've just said that directly, you idiot!" Ivan snapped.

"How could I have said it more directly? I was scared, and I thought you might get angry. I worried that Dmitri Fyodorovitch might cause a scene and take the money—he thought it was his, after all. But who could've guessed it would end in murder? I only thought he'd grab the three thousand rubles from under the mattress. But instead—he killed him! How could you or I have predicted that?"

"But you just said it couldn't have been predicted!" Ivan retorted. "So how was I supposed to know and stay home?"

"You could've guessed it when I sent you to Tchermashnya instead of Moscow," Smerdyakov answered quietly.

"How would that have told me anything?"

Smerdyakov slumped further into the bed, looking exhausted.

"Because Tchermashnya is closer. If you'd gone to Moscow, you'd have been too far away to help. But if you were nearby, Dmitri would've been less bold, knowing you weren't far off. And if anything went wrong, you could've protected me too. I told you about Grigory Vassilyevitch being ill, and I warned you that I might have a seizure. I even explained those knocks—how Dmitri knew them because I told him. I thought you'd realize something bad would happen and stay nearby."

"He makes sense," Ivan thought, though Smerdyakov's mumbling made it hard to follow. "What kind of mental disturbance did Dr. Herzenstube mean?"

"You're playing games with me, aren't you?" Ivan growled, his anger rising.

"I thought you understood at the time," Smerdyakov said calmly. "I thought that's why you left in such a hurry—to avoid trouble and protect yourself."

"Do you think everyone is as much of a coward as you are?" Ivan snapped.

"Forgive me, sir, I assumed you were like me," Smerdyakov answered quietly.

"I should've figured it out," Ivan muttered, frustrated. "And honestly, I did suspect something was going on… but you're lying, aren't you?" Ivan's mind suddenly recalled a detail. "Do you remember what you said to me by the carriage? 'It's always worth talking to a clever man.' You were happy I left, weren't you? You were praising me!"

Smerdyakov sighed again, his pale face flushing slightly.

"If I was pleased," he admitted breathlessly, "it was only because you agreed to go to Tchermashnya instead of Moscow. It was closer. But when I said those words to you, they weren't praise— they were meant as a reproach. You didn't understand."

"A reproach? What for?"

"For abandoning your father when you knew something terrible could happen," Smerdyakov answered slowly. "You left us unprotected, and I could've been arrested at any time for stealing the money."

"Curse you!" Ivan swore, clenching his fists. "Wait—did you tell the prosecutor and investigator about those knocks?"

"I told them everything, just as it happened," Smerdyakov replied steadily.

Ivan's mind raced again.

"I only thought you were planning something evil," he muttered. "I thought Dmitri might kill him, but not steal from him. I never expected theft from Dmitri… but from you, I expected anything. You even bragged to me about faking fits—why did you say that?"

"I said it foolishly, out of simplicity," Smerdyakov explained. "I've never faked a fit in my life. I just wanted to impress you. I liked you back then, so I was open with you."

"My brother accuses you directly of both murder and theft," Ivan said coldly.

"What else can he do?" Smerdyakov replied with a bitter grin. "Who's going to believe him with all the evidence against him? Grigory Vassilyevitch saw the door open—what can Dmitri say to that? But never mind him. All he cares about now is saving himself."

Smerdyakov fell silent for a moment, as though reflecting. Then, suddenly, he added:

"And look here again. He wants to blame me and make it seem like I'm the one who did it—I've heard that already. But think about it: if I were really planning something like this against your

father, would I have been such a fool to tell you beforehand that I could fake a fit? Would I have given myself away like that? And to his own son, no less! It doesn't make sense, does it? No one is hearing this conversation except Providence itself, and if you were to tell the prosecutor and Nikolay Parfenovitch about it, you'd be helping to defend me. After all, who would believe that a criminal would be so open about his plans beforehand? Anyone could see that."

"Well," Ivan said, standing up to end the conversation, struck by Smerdyakov's reasoning, "I don't suspect you at all. In fact, I think it's absurd to even suspect you. I'm grateful to you for clearing things up for me. I'll be going now, but I'll come back again. In the meantime, take care and get well. Is there anything you need?"

"Thank you for everything. Marfa Ignatyevna has been very kind to me and provides whatever I need. Good people visit me every day."

"Good-bye. But I won't say anything about your ability to fake a fit, and I suggest you don't mention it either," Ivan added suddenly.

"I understand completely. And if you don't speak of that, I won't say anything about our conversation at the gate."

As Ivan walked out, he had only taken a few steps down the corridor when he realized there was something insulting in Smerdyakov's last words. He almost turned back, but the impulse passed quickly. Muttering "Nonsense!" to himself, he left the hospital.

His main feeling was one of relief—not because he believed Mitya had committed the murder, but because it wasn't Smerdyakov. Oddly enough, he didn't feel the expected relief that Mitya was guilty. Instead, he had no desire to dig into his emotions and felt an almost physical aversion to thinking about it. It was as though he wanted to forget the whole matter as quickly as possible. Over the following days, Ivan grew more convinced of Mitya's guilt, especially as he became familiar with the overwhelming evidence against him. Even the testimonies of people like Fenya and her mother, who didn't seem important, were hard to dismiss. The accounts of Perhotin, the people in the tavern, Plotnikov's shop, and the witnesses from Mokroe all seemed conclusive. The details were damning, particularly the secret of the knocks, which impressed the lawyers almost as much as Grigory's testimony about the open door. Grigory's wife, Marfa, told Ivan that Smerdyakov had been lying behind the partition wall all night, just a few steps from their bed. She said she woke up several times during the night, despite being a sound sleeper, and heard him moaning. "He was moaning the whole time," she said.

When Ivan spoke to Doctor Herzenstube, suggesting that Smerdyakov wasn't insane but just weak, the old man merely gave him a knowing smile.

"Do you know how he spends his time now?" Herzenstube asked. "He's learning lists of French words by heart. He's got an exercise book under his pillow with the words written out in Russian letters, ha ha!"

Eventually, Ivan pushed aside all his doubts. He couldn't think about Dmitri without feeling disgusted. But one thing still seemed strange: Alyosha remained convinced that Mitya wasn't the murderer, and even suggested that "most likely" Smerdyakov was. Ivan had always valued Alyosha's opinion, so this surprised him. Even stranger was that Alyosha didn't try to talk to him about Mitya. He only answered questions when Ivan asked. This struck Ivan as odd.

However, at that time, Ivan was preoccupied with something else entirely. Ever since he returned from Moscow, he had been consumed by a wild and overwhelming passion for Katerina Ivanovna. This is not the moment to delve into this new chapter of Ivan's life, which had a profound impact on his future—perhaps it's the subject of another story, one I may never write. But I cannot leave out the fact that when Ivan told Alyosha, "I am not keen on her," it was a complete lie. He loved her madly, though at times he hated her so intensely that he might have been capable of harming her. Several factors contributed to these conflicting emotions. Shattered by what had happened with Mitya, Katerina rushed to Ivan as her one hope when he returned. She was deeply wounded, humiliated, and insulted, and the man who had once loved her so ardently had come back (oh, she was well aware of how much he had loved her), a man whose heart and mind she admired, considering him far superior to herself. Yet, despite the Karamazov-like violence of Ivan's passion and the irresistible pull he had over her, the virtuous Katerina did not entirely give herself to him. She was still tormented by guilt over abandoning Mitya, and in moments of tension and rage (and there were many), she would remind Ivan of this directly. These were the "lies upon lies" Ivan had referred to when speaking to Alyosha. Of course, there was a great deal of falsehood in her words, and this angered Ivan more than anything else. But all of that is a story for another time.

For a while, Ivan almost forgot about Smerdyakov, but two weeks after his first visit, the same troubling thoughts began to creep back into his mind. He kept wondering why, on that last night at Fyodor Pavlovitch's house, he had snuck onto the stairs like a thief to listen to what his father was doing downstairs. Why did he feel such disgust when he remembered it? Why had he felt so down the next morning during his journey? Why, when he reached Moscow, had he told himself, "I am a scoundrel"? These nagging thoughts were so consuming that he felt they might even make him forget about Katerina Ivanovna for a time. It was just after having this thought that he ran into Alyosha on the street. Ivan stopped him immediately and asked:

"Do you remember when Dmitri burst in after dinner and beat Father, and later I told you in the yard that I reserved 'the right to desire'? Tell me, did you think then that I wanted Father's death?"

"I did think that," Alyosha answered softly.

"That's right," Ivan said. "It wasn't a guess. But didn't you also think I wanted Dmitri to kill Father? That I thought it would be like one reptile devouring another, and that I might even be willing to help make it happen?"

Alyosha turned pale and silently looked into his brother's eyes.

"Speak!" Ivan demanded. "I need to know the truth—what you really thought. I need the truth!"

He took a deep breath and glared at Alyosha, waiting for his response.

"Forgive me, I did think that, too," Alyosha whispered, without trying to soften his words.

"Thanks," Ivan snapped, then quickly walked away. After that, Alyosha noticed that Ivan started to avoid him and seemed to dislike him. It became so obvious that Alyosha stopped visiting him altogether. Right after that conversation, Ivan didn't go home—he went straight back to see Smerdyakov.

Chapter 7: The Second Visit To Smerdyakov

By the time Smerdyakov was discharged from the hospital, Ivan knew where he was staying—a rundown wooden house divided by a passage. On one side lived Marya Kondratyevna and her mother, and on the other side, Smerdyakov. No one knew for sure what kind of arrangement he had with them—whether he was a friend or just a boarder. Later, people guessed that he might have been staying as Marya Kondratyevna's fiancé, living there temporarily without paying rent or for meals. Both the mother and daughter respected him greatly and considered him far superior to them.

Ivan knocked on the door and went straight into the passage when it opened. Following Marya Kondratyevna's instructions, he entered the better room on the left, which belonged to Smerdyakov. The room was sweltering from the heat of a tiled stove. The blue wallpaper, though cheerful, was worn and peeling in places, and cockroaches swarmed in the cracks, creating a constant rustling. The furniture was sparse: two benches against the walls, two chairs near the table, and a simple wooden table covered with a cloth patterned in pink. Each of the two small windows held a pot of geraniums. In one corner stood a case of icons. On the table sat a small copper samovar, dented and cold, along with a tray and two cups—though Smerdyakov had already finished his tea. He was seated at the table on a bench, writing slowly in an exercise book. A bottle of ink stood beside him, along with a flat iron candlestick holding a cheap, half-melted candle.

As soon as Ivan saw him, it was clear that Smerdyakov had fully recovered from his illness. His face looked healthier and fuller, and his hair, combed neatly back at the sides, stood upright in the front. He wore a colorful but worn and dirty quilted dressing gown. To Ivan's irritation, Smerdyakov had glasses on— something Ivan had never seen him wear before. The sight of him wearing spectacles infuriated Ivan even more: "A man like that, wearing glasses!"

Smerdyakov slowly raised his head and stared through his glasses at Ivan. Then, just as slowly, he removed them and stood up lazily, offering the bare minimum of politeness. His deliberate carelessness made Ivan even more furious. The look in Smerdyakov's eyes was smug, even malicious, as if to say, "Why are you bothering me? We've already settled everything. Why have you come back?" Ivan could hardly contain his anger.

"It's hot in here," Ivan said stiffly, unbuttoning his overcoat. "Then take it off," Smerdyakov replied, making no effort to be welcoming.

With trembling hands, Ivan took off his coat and threw it onto a bench. He dragged a chair to the table and sat down, while Smerdyakov, without hurry, sank back onto his bench.

"First of all, are we alone?" Ivan asked sharply. "Can anyone overhear us?"

"No. You saw the passage; no one can hear a thing," Smerdyakov answered indifferently.

"Now, tell me," Ivan began angrily. "What exactly did you mean when you said, as I was leaving the hospital, that if I kept quiet about your fake seizures, you wouldn't tell the lawyer about everything we talked about at the gate? What were you trying to say? Were you threatening me? Do you think I made some kind of deal with you? Do you think I'm afraid of you?"

Ivan spoke with rising fury, making it clear he wasn't going to play along with any tricks or indirect games. Smerdyakov's eyes gleamed with resentment. His left eye twitched slightly, but his expression remained calm and deliberate.

"If you want things out in the open, fine," Smerdyakov seemed to say with his look. "This is exactly what I meant: You knew ahead of time that your father would be murdered, but you left anyway. I promised not to tell the authorities about that—not because of what it says about your feelings, but because it could suggest something worse, too."

Though Smerdyakov spoke calmly, there was a sharp, defiant edge to his words, and he stared boldly at Ivan. For a moment, Ivan's mind went blank with shock.

"What are you saying? Are you out of your mind?" Ivan demanded. "I'm perfectly sane."

"Do you think I knew about the murder?" Ivan shouted, slamming his fist on the table. "What do you mean by 'something worse'? Speak, you scoundrel!"

Smerdyakov sat silently, continuing to stare at Ivan with the same insolent expression.

"Answer me, you rotten liar! What's the 'something worse' you're hinting at?" Ivan shouted.

"I meant that maybe you also wanted your father dead," Smerdyakov said coldly.

Ivan leapt to his feet and struck Smerdyakov hard on the shoulder, slamming him against the wall. Tears sprang to Smerdyakov's eyes.

"It's shameful to hit a sick man," he muttered, wiping his tears with a dirty, checked handkerchief. He let out a few quiet sobs, then gradually stopped.

"That's enough. Cut it out," Ivan ordered, sitting down again. "Don't make me lose my temper."

Smerdyakov lowered the handkerchief. His thin, twisted face reflected the insult he had just endured.

"So you thought I was in on it with Dmitri—that we both planned to kill my father?" Ivan pressed him.

"I didn't know what was on your mind," Smerdyakov admitted bitterly. "That's why I stopped you at the gate that night—to find out."

"To find out what, exactly?"

"To see if you wanted your father dead."

Ivan seethed with rage at Smerdyakov's smug, insolent tone. "You killed him, didn't you?" Ivan suddenly shouted.

Smerdyakov sneered.

"You know as well as I do that it wasn't me. A smart man like you shouldn't even need to ask."

"Then why did you suspect me?" Ivan demanded, struggling to keep his voice steady.

"Because I was terrified. I suspected everyone. If you wanted the same thing as your brother, I figured I was doomed, too."

"You never mentioned any of this two weeks ago," Ivan said suspiciously.

"I hinted at it in the hospital," Smerdyakov replied coolly. "I thought you were smart enough to understand without me spelling it out."

"Why didn't you just say it clearly?" Ivan snapped. "Answer me! What could I have possibly done to make you think such vile things about me?"

"You wouldn't have killed him yourself," Smerdyakov said with a sly grin. "But you wouldn't have minded if someone else did."

"And why on earth would I want that?" Ivan asked, stunned.

"For the inheritance," Smerdyakov replied with a smirk. "After your father's death, you and your brothers would each get at least forty thousand rubles, maybe more. But if he had married that woman—Agrafena Alexandrovna—all of it would've gone to her. She's smart, and he would've signed everything over to her the moment they married. You and your brothers wouldn't have gotten a single ruble. And believe me, they were this close to getting married. All she had to do was lift a finger, and your father would've gone running to the altar like a dog."

Ivan struggled to keep control over himself.

"Very well," he said at last. "Look at me—I'm not hitting you, not knocking you down, not killing you. Now, keep talking. So, according to you, I planned it all out with Dmitri? I expected him to do it?"

"How could you not expect him to?" Smerdyakov responded calmly. "If he killed your father, he'd lose his noble status, all his property, and end up exiled. That would mean his share of the inheritance would go to you and Alexey Fyodorovitch, split between the two of you. Instead of forty thousand rubles each, you'd both get sixty thousand. There's no question you counted on Dmitri to do it."

"What I have to endure from you!" Ivan muttered through clenched teeth. "Listen, scoundrel. If I had put my hopes in anyone, it would have been you, not Dmitri. I knew something nasty would come from you—I had that feeling at the time."

"I even thought for a moment," Smerdyakov said with a sneering grin, "that you were counting on me. That was the clearest sign of what you had in mind. If you suspected me and still left, it was as if you were saying, 'Go ahead, murder him—I won't stop you.'"

"You wretch! That's what you took it to mean?" Ivan shouted.

"Yes, it was all because of that trip to Tchermashnya. You were supposed to go to Moscow, but you turned down all your father's pleas to go to Tchermashnya. Yet as soon as I mentioned it, you agreed right away. Why would you go to Tchermashnya just because of a silly word from me? That shows you expected something from me."

"I swear I didn't!" Ivan shouted, grinding his teeth.

"Really? Then as your father's son, you should have hauled me off to the police and had me beaten for what I said. Or at least given me a punch in the face right then and there. But you didn't—oh no, not even a little anger from you. Instead, you listened to my foolish advice and left, when you should have stayed to protect your father. What else could I conclude?"

Ivan sat still, fists pressed hard into his knees, a bitter smile on his face.

"I regret not punching you in the face," he said quietly. "I couldn't have arrested you back then—no one would have believed me, and what charge could I have made? But the punch... Yes, I regret not doing that. I should have smashed your disgusting face to pieces."

Smerdyakov smiled, almost as if enjoying Ivan's frustration.

"In normal situations," he began, in the same smug, self-righteous tone he used with Grigory when arguing about religion, "punching someone in the face is illegal. People don't do it anymore. But in extreme situations—well, even in civilized places like France, people still throw punches, just like in the days of Adam and Eve. Some things never change. And yet, even in a situation like this, you didn't dare to hit me."

Ivan shot him a furious glance. "What are you learning French words for?" he snapped, nodding toward the exercise book on the table.

"Why shouldn't I?" Smerdyakov shrugged. "I want to improve myself, in case I ever get the chance to visit those happy parts of Europe."

"Listen, you monster." Ivan's whole body shook with anger. "I'm not scared of anything you say about me. And if I don't kill you right now, it's because I believe you committed that crime—and I'll make sure you're brought to justice. I'll expose you."

"You'd be better off keeping quiet," Smerdyakov replied coolly. "What could you accuse me of? I'm innocent, and no one would believe you anyway. But if you try anything, I'll tell them everything. I have to defend myself, after all."

"You think I'm afraid of you?" Ivan sneered.

"If the court doesn't believe what I've said, the public will," Smerdyakov shot back, his voice steady. "And you'll be humiliated."

"So, it is always worth speaking to a sensible man, right?" Ivan growled.

"You've got it. And it would be smart for you to keep being sensible."

Ivan stood, trembling with rage. He put on his coat and, without another word or even a glance at Smerdyakov, stormed out of the cottage. The cool evening air hit him, and the brightness of the moon made everything look sharp and surreal. His thoughts spun wildly in his mind like a fevered nightmare.

"Should I go straight to the authorities and report Smerdyakov?" Ivan wondered. "But what could I say? He's not guilty—he'll just turn everything back on me. And, really… Why did I go to Tchermashnya that night? Why? Why?"

He stopped in his tracks, as though stabbed by the thought.

"Yes, I was expecting something. He's right! I knew something would happen—I wanted it to happen! I wanted the murder! Did I really want it? Yes, I did. I must kill Smerdyakov. If I don't kill him, there's no point in living."

Ivan didn't go home, but instead went straight to Katerina Ivanovna's, alarming her with his appearance. He looked like a madman. He repeated to her every word of his conversation with Smerdyakov, not leaving out a single syllable. No matter how much she tried to calm him, he couldn't be soothed. He kept pacing back and forth across the room, speaking in strange, disconnected sentences. Finally, he sat down, leaned his elbows on the table, buried his face in his hands, and said this strange sentence: "If it's not Dmitri, but Smerdyakov who is the murderer, then I share in the guilt, because I pushed him to it. Whether I did it knowingly or not, I don't know yet. But if he's the murderer and not Dmitri, then, of course, I'm the murderer too."

When Katerina Ivanovna heard this, she got up silently, walked to her desk, opened a box that was on it, took out a piece of paper, and placed it in front of Ivan. This was the document Ivan would later tell Alyosha about, calling it "the conclusive proof" that Dmitri had killed their father. It was the letter Mitya had written to Katerina Ivanovna when he was drunk, on the very same evening he had met Alyosha at the crossroads on the way to the monastery, after the scene at Katerina Ivanovna's house when Grushenka had insulted her. After parting from Alyosha, Mitya had rushed off to Grushenka. It is uncertain whether he actually saw her, but by the evening, he had ended up at the "Metropolis" tavern, where he got very drunk. While there, he asked for pen and paper and wrote a letter that would have serious consequences for him later. It was a rambling, disjointed, and frenzied letter—exactly the kind you would expect from a man who was both drunk and deeply upset.

It resembled the way a drunk man rants after being insulted, explaining in an incoherent and emotional way how someone had wronged him, what a scoundrel the offender was, how great he was himself, and how he would get back at the one who insulted him. The letter was full of heated but confused thoughts, mixed with drunken tears and fist-pounding. It was written on a dirty, ordinary piece of paper, the cheapest kind, which the tavern had provided, and there were numbers scribbled on the back. He had run out of space and written all over the margins, with the last line scrawled across the rest. The letter went like this:

"FATAL KATYA: Tomorrow I'll get the money and repay your three thousand, and then farewell, woman of great wrath, but farewell, too, my love! Let's make an end of it! Tomorrow I'll try to get it from everyone, and if I can't borrow it, I swear I'll go to my father, bash his head in, and take the money from under his pillow—if only Ivan's gone. Even if I have to go to Siberia for it, you'll get your three thousand. Goodbye. I bow down to the ground before you because I've been a scoundrel to you. Forgive me! No, don't forgive me—you'll be happier if you don't, and so will I. Better Siberia than your love, because I love another woman—and you've gotten to know her all too well today, so how could you forgive? I will kill the man who robbed me! I'll leave you all and go east, so I don't have to see anyone again. Not her either, because you're not my only tormentor—she torments me, too. Goodbye!

P.S.—I curse you, but I adore you! I feel it in my heart. There's one string left, and it's still vibrating. Better to tear my heart in two! I'll kill myself, but first, I'll kill that dog. I'll rip three thousand from him and throw it at you. Even though I've been a scoundrel to you, I'm not a thief! You'll get the three thousand. That dog keeps it under his mattress, tied in pink ribbon. I'm no thief, but I'll murder my thief. Katya, don't look at me with disdain. Dmitri is no thief, but a murderer! He's murdered his father and ruined himself, just to hold his own rather than endure your pride. And he doesn't love you.

P.P.S.—I kiss your feet, farewell! P.P.P.S.—Katya, pray to God that someone will give me the money. Then I won't be drenched in blood. But if no one does—I will be! Kill me!

Your slave and enemy,

D. KARAMAZOV."

When Ivan read this "document," he was convinced. So it was his brother, not Smerdyakov. And if it wasn't Smerdyakov, then it wasn't Ivan either. This letter immediately became, in his mind, undeniable proof of Mitya's guilt. The idea that Mitya might have committed the murder with Smerdyakov never crossed his mind, as such a theory didn't seem to fit the facts. Ivan felt completely reassured. The next morning, he thought of Smerdyakov and his taunts with nothing but contempt, dismissing the intense distress his suspicions had caused him. A few days later, he even wondered how he could have been so consumed by it. He resolved to dismiss Smerdyakov from his mind with contempt and forget about him entirely. A month passed this way. He didn't inquire about Smerdyakov again, but twice, he happened to hear that Smerdyakov was very ill and seemed to be losing his mind.

"He'll end up going mad," said the young doctor Varvinsky, and Ivan remembered this. During the last week of that month, Ivan himself began feeling very ill. He went to see the doctor from Moscow, the one who had been brought in by Katerina Ivanovna just before the trial. Around this time, his relationship with Katerina Ivanovna became more strained than ever. They were like two enemies in love with each other. Her brief but intense changes of heart toward Mitya drove Ivan to a frenzy. Strangely, even during those moments when she defended Mitya, she had never once expressed doubt about his guilt, which Ivan found remarkable. Despite feeling his hatred for Mitya grow each day, he knew it wasn't because of Katerina's shifting emotions. It was because he believed Mitya had killed their father. He admitted this to himself completely.

Still, ten days before the trial, Ivan went to visit Mitya and proposed a plan for him to escape—a plan Ivan had clearly thought through for a long time. Part of his reason for doing this was to heal the wound caused by something Smerdyakov had said about how Mitya's conviction would increase Ivan's and Alyosha's inheritance from forty to sixty thousand roubles. Ivan decided to sacrifice thirty thousand to help Mitya escape. After visiting Mitya, Ivan felt deeply troubled and realized he wanted Mitya to escape not just to ease his guilt about the money, but for another reason: "Is it because I'm as much a murderer at heart?" he asked himself.

Something deep within him seemed to burn and fester. His pride, above all, was wounded terribly during that month. But more on that later...

After his conversation with Alyosha, Ivan found himself standing with his hand on the bell of his lodging, suddenly deciding to go to Smerdyakov's. He acted on a sudden, furious impulse. He had just remembered how Katerina Ivanovna had cried out earlier in Alyosha's presence, "It was you, you who persuaded me of his guilt!" Ivan was stunned when he recalled those words. He had never once tried to convince her that Mitya was the murderer. On the contrary, when he returned from visiting Smerdyakov, he had suspected himself in her presence. She had been the one to produce the "document" proving Mitya's guilt. And now she suddenly cried out, "I've been to Smerdyakov's myself!" When had she gone there? Ivan had known nothing about it. So, she wasn't entirely sure of Mitya's guilt after all! What had Smerdyakov told her? What had he said to her?

His heart burned with violent anger. He couldn't understand how he had let those words pass earlier without reacting, without crying out at the time. Letting go of the bell, he rushed off to Smerdyakov's house. "I might kill him this time," he thought as he hurried on his way.

Chapter 8: The Third and Last Interview with Smerdyakov

As Ivan made his way to Smerdyakov's, the sharp wind that had blown earlier that morning picked up again, and a dry, fine snow began falling heavily. The wind whipped the snow around in the air, forming a chaotic storm that didn't settle on the ground. The streets in this part of town had almost no streetlights. Ivan walked alone through the darkness, paying no attention to the snowstorm, finding his way by instinct. His head throbbed painfully, and his temples ached. His hands twitched uncontrollably, and every step felt heavy.

Near Marya Kondratyevna's house, Ivan suddenly came across a drunk peasant staggering through the street. The man's coarse, patched coat flapped around him as he zigzagged along, mumbling curses to himself. Every now and then, the man burst into a raspy, drunken song:

"Ach, Vanka's gone to Petersburg; I won't wait till he comes back."

But each time, he cut himself off halfway through the second line and returned to swearing under his breath, only to start the song over again. Ivan felt a sudden surge of hatred for the man, even before he had fully noticed him. When Ivan finally realized the peasant's presence, he felt an overwhelming urge to knock him down.

As they crossed paths, the peasant stumbled forward and lurched into Ivan. Furious, Ivan shoved him hard. The man flew backward, hitting the frozen ground with a dull thud. He let out a pitiful "O—oh!" before falling silent. Ivan stepped closer and saw that the man was lying on his back, unconscious and motionless.

"He'll freeze out here," Ivan thought. But instead of helping, he turned and continued his way to Smerdyakov's house.

At the cottage, Marya Kondratyevna came to the door with a candle in hand. In a whisper, she told Ivan that Smerdyakov was very ill. "He's not exactly bedridden," she explained softly, "but he's not himself. He even told us to take away the tea. He wouldn't touch it."

"Is he causing trouble?" Ivan asked harshly.

"Oh, no. He's very quiet," she replied quickly. "But please, don't stay too long." Ivan opened the door and stepped inside the room.

The room was as overheated as before, but a few things had changed. One of the benches along the wall had been removed, and in its place stood an old mahogany sofa covered with worn leather. A bed had been made up on the sofa with surprisingly clean white pillows. Smerdyakov sat on the sofa, still wearing the same frayed dressing gown. A small table had been pushed right up to the sofa, leaving barely any room to move around. On the table sat a thick book with a yellow cover, though it seemed Smerdyakov wasn't reading it. Instead, he sat there idly, staring into space. When he saw Ivan enter, he gave him a slow, silent look, without the slightest hint of surprise.

Ivan immediately noticed how much Smerdyakov's appearance had changed—he looked thinner and more gaunt, his skin a sickly yellow, and his eyes sunken deep into his face with dark blue shadows beneath them.

"You really are sick," Ivan said, stopping just inside the room. "I won't keep you long. I won't even take off my coat. Where can I sit?"

He moved to the other end of the table, dragged a chair closer, and sat down. Smerdyakov shifted slightly on the sofa, meeting Ivan's gaze with the same strange, indifferent expression.

"So why are you just staring at me like that?" Ivan asked impatiently. "I've only got one question, and I swear I won't leave until you answer. Has Katerina Ivanovna been here?"

Smerdyakov kept looking at Ivan without saying a word. Then, with a slow wave of his hand, he turned his face away.

"What's the matter with you?" Ivan demanded. "Nothing."

"What do you mean, 'nothing'?"

"Yes, she was here. But what does it matter to you? Just leave me alone."

"No, I'm not going anywhere. When did she come?"

Smerdyakov gave a mocking smile, as though he had just remembered her. "I'd almost forgotten about her," he sneered, turning back to face Ivan. His gaze was full of burning hatred, the same look he had given Ivan during their last encounter a month ago.

"You look terrible," Smerdyakov added. "Your face is sunken, and you don't seem like yourself."

"Never mind me—just answer my question," Ivan snapped.

"But why are your eyes so yellow? The whites of them are completely yellow. What's eating you up inside?" Smerdyakov chuckled to himself, and then burst into a short, mocking laugh.

"I told you, I'm not leaving without an answer!" Ivan shouted, his irritation rising.

"Why do you keep bothering me? Why are you tormenting me?" Smerdyakov said, his expression full of exhaustion and annoyance.

"I don't care about you," Ivan growled. "Just answer the question, and I'll leave."

"I've got nothing to say to you," Smerdyakov muttered, dropping his gaze.

"Oh, you'll talk, all right," Ivan threatened. "You'll answer me, one way or another."

Smerdyakov looked back at him, not with fear, but with something close to disgust. "Why are you so worked up?" he asked, sneering. "Is it because the trial starts tomorrow? Nothing will happen to you—you know that, right? Just go home, lie down, and sleep easy. You've got nothing to worry about."

"I don't understand you... What should I be afraid of tomorrow?" Ivan asked in confusion, though a strange chill crept over him. Smerdyakov studied him with a sharp, calculating look.

"You don't understand?" Smerdyakov replied slowly, as though scolding him. "It's strange how a smart man like you keeps playing this game."

Ivan stared at him, speechless. The arrogant, dismissive tone from someone who had once been his servant was shocking enough on its own. He hadn't spoken this way even during their last meeting.

"I'm telling you, there's nothing for you to fear. I won't say a word about you—there's no evidence against you. But look at your hands! They're shaking—your fingers are twitching. Why? Relax—you didn't kill him."

Ivan jolted at those words, immediately thinking of Alyosha. "I know it wasn't me," Ivan stammered.

"Do you?" Smerdyakov responded, raising an eyebrow.

Ivan sprang from his seat, grabbing Smerdyakov's shoulder. "Tell me everything, you snake! Tell me everything!"

Smerdyakov didn't flinch. He locked eyes with Ivan, his gaze full of bitterness and hatred.

"Fine, if you want it straight—you killed him," he hissed furiously.

Ivan collapsed back into his chair, as if in deep thought. A bitter laugh escaped him.

"You're talking about me leaving, right? Just like last time?"

"Yes," Smerdyakov replied coldly. "You knew everything back then, and you know it now."

"All I know," Ivan retorted, "is that you've lost your mind."

"Aren't you tired of this? We're face to face—why keep pretending? You want to pin everything on me? But let's not fool ourselves. You are the real murderer. I was only your tool—your obedient servant. I followed your words."

"What are you saying? Did you actually do it?" Ivan felt a wave of cold terror wash over him.

Something in his mind snapped, and a shiver ran down his spine. For the first time, Smerdyakov looked at him curiously, almost confused by Ivan's genuine horror.

"Wait... You really didn't know?" Smerdyakov whispered, doubt creeping into his voice. He searched Ivan's face with a forced, uncertain smile.

Ivan stared at him, unable to speak, as if frozen.

Suddenly, a line from a drunken peasant's song echoed through his mind:

"Ach, Vanka's gone to Petersburg; I won't wait till he comes back."

"I... I think you might be a dream," Ivan muttered. "Just a ghost sitting here."

"There are no ghosts here," Smerdyakov said, his voice steady. "Just the two of us... and one other. He's here, too—right between us."

"Who? What third person?" Ivan shouted, looking around frantically.

"The third is God—Providence. He's here, but don't bother searching. You won't find Him."

"It's a lie!" Ivan cried, his voice rising to a fevered pitch. "You didn't kill him—you're either insane, or you're messing with me!"

Smerdyakov observed him with calm curiosity, seemingly unafraid. He still appeared to believe Ivan knew the truth and was merely trying to pin the crime on him.

"Wait a moment," Smerdyakov said quietly. Slowly, he lifted his left leg from under the table and began rolling up his trouser leg. He wore long white stockings and slippers. Ivan watched, horror building inside him.

"He's mad!" Ivan shouted. He jumped to his feet, backing against the wall in terror. He pressed himself flat against it, staring wildly at Smerdyakov, who remained utterly calm, carefully fumbling in his stocking as if searching for something.

At last, Smerdyakov pulled out a small bundle and placed it on the table.

"Here," he said quietly.

"What is that?" Ivan asked, his voice trembling.

"Take a look," Smerdyakov answered, his tone flat.

Ivan slowly approached the table and reached for the bundle. But as his fingers brushed against it, he recoiled as if he had touched something filthy.

"Your hands are still shaking," Smerdyakov observed coolly. Then, with deliberate slowness, he unwrapped the bundle himself. Inside were three neat packets of hundred-rouble notes.

"All three thousand roubles," Smerdyakov said. "No need to count. They're all here. Go ahead, take them."

Ivan slumped back into his chair, pale as a sheet.

"You scared me... with that stocking," he muttered, managing a strange, weak grin.

"So you really didn't know until now?" Smerdyakov asked again.

"No... I didn't know. I kept thinking it was Dmitri. My brother... Brother! Ach!" Ivan buried his head in his hands, groaning in despair.

"Tell me," he whispered. "Did you do it alone? Or was my brother involved?"

"I did it with your help—and only with yours. Dmitri Fyodorovitch is innocent."

"Fine. We'll talk about me later. Why can't I stop shaking? I can't even speak properly..." Ivan stammered.

"You were bold enough before," Smerdyakov remarked, amused. "You said, 'Everything is lawful.' But look at you now—how scared you've become."

"Do you want some lemonade? It's refreshing. I can ask Marya Kondratyevna to bring us some," Smerdyakov offered, as if nothing unusual had happened. He glanced at the money on the table and moved to cover it. His handkerchief was too dirty, so he grabbed the yellow book Ivan had noticed earlier and placed it over the notes.

The book was The Sayings of the Holy Father Isaac the Syrian.

Ivan read the title without thinking.

"I don't want any lemonade," Ivan muttered. "We can talk about me later. Sit down and tell me exactly how you did it. I need to know everything."

"You'd better take off your coat, or you'll overheat," Smerdyakov suggested.

Ivan seemed to realize for the first time that he was still wearing his coat. He shrugged it off and threw it onto the bench without standing up.

"Now talk. Tell me everything."

He was calmer now, certain that Smerdyakov would tell him everything.

"How it happened?" Smerdyakov sighed. "It was all done exactly the way you said it would be."

"Forget what I said. Just tell me, step by step, how you did it— every detail." Ivan's voice was steady, almost cold. "Don't leave anything out. I need to know it all."

"Well, you left... and then I fell into the cellar."

"In a real fit, or a fake one?"

"Of course, it was fake. I planned the whole thing. I quietly walked down to the bottom of the cellar steps, lay down there, and gave a scream. Then I started thrashing around until they carried me out."

"Wait! Were you pretending the whole time, even afterward, in the hospital?" Ivan asked.

"No, not at all. The next morning, before they took me to the hospital, I had a real attack—worse than I've had in years. I was unconscious for two days," Smerdyakov explained.

"All right, go on."

"They laid me on the bed. I knew they'd put me on the other side of the partition, because whenever I was sick, Marfa Ignatyevna would put me there, close to them. She's been kind to me since I was born. That night, I moaned but quietly. I was waiting for Dmitri Fyodorovitch to come."

"Waiting for him? To come to you?"

"No, not to me. I expected him to come into the house. I had no doubt he'd come that night. Without me and without hearing any news, he'd surely climb over the fence like he always did and do something."

"And if he hadn't come?"

"Then nothing would have happened. I wouldn't have been able to do it without him."

"All right, keep talking. Be clearer—don't rush. Don't leave anything out!" Ivan demanded.

"I expected him to kill Fyodor Pavlovitch. I thought it was certain because I'd prepared him for it in the last few days. He knew about the knocks, which was the key thing. With his suspicions and growing anger, he'd inevitably get into the house using those knocks. So, I was waiting for him."

"Wait," Ivan interrupted, "if he killed him, he would have taken the money and run. You must have thought about that. What would you have done then?"

"He never would have found the money. I only told him it was under the mattress, but that wasn't true. It was actually hidden in a box. Later, I convinced Fyodor Pavlovitch—since I was the only one he trusted—to hide the envelope with the notes behind the icons. No one would have thought to look there, especially in a hurry. So, that's where the envelope was, behind the icons. Keeping it under the mattress would have been ridiculous. The box could be locked, but everyone believed it was under the mattress. It was foolish to think so. So, if Dmitri Fyodorovitch had committed the murder, he wouldn't have found anything. He would have either fled in a panic, like most murderers, or been caught. Either way, I could have taken the money later, and everyone would have blamed Dmitri Fyodorovitch."

"But what if he hadn't killed him, just knocked him out?"

"If he hadn't killed him, of course, I wouldn't have dared to take the money, and nothing would have happened. But I calculated that he would beat him senseless, giving me time to take the money. Then I could have convinced Fyodor Pavlovitch that it was Dmitri who took the money after attacking him."

"Hold on. I'm getting confused. So, it was Dmitri who killed him? You just took the money?" Ivan asked, puzzled.

"No, he didn't kill him. I might as well tell you now that he was the murderer, but I won't lie to you. If you really didn't understand until now—and aren't just pretending to throw the blame on me—then you're still responsible. You knew about the murder, encouraged me to do it, and left, knowing what would happen. That makes you the real murderer, not me, even though I was the one who killed him. You're the true murderer."

"Why? Why am I the murderer? Oh, God!" Ivan exclaimed, finally losing control. He had planned to wait to discuss himself until the end of the conversation but couldn't hold back anymore. "Is this about

Tchermashnya? Tell me, why did you need my consent if you thought me going to Tchermashnya meant I agreed? How do you explain that?"

"If I was sure of your consent, I knew you wouldn't make a fuss about the lost three thousand roubles, even if I were suspected instead of Dmitri or as his accomplice. In fact, you would have protected me. Later, when you received your inheritance, you would have rewarded me for the rest of your life because you'd have gotten the inheritance through me. If Fyodor Pavlovitch had married Agrafena Alexandrovna, you wouldn't have seen a single penny."

"So, you planned to blackmail me for the rest of my life," Ivan sneered. "And what if I hadn't left but had turned you in?"

"What would you have turned me in for? Persuading you to go to Tchermashnya? That's nonsense. After our conversation, you would have either left or stayed. If you'd stayed, nothing would have happened. I would have known you didn't want it to happen, and I wouldn't have gone through with it. But since you left, it was clear that you wouldn't report me, and you wouldn't care about the three thousand. Besides, if you had tried to prosecute me later, I would have told the court that you had encouraged me to commit the theft and the murder, even though I didn't agree to it. That's why I needed your consent—so you couldn't trap me later. What proof would you have had? I could have easily turned it around on you, telling everyone how eager you were for your father's death. People would have believed me, and you would've been ashamed for the rest of your life."

"Was I really that eager?" Ivan growled through clenched teeth.

"Of course you were. By giving me your consent, you silently agreed to everything," Smerdyakov answered, staring at Ivan with conviction. He spoke slowly, exhausted, but something inside him kept pushing him forward. Ivan could sense that Smerdyakov had a purpose, some hidden goal.

"Go on," Ivan urged. "Tell me what happened that night."

"What else do you want to know? I was lying there, and I thought I heard the master cry out. Before that, Grigory Vassilyevitch had suddenly gotten up, gone outside, and then screamed. After that, everything was silent and dark. I lay there, waiting, my heart pounding—I couldn't bear it anymore. So I got up and went out. I saw the window open to the garden, on the left side. I stepped toward it to listen, wondering if the master was still alive, and I heard him moving around and sighing. That's how I knew he was alive. 'Ah,' I thought. I leaned toward the window and said, 'It's me.' He called back, 'He's been here, he's run away.' He meant that Dmitri Fyodorovitch had come. He said, 'He's killed Grigory!' I whispered, 'Where?' and the master pointed toward the corner. He was whispering too.

'I told him, 'Wait a moment.' I went to the corner of the garden to see, and there was Grigory Vassilyevitch, lying by the wall, unconscious and covered in blood. At that moment, I thought to myself, 'So Dmitri Fyodorovitch has been here.' Right then, I decided to finish it. Grigory wouldn't see anything, even if he survived—he was completely unconscious. The only risk was Marfa Ignatyevna waking up. I felt that fear then, but I couldn't hold back the urge to get it done. I could hardly breathe from it.

"I went back to the window and told the master, 'She's here— Agrafena Alexandrovna is here, and she wants to come inside.' He jumped like a child. 'Where is she?' he gasped, not quite believing me. I told him, 'She's right outside. Open the door.' He looked out the window, half believing, half doubting, but too scared to open it. 'So now he's afraid of me,' I thought. And that amused me a little. Then I tapped on the window frame—the signal we had agreed on—as if Grushenka was really there.

"As soon as he heard the taps, he rushed to open the door. When he opened it, I tried to step inside, but he blocked me. 'Where is she? Where is she?' he asked, trembling. I thought, 'If he's this scared of me, things could go wrong.' My legs almost gave out from fear that he might cry out, or Marfa might come, or something

396

else would happen. I whispered, 'She's right under the window. Can't you see her?' He said, 'Go and bring her here.' 'She's scared,' I said. 'She heard the noise and hid in the bushes. Go call her yourself from the study.'

"He ran to the window, holding up the candle, and cried, 'Grushenka! Are you here?' But even as he called out, he didn't want to lean too far out—he was too scared to turn his back on me.

"'Look,' I said, leaning out the window myself. 'There she is, in the bush, laughing at you. Don't you see her?' He believed me then, and he was trembling all over—he was crazy about her. He leaned all the way out of the window, and that's when I grabbed the iron paperweight from the desk—you remember it, the one that weighs about three pounds. I swung it and hit him on the skull. He didn't even cry out—he just crumpled. I hit him again, and then a third time. By the third blow, I knew his skull was broken. He rolled over on his back, his face covered in blood.

"I checked myself. Not a single drop of blood on me. I wiped off the paperweight and put it back on the desk. Then I went to the icons, took the money out of the envelope, and threw the empty envelope and the pink ribbon on the floor. I went into the garden, trembling all over, and headed straight to the apple tree with the hollow—you know the one. I'd planned it in advance, leaving a rag and some paper inside. I wrapped the money in the rag and stuffed it deep into the hollow. I left it there for more than two weeks. I only took it out after I got out of the hospital.

"After hiding the money, I went back to bed. I thought, 'If Grigory dies, I'll be in trouble. But if he survives, it'll be perfect—he'll say Dmitri was here, and everyone will believe Dmitri killed the master and stole the money.' I started groaning, hoping to wake Marfa as soon as possible. Eventually, she got up. When she saw that Grigory wasn't in bed, she ran out to the garden, and I heard her scream. That's when everything started, and I finally felt at ease."

Ivan listened to the whole story in silence, without moving or taking his eyes off Smerdyakov. As he spoke, Smerdyakov occasionally glanced at Ivan but mostly kept his eyes averted. When he finished, his breathing was heavy, and sweat covered his face. It was hard to tell if he felt any remorse or something else entirely.

"Wait," Ivan said slowly, lost in thought. "What about the door? If the master opened the door for you, how did Grigory see it open earlier? He said he saw it open before you went inside."

Smerdyakov gave a twisted smile. "That's just Grigory's imagination. He's as stubborn as a mule. He didn't really see it—he just thought he did. Once an idea gets into his head, it's impossible to change it. It's bad luck for Dmitri, though, because they'll use that to convict him."

Ivan looked puzzled, as if trying to hold on to something slipping from his mind. "I have so many questions, but they keep slipping away..." He rubbed his temples. "Why did you leave the envelope on the floor instead of taking it? When you told the story, it sounded like there was a good reason, but now I don't get it."

"I left it there to make it look real. If someone like me—someone who knew everything—had committed the crime, they wouldn't have wasted time opening the envelope. They'd just take it and go. But Dmitri only knew about the envelope from hearsay. If he'd found it, he'd have ripped it open to make sure the money was inside. He wouldn't have thought about leaving it as evidence because he's not a thief by nature. He's just a desperate man taking what he thought was his. That's why he bragged to everyone that he'd take back what was his from Fyodor Pavlovitch. I didn't tell the prosecutor this outright—I hinted at it, letting him think he figured it out himself. He was thrilled by the idea."

"You thought of all this on the spot?" Ivan asked, stunned.

"How could anyone think of all that so quickly? It was planned out ahead of time."

"It must have been the devil who helped you," Ivan muttered bitterly. "You're much smarter than I thought..."

Ivan stood up, as if intending to walk around the room, but the cramped space between the table and the wall stopped him. Frustrated, he turned and sat back down, gripping his head. His anger boiled over, and he shouted furiously once more.

"Listen, you miserable, pathetic creature! Don't you get it? The only reason I haven't killed you is because I'm keeping you alive for tomorrow's trial. God knows," Ivan raised his hand, "maybe I was guilty, too. Maybe deep down I wanted my father's death. But I swear I'm not as guilty as you think, and maybe I didn't push you to do it at all. No, I didn't! But it doesn't matter—I'll confess everything tomorrow at the trial. I'm determined to tell the truth. I'll reveal everything, every detail. But we'll go together. No matter what you say about me at the trial, I'll face it. I'm not afraid of you. I'll confirm it all myself! But you must confess too! You have to! We'll go together. That's how it's going to be."

Ivan said this solemnly, and his fiery eyes alone showed that he meant it.

"You're sick, I can tell. Your eyes are yellow," Smerdyakov said, not mockingly, but with what seemed like genuine concern.

"We'll go together," Ivan repeated. "And if you won't go, then I'll go alone."

Smerdyakov paused as if he was thinking about it.

"There's not going to be anything like that. And you won't go," he finally said confidently.

"You don't understand me," Ivan exclaimed, frustrated.

"You'll be too ashamed to confess everything. Besides, it wouldn't help. I'll just say I never said anything like that to you. People will think you're either sick—and it sure seems like it—or that you feel so guilty for your brother that you're making it all up, trying to save him. You've always thought of me as nothing more than a fly, and who will believe you anyway? What proof do you even have?"

"Listen, you just showed me those notes to convince me," Ivan said.

Smerdyakov moved a book off the notes and set it aside.

"Take that money with you," Smerdyakov sighed.

"Of course, I'll take it. But why are you giving it to me if you killed for it?" Ivan asked, surprised.

"I don't want it," Smerdyakov said in a shaky voice, pushing it away. "I did think about starting a new life with that money, in Moscow, or better yet, abroad. I dreamed of it, mostly because 'everything is allowed,' just like you taught me. You were right— if there's no God, there's no such thing as virtue, and there's no need for it. You were right about that. So that's how I saw things."

"Did you come to that conclusion on your own?" Ivan asked with a bitter smile.

"With your help."

"And now you believe in God, since you're giving the money back?"

"No, I don't believe," Smerdyakov whispered. "Then why are you giving it back?"

"Just stop it... that's enough!" Smerdyakov waved his hand again. "You used to say everything was allowed, so why are you so upset now? You even want to go and confess against yourself... But it won't happen! You won't testify," Smerdyakov said with certainty.

"You'll see," Ivan replied.

"It's not possible. You're very smart. You like money, I know that. You enjoy being respected because you're proud, and you love women too much. Most of all, you want a peaceful, comfortable life without relying on anyone—that's what you care about. You won't ruin your life by confessing to something like this. You're like Fyodor Pavlovitch. You're more like him than any of his children; you've got the same soul as he did."

"You're not stupid," Ivan said, surprised. His face flushed. "You're being serious now!" he added, looking at Smerdyakov differently.

"Your pride made you think I was stupid. Take the money."

Ivan grabbed the three rolls of notes and stuffed them into his pocket without wrapping them up.

"I'll show them in court tomorrow," he said.

"No one will believe you. You've got plenty of your own money; they'll think you just took this out of your safe and brought it to court."

Ivan stood up.

"I'm telling you again," he said, "the only reason I haven't killed you is that I need you for tomorrow. Remember that!"

"Then kill me. Kill me now," Smerdyakov suddenly said, staring at Ivan in a strange way. "You won't do it! You won't even dare to do anything anymore!" he added, with a bitter smile. "You, who used to be so brave!"

"Till tomorrow," Ivan shouted, moving toward the door. "Wait a moment... show me those notes again."

Ivan pulled out the notes and held them up. Smerdyakov stared at them for ten seconds.

"Okay, you can go," he said, waving his hand. "Ivan Fyodorovitch!" he called out again.

"What do you want?" Ivan stopped but didn't turn around. "Goodbye!"

"Till tomorrow!" Ivan shouted again, and he left the cottage.

The snowstorm was still raging outside. He walked the first few steps confidently, but then he started to stagger. "It's something physical," he thought, grinning to himself. A strange joy began to rise in his heart. He felt a surge of determination; he would finally put an end to the doubt that had been tormenting him for so long. His mind was made up, "and now it won't change," he thought with relief. At that moment, he stumbled over something and almost fell. He stopped and looked down to see the peasant he had knocked over earlier, still lying motionless in the snow. The snow had almost covered his face. Ivan bent down, picked him up, and carried him in his arms. Seeing a light in a nearby house, he knocked on the shutters and asked the man inside to help him take the peasant to the police station, offering him three roubles. The man agreed and came out. I won't go into detail about how Ivan got the peasant to the police station and arranged for a doctor to see him, paying generously for the man's care. I'll just say that it took a whole hour, but Ivan felt satisfied with himself. His thoughts were racing the entire time.

"If I hadn't made up my mind so firmly for tomorrow," he thought with satisfaction, "I wouldn't have spent a whole hour helping that peasant. I would have just walked by and let him freeze. I can still keep an eye on myself," he thought with even more satisfaction, "even though they think I'm losing my mind!"

Just as he reached his house, Ivan stopped abruptly, wondering if he should go straight to the prosecutor and tell him everything right away. He wrestled with the thought, but in the end, he turned back toward his house. "Everything tomorrow, all at once," he whispered to himself. Strangely, almost all the relief and satisfaction he had felt earlier vanished in an instant.

When he stepped into his room, a chill ran through his heart— like a haunting reminder of something agonizing and disgusting that was now present in that room, something that had been there before. He sank heavily onto the sofa. The old woman brought him the samovar, but although he prepared tea, he didn't drink any of it. He sat slumped on the sofa, feeling light-headed and weak, as if his strength had abandoned him. He began drifting off, but then stirred uneasily, got up, and paced across the room to shake off the drowsiness.

At times, he felt as if he might be slipping into delirium, but that wasn't what troubled him the most. He kept scanning the room, as if searching for something, without knowing what. This happened several times— each time, the restlessness tugged at him, and he looked around in confusion. Eventually, his gaze locked onto a single point in the room.

Ivan smiled suddenly, but his face flushed with anger. He remained sitting for a long while, his head resting on both arms. Still, his eyes kept drifting sideways, back to that one spot—toward the sofa against the opposite wall. Something about that spot, some object or presence, seemed to gnaw at him. It irritated him, worried him, and filled him with torment.

Chapter 9: The Devil Ivan's Nightmare

At that moment, Ivan was almost at the door of his house when he suddenly stopped and asked himself whether he should go to the prosecutor immediately and confess everything. After a brief hesitation, he turned back toward the house, whispering to himself, "Tomorrow, I'll do everything at once." Strangely, the sense of satisfaction and relief that had been with him just moments before vanished instantly.

As he entered his room, an unsettling chill ran through his heart, like a sudden memory—or more precisely, a reminder— of something dreadful and repulsive. It was as though the very presence of something vile was lingering there now, just as it had been before. Ivan collapsed wearily onto the sofa. The old woman brought in a samovar, and though he poured himself some tea, he left it untouched. His head was spinning, and he could feel his body growing weaker.

He realized he was unwell, but his thoughts were too scattered to focus on his illness. He kept drifting in and out of a strange, hazy state, only to force himself up from the sofa to shake off the dizziness. He felt as if he might be slipping into delirium, though that wasn't what disturbed him most. His mind kept wandering back to the same unsettling thought—something was off, something was wrong. Several times, he scanned the room as if searching for something specific, though he wasn't sure what. His unease continued to grow, weighing down on him like an invisible burden.

Eventually, his eyes settled on one spot: the sofa against the opposite wall. He sat motionless for a long time, resting his head in his hands, but every now and then, he glanced sideways at that same spot. There was something about that sofa—something irritating, even tormenting him—though he couldn't explain what it was.

And then, just like that, it felt as though someone was sitting there. It was impossible to say how this person had entered the room, as Ivan was certain the room had been empty when he first walked in.

The figure seated on the sofa was a peculiar man—a Russian gentleman of a particular type, perhaps in his fifties, "qui faisait la cinquantaine," as the French would say. His thick, dark hair had streaks of gray, and he wore a small, pointed beard. His outfit gave him an odd appearance: a brownish reefer jacket, well-made but worn and out of fashion, as though it had been stylish three years ago but had since been discarded by more fashionable people. The man's linen clothing and scarf were carefully arranged, but on closer inspection, his linen was not exactly clean, and his scarf was frayed and threadbare. His trousers, though cut well, were too light in color and tight-fitting for current trends. He also wore a soft, white hat, entirely inappropriate for the season.

The overall impression was one of faded gentility. The man appeared to belong to that class of landowners who had once thrived under the old system of serfdom but had since fallen into decline. He seemed like someone who had once mingled with high society, maintaining connections even as his fortunes dwindled.

Perhaps he had spent his later years drifting from one friend's house to another, always welcomed as a charming guest, though never given a place of honor. Such men, pleasant but dependent, often lived solitary lives—either as bachelors or widowers. If they had children, those children were usually raised by distant relatives, and the men rarely mentioned them, perhaps even feeling embarrassed by the connection. Over time, they would lose contact with their children altogether, receiving occasional letters for holidays, which they sometimes answered, but often ignored.

The man's expression was not exactly friendly, but it was adaptable—ready to shift into whatever warmth or charm the situation required. A small, cheap opal ring gleamed on his finger, and a tortoiseshell lorgnette hung from a black ribbon around his neck. Ivan glared at him in silence, unwilling to speak first.

The visitor remained patiently quiet, sitting like a poor relation who had come downstairs for tea, waiting for his host to speak. His expression suggested that he was prepared for a friendly conversation as soon as Ivan was ready, but he sensed that Ivan was too preoccupied and irritable to engage just yet. After a moment, the visitor's face shifted to one of sudden concern.

"By the way," the visitor began, "you went to see Smerdyakov about Katerina Ivanovna, but you left without finding anything out. I suppose you forgot?"

"Ah, yes," Ivan muttered, his face clouded with unease. "I forgot... but it doesn't matter now. Tomorrow will be soon enough." He paused, glaring at the visitor. "And you—don't think for a second that you reminded me! I would have remembered on my own. Why are you meddling, as if I wouldn't have figured it out myself?"

"Then don't believe it," the visitor said with a pleasant smile. "There's no point in believing something against your will. Besides, proof isn't always enough to make people believe— especially material proof. Take Thomas, for example. He didn't believe because he saw Christ risen; he believed because he wanted to believe before he even saw Him. Look at spiritualists, for instance. I rather like them. Imagine—they think they're proving the existence of the afterlife just because some devil waves his horns at them from the other side. That's what they call material proof! But does proving there's a devil mean there's a God? I'd love to join an idealist society—just to lead the opposition! I'd say, 'I'm a realist, but not a materialist.'"

Ivan stood abruptly, gripping his head. "I feel like I'm delirious... In fact, I am delirious. Say whatever nonsense you want—I don't care. You won't drive me mad this time. But I feel ashamed somehow... I need to walk around." He began pacing, muttering to himself, "Sometimes I don't even see you, and other times I can't hear your voice—but I always know what you're saying.

Because it's not really you talking—it's me! I don't even know if I saw you last time or just dreamed it."

He went to the corner, soaked a towel in water, and wrapped it around his head. "Maybe this will make you disappear." With the towel on his head, he resumed pacing.

"I'm glad you feel comfortable enough to treat me so casually," the visitor said cheerfully.

"Fool," Ivan laughed. "Do you think I'd stand on ceremony with you? I'm feeling better now, even though my head's killing me... just don't start rambling about philosophy like last time. If you can't leave, at least gossip—something trivial. That's what poor relations are for. What a nightmare you are! But I'm not afraid of you. I'll outlast you—I won't end up in a madhouse!"

"C'est charmant, a poor relation," the visitor chuckled. "Yes, that's exactly what I am—a poor relation. And it's amusing to see that you're starting to believe I'm real this time. Last time, you insisted I was just a figment of your imagination."

"I've never for a moment believed you were real," Ivan shouted angrily. "You're a lie, you're my sickness, you're a phantom. The problem is, I don't know how to get rid of you, and I know I'll have to suffer through it for a while. You're my hallucination, a reflection of me—but only the worst parts, the stupidest parts of my thoughts and feelings. In that sense, you might be interesting if I had time to waste on you."

"Excuse me, but I've got you there. When you yelled at Alyosha under the streetlamp tonight and said, 'You learned it from him!

How do you know he visits me?' you were thinking about me then. So for that brief moment, you did believe in me," the man said with a calm laugh.

"Yes, that was a moment of weakness... but I couldn't believe in you. I don't even know if I was awake or asleep the last time. Maybe I was just dreaming and didn't see you at all."

"And why were you so angry with Alyosha just now? He's a good soul; I treated him poorly over Father Zossima."

"Don't talk about Alyosha! How dare you, you servant!" Ivan laughed again.

"You scold me, but you laugh—that's a good sign. You're being much more polite than you were last time, and I know why—it's because of that big decision you've made—"

"Don't mention my decision!" Ivan snapped.

"I understand, I understand, it's noble, it's charming—you're going to defend your brother and sacrifice yourself... it's very chivalrous."

"Shut up or I'll kick you!"

"I wouldn't mind that much, actually. If you kick me, then you'll have to believe I'm real—people don't kick ghosts. Joking aside, I don't mind if you scold me, but a bit more politeness wouldn't hurt, even toward me. 'Fool,' 'servant'—such words!"

"When I scold you, I'm scolding myself," Ivan laughed again. "You're just me, with a different face. You only say what I'm already thinking. You can't say anything new!"

"If I think like you, that's to my credit," the man said with dignity.

"You only pick out my worst thoughts, and on top of that, the dumb ones. You're stupid and vulgar. You're so stupid. I can't stand you! What am I supposed to do?" Ivan said through clenched teeth.

"My dear friend, all I want is to behave like a gentleman and be recognized as one," the visitor said, with the apologetic pride typical of a poor relation. "I'm poor, but... well, I won't say I'm honest, but... it's widely accepted that I'm a fallen angel. I can't even imagine how I was ever an angel. If I was, it must have been so long ago that it's not worth remembering. Now, I just care about being seen as gentlemanly and live as best I can, trying to be agreeable. I genuinely love people. I've been misunderstood! When I'm here with you, my life feels more real, and that's what I love most. Like you, I suffer from fantasy, so I enjoy the realism of earth. Here, everything is clear and structured, while where I come from, it's all vague equations. I like to dream. And being here makes me superstitious, believe it or not. Don't laugh! That's what I like, becoming superstitious. I've even adopted some of your habits: I've grown fond of the public baths. Would you believe it? I go and steam with merchants and priests. What I dream of is becoming fully incarnate—permanently—in the form of a merchant's wife weighing about 250 pounds, and believing in everything she does. My ideal is to go to church and light a candle with pure faith. That would end my suffering. I even like being treated by doctors. Last spring, there was a smallpox outbreak, and I went to a hospital to get vaccinated—if only you knew how much I enjoyed that day. I even donated ten rubles to support the Slavs! But you're not listening. By the way, you're not looking well tonight. I know you saw the doctor yesterday... what did he say about your health?"

"Idiot!" Ivan snapped.

"But you're clever, anyway. Are you scolding me again? I didn't ask because I care. You don't have to answer. Oh, and my rheumatism is back—"

"Idiot!" Ivan repeated.

"You keep saying the same thing. I had such a bad case of rheumatism last year that I still remember it."

"Let the devil have rheumatism!"

"Why not? If I take on a physical form, I suffer the consequences.

Satan sum et nihil humanum a me alienum puto."

"What? What was that? Satan sum et nihil humanum... that's not bad for the devil!"

"I'm glad you liked it."

"But you didn't get that from me." Ivan stopped suddenly, as if something struck him. "That never crossed my mind. That's strange."

"Something new, isn't it? I'll be honest with you this time and explain. Listen, in dreams—especially nightmares—whether from indigestion or anything else, people sometimes have such vivid visions, so detailed and real, entire worlds of events woven together with such complexity, with every little thing included, right down to the last button on a shirt. Even Leo Tolstoy never came up with anything so elaborate. And these dreams don't happen to writers alone—ordinary people, like officials, journalists, priests—they all experience them. It's a complete mystery. A statesman once told me that all his best ideas came to him in his sleep. That's what's happening now. Even though I'm your hallucination, just like in a nightmare, I'm saying things that have never crossed your mind before. I'm not just repeating your ideas, though I'm nothing more than your nightmare."

"You're lying. You're trying to convince me you exist apart from me and aren't just my nightmare, but now you're claiming you are a dream."

"My dear fellow, I'm using a special method today. I'll explain it later. Wait, where did I leave off? Oh, yes! I caught a cold back then—not here, but over there."

"Where's 'there'? Tell me, how long are you staying? Can't you leave?" Ivan cried in near despair. He stopped pacing, sat on the sofa, put his elbows on the table, and buried his head in his hands. He yanked off the wet towel and threw it aside in frustration. It had clearly been useless.

"Your nerves are out of order," the man remarked casually, though with perfect politeness. "You're mad at me for catching a cold, but it happened naturally. I was rushing to a diplomatic soirée at a high-ranking lady's house in Petersburg—she was aiming to influence the Ministry. So, I had to wear an evening suit, white tie, and gloves, even though I was, well, far away. I had to fly through space to reach your earth. Of course, it only took a moment, but you know it takes a sunbeam eight minutes to reach the earth. Imagine—an evening suit and an open waistcoat! Spirits don't get cold, but when you're in the flesh, well... to sum it up, I wasn't thinking, so I set off, and you know, in those ethereal spaces, in the waters above the firmament, it's freezing! Not exactly frost, but around 150 degrees below zero. You know how village girls trick people into licking an axe in 30 degrees of frost, and their tongues freeze to it and bleed? That's only in 30 degrees; in 150, just touching an axe would be enough to—well, if there was an axe up there."

"And can there be an axe there?" Ivan interrupted, half-heartedly and disdainfully, struggling not to give in to the delusion and completely lose his mind.

"An axe?" the visitor repeated in surprise.

"Yes, what would happen to an ax out there?" Ivan suddenly shouted with a kind of savage, insistent stubbornness.

"What would happen to an ax in space? What an idea! If it fell a certain distance, it would start, I imagine, flying around the earth without any reason, like a satellite. The astronomers would calculate the times of the ax's rising and setting, and Gatzuk would add it to his calendar, and that would be that."

"You're stupid, incredibly stupid," Ivan said irritably. "If you're going to lie, at least lie better or I won't listen. You're trying to defeat me with realism, trying to make me believe you exist, but I don't want to believe you exist! I won't believe it!"

"But I'm not lying; it's all true. Unfortunately, the truth is rarely entertaining. I can see you're still expecting something big from me, maybe even something impressive. It's a shame because I can only give what I have—"

"Stop talking philosophy, you fool!"

"Philosophy? When my whole right side is numb, and I'm moaning in pain? I've seen every doctor: they can diagnose you beautifully, they have your whole illness figured out, but none of them know how to cure you. There was an enthusiastic young student once who said, 'You might die, but at least you'll know exactly what disease you're dying from!' And what's with sending people to specialists? 'We only diagnose,' they say, 'go to a specialist, he'll treat you.' The old doctor who could cure anything is gone, I tell you. Now it's just specialists, and they all advertise in the newspapers. If something's wrong with your nose, they send you to Paris. There, they say, there's a European specialist who treats noses. When you get there, he'll look at your nose and say, 'I can only treat the right nostril; I don't do the left. You'll need to go to Vienna for that. There's a specialist there who'll handle the left nostril.' What are you supposed to do? I turned to home remedies in the end. A German doctor told me to rub myself with honey and salt in the bathhouse. I went, smeared myself all over, just to get an extra bath, and it didn't help me at all. In desperation, I wrote to Count Mattei in Milan. He sent me a book and some drops, bless him, and, believe it or not, Hoff's malt extract cured me! I bought it by accident, drank a bottle and a half, and I was ready to dance, it worked so well. I wanted to write a thank-you letter to the newspapers out of gratitude, but not a single one would print it. 'That's too reactionary,' they said. 'No one would believe it. The devil doesn't exist. Stay anonymous,' they advised me. But what's the point of a thank-you letter if it's anonymous? I laughed with the newspaper guys and said, 'It's considered reactionary to believe in God these days, but I'm the devil, so people might believe in me.' They agreed, 'Oh, of course, everyone believes in the devil! But still, we can't print it; it might hurt our reputation.' They said I could write it as a joke, but I didn't think that would be funny. So, the letter never got published, and to this day, it still bothers me. Even my best feelings, like gratitude, are denied to me simply because of my position."

"More philosophical reflections?" Ivan snapped bitterly.

"God forbid, but sometimes one has to complain. I've been slandered so much. You constantly insult me, calling me stupid. That's how I know you're still young. My dear fellow, intelligence isn't everything! I have a naturally kind and cheerful heart. 'I write vaudevilles, too,' as they say. You seem to think I'm like Hlestakov from The Government Inspector, just older, but my situation is much more serious. Long ago, by some decree I could never understand, I was destined 'to deny.' But I'm naturally good-hearted and not at all inclined to negativity. 'No, you must deny,' they told me. 'Without denial, there's no criticism. And what would a newspaper be without criticism?' Without criticism, it would just be full of endless praise. But that's not enough for life. Praise has to be tested by doubt, and so on, in that style.

But I didn't create this; it's not my doing. I'm not responsible for it. Still, they've made me the scapegoat. I write the criticism column, and that's how life keeps moving. We all understand the joke. I, for one, would rather disappear. But they say, 'No, you must live, or else there would be nothing.' If everything in the universe made sense, nothing would happen. There would be no events, and we need events. So, I'm forced to create events, even irrational ones, because that's what I'm told to do. And despite all their intelligence, people take this farce seriously, and that's their tragedy. They suffer, but they live a real life, not an imaginary one. Because suffering is life. Without suffering, what's the point of living? Life would turn into one long church service. It would be holy, but dull. And what about me? I suffer, but I don't live. I'm like the unknown in an equation with no solution. I'm a ghost in life, with no beginning and no end, who's forgotten even his own name. You're laughing—no, you're not laughing, you're angry again. All you care about is intelligence. But I tell you again, I'd give up all this super-celestial life, all the ranks and titles, just to be transformed into the soul of a merchant's wife weighing 250 pounds, setting candles in church."

"So, even you don't believe in God?" Ivan said with a hateful smile.

"What can I say?—if you're serious—"

"Is there a God or not?" Ivan cried with the same savage intensity.

"Oh, so you're serious? Honestly, my friend, I don't know. There, I've said it!"

"You don't know, but you see God? No, you're not separate from me. You're just me, nothing else! You're garbage, a product of my imagination!"

"Well, if you prefer, I have the same philosophy as you. That would be true. Je pense, donc je suis. I know that for sure. But everything else—these worlds, God, even Satan—isn't proven to me. Does all that exist by itself, or is it just an emanation of me, a logical progression of my ego that's always existed? But I'd better stop, or you'll jump up and hit me any second."

"Why don't you tell me a story instead?" Ivan said miserably.

"There's a story that fits our conversation, or maybe it's more of a legend than a story. You accuse me of not believing, but you see, I'm not the only one confused. Everything's a mess over where I come from, and it's all because of your science. There used to be atoms, five senses, four elements, and everything made sense somehow. Even the ancients had atoms. But now that you've discovered molecules, protoplasm, and who knows what else, we've had to lower our heads. There's a lot of confusion, and even more superstition and scandal. We have as much gossip as you do, maybe more, and even a secret police for gathering reports. Anyway, this legend comes from our middle ages—not yours, ours—and no one believes it anymore, except for the old ladies. And I don't mean your old ladies, I mean ours. We have everything you have; I'm telling you this as a secret out of friendship, though it's forbidden. This legend is about Paradise. There was once a thinker and philosopher here on earth who rejected everything: laws, conscience, faith, and especially the afterlife. He died, expecting nothing but darkness and death, but instead, he found the afterlife. He was shocked and outraged. 'This goes against everything I believe!' he said. And he was punished for that. Now, forgive me, I'm just repeating what I've heard—it's only a legend—but he was sentenced to walk a quadrillion kilometers in the dark (we've adopted the metric system, you know), and after he completes the journey, the gates of heaven will be opened to him, and he'll be forgiven."

"And what kinds of punishments do you have in the afterlife, besides walking quadrillions of kilometers?" Ivan asked with strange eagerness.

"Punishments? Oh, don't ask. In the old days, we had all kinds of punishments, but now it's mostly moral ones, like guilt and remorse, and all that nonsense. We got that from you, from your softer ways. And who benefits from that? Only the people without a conscience, because how can they be tormented by guilt when they have no conscience? But decent people with honor suffer because of it. Reforms, when they aren't prepared, especially when they're copied from abroad, only cause trouble! The old fire was better. Anyway, the man who was sentenced to walk the quadrillion kilometers just stood there, looked around, and lay down in the road. 'I won't do it. I refuse on principle!' If you mix the soul of an enlightened Russian atheist with the stubbornness of the prophet Jonah, who sulked in the whale's belly for three days, you'll get the character of that thinker lying there."

"What was he lying on?"

"Well, I suppose there was something to lie on. You're not laughing?"

"Bravo!" Ivan shouted, with the same strange eagerness. Now he was listening with unexpected curiosity. "So, is he still lying there?"

"That's the point—he isn't lying there anymore. He lay there for almost a thousand years, then got up and kept going."

"What an idiot!" Ivan said, laughing nervously, though he seemed deep in thought. "What difference does it make whether he lies there forever or walks the quadrillion kilometers? It would take him a billion years to walk it!"

"More than that. I don't have a pencil and paper to figure it out exactly, but he got there long ago, and that's where the story starts."

"He got there? How did he get the billion years to do it?"

"You're still thinking about our earth. But this earth may have repeated itself a billion times. It's been wiped out, frozen, shattered, broken into pieces, turned back into its elements, becoming 'the waters above the firmament,' then a comet, then a sun, and then from the sun, back into the earth again. The same cycle could have repeated endlessly, down to every tiny detail, tediously and unbearably."

"Okay, fine. What happened when he got there?"

"As soon as the gates of Paradise opened and he stepped inside, before even two seconds had passed on his watch (though I'm sure his watch had dissolved into its elements long before then), he shouted that those two seconds were worth walking not just a quadrillion kilometers, but quadrillions upon quadrillions, raised to the quadrillionth power! In fact, he sang 'hosanna' so enthusiastically that some of the high-minded people there didn't want to shake his hand at first. They thought he'd turned into a reactionary too quickly. That's the Russian temperament for you. I remind you, this is just a legend. Take it for what it's worth. But that's the kind of ideas we still have on these matters."

"I've caught you!" Ivan exclaimed, almost childlike in his excitement, as if he'd just remembered something. "That story about the quadrillion years—I made it up myself! I was seventeen then, in high school. I made it up and told it to a classmate named Korovkin, in Moscow... That story is so unique I couldn't have gotten it from anywhere else. I thought I had forgotten it... but now it's come back to me—I remembered it myself, not you! It wasn't you telling it! People remember all sorts of things unconsciously, even when they're about to be executed... it's come back to me in a dream. You are that dream! You're a dream, not a real person!"

"From the way you so passionately deny my existence," the man laughed, "I'm convinced you believe in me."

"Not even a little! I don't have a grain of faith in you!"

"But you have a thousandth of a grain. Homeopathic doses are the strongest. Admit it—you believe, even to a ten-thousandth of a grain."

"Not for a second!" Ivan shouted furiously. "But I wish I could believe in you," he added strangely.

"Aha! That's an admission! But I'm kind-hearted, so I'll help you again. Listen, it was I who caught you, not the other way around. I told you your story, the one you forgot, just to destroy your faith in me completely."

"You're lying. You're here to convince me that you exist!"

"Exactly. But the hesitation, the back-and-forth between belief and disbelief—it can be such torture for a conscientious man like you that it's better to just hang yourself. Since I know you're inclined to believe in me, I threw in some disbelief by reminding you of that story. I lead you between belief and disbelief on purpose, and I have my reasons. It's a new method. As soon as you stop believing in me completely, you'll start telling me to my face that I'm not a dream but a reality. I know you. Then I'll have achieved my goal, which is an honorable one. I'll plant just a tiny seed of belief in you, and it'll grow into a huge oak tree—so big that, sitting on it, you'll long to join the ranks of the 'hermits in the wilderness' and the 'saintly women,' because that's what you secretly want. You'll eat locusts and wander the wilderness to save your soul!"

"So, you're working for the salvation of my soul, are you, you scoundrel?"

"Sometimes one has to do a good deed. Why are you so grumpy?"

"Fool! Did you ever tempt those holy men who ate locusts and prayed in the wilderness for seventeen years until moss grew over them?"

"My dear fellow, I've done nothing but that. You forget the whole world and all the other worlds and focus on just one of those saints because they're rare gems. One soul like that is worth more than a whole constellation sometimes. We have our own way of measuring things, you know. Their conversion is priceless! And some of them, I swear, are just as cultured as you, though you wouldn't believe it. They can believe and doubt so deeply, all at the same time, that sometimes they're a hair's breadth away from 'flipping over,' as the actor Gorbunov puts it."

"Did you get your nose pulled for that?"

"My dear fellow," the man said wisely, "it's better to have your nose pulled than to have no nose at all. As an unfortunate marquis said recently (he must have been treated by a specialist) during confession to his spiritual father—a Jesuit. I was there, it was delightful. 'Give me back my nose!' he cried, beating his chest. 'My son,' said the priest, evading the question, 'everything happens according to the mysterious will of Providence, and what seems like a misfortune often brings unexpected blessings. If fate has taken away your nose, consider it a good thing, for now no one can pull it.' 'Father, that's no comfort,' the marquis cried in despair. 'I'd be happy to have my nose pulled every day of my life if only it were still in its proper place!' 'My son,' sighed the priest, 'you can't expect every blessing at once. Complaining about Providence won't help. Besides, by losing your nose, you've already had your wish granted, in a way—because when you lost your nose, you were led by it!'"

"Fool, how stupid!" Ivan shouted.

"My dear friend, I was only trying to entertain you. But I swear that's real Jesuit reasoning, and I swear that it all happened exactly as I told you. It happened recently and caused me a lot of trouble. That poor young man shot himself that very night when he got home. I stayed with him until the very end. Those Jesuit confessions are truly my favorite distraction when I'm feeling down. Here's another story that happened not long ago. A little blonde Norman girl, about twenty years old—a simple, charming beauty who could make your mouth water—comes to an old priest. She leans down and whispers her sin into the screen. 'Why, my daughter, have you sinned again already?' cries the priest. 'O Holy Mary, what am I hearing? Not with the same man this time, how long will this go on? Aren't you ashamed?' 'Ah, Father,' answers the sinner with tears of guilt, 'it gives him so much pleasure and causes me so little pain!' Imagine an answer like that! I pulled back. It was a cry of nature, more pure than innocence itself, if you ask me. I forgave her on the spot and was about to leave, but I had to stop. I heard the priest through the screen setting up a meeting with her for the evening—even though he was old and tough as stone, he fell instantly! It was nature, the truth of nature showing its power! What, you're frowning again? Angry again? I don't know how to make you happy."

"Leave me alone, you're pounding on my brain like a terrible nightmare," Ivan groaned miserably, helpless against the vision. "You're boring me, it's painful and unbearable. I would do anything to get rid of you!"

"I'm telling you, lower your expectations. Don't expect anything 'grand and noble' from me, and you'll see how well we'll get along," said the man seriously. "You're angry with me because I didn't show up in a blaze of red, with thunder and lightning, with burnt wings. Instead, I came in such a simple form. Your feelings are hurt, first of all, because of your artistic sense, and secondly, because of your pride. How could such a plain devil appear to a great man like you! Yes, you have that romantic side to you, the one Byelinsky made fun of. I can't help it, young man, I was going to show up as a joke dressed like a retired general who served in the Caucasus, with a medal of the Lion and Sun on my jacket. But I didn't dare do it, because you would've beaten me up for wearing the Lion and Sun instead of, at least, the Polar Star or Sirius. And you keep saying I'm stupid, but goodness! I never claimed to be your equal in intelligence. Mephistopheles told Faust he wanted to do evil but only did good. Well, he can say whatever he likes; I'm the opposite. I might be the one being in all creation who truly loves the truth and genuinely wants to do good. I was there when the Word, who died on the cross, ascended to heaven, carrying with Him the soul of the repentant thief. I heard the joyful cries of the cherubim singing and shouting 'hosanna,' and the roaring excitement of the seraphim that shook heaven and all of creation. I swear to you on all that's holy, I wanted to join them and shout 'hosanna' with all my heart. The word almost slipped out, almost escaped my lips... You know how sensitive and artistically impressionable I am. But my common sense— oh, that miserable part of my character—held me back, and I let the moment pass! What would've happened, I thought, what would have happened after my 'hosanna'? Everything on earth would've been wiped out instantly, and no more events could have happened. So, out of a sense of duty and because of my social position, I had to stop that wonderful moment and stick to my miserable job. Somebody else takes all the credit for the good things, and all that's left for me is the nastiness. But I don't envy the honor of a life full of lazy trickery. I'm not ambitious. Why, out of all the beings in the world, am I doomed to be hated by all decent people, even to be kicked? If I take human form, I have to deal with the consequences sometimes. Of course, I know there's a secret to all this, but they won't tell me the secret no matter what, because then, if I understood the meaning of it, I might shout 'hosanna,' and the essential negative part would disappear immediately, and good sense would take over everywhere. And that, of course, would be the end of everything, even magazines and newspapers—because who would still want to read them? I know that at the end of all things, I'll find peace. I'll walk my quadrillion kilometers and learn the secret. But until then, I'm sulking and carrying out my fate, though I hate it—that is, to destroy thousands just to save one. How many souls have had to be ruined, how many honorable reputations destroyed, all for the sake of that one good man, Job, who they made such a fool out of me for in the old days! Yes, until the secret is revealed, I have two kinds of truths—one is their truth up there, which I know nothing about yet, and the other is my own. And there's no telling which one will turn out to be better... Are you asleep?"

"I wish I were," Ivan groaned in frustration. "You're repeating all my old, stupid ideas—things I outgrew and threw away long ago—and you're presenting them like they're something new!"

"Nothing pleases you! And I thought I'd impress you with my writing style. That 'hosanna in the skies' wasn't bad, was it? And what about that ironic tone, like Heine, huh?"

"No, I was never such a flatterer! How could my soul create a flatterer like you?"

"My dear friend, I know a charming and thoughtful young Russian gentleman, a young thinker, and a great lover of literature and art. He's the author of a promising poem called The Grand Inquisitor. I was only thinking of him!"

"I forbid you to mention The Grand Inquisitor," Ivan shouted, his face turning red with shame.

"And the Geological Cataclysm. Do you remember that? Now that was a poem!"

"Shut up, or I'll kill you!"

"You'll kill me? No, excuse me, I'm going to keep talking. I came here just to enjoy this. Oh, I love the dreams of my passionate young friends, full of energy and eager for life! 'There are new people,' you said last spring, when you were thinking about coming here, 'they plan to destroy everything and start with cannibalism. Idiots! They didn't ask for my advice! I believe nothing needs to be destroyed. We just need to destroy the idea of God in man, and that's where we should begin. That's what we have to focus on. Oh, what fools, who can't see the truth! As soon as everyone denies God—and I believe that time will come, like a geological period— the old idea of the universe will collapse on its own, without any cannibalism. Even the old morality will disappear, and everything will start fresh. People will come together to get as much as they can out of life, but only for joy and happiness in the present world. Humanity will rise with divine pride, and the man-god will appear. Hour by hour, he'll expand his control over nature with his will and his science. Man will feel such incredible joy in doing so that it will make up for all the old dreams of heaven's happiness. Everyone will know they're mortal and will face death proudly and calmly, like a god. Their pride will teach them not to regret life being so short, and they'll love their neighbor without needing a reward. Love will only last for a moment, but knowing it's brief will make its flame burn even brighter, instead of wasting away in dreams of eternal love beyond the grave'... and on and on, in the same style. Wonderful!"

Ivan sat staring at the floor, pressing his hands over his ears, but he started trembling. The voice kept going.

"The question now is," the visitor continued, "as this young thinker wondered, is it possible that such a time will ever come? If it does, everything is decided, and humanity's future is set forever. But since people are so incredibly stupid, this can't happen for at least a thousand years. So, anyone who realizes the truth now can live by these new principles. In that sense, 'everything is allowed' for him. What's more, even if this period never comes, since there's no God and no immortality anyway, the new man may become the man-god, even if he's the only one in the whole world. And once he reaches his new level, he can ignore all the barriers of the old morality of the old slave-man if he needs to. There are no laws for a god. Wherever God stands, the ground is holy. Wherever I stand will immediately become the highest place... 'everything is allowed,' and that's the end of it! That's all very inspiring, but if you're going to be dishonest, why do you need moral permission to do it? But that's the modern Russian for you. He can't cheat without a moral excuse. He's so in love with the truth—"

The visitor was getting carried away by his own speech, his voice growing louder and louder, and he looked at Ivan with a mocking expression. But before he could finish, Ivan suddenly grabbed a glass from the table and threw it at him.

"Ah, how foolish!" the man cried, jumping up from the sofa and shaking off the tea that had spilled on him. "He remembers Luther's ink bottle! He thinks I'm just a dream and throws glasses at a dream! Just like a woman! I suspected you were only pretending to block your ears."

A loud, persistent knocking suddenly echoed from the window. Ivan jumped up from the sofa.

"Do you hear that? You should go answer," said the visitor. "It's your brother Alyosha, bringing the most interesting and surprising news, I'm sure!"

"Shut up, liar! I knew it was Alyosha. I could feel he was coming, and of course, he hasn't come for nothing; of course, he's bringing 'news,'" Ivan shouted, frantic.

"Go on, open the window for him. There's a snowstorm out there, and he's your brother. Don't you know what the weather's like? You wouldn't even put a dog outside in this."

The knocking continued. Ivan wanted to rush to the window, but it felt as though his arms and legs were chained. He strained with all his might to break free but couldn't. The knocking on the window grew louder and louder. Finally, the chains broke, and Ivan jumped up from the sofa. He looked around wildly. Both candles had almost burned out, the glass he had thrown at his guest was still sitting on the table, and there was no one on the sofa across from him. The knocking on the window frame continued but was much quieter than it had sounded in his dream—barely a soft tapping.

"It wasn't a dream! No, I swear it wasn't a dream—it all just happened!" Ivan cried out. He rushed to the window and opened the pane.

"Alyosha, I told you not to come!" he yelled to his brother. "What do you want? Say it in two words, do you hear me?"

"An hour ago, Smerdyakov hanged himself," Alyosha called from outside.

"Come around to the steps, I'll let you in," Ivan said, hurrying to open the door for his brother.

Chapter 10: "It Was He Who Said That"

Alyosha entered and told Ivan that a little over an hour ago,

Marya Kondratyevna had rushed to his rooms and informed him that Smerdyakov had taken his own life. "I went in to clear away the samovar, and he was hanging on a nail in the wall." When Alyosha asked her if she had told the police, she said she hadn't told anyone yet. "But I ran straight to you; I've run all the way here." Alyosha said she seemed completely crazed, shaking like a leaf. When Alyosha hurried with her to the cottage, they found Smerdyakov still hanging there. On the table, there was a note that read: "I end my life of my own free will, so no one is to blame." Alyosha left the note on the table and went straight to the police captain to report it. "And from him, I've come straight to you," Alyosha finished, staring intently at Ivan's face. He had kept his eyes fixed on him the whole time, as though noticing something strange in Ivan's expression.

"Brother," he suddenly cried, "you must be really sick. You're looking at me like you don't understand what I'm saying."

"It's good you came," Ivan said absently, as though lost in thought, not really hearing Alyosha's concern. "I already knew he had hanged himself."

"Who told you?" Alyosha asked, surprised.

"I don't know. But I knew. Did I know? Yes, he told me. He just told me now."

Ivan stood in the middle of the room, speaking in the same distant, brooding tone, looking down at the floor.

"Who told you?" Alyosha asked again, glancing around involuntarily.

"He's gone now."

Ivan lifted his head and smiled faintly.

"He was afraid of you, of someone as pure as you. Dmitri calls you a 'cherub.' Cherub!... the thunderous songs of the seraphim. What are seraphim? Maybe a whole constellation. Or maybe that constellation is just a chemical molecule. There's a constellation called the Lion and the Sun, you know that, don't you?"

"Brother, please sit down," Alyosha said in alarm. "For heaven's sake, sit on the sofa! You're delirious. Put your head on the pillow, that's it. Should I get a wet towel for your head? It might help."

"Yes, give me the towel. It's over there on the chair. I threw it down."

"It's not here. Don't worry, I'll find it. I know where it is," said Alyosha, finding a clean, folded towel near Ivan's dressing table in the corner of the room. Ivan looked strangely at the towel, as if recalling something.

"Wait," he said, getting up from the sofa. "An hour ago, I took that towel, wet it, wrapped it around my head, and threw it here... Why is it dry now? There wasn't another one."

"You wrapped this towel around your head?" Alyosha asked.

"Yes, and I walked around the room with it an hour ago... Why have the candles burned down so much? What time is it?"

"Almost midnight."

"No, no, no!" Ivan suddenly shouted. "It wasn't a dream. He was here! He was sitting here, on that sofa. When you knocked on the window, I threw a glass at him... this one." He pointed. "Wait a minute. I was asleep last time, but this dream wasn't a dream. This has happened before. I have dreams now, Alyosha, but they aren't really dreams. They're reality. I walk, talk, and see everything... even though I'm asleep. But he was sitting here, on that sofa there... He's unbelievably stupid, Alyosha, unbelievably stupid." Ivan suddenly laughed and began pacing around the room.

"Who's stupid? Who are you talking about, brother?" Alyosha asked anxiously.

"The devil! He's taken to visiting me. He's been here twice, almost three times. He mocked me, saying I was angry because he was just a regular devil, not Satan with scorched wings, thunder, and lightning. But he's not Satan—that's a lie. He's a fraud. He's just a devil—a petty, trivial devil. He goes to bathhouses. If you undressed him, I bet you'd find he has a tail, long and smooth like a Danish dog's, about a yard long, and the color of dull brown... Alyosha, you're cold. You've been in the snow. Do you want some tea? What? Is it cold? Should I ask her to bring some? C'est à ne pas mettre un chien dehors."

Alyosha hurried to the washstand, wet the towel, and persuaded Ivan to sit back down. He wrapped the wet towel around Ivan's head and sat beside him.

"What were you telling me about Lise?" Ivan asked, becoming more talkative. "I like Lise. I said something mean about her. That wasn't true. I like her... I'm terrified of Katya tomorrow. I'm more scared of her than anything. Because of what's to come. She's going to reject me tomorrow and crush me underfoot. She thinks I'm ruining Mitya out of jealousy for her! Yes, that's what she thinks! But it's not true. Tomorrow will bring the cross, but not the gallows. No, I won't hang myself. You know, I could never commit suicide, Alyosha. Is it because I'm a coward? No, I'm not a coward. Maybe I love life too much? How did I know that Smerdyakov had hanged himself? Yes, it was him. He told me so."

"And you're completely sure that someone was here?" Alyosha asked.

"Yes, he was sitting on that sofa in the corner. You would have driven him away. Actually, you did drive him away. He disappeared as soon as you arrived. I love your face, Alyosha.

Did you know that? I love your face. And he is me, Alyosha. He's everything base in me, everything mean and despicable. Yes, I'm a romantic. He knew it... though he twisted it into a lie. He's so unbelievably stupid; but that works in his favor. He's clever, though, with animal cunning—he knew how to push my buttons. He kept teasing me, saying I believed in him, and that's how he got me to listen. He fooled me like a child. He told me a lot of things about myself that were true, things I would never have admitted on my own. You know, Alyosha," Ivan added in a deeply serious and almost confiding tone, "I would be so relieved to think it was him and not me."

"He's worn you out," Alyosha said softly, looking at his brother with sympathy.

"He's been toying with me. And he's so clever, Alyosha, so clever. 'Conscience! What is conscience?' he said. 'I make it up for myself. Why does it bother me? Just out of habit. Humanity's been used to it for seven thousand years. So let's give it up, and we'll become gods.' That's what he said. That's exactly what he said!"

"And not you, not you?" Alyosha asked earnestly, gazing straight into his brother's eyes. "Forget about him! Leave him behind with everything you hate now, and never let him come back!"

411

"Yes, but he's spiteful. He laughed at me. He was rude, Alyosha," Ivan said, shivering as if offended. "He was unfair to me, unfair about so many things. He lied to my face about me. 'Oh, you're going to commit a great act of virtue—confessing that you killed your father, that the valet did it under your orders.'"

"Brother," Alyosha interposed, "restrain yourself. It was not you murdered him. It's not true!"

"That's what he says, he, and he knows it. 'You are going to perform an act of heroic virtue, and you don't believe in virtue; that's what tortures you and makes you angry, that's why you are so vindictive.' He said that to me about me and he knows what he says."

"It's you say that, not he," exclaimed Alyosha mournfully, "and you say it because you are ill and delirious, tormenting yourself."

"No, he knows what he says. 'You are going from pride,' he says. 'You'll stand up and say it was I killed him, and why do you writhe with horror? You are lying! I despise your opinion, I despise your horror!' He said that about me. 'And do you know you are longing for their praise—"he is a criminal, a murderer, but what a generous soul; he wanted to save his brother and he confessed." ' That's a lie, Alyosha!" Ivan cried suddenly, with flashing eyes. "I don't want the low rabble to praise me, I swear I don't! That's a lie! That's why I threw the glass at him and it broke against his ugly face."

"Brother, calm down, stop!" Alyosha pleaded.

"He knows how to torture me. He's cruel," Ivan continued, ignoring him. "From the start, I had a sense of what he was after. 'Even if it's out of pride, you hoped Smerdyakov would be found guilty and sent to Siberia, and Mitya would go free. You figured you'd only face moral blame for it.' (Did you hear him laugh at that?') 'And some people would even admire you. But now

Smerdyakov is dead—he hanged himself—and who's going to believe just you? Still, you've made up your mind to go. You'll go, even though there's no point. Why are you going now?' That's unbearable, Alyosha. I can't handle these kinds of questions. Who has the right to ask me things like that?"

"Brother," Alyosha interrupted, his heart sinking with fear but still clinging to the hope of bringing Ivan back to his senses, "how could he have told you about Smerdyakov's death before I got here? No one knew yet—there wasn't time for anyone to find out."

"He told me," Ivan said firmly, refusing to doubt. "It's all he talked about. 'It would be fine if you believed in virtue,' he said. 'Even if no one else believes you, you'd still be going for the sake of doing what's right. But you're no better than Fyodor Pavlovitch, so what do you care about virtue? Why do you want to get involved if your sacrifice won't help anyone? You don't even know why you're going! Oh, how much you'd give just to understand your own motives! You haven't made up your mind yet. You'll sit awake all night, thinking about it. But you will go—you know you will. No matter how much you deliberate, the decision isn't yours to make. You'll go because you won't dare not to. But why? That's for you to figure out—that's the riddle!' Then he stood up and left. He called me a coward, Alyosha! That's the answer to the riddle: I'm a coward. 'It's not for eagles like you to soar,' he added—him! And Smerdyakov said the same thing. He must die! Katya despises me—I've seen it for a month now. Even Lise will start despising me. 'You're only going so people will praise you.' That's a vicious lie! And you despise me too, Alyosha. Now I'm going to hate you all over again! And I hate him too—I hate that monster! I don't want to save him. Let him rot in Siberia! He's already started singing hymns! Tomorrow, I'll stand in front of them all and spit in their faces!"

Ivan sprang up in a rage, threw off the towel, and began pacing back and forth in the room again. Alyosha remembered what his brother had said earlier: "It feels like I'm awake, but asleep. I walk, I talk, I see, but I'm still asleep." It seemed just like that now. Alyosha stayed by his side, afraid to leave him alone. The idea of fetching a doctor crossed his mind, but there was no one he could leave Ivan with.

Bit by bit, Ivan drifted into unconsciousness. He kept talking— endlessly—but now his words were jumbled and barely understandable. Suddenly, he swayed, almost falling, but Alyosha caught him in time. Gently, he helped Ivan to bed, somehow undressing him and tucking him in. Alyosha sat with him for another two hours, watching as Ivan slept deeply, breathing softly and steadily. Finally, Alyosha grabbed a pillow and lay down on the sofa without undressing.

As he drifted off to sleep, he prayed for both Mitya and Ivan. A clearer understanding of Ivan's illness began to take shape in his mind. "The agony of a proud decision... an honest conscience." The God Ivan didn't believe in—and the truth that came with Him—were beginning to take hold of his heart, even though Ivan's soul still fought against it. "Yes," Alyosha thought as he lay on the pillow, "if Smerdyakov is dead, no one will believe Ivan. But he'll still testify." Alyosha smiled gently. "God will win," he thought. "Ivan will either rise in the light of truth or... he'll destroy himself in hatred, taking revenge on himself and everyone else for having served a cause he doesn't believe in." With a heavy heart, Alyosha prayed for Ivan once more.

Book 12: A Judicial Error

Chapter 1: The Fatal Day

At ten o'clock in the morning, the day after the events I've described, the trial of Dmitri Karamazov began in our district court. I want to make it clear from the start that I don't consider myself capable of providing a complete account of everything that happened during the trial or even reporting the exact order of events. I imagine that including every detail with proper explanations would take up an entire book—a very large one, at that. So, I hope I won't be criticized for focusing only on what stood out to me. It's possible that I may have paid more attention to things that weren't that important, while missing some essential moments. But I realize now that I'm better off not apologizing. I'll simply do my best, and the reader can judge for themselves that I've put in all the effort I could.

To begin, before even stepping into the courtroom, I must mention the thing that surprised me the most that day. And, as it turned out, it surprised everyone else, too. We all knew that the case had stirred up a lot of interest. People were eagerly waiting for the trial to begin, and for the past two months, it had been the main topic of conversation, speculation, and gossip in local society. We also knew that the case had become widely known throughout

Russia. But none of us expected that it would spark such intense and passionate interest—not only among us locals but across the whole country. This fact became very clear on the day of the trial.

Visitors had arrived not only from our provincial capital but also from several other Russian towns, including Moscow and St. Petersburg. Among them were lawyers, ladies, and even a few prominent figures. Every ticket to the trial had been snatched up as soon as they became available. A special section behind the table where the three judges sat had been set aside for the most important male visitors, with a row of armchairs placed there— something that had never been allowed before. At least half of the audience consisted of women. So many lawyers had come from different places that there wasn't enough room to seat them all. Since every ticket had already been claimed long ago, a partition was hastily erected at the back of the room, where these lawyers were allowed to stand. They considered themselves lucky to even have that standing space since all the chairs had been removed to create more room. The crowd behind the partition stood packed tightly, shoulder to shoulder, throughout the trial.

Some women, especially those who had traveled from far away, showed up in the gallery wearing fancy, elegant outfits. But most of the women didn't seem to care about their appearance. Their faces showed an intense, almost unhealthy level of curiosity. One peculiar thing—confirmed by many observations later—was that nearly all the women, or at least the majority, supported Dmitri and wanted him to be acquitted. This was probably because of his reputation as someone who easily won women's hearts. Everyone knew that two women, both rivals in love, would be involved in the trial. One of them, Katerina Ivanovna, had become the center of much fascination. People told all kinds of extraordinary stories about her and her passion for Dmitri, even though he was on trial for a terrible crime. They particularly talked about her pride and aristocratic connections—after all, she had barely visited anyone in town. There were even rumors that she planned to ask the government for permission to follow Dmitri to Siberia and marry him somewhere in the mines.

Grushenka's appearance in court was just as eagerly anticipated. The public was eager to witness the meeting between the two rivals—the proud aristocratic Katerina and Grushenka, often referred to as "the courtesan." Grushenka was already familiar to the women of the district. Many had seen her before and knew her as the woman blamed for ruining both Fyodor Pavlovitch and his unfortunate son. Almost everyone wondered how both father and son could have fallen so hopelessly in love with what they described as a very ordinary Russian girl—one who wasn't even particularly attractive.

In short, the trial became the topic of endless conversation. I know for a fact that several serious family arguments broke out in town because of Dmitri's case. Many wives had heated arguments with their husbands over their differing opinions about the trial, and naturally, these husbands became even more hostile toward Dmitri. It seemed clear that most of the men in the audience were prejudiced against him, while many of the women supported him. Many of the men's faces were stern, bitter, and even full of resentment. During his time in town, Dmitri had managed to offend quite a few people. Some of the visitors at the trial didn't seem to care much about Dmitri's fate; they were simply there for the spectacle. But the majority of the men were clearly hoping for a conviction, except for the lawyers, who seemed more interested in the legal aspects of the case than the moral ones.

Everyone in the courtroom was buzzing with excitement over the presence of the famous lawyer, Fetyukovitch. His talent was well-known, and he had defended several high-profile cases in the provinces before. Any case he took on instantly became famous and was remembered across Russia for years. There were also plenty of rumors circulating about our prosecutor and the President of the Court. People said that the prosecutor, Ippolit Kirillovitch, was nervous about facing Fetyukovitch because they had been rivals from their early days in St. Petersburg. Kirillovitch, who often felt that his talents hadn't been properly appreciated, was deeply invested in the Karamazov case. He was even dreaming of using this case to rebuild his reputation, but Fetyukovitch was the one obstacle that worried him the most. However, these rumors weren't entirely fair. Kirillovitch wasn't the type to lose his nerve in the face of a challenge. On the contrary, the greater the danger, the more confident he became.

That said, Kirillovitch had a reputation for being impulsive and emotionally sensitive. He had a tendency to throw himself completely into his work, treating each case as if his entire future depended on it. This trait made him the subject of ridicule among his colleagues in the legal world, who thought he was too passionate about psychology. In my opinion, they were wrong to mock him. I believe Kirillovitch was a more complex character than most people realized. Unfortunately, his poor health had held him back early in his career, and he had never fully recovered from that setback.

As for the President of the Court, he was a cultured, humane man with practical experience and progressive views. Although he was somewhat ambitious, he didn't seem too focused on advancing his career. His main goal was to be recognized as a man of modern ideas. He came from a well-connected and wealthy family. As we later found out, the Karamazov case interested him more as a social phenomenon than as a personal tragedy. He saw it as a reflection of society, a product of the national character, and an example of the issues facing the country. However, when it came to the personal aspects of the case—the human tragedy involved, including Dmitri's fate—he remained distant and detached. His attitude toward the case was objective and abstract, which, perhaps, was the proper way for a judge to approach it.

The courtroom was packed and overflowing well before the judges showed up. Our courtroom is the best hall in town— spacious, tall, and great for sound. To the right of the judges, who were sitting on a raised platform, a table and two rows of chairs were set up for the jury. To the left was where the prisoner and the defense counsel sat. In the middle of the courtroom, near the judges, was a table with the evidence. On it lay Fyodor Pavlovitch's white silk dressing gown, stained with blood; the brass pestle used in the supposed murder; Mitya's shirt with a bloody sleeve; his coat, with bloodstains over the pocket where he had put his handkerchief; the handkerchief itself, stiff with blood and now yellow; the pistol Mitya loaded at Perhotin's with plans to kill himself, which was secretly taken from him by Trifon Borissovitch at Mokroe; the envelope containing the three thousand rubles meant for Grushenka, tied with a pink ribbon; and many other items that I can't remember. The seats for the public were a bit further back in the hall. But in front of the balustrade, a few chairs were placed for the witnesses who stayed in the court after giving their testimony.

At ten o'clock, the three judges arrived—the President, an honorary justice of the peace, and another judge. The prosecutor, of course, came in right after them. The President was a short, stout man in his fifties, with a pale complexion, dark hair turning gray and cut short, and a red ribbon from an Order I can't recall. The prosecutor looked particularly pale, almost green. His face seemed thinner, like he had lost weight overnight. I had seen him two days before, and he had looked normal then. The President began by asking if all the jurors were present.

But I can't continue like this, partly because I didn't hear some things, didn't notice others, and have forgotten some parts, but mainly because, as I mentioned before, I don't have enough time or space to mention everything that was said and done. I just know that neither side objected to many of the jurors. I remember the twelve jurors—four were minor town officials, two were merchants, and six were peasants and artisans. I recall that, long before the trial, people, especially the women, were surprised and kept asking, "Can such a delicate, complicated, and psychological case be left to minor officials and even peasants to decide?" and "What could an official, let alone a peasant, understand about such a case?" All four of the officials were, in fact, unimportant men of low rank. Except for one who was younger, they were gray-haired, unknown in society, and had probably spent their lives on meager salaries, with likely elderly, unremarkable wives and large families, maybe even without proper shoes and stockings. At best, they spent their free time playing cards and had likely never read a single book. The two merchants looked respectable but were oddly quiet and stern. One was clean-shaven and dressed in European-style clothes; the other had a small gray beard and wore a red ribbon with some kind of medal around his neck. There's no need to describe the artisans and peasants. The artisans of Skotoprigonyevsk are almost peasants, and some even worked on farms. Two of them also wore European-style clothes, which, maybe for that reason, made them look dirtier and more unappealing than the others. One couldn't help but wonder, as I did the moment I saw them, "What could men like that possibly make of such a case?" Yet their faces left a strangely powerful, almost threatening impression; they were stern and serious.

Finally, the President opened the case of Fyodor Pavlovitch Karamazov's murder. I don't quite remember how he described him. The court usher was instructed to bring in the prisoner, and Mitya entered. The whole room went silent. You could have heard a pin drop. I'm not sure how others felt, but Mitya made a very bad impression on me. He looked overly fancy in a brand-new frock coat. I heard later that he had ordered it in Moscow just for this occasion, from his own tailor, who knew his measurements. He wore spotless black gloves and fine linen. He walked in with long strides, looking straight ahead stiffly, and sat down with an air of complete calm.

At the same time, the defense lawyer, the famous Fetyukovitch, entered, and a soft murmur spread through the courtroom. He was a tall, thin man, with long, skinny legs and very long, thin, pale fingers. His face was clean-shaven, his short hair neatly brushed, and his lips were thin, often curling into a half-smile, half-sneer. He looked about forty. His face would have been pleasant if it weren't for his eyes, which were small and close together, with only a long, thin nose between them. His face had a birdlike quality. He wore evening dress and a white tie.

I remember the President's first questions to Mitya, asking his name, occupation, and other details. Mitya answered sharply, and his voice was unexpectedly loud, making the President start and look at him with surprise. Then followed a list of people who would take part in the proceedings—the witnesses and experts. It was a long list. Four witnesses weren't present—Miüsov, who had testified at the earlier inquiry but was now in Paris; Madame Hohlakov and Maximov, who were both ill; and Smerdyakov, who had recently died, as confirmed by an official police statement. The news of Smerdyakov's death caused a stir in the courtroom. Many in the audience hadn't heard about his sudden suicide. What shocked people the most was Mitya's sudden outburst. As soon as Smerdyakov's death was announced, he shouted from his seat:

"He was a dog and died like a dog!"

I remember how his lawyer rushed over to him and how the President warned him that serious measures would be taken if such behavior was repeated. Mitya nodded and quietly muttered to his lawyer several times, without any sign of regret:

"I won't again, I won't. It slipped out. I won't do it again."

Of course, this brief episode didn't help him with the jury or the public. His character showed itself, speaking volumes. It was under the shadow of this incident that the opening statement was read. It was short but detailed. It laid out the main reasons for Mitya's arrest and why he had to be tried, and so on. Yet it made a big impact on me. The clerk read it loudly and clearly. The whole tragedy unfolded in front of us, concentrated and illuminated in a cruel and unforgiving light. I remember how, right after it was read, the President asked Mitya in a loud, firm voice:

"Prisoner, do you plead guilty?"

Mitya suddenly jumped up from his seat.

"I plead guilty to being a drunk and a scoundrel," he shouted, his voice frenzied, "to being lazy and living badly. I wanted to turn my life around and become an honest man, but just as I was about to, fate struck me down. But I am not guilty of killing that old man, my enemy and father. No, no, I am not guilty of robbing him! I couldn't be. Dmitri Karamazov may be a scoundrel, but he is not a thief."

He sat down again, shaking all over. The President again firmly but briefly told him to only answer the questions asked and not to go off into irrelevant outbursts. Then he ordered the case to continue. All the witnesses were called up to take the oath. I saw them all together. However, the prisoner's brothers were allowed to testify without taking the oath. After a brief speech from the priest and the President, the witnesses were led away and seated as far from each other as possible. Then, one by one, they were called up to testify.

Chapter 2: Dangerous Witnesses

I'm not sure if the President separated the witnesses for the defense and prosecution into groups, or if there was a specific order in which they were called. But I'm certain it must have been planned that way. What I do know is that the witnesses for the prosecution were called first. I'll repeat that I don't plan on describing all the questions one by one. In addition, my account would be somewhat unnecessary, because both the prosecutor's and defense lawyer's speeches later summed up all the evidence, bringing it together in a powerful and meaningful way. I wrote down parts of those two remarkable speeches in full and will quote them when the time comes, along with one surprising and completely unexpected event that happened before the final speeches, which undoubtedly affected the dark and tragic outcome of the trial.

I will simply note that from the very start of the trial, one distinctive feature stood out to everyone: the overwhelming strength of the prosecution compared to the arguments that the defense had to work with. Everyone could tell right away that all the facts started coming together around a single point, and the entire gruesome and bloody crime gradually became clear. From the beginning, everyone likely felt that the case was beyond any dispute, that there was no doubt about it, that no real debate was possible, and that the defense was just a formality—that the prisoner was guilty, clearly and completely guilty. I believe that even the women, who had been eagerly hoping for the acquittal of the fascinating prisoner, were convinced of his guilt. Furthermore, I think they would have felt disappointed if his guilt hadn't been so firmly established, as it would have taken away from the impact of the final scene of the criminal's acquittal. What's more, they all firmly believed up until the very last moment that he would be acquitted. "He's guilty, but he will be acquitted out of mercy, in line with the new ideas and the new feelings that are now popular," and so on, and so on. That's why they were all so eager to crowd into the courtroom. The men, however, were more interested in the duel between the prosecutor and the famous Fetyukovitch. Everyone wondered what even a brilliant lawyer like Fetyukovitch could possibly do with such a hopeless case, and so they followed his every move with intense focus.

But Fetyukovitch remained a puzzle to everyone right up until the end, right up until his final speech. People who were more experienced suspected that he had some hidden strategy, that he was working towards something, but it was nearly impossible to guess what that could be. Still, his confidence and self-assurance were impossible to miss. Everyone also noted with pleasure how, after being in town for only three days, Fetyukovitch had managed to thoroughly master the case and "studied it down to the last detail." Later, people eagerly discussed how skillfully he had questioned all the prosecution's witnesses, trying to confuse them as much as possible and, beyond that, casting doubt on their reputations, reducing the importance of their testimony.

However, it was assumed that he did this more for the sake of his professional pride, to show that he had used every standard tactic in the book. No one thought this would actually help his client in any meaningful way. Everyone knew that Fetyukovitch likely understood this better than anyone, and that he had some secret plan in the background, a hidden defense strategy that he would reveal when the right moment arrived. But in the meantime, confident in his strength, he seemed to be enjoying himself.

For example, when Grigory, Fyodor Pavlovitch's old servant, who had provided the most damaging piece of evidence about the open door, was called to testify, the defense lawyer targeted him the moment it was his turn to cross-examine. It should be noted that Grigory entered the courtroom with a calm and almost dignified air, completely unbothered by the grandeur of the court or the large audience listening to him. He gave his testimony with as much confidence as if he were speaking to his wife Marfa, though perhaps more respectfully. There was no way to get him to contradict himself. The prosecutor was the first to question him, asking detailed questions about the family life of the Karamazovs. The picture that emerged was grim and vivid. It was obvious to everyone listening that Grigory was sincere and impartial. Despite his deep respect for the memory of his deceased master, he testified that Fyodor Pavlovitch had treated Mitya unfairly and "had not raised his children the way he should have. He would have been eaten alive by lice as a child if it weren't for me," he added, referring to Mitya's early childhood. "And it wasn't right of Fyodor to cheat his son out of his mother's inheritance, which should have belonged to him."

In response to the prosecutor's question about what evidence he had to support his claim that Fyodor Pavlovitch had wronged his son financially, Grigory, to everyone's surprise, had no actual proof to present, but he still insisted that the arrangement with Mitya had been "unfair" and that Fyodor should have given him several thousand more rubles. I should note that the prosecutor asked this question—whether Fyodor Pavlovitch had really kept part of Mitya's inheritance—from all the witnesses who could possibly have known about it, including Alyosha and Ivan. However, he received no clear information from anyone. All the witnesses believed it to be true, but none could provide solid evidence. Grigory's description of the scene at the dinner table, when Dmitri burst in, attacked his father, and threatened to kill him, made a chilling impression on the court. The old servant's calm, brief words, and unique way of speaking, were just as effective as the most passionate speech. He even said that he didn't hold any grudge against Mitya for knocking him down and hitting him in the face, adding that he had forgiven him a long time ago. As for the late Smerdyakov, he crossed himself and said that while Smerdyakov was smart, he was also foolish, sickly, and, even worse, an atheist—something he blamed on Fyodor Pavlovitch and his eldest son, who he said had taught Smerdyakov these beliefs. Still, Grigory defended Smerdyakov's honesty almost warmly, recounting how Smerdyakov had once found Fyodor's money in the yard and, instead of keeping it, had brought it to his master. For this, Fyodor had rewarded him with a gold coin and trusted him completely from that day forward. Grigory stubbornly insisted that the door to the garden had been open, but he was asked so many questions that I can't remember them all.

Finally, the defense lawyer began to question him, and his first question was about the envelope in which Fyodor Pavlovitch had supposedly put three thousand rubles for "a certain person." "Did you ever see this envelope, you who had been so close to your master for so many years?" Grigory answered that he had never seen it and hadn't heard anything about the money until everyone started talking about it. Fetyukovitch asked this same question about the envelope to everyone who might have known about it, just as persistently as the prosecutor had asked about Mitya's inheritance, and he received the same answer from all of them—no one had seen the envelope, although many had heard of it. From the very beginning, everyone noticed how determined Fetyukovitch was to focus on this particular subject.

"Now, if you'll allow me, I'd like to ask you a question," Fetyukovitch said, suddenly and unexpectedly. "What was that balm, or rather, that mixture made of, which, according to the preliminary investigation, you used to rub on your back that evening to cure your lumbago?"

Grigory stared blankly at the lawyer, and after a short pause, muttered, "There was saffron in it."

"Only saffron? Don't you remember anything else?"

"There was also yarrow," Grigory added. "And maybe pepper?" Fetyukovitch asked. "Yes, there was pepper too."

"And so on. And it was all mixed with vodka?"

"With alcohol."

There was a quiet chuckle in the courtroom.

"So, it was alcohol. After rubbing your back, if I'm not mistaken, you drank what was left in the bottle, saying a special prayer only known to your wife?"

"I did."

"How much did you drink? Roughly, was it a glass or two?" "Maybe a full tumbler."

"A full tumbler? Could it have been a tumbler and a half?"

Grigory didn't answer. He seemed to realize where the questions were going.

"A glass and a half of straight alcohol—that's quite a bit, wouldn't you say? You might see the gates of heaven open, not just the garden door."

Grigory remained silent. There was more laughter in the courtroom. The President made a small movement.

"Do you know for certain," Fetyukovitch continued, "whether you were really awake when you saw the open door?"

"I was on my feet."

"That's not proof that you were awake." (There was another wave of laughter in the court.) "Could you have answered, at that moment, if someone had asked you a question—like, for example, what year it was?"

"I don't know."

"And do you know what year it is right now?"

Grigory stood there with a puzzled expression, staring straight at his questioner. Strangely enough, he really seemed not to know the year.

"But you can tell me how many fingers you have, right?"

"I'm a servant," Grigory suddenly said in a loud and clear voice. "If my superiors think it's appropriate to make fun of me, it's my duty to endure it."

Fetyukovitch looked a little thrown off, and the President stepped in, reminding him to ask more relevant questions. Fetyukovitch bowed politely and said he had no further questions for the witness. Of course, the audience and jury were left with a slight doubt about the testimony of a man who, while treating himself with alcohol, might have seen "the gates of heaven" and didn't even know what year he was living in. But before Grigory left the witness stand, another moment took place. The President turned to the prisoner and asked if he had any comments on the testimony of the last witness.

"Except for the door, everything he said is true," Mitya cried out in a loud voice. "I thank him for combing the lice off me, and I thank him for forgiving me for hitting him. The old man has been honest all his life, and he was as loyal to my father as seven hundred poodles."

"Prisoner, watch your language," the President warned. "I am not a poodle," Grigory muttered.

"All right, fine, I'm the poodle!" Mitya shouted. "If it's an insult, I'll take it. I beg his pardon. I was a beast, cruel to him. I was cruel to Aesop, too."

"What Aesop?" the President asked sternly.

"Oh, Pierrot... I mean my father, Fyodor Pavlovitch."

The President sternly reminded Mitya once again to be more careful with his words.

"You're damaging yourself in the eyes of your judges."

The defense lawyer was just as clever in handling Rakitin's testimony. It's worth noting that Rakitin was one of the most important witnesses, and the prosecutor relied heavily on him. He seemed to know everything—his knowledge was astonishing. He had been everywhere, seen everything, talked to everyone, and knew every detail about the lives of Fyodor Pavlovitch and all the Karamazovs. About the envelope, though, he had only heard from Mitya himself. But he gave a detailed account of Mitya's wild behavior in the "Metropolis," all his compromising actions and words, and told the story of Captain Snegiryov's "tow." Yet, even Rakitin couldn't offer anything definitive about Mitya's inheritance and instead spoke in vague and scornful terms.

"Who could say who owed what to whom, or who was in the wrong, with their chaotic Karamazov way of confusing everything so badly that no one could figure it out?" He blamed the tragic crime on habits ingrained by centuries of serfdom and the troubled state of Russia due to the lack of proper institutions. He was allowed some freedom in his speech. This was the first time Rakitin showed what he was capable of, and he got attention. The prosecutor knew that Rakitin was planning to write a magazine article about the case, and in his own speech later, as we'll see, he quoted some ideas from the article, showing he had already read it. The picture Rakitin painted was dark and disturbing, and it strongly supported the prosecution's case. Altogether, Rakitin's testimony captivated the audience with its boldness and the impressive nobility of his ideas. There were even two or three moments of applause when he spoke about serfdom and the troubled state of Russia.

But Rakitin, in his youthful excitement, made a small mistake, which the defense lawyer quickly took advantage of. While answering certain questions about Grushenka, and getting carried away by the grandeur of his own emotions and his success, which he was obviously aware of, he went so far as to speak somewhat dismissively of Agrafena Alexandrovna as "the kept mistress of Samsonov." Later, he would have given anything to take back those words, because Fetyukovitch immediately seized on them. And it was all because Rakitin hadn't anticipated that the lawyer could become so intimately familiar with every little detail of the case in such a short time.

"Allow me to ask," began the defense lawyer with the most polite and even respectful smile, "are you, by any chance, the same

Mr. Rakitin who wrote the pamphlet The Life of the Deceased Elder, Father Zossima, published by the diocesan authorities? The one full of profound religious reflections and preceded by an excellent, devout dedication to the bishop? I have just read it with great pleasure."

"I didn't write it for publication... it was published later," muttered Rakitin, suddenly looking flustered and almost ashamed for some reason.

"Oh, how wonderful! A thinker like yourself can, and indeed should, take a broad view of all social questions. Your very instructive pamphlet has been widely circulated through the bishop's patronage and has been of great service... But what I'd really like to know is this: You mentioned earlier that you were quite familiar with Madame Svyetlov." (It should be noted that Grushenka's last name was Svyetlov. I heard it for the first time that day, during the trial.)

"I can't answer for all my acquaintances... I'm a young man... and who can take responsibility for everyone they meet?" Rakitin cried, flushing deeply.

"I understand, I understand perfectly," exclaimed Fetyukovitch, as if he too were suddenly embarrassed and eager to explain himself. "You, like anyone else, might naturally be interested in getting to know a beautiful young woman who was happy to entertain the finest young men in the area, but... I just wanted to know... I've learned that a couple of months ago, Madame Svyetlov was particularly eager to meet the younger Karamazov, Alexey Fyodorovitch, and promised you twenty-five rubles if you brought him to her in his monk's robe. And that meeting actually happened on the evening of the day when the terrible crime we are discussing took place. You brought Alexey Karamazov to Madame Svyetlov, and I'm curious: Did you receive the twenty-five rubles from her as a reward? That's what I would like to hear from you."

"It was just a joke... I don't see how that concerns you... I took it as a joke... intending to return it later..."

"So, you did take the money, but haven't returned it yet... or have you?"

"That's irrelevant," muttered Rakitin, "I refuse to answer that question... Of course, I'll return it."

The President intervened, but Fetyukovitch declared that he had no further questions for the witness. Mr. Rakitin left the witness box with a small blemish on his reputation. The lofty idealism of his earlier speech had lost some of its shine, and Fetyukovitch's expression as he watched Rakitin walk away seemed to say to the audience, "This is an example of the kind of high-minded people who are accusing him." I remember that this incident didn't pass without an outburst from Mitya. Furious at the way Rakitin had spoken about Grushenka, he suddenly shouted, "Bernard!" When the President asked him if he had anything to say after Rakitin's cross-examination, Mitya loudly cried out:

"Since I've been arrested, he's borrowed money from me! He's a shameless Bernard and an opportunist, and he doesn't even believe in God! He fooled the bishop!"

Of course, Mitya was once again scolded for his inappropriate language, but Rakitin's credibility had already been damaged. Captain Snegiryov's testimony was also a failure, but for an entirely different reason. He appeared in ragged, filthy clothes, with muddy boots, and despite the careful supervision of the police officers, he was hopelessly drunk. When asked about Mitya's attack on him, he refused to answer.

"God bless him. Ilusha told me not to say anything. God will make things right in the next life."

"Who told you not to speak? Who are you talking about?"

"Ilusha, my little boy. 'Father, father, how he insulted you!' He said that by the stone. Now he's dying..."

The captain suddenly began sobbing and dropped to his knees in front of the President. He was quickly escorted out, to the sound of laughter from the audience. The dramatic effect that the prosecutor had hoped for was completely lost.

Fetyukovitch continued to take advantage of every opportunity and amazed the public more and more with his detailed knowledge of the case. For example, Trifon Borissovitch made a strong impression—though very damaging to Mitya. He practically counted on his fingers, showing that during Mitya's first visit to Mokroe, he must have spent three thousand rubles, "or just a little less. Just think about how much he spent on those gypsy girls alone! And it wasn't just about giving the peasants half a ruble here or there; he was handing out twenty-five rubles to each of them, at least. He didn't give them less. And so much money was stolen from him! And if anyone did steal it, they didn't leave a receipt. How could you catch a thief when you're throwing money around like that? Our peasants are thieves, you know; they don't care about their souls. And the way he acted with the village girls! They're living well now, let me tell you! They used to be poor." He listed every expense he could remember, adding them all up. So the theory that Mitya had only spent fifteen hundred rubles and saved the rest in a small bag seemed impossible.

"I saw three thousand rubles, as clear as day, in his hands. I saw it with my own eyes. I think I know how to count money," shouted Trifon Borissovitch, eager to impress "his betters."

When Fetyukovitch began cross-examining him, he hardly tried to challenge his testimony but instead asked him about an incident during the first party at Mokroe, a month before the arrest. Timofey and another peasant named Akim had found one hundred rubles on the floor in the hallway, dropped by Mitya when he was drunk. They gave the money to Trifon Borissovitch, and he had given them a ruble each as a reward. "So," asked the lawyer, "did you return that one hundred rubles to Mr. Karamazov?"

Trifon Borissovitch tried to avoid answering, but after the peasants had testified, he was forced to admit that he had found the one hundred rubles. He added that he had returned the entire amount to Dmitri Fyodorovitch "with complete honesty, though it's possible his honor wouldn't remember because he was drunk at the time." However, since he had originally denied the incident of the one hundred rubles until the peasants were called to confirm it, his testimony about returning the money to Mitya was naturally viewed with great suspicion. So once again, one of the most dangerous witnesses brought by the prosecution was discredited.

The same thing happened with the Polish witnesses. They came in acting proud and self-important, loudly declaring that both of them had once served the Crown. They claimed that "Pan Mitya" had offered them three thousand roubles to buy their honor and insisted they had seen a large amount of money in his hands. Pan Mussyalovitch peppered his speech with a lot of Polish words, and when he noticed that this seemed to impress the President and the prosecutor, he became even more pompous. By the end, he was speaking entirely in Polish.

However, Fetyukovitch managed to trap them, too. When Trifon Borissovitch was called back to the stand, he was forced, despite trying to avoid the question, to admit that Pan Vrublevsky had switched the deck of cards during the game, replacing the original pack with his own. Trifon also confirmed that Pan Mussyalovitch had cheated during the game. Kalganov backed this up, and both Poles left the witness stand with their reputations in tatters, accompanied by laughter from the audience.

The same thing happened with nearly every other dangerous witness. One by one, Fetyukovitch found ways to discredit them, dismissing each with subtle mockery. The lawyers and experts watching were deeply impressed by his skill, though they were puzzled about the purpose of it all. Everyone still believed that the prosecution's case was too strong to be overcome. In fact, the case against Dmitri seemed more devastating with each passing moment. Yet, seeing Fetyukovitch's calm and confident demeanor, they couldn't help but trust that he had a plan. They knew that a man of his reputation hadn't traveled all the way from St. Petersburg for nothing—and he certainly wouldn't leave without achieving something significant.

Chapter 3: The Medical Experts and A Pound of Nuts

The testimony of the medical experts also didn't do much to help the prisoner. And later, it became clear that Fetyukovitch hadn't expected it to. The medical defense had only been pursued at the insistence of Katerina Ivanovna, who had brought in a famous doctor from Moscow just for this reason. The defense's case, of course, couldn't lose anything from this, and with some luck, might have gained something. However, there was an element of comedy in it because of the difference in the doctors' opinions. The medical experts included the famous doctor from Moscow, our local doctor Herzenstube, and the young doctor Varvinsky.

The last two also appeared as witnesses for the prosecution.

The first expert called was Doctor Herzenstube. He was a gray- haired and bald old man of seventy, medium height, and solidly built. He was highly respected and admired by everyone in the town. He was a conscientious doctor and a good, pious man, a Moravian Brother or a Hernguter, though I'm not sure which. He had lived in our town for many years and always conducted himself with great dignity. He was kind and humane, treating the poor and peasants for free, visiting them in their dirty homes and leaving money for their medicine. But he was as stubborn as a mule. Once he had an idea in his head, nothing could change it. Almost everyone in the town knew, by the way, that the famous doctor from Moscow had, within his first two or three days in town, made some very offensive remarks about Doctor Herzenstube's abilities. Even though the Moscow doctor charged twenty-five rubles per visit, many people in town rushed to see him, regardless of the cost. Of course, these people had all been patients of Doctor Herzenstube, and the famous doctor had harshly criticized his treatments. He would ask his patients, as soon as he saw them, "Well, who has been filling you up with nonsense? Herzenstube? Heh, heh!" Naturally, Doctor Herzenstube heard all about this, and now all three doctors were called to testify one after the other.

Doctor Herzenstube confidently declared that the prisoner's mental abnormality was obvious. He then gave his reasons for this opinion, which I won't repeat here, and added that this abnormality wasn't just evident in many of the prisoner's past actions but was clear even now, at this very moment. When he was asked to explain how it was obvious right now, the old doctor, with his usual sincerity, pointed out that the prisoner, when entering the courtroom, had "an extraordinary air, quite unusual for the circumstances." He said Mitya had "marched in like a soldier, looking straight ahead," when it would have been more natural for him to look to the left, where the ladies in the audience were seated, especially since Mitya was well known for admiring women and must have been thinking about what they were saying about him now. The old man finished his statement in his usual odd way.

I should add that while he spoke Russian fluently, every sentence he said had a German structure. But this never bothered him because he had always believed that he spoke Russian perfectly— better even than Russians themselves. He loved using Russian proverbs, always insisting that Russian proverbs were the best and most expressive in the world. I should also note that in conversation, he often forgot even the simplest words, though he knew them well. This happened whether he was speaking Russian or German, and when it did, he would wave his hand in front of his face, as if trying to catch the missing word. No one could make him continue speaking until he found it. His remark that the prisoner should have looked at the ladies when he entered the court caused a ripple of laughter in the audience. All the ladies in town were very fond of the old doctor, and they knew that, having been a lifelong bachelor and a deeply religious man, he viewed women as noble beings. So his strange comment seemed even more unusual to everyone.

When the Moscow doctor gave his testimony, he firmly and clearly repeated that he believed the prisoner's mental state to be extremely abnormal. He spoke for a long time, using terms like "aberration" and "mania," and argued that, based on all the evidence, the prisoner had clearly been in a state of mental confusion for several days before his arrest. And if the crime had been committed by him, then even if he had been aware of it, it would have been almost involuntary, as he wouldn't have had the ability to resist the compulsive impulse that had overtaken him.

But beyond this temporary mental confusion, the doctor diagnosed him with mania, which he said would eventually lead to complete insanity. (I should mention that I'm summarizing this in my own words; the doctor used very technical and professional language.) "All of his actions go against common sense and logic," the doctor continued. "Without even mentioning what I didn't witness— the crime itself and the whole catastrophe—but just two days ago, when he was speaking with me, his eyes had an unusual, fixed look. He laughed suddenly, even though there was nothing to laugh at. He showed constant irritation, using strange words like 'Bernard!' and 'Ethics!' and other words that didn't fit the situation." But the doctor believed the strongest proof of mania was that the prisoner couldn't even talk about the three thousand rubles, which he believed had been stolen from him, without becoming extremely upset. And yet, he could speak more calmly about other hardships in his life. In fact, many people said that whenever the subject of the three thousand rubles came up, Mitya would fly into a rage, even though he was generally considered to be a man who didn't care much about money.

"As for my learned colleague's opinion," the Moscow doctor added with a hint of sarcasm, "that the prisoner should have looked at the ladies when he entered the courtroom instead of straight ahead, I must say that while I agree it would be unusual for the prisoner to stare straight ahead in such a fixed way, which could indeed be a sign of mental disturbance, I still think he wouldn't have looked at the ladies. Instead, it would have been far more natural for him to look to the right, where his defense lawyer was seated, as his entire future depends on his lawyer's help." The doctor expressed his opinion firmly and with complete confidence.

But the unexpected testimony of Doctor Varvinsky added the final bit of comedy to the disagreement between the experts. In his opinion, the prisoner was currently, and had always been, in a perfectly normal mental state. Although he admitted that the prisoner must have been in a nervous and highly excited state before his arrest, this could easily be explained by obvious reasons like jealousy, anger, constant drinking, and so on. However, this nervousness didn't mean he was mentally unstable, as the others had suggested. Regarding the debate about whether the prisoner should have looked left or right when entering the court, in his "humble opinion," the prisoner naturally looked straight ahead, as that's where the judges were, and his fate depended on them. So, by looking straight ahead, he actually showed that his mind was perfectly normal. The young doctor finished his "humble" testimony with some passion.

"Bravo, doctor!" Mitya shouted from his seat. "Exactly!"

Mitya, of course, was told to be quiet, but the young doctor's opinion had a big impact on the judges and the audience. As it turned out later, almost everyone agreed with him. But unexpectedly, Doctor Herzenstube's testimony actually helped Mitya. As someone who had lived in the town for many years and knew the Karamazov family well, he provided some important information for the prosecution, but then, as if suddenly remembering something, he added:

"But the poor young man might have had a very different life because he had a kind heart both as a child and later in life, I know that for sure. There's a Russian proverb that says, 'If a man has one head, it's good, but if another clever man comes to visit him, it's even better, because then there are two heads instead of one.'"

"One head is good, but two are better," the prosecutor interrupted impatiently. He knew the old man's habit of speaking slowly and carefully, without worrying about how much time he was taking or the impression he was making. The old man valued his flat, dull, and always cheerfully smug German humor. He loved to make little jokes.

"Oh, yes, that's exactly what I'm saying," the old man continued stubbornly. "One head is good, but two are better. But he didn't meet another clever head, and so he lost his wits. Where did they go? I've forgotten the word." He waved his hand in front of his eyes, as though searching for the word. "Oh, yes, 'spazieren.'"

"Wandering?"

"Yes, wandering. That's what I'm saying. His wits wandered off and fell into such a deep hole that he lost himself. And yet, he was a grateful and sensitive boy. Oh, I remember him very well, a little fellow, about this high, left neglected by his father, running around the backyard without boots, with his little pants held up by one button."

A note of tenderness suddenly came into the honest old man's voice. Fetyukovitch seemed to sense something important and quickly jumped on it.

"Oh, yes, I was a young man back then... I was... well, I was forty-five at the time, and I had only just arrived here. I felt so sorry for the boy back then; I thought to myself, why shouldn't I buy him a pound of... a pound of what? I've forgotten what it's called. A pound of something children really like... what is it?

What is it?" The doctor began waving his hands again. "It grows on trees, and people gather it and give it to everyone…"

"Apples?"

"Oh, no, not apples. You can have a dozen apples, but not a pound. No, there are a lot of them, and they're all small. You put them in your mouth and crack them open."

"Nuts?"

"Yes, that's it, nuts," the doctor said calmly, as if he hadn't been searching for the word. "I bought him a pound of nuts because no one had ever bought him a pound of nuts before. And I raised my finger and said to him, 'Boy, Gott der Vater.' He laughed and said, 'Gott der Vater.' 'Gott der Sohn.' He laughed again and said, 'Gott der Sohn.' 'Gott der heilige Geist.' And he laughed once more and said it as best as he could, 'Gott der heilige Geist.' Then I left, but two days later, when I happened to pass by, he called out to me on his own, 'Uncle, Gott der Vater, Gott der Sohn,' though he had forgotten 'Gott der heilige Geist.' So I reminded him, and I felt sorry for him again. But he was taken away, and I didn't see him again. Twenty-three years passed. One morning, I was sitting in my study, an old man with white hair, when a young man walked in, looking healthy and happy. I never would have recognized him, but he held up his finger and said, laughing, 'Gott der Vater, Gott der Sohn, and Gott der heilige Geist. I've just arrived and came to thank you for that pound of nuts because no one else ever bought me a pound of nuts; only you did.' And then I remembered my happy youth and that poor boy in the yard, without boots on his feet, and my heart was touched. I said, 'You are a grateful young man because you've remembered all your life the pound of nuts I bought you as a child.' And I hugged him and blessed him. I shed tears, and he laughed, but he cried too... because a Russian often laughs when he should cry. But he did cry; I saw it. And now, alas!..."

"And I'm crying now, too, old man, I'm crying now, too, you saintly man," Mitya suddenly cried out.

In any case, the story made a good impression on the audience. But the real turning point in Mitya's favor came with Katerina Ivanovna's testimony, which I will describe shortly. In fact, when the witnesses for the defense started giving their testimonies, luck seemed to suddenly turn in Mitya's favor, and what made it even more surprising was that even the defense lawyer didn't expect it. But before Katerina Ivanovna was called,

Alyosha testified, and he recalled something that seemed to provide solid evidence against one of the prosecution's main arguments.

Chapter 4: Fortune Smiles on Mitya

It was just as much a surprise to Alyosha as it was to everyone else. He wasn't required to take the oath, and I remember both sides spoke to him kindly and with sympathy. It was clear that his reputation for being good had reached everyone already. Alyosha gave his testimony modestly and with restraint, but his deep care for his troubled brother was obvious. In response to one question, he described his brother as a man who could be hot-tempered and driven by his emotions but who was also honorable, proud, and generous, even capable of self-sacrifice when needed. He admitted, however, that his brother's obsession with Grushenka and his rivalry with their father had recently put him in an unbearable situation. But he strongly rejected the idea that his brother could have committed murder for money, though he acknowledged that the three thousand rubles had become an obsession for Mitya. Alyosha explained that Mitya viewed the money as part of the inheritance he believed their father had cheated him out of. While Mitya generally didn't care about money, he couldn't even talk about the three thousand rubles without becoming furious. As for the rivalry between the two "ladies," as the prosecutor called them—Grushenka and Katya—Alyosha answered vaguely and was reluctant to respond to a few of the questions.

"Did your brother ever tell you that he planned to kill your father?" the prosecutor asked. "You can choose not to answer if you feel it's necessary," he added.

"He didn't tell me directly," Alyosha replied. "What do you mean? Did he imply it?"

"He once told me how much he hated our father and that he was afraid that, in a moment of rage... in a moment of madness, he might kill him."

"And did you believe him?"

"I'm afraid I did. But I never doubted that some higher feeling would save him in the end, just as it did, because it wasn't him who killed our father," Alyosha said firmly, in a loud voice that carried across the courtroom.

The prosecutor reacted like a battle-hardened soldier at the sound of a trumpet.

"Let me assure you, I fully believe in the sincerity of your conviction, and I don't attribute it to your affection for your unfortunate brother. Your unique view of this tragic situation has already been made clear during the preliminary investigation. I won't hide from you that your belief is very personal and goes against all the evidence we've gathered. So, I feel it's necessary to ask you to explain what led you to this belief in your brother's innocence and your suspicions about someone else, someone you mentioned during the preliminary inquiry?"

"I only answered the questions I was asked during the preliminary inquiry," Alyosha said slowly and calmly. "I didn't accuse Smerdyakov on my own."

"But you did give evidence against him?"

"My brother Dmitri's words led me to do that. I was told what happened during his arrest and how he had pointed to Smerdyakov before I was questioned. I believe fully in my brother's innocence, and if he didn't commit the murder, then—"

"Then Smerdyakov? Why do you suspect Smerdyakov? And why are you so convinced of your brother's innocence?"

"I can't help but believe my brother. I know he wouldn't lie to me. I could see from his face that he was telling the truth."

"Just from his face? Is that all the proof you have?" "I have no other proof."

"And you have no proof of Smerdyakov's guilt except for your brother's words and the look on his face?"

"No, I have no other proof."

At this point, the prosecutor stopped questioning him. The public was left disappointed by Alyosha's testimony. There had been talk of Smerdyakov before the trial; someone had heard something, someone else had pointed something out, and people had expected Alyosha to have gathered some amazing evidence of his brother's innocence and Smerdyakov's guilt. But in the end, there was nothing—just the natural moral conviction of a brother.

Then Fetyukovitch began his cross-examination. He asked Alyosha when Mitya had told him about his hatred for their father and his fear that he might kill him, and whether he had heard this at their last meeting before the crime. Alyosha seemed to suddenly remember something as he answered, as if it had just become clear to him.

"I remember something now that I had completely forgotten. It didn't make sense to me at the time, but now—" And, clearly struck by a new idea, Alyosha eagerly explained how, during his last conversation with Mitya under the tree on the road to the monastery, Mitya had hit himself on the chest—"the upper part of the chest"—and said several times that he had a way to restore his honor, that the way was here, right here on his chest. "At the time, I thought when he hit his chest, he was saying that the answer was in his heart," Alyosha continued. "I thought he meant that he would find the strength in his heart to stop himself from doing something terrible, something he was afraid to admit to even me. I must admit, I thought he was talking about our father and that the terrible thing he feared was going to see our father and hurting him. But now I remember that he kept pointing to something on his chest, and I realized later that the heart isn't in that part of the chest— it's lower—and he was hitting much higher, just below his neck. I thought my idea was silly at the time, but maybe he was pointing to that little bag he carried with fifteen hundred rubles!"

"That's it!" Mitya shouted from his seat. "That's right, Alyosha, it was the little bag I was hitting!"

Fetyukovitch rushed over to Mitya, urging him to keep quiet, and then quickly turned back to Alyosha. Carried away by his memory, Alyosha passionately shared his theory that the "disgrace" Mitya was referring to was the fifteen hundred rubles, which he could have returned to Katerina Ivanovna as half of what he owed her. But Mitya had decided not to repay her and instead use the money to run away with Grushenka, if she agreed to go with him.

"Yes, that's it, that must be it," Alyosha exclaimed in sudden excitement. "My brother said more than once that half of his shame, half of it (he kept saying 'half') he could fix right away, but that he was so miserable and weak-willed that he couldn't do it... that he knew even before that he wouldn't be able to!"

"And you clearly, confidently remember that he was hitting himself on this part of his chest?" Fetyukovitch asked eagerly.

"Clearly and confidently, because I thought at the time, 'Why is he hitting himself so high when the heart is lower down?' and that thought seemed stupid to me at the time... I remember thinking it was stupid... it flashed through my mind. That's what brought it back to me just now. He meant the little bag when he said he had the means but wouldn't give back the fifteen hundred rubles. And when he was arrested at Mokroe, he cried out—I know because I was told—that he considered it the most disgraceful thing he'd ever done, that when he had the means to pay Katerina Ivanovna back half (half, note!) of what he owed her, he couldn't bring himself to do it. He preferred to remain a thief in her eyes rather than give it back. And what torture, what torture that debt has caused him!" Alyosha exclaimed, finishing with emotion.

The prosecutor, naturally, intervened. He asked Alyosha to recount again exactly how it had happened and pressed several times, asking, "Did the prisoner seem to point to something specific? Or was he simply hitting himself on the chest with his fist?"

"But it wasn't with his fist!" Alyosha cried. "He pointed with his fingers, and he pointed right here, very high up… How could I have forgotten that until now?"

The President then asked Mitya what he had to say in response to the last witness's testimony. Mitya confirmed it, saying that he had indeed been pointing to the fifteen hundred rubles, which were on his chest, just below the neck, and that this was, of course, the disgrace. "A disgrace I cannot deny, the most shameful act of my entire life," Mitya cried out. "I could have paid it back and didn't. I preferred to stay a thief in her eyes rather than return it. And the worst part is that I knew beforehand I wouldn't give it back! You're right, Alyosha! Thank you, Alyosha!"

Thus, Alyosha's cross-examination came to an end. What was significant and striking about it was that one fact had at least been brought to light. Even though it was just one small piece of evidence, merely a suggestion of proof, it did go some way toward showing that the bag had indeed existed, had contained the fifteen hundred rubles, and that the prisoner hadn't been lying when he said at Mokroe that the fifteen hundred rubles were "his own." Alyosha was relieved. His face flushed as he moved back to the seat assigned to him, repeatedly asking himself, "How could I have forgotten that? How could I have forgotten? And what made me remember it now?"

Katerina Ivanovna was then called to the witness stand. As she entered, something extraordinary happened in the courtroom. The ladies clutched their opera glasses and lorgnettes, and there was a stir among the men: some even stood up to get a better view. Everyone said afterward that Mitya had turned "white as a sheet" when she came in. Dressed in all black, she walked forward modestly, almost shyly. It was impossible to tell from her face that she was upset, but there was a determined light in her dark and serious eyes. Many people mentioned afterward that she looked particularly beautiful at that moment. She spoke softly but clearly, so that everyone in the courtroom could hear her. She expressed herself with calmness, or at least tried to appear calm. The President began questioning her with great discretion and respect, as though afraid to touch on any "delicate subjects," showing sensitivity to her deep sorrow. But in response to one of the first questions, Katerina Ivanovna answered firmly that she had once been engaged to the prisoner, "until he left me of his own accord," she added quietly. When asked about the three thousand rubles she had given Mitya to send to her relatives, she answered firmly, "I didn't give him the money simply to send it. I sensed at the time that he was in great need of money… I gave him the three thousand with the understanding that he could send it within a month, if he wished to. He didn't need to worry about that debt after that."

I won't go into every question that was asked or all of her responses in detail. Instead, I will summarize the main points of her testimony.

"I was convinced that he would send the money as soon as he received money from his father," she continued. "I never doubted his honesty… his scrupulous honesty… when it came to money. He felt certain that he would get the money from his father, and he spoke to me about it several times. I knew that he had a serious conflict with his father, and I have always believed that his father treated him unfairly. I don't recall him ever making any threats against his father. He certainly never made such threats in my presence. If he had come to me during that time, I would have immediately eased his worry over that unfortunate three thousand rubles, but he had stopped coming to see me… and I was in such a position myself… that I couldn't invite him. And really, I had no right to demand anything regarding the money," she suddenly added, her voice taking on a tone of resolution. "At one point, I was in debt to him for more than three thousand rubles, and I accepted it, even though I had no idea at the time whether I would ever be able to repay him."

There was a note of defiance in her voice. At this point, Fetyukovitch began his cross-examination.

"Did that happen here, or at the beginning of your acquaintance?" Fetyukovitch asked cautiously, sensing something important. I should mention that, although Fetyukovitch had been brought in from Petersburg partly at Katerina Ivanovna's request, he knew nothing about the episode involving the four thousand rubles Mitya had given her or her "bowing to the ground" before him. She had kept that from him and had said nothing about it, which was strange. It seems almost certain that she herself didn't know until the very last moment whether she would bring it up in court and was waiting for the right moment to decide.

No, I will never forget those moments. She began to tell the story. She revealed everything—the entire episode Mitya had told Alyosha, how she had bowed to the ground before him, and why. She spoke about her father and going to Mitya, but not once did she hint that Mitya had suggested, through her sister, that they "send Katerina Ivanovna" to him to collect the money. She generously kept that part hidden and wasn't ashamed to make it seem as though she had gone to the young officer on her own, relying on something… to beg him for the money. It was an extraordinary moment! I felt a chill and began to tremble as I listened. The courtroom was completely silent, hanging on her every word. It was something unheard of. Even from someone as strong-willed and proudly independent as she was, such an open confession, such a sacrifice, such selflessness seemed unbelievable. And for what? For whom? To save the man who had betrayed and insulted her, to help him, even if just a little, by making a strong impression in his favor. And indeed, the image of the young officer, respectfully bowing to the innocent girl as he handed her his last four thousand rubles—all he had in the world—became very appealing and sympathetic. But I had a troubling feeling in my heart! I feared that her story would be twisted afterward (and indeed, it was). The story spread around town with cruel laughter that perhaps the tale wasn't entirely complete—that something had been left out of the part where the officer had let the young lady leave "with nothing but a respectful bow." People suggested that something had been omitted.

"And even if nothing was left out, even if this was the whole story," some of the most respected ladies in town said, "it's still questionable whether it was appropriate for a young girl to behave like that, even to save her father."

And could Katerina Ivanovna, with her intelligence and sensitive nature, not have known that people would talk about her like that? She must have understood, yet she still decided to tell everything. Of course, all these ugly little suspicions about the truth of her story only came up afterward. At first, everyone was deeply moved by what she said. As for the judges and lawyers, they listened to Katerina Ivanovna with respect, almost ashamed to question her. The prosecutor didn't dare ask a single question about it. Fetyukovitch bowed low to her, nearly triumphant. Much had been accomplished. The idea that the same man who gave his last four thousand rubles out of generosity could murder his father to steal three thousand seemed completely inconsistent. Fetyukovitch felt confident that the charge of theft, at least, had been effectively disproved. The whole case was now seen in a different light, and there was a wave of sympathy for Mitya.

As for Mitya... I was told that once or twice while Katerina Ivanovna was giving her testimony, he jumped up from his seat, only to sit back down and cover his face with his hands. But when she finished, he suddenly cried out in a voice filled with sobs:

"Katya, why have you ruined me?" His sobs echoed through the courtroom. But he quickly pulled himself together and cried again, "Now I am condemned!"

Then he sat still, his teeth clenched, his arms crossed over his chest. Katerina Ivanovna remained in the courtroom, sitting back down in her seat. She looked pale, with her eyes cast down. Those sitting near her said she was trembling all over, as though she had a fever. Then Grushenka was called to testify.

I am now approaching the sudden event that perhaps ultimately led to Mitya's downfall. I'm convinced—so is everyone else, and all the lawyers agreed afterward—that if this incident hadn't happened, the prisoner might have at least been recommended for mercy. But I'll explain that later. First, let me say a few words about Grushenka.

She was dressed in all black, with her stunning black shawl draped over her shoulders. She walked to the witness stand with smooth, quiet steps, moving slightly from side to side as women of fuller figures often do. She looked straight at the President, without glancing to the right or left. To me, she looked very beautiful at that moment—not pale, as some ladies later claimed. They also said her expression was bitter and angry. I think she was simply irritated, painfully aware of the disdainful and prying eyes of our scandal-loving crowd. She was proud and couldn't bear being looked down on. She was the type of person who would flare up at the slightest hint of contempt, eager to retaliate. Of course, there was some nervousness, too, and inward shame over her own nervousness. That's why her tone kept changing. Sometimes it was angry, contemptuous, and harsh; other times, there was a genuine tone of self-blame. Sometimes, she spoke as if taking a bold leap, as if thinking, "I don't care what happens; I'll just say it…"

Regarding her relationship with Fyodor Pavlovitch, she remarked bluntly, "That's all nonsense. Was it my fault that he kept bothering me?" But a moment later, she added, "It was all my fault. I was making fun of both of them—the old man and him—and I caused all of this. It's all because of me."

Samsonov's name came up somehow. "That's nobody's business," she snapped, sounding defiant. "He was my benefactor; he took me in when I didn't even have a shoe to my name, after my family threw me out." The President gently reminded her to stick to answering the questions directly without adding irrelevant details. Grushenka flushed with anger, her eyes flashing.

She said she hadn't seen the envelope with the money in it but had only heard from "that wicked man" that Fyodor Pavlovitch had an envelope with three thousand rubles inside. "But it was all foolishness. I was just laughing. I wouldn't have gone to him for anything."

"To whom are you referring as 'that wicked man'?" the prosecutor asked.

"The servant, Smerdyakov, who killed his master and hanged himself last night."

Naturally, she was immediately asked what made her so sure of that accusation, but it turned out she had no solid proof either.

"Dmitri Fyodorovitch told me so himself; you can believe him. The woman who came between us has ruined him; she's the one behind all of this, let me tell you," Grushenka added, trembling with anger. There was a bitter tone in her voice.

She was asked again who she was referring to.

"The young lady, Katerina Ivanovna, sitting over there. She invited me over, offered me chocolate, and tried to charm me. Let me tell you, she doesn't have much real modesty."

At this point, the President sternly interrupted her, asking her to be more restrained in her language. But Grushenka's heart was full of jealousy and anger, and she didn't care anymore.

"When the prisoner was arrested at Mokroe," the prosecutor asked, "everyone saw and heard you run out of the next room and cry, 'It's all my fault. We'll go to Siberia together!' So, at that moment, did you believe he had killed his father?"

"I don't remember what I felt then," Grushenka replied. "Everyone was shouting that he'd killed his father, and I felt like it was my fault, that he'd done it because of me. But when he said he wasn't guilty, I believed him right away. I still believe him now, and I always will. He's not the kind of man who would lie."

Fetyukovitch began his cross-examination. I remember one of the things he asked was about Rakitin and the twenty-five rubles "you paid him for bringing Alexey Fyodorovitch Karamazov to see you."

"There was nothing strange about him taking the money," Grushenka sneered, full of contempt. "He was always coming to me for money. He used to get at least thirty rubles a month from me, mostly for luxuries. He didn't need me to survive."

"What made you so generous to Mr. Rakitin?" Fetyukovitch asked, even though the President shifted uneasily.

"Why, he's my cousin. His mother and my mother were sisters. But he's always begged me not to tell anyone here about it—he's so ashamed of me."

This fact shocked everyone; nobody in town or even in the monastery, not even Mitya, knew about it. I was told that Rakitin turned bright red with shame where he sat. Grushenka had heard before coming into court that Rakitin had testified against Mitya, and she was furious. The entire effect of Rakitin's noble speech— his eloquent statements, his comments on serfdom and Russia's political troubles—was now completely ruined. Fetyukovitch was satisfied—it was another unexpected advantage. Grushenka's cross-examination didn't last long, and there wasn't anything particularly new in her testimony. She left a very unpleasant impression on the public; hundreds of contemptuous eyes followed her as she finished speaking and sat down again, far away from Katerina Ivanovna. Mitya remained silent throughout her testimony. He sat like a statue, staring at the ground.

Then Ivan was called to testify.

Chapter 5: A Sudden Catastrophe

Ivan was supposed to testify before Alyosha, but the court usher informed the President that Ivan had suffered from some kind of illness or fit and couldn't appear just yet. He would testify once he felt better. At the time, no one seemed to notice this announcement, and it only came up later.

When Ivan finally entered, his arrival caused little stir. The excitement in the courtroom had already peaked, with the two rival women giving their testimonies. The public's curiosity had been satisfied, and now everyone seemed a bit tired. More witnesses were scheduled, but it didn't seem like they would add anything new. Ivan walked in slowly, keeping his head down, lost in thought. Though impeccably dressed, his appearance left a strange and unsettling impression on me—his face looked lifeless, as if he were gravely ill. His eyes were dull, and when he finally raised them to scan the courtroom, he did so sluggishly. Alyosha, seeing his brother, gasped softly, "Ah!"—but no one else noticed.

The President explained to Ivan that, since he was not under oath, he could choose whether or not to answer questions. However, he was expected to tell the truth according to his conscience. Ivan listened blankly, his face slowly softening into a smile. As the President finished speaking, Ivan suddenly laughed out loud.

"And what else?" Ivan asked loudly.

A strange hush fell over the room, and even the President looked uneasy.

"You seem unwell," the President said, glancing toward the usher for help.

"There's no need to worry, your excellency," Ivan responded, his tone suddenly calm and polite. "I'm well enough and I have something interesting to tell you."

"You have some important information?" the President asked, still wary.

Ivan lowered his head, pausing for a few seconds. Then, as if struggling to find the words, he answered, "No... I have nothing important."

They proceeded with questioning, but Ivan responded reluctantly, giving short answers that sounded increasingly annoyed. He answered rationally, but with growing disgust. Many questions were met with "I don't know." He admitted that he didn't care about Dmitri's financial issues with their father. "It wasn't something that interested me," he added flatly. As for the threats Dmitri had made against their father, Ivan acknowledged he had heard them. He also mentioned learning from Smerdyakov about the envelope containing money.

"Again with the same questions," Ivan said suddenly, sounding exhausted. "I don't have anything new to tell you."

The President, trying to remain composed, said gently, "I see you are unwell. Perhaps you need a break."

He was about to turn the questioning over to the prosecutor and defense when Ivan interrupted in a tired voice, "Please, let me go, your excellency. I feel very ill."

Without waiting for a response, Ivan turned and walked toward the door. But after taking a few steps, he stopped. A strange smile spread across his face, and he turned back toward the courtroom.

"I'm like that peasant girl," he said with a sudden grin. "You know the story, don't you? 'I'll stand up if I like, and I won't if I don't.' They were trying to put her in a dress to take her to church to be married, and she said, 'I'll stand up if I like, and I won't if I don't.' It's from one of those books about peasants."

"What are you talking about?" the President asked sternly.

"This," Ivan said, pulling out a bundle of cash. "Here's the money—the notes that were in the envelope." He nodded toward the evidence table. "The same money for which my father was murdered. Where do you want me to put it? Here, Mr. Superintendent, take it."

The usher hurried over, took the money, and handed it to the President.

The President, looking puzzled, asked, "How did this money come into your possession if it's the same money?"

"I got it from Smerdyakov, the murderer," Ivan answered calmly. "Yesterday, just before he hanged himself. It was he who killed my father, not my brother. He did it... and I encouraged him. Who hasn't wished their father dead at some point?"

"Are you in your right mind?" the President asked, unable to hide his shock.

"I think so," Ivan replied. "Just as sane as everyone here—all of you, with your ugly faces." He suddenly turned to the audience, sneering. "My father's dead, and you're all pretending to be horrified. Liars! Every one of you has wished their father dead at some point. One creature eats another, and if there hadn't been a murder, you'd all have gone home disappointed. You wanted a show—panem et circenses! And I'm no different. Water! Can someone give me water, for Christ's sake?" He grabbed his head, looking desperate.

The usher rushed to him, and Alyosha jumped from his seat, crying, "He's sick! Don't believe him—he has brain fever!" Katerina Ivanovna also rose from her seat, frozen with horror, her eyes locked on Ivan. Dmitri stood up as well, staring at his brother with a strange, wild smile on his face.

"Don't worry," Ivan continued, his voice eerily calm. "I'm not insane. I'm just a murderer. You can't expect a murderer to be eloquent." He suddenly laughed—a strange, unsettling sound.

The prosecutor leaned over to the President, clearly disturbed. The other judges whispered among themselves, visibly agitated. Fetyukovitch leaned forward, listening closely, sensing that something critical was unfolding. The room was silent, waiting.

The President, regaining his composure, said, "Witness, your words are confusing and inappropriate here. Calm yourself, if possible, and tell us your story—if you have one. How do you plan to support your claims, assuming you are not delirious?"

"That's just it," Ivan said with a bitter smile. "I have no proof. Smerdyakov won't be sending you evidence from the afterlife in an envelope. All you care about is envelopes—one is enough for you." He paused thoughtfully, as if lost in some private joke. "I have no witnesses... except maybe one."

"And who would that be?" the President asked.

"He has a tail, your excellency, and that would be against the rules! The devil doesn't exist! Don't bother with him; he's just a small, pathetic devil," Ivan suddenly said, stopping his laughter and speaking in a more private tone. "He's probably hiding somewhere—maybe under that table where all the evidence is laid out. Where else would he sit? Listen to me. I told him I won't keep quiet, and he started rambling about geological disasters... pure nonsense! Come on, let the monster loose... he's been singing a hymn, that's because his heart feels light! It's like a drunk man singing on the street about how 'Vanka went to Petersburg,' and I would give a quadrillion quadrillions just for two seconds of joy. You don't really know me! Oh, how foolish all of this is! Come on, take me instead of him! I didn't come here for nothing... Why, why is everything so ridiculous?..."

And he began speaking slowly again, almost as if he was thinking deeply, looking around him. But by this point, the whole courtroom was in a state of excitement. Alyosha ran toward him, but the court usher had already grabbed Ivan by the arm.

"What are you doing?" Ivan yelled, staring at the usher's face. Then suddenly, he grabbed the man by the shoulders and threw him hard to the ground. But the police were quick, and they restrained him. He screamed with rage, shouting something incoherent as they dragged him out.

The entire courtroom was thrown into chaos. I can't recall everything that happened in detail because I was too shaken to follow it all. I only know that later, when things had calmed down and people understood what had taken place, the court usher was reprimanded. He explained, quite reasonably, that Ivan had seemed perfectly fine earlier. The doctor had checked on him just an hour before, after Ivan had felt a bit dizzy, but until he entered the courtroom, he had been speaking clearly and insisted on testifying. No one could have predicted what would happen next.

But before anyone had fully regained their composure and settled down from that scene, another one followed. Katerina Ivanovna had a hysterical fit. She was sobbing and screaming loudly, but she refused to leave the courtroom. She struggled against those trying to move her and begged them not to take her away. Suddenly, she cried out to the President:

"There's more evidence I need to give, right now... right now! Here's a document, a letter... take it, read it quickly, quickly! It's a letter from that monster... that man there!" She pointed directly at Mitya. "He's the one who killed his father! You'll see it right away. He wrote to me about how he was going to kill his father! But the other one is sick, he's ill, he's delirious!" she continued shouting, clearly out of control.

The court usher took the letter she was holding out and handed it to the President. Katerina Ivanovna collapsed into her chair, covering her face with her hands, and began shaking and crying silently, clearly trying to stifle her sobs, afraid she would be removed from the court if she made too much noise. The document she had handed over was the same letter that Mitya had written at the "Metropolis" tavern—the one that Ivan had referred to as "mathematical proof." Sadly, its proof was undeniable, and if it hadn't been for that letter, Mitya might have been saved from the worst of his fate, or at least faced a lesser sentence.

Everything was happening so quickly that it was hard to pay attention to every detail. I assume the President immediately passed the letter to the judges, the jury, and the lawyers from both sides. The next thing I remember is them beginning to question the witness again. The President, speaking gently, asked Katerina Ivanovna if she had recovered enough to continue.

"I'm ready, I'm ready! I can answer all your questions," she replied, still sounding anxious, as though she feared they might not let her finish. She was asked to explain what the letter was about and how she came to receive it.

"I got it the day before the murder happened, but he wrote it the day before that, at the tavern—two days before the crime. Look, it's written on the back of some sort of receipt!" she said breathlessly. "He hated me then because of how he had behaved, because he had been chasing after that woman... and because he owed me that three thousand rubles. He was humiliated because of that money! Let me explain about the three thousand rubles. Please, listen to me. Three weeks before he killed his father, he came to see me. I knew he needed money, and I knew why—he wanted it to win over that woman and run away with her. I knew he had betrayed me and was planning to leave me. And it was me—me—who gave him the money, pretending it was for him to send to my sister in Moscow. And when I gave it to him, I looked him in the eyes and told him, 'You can send it whenever you like, a month later is fine.' How could he not understand what I was really saying? I was basically telling him, 'You need money to betray me and run off with that woman, so here's the money. Take it if you have no honor left.' I wanted to show him exactly what kind of man he was. And what did he do? He took it, spent it all on that woman in just one night! But he knew, he knew that I knew what he was doing. I gave him that money as a test, to see if he would actually take it, and he did—he took my money!"

"That's true, Katya," Mitya suddenly shouted. "I looked into your eyes and knew you were trying to disgrace me, but I still took your money. Go ahead, despise me, everyone! I deserve it!"

"Prisoner," the President warned, "one more word and I'll have you removed!"

"That money tormented him," Katerina went on, speaking quickly. "He wanted to pay me back, he really did. But he needed money for that woman too. So, he killed his father, but he never paid me back. Then he ran off with her to that village where they arrested him. He spent the stolen money there, after killing his father. And the day before the murder, he wrote me this letter. He was drunk when he wrote it. I could tell right away. He wrote it out of spite, fully convinced that I'd never show it to anyone, even if he did kill his father. Otherwise, he wouldn't have written it. He knew I wouldn't want to ruin him. But read it, read it carefully. You'll see he wrote everything down in that letter, everything! He planned it all out—how he would kill his father and where the money was hidden. Look closely, right here: 'I'll kill him as soon as Ivan leaves.' So, he planned it all in advance," Katerina said with a triumphant, bitter smile. It was clear she had studied every word in the letter and picked apart every hidden meaning.

"If he hadn't been drunk, he wouldn't have written to me, but look, it's all in there, just like how the murder happened. It's all written out, a complete plan!" she shouted in desperation.

She was reckless now, not caring about the consequences for herself, even though she had probably thought about them a month ago. Maybe even then, trembling with anger, she had wondered whether or not to show the letter at the trial. But now, she had made the final decision. I remember that the letter was read out loud by the clerk right after this. It left a powerful impact. They asked Mitya if he admitted to writing the letter.

"It's mine, mine!" Mitya cried. "I wouldn't have written it if I hadn't been drunk!... We've hated each other for many reasons,

Katya, but I swear, I swear I loved you even when I hated you, and you didn't love me!"

He collapsed into his seat, wringing his hands in despair. The prosecutor and the defense attorney began questioning her, mostly to find out why she had hidden the letter and had spoken in such a different tone earlier.

"Yes, yes. I was lying before. I lied against my honor and conscience, but I wanted to save him, even though he's hated and despised me so much!" Katya screamed wildly. "Oh, he's despised me terribly! He's always despised me. And you know, he's hated me ever since I bowed down to him for that money. I saw it... I felt it right away, but for a long time, I didn't want to believe it. So many times, I've seen it in his eyes, that look that says, 'You came to me on your own.' Oh, he didn't understand! He couldn't imagine why I ran to him. He could only suspect something bad, thinking everyone is like him!" Katya hissed furiously, in a frenzy. "And he only wanted to marry me because I'd inherited money— because of that, because of that! I always suspected that's why! Oh, he's a brute! He was always sure that I would live in shame before him forever because I went to him back then, and that he had the right to look down on me for the rest of my life. And that's why he wanted to marry me! That's why, that's all it was! I tried to win him over with my love—a love with no limits. I even tried to forgive him for cheating on me, but he understood nothing, nothing! How could he understand anything? He's a monster! I didn't get that letter until the next evening—it was brought to me from the tavern. And just that morning, that same morning, I wanted to forgive him for everything, for everything, even for betraying me!"

The President and the prosecutor, of course, tried to calm her down. I can't help but think they felt a little ashamed for taking advantage of her hysteria and listening to such confessions. I remember hearing them say to her, "We understand how hard this is for you; please believe we feel for you," and other things like that. But they kept pushing her for more information, even as she raved. Finally, she described with surprising clarity—like many people do in such extreme emotional states—how Ivan had nearly driven himself insane in the last two months, trying to save "the monster and murderer," his brother.

"He tortured himself," she shouted. "He kept trying to lessen his brother's guilt and confessed to me that he, too, had never really loved his father and maybe even wished for his death. Oh, he has a sensitive, overly sensitive conscience! He tortured himself with guilt! He told me everything, everything! He came to me every day and talked to me as his only friend. I have the honor of being his only friend!" she suddenly yelled, with a kind of defiance, and her eyes blazed. "He had visited Smerdyakov twice. One day, he came to me and said, 'If it wasn't my brother, but Smerdyakov who committed the murder'—because there was a rumor going around that Smerdyakov had done it—'then maybe I'm guilty, too, because Smerdyakov knew I didn't like my father and probably thought I wanted him dead.' Then I showed him the letter. He was completely convinced that his brother had done it, and it broke him. He couldn't bear the thought that his brother had killed their father! Just a week ago, I could see it was making him sick. These last few days, he's been talking nonsense around me. I saw that he was losing his mind. He was wandering around, raving; people saw him muttering to himself in the streets. The doctor from Moscow checked him at my request the day before yesterday and told me he was on the verge of brain fever—and all because of this monster! All because he wanted to save that monster! And last night, he found out that Smerdyakov was dead! It shocked him so much that it drove him insane... and it's all because of this monster!"

Of course, such a confession, such an outpouring of feelings, only happens once in a lifetime—maybe at the hour of death or on the way to execution! But this was in Katya's character, and it was one of those moments in her life. It was the same impulsive Katya who had thrown herself at the feet of a young scoundrel to save her father; the same Katya who had just sacrificed her pride and modesty in front of all these people, telling them about Mitya's kindness, hoping to soften his fate a little. And now, once again, she sacrificed herself— but this time, it was for someone else. Maybe only now, at this very moment, she realized how much that other person meant to her! She sacrificed herself out of fear for him, suddenly believing that he had ruined himself by confessing to the murder, not his brother. She gave herself up to save him, to protect his name and reputation!

But one terrible question came to mind—was she lying about her past with Mitya? That's what people wondered. No, she hadn't deliberately slandered him when she said Mitya despised her for bowing down to him! She truly believed it. Ever since that moment when she bowed to him, she had been convinced that the simple-hearted Mitya, who had adored her even then, was actually mocking her and despising her. She had loved him with a tortured, prideful love, but that love wasn't like real love—it was more like revenge. Oh! Maybe that wounded love could have turned into real love—maybe that's all Katya had ever wanted—but Mitya's unfaithfulness had cut her too deeply, and her heart couldn't forgive him. The moment of revenge came on her suddenly, and all the pain she had been holding inside for so long exploded out of her all at once, unexpectedly. She betrayed Mitya, but in doing so, she betrayed herself, too. And as soon as she let out all those feelings, the tension broke, and she was overwhelmed with shame. She collapsed into hysterics again, falling to the floor, sobbing and screaming. They had to carry her out. At that moment, Grushenka cried out and rushed towards Mitya before anyone could stop her.

"Mitya," she cried out, "your evil woman has ruined you! There, she's shown you who she really is!" she yelled to the judges, shaking with rage. At a signal from the President, they grabbed her and tried to take her out of the courtroom. She wouldn't let them. She fought and struggled to get back to Mitya. Mitya let out a cry and fought to reach her, but he was overpowered.

Yes, I think the ladies who came to watch the drama must have been satisfied—it had been quite a show. Then I remember the doctor from Moscow showed up. I believe the President had earlier sent the court usher to arrange for medical help for Ivan. The doctor told the court that the sick man was suffering from a serious case of brain fever and needed to be taken away immediately. In response to questions from both the prosecutor and the defense lawyer, the doctor said that the patient had come to him on his own just the day before yesterday. He had warned Ivan that an attack was coming, but Ivan refused to be treated. "He definitely wasn't in a normal state of mind. He told me himself that he saw visions while awake, met people in the street who were dead, and that Satan visited him every evening," the doctor said in conclusion.

After giving his testimony, the famous doctor left. The letter Katerina Ivanovna had produced was added to the other pieces of evidence. After some discussion, the judges decided to continue with the trial and officially record the surprising evidence from Ivan and Katerina Ivanovna.

But I won't go into detail about the other witnesses, who mostly repeated and confirmed what had already been said, though each in their own way. Everything was brought together in the prosecutor's speech, which I'll talk about shortly. Everyone was on edge, electrified by the recent turn of events, and they waited eagerly for the speeches from the prosecution and defense. Fetyukovitch was clearly shaken by Katerina Ivanovna's testimony. But the prosecutor was feeling victorious. Once all the evidence had been presented, the court took a break for almost hour. I think it was just around eight o'clock when the President returned to his seat, and our prosecutor, Ippolit Kirillovitch, began his speech.

Chapter 6: The Prosecutor's Speech. Sketches Of Character

Ippolit Kirillovitch began his speech, trembling with nervousness, cold sweat covering his forehead, feeling both hot and cold by turns. He later described this himself. He considered this speech to be his masterpiece, the crowning achievement of his life, his final, grand work. Indeed, he died just nine months later of rapid consumption, so he had every right to compare himself to a swan singing its last song. He had poured his entire heart and mind into this speech. And poor Ippolit Kirillovitch unexpectedly revealed that, at least, he had some concern for the public good and "the eternal question" buried within him. Where his speech truly excelled was in its sincerity. He genuinely believed the defendant to be guilty; he accused him not only out of a sense of duty but with a burning desire for justice, trembling with real passion "for the security of society." Even the ladies in the audience, who remained hostile toward him, admitted that he made a deep impression on them. He began with a voice that was breaking, but it quickly grew stronger, filling the courtroom to the very end of his speech. But when he had finished, he nearly fainted.

"Gentlemen of the jury," the prosecutor began, "this case has stirred all of Russia. But why are we so surprised, what is so uniquely horrifying for us? We are so used to such crimes! That is what is truly horrifying—that such dark deeds no longer shock us. What should horrify us is not this particular crime, but the fact that we have become so accustomed to it. What are the causes of our indifference, our lukewarm attitude toward such deeds, to such signs of the times, which ominously point to a grim future? Is it our cynicism, the early exhaustion of intellect and imagination in a society that is crumbling, despite its youth? Is it that our moral foundations have been shattered to their very core, or is it, perhaps, that there never were any such foundations among us? I cannot answer these questions; still, they are disturbing, and every citizen must be troubled by them. Our young and still timid press has already done a great service to the public, for without it we would never have known about the horrors of unchecked violence and moral decay, which are continually being made public by the press, not just to those who attend these newly established jury courts, but to everyone. And what do we read about almost every day? Things beside which this case fades and seems almost ordinary. But what is most significant is that most of our national crimes of violence reveal a widespread evil, now so common that it is difficult to fight against.

"One day, we hear about a brilliant young officer from high society, at the very beginning of his career, cowardly and sneakily murdering an official who had once been his benefactor, along with a servant girl, to steal his own IOU and whatever ready money he could find on him; 'it will come in handy for my pleasures in high society and for my career in the future.' After murdering them, he places pillows under the heads of his victims and then leaves.

Next, a young hero 'decorated for bravery' kills the mother of his boss and benefactor, like a robber, and to encourage his friends to join him, he says that 'she loves him like a son, so she will follow all his instructions and take no precautions.' Granted, he is a monster, but I dare not say today that he is unique. Another man may not commit the murder, but he will think and feel like him, and he is just as dishonorable in spirit. Alone with his conscience, he may ask himself, 'What is honor, and is condemning bloodshed just a baseless belief?'

"Perhaps people will cry out against me that I am exaggerating, hysterical, and that what I am saying is a monstrous lie, that I am making too much of this. Let them say it—and heaven knows, I would be the first to rejoice if it were so! Don't believe me, call me morbid, but remember my words; if even a tenth, or only a twentieth, of what I am saying is true—even then, it is terrifying! Look at how our young people take their own lives without ever asking themselves Hamlet's question of what comes after, without even pausing to consider the question, as though everything related to the soul and what awaits beyond the grave has been erased from their minds and buried under the sands. Look at our vice, at our wickedness. Fyodor Pavlovitch, the poor victim in this case, was almost an innocent babe compared to many of them. And yet, we all knew him, 'he lived among us!'

"Yes, one day, perhaps, the brightest minds of Russia and Europe will study the psychology of Russian crime, because it is worth studying. But that study will come later, in calmer times, when all the tragic chaos of today is far behind us, and we can look back on it with more clarity and fairness than I can do now. Today, we either pretend to be horrified or are genuinely shocked, though we secretly revel in the spectacle, craving the strong and strange sensations that stimulate our cynical, jaded lives. Or, like children, we brush away the scary ghosts and bury our heads under the pillow so we can go back to our games and fun as soon as they disappear. But one day, we will have to start living seriously, and we will have to take a look at ourselves as a society; it is time we begin to grasp our social condition, or at least take the first steps in that direction.

"A great writer of the past era compared Russia to a fast troika galloping toward an unknown destination, exclaiming, 'Oh, troika, bird-like troika, who invented you!' He adds, in proud excitement, that all the nations of the world step aside respectfully to let this wild troika pass. Perhaps they do, perhaps they step aside respectfully or not, but in my humble opinion, the great writer ended his book in this way either in a burst of childish, naïve optimism or simply out of fear of the censorship of the time. For if the troika were drawn by his characters, Sobakevitch, Nozdryov, and Tchitchikov, it could reach no sensible destination, no matter who was driving it. And those were the heroes of a previous generation, but ours are worse.

At this point, Ippolit Kirillovitch's speech was interrupted by applause. The liberal meaning of his metaphor was understood. The applause was brief, so the President did not feel the need to warn the crowd, and merely looked sternly in the direction of those clapping. But Ippolit Kirillovitch was encouraged; he had never been applauded before! All his life, he had struggled to get people to listen to him, and now, suddenly, he had caught the attention of all of Russia.

"What, after all, is this Karamazov family, which has gained such infamous recognition across Russia?" he continued. "Perhaps I am exaggerating, but it seems to me that certain fundamental traits of the educated class today are reflected in this family portrait—though, of course, in miniature, like the sun reflected in a drop of water. Think of that wretched, immoral, wild old man, who met such a tragic end—the head of the family! He began life with noble blood, but in poverty and dependence. Then, through an unexpected marriage, he came into a small fortune. He was a petty schemer, a sycophant, and a fool, though not without some intelligence, though undeveloped. But above all, he was a moneylender who grew bolder as he grew richer. His slavish and submissive qualities faded away, but all that was left was his cruel and sarcastic cynicism. He was emotionally underdeveloped, but physically full of vitality. He saw nothing in life beyond sensual pleasure and raised his children to believe the same. He had no sense of duty as a father. He ridiculed such duties. He abandoned his small children to the care of servants and was happy to be rid of them, forgetting them entirely. The old man's motto was 'After me, the flood.' He was an example of everything that is against the idea of civic duty, the very picture of selfishness. His attitude was, 'Let the world burn for all I care, as long as I am doing well.' And he was doing well; he was happy and eager to continue living this way for another twenty or thirty years. He cheated his own son and spent his inheritance trying to steal his son's lover. No, I don't intend to leave the defense entirely to my talented colleague from Petersburg. I will tell the truth myself; I can easily understand the anger he stirred in his son's heart against him."

"But enough, enough about that unfortunate old man; he has paid the price. Let's remember though, that he was a father, one of the typical fathers we see today. Am I being unfair when I say he's a common example of modern fathers? Sadly, many are no different, only they don't openly show such cynicism because they're better educated and more refined, but their mindset is essentially the same. Maybe I'm being too negative, but you said you'd forgive me. So, let's agree right now that you don't have to believe me, but allow me to speak. Let me say what I have to say, and perhaps you'll remember some of my words.

"Now let's talk about the children of this man, this head of the family. One of them is the prisoner we see before us, and the rest of my speech will focus on him. I'll only briefly mention the other two.

"The eldest son is one of those modern young men, highly educated and intelligent, but who has lost faith in everything. He's denied and rejected many things already, just like his father. We've all heard him, and he was a familiar figure in our local society. He never hid his opinions; in fact, he openly shared them, which gives me reason to speak about him now—not as an individual but as a member of the Karamazov family. Another person closely connected to the case took his own life last night. I'm talking about the troubled, mentally ill man who was once a servant, and maybe even the illegitimate son, of Fyodor Pavlovitch, Smerdyakov. During the preliminary investigation, he tearfully told me how Ivan Karamazov had terrified him with his bold ideas. 'Everything is allowed in this world according to him, and nothing should be forbidden in the future—that's what he always taught me,' he said. I believe this idea contributed to driving the man mad, though his epilepsy and the terrible events that took place certainly worsened his mental state. However, he made one very insightful comment, which is why I'm mentioning it: 'If one of Fyodor Pavlovitch's sons is most like him, it's Ivan Fyodorovitch.'

"With that, I'll end my description of his character, as it feels inappropriate to continue. Oh, I don't want to make any harsh predictions or sound like a pessimist about the young man's future. We've seen today in this courtroom that he still has some good feelings in his heart, and that despite his lack of faith and his cynical attitude—which he may have inherited more than developed himself—family loyalty hasn't been completely destroyed in him.

"Now, as for the third son, he's a religious and modest young man who doesn't share his older brother's dark, destructive worldview. He has tried to hold on to 'the people's beliefs,' or at least what some circles of intellectuals consider those beliefs. He nearly became a monk, clinging to the monastery. To me, he represents that early, fearful despair that drives many in our troubled society—those who fear the cynicism and corruption of modern life and who wrongly blame European ideas for all of it—back to their 'native soil,' as they call it. They want to retreat to the comfort of their motherland, as if they were children trying to fall asleep on the worn-out, old lap of their mother, just to escape the frightening world around them.

"I truly hope this fine and talented young man finds success. I hope his youthful idealism and desire to embrace the 'people's ideas' doesn't turn into gloomy mysticism on the moral side, or blind nationalism on the political side—because those two forces are an even greater threat to Russia than the premature decay, caused by misunderstanding and blindly copying European ideas, that his older brother is suffering from."

A few people clapped at his mention of nationalism and mysticism. Ippolit Kirillovitch had really been caught up in his own speech. While much of what he said wasn't directly related to the case and was somewhat unclear, the frail and ill man had been overwhelmed by the desire to express himself fully, maybe for the first time in his life. People later claimed he was driven by petty motives in his criticism of Ivan, because Ivan had out- argued him once or twice, and Ippolit Kirillovitch was trying to get revenge. I'm not sure if that's true. All this, however, was just an introduction, and his speech now moved toward discussing the case itself.

"But let's return to the eldest son," Ippolit Kirillovitch continued. "He's the one on trial here. We have his life and actions laid out before us; the fateful day has arrived, and everything has been exposed. While his brothers represent 'Western ideas' and 'the beliefs of the people,' he seems to embody Russia as she is. Oh, not all of Russia, not by any means! Heaven help us if that were the case! Yet here he is, representing a certain side of our mother Russia—her sound, her scent. He is spontaneous, a fascinating mix of good and evil. He loves high culture and literature, yet he brawls in taverns and tears out his friends' beards. He's capable of great goodness, but only when everything is going his way. And he can be swept up in noble ideals, but only if they fall into his lap effortlessly, requiring no sacrifice on his part. He hates paying for anything, but he loves receiving. That's how he approaches everything in life. Give him every possible pleasure, every advantage, and remove all obstacles, and you'll see how noble he can be. He's not greedy, no, but he needs money, lots of it, and watch how generously, how scornfully, he throws it away in wild extravagance in a single night. But if he doesn't have money, you'll see what lengths he'll go to when he's desperate for it. But we'll get to that later—let's follow the events in order.

"First, we see a poor, neglected child, running barefoot in the backyard, as our respected citizen of foreign background just pointed out. I repeat, I don't refuse to defend the criminal. I'm here to accuse him, but I will also defend him. Yes, I'm human too, and I understand how upbringing and childhood can shape a person's character. But this boy grows up and becomes an officer. After a duel and other reckless behavior, he's sent to one of Russia's distant frontier towns. There, he lived a wild life as an officer. Naturally, he needed money— money above all else. So, after long arguments, he reached a settlement with his father, and the last six thousand rubles were sent to him. There's a letter that proves he gave up his claim to the rest of the inheritance and resolved his dispute with his father over this sum."

Then came his meeting with a young woman of high character and excellent education. Oh, I do not dare to repeat the details; you have only just heard them. There was honor and self-sacrifice involved, and I will remain silent. The image of the young officer, careless and wild, paying tribute to true nobility and a lofty ideal, was presented to us in a very sympathetic way. But immediately after, the other side of the coin was unexpectedly revealed in this very courtroom. Once again, I will not presume to guess why things happened this way, but there were reasons. The same woman, her face wet with long-hidden tears of indignation, claimed that he, of all people, had scorned her for an action that, though rash and perhaps reckless, was still driven by high and generous intentions. He, the woman's fiancé, looked at her with a mocking smile, a smile more

438

unbearable from him than from anyone else. And knowing that he had already deceived her—believing she had to tolerate everything from him, even betrayal—she deliberately offered him three thousand rubles, and very clearly implied that she was offering him money to betray her. "Well, will you take it or not, have you no shame left?" was the silent question in her searching eyes. He looked at her, saw perfectly what was in her mind (he has admitted here before you that he understood everything), took that three thousand rubles without hesitation, and wasted it all in two days on his new lover.

So what are we to believe? The first story of the young officer giving up his last penny in a noble act of generosity, or this other disgusting version? Usually, when there are two extremes, the truth is somewhere in the middle, but that's not the case here. It is likely that in the first instance, he was truly noble, and in the second, he was just as genuinely vile. Why? Because he had the wide-ranging Karamazov nature—capable of holding the most contradictory qualities, able to reach the highest heights and sink to the lowest depths. Remember the insightful remark made by a young man who has seen the Karamazovs up close—Mr. Rakitin: "A sense of their own degradation is just as important to those reckless, unrestrained people as their sense of lofty generosity." And that's true, they need this unnatural mix. They live in two extremes at the same time, or they are miserable, dissatisfied, and incomplete. They are broad, as vast as Mother Russia herself; they take everything in and bear everything.

By the way, gentlemen of the jury, we've just touched on those three thousand rubles, and I will take the liberty of jumping ahead a little. Can you imagine that a man like him, after receiving that money in such a shameful way, would set aside half of it the very same day, sew it up in a small bag, and carry it with him for an entire month, even though he was constantly tempted and in great need of it? Even in his drunken debauchery at the taverns, or when he was desperately trying to get money from who knows where to save his lover from being tempted by his father, he did not touch that little bag! Why, if only to avoid leaving his mistress with the man he was so jealous of, he surely would have opened that bag and stayed close to her, waiting for her to finally say to him, "I'm yours," so they could run away together far from their deadly surroundings.

But no, he did not touch his talisman, and what reason does he give for it? The main reason, as I've already mentioned, was that when she would finally say, "I'm yours, take me wherever you want," he could have the means to take her. But that first reason, according to the prisoner himself, was insignificant compared to the second one. While I have this money on me, he said, I am a scoundrel, not a thief, because I can always go back to my wronged fiancée, and, placing down half of the money I took unjustly, I can always say to her, "You see, I've squandered half of your money, and shown myself to be a weak and immoral man, and, if you wish, a scoundrel" (I am using the prisoner's own words), "but even though I am a scoundrel, I am not a thief, because if I were a thief, I wouldn't have brought back this half of the money, but would have taken it all, just like I did with the other half!" A remarkable explanation! This frantic but weak man, who could not resist the temptation of accepting the three thousand rubles at the cost of such disgrace, suddenly displays the most iron will, carrying around a thousand rubles without daring to touch it. Does this fit with the character we've examined? No, and I dare to tell you how the real Dmitri Karamazov would have behaved in such a situation, if he had indeed set aside that money.

At the first temptation—for example, to entertain the woman with whom he had already wasted half the money—he would have opened his little bag and taken out a hundred rubles, because why should he have returned exactly half the money, that is, fifteen hundred rubles? Why not fourteen hundred? He could have just as easily said at that point that he wasn't a thief, because he brought back fourteen hundred rubles. Then, another time, he would have opened the bag again and taken out another hundred, and then a third time, and a fourth time, and before the month was over, he would have taken out the second-to-last note, thinking that if he returned only a hundred rubles, that would still serve his purpose, since a thief would have taken all of it. Then he would have looked at that last note and said to himself, "It's not really worth it to return just a hundred; let's spend that too!" That is how the real Dmitri Karamazov, as we know him, would have behaved. There is nothing more contradictory to the truth than this story of the little bag. Nothing could be more absurd. But we will come back to that later.

After discussing what had come up during the trial about the financial relationship between father and son, and arguing repeatedly that it was utterly impossible, based on the facts, to determine who was really at fault, Ippolit Kirillovitch turned to the evidence provided by the medical experts regarding Mitya's obsessive belief about the three thousand rubles he believed were owed to him.

Chapter 7: An Historical Survey

The medical experts have tried to convince us that the defendant is insane, that he is, in fact, a maniac. But I argue that he is perfectly sane—and if he weren't, he might have acted more cleverly. As for him being a maniac, I could agree with that on one point only—his obsessive fixation on the three thousand rubles. However, I believe there is a simpler explanation than insanity. Personally, I agree with the young doctor who said that the defendant has always been mentally sound, just irritable and angry. The defendant's outbursts weren't because of the money itself; there was a deeper reason behind them. That reason was jealousy!

At this point, Ippolit Kirillovitch explained in detail the prisoner's dangerous obsession with Grushenka. He started by recalling the moment the defendant went to her apartment, planning "to beat her"—those are his own words, the prosecutor clarified—but instead, he ended up at her feet, overwhelmed by passion. That was where the obsession began. At the same time, the defendant's father also became infatuated with the same woman. It was a strange and tragic coincidence: they both fell for her at the same time, though they had both known her before. And both were consumed by that fiery, wild passion typical of the Karamazovs. According to her own confession, she said, "I was just laughing at both of them." Yes, the idea of playing a joke on them suddenly appealed to her, and she managed to win both men over. The old man, usually obsessed with money, immediately set aside three thousand rubles as a reward for just one visit from her. Soon after, he was even ready to give her everything—his fortune and his name—if she would agree to marry him. We have solid evidence to prove this.

As for the defendant, his tragic story is laid out plainly before us. But this was the "game" the young woman was playing. She gave him no hope until the very end, when he knelt before her, with hands already stained by the blood of his father and rival. It was in this state that he was arrested. At that moment, overwhelmed with guilt, the woman cried out, "Send me to Siberia with him! I brought him to this! It's my fault!"

The clever young man, Rakitin, whom I mentioned earlier, gave a sharp and insightful description of this woman. "She lost her innocence early in life," he said. "She was deceived and abandoned by her fiancé, who seduced her and then left her. Her respectable family disowned her, and she was left in poverty. An older, wealthy man took her in, and though she considers him her benefactor, she became bitter. There may have been good in her heart once, but her misfortunes hardened her. She became cautious with money, sarcastic, and resentful toward society." With this background in mind, it's easy to see how she could have laughed at both father and son, out of spite and malice.

After a month of hopeless love and moral downfall—during which the defendant betrayed his fiancée and misused money entrusted to him—he was driven nearly to madness by jealousy. And who was he jealous of? His own father! What made it worse was that his father was using the very same three thousand rubles—money the defendant saw as rightfully his, part of his inheritance from his mother—to steal away the woman he loved. This betrayal was unbearable. It wasn't just about the money; it was the disgusting way it was being used to destroy his happiness.

The prosecutor then went on to describe how the idea of murdering his father took root in the defendant's mind, supporting his theory with facts.

"At first, he only talked about it—he discussed it openly in taverns throughout that month. The defendant enjoys being surrounded by people and likes sharing all his thoughts with them, even the most dangerous ones. For some reason, he expects those around him to sympathize with his troubles, to agree with him completely, and never to oppose him. If they don't, he loses control, flying into rages and smashing everything around him. (This is where the story about Captain Snegiryov fits in.) Eventually, those who heard him began to realize that his wild threats might turn into real actions."

The prosecutor then described the family meeting at the monastery, the conversations with Alyosha, and the violent scene that followed when the defendant stormed into his father's house after dinner.

"I cannot say for certain," the prosecutor continued, "whether the defendant fully intended to kill his father at that point. But the idea had definitely crossed his mind more than once, and he had thought about it seriously. We have facts, witnesses, and his own words to prove that much. To be honest, gentlemen of the jury, I was unsure until today whether the murder was premeditated. I believed he had imagined the crime in advance, thinking of it as a possibility, but hadn't decided exactly when or how to do it.

"But my uncertainty ended today, when that crucial document was presented in court. You heard the young woman exclaim, 'It's the plan—the plan for the murder!' That's how she described the drunken letter written by the defendant. And, indeed, the letter makes it clear that the murder was premeditated. It was written two days before the crime took place. In it, the defendant swore that if he couldn't get money the next day, he would kill his father and take the envelope of cash from under his father's pillow, as soon as Ivan left the house. 'As soon as Ivan leaves'— those are his own words. He had thought everything through, considering every detail, and then he followed through exactly as he had planned. This is undeniable proof that the crime was premeditated. The murder was committed for the money, and that is clearly stated in the letter. The defendant himself doesn't deny that the signature on the letter is his."

I'll be told that the defendant was drunk when he wrote the letter. But that doesn't make it less important— if anything, it makes it more valuable. When someone writes something drunk, it's usually what they had planned while sober. If he hadn't already thought about it sober, he wouldn't have written it while drunk. Then you might ask: why did he talk about it so openly in taverns?

Usually, someone planning such a crime keeps it secret. But he only talked about it before the plan had fully formed—when it was just a desire, an impulse. Once his plan started to take shape, he talked about it much less. On the night he wrote that letter at the Metropolis Tavern, for example, he acted very differently than usual. Even though he had been drinking, he was silent. He didn't play billiards or chat with anyone. He just sat quietly in a corner. Yes, he did shove a shopkeeper out of his seat, but even that seemed automatic—he couldn't walk into a tavern without causing some sort of trouble.

It's also true that, once he made up his mind, he must have realized he'd said too much in the past. He would have known his earlier words could come back to haunt him and lead to his arrest. But there was no taking them back, and he relied on luck to protect him, just as it always had. He believed in his lucky star. I must admit, though, that he made efforts to avoid the crime from happening. In his own strange words, he wrote: "Tomorrow, I'll try to borrow the money from everyone, and if they won't give it to me, there'll be bloodshed."

Ippolit Kirillovitch then described in detail all the defendant's desperate attempts to borrow money. He told the jury about the defendant's visit to Samsonov and his trip to Lyagavy. Exhausted, mocked, and starving, he even had to sell his watch to pay for the journey—though he claimed to have had fifteen hundred rubles on him, which seems unlikely. On top of that, jealousy tormented him, knowing he had left the woman he loved behind in town. He feared she might visit his father while he was away. But when he returned, he was overjoyed to find that she hadn't gone to his father. In fact, he personally escorted her to her protector,

Samsonov. Strangely, he didn't seem jealous of Samsonov, which is an interesting psychological detail.

After leaving her safely with Samsonov, the defendant rushed back to his hiding place in the gardens, where he discovered that Smerdyakov was having a seizure and the other servant was sick. The coast was clear, and he knew the "signals" for entering the house. What a temptation that must have been! But instead of seizing the opportunity, he went to visit Madame Hohlakov, a respected woman who had been watching his behavior for some time with concern. She gave him sensible advice: to abandon his reckless lifestyle, leave behind the destructive love affair, and stop wasting his youth in drunken debauchery. She suggested that he should head to Siberia and work in the gold mines, where he could channel his restless energy and thirst for adventure into something productive.

After discussing this conversation, the prosecutor described how the defendant discovered that Grushenka had not stayed with Samsonov. The defendant's jealousy and exhaustion overwhelmed him. He was convinced that she had tricked him and was now with his father. The prosecutor emphasized how much luck played a role in what happened next. "If the maid had told him that her mistress was at Mokroe with her former lover, none of this would have happened. But the maid panicked and could only swear she knew nothing. If the defendant didn't kill her on the spot, it was only because he was too focused on chasing after his unfaithful lover."

And yet, even in his frenzy, he grabbed a brass pestle. Why a pestle? Why not some other weapon? But since he had been planning this moment for a month, anything that looked like a weapon would have worked for him. He had been preparing himself, knowing that any object could serve his purpose, and the moment he saw the pestle, he instinctively knew it would do. This wasn't an accident. He knew exactly what he was doing when he picked it up.

Then, we find him in his father's garden. No one was around, the coast was clear, and darkness hid him. Jealousy filled his mind. The thought that Grushenka was inside, with his rival, in his father's arms—perhaps even laughing at him—made it hard for him to breathe. And it wasn't just a suspicion; it was obvious. She had to be there, in that room with the light on, maybe behind the screen. The defendant wants us to believe that he quietly approached the window, peeked inside respectfully, and then left discreetly, fearing he might do something terrible if he stayed. But does he really expect us to believe that? Do we, who know his character and state of mind at the time, think he would have acted that way? He knew the signals to get inside—he could have entered the house whenever he wanted.

At this point, Ippolit Kirillovitch shifted to a thorough discussion of Smerdyakov's possible involvement in the crime. He went into great detail, and although he claimed to dismiss the idea, it was clear that he considered the possibility to be of serious importance.

Chapter 8: A Treatise on Smerdyakov

To begin with, what was the source of this suspicion?" Ippolit Kirillovitch began. "The first person who accused Smerdyakov of committing the murder was the defendant himself, and he did so at the very moment of his arrest. Yet, from that point until now, he has not provided a single piece of evidence to support this accusation—not even the smallest suggestion of proof. The only people who have supported this claim are the defendant's two brothers and Madame Svyetlov. The older brother only expressed his suspicions today, and he is clearly suffering from brain fever. But until now, for the last two months, he has entirely shared the belief in his brother's guilt, and he has not tried to argue against it. We will return to that point later. As for the younger brother, he has admitted that he has no real evidence to support his belief in Smerdyakov's guilt. His only reason for suspecting him comes from the defendant's words and the expression on his face. Remarkably, he has used this as evidence not just once, but twice today. Madame Svyetlov's statement is even more striking: 'What the prisoner tells you must be believed; he is not the sort of person to lie.' That, gentlemen of the jury, is the full extent of the evidence brought against Smerdyakov by these three people, all of whom have a deep interest in the fate of the defendant. Yet this theory of Smerdyakov's guilt has been widely circulated and continues to be upheld. But is it reasonable? Is it even remotely believable?"

At this point, Ippolit Kirillovitch went on to describe Smerdyakov's character, emphasizing that he "ended his life in a fit of madness." He painted a picture of Smerdyakov as a man with limited intelligence, possessing only a little education, whose mind had been thrown off balance by philosophical ideas beyond his grasp. These ideas of duty, both in theory and practice, had come from two sources: from his master, Fyodor Pavlovitch—who may also have been his father—and from Ivan Fyodorovitch, who enjoyed indulging in philosophical conversations, likely to amuse himself when bored at the valet's expense. "Smerdyakov personally described his mental state to me during those last days in his master's house," the prosecutor explained, "and others have testified to it as well—the defendant, his brother, and the servant Grigory—everyone who knew him well."

"In addition to this, Smerdyakov's epilepsy had made him deeply fearful—he didn't have the courage of a chicken. As the defendant himself admitted, 'He fell at my feet and kissed them,' before realizing how damaging this admission would be to his own defense. In his colorful language, the defendant even called him 'an epileptic chicken.' Despite this, the defendant chose Smerdyakov as his confidant and, by his own account, managed to intimidate him into becoming a spy. In this role, Smerdyakov betrayed his master by telling the defendant about the envelope containing the money and revealing the signals for entering the house. How could he have refused to share these secrets? During the investigation, Smerdyakov said, 'He would have killed me—I knew it the moment I looked into his eyes.' He was still trembling as he gave this testimony, even though his tormentor had already been arrested and could no longer harm him. 'He suspected me at every moment. Out of fear, I told him everything—every secret— just to prove I wasn't deceiving him and to save my life.' Those were his exact words, which I recorded and remember clearly. 'Whenever he shouted at me, I would fall on my knees.'"

"Smerdyakov was, by nature, an honest man, and he had earned his master's full trust by once returning some lost money. It's likely that he felt intense guilt for betraying his master, whom he considered his benefactor. According to medical experts, people with epilepsy often suffer from severe, irrational guilt. They become obsessed with their own wickedness and are tormented by their conscience, even when they've done nothing wrong. They often exaggerate or invent faults and crimes they believe they have committed. Here, we have someone just like that—a man driven to wrongdoing out of sheer fear and intimidation."

"He also had a strong sense that something terrible was about to happen. Just before the tragedy, when Ivan Fyodorovitch was preparing to leave for Moscow, Smerdyakov begged him to stay. But he was too frightened to say exactly what he feared, so he only hinted at it, though Ivan didn't understand. It's important to note that Smerdyakov viewed Ivan as a protector. He believed that as long as Ivan was in the house, nothing bad could happen. Remember the defendant's words in his drunken letter: 'I will kill the old man if Ivan leaves.' Everyone believed that Ivan's presence in the house ensured peace and order."

"However, as soon as Ivan left, within an hour, Smerdyakov had an epileptic seizure. This makes perfect sense. Medical experts tell us that epileptics often sense when a seizure is coming, especially during times of extreme stress. While they can't predict the exact moment, they can feel it building. So, when Ivan left, Smerdyakov—feeling scared and vulnerable—went to the cellar, wondering whether the fit would strike him. His fear triggered the tightness in his throat that always preceded his seizures, and he collapsed, unconscious, in the cellar. Some people now suggest that he faked the fit. But if that were true, what would have been his motive? Why would he fake a seizure right before a murder? Wouldn't that only draw attention to him?"

"Gentlemen of the jury, consider this: On the night of the murder, there were five people in Fyodor Pavlovitch's house. First, there was Fyodor Pavlovitch himself—but, obviously, he didn't kill himself. Then, there was Grigory, the servant, but he was almost killed himself. The third person was Grigory's wife, Marfa Ignatyevna, but it's absurd to suggest that she could have murdered her master. That leaves only two people:

the defendant and Smerdyakov. If the defendant is telling the truth and did not commit the murder, then the only other possibility is Smerdyakov—there's no one else it could have been."

"This is why the defendant has made such a cunning and shocking accusation against Smerdyakov, the poor, troubled man who took his own life yesterday. If there had been even the slightest suspicion of someone else's involvement—if there had been any other possible suspect—the defendant would have accused that person instead. But since there was no one else to blame, he has accused Smerdyakov, even though the idea is completely absurd."

Gentlemen, let's put aside psychology, medicine, and even logic. Let's focus only on the facts and see what they tell us. If Smerdyakov killed him, how did he do it? Was he alone or did the prisoner help him? Let's first consider the idea that Smerdyakov did it alone. If he did, it must have been for some reason, for his own gain. But without the kind of motive that the prisoner had— hatred, jealousy, and so on—Smerdyakov could have only done it to steal the three thousand rubles he had seen his master put in the envelope. Yet he told another person, and that person was the one most interested in the money—the prisoner—everything about the money and the signals: where the envelope was, what was written on it, what it was tied with, and, most importantly, told him about the signals to enter the house. Did Smerdyakov do this just to give himself away or to invite someone else, someone who desperately wanted that envelope, to join him? I'll be told, "Yes, but he confessed out of fear." But how can we explain this? A man who could plan and carry out such a bold, violent act would reveal facts that only he knew, and which, if he stayed silent, no one else would ever discover?

No, no matter how cowardly he might be, if he had planned such a crime, nothing would have made him tell anyone about the envelope and the signals, because that would be like giving himself away in advance. He would have made up something, he would have lied if he had to say anything, but he wouldn't have mentioned the money. If, on the other hand, he had said nothing about the money, then committed the murder and stolen it, no one would ever be able to accuse him of murder for robbery, because no one else knew about the money— he was the only one who had seen it, the only one who knew it existed. Even if someone accused him of murder, they would have had to think he did it for some other reason. But since no one saw any such motive in him before, and everyone knew that his master trusted him and treated him well, he would have been the last person anyone suspected. People would first have suspected the man with a motive, the man who had openly admitted having such motives, the one who didn't hide it at all. In fact, they would have suspected the murdered man's son, Dmitri Fyodorovich. If Smerdyakov had killed and robbed him, and Dmitri had been accused, that would have been perfect for Smerdyakov. But are we really supposed to believe that after planning the murder, Smerdyakov would go and tell Dmitri all about the money, the envelope, and the signals? Does that make any sense?

On the day of the murder, which Smerdyakov supposedly planned, we see him falling down the stairs in a fake fit. Why? First, so that Grigory, who was about to take his medicine, would postpone it and stay on guard, seeing that no one else was around to watch the house. Second, his master, knowing there was no one to guard him and fearing a visit from his son, might become even more cautious. And most importantly, Smerdyakov, pretending to be too sick to do anything, could be moved from the kitchen, where he usually slept apart from the others and could come and go as he pleased, to Grigory's room at the far end of the lodge. There, he would be placed behind a screen, three steps away from Grigory's bed, as was the custom whenever he had a fit, established long ago by his master and the kind-hearted Marfa Ignatyevna. Lying behind the screen, he would likely continue the act by groaning, keeping them awake all night, as Grigory and his wife testified. And all this, we're supposed to believe, so he could more easily get up and murder his master!

But I'll be told that he faked the illness to avoid suspicion, and that he told the prisoner about the money and signals to tempt him into committing the murder. Then, after Dmitri killed his father and took the money, making noise and waking people, Smerdyakov got up—what for? To kill his master again and take the money that had already been stolen? Gentlemen, are you laughing? I'm embarrassed to even suggest such an idea, but incredibly, that's exactly what the prisoner claims. He says that after he left the house, knocked Grigory down, and raised the alarm, Smerdyakov got up, went in, killed his master, and stole the money! I won't even mention the fact that Smerdyakov couldn't have planned all this in advance or predicted that the furious, desperate son would simply peek in respectfully, despite knowing the signals, and then retreat, leaving Smerdyakov to take the money. Gentlemen of the jury, I ask you seriously—when could Smerdyakov have committed the crime? Name the moment, or you cannot accuse him.

But maybe the fit was real, and the sick man suddenly recovered, heard the noise, and went outside. So what? He looked around and thought, "Why not go kill my master?" How would he have known what had happened while he was lying unconscious until that moment? There are limits to such wild ideas.

"Exactly," some clever people will say, "but what if they were in on it together? What if they killed him together and split the money—then what?" That's an important question! And the facts supporting it are unbelievable. One of them commits the murder and does all the work while the other fakes a fit, supposedly to raise suspicion in everyone, scare his master, and alarm Grigory.

It would be interesting to hear what possible motives could have made these two plan something so ridiculous.

But maybe Smerdyakov wasn't an active accomplice—maybe he just passively went along with it. Maybe he was too scared to stop it and agreed not to interfere. Maybe, knowing he would be blamed for not crying out for help or stopping the murder, he got Dmitri Karamazov's permission to fake the fit. "Go ahead and kill him; it's none of my business." But since Smerdyakov's attack was sure to cause confusion in the household, Dmitri Karamazov would never have agreed to such a plan. I'll let that go, though. Let's assume he did agree. That would still mean Dmitri Karamazov is the murderer, the one behind it all, and Smerdyakov is only a passive accomplice, if even that.

But what happens? As soon as he's arrested, the prisoner immediately blames everything on Smerdyakov. Not saying they were accomplices, but claiming Smerdyakov was the murderer. "He did it alone," he says. "He killed and robbed him. It was his doing." What kind of accomplices are these, accusing each other right away? And think about the risk for Karamazov. After committing the murder while his supposed accomplice lay in bed, he tries to blame it on the sick man, who could easily resent this and, to save himself, confess the truth. Smerdyakov might have figured out that the court would decide how responsible he was, and he would've realized that if he were punished, it would be far less than the real murderer. In that case, he would have definitely confessed, but he didn't. Smerdyakov never hinted at their involvement together, even though the actual murderer kept accusing him and insisting he had committed the crime alone.

What's more, during the investigation, Smerdyakov himself admitted that he was the one who told the prisoner about the envelope of money and the signals. He said that if it hadn't been for him, Dmitri would have known nothing about it. Now, if Smerdyakov had truly been guilty, would he have so easily confessed to this at the inquiry? Of course not. He would have tried to hide it, twist the facts, or downplay them. But instead, he didn't hide or distort anything. Only an innocent man, who had no fear of being accused of complicity, could have acted the way he did. And yesterday, overwhelmed with sadness due to his illness and the catastrophe, he hanged himself. He even left a note in his own strange writing: "I destroy myself by my own will and desire so that no one else will be blamed." What would it have cost him to add, "I am the murderer, not Karamazov"? But he didn't write that. Did his conscience push him to suicide, but not to confess his guilt?

And what happened next? Notes for three thousand rubles were brought into the court just now, and we were told that they are the same ones that had been in the envelope now on the table before us. The witness said he received them from Smerdyakov the day before. I won't go over the painful scene again, but I will point out a few small details that might not be obvious at first glance. First of all, Smerdyakov must have returned the money and then hanged himself out of guilt. And just yesterday, according to Ivan Karamazov, Smerdyakov confessed his guilt to him. If that's true, why didn't Ivan say something earlier? Why wait until now? If Smerdyakov had truly confessed, then why, I ask again, did he not fully confess in the note he left behind, knowing that an innocent man would face this terrible trial the next day?

The money alone is not proof. A week ago, by pure chance, I and two other people in this court found out that Ivan Fyodorovich had sent two five percent coupons worth five thousand rubles each— ten thousand rubles in total—to the main town in the province to be exchanged. I mention this only to show that anyone can have money, and we can't prove that these notes are the same ones that were in Fyodor Pavlovitch's envelope.

Yesterday, after receiving such important information from the real murderer, Ivan Karamazov did nothing. Why didn't he immediately report it? Why did he wait until the morning? I think I have the right to guess why. His health had been declining for the past week: he told both a doctor and his closest friends that he was suffering from hallucinations and seeing visions of dead people. He was on the verge of a nervous breakdown, which has now overtaken him. In this state, when he suddenly heard of Smerdyakov's death, he might have thought, "The man is dead, I can put the blame on him and save my brother. I have money. I will take a bundle of notes and claim that Smerdyakov gave them to me before he died." You might say that's dishonorable—it's dishonorable to slander even the dead, even to save a brother. True, but what if he slandered him without realizing it? What if, driven by the shock of the valet's death, he truly believed that's how it happened? You saw Ivan's condition just now: he was standing and speaking, but where was his mind?

Then we saw the document, the prisoner's letter written two days before the crime, outlining the whole plan for the murder. So why are we looking for another plan? The crime was committed exactly according to this plan, and by the man who wrote it. Yes, gentlemen of the jury, it went off without a hitch! He didn't run away timidly from his father's window, even though he believed his beloved was inside. No, that's ridiculous! He went in and killed his father. Most likely, he did it in a fit of rage, burning with jealousy, as soon as he saw his hated rival. After killing him, probably with a single blow from the brass pestle, and realizing after searching that his beloved wasn't there, he didn't forget to reach under the pillow and take out the envelope, the torn cover of which lies here on the table before us.

I point this out to draw your attention to one important detail. If he had been an experienced killer, and had committed the murder for the money alone, would he have left the torn envelope on the floor next to the body? If it had been Smerdyakov, for example, killing his master for the money, he would have taken the envelope with him without even bothering to open it over the body. He knew for sure that the money was inside because he saw it put in and sealed. If he had taken the envelope, no one would have ever known about the theft. I ask you, gentlemen, would Smerdyakov have acted like that? Would he have left the envelope behind?

No, this was the act of a frantic murderer, someone who wasn't a thief and had never stolen before. He didn't steal the notes like a thief; he grabbed them as if he were taking back something that was rightfully his from the person who had stolen it. That's how Dmitri Karamazov saw the money—it was almost an insane obsession for him. So, when he found the envelope he had never seen before, he tore it open to check if the money was inside and then ran away with it in his pocket, not even thinking about the fact that he had left a huge piece of evidence behind in the form of that torn envelope. That's because he was Karamazov, not Smerdyakov—he didn't think, he didn't plan. How could he have? He ran off, heard Grigory shout behind him, knocked him down, and struck him with the brass pestle.

The prisoner says that, out of pity, he jumped down to check on Grigory. Would you believe it? He claims he jumped down out of compassion, to see if there was anything he could do to help. Was that really a time to show compassion? No, he jumped down to make sure the only witness to his crime was dead. Any other feeling would be unnatural. Notice that he wiped Grigory's head with his handkerchief, and once he was sure he was dead, he ran to his lover's house, dazed and covered in blood. How could he not have realized he was covered in blood and would be caught immediately? But the prisoner himself assures us he didn't even notice he was covered in blood. And that's believable—it's very possible. That often happens to criminals in moments like this. On one point, they show diabolical cleverness, and on another, they miss something obvious. But at that moment, his mind was on one thing only: where was she? He wanted to know where she was right away, so he ran to her place and found out something shocking: she had gone to Mokroe to meet her first lover.

Chapter 9: The Galloping Troika the End of The Prosecutor's Speech.

Ippolit Kirillovitch had chosen to present his argument in a historical way, a style often used by nervous speakers who like its structure to keep their excitement under control. At this point in his speech, he shifted to talking about Grushenka's "first lover" and shared some interesting ideas on the subject.

"Karamazov, who had been insanely jealous of everyone, seemed to collapse before this first lover. Strangely, he didn't really think of this lover as a serious threat. He had viewed him as a distant problem, and Karamazov always lived in the moment. Perhaps he thought of him as a fantasy. But when his heart realized that the woman had been hiding this new lover from him and deceiving him, it hit him hard, because this man was very real to her—he was her only hope. Understanding this immediately, Karamazov gave in.

"Gentlemen of the jury, I must dwell on this surprising trait in the prisoner's personality. He suddenly shows an intense need for fairness, a respect for women, and an understanding of her right to love. And this happened right after he stained his hands with his father's blood for her sake! The truth is, the blood he spilled was already crying out for revenge, because after destroying his own soul and life, he had to ask himself who he was now and what he could still be to her—the person who meant more to him than his own soul. What could he be compared to her first lover, who had returned, sorry for the past, and offering new love, a fresh start, and the promise of a good life? And he, poor man, what could he offer her now?

"Karamazov felt all of this, realizing that his crime had closed all doors for him and that he was no longer a man with a future, but a criminal facing punishment. This thought crushed him. So, he immediately came up with a desperate plan, which for someone like Karamazov, must have seemed like the only way out. That way was suicide. He ran to get the pistols he had left with his friend Perhotin, and on the way, he pulled the money out of his pocket—the money for which he had killed his father. Now, more than ever, he needed that money. Karamazov would die, Karamazov would shoot himself, and he would make sure everyone remembered! Of course, he was a poet and had always lived recklessly. 'To her, to her!' he thought. 'And there, oh there, I will throw a feast for the whole world, something that will be remembered forever! In the middle of wild celebrations, loud gypsy songs, and dancing, I will raise my glass and drink to the woman I love and her new happiness! Then, right there at her feet, I will shoot myself and pay for what I've done! She will remember Mitya Karamazov, she will see how much Mitya loved her, and she will care for him!'

"Here we see an extreme case of dramatic flair, romantic hopelessness, and the reckless nature of the Karamazovs. Yes, but there's something more, gentlemen of the jury—something that cries out from the soul, that beats constantly in the mind, and that tortures the heart to death. That something is conscience, gentlemen, and its terrible judgment and suffering! The pistol will end everything—the pistol is the only escape! But beyond that— who knows if Karamazov wondered at that moment 'What comes after?' and if Karamazov could, like Hamlet, think 'What comes after?' No, gentlemen of the jury, they have their Hamlets, but we still have our Karamazovs!"

Ippolit Kirillovitch then painted a detailed picture of Mitya's preparations, the scene at Perhotin's house, in the shop, and with the drivers. He quoted several words and actions, all confirmed by witnesses, and the story made a deep impact on the audience. The guilt of this distressed and desperate man became clear and undeniable when all the facts were laid out.

"What use was there for him to be careful? Two or three times, he almost confessed—he hinted at it, nearly said it out loud." (Then followed the evidence from the witnesses.) "He even shouted to the peasant driving him, 'Do you know you're driving a murderer!' But he couldn't admit it, because he had to get to Mokroe and finish his tragic story. But what was waiting for him there? From the very first moment in Mokroe, he realized that his rival, who had seemed unbeatable, wasn't so invincible after all, that the toast to their new happiness was neither wanted nor welcomed. But you know the facts, gentlemen, from the earlier investigation. Karamazov's victory over his rival was total, and his soul entered a new and perhaps the most terrifying phase of its journey.

"We can say with certainty, gentlemen of the jury," the prosecutor continued, "that nature, when violated, and a criminal's heart take their own revenge more fully than any human justice. What's more, justice and punishment on earth actually lighten the burden of nature's punishment and are absolutely necessary for the criminal's soul at such moments to save it from total despair. For I can't even imagine the horror and emotional suffering of Karamazov when he learned that she loved him, that she had rejected her first lover for his sake, that she was calling him, Mitya, to a new life and promising him happiness—and when? When everything was over for him, and nothing was possible!

"Let me also point out something that sheds light on the prisoner's mindset at that time. This woman, his love, had been, until the very moment of his arrest, someone he longed for but couldn't reach—someone he desperately wanted but couldn't have. So why didn't he shoot himself then? Why did he give up on the idea and even forget where his gun was? It was that same burning desire for love, and the hope of finally having it, that stopped him. During the whole party, he stayed close to the woman he adored, who was right there with him, and she was more beautiful and captivating than ever. He never left her side, humbling himself before her in total devotion.

"His passion could easily drown out not only the fear of being arrested but also the guilt eating away at him. For just a moment—oh, only a moment! I can imagine the criminal's state of mind, enslaved by these forces: first, the pull of alcohol, noise, and excitement, of the pounding music and the wild songs and dancing, and of her—drunk, singing, and laughing for him! And second, the hope in the back of his mind that the end wasn't close, that they wouldn't come for him until at least the next morning. So, he had a few hours, and that's something! You can think of a lot in a few hours. I picture him feeling something like what criminals feel on their way to the scaffold. They have another long street to walk down, slowly, past crowds of people. Then there's a turn into another street, and only at the end of that street is the place of execution. I think at the start of the journey, the condemned man, sitting in his disgraceful cart, feels like he still has infinite time left. The houses go by, and the cart moves along—oh, that's nothing, the next street is still far off, and he still looks boldly around at the thousands of cold, curious eyes fixed on him, still thinking he's just like any of them. But then comes the turn into the next street. Oh, that's nothing, nothing! There's still one more street ahead of him, and no matter how many houses he's passed, he'll think there are many more. And that continues all the way to the end, to the very scaffold."

This, I imagine, is how it was with Karamazov at that moment. "They haven't had time yet," he must have thought, "I might still find a way out. There's still time to think of some plan of defense. And now, now—she is so captivating!"

His soul was full of confusion and terror, but somehow, he managed to set aside half of his money and hide it somewhere. I can't explain the disappearance of nearly half of the three thousand rubles he had just taken from his father's pillow any other way. He had been to Mokroe before, more than once, and had already spent two days drinking and carousing there. He knew the old, big house, with all its corridors and outbuildings. I believe that part of the money was hidden in that house, just before the arrest, in some crack or under a floor, in some corner or beneath the roof. For what reason, you may ask? Well, disaster could strike at any moment, of course. He hadn't yet had time to figure out how to face it; his head was throbbing, and his heart was with her, but money—money was essential in any case! With money, a man remains a man. Does such foresight in such a moment seem unnatural to you? But he tells us himself that a month earlier, in a critical and stressful situation, he had split his money and sewn half of it into a little bag. And although that wasn't true, as we will soon prove, it shows that this idea was familiar to Karamazov. He had considered it. Moreover, when he stated during the investigation that he had placed fifteen hundred rubles into a bag (which didn't exist), it's likely that he invented this little bag on the spur of the moment, because two hours earlier, he had divided his money and hidden half of it at Mokroe, simply to avoid having it on him. Remember, gentlemen of the jury, Karamazov could entertain two extreme ideas at once.

We've searched the house, but we haven't found the money. It may still be there, or it may have disappeared the next day and now be in the prisoner's possession. In any case, he was at her side, kneeling before her as she lay on the bed, with his hands outstretched to her. He was so completely absorbed that he didn't even hear the men coming to arrest him. He hadn't had time to prepare any defense in his mind. He was caught off guard, face to face with his judges, the ones who would decide his fate.

Gentlemen of the jury, there are moments in our work that are terrifying to witness, and they are terrifying for the man before us as well! The moment when a criminal sees that all is lost but still fights on, still intends to fight. The moment when every instinct for survival kicks in, and he looks at you with questioning, suffering eyes, studying your face and your thoughts, unsure which way you'll strike. His mind races, forming countless plans in an instant, but he's afraid to speak, afraid of revealing too much! This torment of the soul, this desperate thirst for self- preservation, these humiliating moments of the human spirit are dreadful and sometimes even stir horror and pity in the hearts of the lawyers themselves. This is what we all saw that day.

At first, he was shocked and in his terror blurted out some very incriminating words. "Blood! I deserve it!" But he quickly checked himself. He hadn't prepared what to say or how to respond. He had only a bare denial ready: "I didn't kill my father." That was his first line of defense, behind which he hoped to build some stronger case. He hastened to explain his first compromising outbursts by admitting responsibility only for the death of the servant, Grigory. "Of that blood, I am guilty. But who has killed my father, gentlemen, who has killed him if not I?" Do you hear that, gentlemen? He asked us that—we, who had come to ask him that very question! Do you hear the haste in that phrase, "if not I"—the animal cunning, the childlike impatience of Karamazov? "I didn't kill him, and you mustn't think I did! I wanted to kill him, gentlemen, I wanted to kill him," he rushed to admit (he was in a terrible hurry), "but I'm not guilty—I didn't actually murder him." He admitted that he wanted to kill him, as though saying, "See how honest I am? Now you'll believe even more that I didn't kill him." Oh, in cases like these, criminals are often astonishingly shallow and naïve.

At that point, one of the lawyers casually asked him the simplest of questions: "Wasn't it Smerdyakov who killed him?" And as we expected, he flew into a rage. He was furious that we had guessed his thoughts and brought up Smerdyakov before he could. He immediately swung to the other extreme, as he always does, and started insisting that Smerdyakov could not have killed his father, that Smerdyakov wasn't capable of it. But don't believe him— that was just more of his cunning. He hadn't really given up on the idea of blaming Smerdyakov. On the contrary, he intended to use that defense later, because he had no one else to blame. But for the moment, that option was ruined for him. He would bring it up later, maybe the next day or even a few days later, choosing the right moment to cry out, "You know, I was more skeptical about Smerdyakov than you were—you remember that! But now I'm sure: he killed him. He must have!" But for the time being, he retreated to a gloomy and irritated denial. His impatience and anger led him to make the most absurd and unbelievable claims, like how he peeked into his father's window and respectfully stepped back. The worst part was that he didn't even know the state of things, or about the evidence from Grigory.

We conducted a search of his person. The search angered him, but it also gave him hope, because the full three thousand rubles weren't found on him—only half. And no doubt it was in that moment of angry silence that the idea of the little bag first occurred to him. He must have realized how implausible his story sounded and struggled to make it more believable, to turn it into a tale that might be accepted. In cases like this, the first duty of the investigators is to prevent the criminal from preparing his story, to catch him off guard so that he blurts out his deepest thoughts in all their absurdity and inconsistency. The criminal can only be made to speak by suddenly revealing some new fact, some important piece of evidence that he couldn't have foreseen. We had just such a fact at hand—Grigory's testimony about the open door the prisoner had run through. He had completely forgotten about that door and didn't even suspect that Grigory could have seen it.

The effect was incredible. He jumped up and shouted, "Then Smerdyakov murdered him! It was Smerdyakov!" In that moment, he gave away the defense he had been keeping in reserve, and did so in the most unlikely way, because Smerdyakov could only have committed the murder after Grigory was knocked down and Karamazov had run away. When we told him that Grigory had seen the door open before he fell and had heard Smerdyakov behind the screen when he came out of his bedroom, Karamazov was completely crushed. My esteemed and sharp-witted colleague, Nikolay Parfenovitch, later told me he was almost moved to tears at the sight of him. To make matters worse, the prisoner then hurriedly told us about the much-discussed little bag—so be it, you shall now hear this story!

Gentlemen of the jury, I've already explained why I consider this story not just absurd but the most unlikely invention possible in these circumstances. If someone tried to come up with the most far-fetched tale for a bet, they could hardly think of anything more unbelievable. The worst thing about these stories is that those who triumph in creating them can easily be exposed and defeated by the very details that real life is so full of, and which these unfortunate and unwilling storytellers dismiss as insignificant. Oh, they don't spare any thought for such details, their minds are focused on their grand invention as a whole, and they can't imagine someone daring to question them over some trivial matter! But that's how they get caught.

The prisoner was asked, "Where did you get the material for your little bag, and who made it for you?" "I made it myself," he replied. "And where did you get the linen?" The prisoner was visibly offended, as if the question was beneath him, and would you believe it, his anger was sincere! But they're all like that. "I tore it from my shirt." "Then we'll find that shirt tomorrow, with a piece torn off, among your laundry." And imagine, gentlemen of the jury, if we really had found that torn shirt (and how could we have failed to find it in his chest of drawers or trunk?), that would have been solid evidence to back up his claim! But he didn't think of that. "I don't remember, it might not have been from my shirt, maybe I sewed it from one of my landlady's caps." "What kind of cap?" "It was an old cotton rag of hers lying around." "And you remember that clearly?" "No, I don't." And he was furious, genuinely furious—and yet imagine not remembering it! Even in the most terrifying moments of a person's life, such as when they are being led to execution, they remember these small details. They might forget everything else, but they'll still recall a green roof they passed on the road or a bird perched on a cross—that they will remember. He must have concealed the making of that little bag from everyone in his house, he must have remembered the humiliation he felt at the thought of someone walking in and seeing him with a needle in hand, how at the slightest sound, he would hide behind the screen (and there was a screen in his room).

But, gentlemen of the jury, why am I telling you all this? Why am I focusing on these tiny details, these trivialities?" cried Ippolit Kirillovitch suddenly. "Because the prisoner still clings to these absurdities even now. He hasn't explained anything since that fateful night two months ago. He hasn't added a single real, clarifying fact to his previous fanciful claims; all of them are trivialities. 'You must believe it on my honor.' Oh, we want to believe it, we are eager to believe it, even just on his word of honor! Are we bloodthirsty jackals, craving human blood? Show us one fact in the prisoner's favor, and we'll be happy to celebrate it. But let it be a concrete, real fact, not something based on his brother's impression of his expression, or the claim that when he beat his chest, he must have been referring to the little bag, in the dark, no less! Give us a real fact, and we'll be the first to abandon the accusation, the first to renounce it. But as it stands, justice calls out to us, and we cannot turn back now."

Ippolit Kirillovitch moved on to his final remarks. He looked feverish as he spoke about the blood that cried out for revenge— the blood of a father, murdered by his son, with robbery as the vile motive! He pointed out the tragic and glaring consistency of the facts.

"And whatever you may hear from the skilled and renowned defense attorney," Ippolit Kirillovitch couldn't resist adding, "no matter how eloquent and moving his appeals to your feelings may be, remember that at this moment you are standing in the temple of justice. Remember that you are the protectors of our justice, the defenders of our sacred Russia—of her values, her family, and everything she holds dear! Yes, you represent Russia here and now, and your verdict will echo not only in this courtroom but throughout the entire nation. All of Russia will hear you, as her defenders and her judges, and she will be strengthened or disheartened by your decision. Do not let Russia down. Don't fail her expectations. Our fateful troika races ahead at breakneck speed, perhaps toward disaster, and for a long time now, people across Russia have been reaching out their hands, pleading for a stop to this reckless, furious ride. And if other nations stand aside and let our troika pass, it may not be out of respect, as the poet would like to believe, but out of horror—horror, perhaps even disgust. And it's a good thing they stand aside, but one day, they may stop standing aside. They may form a wall to block the headlong rush of our lawlessness for the sake of their own safety, their own enlightenment, their own civilization. We've already heard cries of alarm from Europe, voices have already begun to rise. Don't provoke them! Don't add fuel to their growing resentment by justifying a son's murder of his father!"

Although Ippolit Kirillovitch was genuinely moved, he ended his speech with this grand appeal—and its impact was extraordinary. When he finished speaking, he hurried out of the room, and as I mentioned earlier, he nearly fainted in the next room. There was no applause in the courtroom, but the more serious attendees were pleased. The ladies, however, weren't as satisfied, though they still admired his eloquence, especially since they had no doubts about the outcome of the trial and fully trusted in Fetyukovitch. "He'll speak soon and, of course, win the day."

Everyone looked at Mitya; he had sat silently through the entire prosecutor's speech, clenching his teeth, with his hands clasped and his head bowed. Occasionally, he would raise his head and listen closely, especially when Grushenka was mentioned. When the prosecutor brought up Rakitin's opinion of her, a smile of contempt and anger flickered across his face, and he muttered audibly, "The Bernards!" When Ippolit Kirillovitch described how he had questioned and tormented him at Mokroe, Mitya lifted his head and listened with intense curiosity. At one point, he seemed ready to leap to his feet and shout out but restrained himself and merely shrugged disdainfully.

Afterward, people talked about the end of the prosecutor's speech, about his performance in questioning the prisoner at Mokroe, and they mocked Ippolit Kirillovitch. "The man couldn't resist bragging about how clever he was," they said.

The court adjourned, but only for a short break, no more than fifteen or twenty minutes. There was a hum of conversation and exclamations from the audience. I still remember some of them.

"A serious speech," remarked a gentleman in one group, speaking gravely.

"He brought in too much psychology," added another voice. "But it was all true, absolutely true!"

"Yes, he's very skilled at it." "He wrapped it all up neatly."

"Yes, and he summed us up, too," joined in another voice. "Do you remember how, at the beginning of his speech, he made us all out to be like Fyodor Pavlovitch?"

"And at the end, too. But that part was nonsense."

"And too vague."

"He got a little too carried away." "It's unfair, really unfair."

"No, it was clever, though. He's waited a long time for this, and now he's had his say, ha ha!"

"What will the defense attorney have to say?" In another group, I overheard:

"He had no right to take a jab at the man from Petersburg like that. 'Appealing to your sensibilities'—do you remember?"

"Yes, that was awkward." "He rushed through it." "He's a nervous man."

"We're laughing, but imagine what the prisoner must be feeling." "Yes, what must it be like for Mitya?"

In a third group, people were saying:

"Who's that lady, the heavyset one with the lorgnette, sitting at the end?"

"She's a general's wife, divorced. I know her."

"That's why she's got the lorgnette." "She's not much good."

"Oh no, she's quite a sharp little woman."

"The woman sitting two seats beyond her, the blonde, is prettier." "They caught him neatly at Mokroe, didn't they?"

"Yes, it was clever enough. We've heard him tell the story at houses before, haven't we?"

"And he couldn't resist telling it again now. That's vanity for you."

"He's a man with a grudge, ha ha!"

"Yes, and easily offended. And there was way too much rhetoric, such long sentences."

"Yes, he kept trying to scare us, over and over. Do you remember the bit about the troika? And 'They have their Hamlets, but we only have Karamazovs so far!' That was a clever line!"

"That was his way of winning over the liberals. He's afraid of them."

"Yes, and he's afraid of the lawyer, too." "What do you think Fetyukovitch will say?"

"Whatever he says, he won't sway our peasants."

"You really think so?"

A fourth group was discussing:

"That bit about the troika was good, the part about the other nations."

"And what he said about other nations not tolerating it was true." "What do you mean?"

"Well, last week in the English Parliament, a member stood up and, while talking about the Nihilists, asked the government if it wasn't time to step in and educate this 'barbaric people.' I know Ippolit was thinking of that. He was talking about it just last week."

"Not an easy task."

"Not an easy task? Why not?"

"Well, we'd just close off Kronstadt and cut off their grain supply. Then where would they get it?"

"From America. They're already getting it from there."

"Nonsense!"

But then the bell rang, and everyone hurried back to their seats. Fetyukovitch took the stand.

Chapter 10: The Speech for The Defense. An Argument That Cuts Both Ways

All was silent as the famous orator's first words echoed through the room. The audience's eyes were fixed on him. He started his speech simply and directly, with confidence, but without a hint of arrogance. He didn't aim for eloquence, emotion, or dramatic expressions. It was as if he were talking to a group of close, understanding friends. His voice was strong and warm, with a natural honesty and simplicity in its tone. Yet, everyone sensed that at any moment, he might shift into true emotion and deliver a powerful blow to the heart. His speech was perhaps less formal than Ippolit Kirillovitch's, but it was free of long phrases and more precise.

There was one thing, however, that didn't sit well with the ladies in the audience: he kept leaning forward at the beginning of his speech, not exactly bowing, but as if he were about to lunge at his listeners, bending his long back almost in half, like a spring that let him bend at right angles.

At the start of his speech, he spoke somewhat disjointedly, without much structure, dealing with facts individually, though by the end, these facts formed a complete argument. His speech could be split into two parts—the first consisting of sharp, sometimes sarcastic, criticism aimed at disproving the accusations. But in the second half, he abruptly changed his tone and manner, rising to emotion. The audience seemed to anticipate this shift and reacted with excitement.

He got straight to the point, explaining that although he practiced law in Petersburg, he had often traveled to smaller towns to defend clients whose innocence he believed in, or at least had an initial sense of. "That is what happened in this case," he said. "From the very first news reports, something struck me that strongly made me lean in the prisoner's favor. What interested me most was a detail that often comes up in legal practice, but rarely in such an extreme and peculiar way as in this case. I should wait until the end of my speech to highlight that detail, but I will mention it at the beginning because I tend to get straight to the point, without holding back my arguments. That may not be the most strategic approach, but at least it's honest. What I'm referring to is this: there's a massive chain of evidence against the defendant, but not a single fact that can withstand close examination on its own. As I followed the case in the papers, this idea grew stronger for me, and then I received a request from the prisoner's family to take on his defense. I immediately came here, and once I did, I became fully convinced. My goal was to dismantle this terrifying chain of evidence and show that each individual piece of evidence is unproven and imaginary. That's why I took on the case."

This was how Fetyukovitch began.

"Gentlemen of the jury," he suddenly declared, "I am new to this area. I have no preconceived notions. The prisoner, a man of passionate and uncontrolled temper, has not offended me. But he has certainly offended many people in this town, prejudicing them against him in advance. Of course, I understand that the moral feelings of local society are justly stirred against him. The prisoner is of a violent and turbulent nature. Yet he was still accepted in society here, even welcomed into the family of my talented colleague, the prosecutor."

(At these words, a few chuckles were heard in the audience, quickly stifled but noticed by everyone. We all knew that the prosecutor had received Mitya unwillingly, only because he had somehow caught his wife's interest—a woman of high virtue and moral worth, but whimsical, capricious, and fond of contradicting her husband, especially over small matters. Mitya's visits, however, had not been frequent.)

"Nevertheless," Fetyukovitch continued, "I dare suggest that despite his independent judgment and fairness, my opponent may have developed an unfair bias against my unfortunate client. Oh, it's completely understandable—my poor client has certainly earned such bias. Morality, and even more so, taste, once offended, is often relentless. In the prosecutor's impressive speech, we heard a strict analysis of the prisoner's character and actions, and his critical approach to the case was obvious. Moreover, he delved into psychological details, something he would not have done if he held any malicious prejudice against the prisoner. But there are things worse than malicious and consciously unfair attitudes in cases like these. It's worse if we are swept up by a creative instinct, driven to craft a story, especially if we are gifted with psychological insight. Before I came here, I was warned in Petersburg—and I already knew myself—that I would face a talented opponent whose psychological insight and skill had earned him considerable fame in legal circles in recent years. But no matter how deep psychology goes, it's a double-edged sword." (Laughter from the audience.) "Forgive me the comparison, of course; I make no claim to eloquence. But let's take any point from the prosecutor's speech as an example.

"The defendant, fleeing through the garden in the dark, climbed over the fence, was caught by the servant, and knocked him down with a brass pestle. Then, he jumped back into the garden and spent five minutes beside the man, trying to determine whether he had killed him or not. And the prosecutor rejects the prisoner's claim that he ran to old Grigory out of pity. 'No,' he says, 'such compassion is impossible in such a moment, it's unnatural. He ran back to see whether the only witness to his crime was dead or alive, proving that he had committed the murder, as he wouldn't have returned otherwise.'

"That's psychology. But let's apply the same method in reverse, and we can come to a conclusion that's just as likely. We're told the murderer ran back to see if the witness was alive or dead, as a precaution, and yet, as the prosecutor himself argues, he had left an incredible piece of evidence in his father's study—a torn envelope with an inscription saying there had been three thousand rubles inside. 'If he had taken the envelope with him, no one would have known it existed, or that the money had been stolen by the defendant.' Those are the prosecutor's words. So, on the one hand, we have a complete lack of precaution—a man panicking and running away, leaving a clue on the floor. But two minutes later, after killing another person, we are asked to believe he suddenly displays cold-blooded, calculated foresight. But even if we accept that, it takes psychological finesse, I suppose, to believe that in one moment I'm as bloodthirsty and sharp-eyed as a hawk, but in the next, I'm as timid and blind as a mole. If I'm so calculating and ruthless that I kill someone and return only to make sure he can't testify against me, why would I spend five minutes tending to my victim, risking the arrival of more witnesses? Why would I soak my handkerchief with blood, wiping his head, just to leave more evidence against myself? If I were truly cold-hearted and calculating, why wouldn't I strike him again with the pestle and kill him outright, relieving myself of any concern about witnesses?

"Furthermore, though he ran back to see whether the witness was alive, he left another piece of evidence along the path—the brass pestle, which he had taken from two women, who could easily recognize it later as theirs and prove that he had taken it. And it wasn't as though he forgot it in a panic or haste. No, he flung the weapon away, as it was found fifteen paces from where Grigory lay. Why would he do that? Simply because he was overcome with grief at having killed an old servant, and he cursed the pestle as a murderous tool. That's the only explanation—what other reason could he have had to throw it so far? And if he was capable of feeling remorse and pity for killing a man, it shows he wasn't guilty of his father's murder. If he had committed that crime, he wouldn't have run back to tend to another victim out of pity. His thoughts would have been consumed by self-preservation, and he would have had no room left for pity. That's beyond doubt. On the contrary, he would have struck the servant's head again, instead of spending five minutes caring for him. There was space for pity only because his conscience had been clear up until then. This presents a completely different psychological picture. I have deliberately used this method, gentlemen of the jury, to demonstrate that psychology can be used to prove anything—it all depends on who's using it. Psychology can easily lead even the most serious people into storytelling, often without them realizing it. I am speaking here about the misuse of psychology, gentlemen."

The sounds of approval and laughter, at the prosecutor's expense, could be heard again throughout the courtroom. I won't recount the entire speech in detail, but I will highlight some of its key passages.

Chapter 11: There Was No Money. There Was No Robbery

There was one point in Fetyukovitch's speech that grabbed everyone's attention. He outright denied the existence of the fatal three thousand rubles and, as a result, the possibility that they had been stolen.

"Gentlemen of the jury," he began. "Any new and unbiased observer would immediately notice a peculiar detail in this case, namely, the accusation of robbery and the absolute impossibility of proving that there was anything to steal. We are told that money was stolen—three thousand rubles—but does anyone even know if these rubles existed? Think carefully: how did we come to hear of this sum, and who actually saw the money? The only person who claimed to have seen it and stated that it had been placed in the envelope was the servant, Smerdyakov. He had spoken about it to the defendant and his brother, Ivan Fyodorovitch, before the incident. Madame Svyetlov had also been informed of it. But none of these three people ever saw the notes themselves—no one but Smerdyakov laid eyes on them.

"Now the question arises: if it's true that the money did exist, and that Smerdyakov saw it, when did he last see it? What if his master had taken the money from under his bed and returned it to his cash box without telling him? Keep in mind that, according to Smerdyakov's account, the notes were kept under the mattress. The defendant would have had to pull them out, but the bed was perfectly undisturbed, as carefully noted in the report. How could the defendant have found the notes without ruffling the bed? And how could he have avoided staining the clean, immaculate linen with his blood-covered hands?

"But I will be asked: What about the envelope that was found on the floor? Yes, let's talk about that envelope. I was somewhat surprised when the highly talented prosecutor declared—he declared, note—that if it weren't for that envelope lying on the floor, no one would have known about its existence or the notes inside it, and therefore, no one would have known the defendant had stolen it. So, by the prosecutor's own admission, this torn piece of paper is the only proof of the robbery charge, 'otherwise, no one would have known about the robbery, or even the money.' But does the fact that this piece of paper was lying on the floor prove that there was money in it, or that the money had been stolen? Yet, the objection will be raised: Smerdyakov saw the money in the envelope. But when did he last see it? I spoke with Smerdyakov, and he told me that he had last seen the notes two days before the incident. So why can't we imagine that Fyodor Pavlovitch, while locked up alone and waiting impatiently for the object of his affection, decided to pass the time by breaking open the envelope and taking out the money? He might have thought to himself, 'What's the use of the envelope? She won't believe the money's in there. But if I show her the thirty rainbow-colored notes all at once, that will have a much stronger effect, it will make her mouth water!' So he tears open the envelope, takes out the notes, and tosses the envelope onto the floor, knowing full well that he's the owner and has nothing to fear from leaving evidence behind.

"Now, gentlemen, could anything be more likely than this scenario? Why is it so unreasonable to believe this could have happened? And if something like this did happen, then the charge of robbery collapses completely—if there was no money, there could be no robbery. If the envelope on the floor is meant to be evidence that money was stolen, why can't I argue that the envelope was on the floor because the money had been taken out of it by its owner?

"But then I will be asked: Where did the money go, if Fyodor Pavlovitch took it out, since it wasn't found when the police searched the house? First of all, part of the money was found in the cash box, and secondly, he could have taken out the remaining amount earlier that morning or the night before, intending to use it for something else, to give it away or send it off. He may have changed his plans without feeling it necessary to inform Smerdyakov in advance. And if there's even the slightest possibility of this, how can the defendant be so confidently accused of having committed murder for the sake of robbery and of actually carrying out the theft? This enters the realm of pure fiction. If we are to claim that something has been stolen, the stolen item must be produced, or at least its existence must be proven beyond any doubt. And yet, no one has ever laid eyes on these notes.

"Not long ago, in Petersburg, a young man, just eighteen years old, who worked as a small-time vendor, entered a moneychanger's shop in broad daylight with an ax. With boldness typical of such criminals, he killed the shopkeeper and stole fifteen hundred rubles. Five hours later, he was arrested, and except for fifteen rubles he had already spent, the full sum was found on him. Additionally, when the shopkeeper returned and reported the robbery, he was able to tell the police not only the exact amount stolen but also the specific notes and coins that made up the sum, and these very notes and coins were found on the young man. Afterward, the killer gave a full confession. Now that is what I call evidence, gentlemen of the jury! In such a case, I know, I see, I touch the money, and I cannot deny its existence. Is it the same in this case? And yet, we are dealing with a question of life or death here.

"Yes, I'll be told, but he was seen spending money that night— fifteen hundred rubles. Where did that money come from? But the fact that only fifteen hundred rubles were found, and not the other half of the supposed three thousand, proves that this money was never in the envelope. Through precise calculations of time, it was shown during the preliminary investigation that the defendant ran directly from the women servants' quarters to Perhotin's without stopping at his home or going anywhere else. He had been in the company of others the whole time and could not have hidden part of the money in town. It is this line of reasoning that has led the prosecutor to assume that the money is hidden somewhere at Mokroe. Why not suggest it's hidden in the dungeons of the castle of Udolpho, gentlemen? Isn't this assumption too far-fetched, too much like a romantic story? And if this assumption falls apart, then the entire charge of robbery falls apart as well, because in that case, where did the other fifteen hundred rubles go? How could they have simply disappeared, since it is proven that the defendant didn't go anywhere else? And yet, we are prepared to destroy a man's life based on such tales!"

"I will be told that he could not explain where he got the fifteen hundred rubles he had, and that everyone knew he was without money before that night. But who exactly knew that? The defendant has given a clear and unwavering account of where that money came from, and if you consider it, gentlemen of the jury, nothing could be more likely or more in line with the defendant's character and spirit than that account. The prosecutor is enchanted by his own story. He tells us that a weak-willed man who accepted the three thousand rubles so insultingly given by his fiancée could not have put half of it aside and sewn it into a bag. And even if he had, he would have undone it every two days to take out a hundred, and he would have spent it all in a month. All of this, you may recall, was delivered in a tone that left no room for contradiction. But what if the events happened differently? What if you've been spinning a tale, but about an entirely different kind of man? That's the issue: you've invented a completely different person!

"I will also be told, perhaps, that there are witnesses who say he spent the entire three thousand rubles given to him by his fiancée on a single day, and so could not have divided it in half. But who are these witnesses? The value of their testimony has already been shown in this court. Moreover, in another person's hands, even a crust of bread looks larger, and none of these witnesses actually counted the money—they only estimated by sight. And the witness Maximov even testified that the defendant had twenty thousand rubles in his hands. You see, gentlemen of the jury, psychology is a double-edged sword. Let me now turn that edge in another direction and see what comes of it.

"A month before the catastrophe, the defendant was entrusted by Katerina Ivanovna with three thousand rubles to send by post. But the question is: was it really handed over in such an insulting and degrading manner as was just claimed? The young lady's first account of the event was completely different—entirely different. In her second account, we only heard cries of anger and vengeance, expressions of long-hidden hatred. The very fact that the witness's first testimony was incorrect gives us reason to believe her second testimony may be incorrect as well. The prosecutor has avoided addressing this story and dares not touch it, as he said himself.

So be it. I won't address it either, but I will say that if a lofty and principled person like that highly esteemed young lady, who is undoubtedly of great moral standing, can suddenly contradict her first statement in court with the obvious intention of ruining the defendant, it's clear that this testimony was not given impartially, not calmly. Do we not have the right to assume that a vengeful woman might have exaggerated? Yes, she may well have exaggerated, particularly regarding the insult and humiliation of offering him the money. No, it was offered in such a way that a man as easy-going as the defendant could have accepted it, especially as he was expecting to soon receive the three thousand rubles that he believed his father owed him. It was thoughtless of him, but it was just his thoughtless nature that made him so sure that his father would give him the money— that he would get it—and so he felt he could always send off the money entrusted to him and repay the debt.

"But the prosecutor refuses to believe that he could have, on that very same day, set aside half of the money and sewn it into a small bag. 'That's not in his nature,' he tells us. 'He couldn't have had such self-control.' And yet the prosecutor spoke of the broad Karamazov nature, exclaiming about how a Karamazov can contemplate two extremes at the same time. A Karamazov is indeed such a two-sided personality, capable of swinging between extremes, so that even in the midst of a wild desire for reckless indulgence, he can rein himself in if something on the other side strikes him. And what was on the other side for the defendant? Love—new love that had ignited in his heart, and for that love, he needed money—oh, far more than for wild parties with his mistress. If she were to say to him, 'I'm yours, I won't go to Fyodor Pavlovitch,' he would need money to take her away. That was far more important to him than indulgence. Could a Karamazov fail to understand that? That very anxiety was what tormented him—so how improbable is it that he would have set aside that money and hidden it for an emergency?

"But time passed, and Fyodor Pavlovitch did not give him the three thousand rubles he had been counting on. Instead, the defendant heard that his father intended to use that money to seduce the woman he, the defendant, loved. 'If Fyodor Pavlovitch doesn't give me the money,' he thought, 'I'll look like a thief in front of Katerina Ivanovna.' Then the idea came to him that he would go to Katerina Ivanovna, lay before her the fifteen hundred rubles still around his neck, and say, 'I am a scoundrel, but not a thief.' So, here we have two strong reasons for him to guard that money like the apple of his eye and not unpick the little bag and spend it bit by bit. Why would you deny the defendant a sense of honor?

Yes, he has a sense of honor, even if it's misplaced or misguided, but it exists, and it's a passionate one, as he has proven.

"But now things get even more complicated. His jealous torment reaches its peak, and two questions plague his fevered mind more and more: 'If I repay Katerina Ivanovna, where will I find the money to run away with Grushenka?' If he acted recklessly, drank, and caused disturbances in taverns during that month, it was perhaps because he was miserable and overwhelmed. These two questions became so pressing that they drove him to despair. He sent his younger brother to beg for the three thousand rubles one last time, but before waiting for an answer, he burst in himself and ended up beating his father in front of witnesses. After that, there was no chance of him getting the money from anyone—his father certainly wouldn't give it to him after being beaten.

"That same evening, he struck himself on the chest—right where the little bag was—and swore to his brother that he had the means to avoid being a scoundrel, but that he would remain one anyway, because he foresaw that he wouldn't use those means, that he wouldn't have the character or the willpower to do it. Why does the prosecutor refuse to believe Alexey Karamazov's testimony, given so genuinely, sincerely, spontaneously, and convincingly? And why, instead, does he force us to believe in money hidden in a crevice, in some dungeon of the castle of Udolpho?

"That same evening, after his conversation with his brother, the defendant wrote that fatal letter, which the prosecutor claims is the key, irrefutable proof that the defendant committed robbery. 'I shall beg from everyone,' he wrote, 'and if I don't get the money, I will murder my father and take the envelope with the pink ribbon from under his mattress as soon as Ivan is gone.' A full plan for the murder, we're told, and so it must have been him. 'Everything happened just as he wrote,' the prosecutor insists.

"But first, that letter was written by a drunken man, in a fit of great anger. Second, he speaks of the envelope based on what he heard from Smerdyakov, as he never saw the envelope himself. Third, yes, he wrote the letter—but how can you prove that he actually carried out what he wrote? Did the defendant take the envelope from under the pillow? Did he find the money? Did that money even exist? And was it money he was after when he ran off that night? Do you remember? He ran off, not to steal, but to find the woman who had crushed him. He wasn't running to follow some plan he had written out, not running for a premeditated robbery— he ran out of a sudden, spontaneous fit of jealous rage. Yes! I will be told that once he got there and murdered his father, he took the money as well. But did he even commit the murder? I reject the charge of robbery with indignation. You cannot accuse a man of robbery if you can't even prove what he's stolen—that's a basic principle. But did he murder his father without robbing him? Did he murder him at all? Is that proven? Or is that also just a story?"

Chapter 12: And There Was No Murder Either"

"Let me remind you, gentlemen of the jury, that a man's life is on the line, and you must be cautious. We heard the prosecutor himself admit that, until today, he hesitated to accuse the defendant of fully and intentionally planning the crime. He only decided to do so after seeing that drunken letter which was shown in court today. 'Everything happened just as it was written,' he said. But, I repeat, the defendant was running to her, just to find out where she was. That is an undeniable fact. If she had been home, he wouldn't have run away—he would have stayed with her, and he wouldn't have done what he promised in the letter. He ran off suddenly, by accident, and by that point, he probably didn't even remember the letter he wrote while drunk. 'He grabbed the pestle,' they say, and we all remember how a whole theory was built around that pestle—how he supposedly had to see it as a weapon, grab it, and so on. A very simple thought comes to mind: What if the pestle hadn't been sitting in plain sight, hadn't been lying on the shelf where the defendant grabbed it, but had been put away in a cupboard? It wouldn't have caught his eye, and he would have run away without it, empty-handed, and certainly wouldn't have killed anyone. So how can we see the pestle as proof of premeditation?

"Yes, but they say he talked about killing his father in the taverns, and two days before, on the evening he wrote his drunken letter, he was calm and only argued with a shopkeeper in the tavern because, apparently, a Karamazov can't help but argue. My response to that is simple: if he had truly been planning such a murder, according to his letter, he certainly wouldn't have gotten into a quarrel with a shopkeeper, and likely wouldn't have gone to the tavern at all. Someone plotting such a crime seeks peace and quiet, hides away, tries not to be seen or heard—not out of calculation, but from instinct. Gentlemen of the jury, psychology is a double-edged sword, and we can use it too. As for all the shouting in the taverns over the month, don't we often hear kids or drunkards coming out of bars yelling, 'I'll kill you'? But they don't actually kill anyone. And that so-called fatal letter—isn't it just drunken irritation? Isn't it like the drunk shouting outside a bar, 'I'll kill you! I'll kill all of you!' Why can't it be that? What reason do we have to call that letter 'fatal' instead of 'ridiculous'? Because his father was found dead, because a witness saw the defendant running from the garden with a weapon, and because he knocked that witness down: that's why we're told everything happened just like he wrote, and the letter wasn't 'absurd' but 'fatal.'

"And now, thank God, we've reached the key point: 'since he was in the garden, he must have killed him.' In those few words— 'since he was, he must have'—lies the entire argument for the prosecution. He was there, so he must have done it. But what if there is no 'must' even if he was there? I admit the chain of events—the coincidences—are suggestive. But look at all these facts separately, without connecting them. For example, why does the prosecution refuse to believe the defendant's claim that he ran away from his father's window? Remember the prosecutor's sarcasm about the sudden respectful and 'pious' feelings that supposedly came over the murderer. But what if there was something like that—a feeling of religious awe, if not filial respect? The defendant said during the investigation, 'My mother must have been praying for me at that moment,' and so he ran away as soon as he realized Madame Svyetlov wasn't in his father's house. 'But he couldn't have figured that out by just looking through the window,' the prosecutor objects. But why couldn't he? Why? The window opened when the defendant signaled. Maybe Fyodor Pavlovitch said something, some exclamation that let the defendant know she wasn't there. Why should we assume things went exactly how we imagine? A thousand things can happen in real life that even the most subtle imagination can't predict.

"'Yes, but Grigory saw the door open, so the defendant must have been inside the house, and therefore, he killed him.' Now, about that door, gentlemen of the jury... Keep in mind that we only have the testimony of one witness about that door, and at the time he was in such a state that— But let's assume the door was open; let's assume the defendant lied about it, out of an instinct of self-defense, which is natural in his situation; let's assume he did go into the house—so what? How does it follow that, because he was there, he committed the murder? He might have rushed inside, run through the rooms, maybe even shoved his father, maybe even hit him. But as soon as he confirmed that Madame Svyetlov wasn't there, he might have run out, relieved that she wasn't there, and that he hadn't killed his father. And perhaps, because he'd resisted the temptation to kill, because his conscience was clear, and he was relieved that he hadn't killed his father, he was able to feel compassion, and leapt over the fence a minute later to help Grigory after accidentally knocking him down in his excitement.

"The prosecutor spoke eloquently about the defendant's mental state at Mokroe—about how love lay before him, calling him to a new life, but love was impossible because of his father's bloodstained corpse, and beyond that, punishment. Yet the prosecutor still allowed him love, explaining it with his theory about the defendant's drunkenness, about a criminal being led to execution, and so on and so forth. But again, I ask the prosecutor: are you not inventing a new personality? Is the defendant really so heartless and cruel that he could be thinking about love and finding ways to avoid punishment, all while his hands were supposedly stained with his father's blood? No, no, no! As soon as it became clear to him that she loved him and was calling him to her, offering him new happiness, I say he would have felt the urge to kill himself double, even triple, if he had his father's murder on his conscience. No! He wouldn't have forgotten where his pistols were! I know the defendant: the cold, stony heartlessness that the prosecutor describes doesn't fit his character. He would have killed himself, no doubt. The only reason he didn't is because 'his mother's prayers saved him,' and he was innocent of his father's blood. That night at Mokroe, he was troubled, he was grieving over old Grigory, and he prayed that the old man would recover, that the blow hadn't been fatal, and that he wouldn't have to suffer for it. Why not accept that version of events? What solid proof do we have that the defendant is lying?

"But then we'll hear it again: 'There's his father's body! If he ran away without killing him, then who did?' This is the entire logic of the prosecution. 'Who else could it be if not him?' They claim there's no one else to blame.

"Gentlemen of the jury, is that really true? Is it positively, absolutely true that there's no one else? We heard the prosecutor list everyone who was in the house that night. There were five people; I agree that three of them couldn't have done it— the victim himself, old Grigory, and his wife. That leaves the defendant and Smerdyakov, and the prosecutor dramatically says that the defendant accused Smerdyakov because there was no one else. He says if there had been a sixth person, even a phantom, the defendant would have immediately blamed them instead of Smerdyakov. But, gentlemen of the jury, why can't I come to the opposite conclusion? There are two people left: the defendant and Smerdyakov. Why can't I say that you accuse my client simply because you have no one else? And you have no one else because you've already decided to rule Smerdyakov out."

"It's true that Smerdyakov is only accused by the prisoner, his two brothers, and Madame Svyetlov. But there are others who also hint at his guilt: vague rumors, suspicions, unclear reports, and a feeling of expectation. Finally, there are a number of facts which, while not conclusive, are very suggestive. First, there's the matter of his fit on the day of the murder, which the prosecutor took great care to defend as genuine. Then, there's his sudden suicide right before the trial. And, of course, we've heard today's surprising testimony from the defendant's elder brother, who up until now believed in his guilt but today presented new evidence and proclaimed Smerdyakov as the murderer. Yes, I fully agree with the court and the prosecutor that Ivan Karamazov is suffering from brain fever, and that his statement could very well be the result of a desperate, feverish attempt to save his brother by blaming a dead man. But again, Smerdyakov's name has surfaced, stirring more mystery. There's something here that's still unexplained, something incomplete. Maybe, one day, it will all come to light. But we won't discuss that right now. We'll get to it later.

"The court has decided to continue the trial, but before moving on, I'd like to take a moment to comment on the prosecutor's character portrayal of Smerdyakov, which he delivered with great skill. While I admire his talent, I cannot agree with his depiction. I personally visited Smerdyakov, spoke with him, and I was left with a very different impression. Yes, he was physically weak, but his character was nothing like the timid, simple-minded person the prosecutor has made him out to be. I found no trace of the timidity that the prosecutor emphasized. Nor did I see any innocence. On the contrary, what I sensed was a deep mistrustfulness, hidden behind a mask of naivety, along with a sharp and calculating intelligence. The prosecutor was too quick to dismiss him as weak-minded. My own impression of him was very clear: Smerdyakov is a distinctly spiteful, ambitious, vindictive, and deeply envious person. I made some inquiries: he resented his low birth, was ashamed of it, and would clench his teeth when reminded that he was the son of 'stinking Lizaveta.' He showed no respect for Grigory and his wife, who had cared for him in his youth. He cursed and mocked Russia and often dreamed of escaping to France, where he wanted to become a Frenchman. He frequently complained that he didn't have the means to achieve this dream. It seemed to me that he had no love for anyone but himself and held an inflated view of his own worth. His understanding of culture was limited to fine clothes, clean shirts, and polished boots. Believing himself to be the illegitimate son of Fyodor Pavlovitch (there is some evidence to support this belief), he likely resented his position compared to Fyodor's legitimate sons. They had everything; he had nothing. They had rights and inheritance, while he was just the cook. He told me personally that he helped Fyodor Pavlovitch put the money into the envelope. The purpose of that money— money that could have changed his life—must have been deeply upsetting to him. And he saw three thousand rubles in brand-new, brightly colored notes. (I asked him specifically about this.) Oh, be careful when showing an ambitious, envious man a large sum of money all at once! It was the first time he had ever seen so much money in one person's hands. The sight of those rainbow-colored notes might have made a disturbing impression on his mind, even if there were no immediate consequences.

"The talented prosecutor, with great skill, laid out all the arguments for and against Smerdyakov's guilt, and asked why he would have faked a fit. But perhaps he didn't fake it at all. The fit could have been real, and he might have naturally recovered—not fully, but enough to regain consciousness, as often happens with epileptics.

"The prosecutor also asks when Smerdyakov could have committed the murder. It's easy to pinpoint that moment. He could have woken up from a deep sleep (an epileptic fit is always followed by a deep sleep) right when old Grigory shouted 'Parricide!' at the top of his lungs. That shout, piercing through the dark and the stillness, could have woken Smerdyakov, whose sleep may have been lighter at that particular moment. He could have woken up even an hour earlier.

"Getting out of bed, he might have wandered out, almost unconsciously, toward the sound, trying to figure out what was going on. His mind was still foggy from the fit, and he was half asleep. But once he reached the garden, he overheard terrible news from his frightened master. His mind could have immediately started working, and a terrible but irresistible idea could have formed in his head—to kill the old man, take the three thousand rubles, and frame his young master. A sudden, overwhelming desire for money, for fortune, might have overtaken him, especially when he realized how unlikely it would be that anyone would suspect him. These sudden, uncontrollable impulses often arise when the opportunity is just right, especially with murderers who hadn't originally planned to kill. And Smerdyakov could have gone ahead with it. With what weapon? Any rock lying around in the garden. And why? For the three thousand rubles that could have changed his life. I'm not contradicting myself— the money may very well have existed, and perhaps Smerdyakov was the only one who knew where it was kept. And as for the torn envelope found on the floor?

"When the prosecutor explained his clever theory—that only an inexperienced thief like Karamazov would leave the envelope on the floor, while someone like Smerdyakov would have avoided leaving any evidence—I couldn't help but think that I'd heard that argument before. And, would you believe it, I heard that exact theory, that exact suggestion of how Karamazov would have behaved, from Smerdyakov himself just two days earlier. What's more, I remember thinking at the time that Smerdyakov's explanation seemed oddly calculated, as if he was trying to push that idea onto me, hoping I'd think it was my own. He was planting the idea in my mind, subtly. Didn't he suggest the same thing during the investigation, planting the idea in the prosecutor's mind too?

"You may ask, 'What about Grigory's wife? She said she heard Smerdyakov groaning all night.' Yes, she did, but her testimony is highly unreliable. I once knew a woman who swore she'd been kept awake all night by a dog barking in the yard. But it turned out the dog had only barked once or twice. That's a normal reaction. When someone is asleep and hears a noise, they wake up, annoyed at being disturbed, but they fall back asleep quickly. A couple of hours later, they hear another noise, wake up again, and fall asleep once more. By morning, they feel as if they've been kept awake all night. It seems to them as if the noise lasted all night, but really, they only remember the few moments when they were awake, not the hours of sleep in between."

"But why, why, asks the prosecutor, did Smerdyakov not confess in his final letter? Why did his conscience lead him to take one step, but not both? But, pardon me, conscience means remorse, and the suicide may not have felt remorse at all, only despair. Despair and remorse are two very different things. Despair can be vengeful and unyielding, and the person who takes his own life may have harbored even greater hatred toward those he envied throughout his life.

"Gentlemen of the jury, beware of a miscarriage of justice! What is so unlikely about the explanation I've just given you? Point out the flaw in my argument; find where it is impossible or absurd. And if there is even the slightest possibility, the slightest hint of probability in what I've proposed, you cannot condemn him. But is it only a hint? I swear by all that is sacred, I fully believe the explanation of the murder that I've presented to you. What troubles and outrages me is that in all the overwhelming facts piled up by the prosecution against the defendant, there isn't a single one that is certain or undeniable. Yet this unfortunate man is on the verge of ruin because of these accumulated facts. Yes, the combined effect is terrifying: the blood, the blood dripping from his fingers, the bloodstained shirt, the cry of 'Parricide!' ringing through the dark night, and the old man falling with his head crushed. And then, all the phrases, the declarations, the gestures, the shouts! Oh! All of this has such an impact, it can cloud the mind. But, gentlemen of the jury, can it cloud your minds? Remember, you've been given the absolute power to bind and to free, but the greater the power, the greater the weight of responsibility.

"I stand by every word I have said, and I won't retreat from a single point, but let's suppose for a moment that I agree with the prosecution—that my poor client did indeed stain his hands with his father's blood. This is purely hypothetical, I repeat; I never for a moment doubt his innocence. But, for the sake of argument, let's assume that my client is guilty of parricide. Even then, hear me out. I have something more to say to you, because I believe there must be a great struggle going on in your hearts and minds. Forgive me for mentioning your hearts and minds, gentlemen of the jury, but I want to be truthful and sincere to the very end. Let us all be sincere!"

At this point, the speech was interrupted by a burst of applause. The last words were spoken with such sincerity that everyone felt he had something significant to say, and that what would follow might be crucial. But the President, upon hearing the applause, sternly threatened to clear the court if such disruptions occurred again. The room fell silent, and Fetyukovitch continued, his voice now filled with emotion, quite different from the tone he had used before.

Chapter 13: A Corrupter of Thought

"It's not just the accumulation of facts that threatens my client's life, gentlemen of the jury," he began, "what truly condemns my client is one undeniable fact—the dead body of his father. If this had been an ordinary murder case, you would have dismissed the charge based on the triviality, the incompleteness, and the wild nature of the evidence, if you examined each part of it separately. Or at least, you would have hesitated to destroy a man's life simply due to the prejudice against him, which, unfortunately, he may have deserved. But this is not a regular murder case—it is a case of parricide. And that word weighs heavily on people's minds, to the point that the trivial evidence becomes less trivial, the incomplete evidence less incomplete, even to an unbiased mind. How can a prisoner like this be acquitted? What if he committed the murder and walks free? That's the thought everyone, almost instinctively, has at the back of their minds.

"Yes, it's a horrible thing to kill one's father—the father who gave me life, who loved me, who sacrificed for me, worried for me when I was sick, worked for my happiness, and took joy in my successes. To kill a father like that—it's unthinkable. But, gentlemen of the jury, what is a father—truly? What is the meaning behind that word? What does it represent? We've just touched upon the ideal of what a real father should be. In this case we're discussing, Fyodor Pavlovitch Karamazov did not live up to that idea of a father. That's the tragedy. And the truth is, some fathers are a tragedy. Let us examine this closely, gentlemen, without shying away from any painful truths. We mustn't avoid difficult questions, as the talented prosecutor suggested we might do.

"In the midst of his passionate speech, my esteemed opponent exclaimed multiple times, 'I won't leave the defense of the prisoner to the lawyer from Petersburg. I accuse, but I also defend!' He repeated this several times but conveniently left out the fact that if this terrible prisoner had been so deeply grateful for a handful of nuts given to him in childhood, might not such a man have also remembered, for twenty-three years, how he had run around in his father's yard, 'barefoot and with his trousers barely hanging on,' as the kind-hearted Dr. Herzenstube so vividly described?

"Oh, gentlemen, why must we examine this misfortune further, why go over what we all know already? What did my client find when he returned to his father's home? Why is he being painted as a heartless monster? Yes, he's wild, he's unruly—we're not denying that. But who is responsible for how he turned out? Who is to blame for the way he was raised, despite his good heart? Did anyone try to teach him reason? Did he have the benefit of education? Did anyone show him love, even just a little, in his youth? He was left to grow up like an animal, with only Providence looking after him. Perhaps he longed to see his father after years of separation. Perhaps he fought against the terrible memories of his childhood and longed to embrace his father and forgive him. But what did he face? He was greeted with mockery, suspicions, and arguments over money. He was surrounded by filthy talk and corrupt ideas, and then he saw his father trying to seduce the woman he loved with money that belonged to him. Gentlemen, that is beyond cruel! And the old man constantly complained about his son's lack of respect. He slandered him, ruined his reputation, bought up his debts just to have him thrown in prison.

"Gentlemen of the jury, people like my client—those who seem fierce and out of control on the outside— are often the most tender-hearted inside. They just don't show it. Don't laugh at this idea! The prosecutor mocked my client for loving Schiller, for loving beauty and the sublime. But I wouldn't have laughed at that. These types of people—let me defend them, they're often misunderstood—long for goodness, tenderness, and justice, often in contrast to their own wild behavior. Passionate and intense on the surface, they're capable of deep love, spiritual and pure. Don't laugh at me—this is often the case with people like him. But they can't hide their coarser passions, and that's what stands out to everyone. But inside, they are full of inner turmoil. Their outward passion burns out quickly, but when they're around someone noble, they long to be better, to change, to become honorable and good. They seek to be 'sublime and beautiful,' as the phrase goes, even though people make fun of it.

"I mentioned earlier that I wouldn't speak much about my client's engagement, but let me add this. What we just heard wasn't evidence—it was the outburst of a woman blinded by anger and revenge. And it wasn't her place—not hers—to accuse him of betrayal, for she was the one who betrayed him. If she had taken a moment to reflect, she would never have said what she did. Don't believe her! My client is not the monster she called him!

"On the eve of His Crucifixion, Christ said, 'I am the Good Shepherd. The good shepherd lays down his life for his sheep, so that none of them may be lost.' Let's not allow a man's soul to be lost because of us!

"I asked earlier what 'father' means, and I said it's a great word. But we must be honest with our words, gentlemen. A father like Fyodor Pavlovitch Karamazov doesn't deserve that title. Filial love for a father like that is impossible. Love cannot be created from nothing; only God can create something from nothing.

"'Fathers, do not provoke your children to anger,' the apostle writes, from a heart full of love. I'm not quoting this for my client's sake—I mention it for the sake of all fathers. Who gave me the right to speak to fathers? No one. But as a man and a citizen, I make this plea. We don't have much time on this earth. We do many wrongs, say many wrong things. So let's use this moment, while we are all together, to say something good to each other. That's what I'm doing. While I stand here, I take advantage of this opportunity. Not for nothing is this platform given to us by the highest authority—our words are heard all across Russia! I am not speaking only to the fathers here today, but to all fathers: 'Fathers, do not provoke your children to anger.' Yes, let us first follow Christ's teaching ourselves before we expect our children to follow it. Otherwise, we are not fathers, but enemies to our children, and they are not our children, but our enemies—enemies we created ourselves. 'The measure you use will be measured back to you'—those aren't my words; that's from the Gospel.

How can we be angry at our children for treating us as we've treated them?"

"Not long ago in Finland, a servant girl was suspected of secretly giving birth to a child. She was closely watched, and eventually, a box that no one knew about was found in the corner of a loft, hidden behind some bricks. When the box was opened, the body of a newborn child, whom she had killed, was discovered. Along with it, the skeletons of two other babies were found, and she confessed to killing them right after their birth.

Gentlemen of the jury, was she a mother to these children? She did indeed give birth to them, but was she truly their mother? Could anyone dare to give her the sacred title of 'mother'? Let us be bold, gentlemen. Let us be audacious, as it is our duty at this moment to face certain ideas and words without fear, unlike the women in Ostrovsky's play who are frightened by certain expressions. No, we must show that the progress of recent years has influenced us as well. Let us say plainly: a father is not simply the one who begets a child, but the one who begets it and fulfills his duty to it.

Of course, there is another interpretation of the word 'father,' which insists that any father—no matter if he is a monster or the enemy of his children—remains a father simply because he begot them. But this is a mystical understanding that I cannot grasp intellectually. I can only accept it through faith, like many other things I do not understand but which religion instructs me to believe. But if this is the case, it should remain outside the realm of everyday life. In actual life, which has its own rights but also imposes great duties and obligations on us, if we want to be humane—Christian even—we must act based on convictions that are justified by reason and experience. These convictions should have gone through the crucible of analysis. In short, we must act rationally, not as though in a dream or delirium, in order to avoid harming others or unjustly ruining a man. That would be truly Christian work—both rational and philanthropic."

There was a loud burst of applause at this point, coming from several parts of the court. Fetyukovitch waved his hands, pleading with the audience to let him finish without interruption. The room quickly grew silent again, and the orator continued.

"Do you think, gentlemen, that our children, as they grow and begin to reason, can avoid asking these questions? No, they cannot, and we cannot impose impossible restrictions on them. The sight of an unworthy father naturally raises tormenting questions in a young person, especially when he compares his father with the excellent fathers of his friends. The conventional answer to such questions is: 'He gave you life; you are his flesh and blood, so you must love him.' But the young man wonders: 'Did he love me when he fathered me?' And he starts asking more questions. 'Did he have me for my sake? He didn't even know me then, not my sex, not my character. It could have been a moment of passion, maybe even inflamed by wine, and all he passed on to me was his propensity for drunkenness. Why am I bound to love him simply because he begot me when he's cared nothing for me my whole life since?'

"Perhaps these questions seem harsh and cruel, but don't expect an impossible restraint from a young mind. 'Drive nature out of the door, and it will fly in through the window.' Above all, we must not be afraid of words. Let us decide this question based on reason and humanity, not mystical ideas. How should it be decided? Like this: let the son stand before his father and ask, 'Father, tell me, why must I love you? Show me that I must love you.' If the father can answer and give him a good reason, then we have a real, healthy parental relationship, based on reason and responsibility, not on mystical prejudice. But if he cannot answer, then the family bond is broken. He is not a father, and the son has the right to see him as a stranger, or even an enemy. Our courtroom, gentlemen of the jury, should be a school for sound and true ideas."

(At this point, the speaker was interrupted by wild applause. It wasn't the entire audience, but at least half of them joined in. Fathers and mothers applauded, and there were shouts and exclamations from the gallery where the ladies sat. Handkerchiefs were waved in the air. The President began ringing his bell furiously, clearly irritated by the behavior of the audience, but he did not dare to clear the courtroom as he had previously threatened. Even those in high positions—old men with medals on their chests, seated in the reserved section behind the judges—applauded and waved handkerchiefs. When the noise finally died down, the President reiterated his stern warning to clear the court if such an incident occurred again. Fetyukovitch, excited and triumphant, resumed his speech.)

"Gentlemen of the jury, you recall the dreadful night we have spoken about so much today, the night when the son climbed over the fence and stood face to face with the enemy and persecutor who had fathered him. I insist strongly that he did not run to his father's house for money. The charge of robbery is absurd, as I've already proven. And he didn't break into the house with the intention of murder—oh no! If he had meant to kill his father, he would at least have armed himself in advance. The brass pestle he picked up was grabbed instinctively, without thinking. Yes, he tricked his father by knocking on the window. Yes, he entered the house—but as I've said before, I don't believe this story for a second. But let's suppose for a moment that it's true. Gentlemen, I swear by all that's holy: if the person inside had been just a regular enemy, not his father, then after running through the rooms and confirming that the woman wasn't there, he would have run away without harming anyone. He might have struck the man, pushed him away maybe, but nothing more. He wasn't focused on hurting anyone—he just wanted to find out where she was. But it was his father! The mere sight of his father, the man who had hated him since childhood, who had been his enemy, his tormentor, and now his rival in love—seeing him was enough! An overwhelming, uncontrollable hatred took hold of him, clouding his reason. It all surged up in him in an instant—madness, but also a primal instinct of revenge for the violation of nature's eternal laws.

But even then, the prisoner did not kill him—I stand by that! I shout it out loud! He merely swung the pestle in a burst of disgust and rage. He didn't intend to kill his father; he didn't know he would kill him. If the pestle hadn't been in his hand, he might have only knocked his father down, but wouldn't have killed him. As he fled, he didn't know whether the old man was dead or alive. This was not premeditated murder, nor was it true parricide. A father like that cannot be murdered in cold blood; such a killing is only seen as parricide by those blinded by prejudice.

But again, I ask you, from the depths of my soul—did this murder even happen? If we convict him and send him to punishment, he'll say to himself: 'These people did nothing to raise me, nothing to educate me, nothing to improve my lot in life. They gave me no food, no drink, and now they've sent me to prison. I owe them nothing, and I will owe no one anything for the rest of my life. They are cruel, and so I will be cruel.' That is what he'll think, gentlemen. And by condemning him, you'll only ease his conscience. He will curse the blood he spilled, but he will not regret it. At the same time, you will destroy any chance of him becoming a better man, for he will stay lost in his wickedness for the rest of his life.

But if you truly wish to punish him, to crush him with the most terrible punishment imaginable, and at the same time save him, show him mercy! Overwhelm him with it, and watch how he trembles, how his heart shatters. He will ask himself, 'How can I bear this mercy? How can I endure such love? Do I deserve this?' That's what he will cry out.

Oh, I know this heart—this wild but grateful heart, gentlemen! It will bow down before your mercy; it longs for some great act of kindness, and it will melt. This heart, once full of bitterness, will soften and grow, seeing that both God and men are good and just. Remorse will crush him, and he will no longer think, 'I'm free of them.' Instead, he will say, 'I am more guilty than anyone else.' With tears of repentance and agony, he will cry out: 'Others are better than I am. They wanted to save me, not destroy me!' Oh, such an act of mercy is easy for you! Without solid evidence, how can you declare, 'Yes, he is guilty'?"

"Better to let ten guilty men go free than to condemn one innocent man! Can you hear it, that powerful voice from the past century of our proud history? It is not my place to remind you, but I must say that the Russian court exists not only to punish, but also to save the criminal! Let other nations focus on retribution and the strict letter of the law; we will uphold the spirit and true meaning—salvation and the reformation of the lost. If this is the case, if Russia and her justice are truly like this, then she may continue forward with confidence! Do not try to frighten us with the image of runaway troikas, which all other nations stand aside from in disgust. Russia is not a runaway troika, but a grand and stately chariot, moving calmly and with dignity toward her goal. The fate of my client rests in your hands, but so does the fate of Russian justice. You will defend it, you will save it, and you will prove that there are men who watch over it, men who will keep it safe in their care!"

Chapter 14: The Peasants Stand Firm

This was how Fetyukovitch ended his speech, and the audience erupted with overwhelming enthusiasm, like a storm that couldn't be stopped. The excitement was so intense that no one tried to contain it: women were crying, and even many of the men wept, including two important figures. The President gave in to the moment and even delayed ringing his bell to restore order. The crowd's emotions felt sacred to them—something that couldn't be silenced, as many women later said. Even the speaker, Fetyukovitch, was deeply moved.

At that moment, Ippolit Kirillovitch stood up to raise objections. The crowd turned on him instantly, filled with hatred. "What? He's actually going to object?" the women whispered angrily. But nothing could have stopped him—not even his wife, if she had tried. He looked pale, trembling with emotion, and at first, his words were barely understandable. His breathing was unsteady, and he seemed unable to speak clearly, stumbling over his thoughts. However, he soon pulled himself together. I'll only quote a few of the key points from his new speech.

"They accuse me of creating a made-up story, but isn't this defense just another story piled on top of mine? All it's missing is poetry. They claim that Fyodor Pavlovitch, while waiting for his mistress, tore open an envelope and carelessly tossed it on the floor—and they even tell us exactly what he said as he did it. Isn't that pure imagination? And what proof is there that he took the money from that envelope? Who heard him? The weak- minded Smerdyakov, who they've turned into some sort of tragic, rebellious hero seeking revenge for his illegitimate birth—doesn't that sound like a made-up drama? And then we have the son, who breaks into his father's house, supposedly kills him, but somehow doesn't kill him at the same time. This isn't just a story; it's a riddle that even the storyteller can't solve. If he killed him, then he killed him—so what does it mean to say he killed him without killing him? How are we supposed to make sense of that?

"Then we're told that this courtroom is a place for reasonable and sound ideas. But what do we hear from this place of reason? A bold claim that calling the murder of a father 'parricide' is just an outdated prejudice. And if killing a parent is just a prejudice, what's next? Are children going to ask why they should love their parents at all? What will happen to society, to families? They dismiss parricide as nothing more than a silly superstition among old merchants' wives from Moscow. And to make things worse, they twist the most important principles that protect our legal system, all for the sake of excusing a crime that can't be excused. The defense urges us to 'crush him with mercy,' but isn't that exactly what the criminal hopes for? We'll see tomorrow just how much he's 'crushed' by it. And is the defense attorney being too modest by only asking for the defendant's acquittal? Why not go further—why not set up a charity in the criminal's name to honor his crime for future generations?

"Even religion and the teachings of the Gospel are being twisted. They dismiss faith as just mysticism and claim that their version of Christianity—one based on logic and reason—is the only true one. They present us with a false image of Christ! The defense lawyer quotes, 'What measure you give will be the measure you get,' and then twists it to suggest that Christ taught us to treat others the way they treat us. And they say this from the same place that claims to stand for truth and reason! But that's not what Christ teaches us. He warns us not to act like the wicked world around us. He tells us to forgive, to turn the other cheek, not to repay evil with evil. That's what God asks of us—not to pretend that forbidding children from killing their parents is just some outdated prejudice. And we won't stand by while someone rewrites the Gospel of our Lord, who is called by the defense attorney the 'crucified lover of humanity,' as if that's all He is. In truth, we call to Him, saying, 'For You are our God!'"

At this point, the President stepped in, urging Ippolit Kirillovitch not to exaggerate or go beyond acceptable limits, as officials often do in these situations. The audience grew uneasy, with murmurs of frustration spreading through the crowd. There were even angry outbursts. Fetyukovitch did not directly respond to the prosecutor. Instead, he calmly walked up to the podium, placed a hand over his heart, and spoke a few dignified words in an offended tone. He briefly and sarcastically mentioned the accusation of "storytelling" and "psychology," and at the perfect moment, he quoted the line, "Jupiter, you are angry, therefore you are wrong," which made the audience burst into laughter, as everyone could see that Ippolit Kirillovitch was nothing like Jupiter.

As for the prosecutor's suggestion that he was teaching young people to kill their parents, Fetyukovitch responded with quiet dignity, saying the accusation wasn't even worth addressing. When the prosecutor hinted that Fetyukovitch had expressed unorthodox views, the defense lawyer implied that it was a personal attack and that he had expected better from a court of law—a place where his reputation as a citizen and loyal subject should not have been questioned. However, at this point, the President interrupted him too, and Fetyukovitch ended his speech with a respectful bow, leaving the courtroom filled with a hum of approval. The audience, especially the women, believed that Ippolit Kirillovitch had been completely defeated.

Finally, the defendant, Mitya, was allowed to speak. He stood up but said very little. He was completely drained, both physically and emotionally. The strength and confidence he had shown in the morning were gone. It was as if the day's events had taught him a hard lesson—one that would stay with him for the rest of his life. His voice was faint, and he no longer shouted. There was a new tone in his words—one of humility, defeat, and acceptance.

"What can I say, gentlemen of the jury? My judgment has come. I feel God's hand on me. This is the end for a man who lost his way. But before God, I swear to you—I didn't kill my father! I say it again, I didn't kill him! I made mistakes, but I wanted to do good. I tried, even though I lived like a wild animal. I'm grateful to the prosecutor—he showed me things about myself I hadn't realized. But he's wrong—I didn't kill my father. I thank my lawyer too. I cried when I listened to him. But he also guessed wrong—I didn't do it. And don't listen to the doctors. I'm not insane—my heart is just heavy.

"If you spare me, if you let me go, I'll pray for you. I'll become a better man. I swear to God I will. But if you condemn me, I'll break my sword over my head and kiss the pieces. Just don't take my God away from me. I know myself too well—I'll rebel if I lose Him. My heart feels so heavy. Please, gentlemen... show me mercy."

He nearly collapsed back into his seat; his voice gave out, and he could barely get out his last words. Afterward, the judges began asking both sides to present their final arguments and conclusions. But I won't go into all the details. Finally, the jury stood and left the room to deliberate. The President, exhausted, gave them a weak final reminder: "Stay impartial, don't let yourselves be swayed by the defense's eloquence, but also carefully consider the arguments. Remember, you carry a great responsibility," and so on.

With that, the jury withdrew, and the court adjourned. People stood, stretched, and moved around, exchanging their thoughts and grabbing refreshments from the buffet. It was late—almost one in the morning—but no one wanted to leave. The tension was too high, and resting wasn't an option. Everyone waited with heavy hearts, though to say that might be an exaggeration. The women, more accurately, were overwhelmed by restless impatience, not real worry. They all felt certain that Mitya would be acquitted. They were already preparing themselves for an outpouring of joy at the final verdict. Many of the men felt the same way. Some were pleased by the prospect, others frowned in disapproval, and a few looked defeated, clearly hoping he would be found guilty. Fetyukovitch was confident in the outcome, standing in the middle of a crowd of people congratulating and praising him.

"There are invisible threads that connect a defense lawyer to the jury," Fetyukovitch told one group, as I later heard. "You can feel them forming during your speech. I felt them today—our case is won. You can relax."

"What will our peasants think of this?" asked a grumpy, pock-marked landowner as he approached a group in conversation.

"They're not all peasants," someone replied. "There are four government clerks on the jury."

"Yes, that's right," added a member of the district council.

"And don't forget about Nazaryev, the merchant with the medal— he's a juror too."

"Is he really?"

"Yes, and he's no fool either." "But he hardly says anything."

"That's true, but maybe that's a good thing. He doesn't need any fancy talk from city folk—he could teach them all a thing or two. He's got twelve kids, after all! Imagine that!"

"Surely they'll acquit him, right?" one young official burst out.

"Of course they will," a confident voice replied.

"It would be outrageous not to!" added the official. "Even if he did kill his father—well, fathers aren't all the same. And besides, he was in such a state! Maybe he just swung the pestle in the heat of the moment and accidentally knocked the old man over. Honestly, dragging the valet into it was ridiculous. If I were Fetyukovitch, I'd have just said outright: 'He killed him, but he's not guilty—simple as that!'"

"That's pretty much what he said, just without those exact words." "No, no—he practically said it!" added another voice. "Remember the actress in Lent? She got off after cutting her lover's wife's throat."

"Yeah, but she didn't quite finish the job." "What's the difference? She started it, didn't she?"

"And what about the bit about children—wasn't that something?" "Brilliant!"

"And all that stuff about mysticism, too!"

"Please, enough about mysticism!" someone else groaned. "Think about poor Ippolit—his wife's going to claw his eyes out over this Mitya business."

"Is she here?"

"Not a chance! If she were, she'd have done it right here in court. She's at home with a toothache."

"He he he!"

"He he he!"

In another group, someone muttered, "They might actually let Mitya off, after all."

"If they do, he'll probably turn the whole town upside down tomorrow—he'll be on a drinking spree for ten days straight!"

"Oh, the devil will have his way."

"Of course! Where else would the devil be but here?"

"Well, I'll admit, the defense was persuasive. But still, you shouldn't go smashing your father's head in with a pestle. Where's the line?"

"Do you remember the cart?"

"Yes, how he turned it into a chariot!"

"And tomorrow, he'll turn it back into a cart, just because it suits him."

"These lawyers are clever, aren't they? Can we even expect justice in Russia these days?"

Then, the bell rang. The jury had deliberated for exactly one hour—no more, no less. Everyone quickly returned to their seats, and the courtroom fell into complete silence. I still remember the moment the jury returned. It was finally time. I can't recall the specific questions they were asked, but I remember the answer to the first and most important one: "Did the defendant commit the murder for the purpose of robbery and with premeditation?" (Though those may not have been the exact words.) The room held its breath as the foreman, the youngest of the clerks, spoke clearly:

"Yes, guilty."

He repeated the same verdict for every question: "Yes, guilty," without adding any recommendation for mercy. No one had expected that. Almost everyone thought the jury would at least ask for leniency. For a moment, the courtroom was frozen. Both those hoping for a conviction and those praying for an acquittal sat in stunned silence. But the stillness only lasted a second before chaos erupted. Some men grinned, rubbing their hands together in satisfaction. Those unhappy with the outcome seemed crushed, shrugging and whispering to each other, struggling to comprehend what had just happened.

As for the women, they were on the verge of starting a riot. At first, they didn't believe their ears. Then, the whole room was filled with exclamations: "What does this mean? What's going on?" They jumped from their seats, as if expecting the verdict to be overturned on the spot.

In the midst of the uproar, Mitya suddenly stood up, stretching his arms toward the crowd and crying out in anguish:

"I swear by God and the Judgment Day—I am not guilty of my father's blood! Katya, I forgive you! Brothers, friends—show mercy to the other woman!"

He broke down, sobbing so violently that his wails echoed through the entire courtroom. It was as if the voice coming from him wasn't his own. From the farthest corner of the gallery, a piercing scream rang out—it was Grushenka. She had managed to sneak back into the courtroom before the lawyers gave their closing arguments.

Mitya was taken away, and the sentencing was postponed until the next day. The room was still in chaos, but I didn't stay to hear any more. On my way out, I overheard a few final remarks:

"He'll get twenty years in the mines!" "At least twenty."

"Well, the peasants stood firm."

"And they've sealed Mitya's fate."

Epilogue

Chapter 1: Plans For Mitya's Escape

At nine in the morning, five days after the trial, Alyosha went to Katerina Ivanovna's house to discuss an important matter and deliver a message. They talked in the same room where she had once received Grushenka. In the next room, Ivan Fyodorovich lay unconscious, burning with a high fever. After the scene in the courtroom, Katerina Ivanovna had ordered Ivan to be brought to her home, ignoring the inevitable gossip and disapproval from others. One of her two relatives had left for Moscow right after the trial, but the other stayed behind. Even if both had left, Katerina would have stuck to her decision—she was determined to care for Ivan, day and night. Doctors Varvinsky and Herzenstube attended to him. The famous specialist, however, had returned to Moscow, unwilling to predict how the illness would end. Though the doctors tried to encourage her and Alyosha, it was clear they could offer no real hope for recovery.

Alyosha visited his brother twice a day, but this time he had urgent business. He knew the topic would be difficult to bring up, yet there was no time to delay. He had another appointment that morning that could not wait. For about fifteen minutes, they had been talking. Katerina Ivanovna was pale and looked utterly exhausted, though she was also agitated, her emotions on edge. She seemed to guess why Alyosha had come.

"Don't worry about his decision," she said firmly. "One way or another, he'll come to it. He has to escape. That poor man, that hero—no, not Dmitri Fyodorovich, but the man in the next room, the one who has sacrificed himself for his brother," she added, her eyes flashing. "He told me the whole escape plan long ago. You know, he's already started making arrangements. I mentioned it to you before... It'll likely happen at the third stage, on the way to Siberia, when the prisoners are being transported. But it's still a long way off. Ivan Fyodorovich has already spoken to the officer in charge of the third stage. We just don't know yet who'll lead the prisoner escort—it's too early to find that out. Maybe tomorrow, I'll show you all the details of the plan. Ivan left them with me on the eve of the trial, just in case. That was when—do you remember?—you found us quarreling. He had gone downstairs, but I called him back when I saw you. Do you remember? Do you know what we were fighting about?"

"No, I don't," Alyosha answered.

"Of course, he didn't tell you. It was about the escape plan. He told me the idea three days earlier, and we started arguing about it right away. We fought for three days straight. He told me that if Dmitri was convicted, he would escape abroad with that... woman. And when I heard that, I got furious. I can't even explain why— I don't know myself. I was furious that she would go abroad with Dmitri!" Katerina Ivanovna exclaimed suddenly, her lips trembling with anger. "As soon as Ivan saw how angry I was about her, he assumed I was jealous of Dmitri and still in love with him. That's how our first fight started. I wouldn't explain myself or apologize—I couldn't stand the idea that he might think I still had feelings for Dmitri, especially when I had told him, long ago, that I didn't love anyone but him! It was just my anger toward her that made me so upset.

"Three days later, that evening when you came by, he gave me a sealed envelope. He told me to open it only if something happened to him—he must have sensed he would fall ill. Inside, he said, were the full details of the escape plan, and if he died or became too sick, it would be up to me to save Mitya on my own. He also left me nearly ten thousand rubles—the same money the prosecutor mentioned in court, the money Ivan had sent to be exchanged. I was amazed that Ivan, even though he was jealous of me and still believed I loved Mitya, didn't give up on saving his brother. He trusted me with the plan. Oh, what a sacrifice that was! You have no idea, Alyosha, how much it meant! I wanted to throw myself at his feet in gratitude, but I knew if I did, he'd only think I was happy about Mitya being saved—and of course, he'd believe that! Just the thought of him thinking that way made me furious all over again. So instead of kissing his feet, I lost my temper! Oh, I'm such an unhappy person! It's my awful, wretched nature! I'll drive him away, just like I did with Dmitri. He'll leave me for someone else—someone he can be happy with. And if that happens... I won't survive it. I'll end it all!"

Her voice trembled, and she covered her face with her hands for a moment. Then, as if the memory hit her with full force, she continued, "Do you remember? When you came in that evening, and I called Ivan back, I was so furious at the way he looked at me—with contempt and hatred—that I told you it was he who convinced me Dmitri was a murderer! I only said it to hurt him. He never said anything of the sort—it was me! I was the one who persuaded him! It's my vile temper that caused everything— everything that happened in court. Ivan only wanted to show me that he was an honorable man, that even if I loved Dmitri, he wouldn't destroy him out of jealousy or revenge. That's why he went to the trial. All of this… it's all my fault! I alone am to blame!"

Katya had never spoken to Alyosha like this before, and he knew she was at the breaking point, where even the proudest heart collapses under the weight of grief. Alyosha also sensed the real reason behind her suffering—a reason she had carefully hidden from him since the trial. She was tormented by guilt over her betrayal at the trial. Alyosha knew that her conscience was urging her to confess everything to him, to collapse in tears and beg for forgiveness. But the thought of her reaching such a low point pained him, and he wanted to spare her from it. Yet it made the reason for his visit even harder to bring up.

He tried to steer the conversation back to Mitya.

"Don't worry about him! It's going to be fine!" she said sharply, her voice stubborn and insistent. "I know him too well. He'll agree to escape. It won't happen right away—he'll have time to come to terms with it. Ivan will recover by then and take care of everything, so I won't have to be involved. Don't worry—Mitya will go through with it. He's already agreed, hasn't he? Do you think he'd give up on her? And they won't let her visit him, so he has no choice but to escape.

"But he's scared of you most of all. He's afraid you'll disapprove of him escaping on moral grounds. But you must give your blessing, Alyosha—if that's what it takes to convince him," she added with a bitter smile.

"He talks about some hymn," Katya said again, "some cross he has to bear, some duty. I remember Ivan Fyodorovich telling me a lot about it—oh, if only you knew how he talked!" She suddenly cried out, unable to hold back her emotions. "If only you knew how much he loved that miserable man in the moment he told me, and how he hated him at the same time, maybe just as much! And I listened to his story, to his tears, with nothing but scorn. Like a brute! Yes, I am a brute. I'm the reason he's sick with this fever. But that man in prison—he doesn't know what it means to suffer," she snapped irritably. "Can someone like him really suffer? Men like him never suffer!"

Her voice was sharp with hatred and disgust. Yet, she had been the one who betrayed him. Alyosha wondered if the hatred she felt was because of the guilt she carried. "Maybe she hates him because she knows she's wronged him," Alyosha thought. But he hoped it was only in fleeting moments. He sensed a challenge in her words but chose not to respond to it.

"I asked you here today to get you to promise to persuade him yourself," Katya continued, her tone growing sharper. "Or do you think escaping would be dishonorable, cowardly… or maybe even unchristian?"

"No, not at all. I'll tell him everything," Alyosha muttered. Then, looking her straight in the eyes, he added suddenly, "He wants you to come see him today."

"Me? Are you serious?" Katya whispered, her face turning pale as she pulled back slightly on the sofa.

"Yes, it's true—and you must," Alyosha answered with growing urgency. "He needs you now more than ever. I wouldn't have brought it up if it weren't necessary. He's not well; he's losing his grip. He keeps asking for you—not to make peace or settle things between you, but just for you to show yourself at his door. So much has happened to him since that day. He knows now how deeply he hurt you. He doesn't even ask for your forgiveness—he told me himself, 'It's impossible for her to forgive me.' All he wants is for you to stand at his door."

"It's all happening so fast…" Katya whispered, her voice shaky. "I had a feeling you would come with this message. I knew he would ask me to come. But it's impossible!"

"Even if it feels impossible, you need to do it. Think about it— he's only just now realizing how much pain he caused you. He's never understood it until now. He said, 'If she refuses to come, I'll be miserable for the rest of my life.' Do you hear that? Even though he's been sentenced to twenty years of hard labor, he's still hoping to find some happiness. Isn't that heartbreaking? Please— you must see him, even if only for a moment. He's ruined, but he's innocent." Alyosha's voice was charged with urgency. "His hands are clean—there's no blood on them! For the sake of the suffering that lies ahead for him, you have to go. Stand at his door, meet him on his way into the darkness. It's what you ought to do!" Alyosha pressed the word ought with firm conviction.

"I know I should… but I can't," Katya moaned. "What if he looks at me? I can't bear it."

"You need to meet his eyes. How will you live with yourself if you don't do it now?"

"Better to suffer for the rest of my life," Katya murmured.

"No—you must go, you must," Alyosha repeated relentlessly.

"Why today? Why right now?" she protested. "I can't leave Ivan—he needs me."

"You only need to go for a moment," Alyosha insisted. "If you don't come, he'll be delirious by tonight. I wouldn't lie to you— please, have pity on him!"

"Have pity on me!" Katya cried bitterly, bursting into tears.

"You will come," Alyosha said firmly, seeing her break down.

"I'll go tell him you'll be there soon."

"No! Don't tell him that!" she cried out in alarm. "I will come— but don't promise him anything. I might go to the prison, but I might not go inside. I just… I don't know yet." Her voice faltered, and she struggled to catch her breath.

Alyosha rose to leave.

"What if I run into someone?" Katya asked suddenly, her voice low and fearful, her face going pale again.

"That's exactly why you need to go now—so you won't run into anyone," Alyosha assured her. "I promise there will be no one there. You can trust me on that. We'll be waiting for you," he added firmly, and with that, he left the room.

Chapter 2: For A Moment the Lie Becomes Truth

He hurried to the hospital where Mitya was now staying. The day after his sentence, Mitya had fallen ill with a nervous fever and was transferred to the prison section of the town hospital. However, thanks to requests from several people— Alyosha, Madame Hohlakov, and Lise—Doctor Varvinsky arranged for Mitya to be placed in a private room, the same one Smerdyakov had been in. While a guard was stationed at the far end of the corridor and the window was barred, Varvinsky felt justified in showing this kindness, even if it wasn't strictly by the rules. He was a compassionate young man and understood how hard it would be for someone like Mitya to adjust immediately to life among criminals and murderers. He believed it would be better for him to ease into it gradually. Family and friends were allowed to visit with the informal consent of the doctor, the hospital overseer, and the police captain. However, only Alyosha and Grushenka had come to see Mitya so far. Rakitin had tried to visit twice, but Mitya had begged Varvinsky not to let him in.

Alyosha found Mitya sitting on the bed in a hospital gown, looking feverish. A towel soaked in vinegar and water lay across his head.

When Mitya saw Alyosha enter, he gave him a strange look, a mixture of confusion and dread. He had been deeply preoccupied ever since the trial, spending long stretches in silence, lost in heavy, painful thoughts. Even when he did speak, it was abrupt, as if he couldn't express what he really wanted to say. At times, he looked at his brother with visible pain on his face, though he seemed more at ease around Grushenka. He hardly spoke to her either, but the moment she walked into the room, his face would light up with joy.

Alyosha sat beside him in silence. Mitya was waiting for him anxiously, but he didn't dare ask the question that was burning in his mind. The idea that Katya might actually come felt too unreal to hope for, but the thought that she might not come at all was unbearable. Alyosha could sense his brother's inner struggle.

"Trifon Borissovitch," Mitya began nervously, "he's torn his whole inn apart, or so they tell me. Pulled up the floors, ripped out the planks, even dismantled the gallery. All because he's still looking for that fifteen hundred rubles the prosecutor said I'd hidden there. They say he started as soon as he got home. Serves him right, the crook! The guard here told me about it yesterday— he's from the same town."

Alyosha leaned closer. "Listen. She's going to come, Mitya, but I don't know when. Maybe today, maybe in a few days—I can't say for sure. But she will come. That much is certain."

Mitya jolted slightly at the words and opened his mouth as if to speak, but then fell silent again. The news affected him deeply. He was desperate to know what had been said, yet too afraid to ask. If Katya came with harsh words or contempt, it would crush him.

"She said," Alyosha continued carefully, "that I must make sure your conscience is at ease about the escape. If Ivan isn't well by then, she will handle everything herself."

"You've mentioned that before," Mitya said, lost in thought. "And you told Grusha about it," Alyosha added.

"Yes," Mitya admitted softly. "She won't come this morning, though." He glanced anxiously at his brother. "She said she'd come later, in the evening. When I told her yesterday that Katya was making arrangements, she didn't say much. She just whispered, 'Let her.' She knows it's important. I didn't press her. I think she realizes now that Katya doesn't care for me anymore—that she loves Ivan instead."

"Does she?" Alyosha asked quietly, startled.

"Maybe not. But she knows Katya doesn't love me. At least, she isn't coming this morning." Mitya's voice grew more urgent. "I asked Grusha to do something for me. You know, Ivan is better than all of us. He deserves to live. He has to get well."

"Katya is worried about him, but she's certain he'll recover," Alyosha offered.

"That means she thinks he'll die," Mitya said grimly. "That's what people believe when they're scared—if they say he'll get better, it's because they fear the worst."

"I think Ivan will recover," Alyosha said firmly. "He's strong.

There's every reason to hope."

"Yes, he'll get better," Mitya agreed quietly. "But Katya still thinks he'll die. She's carrying a lot of sorrow…"

A heavy silence fell between them. Mitya's face twisted with anxiety, and suddenly he spoke in a trembling voice, thick with emotion.

"Alyosha, I love Grusha so much."

"They won't let her go with you," Alyosha said gently.

Mitya's expression darkened. "There's something else I need to tell you," he said abruptly, his voice sharp and determined. "If they beat me—on the way there, or when I get to Siberia—I won't stand for it. I'll kill someone, and they'll shoot me for it. Twenty years of that... no, I won't survive it. They've already started treating me badly. I've been lying here all night, thinking it over, judging myself. I thought I could endure it, that I'd sing a hymn to keep my spirits up. But if a guard insults me, I won't be able to take it. For Grusha, I could endure anything—anything but the blows. But they won't even let her come to me."

Alyosha smiled softly.

"Listen, brother, once and for all," Alyosha began calmly. "Here's what I think, and you know I wouldn't lie to you. You're not ready for this, Mitya. A cross like this—it's not for you. And you don't need to carry such a burden if you're not ready. If you had killed our father, it would trouble me deeply to see you avoid your punishment. But you're innocent, and this cross is too much for you. You wanted to remake yourself through suffering, but listen—just keep that desire alive in your heart, wherever you go, for the rest of your life. That will be enough. Not accepting this burden will make you feel a deeper sense of duty throughout your life. And that constant awareness will change you more than if you went to Siberia. There, you wouldn't last—you'd resent it and, in the end, say, 'I've paid my debt.' The lawyer was right about that. Some people can't bear that kind of weight. For some, it's impossible. These are my thoughts, if you want to hear them."

He smiled slightly. "If your escape would cause harm to others— if soldiers or officers had to answer for it—I wouldn't allow it. But Ivan spoke with the superintendent of the third étape, and he said it could be done quietly, without a major investigation. And while bribing people isn't exactly right, I'm not here to judge that. If Ivan and Katya asked me to help you escape, I know I would use bribes myself. I'm just being honest with you. So I can't judge your decision, either. But I promise you this—I will never condemn you for it. It would be strange if I did. Now, I think I've said everything I needed to."

"But I condemn myself!" Mitya cried. "I'm going to escape— that's been decided with or without you. What else could Mitya Karamazov do but run away? But I'll carry the guilt with me forever. I'll pray for forgiveness for the rest of my life. Isn't that what the Jesuits teach? Isn't this exactly how they think?"

"Yes," Alyosha replied with a gentle smile.

"I love you for always being so honest," Mitya said, laughing suddenly. "You never hide anything from me. I've caught you being Jesuitical, Alyosha! I should kiss you for that." He grinned, then grew serious. "Now, let me tell you the rest. If I escape, even with money and a passport—even if I make it to America—I'll only find some new kind of exile, just as bad as Siberia. Maybe even worse. I hate America already. Even if Grusha is with me... just look at her. She's no American! She's Russian to her core. She'll be homesick every day, and I'll have to watch her suffer because of me. What harm has she done to deserve that? And how will I stand being surrounded by strangers, even if they're better people than I am? I hate America! They may be geniuses with machines, but they're not part of my soul. I love Russia, Alyosha. I love the Russian God, even if I am a scoundrel. I'll choke over there!" His eyes blazed with emotion, and his voice quivered with tears.

"So here's my plan," he continued, regaining control. "Once Grusha and I get to America, we'll move to the most remote place we can find—out in the wilderness, with bears if we have to. There are still wild places there, I've heard. Maybe we'll live where the last of the Mohicans once roamed." He smiled faintly at the thought. "We'll get to work on the land, just the two of us. We'll study English until we speak it perfectly. It'll take three years, I bet. But once we've learned it—goodbye, America! We'll come back here as American citizens.

"Don't worry—we won't come back to this town. We'll go somewhere far away, north or south. We'll be different people by then—Grusha and I. Maybe the doctors will give me a fake wart or something—if they're so good with machines, why not? Or I'll pluck out an eye, grow a long beard, and go gray thinking about Russia.

No one will recognize us. And if they do, they can send us to Siberia—it will mean that was our fate all along. We'll still work the land, somewhere in the wilds. I'll live as an American for the rest of my days, but I'll die on Russian soil. That's my plan, and I won't change it. What do you think?"

Alyosha nodded. "Yes," he said softly, not wanting to disagree.

Mitya paused for a moment, then said suddenly, "They really put on a show at the trial, didn't they?"

"If they hadn't, you would've been convicted just the same," Alyosha sighed.

"Yes, people are sick of me here. God bless them, but it's hard," Mitya muttered, his voice heavy with sadness.

There was another long silence before Mitya broke it, his tone urgent and anxious. "Alyosha, put me out of my misery—tell me! Is she coming or not? What did she say? How did she say it?"

"She said she would come," Alyosha answered carefully, "but I don't know if it'll be today. It's hard for her, you know." He glanced at his brother with concern.

"Of course it's hard for her! Alyosha, this waiting will drive me mad. Grusha keeps watching me—she understands. My God, calm my heart! What do I even want? I want Katya! But do I really know what I want? It's the cursed Karamazov nature—reckless and wild! I'm not fit for this suffering. I'm just a scoundrel. That's all."

"Here she is!" Alyosha suddenly cried.

Katya appeared in the doorway, standing still for a moment, staring at Mitya with a dazed expression. Mitya leapt to his feet, his face pale and fearful. But almost immediately, a timid, pleading smile crept across his lips, and with an impulsive gesture, he held out both hands to her.

Without hesitation, Katya rushed toward him, grabbed his hands, and almost forced him to sit back down on the bed. She sat beside him, pressing his hands tightly in hers. They both tried to speak several times but stopped, smiling strangely as they gazed into each other's eyes.

Two minutes passed in silence.

"Have you forgiven me?" Mitya whispered at last. Then, turning to Alyosha with joy breaking across his face, he exclaimed, "Did you hear that? Did you hear what I just asked?"

"That's what I loved you for, that you are generous at heart!" broke from Katya. "My forgiveness is no good to you, nor yours to me; whether you forgive me or not, you will always be a sore place in my heart, and I in yours—so it must be...." She stopped to take breath. "What have I come for?" she began again with nervous haste: "to embrace your feet, to press your hands like this, till it hurts—you remember how in Moscow I used to squeeze them—to tell you again that you are my god, my joy, to tell you that I love you madly," she moaned in anguish, and suddenly pressed his hand greedily to her lips. Tears streamed from her eyes. Alyosha stood speechless and confounded; he had never expected what he was seeing.

"Love is over, Mitya!" Katya began again, "but the past is painfully dear to me. Know that you will always be so. But now let what might have been come true for one minute," she faltered, with a drawn smile, looking into his face joyfully again. "You love another woman, and I love another man, and yet I shall love you for ever, and you will love me; do you know that? Do you hear? Love me, love me all your life!" she cried, with a quiver almost of menace in her voice.

"I shall love you, and ... do you know, Katya," Mitya began, drawing a deep breath at each word, "do you know, five days ago, that same evening, I loved you. When you fell down and were carried out All my life! So it will be, so it will always be—"

So they murmured to one another frantic words, almost meaningless, perhaps not even true, but at that moment it was all true, and they both believed what they said implicitly.

"Katya," cried Mitya suddenly, "do you believe I murdered him? I know you don't believe it now, but then ... when you gave evidence. Surely, surely you did not believe it!"

"I did not believe it even then. I've never believed it. I hated you, and for a moment I persuaded myself. While I was giving evidence I persuaded myself and believed it, but when I'd finished speaking I left off believing it at once. Don't doubt that! I have forgotten that I came here to punish myself," she said, with a new expression in her voice, quite unlike the loving tones of a moment before.

"Woman, yours is a heavy burden," broke, as it were, involuntarily from Mitya.

"Let me go," she whispered. "I'll come again. It's more than I can bear now."

She was getting up from her place, but suddenly uttered a loud scream and staggered back. Grushenka walked suddenly and noiselessly into the room. No one had expected her. Katya moved swiftly to the door, but when she reached Grushenka, she stopped suddenly, turned as white as chalk and moaned softly, almost in a whisper:

"Forgive me!"

Grushenka stared at her and, pausing for an instant, in a vindictive, venomous voice, answered:

"We are full of hatred, my girl, you and I! We are both full of hatred! As though we could forgive one another! Save him, and I'll worship you all my life."

"You won't forgive her!" cried Mitya, with frantic reproach.

"Don't be anxious, I'll save him for you!" Katya whispered rapidly, and she ran out of the room.

"And you could refuse to forgive her when she begged your forgiveness herself?" Mitya exclaimed bitterly again.

"Mitya, don't dare to blame her; you have no right to!" Alyosha cried hotly.

"Her proud lips spoke, not her heart," Grushenka brought out in a tone of disgust. "If she saves you I'll forgive her everything—"

She stopped speaking, as though suppressing something. She could not yet recover herself. She had come in, as appeared afterwards, accidentally, with no suspicion of what she would meet.

"Alyosha, run after her!" Mitya cried to his brother; "tell her ... I don't know ... don't let her go away like this!"

"I'll come to you again at nightfall," said Alyosha, and he ran after Katya. He overtook her outside the hospital grounds. She was walking fast, but as soon as Alyosha caught her up she said quickly:

"No, before that woman I can't punish myself! I asked her forgiveness because I wanted to punish myself to the bitter end. She would not forgive me. I like her for that!" she added, in an unnatural voice, and her eyes flashed with fierce resentment.

"My brother did not expect this in the least," muttered Alyosha. "He was sure she would not come—"

"No doubt. Let us leave that," she snapped. "Listen: I can't go with you to the funeral now. I've sent them flowers. I think they still have money. If necessary, tell them I'll never abandon them.... Now leave me, leave me, please. You are late as it is—the bells are ringing for the service. Leave me, please!"

Chapter 3: Ilusha's Funeral. The Speech at The Stone

He really was late. They had waited as long as they could and had decided to carry the little flower-covered coffin to the church without him. It was Ilusha's coffin. The poor boy had died just two days after Mitya's sentencing. At the gate of the house, Alyosha was greeted by the shouts of Ilusha's schoolmates. They had been waiting impatiently for him, and now that he'd arrived, they ran to him with relief. There were about twelve boys, each with schoolbags or satchels slung over their shoulders. "Stay with Father," Ilusha had told them in his final moments, and they had taken his words to heart. Kolya Krassotkin stood at the front of the group.

"I'm so glad you've come, Karamazov!" Kolya exclaimed, grabbing Alyosha's hand. "It's awful—just awful in there. Snegiryov hasn't touched a drop of alcohol today, we know that for sure, but it's like he's drunk... I try to act manly, but it's unbearable. Karamazov, can I ask you one thing before you go in?"

"What is it, Kolya?" Alyosha asked.

"Is your brother innocent or guilty? Did he kill your father, or was it the valet? I haven't slept in four nights thinking about it—tell me the truth!"

"The valet killed him. My brother is innocent," Alyosha answered calmly.

"That's what I thought!" cried Smurov from among the boys.

"So, he'll die an innocent man!" Kolya exclaimed. "He's ruined, but happy! I almost envy him!"

"Envy him? Why would you say that?" Alyosha asked in surprise. "Oh, to give everything for the sake of truth—that's what I want!

I want to sacrifice myself, too." Kolya's eyes sparkled with enthusiasm.

"But not like this. Not in disgrace and horror," Alyosha warned gently.

"Of course not," Kolya agreed. "But I wouldn't mind dying for humanity, even if it meant disgrace. I don't care if my name is forgotten. I respect your brother!"

"And so do I!" shouted another boy suddenly—the same one who had once bragged about knowing who founded Troy. His face turned bright red with embarrassment, just as it had on that day.

Alyosha entered the house quietly. Ilusha lay in a small blue coffin, his hands folded over his chest, surrounded by flowers. His face had barely changed, and strangely, there was no odor of decay. His expression was calm, almost thoughtful, as if lost in a peaceful dream. His hands, crossed over his heart, looked as if they had been carved from marble. The coffin was adorned with flowers inside and out, some sent that morning by Lise Hohlakov, and others by Katerina Ivanovna. As Alyosha opened the door, Captain Snegiryov stood beside the coffin, holding a handful of flowers with trembling hands, scattering them over his son again and again.

The captain barely acknowledged Alyosha's presence and refused to look at anyone, not even his hysterical wife, who kept trying to stand on her crippled legs for one last look at their boy. Nina had been pushed close to the coffin in her chair, resting her head against it, quietly crying. Snegiryov's face was a mix of bewilderment and sorrow, his actions erratic, and his words confused. "Old man, my dear old man!" he kept muttering as he gazed down at Ilusha. He had called Ilusha "old man" as a term of endearment when the boy was alive.

"Father, give me a flower," the mother whimpered, reaching toward the little white rose tucked into Ilusha's hand. "Give me the white one." Whether she wanted it as a keepsake or was simply drawn to its beauty, she reached out for it again and again.

"No!" Snegiryov shouted, clutching the flowers tightly. "They're his, not yours! Everything here belongs to him!"

"Father, please give her a flower," Nina pleaded softly, her face wet with tears.

"I won't give anything to her—especially not to her!" Snegiryov cried bitterly. "She didn't love him! She took away his little cannon, and he gave it to her." He burst into loud, uncontrollable sobs, overwhelmed by the memory of Ilusha surrendering his beloved toy to his mother. The poor woman buried her face in her hands, her silent tears flowing freely.

The boys gathered around the coffin in a close circle, ready to carry it out. Seeing that the captain would not leave his son's side, they prepared to lift the coffin.

"I won't let him be buried in the churchyard!" Snegiryov wailed suddenly. "He told me—he said to bury him by the stone! I won't let him be taken anywhere else!"

For the past three days, he had insisted on burying Ilusha by the stone, but Alyosha, Kolya, the landlady, her sister, and all the boys had tried to dissuade him.

"What nonsense—bury him by a stone, as if he'd hanged himself?" the old landlady had scolded. "He'll be laid to rest in holy ground, where prayers will be said over him. He'll hear the singing from the church, and the deacon will read for him as if it were over his grave."

At last, the captain gave in with a despairing wave of his hand, as if to say, "Do what you want."

The boys gently lifted the coffin. As they passed the mother, they lowered it briefly so she could say goodbye. But when she saw her son's face up close for the first time in days, she trembled violently. Her gray head twitched uncontrollably above the coffin, as if she were a broken puppet.

"Mother, bless him. Cross yourself and kiss him," Nina begged, her voice breaking. But the grieving woman could only strike her chest with her fists, her face twisted in silent agony.

The boys carried the coffin past her. Nina pressed her lips to her brother's for the last time as they bore him away.

On his way out, Alyosha asked the landlady to look after those left behind. She interrupted him before he could finish.

"Of course I'll stay. We're Christians, too," she said, her voice thick with tears.

They didn't have far to carry the coffin to the church, only about three hundred steps. The day was calm and clear, with a slight chill in the air. The church bells were still ringing. Snegiryov ran around in a panic, fussing over the coffin in his old, thin summer coat, his head bare, holding his worn-out wide-brimmed hat in his hand. He seemed confused and worried. One moment, he reached out to hold the head of the coffin, but only got in the way of the people carrying it. The next, he ran beside them, trying to find a place to help. A flower fell into the snow, and he rushed to pick it up as if losing that flower would be the worst thing in the world.

"We forgot the piece of bread!" he suddenly cried in panic. But the boys quickly reminded him that he had already taken the bread and put it in his pocket. He immediately pulled it out, relieved.

"Ilusha told me to bring it," he explained to Alyosha right away. "I was sitting with him one night, and he suddenly said, 'Father, when they fill up my grave, crumble a piece of bread on it so the sparrows can come. I'll hear them, and it will make me happy not to be alone.'"

"That's a good idea," said Alyosha. "We should do it often."

"Every day, every day!" the captain quickly responded, feeling comforted by the thought.

They finally reached the church and placed the coffin in the center. The boys gathered around it, standing respectfully throughout the service. It was an old, modest church, and many of the icons had no fancy coverings, but such simple churches are the best for praying. As the mass went on, Snegiryov calmed down a little, though at times, he still seemed lost and anxious. Once, he went to the coffin to adjust the cover or the wreath, and when a candle fell from the holder, he rushed to fix it, fumbling nervously. After that, he stood quietly by the coffin, his face showing blank confusion.

After the Epistle, he whispered to Alyosha, who stood beside him, that the reading hadn't been done properly, but he didn't explain what he meant. During the "Like the Cherubim" prayer, he joined in the singing but didn't finish. He fell to his knees, pressing his forehead against the stone floor, and stayed like that for a long time.

Finally, the funeral service began, and candles were passed around. The distracted father began moving about again, but the touching, heartfelt prayers seemed to reach him. He suddenly became smaller, shaking with short, quick sobs. At first, he tried to hold them back, but eventually, he cried openly. When it was time to say goodbye and close the coffin, he threw himself over it, as if he wouldn't let them cover Ilusha, kissing his son's cold lips again and again. It took a while, but they finally convinced him to step back. Then, out of nowhere, he grabbed a few flowers from the coffin. He looked at them as if he had just thought of something new and, for a moment, seemed to forget his sorrow. He slowly drifted into deep thought and didn't fight back when the coffin was lifted and carried to the grave.

The grave was near the church, and it was a costly one that Katerina Ivanovna had paid for. After the usual rites, the gravediggers lowered the coffin. Snegiryov, still holding his flowers, leaned so far over the open grave that the boys grabbed his coat in fear and pulled him back. He didn't seem to fully understand what was happening. When they started filling the grave with dirt, he suddenly pointed at the earth and tried to say something, but no one could understand him, and he stopped. Then he remembered the bread. He got very excited, grabbed the bread, and started tearing it into pieces, tossing them onto the grave.

"Come on, birds, come on, sparrows!" he muttered anxiously. One of the boys noticed it was hard for him to crumble the bread with the flowers in his hands and suggested he hand the flowers to someone else for a bit. But he refused, suddenly becoming worried about the flowers, as if afraid they were trying to take them away from him completely. After making sure the bread was crumbled and everything was done, he surprised everyone by turning calmly and starting to walk home. But his pace quickened until he was almost running. Alyosha and the boys kept up with him.

"The flowers are for Mama, the flowers are for Mama! I wasn't nice to her," he started saying suddenly.

Someone reminded him to put on his hat because of the cold, but he angrily threw it into the snow, saying, "I won't wear it, I won't wear it." Smurov picked up the hat and carried it for him. All the boys were crying, with Kolya and the boy who had talked about Troy crying the hardest. Even Smurov, with the captain's hat in his hand, was crying heavily, but he still managed to pick up a piece of red brick from the snowy path and throw it at a flock of sparrows flying by. He missed, of course, and kept crying as he ran.

Halfway home, Snegiryov suddenly stopped, standing still for a moment as if something had struck him. Then, without a word, he turned around and ran back toward the empty grave. But the boys quickly caught up to him and grabbed him. He fell onto the snow like he had been knocked over and started crying out, "Ilusha, my boy, my dear boy!" Alyosha and Kolya tried to help him up, soothing and comforting him.

"Come on, Captain, show some strength," Kolya murmured. "A brave man has to stay strong."

"You'll ruin the flowers," Alyosha added. "And Mama is waiting for them. She's sitting at home crying because you didn't give her any earlier. Ilusha's little bed is still there—"

"Yes, yes, Mama!" Snegiryov suddenly remembered. "They'll take the bed away, they'll take it away," he said in a panic, as though someone really might. He jumped up and ran toward home again. It wasn't far, so they all got there together. Snegiryov hurried to open the door, calling out to his wife, with whom he had fought so bitterly just before:

480

"Mamma, my poor, sweet crippled one, Ilusha sent you these flowers," Snegiryov cried, holding out the small bunch of flowers he had struggled to keep while stumbling through the snow. They were frozen and crushed, but he offered them with trembling hands. As he looked toward the corner of the room, his eyes fell on Ilusha's little boots, neatly placed by the bed. The landlady had tidied them, setting them side by side. Seeing the old, patched boots, stiff with wear, Snegiryov let out a gasp, raised his hands, and rushed over to them. Dropping to his knees, he grabbed one boot and kissed it over and over, pressing it desperately to his lips.

"Ilusha, my boy, my dear old man! Where are your little feet?" he sobbed. "Where have they taken you? Where?" he cried out in anguish, his voice raw with grief.

Nina broke into loud sobs, and Kolya ran from the room, unable to bear it. The other boys followed, their emotions too overwhelming to stay. Finally, Alyosha quietly stepped out as well.

"Let them cry," Alyosha said softly to Kolya. "There's no point trying to comfort them right now. We'll give them a minute, and then we can go back."

"No, it's too much—this is unbearable," Kolya agreed, lowering his voice so no one could hear. "Karamazov, if I could bring him back, I'd give anything—anything in the world."

"So would I," Alyosha whispered.

"Do you think we should come back here tonight? The captain will probably be drunk," Kolya murmured.

"Maybe," Alyosha admitted. "But we should come, just the two of us. If we all go together, it will stir up too many memories. It'll be better if we quietly spend some time with his mother and Nina."

"The landlady is already setting the table," Kolya added. "There'll be some kind of funeral meal, and the priest is coming. Should we go back for that?"

"Of course," Alyosha replied.

"It's strange, isn't it?" Kolya continued thoughtfully. "We go from this deep sorrow, and then suddenly there are pancakes. It feels so out of place, like it doesn't belong in our religion."

"They're having salmon too," the boy who had discovered who founded Troy remarked loudly.

"Kartashov, for the love of everything, stop with your stupid comments!" Kolya snapped irritably. "No one's talking to you, and no one cares whether you exist or not."

Kartashov's face flushed red with embarrassment, but he said nothing.

They kept walking slowly along the path. After a moment, Smurov pointed ahead and exclaimed, "There's Ilusha's stone—the one they wanted to bury him under!"

They all stopped, standing still around the large stone. Alyosha stared at it, and the memory of Snegiryov's story flooded his mind—how Ilusha had clung to his father, sobbing, "Father, how could they insult you like that?" The scene played vividly in Alyosha's imagination, as if it were happening all over again.

A sudden impulse stirred in Alyosha's heart. He looked earnestly at each of the boys' bright, familiar faces. Then, with a serious expression, he said, "Boys, I'd like to say something here, at this spot."

The boys gathered around him, giving him their full attention, their eyes wide with expectation.

"Boys, we're going to part ways soon. I'll be with my two brothers for a while—one is going to Siberia, and the other is terribly ill. After that, I'll leave this town, maybe for a long time. So let's make a promise here, at Ilusha's stone, that we will never forget Ilusha or each other. No matter what happens in our lives—whether we meet again in twenty years or never at all—let's always remember how we buried this boy, the same boy we once threw stones at by the bridge. Remember how we grew to love him afterward. He was a brave and kind boy. He cared deeply about his father's honor and stood up for him when others were cruel.

"So first and foremost, let's agree to always keep Ilusha in our hearts. And even if life takes us to places far away—whether we achieve great success or face terrible hardships—let's hold on to this memory. Let's not forget how good it felt to stand here together, united by kindness and love. For those moments, we were better than we usually are." Alyosha smiled warmly at them. "My little doves—yes, let me call you that. You remind me of those soft, blue birds right now, with your kind, sweet faces.

"Maybe my words don't make much sense to you today. Maybe I'm speaking too strangely. But I believe you'll remember this one day, and you'll agree with me. There's nothing better or more important in life than a good memory, especially one from childhood, from home. People talk a lot about education, but I think having good memories like this is the best education of all. If a person carries memories like these through life, they will be safe, no matter what. Even if they have only one good memory, that could be enough to save them someday.

"Yes, we might grow up and make mistakes—we might even become wicked. We could become so bitter that we laugh at other people's tears, or mock someone like Kolya, who just said, 'I want to suffer for all humanity.' We might even mock ourselves. But no matter how far we fall—and may God prevent that—if we remember today, if we remember Ilusha and how we loved him, even the cruelest among us will feel ashamed of having once been kind.

"And that one memory might stop us from doing something terrible. It will remind us, 'I was good and brave once. I was honest.' And even if we laugh at that kindness, deep down, we'll know it's no joke. We'll realize that we were wrong to laugh. And that thought alone might keep us from falling too far."

"I understand you, Karamazov!" Kolya exclaimed, his eyes bright with emotion.

The boys were filled with excitement, each of them wanting to speak, but they held back, watching Alyosha with deep attention and feeling.

"I say these things in case we ever lose our way," Alyosha continued. "But there's no reason for us to turn bad, is there, boys? Let's make a promise—first and foremost, let's be kind. Then, let's be honest. And most importantly, let's never forget each other. I'll say it again—I promise that I'll never forget any of you. Every face I see right now, I'll carry with me, even thirty years from now.

"Just earlier, Kolya told Kartashov that we didn't care if he existed or not. But that's not true. I'll never forget that Kartashov exists. Right now, instead of blushing like he did when he told us about the founders of Troy, he's looking at me with those joyful, kind eyes of his." Alyosha smiled warmly. "Boys, my dear boys, let's be brave and generous like Ilusha. Let's be smart and courageous like Kolya—although I know Kolya will be even wiser when he grows up. And let's all try to be as sweet, modest, and thoughtful as Kartashov.

"But why am I only mentioning those two? You're all dear to me. From this day forward, each one of you has a place in my heart, and I hope you'll keep a place for me in yours. And who brought us together, making us feel this kindness and love we'll carry with us for the rest of our lives? It was Ilusha—the good, dear boy, who will always be precious to us. Let's make sure we never forget him. May his memory live forever in our hearts from this day on!"

"Yes, forever! Forever!" the boys cried out, their faces softening with emotion.

"Let's remember everything about him—his face, his clothes, his little boots, his coffin, and even his poor, troubled father. And let's never forget how bravely he stood up for his father, all by himself, against the whole school."

"We'll remember, we'll remember!" the boys shouted. "He was brave! He was good!"

"I loved him so much!" Kolya exclaimed.

"Ah, children, my dear friends, don't be afraid of life," Alyosha said gently. "Life is so good when we do what is right and kind."

"Yes, yes!" the boys echoed enthusiastically.

"Karamazov, we love you!" someone called out—it was probably Kartashov.

"We love you! We love you!" the boys repeated, their voices full of feeling. Some of them had tears in their eyes.

"Hurrah for Karamazov!" Kolya shouted joyfully.

"And may the memory of our dear friend live forever!" Alyosha added, his voice full of emotion.

"Forever!" the boys repeated in unison.

"Karamazov," Kolya asked suddenly, "do you think it's true, what we learn in religion? Will we all rise from the dead and see each other again, even Ilusha?"

"Yes, absolutely," Alyosha answered, his voice light with both joy and faith. "We will rise again, and we'll meet each other with joy. We'll tell each other everything that's happened, and we'll be so happy!"

"Oh, how wonderful that will be!" Kolya cried out in delight.

"Now, let's finish our talk," Alyosha said, smiling. "It's time to go to the funeral dinner. Don't worry about eating pancakes— they're part of an old tradition, and there's something nice about that." He gave a small laugh. "Come on, let's go! And let's walk hand in hand."

"And always, all our lives, hand in hand!" Kolya declared passionately. "Hurrah for Karamazov!"

"Hurrah for Karamazov!" the boys shouted again, their voices ringing with excitement and unity.

The End

Thank you for Reading

You've Just Read a Piece of the Greatest Library Ever Rebuilt

Thank you for reading.

This book is one of thousands we're restoring, reimagining, and translating as part of the **Modern Library of Alexandria** — a global movement to preserve and share humanity's most important ideas.

What was once lost to fire and time is now rising again — not just as memory, but as living, breathing knowledge, freely accessible to all.

What You Can Do Next:

- **Keep Reading.**

  Discover more legendary works — in beautiful print, audiobook, or digital form — at LibraryofAlexandria.com.

- **Build Your Own Library.**

  Every title is available as a paperback, hardcover, or collectible boxset — at true printing cost. Craft a personal library worthy of display.

- **Spread the Light.**

  Share this book. Tell others about the movement. Help us translate every timeless work into every language, so no reader is ever left behind.

By finishing this book, you've already taken part in something extraordinary.

Join us at LibraryofAlexandria.com

Together, we're rebuilding the greatest library the world has ever known.

With appreciation,
The Modern Library of Alexandria Team

Visit:

www.libraryofalexandria.com

Or scan the code below: